Lecture Notes in Computer Science   2412

Edited by G. Goos, J. Hartmanis and J. van Leeuwen

T0140282

Springer
*Berlin
Heidelberg
New York
Barcelona
Hong Kong
London
Milan
Paris
Tokyo*

Hujun Yin   Nigel Allinson
Richard Freeman John Keane
Simon Hubbard (Eds.)

Intelligent Data Engineering and Automated Learning– IDEAL 2002

Third International Conference
Manchester, UK, August 12-14, 2002
Proceedings

 Springer

Series Editors

Gerhard Goos, Karlsruhe University, Germany
Juris Hartmanis, Cornell University, NY, USA
Jan van Leeuwen, Utrecht University, The Netherlands

Volume Editors

Hujun Yin
Nigel Allinson
Richard Freeman
UMIST, Department of Electrical Engineering and Electronics
Manchester, M60 1QD, UK
E-mail: {h.yin/allinson}@umist.ac.uk
E-mail: rics@swift.ee.umist.ac.uk

John Keane
UMIST, Department of Computation
Manchester, M60 1QD, UK
E-mail: jak@co.umist.ac.uk

Simon Hubbard
UMIST, Department of Biomolecular Science
Manchester, M60 1QD, UK
E-mail: sjh@bms.umist.ac.uk

Cataloging-in-Publication Data applied for

Die Deutsche Bibliothek - CIP-Einheitsaufnahme

Intelligent data engineering and automated learning : IDEAL 2002 ;
third international conference, Manchester, UK, August 12 - 14, 2002 ;
proceedings / Hujun Yin ... (ed.). - Berlin ; Heidelberg ; New York ; Barcelona ;
Hong Kong ; London ; Milan ; Paris ; Tokyo : Springer, 2002
   (Lecture notes in computer science ; Vol. 2412)
   ISBN 3-540-44025-9

CR Subject Classification (1998): H.3, I.2, H.4, H.5, I.4, J.1, H.2

ISSN 0302-9743
ISBN 3-540-44025-9 Springer-Verlag Berlin Heidelberg New York

Springer-Verlag Berlin Heidelberg New York,
a member of BertelsmannSpringer Science+Business Media GmbH

http://www.springer.de

© Springer-Verlag Berlin Heidelberg 2002
Printed in Germany

Typesetting: Camera-ready by author, data conversion by PTP-Berlin, Stefan Sossna e.K.
Printed on acid-free paper   SPIN: 10873722   06/3142   5 4 3 2 1 0

Preface

Data analysis and engineering, and associated learning paradigms, are playing increasingly important roles in an increasing number of application fields. Developments and specialities will benefit many scientific and engineering domains from knowledge/information discovery, data mining and analysis, agents and Internet applications to financial management and bio-informatics.

Intelligent Data Engineering and Automated Learning (IDEAL) is a biennial conference dedicated to emerging and challenging topics in intelligent data analysis and engineering and associated learning paradigms. Following the highly successful IDEAL'98 and IDEAL'00 conferences, both held in Hong Kong, the third conference in this series, IDEAL'02, attracted researchers, scientists and practitioners from all over the world, who came together in Manchester to present their findings and theories, to exchange ideas, and to share their successes. IDEAL has proven to be an *ideal* forum for revealing and developing the latest theoretical advances and practical applications in intelligent data engineering and automated learning. It is becoming a major international and interdisciplinary event. The themes of IDEAL'02 are Document Analysis and Management, Data Mining, Financial Engineering, Agent Technologies, and Bio-informatics. Over 150 papers were submitted to the conference and they were reviewed by the Program Committee and the additional reviewers. We finally selected about 80 high-quality papers. A special session on Autonomous Mining also contributed a number of excellent papers.

We would like to thank the International Advisory Committee for their guidance and advice, and the Program Committee and additional reviewers for their efficient reviewing of the contributed papers and their helpful comments for the authors. The Asia and America Liaisons did also an excellent job in publicizing the event. We would also like to express our gratitude to the IEEE Neural Networks Society, the UK Engineering and Physical Sciences Research Council (EPSRC), the publisher, Springer-Verlag, and the Manchester Conference Centre for their support throughout.

University of Manchester Institute of Science and Technology (UMIST)
Manchester, UK

June 2002

Hujun Yin
Nigel M. Allinson
Richard Freeman
John Keane
Simon Hubbard

Organization

General Co-Chairs

Hujun Yin	UMIST, UK
Nigel Allinson	UMIST, UK
Lei Xu	Chinese University of Hong Kong

International Advisory Committee

Lei Xu (Chair)	Chinese University of Hong Kong
Yaser Abu-Mostafa	CALTECH, USA
Shun-ichi Amari	RIKEN, Japan
Michael Dempster	University of Cambridge, UK
Nick Jennings	University of Southampton, UK
Erkki Oja	Helsinki University of Technology, Finland
Lalit M. Patnaik	Indian Institute of Science, India
Burkhard Rost	Columbia University, USA

Organizing Committee

Hujun Yin (Chair)	UMIST, UK
Nigel Allinson	UMIST, UK
Richard Freeman	UMIST, UK
Simon Hubbard	UMIST, UK
John Keane	UMIST, UK

Asia Liaison

Yiu-ming Cheung	Hong Kong Baptist University, Hong Kong

America Liaison

Malik Magdon-Ismail	Rensselaer Polytechnic Institute, USA

Special Session Organizers

Yiu-ming Cheung	Hong Kong Baptist University, Hong Kong
Jiming Liu	Hong Kong Baptist University, Hong Kong

Program Committee

Nigel Allinson (Chair)	UMIST, UK
Jim Austin	University of York, UK
Hamid Bolouri	University of Hertfordshire, UK
Max Bramer	University of Portsmouth, UK
Laiwan Chan	Chinese University of Hong Kong
Tom Downs	University of Queensland, Australia
Colin Fyfe	University of Paisley, UK
Joydeep Ghosh	University of Texas, USA
Tony Holden	University of Cambridge, UK
Simon Hubbard	UMIST, UK
David Jones	University College London (UCL), UK
Samuel Kaski	Helsinki University of Technology, Finland
John Keane	UMIST, UK
Martin Kersten	CWI Amsterdam, The Netherlands
Irwin King	Chinese University of Hong Kong
Chris Kirkham	AXEON Ltd., UK
Jimmy Lee	Chinese University of Hong Kong
Kwong S. Leung	Chinese University of Hong Kong
Malik Magdon-Ismail	Rensselaer Polytechnic Institute, USA
Luc Moreau	University of Southampton, UK
Jose Principe	University of Florida, USA
Omer Rana	University of Wales, Cardiff, UK
Vic Rayward-Smith	University of East Anglia, UK
Jennie Si	Arizona State University, USA
Ben Stapley	UMIST, UK
Atsuhiro Takasu	National Institute of Informatics, Japan
Marc van Hulle	K. U. Leuven, Belgium
Lipo Wang	Nanyan Technological University, Singapore
Olaf Wolkenhauer	UMIST, UK
Andy Wright	BAE Systems, UK
Xin Yao	University of Birmingham, UK
Xinfeng Ye	University of Auckland, New Zealand
Hujun Yin	UMIST, UK
Hans-Georg Zimmermann	Siemens, Germany

Additional Reviewers

Sophia Ananiadou	Salford University, UK
Zuhair Bandar	Manchester Metropolitan University, UK
Songcan Chen	Nanjing University of Aeronautics and Astronautics, China
Keeley Crockett	Manchester Metropolitan University, UK
Christie Ezeife	University of Windsor, Canada
Richard Freeman	UMIST, UK
Jonathan Gabbai	UMIST/BAE Systems, UK
Ann Gledson	UMIST/Premier Systems Technology, UK
Cefn Hoile	British Telecommunications, UK
Huosheng Hu	Essex University, UK
Yoo-Shin Kim	Pusan National University, Korea
Paulo Lisboa	Liverpool John Moores University, UK
Yuchang Lu	Tsinghua University, China
Farid Meziane	Salford University, UK
Emanuela Moreale	Open University, UK
Andy Nisbet	Trinity College Dublin, Ireland
Ilias Petrounias	UMIST, UK
Ben Russell	UMIST/Premier Systems Technology, UK
Jeevandra Sivarajah	UMIST, UK
Goran Trajkvski	Towson University/West Virginia University, USA
Wenjia Wang	Bradford University, UK
Zhen Rong Yang	Exeter University, UK
Qingfu Zhang	Essex University, UK

Table of Contents

Data Mining

Knowledge Engineering

Text and Document Processing

Internet Applications

Agent Technologies

Special Session on Autonomous Mining

Financial Engineering

Bio-Informatics

Learning Systems

Pattern Recognition

Mining Frequent Sequential Patterns under a Similarity Constraint

Matthieu Capelle, Cyrille Masson, and Jean-François Boulicaut[*]

Institut National des Sciences Appliquées de Lyon
Laboratoire d'Ingéniérie des Systèmes d'Information
F-69621 Villeurbanne Cedex, France
{cmasson,jfboulic}@lisi.insa-lyon.fr

Abstract. Many practical applications are related to frequent sequential pattern mining, ranging from Web Usage Mining to Bioinformatics. To ensure an appropriate extraction cost for useful mining tasks, a key issue is to push the user-defined constraints deep inside the mining algorithms. In this paper, we study the search for frequent sequential patterns that are also similar to an user-defined reference pattern. While the effective processing of the frequency constraints is well-understood, our contribution concerns the identification of a relaxation of the similarity constraint into a convertible anti-monotone constraint. Both constraints are then used to prune the search space during a levelwise search. Preliminary experimental validations have confirmed the algorithm efficiency.

1 Introduction

Many applications domains need for the analysis of sequences of events, like the design of personalized interface agents [5]. The extraction of frequent sequential patterns in huge databases of sequences has been heavily studied since the design of apriori-like algorithms [1,6]. Recent contributions consider the use of other criteria for the objective interestingness of the mined sequential patterns. Other kinds of user-defined constraints (e.g., enforcing a minimal gap between events) have been defined [3,10]. Provided a conjunction of constraints specifying the potential interest of patterns, the algorithmic challenge is to make use of these constraints in order to efficiently prune the search space.

In this paper, we are interested in the conjunction of two constraints: a *frequency constraint* and a *similarity constraint*. Two patterns are considered similar if the similarity measure between them is smaller than some threshold. Many research have been done in that field (for a survey, see, e.g., [7]), and the similarity measure we use allows us to identify a constraint that can be efficiently used inside our levelwise mining algorithm. Indeed, by mining sequential patterns satisfying a conjunction of an anti-monotone constraint (the frequency one) and a convertible anti-monotone constraint (the similarity one), we improve the global pruning efficiency during a levelwise exploration of the candidate patterns.

---

[*] Research partially funded by the European contract cInQ IST 2000-26469.

H. Yin et al. (Eds.): IDEAL 2002, LNCS 2412, pp. 1–6, 2002.

In Section 2, we introduce the sequential patterns and some useful properties of constraints. In Section 3, we define the distance measure and the similarity constraint we use. In Section 4, we demonstrate the relevancy of the approach by practical experiments. Section 5 is a short conclusion.

2   Basic Notions

Given a finite alphabet Σ, a sequential pattern M is an ordered list of symbols of Σ. L_M denotes the set of patterns that can be built using symbols of Σ. A sequential pattern M will be denoted $M_1 \rightarrow \ldots \rightarrow M_n$ where M_i is the ith symbol of M and n is the *length* of M. $M_i \rightarrow M_{i+1}$ means that the element M_i preeceds the element M_{i+1}. $M' = M_1' \rightarrow \ldots \rightarrow M_m'$ is a *sub-pattern* of $M = M_1 \rightarrow \ldots \rightarrow M_n$ if there exist some integers $i_1 < \ldots < i_m$ such that $M_1' = M_{i_1}, \ldots, M_m' = M_{i_m}$. An *event* is denoted by a pair (A, t) where $A \in \mathcal{P}(\Sigma) \backslash \emptyset$ and $t \in \mathbb{N}$ (occurrence time of A). Several events can occur at the same time. An *event sequence* is a list of events sorted by increasing occurrence times. Generally, the *support* of a pattern M is its occurring rate in the data and a pattern is said *frequent* if its support exceeds an user-defined threshold.

Classical methods for frequent sequential pattern mining relies on an adaptation of the `apriori` paradigm [1,6]. The extraction process consists in several iterations of a levelwise algorithm, composed of three steps: generation of new candidates of length k, safe pruning of this set by using the frequency constraint (i.e., the extension of an infrequent pattern cannot be frequent), and counting the support of the remaining candidates. At each iteration, we extract longer patterns and it stops when no more candidates can be generated. Tractability can then be obtained by increasing the frequency threshold. However, considering only a frequency constraint often leads to a lack of focus. Indeed, if the user has an idea of some specific properties on the desired patterns, he might be overwhelmed by many useless results. A naive approach would be to check them in a post-processing phase: it means that the mined patterns will be among the frequent ones for a given frequency threshold. The challenge is to make an active use of the constraints, i.e., pushing them into the different steps of the extraction process. For that purpose, the constraints must satisfy some properties.

A constraint C_{am} is **anti-monotone** if, for all pattern M verifying C_{am}, all its sub-patterns verify C_{am}. For instance, the frequency constraint is anti-monotone thanks to safe pruning. Pushing anti-monotone constraints leads to quite effective algorithms [8,6]. However, this strong property only characterizes a few constraints. The concept of convertible constraint [9] allows to relax this definition while keeping an efficient pruning. In the following, we consider an equivalence relation R on the patterns. A constraint C_{cam} is **convertible anti-monotone** if, for all pattern M verifying C_{cam}, all its sub-patterns equivalents to M by R verify C_{cam}. When considering the prefix equivalence relation, such a constraint can be characterized with prefix decreasing functions [9] defined on L_M. Let $M, M' \in L_M$ such that M' is a prefix of M, f is a prefix decreasing function iff $f(M') \leq f(M)$.

Pushing non (convertible) anti-monotone constraints has been studied but the benefit cannot be guaranteed [3]. In this paper, given a collection of event sequences D and $C = C_{freq} \wedge C_{sim}(M_R)$ where C_{freq} denotes the frequency constraint and $C_{sim}(M_R)$ denotes a similarity constraint w.r.t. a reference pattern M_R, find the collection of patterns from L_M occurring in D and verifying C.

3 Similarity Constraint

Let us consider an user-defined reference pattern M_R and a set of operations $O_S = \{Ins, Del, Sub\}$ to which we associate costs depending on the position and the symbol on which they are applied. $C_{Ins}(X, i)$ is the insertion cost of symbol X at position $i, 0 \leq i \leq |M_R|$, $C_{Del}(X, i)$ is the deletion cost of X at position $i, 1 \leq i \leq |M_R|$, and $C_{Sub}(X, Y, i)$ is the substitution cost of X by Y at the position $i, 1 \leq i \leq |M_R|$. Costs values belong to the interval $[0, 1]$. The more its cost is close to 0, the more we consider the operation costly. Let $M \in L_M$, the cost $c(a_{M,M_R})$ of a_{M,M_R}, an alignment of M and M_R, is the product of all costs of its operations. The similarity score of a pattern M w.r.t. a pattern M_R is $sim(M, M_R) = max\{c(a_{M,M_R})|a_{M,M_R}$ is an alignment of M and $M_R\}$. Notice that the maximal similarity of two patterns is 1. The algorithm that computes $sim(M, M_R)$ looks like the one used for editing distances [4]. It uses a matrix $\mathcal{M}$. However, we consider more complex operations and the cell $\mathcal{M}(0, 0)$ is initialized to 1 (we need a maximization criterion instead of a minimization criterion). More precisely, computing $\mathcal{M}$ relies on the following equations:

$$\forall j \in \{1, \ldots, |M|\}, \mathcal{M}(0, j) = \mathcal{M}(0, j-1) * C_{ins}(M[j], 0)$$
$$\forall i \in \{1, \ldots, |M_R|\}, \mathcal{M}(i, 0) = \mathcal{M}(i-1, 0) * C_{del}(M_R[i], i)$$
$$\mathcal{M}(i, j) = max \begin{cases} \mathcal{M}(i-1, j-1) * C_{sub}(M_R[i], M[j], i) \\ \mathcal{M}(i, j-1) * C_{ins}(M[j], i) \\ \mathcal{M}(i-1, j) * C_{del}(M_R[i], i) \end{cases}$$

Finally, the similarity score is the value $\mathcal{M}(|M_R|, |M|)$. To compute it, we can use dynamic programming: $\mathcal{M}(i, j)$ is determined by $\mathcal{M}(i-1, j-1), \mathcal{M}(i-1, j)$ and $\mathcal{M}(i, j-1)$. Thus, we can compute $sim(M, M_R)$ given the similarity score of its prefixes of length $|M| - 1$ The complexity of the algorithm is in $\mathcal{O}(|M_R|)$.

Table 1. Computation of $sim(A \rightarrow B \rightarrow E \rightarrow C \rightarrow D, A \rightarrow B \rightarrow C)$

		A	B	E	C	D
(0)	1	$\rightarrow 0.01$	$\rightarrow 0.001$	$\rightarrow 10^{-4}$	$\rightarrow 10^{-5}$	$\rightarrow 10^{-6}$
A(1)	$\downarrow 0.01$	$\searrow 1$	$\rightarrow 0.75$	$\rightarrow 0.56$	$\rightarrow 0.42$	$\rightarrow 0.32$
B(2)	$\downarrow 7, 5.10^{-3}$	$\downarrow 0.75$	$\searrow 1$	$\searrow 0.67$	$\downarrow 0.32$	$\rightarrow 0.24$
C(3)	$\downarrow 7, 5.10^{-5}$	$\downarrow 7, 5.10^{-3}$	$\downarrow 0.01$	$\searrow 0.01$	$\searrow 0.67$	$\rightarrow 0.60$
sim	$7, 5.10^{-5}$	$7, 5.10^{-3}$	0.01	0.01	0.67	0.60
sim-pot	1	1	1	0.67	0.67	0.60

Example. Let $M_R = A \to B \to C$ and assume the costs given below, table 1 describes a computation of $sim(M, M_R)$.

$\forall X \in \Sigma, c_{Del}(X, 1) = 0.01, c_{Del}(X, 2) = 0.75, c_{Del}(X, 3) = 0.01$
$\forall X \in \Sigma, c_{Ins}(X, 0) = 0.01, c_{Ins}(X, 1) = 0.75, c_{Ins}(X, 2) = 0.01, c_{Ins}(X, 3) = 0.9$
$$\forall i \in \{1, 2, 3\}, c_{Sub}(X, Y, i) = \begin{cases} 1 \text{ if } X = Y \\ 0.9 \text{ if } (X, Y) \in \{(A, D), (D, A), (B, E), (E, B)\} \\ 0.01 \text{ else} \end{cases}$$

Given a reference pattern $M_R \in L_M$, operations costs and a similarity threshold $min\text{-}sim \in [0, 1]$, a pattern M is similar to M_R if $sim(M, M_R) \geq min\text{-}sim$. We can now define the similarity constraint $C_{sim}(M_R)$ as follows: $M \in L_M$ satisfies $C_{sim}(M_R)$ iff M is similar to M_R.

Our algorithm (see [2] for details) is a variant of cSPADE [10]. However, it differs from it on some points:

- It does not consider any non (convertible) anti-monotone constraints.
- It supports the potential similarity constraint (defined below), i.e. a relaxation of $C_{sim}(M_R)$.
- It uses the prefix equivalence classes, instead of the suffix ones. This choice is due to the fact that our similarity constraint is based on prefix relations.

However, our constraint $C_{sim}(M_R)$ is neither anti-monotone, nor convertible anti-monotone. We have been looking for a relaxation of $C_{sim}(M_R)$ that would be convertible anti-monotone. Assume R_p denotes the equivalence relation "is prefix of". We define the potential similarity of a pattern M w.r.t. M_R as the maximal similarity score that its extensions can reach. Formally, $sim\text{-}pot(M, M_R) = \max\{sim(M', M_R)|M' \in L_M \text{ and } R_p(M, M')\}$. A corollary of this definition is that for all $M' \in L_M$ $sim\text{-}pot(M', M_R) \geq sim(M', M_R)$. To compute $sim\text{-}pot(M, M_R)$, we can take the largest value of the $(|M| + 1)th$ column of $\mathcal{M}$. Indeed, it is not possible to increase this value since the cost of a further editing operation on M is smaller than 1.

Our first idea was to consider the potential similarity of a pattern as the result of the *sim-pot* function. As it can be shown that *sim-pot* is a prefix anti-monotone function, that would have lead to a convertible anti-monotone constraint ensuring a safe pruning, i.e. without affecting the correction of the mining algorithm. However, we have shown that its completeness is lost (see [2] for details). Thus, we defined a new function *sim-pot-comp* based on *sim-pot*. The idea is to consider this "complete" potential similarity of a pattern M as the potential similarity of its prefix of length $|M| - 1$. Let $M', M \in L_M$ such that $R_p(M', M)$ and $|M| = |M'| + 1$, the function *sim-pot-comp* is defined by: *sim-pot-comp*$(M, M_R) = sim\text{-}pot(M', M_R)$. Given a similarity threshold $min\text{-}sim$, we now say that a pattern $M \in L_M$ is potentially similar to M_R if *sim-pot-comp*$(M, M_R) \geq min\text{-}sim$. Thus, we can define a similarity constraint as follows: $\forall M \in L_M$, M satisfies $C_{sim-pot}(M_R)$ iff M is potentially similar to M_R. *sim-pot-comp* is still a prefix anti-monotone function, and thus $C_{sim-pot}(M_R)$, which is a relaxation of the initial constraint $C_{sim}(M_R)$, is convertible anti-monotone and is used in our complete and correct extraction algorithm.

Table 2. Files used for our experiments

Parameter	Description of the parameter	File F1	File F2	File F3
$|D|$	Number of event sequences	25k	50k	100k
$|C|$	Average number of elements per event sequence	10	10	10
$|T|$	Average element size	10	10	10
$|S|$	Average size of maximal sequential patterns	10	10	10
$|N_S|$	Number of maximal sequential patterns	5k	5k	5k
$|N|$	Number of items	100	100	2k

4 Experiments

Our prototype has been implemented in JAVA and experiments have been run on a Pentium III 800 Mhz with 512Mb of memory. We used 3 synthetic data sets (Table 2) obtained with the Quest generator [1]. Experiments aim at showing the relevancy of the active use of the conjunction of similarity and frequency constraints, compared to its use during post-processing. To simplify, we consider a fixed frequency threshold and only inclusions and deletions operations with uniform costs. Thus, the similarity threshold corresponds to a maximum number of operations allowed to align a pattern on the reference one. We are mainly interested in execution time, number of constrained and generated candidates, and respective selectivities of C_{freq} and $C_{sim}(M_R)$ constraints. Results are depicted on Figure 1. When the similarity threshold is 0, it means that the similarity constraint is taken into account in a post-processing phase. When it is equal to 1, it means that no editing operations are allowed. First, we can remark that the higher the similarity threshold is, the better the performances are. Moreover, we can see that the number of generated candidates and the execution time globally follow the same trends. Notice an exception for the file F3 with a similarity threshold of 1. Indeed, performances increase whereas the number of generated candidates remains the same. We can explain that by the decrease of the selectivity of support-based pruning and the increase of the selectivity of similarity-based pruning, whose validity is not difficult to check. Finally, we observe that the selectivity of the similarity-based constraint is inversely proportional to the selectivity of the support-based constraint.

5 Conclusion

We studied how to push a similarity constraint into a frequent sequential patterns mining algorithm. Experimental results confirm the relevancy of the approach. There are many possible extensions of this work: first, it worths to study the impact of more complex alignments methods (such as the `Viterbi` algorithm). Moreover, we have to use the prototype against real data sets and study the influence of the choice of editing operations costs.

---

[1] http://www.almaden.ibm.com/cs/quest/index.html

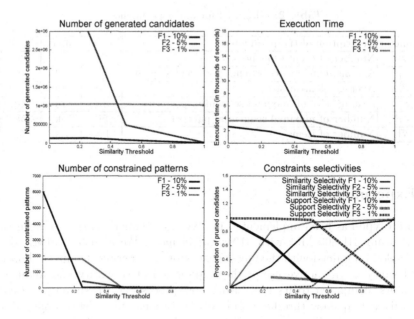

Fig. 1. Extractions results on the three files

References

1. R. Agrawal and R. Srikant. Mining sequential patterns. In *Proc. ICDE'95*, pages 3–14. IEEE Press, March 1995.
2. Matthieu Capelle. Extraction de motifs séquentiels sous contraintes (in french). Master's thesis, DEA ECD, INSA Lyon, Villeurbanne, France, September 2001.
3. M. N. Garofalakis, R. Rastogi, and K. Shim. SPIRIT: Sequential Pattern Mining with Regular Expression Constraints. In *Proc. VLDB'99*, pages 223–234. Morgan Kaufmann, September 1999.
4. Levenshtein. Binary codes capable of corecting deletions, insertions, and reversals, 1966.
5. J. Liu, Kelvin Chi Kuen Wong, and Ka Keung Hui. Discovering user behavior patterns in personalized interface agents. In *Proc. IDEAL 2000*, pages 398–403. Springer Verlag LNCS 1983, December 2000.
6. H. Mannila, H. Toivonen, and A. I. Verkamo. Discovery of frequent episodes in event sequences. *Data Mining and Knowledge Discovery*, 1(3):259–289, 1997.
7. P. Moen. *Attribute, Event Sequence, and Event Type Simarity Notions for Data Mining*. PhD thesis, Dept. of Computer Science, University of Helsinki, Finland, February 2000.
8. R. T. Ng, L. V.S. Lakshmanan, J. Han, and A. Pang. Exploratory mining and pruning optimizations of constrained associations rules. In *Proc. SIGMOD'98*, pages 13–24. ACM Press, June 1998.
9. J. Pei, J. Han, and L. V.S. Lakshmanan. Mining frequent itemsets with convertible constraints. In *Proc. ICDE'01*, pages 433–442. IEEE Computer Press, April 2001.
10. M. J. Zaki. Sequence mining in categorical domains: Incorporating constraints. In *Proc. CIKM'00*, pages 422–429. ACM Press, November 2000.

Pre-pruning Classification Trees to Reduce Overfitting in Noisy Domains

Max Bramer

Faculty of Technology, University of Portsmouth, UK
Max.Bramer@bcs.org.uk
http://www.btinternet.com/~Max.Bramer

Abstract. The automatic induction of classification rules from examples in the form of a classification tree is an important technique used in data mining. One of the problems encountered is the overfitting of rules to training data. In some cases this can lead to an excessively large number of rules, many of which have very little predictive value for unseen data. This paper describes a means of reducing overfitting known as *J-pruning*, based on the *J-measure*, an information theoretic means of quantifying the information content of a rule. It is demonstrated that using J-pruning generally leads to a substantial reduction in the number of rules generated and an increase in predictive accuracy. The advantage gained becomes more pronounced as the proportion of noise increases.

1 Introduction

The growing commercial importance of knowledge discovery and data mining techniques has stimulated new interest in the automatic induction of classification rules from examples, a field in which research can be traced back at least as far as the mid-1960s [1].

A problem that arises with all methods of generating classification rules is that of *overfitting* to the training data. In some cases this can result in excessively large rule sets and/or rules with very low predictive power for previously unseen data. A smaller number of more general rules may have greater predictive accuracy on unseen data, at the expense of no longer correctly classifying some of the instances in the original training set. Alternatively, a similar level of accuracy may be achieved with a more compact set of rules.

Most work in this field to date has concentrated on generating classification rules in the intermediate form of a decision tree using variants of the TDIDT (Top-Down Induction of Decision Trees) algorithm [2].

A method for reducing overfitting in classification rules known as *J-Pruning* has previously been reported [3]. The method makes use of the value of the *J-measure*, an information theoretic means of quantifying the information content of a rule. The rules are *pre-pruned*, i.e. pruned as they are being generated.

In this paper the robustness of this technique in the presence of noise is examined.

H. Yin et al. (Eds.): IDEAL 2002, LNCS 2412, pp. 7-12, 2002.

A comparison is made between the results obtained from the unpruned and J-pruned versions of TDIDT for varying levels of noise added in a systematic fashion to three datasets from the UCI Repository of Machine Learning Datasets [4].

2   Overfitting of Classification Rules to Data

One approach to reducing overfitting, known as *post-pruning*, which is often used in association with decision tree generation, is to generate the whole set of classification rules and then remove a (possibly substantial) number of rules and terms, by the use of statistical tests or otherwise. An empirical comparison of a number of such methods is given in [5]. An important practical objection to post-pruning methods is that there is a large computational overhead involved in generating rules only then to delete a high proportion of them, especially if the training sets are large.

Pre-pruning a classification tree involves truncating some of the branches prematurely as they are being generated. Each incomplete branch (rule) such as

IF x = 1 AND z = yes AND q > 63.5 …. THEN …

corresponds to a subset of instances currently 'under investigation'. If not all the instances have the same classification the TDIDT algorithm would normally extend the branch to form a subtree by selecting an attribute to split on.

When following a pre-pruning strategy the subset is first tested to determine whether or not a termination condition applies. If it does not, a 'splitting attribute' is selected as usual. If it does, the branch (rule) is *pruned*, i.e. it is treated as if no further attributes were available and the branch is labeled with the most frequently occurring classification for the instances in the corresponding subset.

Reference [6] reports on experiments with four possible termination conditions for pre-pruning rules as they are generated by TDIDT, e.g. truncate each rule as soon as it reaches 4 terms in length. The results obtained clearly show that pre-pruning can substantially reduce the number of terms generated and in some cases can also increase the predictive accuracy, in all cases with a considerable reduction in computation time compared with generating complete trees. Although the results also show that the choice of pre-pruning method is important, it is not clear that (say) the same length limit should be applied to each rule, far less which of the termination conditions is the best one to use or why. There is a need to find a more principled choice of termination condition to use with pre-pruning, if possible one which can be applied completely automatically without the need for the user to select any 'threshold value' (such as the maximum number of terms for any rule). The *J-measure* described in [6] provides the basis for a more principled approach to pre-pruning.

3   Using the J-measure for Pre-pruning Classification Trees

The *J-measure* was introduced into the rule induction literature by Smyth and Goodman [7] who give a strong justification of its use as an information theoretic means of quantifying the information content of a rule that is soundly based on theory.

Given a rule of the form **If Y=y, then X=x**, the (average) information content of the rule, measured in bits of information, is denoted by $J(X;Y=y)$. The value of this quantity is the product of two terms:

- $p(y)$ The probability that the hypothesis (antecedent of the rule) will occur - a measure of *hypothesis simplicity*
- $j(X;Y=y)$ The *cross-entropy* - a measure of the *goodness-of-fit* of a given rule.

In what follows, it will be taken as a working hypothesis that a rule with a high J value (i.e. high information content) is also likely to have a high level of predictive accuracy for previously unseen instances.

There are several ways in which J values can be used to aid classification tree generation. One method, which will be called *J-pruning*, is to prune a branch as soon as a node is generated at which the J value is less than that at its parent.

Thus for example consider an incomplete rule

IF attrib1 = a AND attrib2 = b .... (with J-value 0.4)

which is expanded by splitting on categorical attribute *attrib3* into the three rules

IF attrib1 = a AND attrib2 = b AND attrib3 = c1 .... (with J-value 0.38)
IF attrib1 = a AND attrib2 = b AND attrib3 = c2 .... (with J-value 0.45)
IF attrib1 = a AND attrib2 = b AND attrib3 = c3 .... (with J-value 0.03)

Assuming that none of the new rules is complete (i.e. corresponds to a subset of instances with only one classification) all three would be considered as candidates for J-pruning. As the J-values of the first and third are lower than that of the original (incomplete) rule each rule would be truncated, with all the corresponding instances classified as belonging to the class to which the largest number belong. For example, the first new rule might become

IF attrib1 = a AND attrib2 = b AND attrib3 = c1 THEN Class = 5

The second new rule has a larger J-value than the original rule and in this case the TDIDT algorithm would continue by splitting on an attribute as usual.

The difficulty in implementing this method is to know which classification to use when calculating the J-value of an incomplete rule. If there are only two classes the value of J is the same whichever is taken. When there are more than two classes an effective heuristic is to generate the J-value for each of the possible classes in turn and then to use the largest of the resulting values.

Reference [3] compares the results obtained using the TDIDT algorithm both with and without J-pruning for 12 datasets, mainly taken from the UCI Repository [4]. The results were calculated using 10-fold cross-validation in each case. TDIDT was used with the Information Gain attribute selection criterion throughout.

For many of the datasets a considerable reduction in the number of rules was obtained using J-Pruning (e.g. from 357.4 unpruned to 25.9 J-pruned for *genetics* and from 106.9 unpruned to 29.6 J-pruned for *soybean*). Averaged over the 12 datasets the number of rules was reduced from 68.5 to only 19.1. The effect on the predictive accuracy of the generated rulesets varied considerably from one dataset to another, with J-pruning giving a result that was better for 5 of the datasets, worse for 6 and unchanged for one, the average being slightly lower with J-Pruning than without.

Although these results were very promising, an important criterion, not discussed in [3], for evaluating any classification rule generation algorithm is its *robustness*, particularly when noise is present in the data. This forms the topic of the next section.

4 Experiments with Noisy Datasets

Many (perhaps most) real-world datasets suffer from the problem of *noise*, i.e. inaccurately recorded attribute or classification values. Although the user of a rule generation algorithm will generally be unaware that noise is present in a particular dataset, far less the proportion of values that are affected, the presence of noise is likely to lead to an excessively large number of rules and/or a reduction in classification accuracy compared with the same data in noise-free form.

The robustness of the unpruned and J-pruned versions of the TDIDT algorithm to noise was investigated using the *vote* dataset from the UCI Repository [4]. The dataset comprises information about the votes of each of the members of the US House of Representatives on 16 key measures during 1984. The dataset has 300 instances, each relating the values of 16 categorical attributes to one of two possible classifications: *republican* or *democrat*. It seems reasonable to suppose that the members' votes will have been recorded with few (if any) errors, so for the purpose of these experiments the *vote* dataset in its original form will be considered noise-free.

From this dataset further datasets were created by contaminating the attribute values with progressively higher levels of noise. There were eight such datasets, named *vote_10*, *vote_20*, ..., *vote_80*, with the numerical suffix indicating the percentage of contaminated values.

The methodology adopted in the case of say *vote_30* was to consider the possibility of contaminating each attribute value in each instance in turn. For each value a random number from 0 to 1 was generated. If the value was less than or equal to 0.30 the attribute value was replaced by another of the valid possible values of the same attribute, selected with equal probability. The original classification was left unchanged in all cases. As the level of noise contamination increases from zero (the original dataset), through 10%, 20%, ... up to 80%, it is to be expected that (with any method) the predictive accuracy of any ruleset generated will decline, possibly severely.

Figure 1 shows the number of rules generated using the TDIDT algorithm (with the 'Information Gain' attribute selection criterion) in its standard 'unpruned' form and with J-pruning for each of the datasets *vote_10*, *vote_20*, ... *vote_80*. Figure 2 shows the corresponding levels of predictive accuracy for the two forms of the algorithm for the nine versions of the *vote* dataset. All results were calculated using 10-fold cross-validation. The J-pruned algorithm clearly produces substantially fewer rules with at least as good predictive accuracy as the unpruned version.

This experiment was repeated for two further datasets taken from the UCI Repository: *genetics* and *agaricus_lepiota*. The *genetics* dataset comprises 3,190 instances, each with 60 categorical attributes and 3 possible classifications. The *agaricus_lepiota* dataset comprises 5,644 instances (after those containing any missing values were removed), each with 22 categorical attributes and 2 possible classifications. These datasets were chosen partly because all the attributes were categorical. It was considered that categorical values were less likely to be wrongly (or imprecisely) recorded than continuous ones.

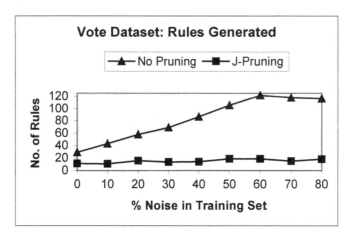

Fig. 1. Comparison of Number of Rules Generated: *vote* Dataset

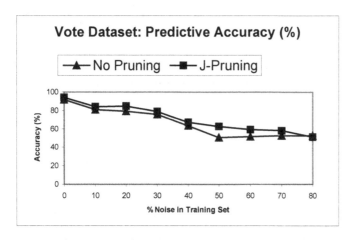

Fig. 2. Comparison of Predictive Accuracy: *vote* Dataset

The results of the experiments for these datasets (again calculated using 10-fold cross-validation) are given in Table 1, with values rounded to the nearest integer.

The reduction in the number of rules obtained using J-pruning increases substantially as the percentage of noise in the data increases. In the most extreme case, for *agaricus_lepiota_80*, the unpruned version of TDIDT gives 2916 rules and the J-pruned version only 19. The predictive accuracy obtained using J-pruning was better than that for the unpruned version of TDIDT in all cases where the proportion of noise exceeded 10%.

Table 1. Rules Generated and Predictive Accuracy: *genetics* and *agaricus_lepiota*

Noise	genetics				agaricus_lepiota			
	Rules		Accuracy (%)		Rules		Accuracy (%)	
%	Un-pruned	Pruned	Un-pruned	Pruned	Un-pruned	Pruned	Un-pruned	Pruned
0	357	26	89	78	15	10	100	100
10	918	122	73	72	349	96	96	95
20	1238	158	60	67	794	128	89	91
30	1447	185	54	64	1304	149	81	86
40	1652	175	44	60	1827	159	72	80
50	1815	163	36	55	2246	167	64	76
60	1908	165	33	52	2682	167	55	71
70	1998	153	29	51	3003	184	48	67
80	2074	179	27	48	2916	19	52	74

5 Conclusions

Overall these results clearly demonstrate that the J-pruning technique is robust in the presence of noise. Using J-pruning rather than the unpruned form of TDIDT (with attribute selection using Information Gain) will generally lead to a substantial reduction in the number of classification rules generated. This will often be accompanied by a gain in predictive accuracy. The advantage gained by using J-pruning becomes more pronounced as the proportion of noise in a dataset increases.

References

1. Hunt, E.B., Marin J. and Stone, P.J. (1966). Experiments in Induction. Academic Press
2. Quinlan, J.R. (1993). C4.5: Programs for Machine Learning. Morgan Kaufmann
3. Bramer, M.A. (2002). An Information-Theoretic Approach to the Pre-pruning of Classification Rules. Proceedings of the IFIP World Computer Congress, Montreal 2002.
4. Blake, C.L. and Merz, C.J. (1998). UCI Repository of Machine Learning Databases [http://www.ics.uci.edu/~mlearn/MLRepository.html]. Irvine, CA: University of California, Department of Information and Computer Science
5. Mingers, J. (1989). An Empirical Comparison of Pruning Methods for Decision Tree Induction. Machine Learning, 4, pp. 227-243
6. Bramer, M.A. (2002). Using J-Pruning to Reduce Overfitting in Classification Trees. In: Research and Development in Intelligent Systems XVIII. Springer-Verlag, pp. 25-38.
7. Smyth, P. and Goodman, R.M. (1991). Rule Induction Using Information Theory. In: Piatetsky-Shapiro, G. and Frawley, W.J. (eds.), Knowledge Discovery in Databases. AAAI Press, pp. 159-176

Data Mining for Fuzzy Decision Tree Structure with a Genetic Program

Dr. James F. Smith III

Naval Research Laboratory, Code 5741
Washington, D.C., 20375-5000
Telephone: 202.767.5358
jfsmith@drsews.nrl.navy.mil

Abstract. A resource manager (RM), a fuzzy logic based expert system, has been developed. The RM automatically allocates resources in real-time over many dissimilar agents. A new data mining algorithm that uses a genetic program, an algorithm that evolves other computer programs, as a data mining function has been developed to evolve fuzzy decision trees for the resource manager. It not only determines the fuzzy decision tree structure it also creates fuzzy rules while mining scenario databases. The genetic program's structure is discussed as well as the terminal set, function set, the operations of cross-over and mutation, and the construction of the database used for data mining. Finally, an example of a fuzzy decision tree generated by this algorithm is discussed.

1 Introduction

Modern naval battleforces generally include many different platforms, e.g., ships, planes, helicopters, etc. Each platform has its own sensors, e.g., radar, electronic support measures (ESM), and communications. The sharing of information measured by local sensors via communication links across the battlegroup should allow for optimal or near optimal decisions. The survival of the battlegroup or members of the group depends on the automatic real-time allocation of various resources.

A fuzzy logic algorithm has been developed that automatically allocates electronic attack (EA) resources in real-time. In this paper EA refers to the active use of electronic techniques to neutralize enemy equipment such as radar [1]. The particular approach to fuzzy logic that will be used is the fuzzy decision tree, a generalization of the standard artificial intelligence technique of decision trees [2].

The controller must be able to make decisions based on rules provided by experts. The fuzzy logic approach allows the direct codification of expertise forming a fuzzy linguistic description [3], i.e., a formal representation of the system in terms of fuzzy if-then rules. This has proven to be a flexible structure that can be extended or otherwise altered as doctrine sets, i.e., the expert rule sets change.

The fuzzy linguistic description will build composite concepts from simple logical building blocks known as root concepts through various logical connectives: "or", "and", etc. Optimization has been conducted to determine the form of the membership functions for the fuzzy root concepts and fuzzy decision tree structure.

H. Yin et al. (Eds.): IDEAL 2002, LNCS 2412, pp. 13-18, 2002.

The rule discovery procedure employed here is a type of data mining. Data mining is defined as the efficient discovery of valuable, non-obvious information embedded in a large collection of data [4]. A genetic program is used as a data mining function. A genetic program is a computer program that evolves other computer programs.

To be consistent with terminology used in artificial intelligence and complexity theory [5], the term "agent" will sometimes be used to mean platform, also a group of allied platforms will be referred to as a "meta-agent." Finally, the terms "blue" and "red" will refer to "agents" or "meta-agents" on opposite sides of a conflict, i.e., the blue side and the red side.

Section 2 briefly introduces the ideas of fuzzy set theory, fuzzy logic, fuzzy decision trees, and the five major components of the resource manager (RM). Section 3 discusses data mining and the use of a genetic program as a data mining function. Section 4 introduces the basic concepts of genetic programs. Section 5 describes the application of a genetic program as a data mining function that automatically determines fuzzy decision tree structure, i.e., how vertices and edges are connected and labeled in a fuzzy decision tree. This is equivalent to automatically generating fuzzy if-then rules. Section 5 concludes with a discussion of experimental results. Finally, section 6 provides a summary.

2   A Brief Introduction to Fuzzy Sets, Fuzzy Logic, and the Fuzzy RM

The RM must be able to deal with linguistically imprecise information provided by an expert. Also, the RM must control a number of assets and be flexible enough to rapidly adapt to change. The above requirements suggest an approach based on fuzzy logic. Fuzzy logic is a mathematical formalism that attempts to imitate the way humans make decisions. Through the concept of the grade of membership, fuzzy set theory and fuzzy logic allow a simple mathematical expression of uncertainty [6]. The RM requires a mathematical representation of domain expertise. The decision tree of classical artificial intelligence provides a graphical representation of expertise that is easily adapted by adding or pruning limbs. The fuzzy decision tree, a fuzzy logic extension of this concept, allows easy incorporation of uncertainty as well as a graphical codification of expertise [2]. Finally, a detailed discussion of the particular approach to fuzzy logic and fuzzy decision trees used in the RM is given in the literature [7].

The resource manager is made up of five parts, the isolated platform model, the multi-platform model, the communication model, the fuzzy parameter selection tree and the fuzzy strategy tree. As previously discussed the isolated platform model provides a fuzzy decision tree that allows an individual platform to respond to a threat. The multi-platform model allows a group of platforms to respond to a threat in a collaborative fashion. The communication model describes the means of communication or interaction between the platforms. The fuzzy parameter selection tree is designed to make optimal or near optimal selections of root concept parameters from the parameter database assembled during previous optimization with the genetic algorithm (GA) [7,8]. Finally, the strategy tree is a fuzzy tree that an agent uses to try to predict the behavior of an enemy. A more detailed discussion of the structure of the RM as well as explicit forms for fuzzy membership functions can be found in the literature [7,9].

3 Data Mining with Genetic Programs

The rule discovery procedures employed here are a component of a data mining operation. Data mining is defined as the efficient discovery of valuable, non-obvious information embedded in a large collection of data [4].

In previous papers [7,9] a GA was used as a data mining function to determine parameters for fuzzy membership functions. This section discusses a different data mining function, a genetic program [10] (GP). The GP data mines fuzzy decision tree structure, i.e., how vertices and edges are connected and labeled in a fuzzy decision tree. Whereas the GA based data mining procedures determine the parameters of and hence the form of fuzzy membership functions, the GP based procedure actually data mines fuzzy if-then rules.

The genetic program based techniques used here are efficient. The fuzzy rules extracted are certainly not a priori obvious, and the information obtained is valuable for decision-theoretic processes.

The application of the genetic program is actually part of the second step in a three-step data mining process. The first step is the collection of data and its subsequent filtering by a domain expert, to produce a scenario database of good quality. The second step involves the use of various data mining functions such as clustering and association, etc. During this step, the genetic program based approach is used to mine fuzzy rules from the database. These rules allow the fuzzy decision tree to form optimal conclusions about resource allocation. In the third and final step of the data mining operation, the RM's decisions are analyzed by a domain expert to determine their validity.

4 Genetic Programs

A genetic program is a problem independent method for automatically creating computer programs. Like a genetic algorithm it evolves a solution using Darwin's principle of survival of the fittest. Unlike the genetic algorithm, of which it can be considered an extension: its initial, intermediate, and final populations are computer programs.

Like a genetic algorithm the fittest individuals in the population are copied and subject to two operations, crossover and mutation. Crossover corresponds to sexual recombination, a kind of mating between parent computer programs. The crossover operation is constrained to produce structurally valid offspring. Finally, the mutation operation is a random change in a computer program that is part of the evolving population.

A genetic program requires the completion of five major steps before it can be used. The first step involves specifying a set of terminals. The terminals are the actual variables of the problem. These can include a variable like "x" used as a symbol in building a polynomial and also real constants. In the case the computer programs to be built are actually fuzzy decision trees, the terminal set might consist of root concepts that label the leaves of the tree. This is discussed in more detail in section 5.

5 Evolving the Fuzzy Kinematic-ID Subtree

This section discusses the automatic generation of a subtree of the RM's isolated platform decision tree (IPDT) using a GP to data mine a data base of military scenarios. The IPDT of the fuzzy RM has been extensively discussed [7,9]. The IPDT uses sensor data to make decisions about the threat status of an incoming platform. A platform may be an airplane, helicopter, ship, etc. Previous versions of the IPDT were constructed by hand based on human expertise.

Due to space limitations the fitness function, termination criteria, and population initialization are not discussed here. They will be described in detail in reference [11].

5.1 Data Base Construction

As in any data mining operation the first step is the construction of the data base that will be mined. The data base used for automatic construction of subtrees of the IPDT consists of sensor output for the various platforms involved in the engagement. Each record contains the range, bearing, elevation, ID information for the emitting platforms involved, etc. It also contains a number between zero and one, which represents an expert's opinion as to whether or not the emitter is attacking.

5.2 Terminal and Function Sets

To use the genetic program it is necessary to construct terminal and function sets relevant to the problem. The terminal sets used for construction of subtrees of the IPDT typically consist of one or more fuzzy root concepts [7]. A typical terminal set might be

$$T=\{close, heading\_in, ranging, banking, friend, lethal\} \ . \tag{1}$$

The root concept "close" is explained in reference [7]. The root concept of "heading_in" is similar to "close", but with range replaced by the emitter's heading in the root concept's membership function. "Ranging" and "banking" have fuzzy membership functions that are functions of the second time derivative of range and heading, respectively. The fuzzy membership function for "friend" gives the degree of membership of the detected platform in the concept "friend", i.e., how much confidence does blue have that the emitter is a friend. Finally, the membership function for the root concept "lethal" is found by summing the membership functions for all the foe classes. These concepts are explained in greater detail in the literature [9].

The function set, F, consist of the logical operations of "AND" and "OR" as well as the logical modifier "NOT", i.e.,

$$F=\{AND, OR, NOT\} \ . \tag{2}$$

5.3 Genetic Program Evolved IPDT Subtrees

Fig. 1 depicts the IPDT subtree considered for construction using GP based data mining. This subtree was originally drawn based on experts' intuition. A line on a vertex denotes the logical connective "AND", a vertex without a line indicates the logical connective "OR", and a circle on an edge denotes the logical modifier "NOT". The tree is read as "if close and not a friend or heading_in and not a friend then attacking." The root concepts are "close", "heading_in" and "friend". The composite concept is "attacking".

This subtree of the IPDT has been rediscovered by data mining a data base of military scenarios using a GP. Other more sophisticated trees have been discovered by GP based data mining, but this simple tree is considered here to illustrate the process. The fact that concepts like "ranging" and "banking" do not appear on the tree is related to the database used for the data mining procedure. There were no scenarios in the database that would make use of the "ranging" and "banking" concepts. The GP in many different runs was successful in constructing this subtree as expected, however, it did not always construct the same tree. Also, using different random seeds for each run, the number of generations required for the GP to stop varied. The GP's ability to construct the same subtree as that written down based on experts' rules provides a form of support for the subtree since it can be found in multiple ways. Finally, the GP's ability to construct other trees points up the potential non-uniqueness of the subtree.

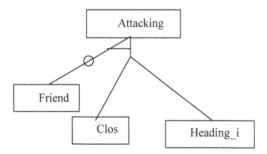

Fig.1. The IPDT subtree constructed by the GP

In one class of experiments the smallest number of generations required to generate the tree in Fig. 1 was three and the maximum 30. The maximum number of generations the GP could have run was 100. The GP, in one case, generated a tree different from the anticipated result in Fig. 1. This tree is under current examination and may prove to be superior to the subtree in Fig. 1.

The GP's ability to find different fuzzy decision trees for the same problem most likely relates to the military data base that is being data mined, the fitness function and the parameters characterizing convergence. These are subjects of current research.

6 Summary

A method for data mining fuzzy decision tree structure, and hence fuzzy if-then rules from military databases is introduced. This method uses a genetic program, an algorithm that automatically creates other computer programs, as a data mining function. The genetic program's structure is discussed as well as the terminal set, function set and the construction of the data base used for data mining. Finally, an example of a fuzzy decision tree generated by this algorithm is discussed.

Acknowledgements. The Office of Naval Research sponsored this project.

References

1. Schleher, D. C.: Electronic Warfare in the Information Age, Artech House, Boston (1999) Chapter 1
2. Molina Lopez, J.M., Jimenez Rodriguez, F.J., Casar Corredera, J.R.: Symbolic Processing for Coordinated Task Management in Multiradar Surveillance Networks in Fusion98, Proceedings of the International Conference on Multisource-Multisensor Information Fusion, Vol . II, CSREA Press, Las Vegas (1998) 725-732
3. Tsoukalas, L.H,. Uhrig, R.E.: Fuzzy and Neural Approaches in Engineering, John Wiley and Sons, New York (1997) Chapter 5
4. Bigus, J.P.: Data Mining with Neural Nets, McGraw-Hill, New York (1996) Chapter 1
5. Holland, J. H.: Hidden Order How Adaptation Builds Complexity, Perseus Books, Reading (1995) 1-15
6. Zimmerman, H. J.: Fuzzy Set Theory and its Applications, Kluwer Academic Publishers Group, Boston (1991) 11
7. Smith III, J.F, Rhyne, II, R.: A Resource Manager for Distributed Resources: Fuzzy Decision Trees and Genetic Optimization in Proceedings of the International Conference on Artificial Intelligence, IC-AI'99, Vol. II, CSREA Press, Las Vegas (1999) 669-675
8. Goldberg, D.E.: Genetic Algorithms in Search, Optimization and Machine Learning, Addison-Wesley, Reading (1989)
9. Smith III, J.F., Rhyne II, R. D.: Fuzzy logic resource manager: tree structure and optimization in Signal Processing, Sensor Fusion, and Target Recognition X, Vol. 4380, SPIE Proceedings, Orlando (2001) 312-323
10. Koza, J.R., Bennett III, F.H., Andre, D., Keane, M.A.: Genetic Programming III: Darwinian Invention and Problem Solving. Morgan Kaufmann Publishers, San Francisco (1999) Chapter 2
11. Smith III, J.F.: Genetic Program Based Data Mining, NRL Formal Report, Naval Research Laboratory, Washington D.C. 20375-5000, to be published, 2003.

Co-evolutionary Data Mining to Discover Rules for Fuzzy Resource Management

Dr. James F. Smith III

Naval Research Laboratory, Code 5741
Washington, D.C., 20375-5000
Telephone: 202.767.5358
jfsmith@drsews.nrl.navy.mil

Abstract. A fuzzy logic based expert system has been developed that automatically allocates resources in real-time over many dissimilar platforms. An approach is being explored that involves embedding the resource manager in an electronic game environment. The game allows a human expert to play against the resource manager in a simulated battlespace with each of the defending platforms being exclusively directed by the fuzzy resource manager and the attacking platforms being controlled by the human expert or operating autonomously under their own logic. This approach automates the data mining problem. The game automatically creates a database reflecting the domain expert's knowledge, it calls a data mining function, a genetic algorithm, for data mining of the data base as required. The game allows easy evaluation of the information mined in the second step. The criterion for re-optimization is discussed. The mined information is extremely valuable as indicated by demanding scenarios.

1 Introduction

A fuzzy logic algorithm has been developed that automatically allocates electronic attack (EA) resources in real-time. In this paper EA refers to the active use of electronic techniques to neutralize enemy equipment such as radar [1]. The particular approach to fuzzy logic that will be used is the fuzzy decision tree, a generalization of the standard artificial intelligence technique of decision trees [2].

The controller must be able to make decisions based on rules provided by experts. The fuzzy logic approach allows the direct codification of expertise forming a fuzzy linguistic description [3], i.e., a formal representation of the system in terms of fuzzy if-then rules. This will prove to be a flexible structure that can be extended or otherwise altered as doctrine sets, i.e., the expert rule sets change.

The fuzzy linguistic description will build composite concepts from simple logical building blocks known as root concepts through various logical connectives: "or", "and", etc. Optimization has been conducted to determine the form of the membership functions for the fuzzy root concepts.

The optimization procedures employed here are a type of data mining. Data mining is defined as the efficient discovery of valuable, non-obvious information embedded in a large collection of data [4]. The genetic optimization techniques used here are efficient, the relationship between parameters extracted and the fuzzy rules

H. Yin et al. (Ed.): IDEAL 2002, LNCS 2412, pp. 19-24, 2002.

are certainly not a priori obvious, and the information obtained is valuable for decision-theoretic processes. Also, the algorithm is designed so that when the scenario databases change as a function of time, then the algorithm can automatically re-optimize allowing it to discover new relationships in the data. The resource manager (RM) can be embedded in a computer game that EA experts can play. The software records the result of the RM and expert's interaction, automatically assembling a database of scenarios. After the end of the game, the RM makes a determination of whether or not to re-optimize itself using the newly extended database.

To be consistent with terminology used in artificial intelligence and complexity theory [5], the term "agent" will sometimes be used to mean platform, also a group of allied platforms will be referred to as a "meta-agent." Finally, the terms "blue" and "red" will refer to "agents" or "meta-agents" on opposite sides of a conflict, i.e., the blue side and the red side.

Section 2 will briefly introduce the ideas of fuzzy set theory, fuzzy logic, fuzzy decision trees, and five major components of the RM. Section 3 discusses optimization with a focus on genetic algorithms and data mining. Section 4 discusses co-evolution, related software, the co-evolutionary re-optimization criterion, the co-evolutionary stopping criterion and experimental results. Section 5 discusses examples of the RM's response for multi-platform scenarios that show the information data mined is extremely valuable. Finally, section 6 provides a summary.

2   A Brief Introduction to Fuzzy Sets, Fuzzy Logic, and the Fuzzy RM

The RM must be able to deal with linguistically imprecise information provided by an expert. Also, the RM must control a number of assets and be flexible enough to rapidly adapt to change. The above requirements suggest an approach based on fuzzy logic. Fuzzy logic is a mathematical formalism that attempts to imitate the way humans make decisions. Through the concept of the grade of membership, fuzzy set theory and fuzzy logic allow a simple mathematical expression of uncertainty [6]. The RM requires a mathematical representation of domain expertise. The decision tree of classical artificial intelligence provides a graphical representation of expertise that is easily adapted by adding or pruning limbs. The fuzzy decision tree, a fuzzy logic extension of this concept, allows easy incorporation of uncertainty as well as a graphical codification of expertise [2]. Finally, a detailed discussion of the particular approach to fuzzy logic and fuzzy decision trees used in the RM is given in reference [7].

Five major components of the RM are the isolated platform model, the multi-platform model, the communication model, the fuzzy parameter selection tree and the fuzzy strategy tree. As previously discussed the isolated platform model provides a fuzzy decision tree that allows an individual platform to respond to a threat [7]. The multi-platform model allows a group of platforms to respond to a threat in a collaborative fashion. The communication model describes the means of communication or interaction between the platforms. The fuzzy parameter selection tree is designed to make optimal or near optimal selections of root concept parameters from the parameter database assembled during previous optimization with the genetic algorithm. Finally, the strategy tree is a fuzzy tree that an agent uses to try to predict the behavior of an enemy. A more detailed discussion of the structure of the RM as well as explicit forms for fuzzy membership functions can be found in reference [7].

3 Optimization of the Root Concept's Parameters Using a Genetic Algorithm for Data Mining

The parameters of the root concept membership function are obtained by optimizing the RM over a database of scenarios using a genetic algorithm [8] (GA). Once the root concept membership functions are known, those for the composite concepts [7] follow immediately. At this point the necessary fuzzy if-then rules for the RM have been fully determined. A detailed discussion of the GA for data mining as well as the construction of the chromosomes and fitness functions are given in reference [7].

The application of the genetic algorithm is actually part of the second step in a three-step data mining process. The first step is the collection of data and its subsequent filtering by a domain expert, to produce a scenario database of good quality. The second step involves the use of various data mining functions such as clustering and association, etc. During this step, the genetic algorithm based optimization is used to mine parameters from the database. These parameters allow the fuzzy decision tree to form optimal conclusions about resource allocation. In the third and final step of the data mining operation, the RM's decisions are analyzed by a domain expert to determine their validity.

An alternate approach to constructing a database for re-optimization involves embedding the RM in a computer game. The game is designed so human EA experts can play it, in real-time against the RM. The game also allows the RM to be matched against computerized opponents running under their own autonomous logic. The game software records the events of the game for both cases, i.e., the RM's opponent is a human expert or a computerized agent. This record contributes to a database for re-optimization. Such a database is purer than one born of sensor data since environmental noise, sensor defects, etc., are not contaminating the data. This offers the advantage that the filtering stage of the data mining operation is simplified. The obvious disadvantage is that the database will be less representative of events in the real world, than one born of real sensor data taken during battle.

4 Co-evolutionary Data Mining

In nature a system never evolves separately from the environment that contains it. Both biological system and environment simultaneously evolve. This is referred to as co-evolution [9]. In a similar manner the fuzzy resource manager should not evolve separately from its environment, i.e., enemy tactics should be allowed to simultaneously evolve. Certainly, in real world situations if the enemy sees the resource manager employ a certain range of techniques, they will evolve a collection of counter techniques to compete more effectively with the resource manager.

4.1 Tools for Visualization of Data Mined Information

To facilitate data mining, co-evolution and validation of the RM, a software tool known as the scenario generator (SG) has been created. It automatically creates simulated blue and red platforms with user defined assets. It also creates a map or battlespace and automatically places the red and blue platforms in this space where they can interact. Each blue platform is controlled by its own copy of the fuzzy RM.

The SG has two modes of operation. In the computer vs. computer (CVC) mode each red platform is controlled by its own controller distinct from the fuzzy RM used by the blue platforms. In the second mode, the human vs. computer (HVC) mode, a human player controls a red platform through an interactive graphics user interface (GUI). There can be multiple red platforms. At each time step, the human player can control any of the red platforms, but only one of them per time step. Those red platforms not under human control run under their own logic as in the CVC mode.

4.2 Criterion for Re-optimization

The criterion for re-optimization is formulated based upon a determination that a particular parameter set has become ineffective. In the EA community, failure to delay, disrupt, or deny information that an enemy seeks can be the basis for labeling a parameter set ineffective. Outright loss of platforms is another simple measure of ineffectiveness that can be employed. Kindred to how humans change and replace strategies, the RM uses the re-optimization criteria as a point of re-building and re-construction of strategies. When the re-optimization criterion is triggered, a GA is called to re-optimize the root concepts of the decision and strategy trees. An explicit example of the re-optimization criterion for red and blue is discussed in subsection 4.4.

4.3 Stopping Criterion for Co-evolution

Just as with a genetic algorithm, in a co-evolutionary game based optimization, a stopping criteria must be defined. Upon completion of the game, several iterations of a particular scenario can be played. A criterion for re-optimization determines when the RM will re-optimize its parameters. This optimization is kindred to the scenario-based optimization discussed in reference [7], however the scenarios optimized over are recordings of the previous games since the last optimization. Since the re-optimization criterion determines how many scenarios the optimization is taking into account, this criterion is non-trivial.

4.4 A Simple Example of Co-evolutionary Optimization Using the Fuzzy Concept "close"

This subsection provides a simple example of co-evolutionary data mining using the fuzzy root concept "close." CVC and HVC co-evolution are considered as well as a comparison between the techniques.

The fuzzy membership function for the root concept close is discussed in detail in reference [7]. This membership function has three parameters to be determined. The parameters for close were initially determined using a genetic algorithm [7]. The fitness function used for initial optimization, i.e., before the beginning of the co-evolutionary process is described in references [7]. This fitness function is the zeroth' order fitness function for co-evolution.

For both HVC and CVC modes a loss by blue results in immediate re-optimization of blue's parameter set. In CVC mode a loss by red results in an immediate re-optimization of red's parameter set. The stopping criterion for re-optimization for both modes is a maximum number of co-evolutionary generations. A co-evolutionary generation refers to a single battle followed by re-optimization of red or blue.

A blue loss occurs if one of blue's agents is disabled, due to the successful delivery of a red missile. A probabilistic model determines the effectiveness of the fired missile. A blue win occurs if the blue agent group is able to delay red a certain number of time steps t. Finally, a red loss occurs if blue wins.

In HVC mode, the human player acting as a red agent can locate blue agents using a simulated radar display known as a PPI display. When a blue agent is located on the screen, the user clicks on the target region and presses the fire button located in the lower right hand corner to launch a missile.

It is found through computational experiments that the RM rapidly learns to beat human experts in HVC mode. Finally, in CVC mode the RM takes longer to learn to beat a computerized enemy than a human enemy, but the RM is exposed to many more strategies providing a more robust RM.

5   Improvements in the RM's Response through Data Mining

In this section examples of the fuzzy RM's ability to optimally allocate electronic attack resources are referenced. Examples of the RM's performance have been published [10] that show the information data mined is extremely valuable. The software described in subsection 4.1 is extremely useful for evaluation of the RM and determination of the value of information data mined in the second data mining step. By observing the RM's operation in movies, it can be seen that the RM's response is faster and more adaptive to change when the best parameter sets are used. In particular the ability of the RM to respond to late arriving threats, disabled allies and outright loss of platforms is greatly improved.

6   Summary

A fuzzy logic based resource manager (RM) for optimal allocation and scheduling of electronic attack resources distributed over many platforms is under development. Five components of the RM are discussed. Genetic algorithm based co-evolutionary data mining is introduced. Co-evolution refers to a process where both friend and foe agents and meta-agents simultaneously evolve in a complex simulated environment perceived by various sensors. Construction of the database, which is used for data mining and optimization was summarized. Two methods of co-evolution, computer versus computer (CVC) and human versus computer (HVC) were presented. CVC optimization involves evolution with a computer-controlled opponent; HVC optimization, with a human-controlled opponent or a human opponent and computerized opponents. Experimental results for each form of co-evolutionary optimization were discussed and a comparison of both methods was outlined. It was found in HVC optimization that the RM quickly learned to beat its human opponent. In CVC optimization, the RM's computerized opponent proved more resilient than a human player. The more resilient computerized opponent in CVC mode exposed the RM to more types of strategies with the potential for a more adaptive and robust RM. Examples of the resource manager's multi-platform response are referenced to illustrate the RM's excellent performance and as a method of determining the value of the information data mined.

Acknowledgements. This work was sponsored by the Office of Naval Research.

References

1. Schleher, D. C.: Electronic Warfare in the Information Age, Artech House, Boston (1999) Chapter 1
2. Molina Lopez, J.M., Jimenez Rodriguez, F.J., Casar Corredera, J.R.: Symbolic Processing for Coordinated Task Management in Multiradar Surveillance Networks in Fusion98, Proceedings of the International Conference on Multisource-Multisensor Information Fusion Vol . II, CSREA Press, Las Vegas, Nevada (1998) 725-732
3. Tsoukalas, L.H., Uhrig, R.E.: Fuzzy and Neural Approaches in Engineering, John Wiley and Sons, New York (1997) Chapter 5
4. Bigus, J.P.: Data Mining with Neural Nets, McGraw-Hill, New York (1996) Chapter 1
5. Holland, J. H.: Hidden Order How Adaptation Builds Complexity, Perseus Books, Reading (1995) 1-15
6. Zimmerman, H. J.: Fuzzy Set Theory and its Applications, Kluwer Academic Publishers Group, Boston (1991) 11
7. Smith III, J.F, Rhyne II, R.: A Resource Manager for Distributed Resources: Fuzzy Decision Trees and Genetic Optimization in Proceeding of the International Conference on Artificial Intelligence, IC-AI'99, Vol. II, CSREA Press, Las Vegas (1999) 669-675
8. Goldberg, D.E.: Genetic Algorithms in Search, Optimization and Machine Learning, Addison-Wesley, Reading (1989)
9. Cliff, D., Miller, G. F.: Co-evolution of Pursuit and Evasion II: Simulation Methods and Results in Proceedings of the Fourth International Conference on Simulation of Adaptive Behavior (SAB96), MIT Press Bradford Books, Cambridge (1996) 1-10
10. Smith III, J.F. Rhyne II, R.D.: A Fuzzy Logic Algorithm for Optimal Allocation of Distributed Resources in *Fusion 99: Proceednings of the Second International Conference on Information Fusion,* International Society of Information Fusion, San Jose (1999) 402-409

Discovering Temporal Rules from Temporally Ordered Data

Kamran Karimi and Howard J. Hamilton

Department of Computer Science
University of Regina
Regina, Saskatchewan
Canada S4S 0A2
{karimi, hamilton}@cs.uregina.ca

Abstract. We introduce a method for finding temporal and atemporal relations in nominal, causal data. This method searches for relations among variables that characterize the behavior of a single system. Data are gathered from variables of the system, and used to discover relations among the variables. In general, such rules could be causal or acausal. We formally characterize the problem and introduce RFCT, a hybrid tool based on the C4.5 classification software. By performing appropriate preprocessing and postprocessing, RFCT extends C4.5's domain of applicability to the unsupervised discovery of temporal relations among temporally ordered nominal data.

1 Introduction

We consider the problem of discovering relations among a set of variables that represent the state of a single system as time progresses. Given a sequence of temporally ordered records, with or without an explicit time variable, the goal is to identify as many cases as possible where two or more variables' values depend on each other. We may want to describe the system, predict future behavior, or control some of the variables by changing the values of other variables. For example, a description might be based on the observation that ($y = 5$) is always true when ($x = 2$). From this description, we could predict the value of y as 5 when we see that x is 2. This description is an example of *association* between two values, where observing the value of one variable allows us to predict the value another variable, without one necessarily causing the other. Alternatively, from the description, we could devise the rule: **if** {($x = 2$)} **then** ($y = 5$), and use forward chaining to predict that setting the value of x to 2 will result in y becoming 5. This rule can be interpreted as a *causal relation*.

Previous research has emphasized causality mining, time series, and event sequences. A *causality miner* attempts to generate a description of the causal relations in the data. TETRAD [13] and CaMML [8, 16] are two causality miners based on Bayesian networks [3]. The suitability of using Bayesian networks for mining causality is a continuing source of debate [4, 10, 15]. In [11] the author claims that it is possible to discover and express causality with mathematical tools, while in [2] the claim is that the ability to extract correct causal relations from any given set of

H. Yin et al. (Eds.): IDEAL 2002, LNCS 2412, pp. 25–30, 2002.
© Springer-Verlag Berlin Heidelberg 2002

observed data is doubtful. At the least, considerable disagreement exists about the concept of causality.

Interpreting association relations as causal relations, as done by applications such as TETRAD, requires justification. The main trend in causality mining involves using the statistical concept of conditional independence as a measure of the control one variable may have over another. For example, given the three variables x, y, and z, if x is independent from y given z, that is, $P(x, y \mid z) = P(x \mid z)$, then we can conclude that x is not a direct cause of y, and y is not a direct cause of x. In other words, z separates x and y from each other. This basic concept is used in Bayesian Networks to build graphs that show the conditional dependence of the variables under observation. This graph is then *interpreted* as signifying causal relations. The notion of conditional independence is void of time. The proponents of this mainstream method use temporal information, if it is available, to place constraints on the relationships among the variables (e.g., if we know x always appears before y, then y cannot be a cause of x), but time is not essential to the working of their algorithms. Leaving out time when dealing with the notion of causality seemed counterintuitive to us.

In this paper, we introduce the principles of RFCT's operation. RFCT [9] is a new hybrid tool based on the C4.5 classification software [12]. The name RFCT is a loose acronym for "Rotate, Flatten, apply C4.5, and enforce Temporal constraints." By performing appropriate preprocessing (rotation, and flattening) and postprocessing (applying temporal constraints), RFCT extends C4.5's domain of applicability to the unsupervised discovery of temporal relations among nominal data. We chose C4.5 because it is available in source code, and has been used widely in the literature.

The remainder of this paper is organized as follows. Section 2 formally presents the problem and the notation used in this paper. Section 3 introduces the RFCT method and software, and Section 4 concludes the paper.

2   Formal Representation of the Problem

Given a set of temporally ordered observation records $\mathbf{D} = \{d_1, \ldots, d_r\}$, the problem is to find a set of relations, as described in more detail below. Each record $d_t = <d_{t1}, \ldots, d_{tm}>$ gives the values of a set of variables $V = \{v_1, \ldots, v_m\}$ observed at time step t. Each relation predicts or constrains the value of one variable v_j, $1 \leq j \leq m$. The data values are assumed to be nominal, that is, symbolic values such as "yes," or numeric values, such as "1," representing different categories with no ordering defined among the values. It is assumed that no variable explicitly holds a time value. Unlike the real-world data studied by many researchers [1, 2, 14], we assume that a temporal order exists among the records.

The goal is to discover relationships among the past and present values of the variables. Of particular interest is any relation that can be specified as a rule that determines the value of some variable v_j at time t based on the previous or current values of the variables. The current value of v_j may not be used to determine its own value. If a rule predicts v_j's value at time step t based only on the values of other variables observed at time step t, then the rule is an *atemporal rule*. Alternatively, if the rule is based on the value of variables from previous time steps, it is called a *temporal rule*. Since one common sense definition of a causal relation involves the passage of time between the cause and the effect, we arbitrarily define such rules to specify causal relations. By this assumption, for a rule to be causal, the variables from the past must be indispensable; otherwise it will turn into an atemporal rule.

For any t, $1 \leq t \leq T$ we distinguish between the current time step t, and the previous time steps. We define the previous set $P(t) = \{d_{ki} \mid 1 \leq k \leq t, 1 \leq i \leq m\}$ to represent all observations made from time 1 to time t.

For practical reasons, we concentrate on a limited window of past observations. For any given time step t, the *window* includes the preceding w-1 time steps, plus the current time step, for a total of w time steps. We assume that only information in this window is relevant to predicting the value of some variable v_j at time t. The *window set* $P_w(t) = \{d_{ki} \mid w \leq t \ \& \ t\text{-}w+1 \leq k \leq t, 1 \leq i \leq m\}$ represents all observations in the window.

The *flattening* operator $F_w(t,D)$ takes as input a window size w, a current time t, $t \geq w$, and the input records D, and gives a single flattened record $z = \{z_{ki} \mid d_{pi} \in P_w(t) \ \& \ k = w\text{-}t+p \ \& \ z_{ki} = d_{pi}\}$. The flattened record contains the most recent w records. Given T input records, F_w can be applied with any t, $w \leq t \leq T$, thus turning the original T records into T-w+1 flattened records. Each flattened record contains mw fields.

The F_w operator renames the time index values so that in each record, time is measured relative to the start of that record only. In each flattened record, the time index ranges from 1 to w. The flattened records are thus independent of the time variable t. To create a variable corresponding to each member of a flattened record, we define the set $V_w = \{v_{ki} \mid 1 \leq k \leq w, 1 \leq i \leq m\}$. The variables in V_w correspond to w consecutive values of the variables in the set V. With mw members, V_w has a one to one correspondence with every flattened record z.

To use tools that do not consider any temporal order to be present among the input records, we flatten the T records and use the new T-w+1 records as input. Each flattened record contains all information available in a window of w time steps. The flattened records can thus be processed by a tool that ignores temporal relationships. Before flattening, time goes "down" to the next record, but after flattening, time moves horizontally within the same record, hence the name "flattening."

We look for a relation $R: S \rightarrow \{v_j\}$. The only restriction is that $v_j \notin S$. We consider S to be minimal, that is, there is no S' such that $S' \subset S$ and $R: S' \rightarrow \{v_j\}$. We define R to be of two different types:

- Atemporal: $R: S \rightarrow \{v_j\}, S \subseteq V - \{v_j\}$.
- Temporal: $R: S \rightarrow \{v_{wj}\}, S \subseteq V_w - \{v_{wj}\} \ \& \ S \cap (V_w - \{v_{w1}, ..., v_{wm}\}) \neq \emptyset$.

If S includes variables from only the current time step then we call R an atemporal relation. If S includes variables from previous time steps, then we call R a temporal relation. For such relations to be discovered, we assume that relations among data persist over time, and thus are repeatable. For the use of a time window to be justified, we assume that each relation is of limited duration. If we cannot prove that set S is minimal, then a specified temporal relation may actually be equivalent to an atemporal relation that can be found by eliminating unnecessary variables. In addition, we require the relation to obey the temporal order by referring to the variables according to the order of their appearance. This is clarified in Section 3.

3   Method

In this section, we describe RFCT's method for finding relations among variables in a single system. For a practical comparison of this method with TETRAD, see [5]. RFCT is an unsupervised variant of C4.5, a well-known decision rule and tree discoverer. Another rule discoverer could be used in RFCT instead of C4.5.

C4.5 first creates a decision tree that can be used to predict the value of one variable (the *decision attribute*) from the values of other variables (the *condition attributes*). C4.5 uses a greedy algorithm with one look-ahead step, based on information entropy of the condition attributes, to build a decision tree. Decision rules are derived from the decision tree with a program called "c4.5rules." After the rules have been created, the *consult* program in the C4.5 package can be used to execute the rules. It prompts for the condition attributes and then outputs the appropriate value of the decision attribute.

Each decision rule generated by C4.5 is equivalent to a simple predicate, such as **if** $\{(a = 1)$ **and** $(b = 2)\}$ **then** $\{(class = 4)\}$ [83.2%]. The variables a and b may be causing the value of *class*, or they may be associated with it because of some other reason. A certainty value, assigned to each rule, specifies the confidence of that rule. In the example rule just given, the certainty value is 83.2%. C4.5 has been modified to output its rules as Prolog statements, which can be executed by a Prolog Interpreter with little or no change [6, 7].

For our research, we created a modified version of C4.5, called C4.5T, which ensures that each decision rule references condition attributes in temporal order, and adds temporal annotations to both condition and decision attributes. An implicit assumption in C4.5 is that all condition attributes are available at the same time. As a decision tree is being built, the condition attributes may be used in any order. C4.5T performs two additional steps (listed below). To illustrate these steps, suppose the input consists of data records that contain the values of 4 variables: $<a, b, c, d>$, flattened with a time window of $w = 3$. Suppose C4.5 generates the decision rule: **if** $\{(a = 3)$ **and** $(b = 2)$ **and** $(c = 6)\}$ **then** $(d = 8)$, where condition attributes a and c are derived from the first unflattened record in the window, condition attribute b is derived from the second time step, and the decision attribute d is derived from the third. The two additional steps performed by C4.5T are as follows.

1.   Reorder the arguments in the rule, so that the attributes appear in the same temporal order as their respective unflattened records. For example, reorder the rule given above as: **if** $\{(a = 2)$ **and** $(c = 6)$ **and** $(b = 3)\}$ **then** $(d = 8)$.
2.   Add "At Time n:" before the attributes that happen at time step n in the flattened record. Intuitively, this can be considered the reverse of the flattening operation. For example, annotate the rule given above as follows:
     if {At Time 1: $(a = 2)$ **and** $(c = 6)$ **and** At Time 2: $(b = 3)$} **then** At Time 3: $(d = 8)$.

C4.5T has been implemented as a modification to c4.5rules, a program in the C4.5 Release 8 package that generates rules from decision trees, to output temporal rules. The user can specify the number of records involved in the flattening process via a new option -T (Time window). The modified c4.5rules program then generates the rules as usual, but before outputting them, it sorts the decision attributes of each rule according to their time of occurrence. It then prints out the rules, along with the temporal information as outlined in the example given above. We have also modified the c4.5 program (C4.5's decision tree builder) to consider the temporal order while building the tree [9].

The RFCT algorithm is introduced here.

Algorithm RFCT.

Input: a set of m variables V; a data set D consisting of T records with m values; and a window size w.

Output: a set of decision rules R.

for $j = 1$ to m

    D' = rotate the values in each record $d \in D$ such that value in v_j is the last member of d.

    $Flat$ = the sequence of values yielded by $F_w(t,D')$, for all t, $w \leq t \leq T$.

    $R = R \cup$ C4.5T($Flat$)

end for

return R

Since C4.5 is a supervised algorithm, the user must specify the decision attribute. To avoid providing this supervision, RFCT is set to apply C4.5T to every possible decision attribute in turn. Alternatively, the user can choose exactly which attributes should be considered as decision attributes. To allow temporal relations of up to w steps to be discovered, preprocessing using the flattening operator with window size w, is applied to the input. RFCT provides the user with temporal rules as its output.

4 Concluding Remarks

We introduced a new unsupervised learning tool called RFCT, which is based on C4.5 and relies on straightforward methods to extend its abilities. It is specifically meant for cases where data is generated sequentially by a single source. RFCT is not meant to replace software such as TETRAD, as its domain of applicability is more restrained (temporal output from a single source vs. data generated by many sources with no regard to the order in which they were gathered). RFCT is written in Java and runs in any environment that supports the Java runtime environment and has a graphical user interface, including Microsoft Windows and XWindow. The package includes full source code and online help, and is freely available from http://www.cs.uregina.ca/~karimi/downloads.html or by contacting the authors.

References

1. Bowes, J., Neufeld, E., Greer, J. E., Cooke, J., A Comparison of Association Rule Discovery and Bayesian Network Causal Inference Algorithms to Discover Relationships in Discrete Data, Proceedings of the Thirteenth Canadian Artificial Intelligence Conference (AI'2000), Montreal, Canada, 2000.
2. Freedman, D., Humphreys, P., Are There Algorithms that Discover Causal Structure?, Technical Report 514, Department of Statistics, University of California at Berkeley, 1998.
3. Heckerman, D., A Bayesian Approach to Learning Causal Networks, Microsoft Technical Report MSR-TR-95-04, Microsoft Corporation, May 1995.

4. Humphreys, P., Freedman, D., The Grand Leap, British Journal of the Philosophy of Science 47, pp. 113-123, 1996.
5. Karimi, K. and Hamilton, H.J., Finding Temporal Relations: Causal Bayesian Networks vs. C4.5, The Twelfth International Symposium on Methodologies for Intelligent Systems (ISMIS'2000), Charlotte, NC, USA, October 2000.
6. Karimi, K., Hamilton, H.J., Learning With C4.5 in a Situation Calculus Domain, The Twentieth SGES International Conference on Knowledge Based Systems and Applied Artificial Intelligence (ES2000), Cambridge, UK, December 2000.
7. Karimi, K., Hamilton, H.J., Logical Decision Rules: Teaching C4.5 to Speak Prolog, The Second International Conference on Intelligent Data Engineering and Automated Learning (IDEAL 2000), Hong Kong, December 2000.
8. Kennett, R.J., Korb, K.B., Nicholson, A.E., Seabreeze Prediction Using Bayesian Networks: A Case Study, Proc. Fifth Pacific-Asia Conference on Knowledge Discovery and Data Mining (PAKDD'01). Hong Kong, April 2001.
9. Karimi, K., Hamilton, H.J., RFCT: An Association-Based Causality Miner, The Fifteenth Canadian Conference on Artificial Intelligence (AI'2002), Calgary, Alberta, Canada, May 2002.
10. Korb, K. B., Wallace, C. S., In Search of Philosopher's Stone: Remarks on Humphreys and Freedman's Critique of Causal Discovery, British Journal of the Philosophy of Science 48, pp. 543-553, 1997.
11. Pearl, J., Causality: Models, Reasoning, and Inference, Cambridge University Press. 2000.
12. Quinlan, J. R., C4.5: Programs for Machine Learning, Morgan Kaufmann, 1993.
13. Scheines, R., Spirtes, P., Glymour, C. and Meek, C., Tetrad II: Tools for Causal Modeling, Lawrence Erlbaum Associates, Hillsdale, NJ, 1994.
14. Silverstein, C., Brin, S., Motwani, R., Ullman, J., Scalable Techniques for Mining Causal Structures, Proceedings of the 24th VLDB Conference, pp. 594-605, New York, USA, 1998.
15. Spirtes, P., Scheines, R., Reply to Freedman, In McKim, V. and Turner, S. (editors), Causality in Crisis, University of Notre Dame Press, pp. 163-176, 1997.
16. Wallace, C. S., Korb, K. B., Learning Linear Causal Models by MML Sampling, Causal Models and Intelligent Data Management, Springer-Verlag, 1999.

Automated Personalisation of Internet Users Using Self-Organising Maps

Yrjö Hiltunen and Mika Lappalainen

Pehr Brahe Software Laboratory, University of Oulu,
Rantakatu 8, FIN-92100 RAAHE, Finland
{yrjo.hiltunen, mika.lappalainen}@ratol.fi
http://www.pbol.org

Abstract. Automated personalisation offers a major improvement in the use of large Web sites. These systems learn from a user and suggest where on the Web site a user might move. Self-organising maps (SOM) may also be considered as a potential tool for Web data analysis. In this paper, the use of SOM analysis for automated personalisation of Internet users is demonstrated. The map was obtained by training a self-organising network with user demographics; click stream data were used to calculate the probabilities of user behaviour on the Web site. Thus, the map can be used for personalisation of users and to calculate the probabilities of each neuron in predicting where the user will next move on the Web site. The results indicate that SOM analysis can successfully process Web information.

1   Introduction

Personalisation involves designing a Web site to be more responsive to the unique and individual needs of each user [1-2]. Many of the largest commercial Web sites are already using systems to help their customers find products to purchase. These systems may be based on the demographics of the customer or on an analysis of the past buying behaviour of the customer as a prediction for future behaviour. One method of personalisation is to use artificial neural networks.

Recent applications have demonstrated that an artificial neural network (ANN) can provide an efficient and highly automated alternative data analysis [3-4]. Self-organising maps (SOM) are an efficient means of handling complex multidimensional data [5]. The aim of a SOM is to transform an n-dimensional input vector into a two-dimensional discrete map. The input vectors, which have common features, are projected to the same area of the map, e.g. to the same or neighbouring neurons. In this unsupervised ANN methodology the classes do not need to be pre-specified by the user, thus the SOM can be classified without previous *a priori* knowledge [5].

In this study, we applied self-organising maps to the automated personalisation of the Internet users on the basis of user demographics and clickstream data. This application is a good example of the capabilities of unsupervised neural network analysis.

H. Yin et al. (Eds.): IDEAL 2002, LNCS 2412, pp. 31-34, 2002.

2 Methods

2.1 Data Sets

Two different data sets were included in the study: (a) a database consisting of over 250 000 user demographics such as age, sex, education, profession, and dwelling place. The users described these demographics on their first visit to the Web site. (b) A logfile based on a sample of about 400 000 Web sessions over a period of 10 days. The Web site includes seven different pages as well as the mode of exit from the site, so each record in the file contains the complete set of pages visited in any session. The number of page visits during one session varied between 1 and 34. The logfile data were divided into two subsets. The first subset (the data of the first five days) was used for computing the access probabilities of each neuron. The second subset (the rest of the data) was the test set.

2.2 SOM Analysis

The user demographics were coded into 30 inputs for the SOM. All input values were between 0 and 1. One SOM was designed for personalisation, this had 100 neurons in a 10x10 hexagonal arrangement. Linear initialisation and batch training algorithms were used in the training of the map. A Gaussian function was used as the neighbourhood function. The map was trained with 50 epochs and the initial neighbourhood had a value of 3. The k-means algorithm was applied to the clustering of the map. The SOM Toolbox program (Version 2.0beta) was used in the analysis under a Matlab-software platform (Mathworks, Natick, MA, USA).

3 Results and Discussion

In this study, we used SOM analysis for personalisation of Internet users. The map for the demographic data presenting the total number of hits for each neuron is shown in Figure 1, together with the main clusters calculated by the k-means method. The main clusters consist of different types of users such as young students, well-educated males, people living in the countryside etc.

The page request probabilities of the site were determined using the logfile of the five days. The users of the file were personalised by the SOM based on their demographic data and at the same time the mean values of page access were upgraded during each session. The probabilities of each neuron were calculated for the 20 first accesses forming a 100*20*8 table. These probabilities make it possible to predict the user's behaviour before each page request. Thus, the number of the page access (between 1 and 20) and the best matching neuron (between 1 and 100) are used to choose the probabilities from the table. The probabilities of a page are shown in Figure 2. The size of each neuron visualises the probability values of this page. These values form two distinctly different areas. The first one is comprised of clusters 1 and 4 and the other one of clusters 2, 3, 5, 6 and 7 in Figure 1. This suggests that males are three times more likely to choose this page than females.

Using SOM analysis the demographic data have been linked to the logfile information. This model describes how the user with a certain profile will behave on average during any session. To test the model, the probabilities were also calculated using the other data set. These values were agreed with the previous ones, suggesting that the models are likely to be generic.

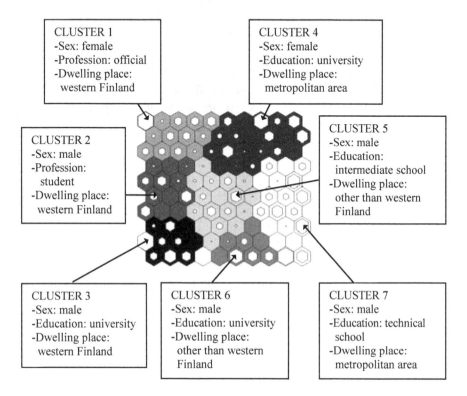

CLUSTER 1
-Sex: female
-Profession: official
-Dwelling place:
    western Finland

CLUSTER 4
-Sex: female
-Education: university
-Dwelling place:
    metropolitan area

CLUSTER 2
-Sex: male
-Profession:
    student
-Dwelling place:
    western Finland

CLUSTER 5
-Sex: male
-Education:
    intermediate school
-Dwelling place:
    other than western
    Finland

CLUSTER 3
-Sex: male
-Education: university
-Dwelling place:
    western Finland

CLUSTER 6
-Sex: male
-Education: university
-Dwelling place:
    other than western
    Finland

CLUSTER 7
-Sex: male
-Education: technical
    school
-Dwelling place:
    metropolitan area

Fig. 1. SOM of the demographic data showing the number of the hits on the size of the depicted neuron. The background colours visualise the main clusters of the map. Some example reference profiles related to the main clusters are shown.

Our SOM-based method provides a possible tool for personalisation and prediction of a user's behaviour. This method could be routinely utilised in the analysis of data and requires no extensive knowledge of neural nets. Thus, it can be included in any kind of Internet software; indeed, only reference vectors and a probability table are needed for this type of application. Furthermore, the SOM could be retrained, if new types of users visit the Web sites and the sites can then better serve the users. One further possibility is to make the service anonymous i.e. the user's profile is only on the user's computer not on the server. Thus, the users could not be identified, but the service providers would get statistical information from their customers.

4 Conclusion

Recent applications have shown that artificial neural network analysis can provide an efficient and highly automated method for data analysis [3-5]. Indeed, the analyses presented here demonstrate that ANN analysis can also be used for handling Internet information. The results demonstrate that SOM analysis allows extension of the automation procedure for personalisation of Internet users.

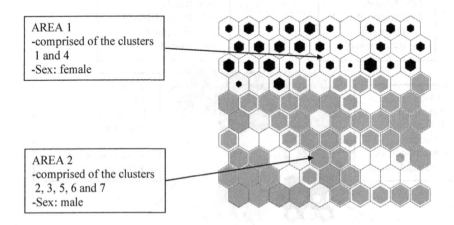

AREA 1
-comprised of the clusters 1 and 4
-Sex: female

AREA 2
-comprised of the clusters 2, 3, 5, 6 and 7
-Sex: male

Fig. 2. The probabilities of a Web page showing the size of the depicted neuron. The background colours visualise the areas of different probabilities.

Acknowledgments. This study was supported by the Jenny and Antti Wihuri Foundation.

References

1. Schafer, J. B., Konstan, J., Riedi, J.: Recommender systems in e-commerce. Proceedings of first ACM conference on Electronic commerce (1999) 158-166
2. Sarwar, B., Karypis, G., Konstan, J., Riedi, J.: Analysis of recommendation algorithms for e-commerce. Proceedings of 2nd ACM conference on Electronic commerce (2000) 158-167
3. Kaartinen, J.; Hiltunen, Y.; Kovanen, P. T.; Ala-Korpela, M.: NMR Biomed. **11** (1998) **1** 168-176
4. Hyvönen, M., Hiltunen, Y., El-Deredy W., Ojala, T., Vaara, J., Kovanen, P., Ala-Korpela, M.: Application of Self-Organizing Maps in Conformational Analysis of Lipids. J. Am. Chem. Soc. **123** (2001) 810-816
5. Kohonen, T.: Self-organizing Maps. Springer-Verlag, Berlin Heidelberg New York (2001)

Data Abstractions for Numerical Attributes in Data Mining

Masaaki Narita, Makoto Haraguchi, and Yoshiaki Okubo

Division of Electronics and Information Engineering
Hokkaido University
N-13 W-8, Sapporo 060-8628, Japan
{makoto,yoshiaki}@db-ei.eng.hokudai.ac.jp

Abstract. In this paper, we investigate *data abstractions* for mining association rules with numerical conditions and boolean consequents as a target class. The act of our abstraction corresponds to joining some consecutive primitive intervals of a numerical attribute. If the *interclass variance* for two adjacent intervals is less than a given admissible upper-bound ϵ, then they are combined together into an extended interval. Intuitively speaking, a low value of the variance means that the two intervals can provide almost the same posterior class distributions. This implies few properties or characteristics about the class would be lost by combining such intervals together. We discuss a bottom-up method for finding maximally extended intervals, called *maximal appropriate abstraction*. Based on such an abstraction, we can reduce the number of extracted rules, still preserving almost the same quality of the rules extracted without abstractions. The usefulness of our abstraction method is shown by preliminary experimental results.

1 Introduction

When data values processed by data mining algorithms are too concrete or too detailed, the computational complexity needed to find useful rules generally increases. At the same time, we find some difficulties in reading and analyzing the output rules, as they are written in terms of original data values. A notion of data abstraction seems useful to solve the problem of this kind. Here, by the term *data abstraction*, we mean an act of disregarding the differences among similar attribute values, where two or more attribute values are said similar if they share the properties needed to achieve the data mining task. In case of numerical attributes, a result of abstraction is normally represented by a family of wider intervals of consecutive primitive intervals [9]. Each extended interval after abstraction is viewed as an abstract value. Thus, data mining algorithms are required to extract some intervals with wider ranges and the rules should be described in terms of such extended intervals, as long as we consider data mining processes based on abstraction strategy.

The authors have already developed a method for abstracting categorical data expressed by nouns [7] and for revising a knowledge source for the abstraction [8]. This paper, on the other hand, aims to provide a method for abstracting numerical values, based on the same idea of data abstraction for categorical

H. Yin et al. (Eds.): IDEAL 2002, LNCS 2412, pp. 35–42, 2002.
© Springer-Verlag Berlin Heidelberg 2002

data. Actually, we consider a problem of finding association rules [1] of the form $A \in [a, b], \ldots \Rightarrow C = c$, where A is a numerical attribute, $[a, b]$ is an interval of real numbers, c is a class in a target attribute C for which we extract classification rules as in the above. To make our arguments simple, we assume without loss of generality that C is boolean and c is "yes/true".

Our basic strategy for data abstraction can be stated as follows:

Abstraction Formation Process: When posterior class distributions given primitive intervals are similar, we have no particular reason to distinguish them, provided every property or characteristic about the classes are captured by the class distributions. An abstraction that integrates some consecutive primitive intervals with their similar class distributions into an extended one is therefore considered to be *appropriate*.

Generalization of Database: We choose an appropriate abstraction, and obtain a generalized database [6] by replacing primitive intervals with the corresponding extended ones in the chosen abstraction.

Extracting Association Rules: Association rules with higher confidence values are extracted from the generalized database.

The actual performance of the above strategy depends on how we define the similarity notion. We can define it in various ways by using metric, mean squared error, interclass variance, conditional entropy, and so on. However, we choose in this paper the *interclass variance* by the following reasons: (P1) It can be easily computed. (P2) It can ignore minor distributions with low probability (weight). (P3) Both the mean squared error and the conditional entropy show similar behaviors to the interclass variance. The property (P2), not possessed by standard metric measures, is particularly important, as it contributes for obtaining a larger interval by ignoring minor and exceptional intervals.

Furthermore, we suppose a non-negative parameter, ϵ, as an allowable upper-bound of similarity error, the interclass variance, caused by connecting distinct intervals together. If $\epsilon = 0$, then nothing happens in our abstraction. On the other hand, as ϵ grows, the number of consecutive primitive intervals to be joined together increases. Particularly, minor intervals with low probabilities can be joined to the optimal intervals whenever the join operation still satisfies the allowable error bound, while the extension in this case violates the optimality as the confidence of the joined interval is less than the confidence of optimal interval. This is another point distinguishing our approach from the strategies based on optimality notions. The notion of appropriate abstraction is now defined as a grouping of consecutive primitive intervals within the allowable similarity error. User gives ϵ, and our system searches for a maximal appropriate abstraction in the lattice of possible abstractions. The lattice size is single exponential with respect to the number of primitive intervals of equal length. Our experimental results show that, given an adequate error bound ϵ, some meaningful abstractions are really found by putting the necessary part of lattice on memory in a 8G bytes machine.

2 Related Works

We can understand that some previous studies, [2,4,5] for example, perform abstraction of primitive intervals.

In [2], desirable intervals of numerical attributes are determined based on a parameter K (≥ 1), called a *partial completeness level*. Briefly speaking, an interval I is obtained by combining several consecutive base intervals $I_1, \cdots, I_l$ such that for each I_i, the support of I is at most K times the support of I_i, where I is referred to as a *generalization* of I_i. It has been proved that for any association rule R in terms of base intervals, there exists an association rule R' in terms of their generalizations. It should be noted here that the $sup(R)$ and $conf(R)$ are within ranges evaluated by $sup(R')$, $conf(R')$ and K. In this sense, the parameter K affects the amount of information loss w.r.t. support and confidence values of the original rules, caused by interval generalizations. The more K approaches to 1, the more the information loss decreases. Thus the process of generalizing (combining) intervals is controlled by just giving K.

However, the method by Srikant and Agrawal often suffers from base intervals containing small numbers of data. Let us assume we have two consecutive base intervals I_1 and I_2 and two association rules; $R_1 : A \in I_1 \Rightarrow C =$ yes and $R_2 : A \in I_2 \Rightarrow C =$ yes. If $sup(A \in I_2)$ is much smaller than $sup(A \in I_1)$, then I_1 and I_2 are never generalized. In such a case, however, we often prefer to have the generalized interval $I_1 \cup I_2$ and obtain a rule $R' : A \in I_1 \cup I_2 \Rightarrow C =$ yes, considering the data belonging to I_2 and $C =$ yes as *exceptions*. The generalization is never allowed in their method unless a large K is given. According to our method, on the other hand, such minor data are adequately considered as exceptions and are absorbed into such a generalized interval. It is a remarkable advantage of our method.

The literature [4,5] also perform abstractions of primitive intervals by using the following notions of optimality:

Optimized Range [4]: Given a series of consecutive primitive intervals $I_1, ..., I_n$ in the order of numerical values, find a range, a union of sequential intervals $I = \cup_{i=j}^{k} I_i$, such that it maximizes the *interclass variance* of C_I and C_{I^c}, where C_J denotes a posterior class distribution given an interval J.

Optimized Confidence Rule [5]: Given a minimum support $minsup$, find an interval of consecutive buckets such that it has the maximum confidence among those whose support is greater than $minsup$, where the buckets are primitive intervals involving almost the same number of data in them.

The extraction processes of intervals based on theses criterions include an operation for joining several consecutive small intervals or buckets sharing similar posterior class distributions. In case of optimized confidence rules, consecutive buckets $I_\ell, I_{\ell+1}, ..., I_k$ of high confidence have similar posterior class distributions, and they form a joined interval $I_\ell \cup I_{\ell+1} \cup \cdots \cup I_k$ to be described in the output rule. However, some intermediate buckets with low confidence, dissimilar to the buckets with high confidence, may be included in the joined intervals to achieve the minimum support condition. Completely similar situations are also incidental to the problem of finding the optimized range. In spite of these facts, we pay our attention to more about the function of putting similar buckets or primitive intervals together. This is simply because we regard the similarity notion as a semantic constraints to form *semantically meaningful* intervals, not captured by the standard criterion described in terms of support and confidence.

Data abstractions are closely related to the task of *data clustering* in the sense that both of them try to find meaningful groups of data. A distinct difference can be stated as follows. Although many clustering methods have been proposed, e.g. see [11], each of them usually computes just one clustering result (grouping) at once. On the other hand, our method can obtain a number of maximal abstractions, that is, several ways of groupings. Such a behavior is a remarkable advantage over clustering methods, since it can provide several interpretations of the data for users and they will understand the data from several viewpoints.

3   Preliminaries

Let $R = (A_1, \dots, A_n)$ be a relational schema, where A_i is a *numerical attribute*. We consider in this paper a relational database $\mathcal{D}_R$ that is given as a set of tuples $t = (v_1, \dots, v_n)$ such that $v_i \in \mathcal{I}_{A_i}$, where $\mathcal{I}_{A_i}$ is the interval of A_i. For a tuple t in $\mathcal{D}_R$, its value of A_i is referred to as $t[A_i]$. We additionally assume a boolean attribute C with the domain $\{\text{yes}, \text{no}\}$, called a *target attribute*, and each tuple $t \in \mathcal{D}_R$ has its C-value. A tuple t is said to belong to the *class* of yes (no) iff $t[C] = \text{yes}$ ($t[C] = \text{no}$). For a numerical attribute A, we assume that $\mathcal{I}_A$ is given as an ordered set of m *primitive intervals*, $I_1, \dots, I_m$, in the order of numerical values. A subset I of $\mathcal{I}_A$ defined as a concatenation of some consecutive primitive intervals is called a *subinterval* of $\mathcal{I}_A$, that is, $I = \cup_{i=j}^{k} I_i$.

The probability of a tuple $t \in \mathcal{D}_R$, $\Pr(t)$, is given by a uniform distribution, $\Pr(t) = 1/|\mathcal{D}_R|$, where $|S|$ is the number of elements in a set S. Then, each attribute A in the relational schema is regarded as a random variable: $\Pr(A \in I) = \Pr(\{t \in \mathcal{D}_R \mid t[A] \in I\}) = |\{t \in \mathcal{D}_R \mid t[A] \in I\}|/|\mathcal{D}_R|$, where I is a subinterval of $\mathcal{I}_A$. The value $\Pr(A \in I)$ is often referred to as the *support* of I, denoted by $sup(I)$. The event $A \in I$ is also called a *numerical condition* and A is called a *condition attribute*. We say that a tuple $t \in \mathcal{D}_R$ *satisfies* the condition iff $t[A] \in I$.

Given a target attribute C, we try to find *association rules* of the form $r = C_1 \wedge \cdots \wedge C_l \Rightarrow (C = \text{yes})$, where C_i is a numerical condition. The *support* of r, $sup(r)$, is defined as $sup(r) = \Pr(\bigcap_{i=1}^{l} C_i \cap C = \text{yes})$. Furthermore, the *confidence* of r, $conf(r)$, is defined as $conf(r) = \Pr(\bigcap_{i=1}^{l} C_i \cap C = \text{yes}) / \Pr(\bigcap_{i=1}^{l} C_i)$, that is, the conditional probability of $C = \text{yes}$ given the numerical conditions.

4   Mining Association Rules with Data Abstractions

We discuss here a method for mining association rules with data abstractions for numerical attributes.

4.1   Selecting Condition Attributes

In order to find useful association rules, we have to decide which attributes should be used for their numerical conditions. Our selection of condition attributes is carried out based on the notion of *information gain* [1], as has been adopted in C4.5 [3].

Let C be a target attribute and A be a numerical attribute with its interval consisting of m primitives, $I_1, \ldots, I_m$. The *information gain* of C given A, denoted by $I(C; A)$, is defined as the difference the entropy of C minus the conditional entropy C given A: $I(C; A) = H(C) - H(C|A)$, where $H(C) = -\Pr(C = \text{yes}) log_2 \Pr(C = \text{yes}) - \Pr(C = \text{no}) log_2 \Pr(C = \text{no})$ and $H(C|A) = \sum_{i=1}^{m} \Pr(A \in I_i) H(C|A \in I_i)$. Intuitively speaking, an attribute providing a higher gain has more potential ability to discriminate the classes. Thus, as a condition attribute, we select A^* from our relational schema $R = (A_1, \ldots, A_n)$ such that $A^* = \arg \max_{A_i \in R} I(C; A_i)$.

4.2   Finding Appropriate Data Abstractions

Let A be a condition attribute with its interval consisting of m primitive intervals, $I_1, \ldots, I_m$. Here, we try to make numerical conditions for A.

Although for each primitive interval I_i, we can consider a numerical condition $A \in I_i$, the rules with such conditions would be undesirable in the sense that they are too concrete or too detailed. In order to extract useful rules, it is required to adequately divide the whole interval into a number of subintervals that can provide more meaningful conditions. Such an interval division can be viewed as a *data abstraction for A*.

A data abstraction for A, φ_A, is considered as a grouping of the primitive intervals, that is, a partition of the set of primitive intervals, $\{g_1, \ldots, g_l\}$, where each group g_i consists of a number of consecutive primitives, $I_j, \ldots, I_k$, and gives a subinterval $I_{g_i} = \bigcup_{i=j}^{k} I_i$.

For a data abstraction φ, if a data abstraction φ' can be obtained by combining two adjacent subintervals in φ, then we say that φ precedes φ', denoted by $\varphi \preceq \varphi'$. The set of possible data abstractions forms a lattice, called an *abstraction lattice*, under the ordering. By searching in the lattice, we can find useful abstractions with meaningful subintervals. The number of possible abstractions for A is given by $\sum_{i=0}^{m-1} {}_{m-1}C_i = 2^{m-1}$, where m is the number of primitive intervals of A. Although the order is exponential, the authors consider that the search space might be often tractable, since even a personal computer often has its main memory of a few G-bytes nowadays.

Our actual search in the lattice is carried out in a bottom-up manner. That is, any two adjacent intervals is combined together step-by-step to form an extended interval. In order to obtain meaningful extension, our process of combining intervals is basically performed as follows: if two adjacent intervals give similar class

---

[1] It is also known as *mutual information*.

distributions [2], then they are combined together into an extended interval. It should be noted here that such an extended interval can give a class distribution that is almost the same as ones by the original two intervals. In this sense, no property or characteristic about the class would be lost by the abstraction.

Our similarity measure of class distributions is based on a variance between classes of intervals, called an *interclass variance* [4]. Let A be an attribute with an interval consisting of m subintervals, $I_1, \ldots, I_m$. Consider a 2-partition of $\{I_1, \ldots, I_m\}$, $\{C, D\}$, where C and D are called *interval classes*. Then the interclass variance between C and D, denoted by $V(C, D)$, is defined as $V(C, D) = \frac{sup(C)(conf(C) - conf(C \cup D))^2 + sup(D)(conf(D) - conf(C \cup D))^2}{sup(C) + sup(D)}$, where for an interval class S, $sup(S) = \sum_{I \in S} sup(I)$ and $conf(S) = conf(A \in \bigcup_{I \in S} I \Rightarrow C = \text{yes})$.

Given two intervals I and J we try to combine, we compute the variance $V(\{I\}, \{J\})$. If the value is less than a given threshold ϵ, then they are combined into an extended interval $I \cup J$. This combining process is iterated until no adjacent intervals can be combined together and the *maximal* ones are output as most *appropriate* in the sense that they provide meaningful intervals as wide as possible. Among maximal ones, we select one with the fewest subintervals.

4.3   Extracting Association Rules

Let A be an attribute with its interval $\mathcal{I}$ and $\varphi^* = \{g_1, \ldots, g_k\}$ be a maximal abstraction for A obtained at the previous step. In order to identify numerical conditions for association rules, we first try to divide the intervals I_{g_i} into two classes for which the interclass variance is maximized. More precisely speaking, it corresponds to finding a boundary δ^* such that $\delta^* = \arg\max_{\delta \in \mathcal{I}} V(C_{\geq \delta}, C_{< \delta})$, where $C_{\geq \delta} = \{I_{g_i} \mid g_i \in \varphi^* \wedge conf(\{I_{g_i}\}) \geq \delta\}$ and $C_{< \delta} = \{I_{g_i} \mid g_i \in \varphi^* \wedge conf(\{I_{g_i}\}) < \delta\}$. Then a number of association rules are extracted based on the interval class $C_{\geq \delta^*}$. For each $I \in C_{\geq \delta^*}$, we construct an association rule of the form $A \in I \Rightarrow C = \text{yes}$.

4.4   Extracting Rules with Multiple Conditions

Association rules with multiple conditions can be easily obtained. Suppose we have a rule $C_1 \Rightarrow C = \text{yes}$, where C_1 is a numerical condition. In order to identify one more condition attribute, we consider $C_1 \wedge C = \text{yes}$ as a target class. For the new target class, the same procedure for attribute selection can be performed and then a condition attribute A' is obtained. Introducing a condition C' for A', we will obtain a rule $C_1 \wedge C' \Rightarrow C = \text{yes}$.

5   Experimental Results

This section presents our preliminary experimental results. Our system based on the abstraction method has been implemented in C and run on a Sun Blade 1000

---

[2] A *class distribution* given by an interval I is a conditional probability of $C = \text{yes}$ given the interval. That is, it corresponds to the confidence of an association rule $A \in I \Rightarrow C = \text{yes}$.

Table 1. Confidence values

Num. of conditions	1	2	3
System in [4]	56.30 %	59.06 %	61.30 %
Our system	56.30 %	62.95 %	63.50 %

workstation (UltraSPARC-III 750MHz, 8GB memory). We try to extract association rules from a database, *Forest Cover Type*, in *The UCI KDD Archive* [10]. The database consists of 581012 tuples with 54 attributes of which 10 attributes are numerical. Association rules for a target class Rawah_Wilderness_Area = yes with at most three numerical conditions are extracted, where the interval of each attribute consists of 50 primitives and the threshold of admissible interclass variance ϵ is set to 0.0003. Our rules are compared in confidence values with ones extracted by a system previously proposed in the literature [4]. For each attribute, the system computes a data abstraction with just two subintervals by which the interclass variance is maximized. As shown in Table 1, our method could find more confident rules for each case.

6 Concluding Remarks

We investigated *data abstractions* for numerical attributes. A method for finding maximal abstractions in a bottom-up manner was discussed. The basic idea of our data abstraction is to combine adjacent intervals giving similar class distributions into an extended interval. The similarity is measured by the interclass variance between interval classes. Since a low value of the variance means that the interval classes show similar class distributions, combining them together loses few properties or characteristics about the target class. The combining process can be controlled by giving an adequate threshold ϵ for our admissible variance. Some preliminary experimental results showed an effectiveness of our abstraction framework.

We are currently investigating relationships among the methods in [2,4,5] and ours from empirical and theoretical viewpoints further. By the investigation, we will be able to give more convincing characterization of our method.

References

1. R. Agrawal, R. Srikant: Fast Algorithms for Mining Association Rules, *Proc. of the 20th Int'l Conf. on Very Large Data Bases,* pp. 478–499, 1994.
2. R. Srikant and R. Agrawal: Mining Quantitative Association Rules in Large Relational Tables, Proc. of the ACM SIGMOD Int'l. Conf. on Management of Data, pp. 1–12, 1996.
3. J. R. Quinlan: *C*4.5: Programs for Machine Learning, *Morgen Kaufmann,* 1993
4. Y. Morimoto, H. Ishii and S. Morishita: *Efficient Construction of Regression Trees with Range and Region Splitting, Proc. of the 23rd VLDB Conf.,* pp.166-175, 1997.
5. T. Fukuda, Y. Morimoto, S. Morishita and T. Tokuyama: Mining Optimized Association Rules for Numeric Attributes, *Proc. of the 15th ACM symposium on Principles of Database Systems,* pp. 182–191, 1996.

6. J. Han and Y. Fu: *Attribute-Oriented Induction in Data Mining.* In Advances in Knowledge Discovery and Data Mining (Fayyad, U.N. et.al. eds.), pp.399-421, 1996.

7. Y. Kudoh and M. Haraguchi: Detecting a Compact Decision Tree Based on an Appropriate Abstraction Proc. of 2nd Int'l. Conf. on Intelligent Data Engineering and Automated Learning, LNCS-1983, pp.60–70, 2000.

8. Y. Okubo, Y. Kudoh and M. Haraguchi: Constructing Appropriate Data Abstractions for Mining Classification Knowledge Proc. of the 14th Int'l. Conf. on Application of Prolog, pp.275–284, 2000.

9. M. P. Wellman and CL. Liu: State-Space Abstraction for Anytime Evaluation of Probabilistic Networks, *Uncertainty in Artificial Intelligence,* pp. 567–574, 1994.

10. S. Hettich and S. D. Bay: The UCI KDD Archive, http://kdd.ics.uci.edu, Univ. of California, Dept. of Information and Computer Science, 1999.

11. D. Fasulo: An Analysis of Recent Work on Clustering Algorithms, http://www.cs.washington.edu/homes/dfasulo/clustering.ps, 1999.

Calculating Aggregates with
Range-Encoded Bit-Sliced Index

Kashif Bhutta

University of Windsor, bhutta@uwindsor.ca

Abstract. This paper proposes, for query optimizing on Data warehouses, the use of range-encoded bitmap index to calculate aggregates. By using space optimal range-encoded bitmap index for range and aggregate predicates, the need of separate indexes for these operations can be eliminated. The proposed algorithm also uses the population ratio of 1's in a bitmap to decide whether the bitmap has to be scanned from the disk at all; thus exploiting the opportunity of skipping many bitmap scans since processing them does not affect the solution. These optimizations result in significant improvement in query evaluation time.

1 Introduction

Database management systems are widely accepted as standard tools for manipulating large volumes of data. To enable fast access to stored data according to its content, databases use structures known as indexes. The disk access is the most expensive operation of query evaluation process. The goal of indexing is to minimize the number of disk access operations either by minimizing the number of accesses for reading the data or by evaluating query by indexes only, without accessing the database at all. Bit-Sliced index and the projection index are such examples of indexes.

1.1 Bit-Sliced Index

A bit-sliced index (also referred to as binary bit-sliced index) of an attribute is a bit-wise projection of that attribute. The projection index simply is the projection of an attribute with duplicates preserved and stored with the same Record ID (RID) numbers. The bit-sliced index stores a set of bitmap slices, which are orthogonal to the data held in a Projection index. The following example illustrates Bit-sliced index:

Consider a table *SALE* that contains all records about sales made during the past month by individual stores of a large chain. The table has an attribute *dollar_amt* representing the transaction amount of a sale. For simplicity, without losing generality we assume that *dollar_amt* attribute has a *short* data type. A small fact table *SALE* is presented in figure 1 with 20 tuples. A bit-sliced index on *dollar_amt* attribute is presented in figure 2.

In bit-sliced index the values of a projection index are represented in their binary equivalent and they are stored in slices of bits on disk. The number of bitmaps in a

H. Yin et al. (Eds.): IDEAL 2002, LNCS 2412, pp. 43-49, 2002.

binary bit-sliced index is equal to the length of the attribute's data type in bits, and the length of each bitmap is equal to the cardinality of the indexed table. In our example, a *short* data type is 16 bits long, so the bit-sliced index on *dollar_amt* attribute has 16 bitmaps with each having a length of 20 bits, since the cardinality of fact table is 20.

1.2 Bitmap Encoding Schemes

The bitmap indexes are stored by different encoding schemes to optimize their performance. The most important encoding schemes are the *equality-encoding* and *range-encoding*. If an attribute has cardinality b_i, the representation of value v_i in an *equality-encoding* scheme has bi bits, one for each possible value. The representation of value v_i has all bits set to 0, except for the bit corresponding to v_i, which is set to 1. For a *range-encoding* scheme, there are b_i bits again, one for each possible value. The representation of value v_i has the v_i rightmost bits set to 0 and the remaining bits (starting from the one corresponding to v_i and to the left) set to 1. Intuitively, each bitmap b_{vi} has 1 in all records whose i^{th} value is less than or equal to v_i. Since the bitmap B_{bi-1} has all bits set to 1, it is not needed to be stored. So, a range-encoded index consists of $(b_i - 1)$ bitmaps. See [2] for more comprehensive examples of encoding schemes. The bitmap indexes can be split into more than one component for optimization purposes.

RID	product_Id	customer_Id	dollar_amt
001	120	C25	970
002	122	C25	860
003	120	C26	950
004	121	C28	041
005	120	C25	870
006	130	C37	859
007	123	C22	847
008	120	C40	272
009	125	C32	182
010	130	C10	945
011	123	C28	864
012	120	C40	NULL
013	120	C20	950
014	121	C28	027
015	125	C33	426
016	130	C18	994
017	130	C32	559
018	123	C02	NULL
019	120	C44	283
020	125	C30	782

Fig. 1. Fact table SALE with 20 tuples

B_{15}	B_{14}	B_{13}	B_{12}	B_{11}	B_{10}	B_9	B_8	B_7	B_6	B_5	B_4	B_3	B_2	B_1	B_0
0	0	0	0	0	0	1	1	1	1	0	0	1	0	1	0
0	0	0	0	0	0	1	1	0	1	0	1	1	1	0	0
0	0	0	0	0	0	1	1	1	0	1	1	0	1	1	0
0	0	0	0	0	0	0	0	0	0	1	0	1	0	0	1
0	0	0	0	0	0	1	1	0	1	1	0	0	1	1	0
0	0	0	0	0	0	1	1	0	1	0	1	1	0	1	1
0	0	0	0	0	0	1	1	0	1	0	0	1	1	1	1
0	0	0	0	0	0	0	1	0	0	0	1	0	0	0	0
0	0	0	0	0	0	0	0	1	0	1	1	0	1	1	0
0	0	0	0	0	0	1	1	1	0	1	1	0	0	0	1
0	0	0	0	0	0	1	1	0	1	1	0	0	0	0	0
0	0	0	0	0	0	0	0	0	0	0	0	0	0	0	0
0	0	0	0	0	0	1	1	1	0	1	1	0	1	1	0
0	0	0	0	0	0	0	0	0	0	0	1	1	0	1	1
0	0	0	0	0	0	0	1	1	0	1	0	1	0	1	0
0	0	0	0	0	0	1	1	1	1	1	0	0	0	1	0
0	0	0	0	0	0	1	0	0	0	1	0	1	1	1	1
0	0	0	0	0	0	0	0	0	0	0	0	0	0	0	0
0	0	0	0	0	0	0	1	0	0	0	1	1	0	1	1
0	0	0	0	0	0	1	1	0	0	0	0	1	1	1	0

Fig. 2. Bit-Sliced index on dollar_amt for fact table SALE

The number of components and encoding scheme can be decided at design time to optimize the performance of an index.

2 Evaluating Range and Aggregates with Bit-Sliced Index

O'Neil and Quass [5] have proposed an algorithm for efficiently evaluating *sum, count*, and *average* of an attribute using bit-sliced index. In most cases, bit-sliced index is more space efficient and outperforms the traditional value-list and projection indexes. When it comes to evaluating *sum, average*, or *count* aggregates like *SELECT SUM (dollar_amt) FROM SALES WHERE <condition>*, bit-sliced index gives the best performance.

For the rest of our discussion, we assume that we are given the fact table *SALE* presented in figure 1 and bit-sliced index on *dollar_amt* attribute presented in figure 2. When the algorithm is executed, the bitmaps B_f and B_{nn} are scanned from the disk and if a non-null value is present in the foundset, all 16 bitmaps of bit-sliced index are scanned one by one. Since it is assumed that B_f remains in memory for the rest of the processing, so there are total of eighteen bitmap scans. There are total seventeen *AND* operations performed on those bitmaps and then seventeen *COUNT* operations on the result of those *AND* operations. Since these operations are much less expensive than a bitmap scan, especially the *COUNT* operation, so these operations have less significant effect on the performance of an indexing scheme. This algorithm performs best for aggregates; refer to [5] for the comparative analysis of bit-sliced index with other techniques. The main disadvantage of this algorithm is that it scans all the bitmaps whether they are needed or not. For example if a bitmap is stored in index and has all zero's in it, scanning and processing of that bitmap does not affect the solution (*SUM*) and that could have been avoided.

The binary base bit-sliced index does not provide a good performance for range queries of the type (i.e., A *op* v | *op* $\in \{<,>,<=,>=\}$), so [5] proposed another algorithm to evaluate range queries with a non-binary base range-encoded bit-sliced index. The Algorithm evaluates each range predicate operator by computing two bitmaps: the B_{EQ} bitmap and either the B_{LT} or B_{GT} bitmap. For example if the predicate is ">=", then the result bitmap B_{GE} is obtained by computing the bitmaps B_{EQ} and B_{GT}, steps that involve B_{LT}, B_{LE} or B_{NE} are not required. The final result bitmap that is returned is either B_{LT}, B_{LE}, B_{GT}, B_{GE}, B_{EQ}, or B_{NE} corresponding to the predicate operator "<", "<=", ">", ">=", "=", "≠", respectively. The performance of the algorithm varies by different factors. It primarily depends on the type of predicate being evaluated, the number of components, and the base of each component. We evaluate the performance of this algorithm with a 3-component uniform base-10 range-encoded bit-sliced index for predicate *"dollar_amt <= 864"*. For this predicate, the algorithm performs 6 bitmap scans and 10 bitmap operations. See [4] for a detailed discussion of this example.

The two step process of evaluation is eliminated by Chan and Ioannidis [4]. They proposed an optimized range evaluation algorithm called *RangeEval_Opt*. Algorithm *RangeEval_Opt* reduces the bitmap operations by about 50% and requires one less bitmap scan for a range predicate evaluation. Algorithm *RangeEval_Opt* avoids the intermediate equality predicate evaluation. Evaluating the same predicate (*dollar_amt <= 864*) with *RangeEval_Opt* costs about 5 bitmap scans and 5 bitmap operations [4]. Further improving upon *RangeEval-Opt*, Wu [3] proposed an execution tree reduction technique. Taking the same example, given are a 3-component range-encoded index with decimal base on attribute *"dollar_amt"* and the predicate *"dollar_amt <= 864"*. Suppose that for some certain running state of a database, the second digit of all the values of *dollar_amt* is no larger than 5, i.e., in the component-2 of the index, the bit vectors b_2^5, b_2^6, b_2^7 and b_2^8 are all set to "1". By replacing the corresponding bit vectors with '1'-vectors, and by applying $x \cdot 1 = x$ (identity law) and $x + 1 = 1$ (domain law) of Boolean algebra, the execution tree is reduced down to one node, i.e., instead of 5 bitmap scans plus 4 logical operations, only one bitmap (the bit vector b_3^8 of component-3) is read, see [3] for details. To be able to apply such a reduction, the information about the percentage of population of each bit vector is needed. Without much extra cost, this information can be computed at the time of index creation and can be synchronized every time the index is changed [3].

The improved algorithm presented by Wu [3] performs at-least as good as the *RangeEval_Opt* with a chance of improvement in certain situations; it processes a bitmap only if it does not have all 1's in it. If a bitmap has all 1's in it, or its ratio of population is 1, scanning and processing it does not make a difference and can be avoided. Evaluating the range predicate "*dollar_amt <= 864*" with the index of figure 4 and with the assumption that all the digits in component 3 are less or equal to seven for some state of data warehouse fact table. So B_3^8 and B_3^7 have all 1's when this query is evaluated. By using tree reduction technique, the above query can be answered with the same bit-sliced index by scanning only 3 bitmaps and performing only two operations on them. See [1] for more details.

3 The Limitations of the Previous Techniques

The bit-sliced index proposed by [5] for aggregate calculation is known for best performance for *sum*, *average*, and *count* aggregates, despite that it scans all the bitmaps of a bit-sliced index. For evaluating range predicates, [5] proposed range-encoded bit-sliced index with multiple components. This technique was improved significantly by Chan and Ioannidis [4] with reduction in number of bitmap scans and operations on them and was further improved by Wu [3] with the idea of using tree reduction technique. The two later techniques address the problem of evaluating the range predicates and require that the bit-sliced index be available in range bit-encoding. This has been assumed that binary bit-sliced index is also stored and can be used for aggregates by the use of algorithm proposed by [5]. The space and maintenance overheads remain a problem for these techniques and having multiple indexes worsen this problem. In this paper, an algorithm is proposed to calculate aggregates with the range-encoded bit-sliced index that results in an improvement in performance without increase in space. Since, the proposed bit-sliced index is a range-encoded index, it can efficiently be used by the latest algorithms to answer range queries. The proposed method will also eliminate the need of maintaining separate indexes for range and aggregate predicates, which will reduce the space requirements and maintenance overheads considerably.

4 Calculating Aggregates with Range-Encoded Bit-Sliced Index

There are two challenges faced by data warehouse designers. First, the space of the bitmap index so that maintaining cost should be as low as possible. Second, low time complexity so that the query should be answered as quickly as possible. This paper is presenting an algorithm to perform aggregate operations with a space optimized range-encoded bitmap index. The algorithm improves the response time by reducing the number of bitmap scans significantly. The proposed index is a space optimized range-encoded bit-sliced index, which can be efficiently used by the latest techniques for evaluating range predicates. We will calculate both, aggregates and range predicates in our evaluation of this technique and will compare its performance with the other techniques.

A space optimized range-encoded bit-sliced index on *dollar_amt* will have 16 components in it, for each binary digit of a *short* data type. Each component has a uniform base-2. As binary base or base-2 numbers have only two digits, either 0 or 1. So, for a space optimized range-encoded bit-sliced index of binary base, we need to have two bitmaps in each of the sixteen components. In a range-encoding scheme, we do not have to store the bitmap for the most significant digit, which is 1 in this case, so we need to store the bitmap for digit 0 in each component. The index has been presented in figure 4. As obvious, this index consumes the same space as the bit-sliced index of figure 2. The difference is that this is a range-encoded bitmap index of 16 components of one bitmap each. Note that this index is exactly the complement of bit-slice index of figure 2. Figure 3 presents the algorithm to calculate aggregates with range-encoded index of figure 4 and an overview of the algorithm is presented next followed by a comparative analysis.

Input: We are given a n-component base-2 Bit-Sliced index for an attribute, n is the number of components in the range-encoded index (n= 16 in this case). B_f is the bitmap of foundset, B_{nn} represent the bitmap of non-null values, B_i^j denotes the j-th bit vector of i-th component and for a bit vector B_i^j , $\theta(B_i^j)$ denotes the percentage of 1's in B_i^j

Output: The sum of the attribute values satisfying the found set

```
If ( COUNT (B_f AND B_nn ) == 0 ) Return null;
CNT = COUNT(B_f); SUM = 0.00;
For i = 1 to n
    If (θ(B_i^0) ≠ 1) then SUM += 2^(i - 1) *(CNT - COUNT (B_i^0
    AND B_f ));
Return SUM;
```

Fig. 3. Aggregates with range-encoded index

Overview: First of all two bitmaps B_f and B_{nn} are scanned from the disk. The algorithm performs an *AND* operation on them. If all the tuples in the foundset have null values in their required attribute, the algorithm will return null and finish. If any tuple in the foundset has a non-null value, it performs a *COUNT* operation on the foundset and stores the result in a variable named *CNT*. It initializes the *SUM* and goes into the *FOR* loop. The *FOR* loop will by executed for the same number of times as there are components. Since the component itself consists of only one bitmap each, so only one bitmap will be scanned from each component. In each execution of the loop, the bitmap is scanned only if it does not have all 1's in it or its population ratio is not 1. In other words, if it satisfies the condition of the *if* statement provided in the single statement of the *FOR* loop. If the bitmap of a component has all 1's in it, is not needed to be scanned and operated upon, since that bitmap has all zeros in its all attribute values for that digit, it does not affect the value of *SUM*. If a bitmap is scanned, it will be *ANDed* with the foundset B_f, which stays in memory for the rest of the processing after it has been scanned from the disk the first time. Then a *COUNT* operation is performed on the result of that *AND* operation. This count is subtracted from the variable *CNT* and the resultant figure is multiplied with the appropriate exponent of 2. The *SUM* is then returned to the calling module.

B_{16}^0	B_{15}^0	B_{14}^0	B_{13}^0	B_{12}^0	B_{11}^0	B_{10}^0	B_9^0	B_8^0	B_7^0	B_6^0	B_5^0	B_4^0	B_3^0	B_2^0	B_1^0
1	1	1	1	1	1	0	0	0	0	1	1	0	1	0	1
1	1	1	1	1	1	0	0	1	0	1	0	0	0	1	1
1	1	1	1	1	1	0	0	0	1	0	0	1	0	0	1
1	1	1	1	1	1	1	1	1	1	0	1	0	1	1	0
1	1	1	1	1	1	0	0	1	0	0	1	1	0	0	1
1	1	1	1	1	1	0	0	1	0	1	0	0	1	0	0
1	1	1	1	1	1	0	0	1	0	1	1	0	0	0	0
1	1	1	1	1	1	1	0	1	1	1	0	1	1	1	1
1	1	1	1	1	1	1	1	0	1	0	0	1	0	0	1
1	1	1	1	1	1	0	0	0	1	0	0	1	1	1	0
1	1	1	1	1	1	0	0	1	0	0	1	1	1	1	1
1	1	1	1	1	1	1	1	1	1	1	1	1	1	1	1
1	1	1	1	1	1	0	0	0	1	0	0	1	0	0	1
1	1	1	1	1	1	1	1	1	1	1	0	0	1	0	0
1	1	1	1	1	1	0	0	1	0	1	0	1	0	0	1
1	1	1	1	1	1	0	0	0	0	0	1	1	1	0	1
1	1	1	1	1	1	0	1	1	1	0	1	0	0	0	0
1	1	1	1	1	1	1	1	1	1	1	1	1	1	1	1
1	1	1	1	1	1	1	1	0	1	1	1	0	1	0	1
1	1	1	1	1	1	0	0	1	1	1	1	0	0	0	1

Fig. 4. A 16-component range-encoded index on *dollar_amt*

Comparative Analysis: To keep our analysis simple, we are using the fact table *SALE* of figure 1 and bitmap index on its *dollar_amt* attribute from figure 4. For more comprehensive analysis with real life examples, please refer to [1]. Consider the evaluation of the query *"find the total amount of sale for the products where product_id is 120 or product_id is 122"* with the index of figure 4 and fact table of figure 1. We assume that B_f and B_{nn} are already available and the ratios of the population of all bitmaps are stored. The algorithm scans the two bitmaps B_f and B_{nn}, *AND* them and then count the number of 1's in resultant. Then a *COUNT* on B_f is performed and the result is stored in variable *CNT*, which is 8 in this case. Next the *SUM* is initialized to 0 and *FOR* loop is executed. In this case, only 10 bitmaps satisfy the *if* condition, so only 10 bitmaps are scanned and two operations are performed on all of them. The total execution takes place with 12 bitmap scans and 23 bitmap operations, while with the previous technique [5], it would be 18 bitmap scans and 34 operations on them. This is a significant improvement over the previous algorithm. For the range query like *"dollar_amt <= 864"*, the algorithm of [3] can be applied. There are only 10 bitmaps that will pass the *if* condition so only 10 bitmaps will be scanned and the algorithm will perform only one operation on each bitmap. The above query can be evaluated with 10 bitmap scans and 11 bitmap operations, which is a huge improvement over previous technique [5] in terms of number of operations for the index of same size.

In worst case, with the total of 18 bitmap scans and 35 bitmap operations, the proposed algorithm gives as good performance as one proposed by [5]. Practically, this is less likely that the bitmap will have to be scanned from all components for any data type. Also, the proposed index is a space optimized range-encoded index and can be used with the latest evaluation techniques for the range queries. In worst case, evaluating range using *RangeEvalOpt* with tree reduction technique [3] will take only 16 bitmap scans and 17 bitmap operations where as range with the index of figure 2 takes the same number of bitmap scans and perform 64 operations on them.

Experimentation was conducted on a fact table of 1.9 million records. Both types of indexes were constructed on the *dollar_amt* attribute of that table. About 200 queries were evaluated using the same foundset with both indexes. A different foundset was used in each query. A statistical analysis was performed and it was concluded with 95% confidence that both indexes give same performance for aggregates. The similar statistical analysis was done for their performance for range queries and it was concluded with the 95% confidence that space optimal range-encoded index of figure 4 performs significantly faster than bit-sliced index [5] of figure 2.

5   Conclusions

A space optimal range-encoded bitmap index is proposed to replace the bit-sliced index [5]. The proposed algorithm gives at least similar performance for the aggregate evaluations with the opportunity of easy maintenance and using it for range predicates more efficiently. The option of multiple indexes is still there for better performance for range queries with an index of higher base components.

References

1. K. Bhutta, Calculating Aggregates with Range-Encoded Bit-Sliced Index, School of Computer Science, University of Windsor, Canada, 2002, http//cs.uwindsor.ca
2. C. Y. Chan, Y. E. Ioannidis, An Efficient Bitmap Encoding Scheme for Selection Queries. In Proc. of the ACM SIGMOD Conference on Management of Data, 1999, pages 215-226
3. M.-C. Wu, Query Optimization for Selections Using Bitmaps. In Proc. of the ACM SIGMOD Conference on Management of Data, 1999, pages 227-238.
4. C-Y. Chan and Y. E. Ioannidis, Bitmap Index Design and Evaluation, . In Proc. of the ACM SIGMOD Conference on Management of Data, 1998, pages 355-366.
5. P. O'Neil and D. Quass, Improved query performance with variant indexes. Proc. ACM SIGMOD Intl. Conference on Management of Data, 1997, Pages 38-49.

T3: A Classification Algorithm for Data Mining

Christos Tjortjis and John Keane

Department of Computation, UMIST, P.O. Box 88, Manchester, M60 1QD, UK
{christos, jak}@co.umist.ac.uk

Abstract. This paper describes and evaluates T3, an algorithm that builds trees of depth at most three, and results in high accuracy whilst keeping the size of the tree reasonably small. T3 is an improvement over T2 in that it builds larger trees and adopts a less greedy approach. T3 gave better results than both T2 and C4.5 when run against publicly available data sets: T3 decreased classification error on average by 47% and generalisation error by 29%, compared to T2; and T3 resulted in 46% smaller trees and 32% less classification error compared to C4.5. Due to its way of handling unknown values, T3 outperforms C4.5 in generalisation by 99% to 66%, on a specific medical dataset.

1 Introduction

Classification produces a function that maps a data item into one of several predefined classes, by inputting a training data set and building a model of the class attribute based on the rest of the attributes. Decision tree classification has an intuitive nature that matches the user's conceptual model without loss of accuracy [4]. However no clear winner exists [5] amongst decision tree classifiers when taking into account *tree size, classification* and *generalisation accuracy*[1].

This paper describes and evaluates T3, an algorithm that builds trees of depth at most three, and results in high accuracy whilst keeping the size of the tree reasonably small. T3 outperforms C4.5 and T2 on average. The key concepts where T3 differs from T2 are the maximum *depth* of the tree permitted to be built and the *Maximum Acceptable Error* (MAE) allowed at any node as a tree building stop criterion.

The paper is structured as follows: C4.5 and T2 are briefly described and compared in sections 2 and 3; T3 is presented in section 4; experimental results are given in section 5 and evaluated in section 6; conclusions and future work are presented in section 7.

2 Description of C4.5 and T2

C4.5 is a well-known classification algorithm that constructs decision trees of arbitrary depth in a top-down recursive divide-and-conquer strategy with splits

---

[1] *Tree size* is measured by counting the number of its nodes, *classification accuracy* is the proportion of records in the training set that are correctly classified and *generalisation accuracy* is the proportion of records in the test set that are correctly classified.

H. Yin et al. (Eds.): IDEAL 2002, LNCS 2412, pp. 50–55, 2002.

maximising the *Gain Ratio* [7]. It is biased, however, in favour of continuous attributes, a weakness partly addressed by later improvements [8]. C4.5 employs a pruning technique that replaces subtrees with leaves, thus reducing overfitting. In a number of datasets the accuracy achieved by C4.5 was comparatively high [7, 8].

T2 calculates optimal decision trees up to depth 2 using two kinds of decision nodes: (1) discrete splits on a discrete attribute, where the node has as many branches as there are possible attribute values, and (2) interval splits on continuous attributes where the node has as many branches as there are intervals and the number of intervals is restricted to be either at most as many as the user specifies if all the branches of the decision node lead to leaves, or otherwise to be at most 2 [2]. The attribute value "unknown" is treated as a special attribute value and each node has an additional branch, that takes care of unknown attribute values.

3 Comparing T2 with C4.5

T2 was reported to perform better than C4.5 in terms of accuracy in 5 out of 15 data sets, of size up to 3196 records and number of attributes varying between 4 and 60 [2]. C4.5 resulted in a higher accuracy of 4% on average.

These experiments have been verified using 8 of the publicly available datasets from the UCI repository [9] used in [2]. The pruned version of C4.5 trees is used to compare generalisation accuracy, as C4.5 unpruned trees have lower performance. Table 1 illustrates the results in terms of generalisation accuracy. The last column is the quotient of T2's accuracy over that of C4.5. T2 performed better in only 1 out of 8 datasets having on average a 6.3% worse generalisation accuracy than C4.5. T2 performed 2.7% on average worse than C4.5 in terms of classification accuracy.

Table 1: Comparing the generalisation accuracy of T2 and C4.5 pruned trees

Data sets	Generalisation Accuracy (%)		T2 over C4.5 pruned
	T2	C4.5 pruned	
Iris	94.0	92.0	1.02
Hepatitis	67.3	80.8	0.83
Breast-cancer	70.5	74.7	0.94
Cleve	70.3	77.2	0.91
Crx	75.5	83.0	0.91
Pima	76.6	76.6	1.00
Hypotheroid	99.1	99.2	1.00
Chess	86.6	99.5	0.87

4 T3: An Enhancement of T2

Despite its simplicity and its ability to produce reasonably accurate results, T2 has deficiencies such as decreased efficiency when dealing with data sets containing many categorical attributes [1, 3] caused by the greedy approach used for discrete splits; problems when the classification task involves more than four classes [3];

inability to cope with very large data sets [3, 8]; the lack of useful information derived when data sets present complex interrelations, that cannot be fully described by a two-level decision tree; and possible overfitting of the training set [1].

T2's behaviour for various data set sizes has been studied and the maximum depth of 2 restricts its efficiency when dealing with large sets. Hence, the approach here is to enhance T2 with the ability to build trees of depth up to 3. This enhancement is termed *T3* and uses the same building tree approach. The cost of allowing T3's trees to grow bigger, needs to be balanced by limiting the tree size to only that necessary.

The approach taken introduces a new parameter called *Maximum Acceptable Error* (MAE). MAE is a positive real number less than 1, used as a stopping criterion during tree building. The idea is based on the observation that T2 uses a greedy tree building approach meaning that further splitting at a node would stop only if the records already classified in this node, belonged to a single class.

However, this greedy approach is not optimal, as minimising the error in the leaf nodes does not necessarily result in minimising the overall error in the whole tree. In fact, it has been proved that a strategy choosing locally optimal splits necessarily produces sub-optimal trees [6]. Furthermore, even minimising classification error does not always cause minimisation of the generalisation error, due to overfitting.

By introducing MAE, the user can specify the level of "purity" in the leaves and stop further building of the tree, concerning a potential node split. MAE has been set to have 4 distinct values, namely 0.0, 0.1, 0.2 and 0.3, meaning that splitting at a node stops even if the error in that node is equal to or below a threshold of 0, 10, 20 or 30% respectively[2].

More precisely, building the tree would stop at a node in two cases: (1) when the maximum depth is reached; (2) at that node when all the records remaining there to be classified belong to the same class in a minimum proportion of 70, 80, 90 or 100%.

5   Experimental Results

Several experiments have been done using 22 data sets from the UCI repository that were converted to MLC++ format [5] and one real stroke register data set[3]. The selection included the data sets used in section 3 plus other sets with different number of records, attributes, classes, missing values and different proportions of continuous and discrete attributes. Table 2 displays the selected data sets together with the number of records, attributes, continuous attributes and classes.

The following naming convention is used: T3.0, T3.1, T3.2 and T3.3 are the versions of T3 with depth 3 and MAE set to 0.0, 0.1, 0.2 and 0.3 respectively, while T2.0, T2.1, T2.2 and T2.3 are the versions of T3 with depth 2 and MAE set to 0.0, 0.1, 0.2 and 0.3 respectively. Hence, T2.0 is actually the original T2.

The 8 different versions of T3 were run against all 23 data sets. In 7 of them results were identical for all versions of T3. Those were namely: Breast, Diabetes, Heart,

---

[2] Higher values of MAE were also used but resulted in lower accuracy and/or trivial trees built.

[3] *Med_123* was provided by Dr Theodoulidis & Dr Saraee, Department of Computation, UMIST. Their contribution to the evaluation of results is also acknowledged.

Pima, Iris, Waveform-21 and Waveform-40. The following discussion concerns the rest of the data sets.

In the remaining 16 data sets T2.3 was the best version in terms of generalisation accuracy, resulting in higher performance on 7 sets. T2.2 was second best achieving highest performance 6 times out of 16. In terms of classification accuracy, T3.0 was a clear winner in all of the 16 sets. The second best version was T3.1 achieving equal to T3.0 performance in 11 cases. Finally, in terms of tree size, T2.3 resulted in smaller trees in 16 out of 16 sets, leaving T2.2 in the second place, as it achieved equally small trees in 8 cases.

Table 2: The data sets used for experimenting with T3

Data sets	Rec.	Att.	Cont	Cl.	Data sets	Rec.	Att.	Cont	Cl.
Lenses	24	4	-	3	Soybean	683	35	-	19
Lymphography	148	18	3	4	Australian	690	14	6	2
Iris	150	4	4	3	Crx	690	15	6	2
Hepatitis	155	19	6	2	Breast	699	10	10	2
Heart	270	13	13	2	Diabetes	768	8	8	2
Breast-cancer	286	9	-	2	Pima	768	8	8	2
Cleve	303	13	6	2	Med_123	795	37	11	2
Monk1	556	6	-	2	Hypotheroid	3163	25	7	2
Monk2	601	6	-	2	Chess	3196	36	-	2
Monk3	554	6	-	2	Waveform-40	5000	40	40	3
Vote	435	16	-	2	Waveform-21	5000	21	21	3
					Mushroom	8124	22	-	2

6 Performance Evaluation

T2.3 had the best performance in all 16 cases in terms of size and in 8 out of 16 cases in terms of generalisation accuracy. That means that T2.3 is by far the best version of T3. However, as expected, T3.0 is better for classification accuracy in all 16 cases. Furthermore in no case did T3.0 result in minimal trees. T3.1, T3.2 and T3.3 resulted in minimal trees in 1, 1 and 3 cases respectively out of 16. A conclusion to be drawn from this is that the less greedy is the approach the smaller is the tree. An explanation is that less greedy approaches, i.e. higher values for maximum acceptable error, cause a "premature" stop to the tree building phase. This argument is also justified by the fact that T2.0, T2.1 and T2.2 resulted in minimal trees in 5, 7 and 8 cases respectively out of 16. A general conclusion is that increasing the size of a tree, increases the classification accuracy, but results in decrease of generalisation accuracy.

Table 3 displays the best version of T3 for each of the 16 data sets, with the relevant tree size, classification and generalisation error of them, in comparison to T2. The table illustrates that classification error is on average decreased by 47% and the generalisation error, decreased on average by 29%, while the relevant trees are on average double the size of the ones built by T2.

Comparing the best overall versions of T3 and C4.5 for classification accuracy, namely T3.0 and C4.5 unpruned, shows that in 9 out of 16 cases T3.0 performed better than C4.5 unpruned, and they were equal twice. On average T3.0 resulted in

32% less classification error than C4.5 unpruned. Similarly the 'best' versions can be compared for tree size and generalisation accuracy, that is T2.3 and C4.5 pruned. T2.3 resulted in smaller trees 12 out of 16 times. It also resulted in higher generalisation accuracy in 4 out of 16 cases and was equal 3 times. On average T2.3 resulted in 46% smaller trees but 15% more generalisation error than C4.5 pruned. Results are presented in Table 4.

Table 3: *An evaluation of how much T3 improves T2's performance*

Data sets		T3			T2			T3 over T2		
	best	size	class	gen	size	class	gen	size	class	gen
Lenses	3.0	20	0.0	62.5	10	12.5	62.5	2	0	1
Lymphography	2.0	28	15.3	22.0	28	15.3	22	1	1	1
Hepatitis	3.0	33	1.0	26.9	12	6.8	32.7	2.8	0.15	0.82
Breast-cancer	2.3	46	22	25.3	99	19.9	29.5	0.5	1.11	0.86
Cleve	3.1	49	5.9	22.8	20	15.8	29.7	2.5	0.37	0.77
Monk1	3.0	47	0	0	17	16.9	16.7	2.8	0	0
Monk2	3.0	48	20.0	38.9	14	33.7	39.4	3.4	0.59	0.99
Monk3	2.0	15	6.6	2.8	15	6.6	2.8	1	1	1
Vote	3.1	45	2.7	3.7	17	4	3.7	2.6	0.68	1
Soybean	3.3	72	11.9	12.7	28	28.6	33.8	2.6	0.42	0.38
Australian	3.3	49	12.0	14.3	60	12.6	19.1	0.8	0.95	0.75
Crx	2.2	27	11.8	17.5	65	11.4	24.5	0.4	1.04	0.71
Med_123	3.2	54	0	0.4	18	0.2	0.8	3	0	0.5
Hypotheroid	3.0	24	0.5	0.9	11	0.7	0.9	2.2	0.71	1
Chess	3.0	19	5.9	6.8	10	12.9	13.4	1.9	0.46	0.51
Mushroom	3.0	124	0	0	75	0.5	0.7	1.7	0	0

Of particular interest is the performance of T3 when used on real stroke register data compared to C4.5. More specifically, T3.0 resulted in 0% and 0.8% classification and generalisation error as compared to the respective 20.9% and 33.6% achieved by C4.5. This indicates that T3 may have much potential when used on "real" data that have not been extensively pre-processed like the sets found in [9].

7 Conclusions and Future Work

Experimental results have shown that T3 produces relatively small sized and comprehensible trees with high accuracy in generalisation and classification. It improves the performance of T2, in terms of both generalisation accuracy and particularly classification accuracy. T3 also outperforms C4.5 in terms of tree size and classification accuracy. However, T3's generalisation accuracy remains lower than that of C4.5. It should be noted that T3 performed exceptionally well on "real" data. T3 addresses T2's deficiency when dealing with data sets containing many categorical attributes by using a less greedy approach for discrete splits. This is demonstrated by the results for the *Mushroom* and *Breast-cancer* data sets containing many multi-valued discrete attributes. Another reported weakness of T2, that of dealing with data sets that have more than four classes, is addressed by building larger trees as indicated by results for *Soybean-Large*. T3 also partly tackles the potential problem of T2 in capturing less useful information when used on data sets presenting complex interrelations that cannot be fully described by a two-level decision tree. Further work will address the way continuous attributes are treated, as the current algorithm does not improve on T2 in this respect. Scalability is another known weakness of T2 that has not been addressed yet by T3. T3, as T2, seems to achieve better performance for small or medium size data sets.

Table 4: A comparison between T3 and C4.5

Data set	T2.3		C4.5 pr.		T3.0		C4.5 unpr.	
	size	gen	size	gen	size	class	size	class
Lenses	1	62.5	7	37.5	20	0	7	6.2
Lymphography	19	22.0	21	24.0	74	2.0	25	6.1
Hepatitis	1	13.5	11	19.2	33	1.0	17	4.9
Breast-cancer	42	25.3	41	25.3	257	7.9	120	12.6
Cleve	12	26.7	27	22.8	53	5.4	55	5.0
Monk1	17	16.7	18	24.3	47	0	43	9.7
Monk2	14	39.4	31	35.0	48	20.0	73	14.2
Monk3	15	2.8	12	2.8	55	4.1	25	3.3
Vote	9	3.0	7	3.0	45	2.0	25	2.7
Soybean-large	28	33.8	68	10.5	82	10.5	150	3.5
Australian	11	13.9	58	13.0	140	4.6	124	5.0
Crx	33	19.0	58	17.0	171	3.7	90	3.9
Med_123	18	0.8	1	33.6	39	0	186	20.9
Hypotheroid	1	5.2	7	0.8	24	0.5	17	0.5
Chess	7	22.1	53	0.5	19	5.9	63	0.3
Mushroom	16	1.8	30	0	124	0	30	0

References

1. Aha, D.W., Breslow, L.A: Comparing Simplification Procedures for Decision Trees on an Economics Classification, NRL/FR/5510 98-9881, (Technical Report AIC-98-009), May 11, 1998.
2. Auer, P. Holte, R.C., Maass, W.: Theory and Applications of Agnostic PAC-Learning with Small Decision Trees, Proc. 12th Int'l Machine Learning Conf. San Francisco, Morgan Kaufmann 1995, pp. 21-29.
3. Breslow, L., Aha, D.W.: Comparing Tree-Simplification Procedures, Proc. 6th Int'l Workshop Artificial Intelligence and Statistics, Ft. Lauderdale, 1997, pp. 67-74.
4. Ganti, V., Gehrke, J., Ramakrishnan, R.: Mining Very Large Databases, IEEE Computer, Special issue on Data Mining, August 1999.
5. Kohavi, R., Sommerfield, D., Dougherty, J.: Data Mining using MLC++: A Machine Learning Library in C++, Tools with AI, 1996.
6. Murthy, S., Saltzberg, S.: Decision Tree Induction: How effective is the Greedy Heuristic?, Proc. 1st Int'l Conf. on KDD and DM, 1995, pp. 156-161.
7. Quinlan, J.R.: C4.5: Programs for Machine Learning, San Mateo, Morgan Kaufmann, 1993.
8. Quinlan, J.R.: Improved Use of Continuous Attributes in C4.5, Journal of AI Research 4, Morgan Kaufmann 1996, pp. 77-90.
9. http://www.ics.uci.edu/~mlearn/MLRepository.html UCI Machine Learning Repository data sets converted to MLC++ format, http://www.sgi.com/tech/mlc/db/ (last accessed 5/02).

A Hierarchical Model to Support Kansei Mining Process

Tomofumi Hayashi, Akio Sato, and Nadia Berthouze

Database Systems Lab, University of Aizu
Aizu Wakamatsu, 965-8580, Japan

Abstract. Image retrieval by subjective content has been recently addressed by the Kansei engineering community in Japan. Such information retrieval systems aim to include subjective aspects of the users in the querying criteria. While many techniques have been proposed in modeling such users' aspects, little attention has been placed on analyzing the amount of information involved in this modeling process and the multi-interpretation of such information. We propose a data warehouse as a support for the mining of the multimedia user feedback. A unique characteristic of our data warehouse lays in its ability to manage multiple hierarchical descriptions of images. Such characteristic is necessary to allow the mining of such data, not only at different levels of abstraction, but also according to multiple interpretation of their content. The proposed data warehouse has been used to support the adaptation of web-based image retrieval systems by impression words.

1 Introduction

Image retrieval by subjective interpretation has been recently addressed by the kansei engineering community in Japan. Various web search engines [1], art appreciation systems [2] and design support systems [3] have been proposed to allow the retrieval of images on the basis of the subjective impression (kansei in Japanese) they convey to a human observer. An example of query to such search engines could be "retrieve romantic images of airplanes".

These systems query the web database using models of impression words. These models, called Kansei User Models, are mathematical functions that map low level features (e.g. color, texture, shape, etc.), characterizing an image, into the word used to label the subjective impression conveyed to the user by this image. These models are generally tailored to the subjectivity of each person or to groups of persons sharing a similar profile. The tailoring is based upon relevance feedback [4] entered by the person to assess the system's.

While techniques for creating and adapting Kansei User Models have been widely explored, the analysis of the user feedback has been largely ignored. As a consequence, the results obtained so far have not been very encouraging. One reason behind this failure can be attributed to a static pre-processing and analysis of the user feedback. Such approach is inappropriate to account for the complexity and variability of users' subjective impressions. Images allow for a

H. Yin et al. (Eds.): IDEAL 2002, LNCS 2412, pp. 56–61, 2002.

multiple interpretation of their content because of the attention and selection mechanisms that our brain uses in filtering information. These mechanisms are triggered by external factors such as mood, experience, goals, etc. Thus feedback must be analyzed and processed with these mechanisms in mind in order to explore: a) multiple interpretation, i.e. subjective perceptions, of the information contained in multimedia data; b) the dynamic selection of salient (to a certain subjective impression) image features; and c) the fuzziness and limits in the meaning of the words used to label a given subjective impression.

In this paper, we present a hierarchical model for low-level features aggregation to support the mining of multimedia user feedback aimed at adapting Kansei User Model for Image Retrieval. The paper is organized as follows. First we briefly describe the type of data involved in Kansei User Modeling and the requirements for their mining. Finally we propose a hierarchical data model to store and manage multiple hierarchical descriptions of images.

2   Requirements for Kansei User Model Adaptation

Images can be described both in terms of their low-level features and their higher level content, for example a smiling face. While both are playing a role in the impression conveyed by the images, in this paper we focus only on the low-level features.

In our brain, the low-level information is filtered and aggregated in various ways [8],[7]. Our state of mind, goal and/or past experience direct our attention to some aspects of an image, at different levels of abstraction. For example, different areas of the sea landscape shown in Figure 1 (left) might convey opposite impressions: the wide blue sea may convey an impression of freedom while the dark wall of leaves may convey the opposite.

One of the main reasons for the low performance of Kansei User Models is their static handling of this low-level information. Generally, the adaptation

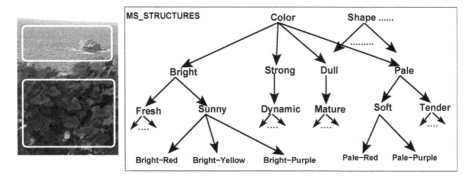

Fig. 1. Left) The focus of attention on this image can change the visual impression conveyed. Right) An example of hierarchical aggregation of color features into higher level tonality concepts.

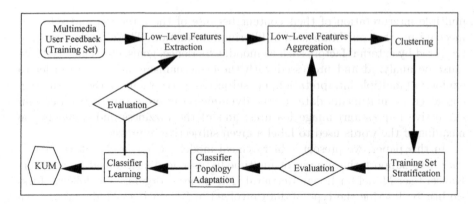

Fig. 2. Kansei User Model adaptation process.

of a Kansei User Model is obtained by adjusting the weights of each features following user feedback. This type of adaptation does not generally improve the performance because it does not change the level of aggregation and interpretation of such features. Figure 1 (right) shows an example of hierarchical aggregation of low-level features. In this particular structure, color dimensions (low-level) are aggregated into higher level concepts that capture the feeling conveyed by tonality aspects of color, more than by its hues [10]. According to this hierarchical schema, a same bright red region could be considered as: 1) red, or 2) bright or 3) sunny. Its level of description could lead to very different results in the mining process.

Figure 2 shows an example of the Kansei User Modeling process taking into account such level of interpretation. At first, user feedback is analyzed and described in order to extract the low-level features of the images. The second step consists in aggregating those features into higher level concepts, by using Attribute Relevance Analysis for example. The resulting aggregated features are used to create a stratified sampling of the set of feedback (training set for the classifier). The quality of the clusters produced would be a measure of the validity of the aggregation process.

Figure 3 shows an example of the clustering of the same set of images, performed by using a different level of abstraction for the impression "enchanting landscape". The clustering with the highest confidence could be selected to redefine the topology of the classifier. The adaptation of the topology of the classifier would then be based on the aggregated features used in the selected clusters. In our preliminary results, this adaptation process shows to improve the performance of the classifier both in quality and in learning time.

Fig. 3. Clustering using the Clique algorithm [9] on two different signatures structure of the same set of images

3   Hierarchical Meta Schemas to Support Multimedia Data Mining Processes

We propose to support such complex mining process by dynamically storing in the data warehouse a set of hierarchical meta-schema that support the aggregation of low level features according to various interpretations of an image content. In order to allow for hierarchical meta-schema with variable depth, we adopt the following structure: each node of a hierarchy is characterized by a name, a depth and a value. The name indicates not only the concept but also the parent name of the concept. For example, the node "soft" will be identified by the name "Color.Pale.Soft".

Concepts can have values of different type. For example, the concept describing the percentage of a color in an image will have values of type float, while shape concepts describing the main shapes detected in an image can use the polygonal type (a set of points). In order to allow the storage of values of different types (numerical, polygonal, etc.) we use the inheritance mechanism offered by the extention of SQL for Object-Relational Database Management (O-RDBM) Systems (in our particular case we used PostgresSQL[1]). We create 2 types of tables to store concepts and their values: MS_Structure table and < *type* >Value tables. The value of each concept is stored in a < *type* > Value table according to the type of its values. Hence each < *type* >Value table has an attribute "value" to store the value of a concept, and all the attribute of MS_Structure table. Table 1 shows an example of < *type* >Value table containing the color signatures of images. Each row of this table corresponds to a concept (node) in the hierarchical structures of Figure 1 for the signature of

---

[1] http://www.postgresql.org/

the image 'img456'. The second attribute of the table indicates the hierarchical structure used. The third attribute indicates the complete path in the hierarchy.

Table 1. An example of Value table for signatures with numerical values.

imageID	hierarchy	nodePath	value
img456	Tone	Color.Bright.Sunny.BrightRed	0.09
img456	Tone	Color.Bright.Sunny.BrightYellow	0.1
img456	Tone	Color.Bright.Sunny.BrightPurple	0.02
img456	Tone	Color.Bright.Sunny	0.4
img456	Tone	Color.Bright.Fresh.BrightCyan	0.01
img456	Tone	Color.Bright.Fresh.BrightGreen	0.1
img456	Tone	Color.Bright.Fresh.White	0.03
img456	Tone	Color.Bright.Fresh	0.15
img456	Tone	Color.Bright	0.4
img456	.....	.....	.....

4   Conclusion

We proposed a data warehouse to support the mining of kansei multimedia feedback. The mining activity aims at creating Kansei User Model to retrieve images from the Web on the basis of their visual impressions. Such data warehouse supports the storage and management of multiple hierarchical descriptions of images allowing the mining of image data at different levels of abstraction and details. In this way the modeling process can take into account the attention and selection mechanisms that are typical of our brain when interpreting complex information. The data model allows also to store image descriptions with different types of value, such as numerical, textual or geometrical. It is performed in a transparent way for the user by exploiting the inheritance mechanism offered by O-RDBMS. Mining software application accesses the O-RDBMS server through a library interface which offers logical independence from the data model implemented.

References

1. Inder, R., Bianchi-Berthouze, N., Kato, T.: K-DIME: A Software Framework for Kansei Filtering of Internet Material. Proceedings of IEEE International Conference on Systems, Man and Cybernetics, Vol. 6, 241-246, Japan (1999).
2. Hattori, R., Fujiyoshi, M., Iida, M.: An Education System on WWW for Study Color Impression of Art Paintings Applied NetCatalog. IEEE International Conference on Systems Man and Cybernetics '99, Vol.6, 218-223, Japan (1999).
3. Lee, S., Harada, A.: A Design Approach by Objective and Subjective Evaluation of Kansei Information Proceedings of International Workshop on Robot and Human Communication, IEEE Press, pp. 327-332, Hamamatsu, Japan, 1998.

4. Rui, Y., T. S. Huang, M. Ortega, and S. Mehrotra.: Relevance Feeback: A power tool in interactive content-based image retrieval. IEEE Transaction on Circuits and Systems for Video Technology, 8(5):644–655, 1998.
5. Bianchi-Berthouze, N.: Mining Multimedia Subjective Feedback. International Journal of Information Systems, Kluwer Academic Plublishers, 2002
6. Bianchi-Berthouze, N. and L. Berthouze.: Exploring Kansei in Multimedia Information. International Journal on Kansei Engineering, 2(1):1–10, 2001.
7. Pashler, H.: Attention and Visual Perception: Analysing Divided Attention. S.M Kosslyn, D.N.Osherson editors, International Journal of Visual Cognition, 2:71–100, MIT Press , 1996.
8. Bianchi-Berthouze, N. and C. Lisetti.: Modeling Multimodal Expression of Users's Affective Subjective Experience. Fiorella De Rosis Editors, International Journal on User Modeling and User-Adapted Interaction: Special Issue on User Modeling and Adaptation in Affective Computing, 12(1):49–84, 2002.
9. Agrawal, R., Gerhrke, J., Gunopulos, D., Raghavan, P.: Automatic Subspace Clustering of High Dimensionla Data for Data Mining Applications. Proceedings of ACM SIGMOD International Conference on Management of Data, Seattle, Washington, 1998.
10. Kobayashi, S.: Colorist: a practical handbook for personal and professional use. Kodansha Press, 1998

Evolving SQL Queries for Data Mining

Majid Salim and Xin Yao

School of Computer Science, The University of Birmingham
Edgbaston, Birmingham B15 2TT, UK
{msc30mms,x.yao}@cs.bham.ac.uk

Abstract. This paper presents a methodology for applying the principles of evolutionary computation to knowledge discovery in databases by evolving SQL queries that describe datasets. In our system, the fittest queries are rewarded by having their attributes being given a higher probability of surviving in subsequent queries. The advantages of using SQL queries include their readability for non-experts and ease of integration with existing databases. The evolutionary algorithm (EA) used in our system is very different from existing EAs, but seems to be effective and efficient according to the experiments to date with three different testing data sets.

1   Introduction

Data mining studies the identification and extraction of useful knowledge from large amounts of data [5]. There are a number of different fields of inquiry within data mining, of which classification is particularly popular. Machine learning algorithms that can learn to classify datum correctly can be applied to a wide variety of problem domains, including credit card fraud detection and medical diagnostics [1,2,3]. An important aspect of such algorithms is ensuring that they are easy to comprehend, to facilitate the transfer of machine discovered knowledge to people easily [4]. This paper will present a framework for discovering classification knowledge hidden in a database through evolutionary computation techniques, as applied to SQL queries. The task is related to but different from the conventional classification problem. Instead of trying to learn a classifier for predicting an unseen example, we are most interested in discovering the underlying knowledge and concept that best describes a given set of data from a large database.

SQL is a standardised data manipulation language that is widely supported by database vendors. Constructing a data mining framework using SQL is therefore very useful, as it would inherit SQL's portability and readability.

Ryu and Eick [7] proposed a genetic programming (GP) based approach to deriving queries from examples. However, there are two major differences between the work presented here and theirs. First, the query languages used are different and, as a result, the chromosome representations are different. Our use of SQL has made the whole system much simpler and more portable. Second, the evolutionary algorithms used are different. While Ryu and Eick [7] used GP, we

H. Yin et al. (Eds.): IDEAL 2002, LNCS 2412, pp. 62–67, 2002.

have developed a much simpler algorithm which does not use any conventional crossover and mutation operators. Instead, the idea of self-adaptation at the gene level is exploited. Our initial experimental studies have shown that such a simple scheme is very easy to implement, yet very effective and efficient.

The rest of this paper is structured as follows. Section 2 describes the architecture of the proposed framework, justifying design decisions made and explaining the benefits and drawbacks that were perceived in the process. Section 3 presents initial results obtained with the framework, and Section 4 concludes the paper with a brief discussion of future work that is planned.

2 Evolving SQL Queries

It was necessary to find a way of representing SQL queries genotypically, to allow for the application of evolutionary search operators. Another issue was the design of a fitness function to apply evolutionary pressure to the queries, to guide them towards the correct classification rules.

Genotypes were required to encode the list of conditional constraints that specify the criterion by which records should be selected. Each conditional constraint in SQL follows the structure [attribute name] [logical operator] [value]. This sequence was chosen as the basic unit of information, or 'gene', from which genotypes would be constructed. Genotypic representations varied randomly in length.

2.1 Evolutionary Search

The algorithm that was implemented is described in this section. 100 genotypes were constructed by randomly selecting attribute names, logical operators and values. Each attribute in the dataset began with a 0.5 probability of being included in any given genotype. Genotypes were then translated into SQL by initialising a String with the value 'SELECT * FROM [tablename] WHERE', and then appending each gene in the genotype to the end of the String. For example, a genotype such as this:

```
(LEGS = 4) (PREDATOR = TRUE) (FEATHERS = FALSE)
(VENOMOUS = FALSE)
```

would be translated into the following SQL query, through the random addition of AND and OR conditionals:

```
SELECT * FROM Animals WHERE LEGS = 4 AND PREDATOR = true
AND FEATHERS = false OR VENOMOUS = false
```

Such SQL queries, once constructed, were sent to the database, and the results analysed.

Each genotype was assigned a fitness value according to the extent to which its results corresponded with a target result set T. The fitness function used was

```
fitness = 100 - falsePositives - (2 * falseNegatives),
```

where 100 was an arbitrarily chosen constant. This fitness function was adapted from a paper by Ryu and Eick [7], dealing with deriving queries from object oriented databases. `falsePositives` is the number of records that were incorrectly identified as belonging to T, and `falseNegatives` is the number of records that should have been included T, but were not. The fitness function punishes false negatives more than it punishes false positives. If a query returns no false negatives, but several false positives, it can be seen to be correctly identifying the target result set, but generalising too much, whereas a query that returns false negatives is simply incorrect. By punishing false negatives more, it was hoped to apply evolutionary pressure that would favour queries that better classified the training data.

After assigning fitness values for the 100 queries, the best and worst three were selected. If a perfect classifier was found (with fitness of 100) the evolution would terminate, otherwise the attributes would have their probabilities re-weighted. Every attribute that appeared in the top three fittest genotypes had its selection probability incremented by 1%. Every attribute in the worst three genotypes had its probability decremented by 1%.

The old genotypes were then discarded, and a new set of 100 genotypes were randomly created using the self-adapted probabilities. Over a period of generations, attributes that contributed to higher fitness values came to dominate in the genotype set, whereas attributes that contributed little to a genotype featured less and less.

2.2   Discussions

Our algorithm departs from the metaphor commonly used in evolutionary algorithms; however it does offer a mechanism through which the genotypes are iteratively converging on the sector of the search space that offers the greatest classification utility. Although genetic information of parents are not inherited directly by offspring, the genetic information in the whole *population* is inherited by the next *population*. Such inheritance is biased toward more useful genetic materials probabilistically. Hence, more useful genetic materials will occur more frequently in a population. It is hoped that classification rules may be discovered as a consequence of this.

3   Experimental Studies

Several experiments have been carried out to evaluate the effectiveness and efficiency of the proposed framework. All datasets were downloaded from the UCI Machine Learning Repository [1]. Each dataset was tested with 20 independent runs. If after 100 generations a perfect classifier was not found, the best classifier found to date was returned. The results were averaged over the 20 runs, and are presented below.

---

[1] http://www1.ics.uci.edu/ mlearn/MLRepository.html

3.1   The Zoo Dataset

The Zoo dataset contains data items that describe animals. In total 14 attributes are provided, of which 13 are boolean and one has a predefined integer range. The animals are classified into 7 different types. Table 1 describes the results from the Zoo dataset. 'ANG' refers to the average number of generations that it took for our algorithm to find a perfect classifier.

Table 1. Results for the Zoo dataset, showing performance of the evolved classifying queries for each animal type. The results were averaged over 20 runs.

Type	False Positives	False Negatives	ANG	Accuracy
1	0	0	0.8	100.0%
2	0	0	0.7	100.0%
3	1	0	n/a	83.3%
4	0	0	4.7	100.0%
5	0	0	21.0	100.0%
6	0	0	44.5	100.0%
7	2	0	n/a	83.3%

It can be seen that our algorithm performed well on most of the classification tasks. The two instances in which it failed to find perfect classifiers are the most difficult tasks within the dataset, as both tasks involve a very small set of animals. In both cases, however, the best queries did not include false negatives.

3.2   Monk's Problems

The Monks Problem dataset involves data items with six attributes, all of which are predefined integers between 1 and 4. The first Monk's problem is the identification of data patterns where (B=C) or (E=1). The second problem is the identification of all data patterns that feature exactly two of (B = 1, C = 1, D =1, E = 1, F = 1 or G = 1). The third Monk's problem is the identification of data patterns where (F = 3 and E = 1) or (F != 4 and C != 3), and features 5% noise added to the training set. The results averaged over 20 runs are summarised in Table 2.

Our algorithm performed perfectly on the first problem, and very well on the third, but performed poorly on the second problem. Part of the reason lies in SQL's inherent difficulty in expressing the desired conditions. The second Monks Problem requires a solution that compares relative attribute values, whereas SQL is usually used to select records according to a set of disjunctive attribute constraints.

Table 2. Results for Monks Problem datasets, showing performance of the best queries for each problem. 'ANG' refers to the average number of generations that it took for our algorithm to find a perfect classifier.

Type	False Positives	False Negatives	ANG	Accuracy
Problem 1	0	0	40.6	100.0%
Problem 2	85	0	n/a	16.9%
Problem 3	5	3	n/a	94.7%

3.3   Credit Card Approval

The credit card approval dataset contains anonymised information on credit card application approvals and rejections. The dataset contains a variety of attribute types, with some attributes having predefined values and others having continuous values. The dataset also features 5% noise.

Our algorithm succeeded in correctly identifying, on average, 82.9% of the rejections. However, this relative success is countered by the fact that this classifier also included a large number of false positives - 101 on average, accounting for nearly 20% of the dataset size.

3.4   Discussion of the Results

The results for the Zoo and Monk's Problem datasets are encouraging. Our algorithm demonstrates the poorest performance on the second Monk's problem, which may be because the problem is not structurally conducive to an SQL based classification rule, although future refinements of our algorithm will hopefully improve upon these results.

The results with the credit card approval dataset also show room for improvement. This may be due to its inclusion of continuous variables. Our algorithm performs poorly with continuous valued attributes because, although it can identify attributes that are valuable in making a classification, it cannot make the same distinction for logical operators or values. It is necessary for the algorithm to find the variable values as well as attribute values that are necessary for good classification. It is proposed that logical operators will be given initial selection probabilities as well, which will decrement or increment according to the effect they play upon the fitness value of their genotype.

4   Conclusions

By using evolutionary computation techniques to evolve SQL queries it is possible to create a data mining framework that both produces easily readable results, and also can be applied to any SQL compliant database system. The problem considered here is somewhat different from the conventional classification problem. The key question we are addressing here is: Given a subset of data in a large database, how can we gain a better understanding of them? Our solution is to evolve human comprehensible SQL queries that describe the data.

The algorithm proposed in this paper differs from many traditional evolutionary algorithms, in that it does not use the metaphor of selection, whereby the fittest individuals have their traits inherited by the new generation of individuals, through operations such as crossover or mutation. Rather, it rewards the attributes that make individuals successful, and then iterates the initial step of creation. In other words, rather than survival of the fittest, this work operates upon the principle of survival of the qualities that make the fittest fit. Although many genetic algorithms feature mutation, it is usually scaled down so that it does not destroy any useful structures that evolution may have already constructed. This approach differs in that it divorces the importance of the attribute from the values that the attribute happens to have in a given gene. As such it effects an 'evolutionary liquidity' that in turn results in an appealingly diverse population, more likely to distribute itself over an entire search space than it is to converge on some local optima.

Although our preliminary experimental results are promising, they also offer room for improvement. It is hoped that future improvements with regard to dealing with continuous variables will improve performance.

References

1. X. Yao and Y. Liu, 'A new evolutionary system for evolving artificial neural networks,' *IEEE Transactions on Neural Networks*, 8(3):694-713, May 1997.
2. X. Yao and Y. Liu, 'Making use of population information in evolutionary artificial neural networks,' *IEEE Transactions on Systems, Man and Cybernetics, Part B: Cybernetics*, 28(3):417-425, June 1998.
3. Y. Liu, X. Yao and T. Higuchi, 'Evolutionary ensembles with negative correlation learning,' *IEEE Transactions on Evolutionary Computation*, 4(4):380-387, November 2000.
4. J. Bobbin and X. Yao, 'Evolving rules for nonlinear control', In *New Frontier in Computational Intelligence and its Applications*, M. Mohammadian (ed.), IOS Press, Amsterdam, 2000, pp.197-202.
5. A. A. Freitas, 'A genetic programming framework for two data mining tasks: classification and knowledge discovery', *Genetic Programming 1997: Proc. 2nd Annual Conference*, pp 96-101, Stanford University, 1997
6. A. A. Freitas, 'A survey of evolutionary algorithms for data mining and knowledge discovery', In: A. Ghosh, S. Tsutsui (eds.), *Advances in Evolutionary Computation*, Springer-Verlag, 2001
7. T. W. Ryu, C. F. Eick, 'Deriving queries from results using genetic programming', *Proc. 2nd International Conference, Knowledge Discovery and Data Mining*, pp 303-306, AAAI Press, 1996

Indexing and Mining of the Local Patterns in Sequence Database[1]

Xiaoming Jin, Likun Wang, Yuchang Lu, and Chunyi Shi

The State Key Laboratory of Intelligent Technology
and System Computer Science and Technology Dept.
Tsinghua University, Beijing, China
{xmjin00,wlk99}@mails.tsinghua.edu.cn,
lyc@tsinghua.edu.cn, scy@est4.cs.tsinghua.edu.cn

Abstract. Previous studies on frequent pattern discovery from temporal sequence mainly consider finding global patterns, where every record in a sequence contributes to support the patterns. In this paper, we present a novel problem class that is the discovery of local sequential patterns, which only a subsequence of the original sequence exhibits. The problem has a two-dimensional solution space consisting of patterns and temporal features, therefore it is impractical that use traditional methods on this problem directly in terms of either time complexity or result validity. Our approach is to maintain a suffix-tree-like index to support efficiently locating and counting of local patterns. Based on the index, a method is proposed for discovering such patterns. We have analyzed the behavior of the problem and evaluated the performance of our algorithm on both synthetic and real data. The results correspond with the definition of our problem and verify the superiority of our method.

1 Introduction

Recently, there has been increased interest in using data mining techniques to extract frequent patterns from temporal sequences, e.g. sales records, stock prices, weather data, medical data, etc. Previous studies on frequent pattern discovery have mainly considered finding global patterns, where every record in a temporal sequence contributes to the pattern [1][2][3].

However, local patterns, which are frequent only in a time period, i.e. in a subsequence of the entire sequence, are actually very common in practice. For example, "a customer always buys biscuits followed by soda in summer, but followed by milk in winter." Compared with global patterns, local patterns reveal another kind of knowledge. Knowing which pattern and in which time period is frequent could be equally if not more useful than simply knowing whether a pattern is frequent. Stock market trading may have such a pattern like, "In summer, if the stock price of a game producer goes up and stays about level for two days, then it will go up the third day". The analysts observe that there may be some correlation of price behavior from July to September so that they could plan their buy-sell strategies appropriately in that season

---

[1] The research has been supported in part of Chinese national key fundamental research program (No. G1998030414) and Chinese national fund of natural science (No. 79990580)

H. Yin et al. (Eds.): IDEAL 2002, LNCS 2412, pp. 68-73, 2002.

while they will not be confused by this pattern when they make a decision for the rest time.

This problem has not been well considered in the KDD field. The issue of temporal association rules [4][5], partial periodic patterns [6] and sequential patterns [7] seems alike to the problem we consider, but in fact the formats of either the raw data or the knowledge is essentially different.

In this paper, we introduce a problem class that is the discovery of local sequential patterns. The problem has a two-dimensional solution space consisting of patterns and temporal features, therefore it is impractical that use traditional methods on this problem directly in terms of either time complexity or result validity. A practicable approach is to slide a window through the sequence, and mine for global patterns in each window. The time complexity of it is not bad. But it can only find a small portion of local patterns, which are of the same valid subsequence length. A method that finds all local patterns can be derived by retrieving all the possible subsequences, and using previous algorithms to discover global patterns in each subsequence. However, the time complexity of it is extremely poor.

Our approach is to construct a suffix-tree-like index to support efficient locating and counting of local patterns. Based on the proposed index, we present a "*divide and discovery*" mining method for local sequential patterns, of which the time and storage growing is restricted. We have analyzed the behavior of the problem and evaluated the performance of our algorithm on both synthetic and real data. The results correspond with the definition of our problem and verify the superiority of our method.

2 Problem Definition

A sequence $S = A_1, A_2, \ldots, A_n$ is a list of records ordered by position number. Without losing generality, we represent S by a \$-terminated sequence of symbols from an alphabet $\Sigma = \{a_1, \ldots, a_k\}$, where each symbol uniquely represents a record at a time point. $|S|$ denotes the length of S, and $S[m,n]$ denotes the subsequence of S, which is a continuous part of S, from position m to n.

Given a subsequence s of S, we use the sequential pattern format $A \rightarrow B(s)$: B follows A in s where A and B are two subsequence of s.

The *local frequency* of A in subsequence s, denoted as $\mathrm{Lf}(A, s)$, is the number of occurrences of A in s, i.e.

$$\mathrm{Lf}(A,s) = |\{i \mid s[i,i+|A|-1] = A\}|$$

The *local support* of A is:

$$\delta(A) = \min\left(\{m \mid A[1,m] = A[|A|-m+1,|A|]\} \cup \{|A|\}\right)$$
$$\mathrm{Lsupp}\,(A,s) = \mathrm{Lf}(A,s)\,\delta(A)/|s|$$

Here, $\delta(A)$ is used to ensure the *local support* of patterns with different length comparable. The *local support* of the pattern $A \rightarrow B(s)$ is the support of subsequence AB in s, i.e.

$$\mathrm{Lsupp}\,(A \rightarrow B(s)) = \mathrm{Lsupp}\,(AB, s)$$

The *local confidence* of the pattern $A \rightarrow B(s)$ is the ratio of the *local frequency* of AB to the *local frequency* of A, i.e.

$$\text{Lconf}\,(A{\rightarrow}B(s))=\text{Lf}\,(AB,s)/\,\text{Lf}\,(A,s)$$

Given *a minimum support* **ms** and *a minimum confidence* **mc**, if the *local support* of pattern $A{\rightarrow}B(s)$ is no less than **ms** and the *local confidence* of that pattern is no less than **mc**, we consider the pattern as a *local sequential pattern* (LSP).

Based on the above definitions, the problem of LSP discovery is: given a long sequence, to find all LSPs through searching in the sequence, i.e. find all $<A,B,s>$ that are satisfied with:

$$\text{Lsupp}\,(A{\rightarrow}B\,(s)) \geq \textbf{ms} \wedge \text{Lconf}\,(A{\rightarrow}B\,(s)) \geq \textbf{mc}.$$

For example, S="dsdsududududdsdsusussuudu\$", **ms**=0.5, **mc**=0.5, we could find u$\rightarrow$d ("udududud") is a LSP, because δ("ud")=2, Lsupp (u$\rightarrow$d ("udududud")) =5·2/10=1≥**ms** and Lconf(u$\rightarrow$d ("udududud"))=5/5=1≥**mc**. There are some other LSPs, e.g. s$\rightarrow$u("susussu") with δ("su")=2, Lsupp (s$\rightarrow$u ("susussu"))= 3·2/7≈0.86, and Lconf (s$\rightarrow$u ("susussu")) = 3/4 = 0.75.

3 Method for Discovering LSPs

Our method for discovering LSPs consists of a suffix-tree-like index and a "divide and discover" strategy.

A suffix tree [8], also known as a position tree or a sub-word tree, is a tree for storing strings in leaf nodes. Each internal node corresponds to one common prefix. Any sequence S is mapped to a suffix tree T whose paths are the suffixes of S, and whose leaf nodes correspond uniquely to positions within S, whereupon any common subsequence can be spelled out according to the path from the root to a unique internal node. For the rest of this paper, we shall use the following notational conventions: *locus*(A) denotes the first node in the suffix tree encountered after A is spelled out; *subsequence*(t) denotes the subsequence spelled out in the suffix tree by following the path from root to node t; $T(A)$ denotes the sub-tree of T of which the root is *Locus*(A) and $T(t)$ is the sub-tree of which the root is node t; $\{Leaf\,(t)\}$ denotes the set of all leaf nodes of $T(t)$.

In our proposed method, a modified suffix tree that includes a standard suffix tree and a leaf chain is used. The leaf chain is added in order to improve the efficiency. A internal node t of the indexing tree has the following data structure (*t.Child, t.Ancestor, t.Next, t.Start, t.End, t.FirstLeaf, t.LastLeaf, t.offset*). *t.Start* and *t.End* indicate the starting position and ending position of the subsequence associated with the branch to t, *t.Child* stores the pointer to the first child of node t, *t.Ancestor* stores the pointer to ancestor node of t, *t.Next* stores the pointer to the next node with the same ancestor node of t. In order to support efficient locating and counting of the leaf nodes, all the leaves are linked, forming a leaf chain. *t.FirstLeaf* and *t.LastLeaf* store the pointer to the first leaf node and the last leaf node of the sub-tree $T(t)$. Finally, $\delta(subsequence(t))$ is stored in *t.offset* when t is created for avoiding repeated calculation of it.

The data structure of a leaf node is (*t.Ancestor, t.Next, t.Position, t.NextLeaf*) where *t.Ancestor* and *t.Next* have the same meaning as that of an internal node, *t.Position* is the position of corresponding suffix in S, *t.NextLeaf* is the next leaf node in the leaf chain.

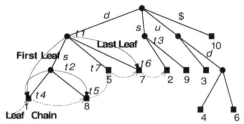

Fig. 1. Suffix tree for "dsuududds$", together with the leaf chain

Suppose A and B are two subsequences and the indexing tree for the sequence has been created, the *local frequency* of A in any subsequence $S[m,n]$ can be calculated by counting the number of leaf nodes of the sub-tree $T(A)$ that satisfies the position restrictions. That is:

$$Lf(A,S[m,n]) = |\{leaf(t_A)|m\leq leaf(t_A).Position\leq n-|A|+1\}|$$
$$Lf(AB,S[m,n]) = |\{leaf(t_B)|m\leq leaf(t_B).Position\leq n-|AB|+1\}|$$

where $t_A = locus(AB)$, $t_B = locus(AB)$. Benefiting from maintaining the leaf chain, the number of leaf nodes can be easily and efficiently obtained by a simple traverse in the leaf chain between $t.Firstleaf$ and $t.Lastleaf$.

After the *local frequency* has been obtained, the *local support* of A and the *local confidence* of $A\rightarrow B(S[m, n])$ can be calculated as:

$$Lsupp(A,S[m, n])=Lf(A,S[m,n])\cdot t_A.offset/(n-m+1)$$
$$Lconf(A\rightarrow B(S[m, n]))=Lf(AB, S[m, n])/Lf(A, S[m, n])$$

An example indexing tree for the sequence "dsuududds$" is shown in Fig. 1. Given the local pattern d$\rightarrow$s("dsuud"), the *local support* and the *local confidence* can be calculated as follows: *Locus* ("d")=$t1$, *locus* ("ds")=$t2$, *leaf*($t1$)={$t4,t5,t6,t7$}, *leaf*($t2$)={$t4,t5$}, Lf(d,"dsuud") = $|\{leaf(t1)|1\leq leaf(t1).Position\leq 5-|\text{"d"}|+1\}| = |\{t4,t7\}|$ = 2, Lf (ds,"dsuud") = $|\{leaf(t2)|1\leq leaf(t2).Position\leq 5-|\text{"ds"}|+1\}| = |\{t4\}| = 1$, Lsupp(d$\rightarrow$s, "dsuud") = Lf (ds, "dsuud")$\cdot$2/5 = 0.4, Lconf (d$\rightarrow$s, "dsuud") = Lf(ds, "dsuud")/Lf(d, "dsuud") = 0.5.

Based on the index, a *"divide and discover"* strategy could be applied to mine for LSPs. The detail of the strategy is as follows:

First, the sequence S is divided into a set of continuous segments (Sp) with the same length so that $S=S1S2...Sp...$. For each segment, an indexing tree is initialized. Then go through each segment Sp and insert each subsequence $Sp[n,...,|Sp|]$ ($1\leq n\leq|Sp|$) into the indexing tree. The insertion method is similar to that for a standard suffix tree [8]. The only difference is that the relative leaf chain pointers are updated when a node is inserted.

After a leaf node t is inserted, only the *local support* and *local confidence* of all the patterns stored in the ancestor of t will change. So we need only search the nodes in the path of traveling from node t to root. For each node t_1 in the travel path, find all the possible subsequences D such that the *local support* of *subsequence*(t_1)(D) is no less than the minimal support. We call these <*subsequence*(t_1), D> LSP-candidates. Let ($p_1,p_2,....p_n$) denote the starting positions of subsequence A. Given any p_m ($1\leq m\leq n$) and a position q ($p_{m-1}<q<p_{m+1}$), the support value of A in the subsequence from p_m to the current position n will not be less than the support value of A in the

subsequence from q to n. Therefore we need only consider the subsequences whose starting positions are p_m instead of scanning all the possible subsequences. It reduces the time complexity dramatically without losing LSP compared to the naïve methods.

For each candidate, consider all its ancestor nodes t_2. The pattern $subsequence(t_2)$ $\rightarrow$ $subsequence(t_1)$-$subsequence(t_2)$ (D) is outputted as an LSP if and only if the *local confidence* of it is no less than the minimal confidence.

In addition to the above common strategy, we should consider another special pattern class individually: for a node t, if $|S[t.Start,t.End]|>1$, $S[t.Start,t.End]$ can be split into two subsequences, which form a set of LSPs whose local confidences equal to 1.

The number of nodes of the indexing tree is at most $2|Sp|$ - 1 [8]. The time complexity for mining LSPs in one segment is approximately $O(|Sp|^2)$. By using the dividing strategy, the indexing tree is re-initialized in each segment. Therefore the size of the indexing tree is restricted, and then the time for searching through the tree is also reduced to $O(|S|)$ approximately. This strategy makes our approach scaleable. As the tradeoff, a few LSPs, of which the duration is in more than one segments, are neglected. Since the length of the segments won't be too small, the number of missing LSPs is very small. So we can treat the missing patterns individually by a simple counting method.

4   Experimental Results

The real data were extracted from stock market. The data are a set of time series, which are sequences of real numbers representing daily closing price, collected from 10/1/1997 to 8/1/2000. First, we use the clustering windows method [9] to discretize it into a symbol sequence in which each symbol represents the series behavior at that time point. Due to the space limitation, we show the resulting LSPs of only one dataset in Table 1. From it, we can get several interesting observations such as: during the time [20,63] a period of surging was always followed by falls ($j \rightarrow g$ [20,63], Lsupp=0.20, Lconf=0.64); during [26,34] this happened more frequently ($j \rightarrow g$ [26,34] , Lsupp=0.33, Lconf=0.75), whereas during [76,84] a period of surging was always followed by another surging (LSP: $j \rightarrow j$ [76,84]), etc. Such knowledge could benefit the analysis of the stock market. Furthermore, it is possible to obtain other novel knowledge through the comparisons with the LSPs derived from the market environment or price movement of other stocks, which is relative to the discovered time region.

For the purpose of performance comparison, we also implemented the naïve algorithm that counted every possible subsequence (introduced in section 1), and carried out two sets of experiments using both the proposed method and the naïve one on generated sequences with varying length. From the experiment, we drew some conclusions. First of all, our method successfully discovered all the potential LSPs. Secondly, our approach outperformed the naïve one by up to 15 times in term of time expense. Finally, there are some additional patterns that had also been found. It came from the randomness of the method of generating the experimental data.

Table 1. Experimental results on real data

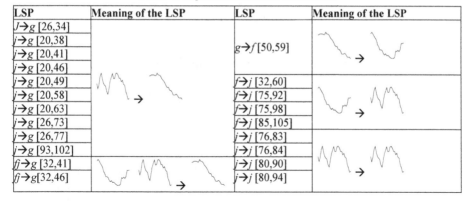

LSP	Meaning of the LSP	LSP	Meaning of the LSP
J→g [26,34]			
j→g [20,38]		g→f [50,59]	
j→g [20,41]			
j→g [20,46]			
j→g [20,49]		f→j [32,60]	
j→g [20,58]		f→j [75,92]	
j→g [20,63]		f→j [75,98]	
j→g [26,73]		f→j [85,105]	
j→g [26,77]		j→j [76,83]	
j→g [93,102]		j→j [76,84]	
fj→g [32,41]		j→j [80,90]	
fj→g[32,46]		j→j [80,94]	

5 Conclusions

In this paper, we present a data-mining problem: discovery of local sequential patterns. Such patterns are actually very common in practice, and the efficient discovery will benefit KDD in many real applications. Since the problem has a two-dimensional solution space consisting of patterns and temporal features, previous algorithms are either inapplicable or have extremely poor time complexity for discovering such patterns. In our approach, prerequisite searching and counting of patterns instances are accelerated by using an indexing tree, and all LSPs are discovered after one scan of the sequence. In addition, the proposed "*divide and discover*" strategy keeps the growing of the storage expense under a threshold and makes the time expense scale linearly. We evaluated the behavior of our problem and the performance of our algorithm on both synthetic and real data. The results corresponded with the definition of our problem and verified the superiority of our method to the naïve one.

References

1. Wang, K., Tan., J., Incremental discovery of sequential patterns. ACM SIGMOD Workshop on Research Issues on Data Mining and Knowledge Discovery, Montreal, Canada. 1996.
2. Mannila, H., Toivonen, H., Verkamo, A.I., Discovering frequent episodes in sequences. The First International Conference on Knowledge Discovery and Data Mining, Canada. 1995.
3. Kam, P.-s., Fu., A.W.-C., Discovering temporal patterns for interval-based events. DaWaK 2000, London, UK. 2000.
4. Chen, X., Petrounias, I., An integrated query and mining system for temporal association rules. DaWaK 2000, London, UK. 2000.
5. Tansel, A., Ayan, N., Discovery of association rules in temporal databases. KDD'98, Distributed Data Mining Workshop, NewYork, USA, 1998.
6. Han, J., Dong, G., Yin, Y., Efficient mining of partial periodic patterns in time series database. The Fifteenth International Conference on Data Engineering, Australia. 1999.
7. Srikant, R., Agrawal, R., Mining sequential patterns: generalizations and performance improvements. EDBT'96, Avignon, France, 1996.
8. Weiner, P., Linear pattern matching algorithms. Conference Record, The IEEE 14th Annual Symposium on Switching and Automata Theory, 1973.
9. Das, G., Lin, K., Mannila, H., Renganathan, G., Smyth, P., Rule discovery from time series. The 4th International Conference on Knowledge Discovery and Data Mining. 1998.

A Knowledge Discovery by Fuzzy Rule Based Hopfield Network

Thanakorn Sornkaew and Yasuo Yamashita

Department of Industrial Engineering and Management
Nihon University 1-2-1 Izumicho, Narashino, Chiba, Japan 275-8575
thanabiz@yahoo.com

Abstract. In this paper, a new method for discovering knowledge from empirical data is proposed. This model consists of five steps. Firstly, we find the centers of fuzzy membership functions using adapted self-organizing feature map (SOFM). Secondly, we use the centers of Gaussian membership functions derived from previous step to determine the widths of Gaussian membership functions by means of the first-nearest-neighbor heuristic. Thirdly, it builds a weight network of Hopfield network so that weights reflect the importance of the network's connections. Fourthly, Hopfield network is operated to get output values. The final step is to extract rules or knowledge via our proposed algorithm. In this algorithm, the irrelevant candidate rules are deleted so that the number of fuzzy rules and the number of antecedents can be defined. Therefore, it extracts fuzzy rules from the network. The experiments on wine recognition data show good performance concerning predictive accuracy.

1 Introduction

An important goal of knowledge discovery is to turn data into knowledge. For instance, knowledge acquired through knowledge discovery methods on a medical database can be used to make a diagnosis of cancer. The knowledge discovery is usually represented in rule formats. Researchers have defined a series of steps that provide a framework for knowledge discovery processes such as in [7]. These processes include developing an understanding of the application domain, creating a target data set and selecting a data set or focusing on a subset of variables or data samples, cleaning and preprocessing data, reducing and transforming data, choosing the data mining task, mining data, evaluating the output, and consolidating discovered. The approaches for discovering knowledge from two specific medical databases were introduced in [6]. The two different representations of knowledge called rules and causal structures were learned. Rules captured interesting patterns and regularities in the database.

Fuzzy modeling uses a natural description language to form a system model based on fuzzy logic with fuzzy predicates. We consider a multi-input single-output (MISO) fuzzy model based on the collection of rules which was developed by [8] and used by many researchers such as [1,2,3]. This knowledge representation in fuzzy modeling is written in following format:

$$IF \ X_1 \ is \ A_1 \ AND \ X_2 \ is \ A_2 \ AND,\ldots, \ AND \ X_b \ is \ A_b \ THEN \ Class \ is \ V_q$$

H. Yin et al. (Eds.): IDEAL 2002, LNCS 2412, pp. 74–79, 2002.

Fuzzy sets are defined by many fuzzy membership functions, for instance, trape-zoidal, triangular, bell-shaped or Gaussian membership functions. The use of this rule format has many advantages. The consequent parts are presented by linguistic terms which make this model more intuitive and understandable and give more insight into the model structure. Also, this modeling is easy to implement [4].

This paper introduces an new method for inducing symbolic knowledge from em-pirical data. The remaining part is organized as follows. The fuzzy rule based Hopfield network is formalized in Section 2. In Section 3 the proposed rule extraction algorithm is described, The experimental results are presented in Section 4.

2   Fuzzy Rule Based Hopfield Network

2.1   Learning for Determining the Parameters of Gaussian Membership Functions

Kohonen's self-organizing feature map algorithm is adapted to find the centers of the Gaussian membership function [1]. To achieve this goal, an initial form of the neuron-fuzzy network is constructed. When attribute value ξ_i of the i th attribute of each teaching pattern is presented, neurons will compete and the the neuron c whose weight m_i^c is the closest to input value ξ_i is chosen as the winner. Then, the connection weight of the winning neuron is modified. The algorithm is as follows:

For each attribute i,

1. Take a sample ξ_i from a normalized data set.
2. Determine the winning neuron c using the following function:

$$\|\xi_i - m_i^c(t)\| = min_{1 \le k \le K}\left(\|\xi_i - m_i^k(t)\|\right). \tag{1}$$

3. Update weight vector of the winning neuron according to:

$$m_i^c(t+1) = m_i^c(t) + \alpha(t)\left(\xi_i - m_i^c(t)\right). \tag{2}$$

4. The other neurons are not updated as

$$m_i^k(t+1) = m_i^k(t) \qquad \forall \ k \ne c. \tag{3}$$

5. If the change rate of connection weight is lower than v then stop else go to step 1.

Here, $\alpha(t)$ is a learning rate, K is the number of membership functions, m_i^k is a weight vector or the center of the i th attribute at the k th Gaussian membership function, and m_i^c is the closest weight vector of the i th attribute. The K fuzzy sets consist of five linguistic terms: very low (VL), low (L), medium (M), high (H), very high (VH).

Once the centers of Gaussian membership functions are obtained, their widths are simply determined by the first-nearest-neighbors heuristic as

$$\sigma_i^k = \left|\frac{m_i^k - m_i^c}{r}\right| \tag{4}$$

where r is an overlap parameter that usually ranges from 1.0 to 2.0.

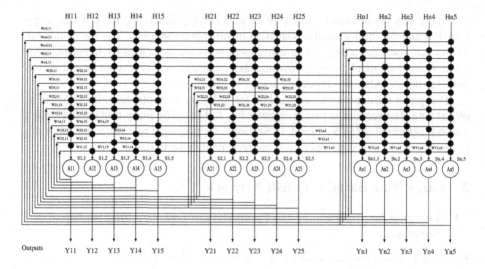

Fig. 1. Fuzzy Hopfield network.

2.2 Fuzzy Hopfield Network

The Hopfield network can be viewed as a nonlinear associative memory. The primary function of this associative memory is to retrieve a pattern which is stored in the memory in response to the presentation of a noisy pattern.

As shown in Fig. 1, the circles show neurons of Hopfield network and the black dots describe the network's connection weights. Hopfield neurons receive input state and convert it to output. For a network made up of neurons, the state of the network is thus defined by the vector.

$$S = [S_{1,1}, S_{1,2}, S_{1,3}, S_{1,4}, S_{1,5}, \ldots, S_{n,1}, S_{n,2}, S_{n,3}, S_{n,4}, S_{n,5}]^T \tag{5}$$

where, the superscript T denotes matrix transposition, and n is the total number of attributes. A pair of neurons ik and jl in the network are connected by a synaptic weight $W_{ik,jl}$. The rate of change in the network states $S_{i,k}(t)$ is determined by

$$\frac{dS_{i,k}(t)}{dt} = -\frac{S_{i,k}(t)}{\tau} + \sum_{j=1}^{M}\sum_{l=1}^{K} W_{ik,jl} Y_{j,l}(t) + H_{i,k} \tag{6}$$

where τ is a constant, $H_{i,k}$ is threshold of the the i th attribute at the k th fuzzy membership function, K is the number of fuzzy membership functions for each attribute ($K = 5$), and M is the number of attributes.

According to the above equation, the network states $S_{i,k}(t)$ are gradually changed with time. The resulting output vector $Y_{i,k}(t)$ of the network depending on the values of $S_{i,k}(t)$ is

$$Y_{i,k}(t) = \frac{1}{1 + e^{(S_{i,k}(t)/\Gamma)}} \tag{7}$$

where Γ is the temperature of neuron.

According to the outer product rule of storage, that is, the generalization of Hebb's postulate of leaning, the synaptic weight from neuron ik to neuron jl is calculated by

$$W_{ik,jl} = \frac{1}{N} \sum_{\mu=1}^{P} \xi_{\mu,ik} \xi_{\mu,jl} \tag{8}$$

where N is the total number of neurons, P is the total number of teaching patterns, and $\xi_{\mu,ik}$ is the i th attribute value of teaching pattern μ at the k th fuzzy membership function.

There are three conditions for synaptic weight $W_{ik,jl}$.

1. The output of each neuron in the network is fed back to all other neurons. Also, the states of neurons are asynchronously updated at any iteration.
2. The influence of neuron ik on neuron jl is equal to the influence of neuron jl on neuron ik.
3. For every neuron, there is no self-feedback.

The initial states of neurons are given through Gaussian membership function which is defined by Kohonen's network:

$$S_{i,k}(0) = exp\left\{ -\left(\frac{\|x_i - m_i^k\|^2}{\sigma_i^{k2}} \right) \right\} \tag{9}$$

where m_i^k and σ_i^k are the center and the width of the k th Gaussian membership function at the i th attribute, x_i is the value of the i th attribute.

3   Proposed Rule Extraction Algorithm

After we trained the network with the training set, fuzzy rules can be extracted via following procedures:

1) Initialize: make candidate rules $Q = \{R_1, R_2, R_3, \ldots, R_N\}$ equal to the number of neurons.
2) For each attribute i, and for each fuzzy membership function k,
   - compute the sum of output value $Y_{i,k}$ of the neuron ik derived from trained neural network for all pattern μ,

$$O_{i,k} = \sum_{\mu=1}^{P} Y_{i,k}^{\mu}. \tag{10}$$

3) The following algorithm is operated in order to determine the number of rules. For each attribute i,
   - create ranking of the output $O_{i,k}$ for each attribute i according to the k th fuzzy membership function.

- select the highest output value and remove other output values $O_{i,k}$ of each output ranking from list Q

4) Once the number of rules are defined, we can calculate the number of antecedences b for each rule and define fuzzy value A_b^q for each antecedences at the q th rule.
   For each candidate rule in list Q, and for each attribute i,
   - create ranking of the connection weight $W_{ik,jl}$ based on the absolute value of weight.
   - select the connection weights which are in the top b ranking.

5) For each candidate rule in list Q, our algorithm generates fuzzy rules in the format:

$$R_q : IF \ X_1 \ is \ A_1^q \ AND \ X_2 \ is \ A_2^q \ AND, \dots, \ AND \ X_b \ is \ A_b^q$$
$$THEN \ Class \ is \ V_q. \tag{11}$$

where R_q is the q th rule, X_b are input values of the b th antecedent fuzzy variable, A_b^q are fuzzy sets of the b th antecedences at the q th rule, V_q is a fuzzy output variable of the q th rule.

4   Experimental Results

We used data set which is called "wine recognition data" from machine learning databases of UCI for this study. This data set contains 178 instances: 59 for class 1 and 71 for class 2 and 48 for class 3. Each instance consists of 13 attributes which are alcohol, malic acid, ash, alkalinity of ash, magnesium, total phenols, flavanoids, nonanthocyanins phenols, proanthocyanians, color intensity, hue, OD280/D315 of diluted wines, proline. These instances are divided into a training set of size 108 and a test set of size 70. The neural network has 65 neurons: 5 membership functions for 13 attributes. We used the same neural network structure in three learning tasks.

The performance is evaluated by accuracy rate which is simply the ratio of the number of correctly classified test examples over the total number of test examples. We tested 23 samples of class 1 and achieved 22 correct classification. 29 samples of class 2 are tested and 28 samples are correctly classified. For class 3, 17 examples of 18 are correctly classified then the total number of correct classification are 67 examples. The experimental results show good performance at accuracy rate of 95.7 percent compared to 96.1 percent of 3 layers neural network.

5   Conclusions

In this paper, we have proposed a new method which can extract rules or discover knowledge from empirical data. We first determine the centers of Gaussian membership functions by means of adapted self-organizing feature map. Then, we use these centers in the first nearest-neighbor heuristic to determine the widths of Gaussian membership function. Fuzzy rule based Hopfield network is trained using Hebb's postulate learning and run in order to get output values. Thus, we proposed rule extraction algorithm for discovering knowledge or extracting symbolic rules. We used wine recognition data to evaluate our proposed technique. According to our experiments, our method is able to extract meaningful rules for wine recognition database, where no preexisting rules are available. Despite the small number of examples available in our application domain, the results of our experiments can be considered very promising.

References

[1] C. T. Lin and C. S. G. Lee, "Neural-network-based Fuzzy Logic Control and Decision System," *IEEE Trans. Comput.*, vol. 40, pp. 1320-1336, 1991.

[2] W. A. Farag, V. H. Quintana, and G. Lambert-Torres, "A genetic-based neuro-fuzzy approach for modeling and control of dynamical systems," *IEEE Trans. Neural Networks*, vol. 9, pp. 756-767, 1998.

[3] M. Sugeno and T. Yasukawa, "A fuzzy-logic-based approach to qualitative modeling," *IEEE Trans. Fuzzy Syst.*, vol. 1, pp. 7-31, Feb. 1993.

[4] I. A. Taha and J. Ghosh, "Symbolic interpretation artificial neural network," *IEEE Trans. Knowledge and Data Eng.*, vol. 11, pp. 448-463, 1999.

[5] K. J. Cios, A. Teresinska, S. Konieczna, J. Potocka, and S. Sharma, "A knowledge discovery approach to diagnosing myocardial perfusion," *IEEE Engineering in Medicine and Biology*, vol. 19, pp. 17-25, 2000.

[6] M. L. Wong, W. Lam, K. S. Leung, P. Sh. Ngan, and J. C.Y. Cheng, "Discovery knowledge from medical databases using evolutionary algorithms," *IEEE Engineering in Medicine and Biology*, vol. 19, pp. 45-55, 2000.

[7] U. M. Fayyad, "Data mining and knowledge discovery: making sense out of data," *IEEE Expert*, vol. 11, pp. 20-25, 1996.

[8] E. Mamdani, "Advances in the linguistic synthesis of fuzzy controllers," *Int. J. Man-Machine Studies*, vol. 8, pp. 669-678, 1976.

Fusing Partially Inconsistent Expert and Learnt Knowledge in Uncertain Hierarchies

Jonathan Rossiter

AI Group, Dept. of Engineering Mathematics
University of Bristol, Bristol, BS8 1TR, UK
Jonathan.Rossiter@bris.ac.uk

Abstract. This paper presents an approach to reasoning with learnt and expert information where inconsistencies are present. Information is represented as an uncertain taxonomical hierarchy where each class is a concept specification either defined by an expert or learnt from data. We present this as a good framework within which to perform information fusion. We show through a simple example how learnt information and uncertain expert knowledge can be represented and how conclusions can be reasoned from the fused hierarchy. This reasoning mechanism relies on a default assumption to rank conclusions based on the position of contributing information in the class hierarchy.

1 Introduction

In this paper we present a practical approach to the fusion of expert and learnt information. The fusion itself takes place within an uncertain class hierarchy [4] within which both expert and learnt information are represented. Uncertainty is important here as a vital component for the specification of expert knowledge and also as a means of fusing transparent learnt models. We explain the problem of maintaining consistency when reasoning with uncertain class hierarchies and we describe the implementation of a default reasoning algorithm that has been shown to work in polynomial time. The focus of this work is within the general area of 'modelling with words', and more specifically 'fusing learnt end expert models with words'. For more discussion on modelling with words in taxonomical hierarchies see [3].

2 Learnt and Expert Knowledge

It is the nature of human communication to summarise knowledge using terms which, in some way, represent uncertainty. For example, a medical diagnosis of lung disease could contain expressions such as 'evidence of widespread emphysematous disease with some basal fibrosis in the lower zones'. Here the words 'some', 'lower', and 'widespread' are imprecise terms. It is also the case that many technical terms such as 'emphysema' and 'fibrosis' are not crisply related

H. Yin et al. (Eds.): IDEAL 2002, LNCS 2412, pp. 80–86, 2002.

to the data at hand, and hence have some vague qualities. It would seem natural therefore to model expert knowledge in a framework that can handle this vagueness through linguistic terms. In this paper we model vague words through labels such as 'small', 'medium' and 'large' which are matched to fuzzy set definitions. Expert knowledge can be represented as simple rules based on these fuzzy set labels such as 'if a region of the lung scan is very dark then it is quite likely to be diseased'. Such rules allow knowledge to be represented with a high degree of transparency. In other words, non-technical observers can elicit useful information from the representation.

Learnt knowledge, on the other hand, can be represented in any number of ways depending on the learning mechanism used. Common representations are graphical, numeric or connectionist. One focus of machine learning that has relevance to transparent information fusion is machine learning within a framework of computing with words. We have presented such a learner in [3].

2.1 An Uncertain Hierarchical Representation of Knowledge

In this paper we will work in the framework of an uncertain class hierarchy where uncertainties are represented by fuzzy sets and interval probabilities. Hierarchies are, in themselves, consistent with expert and real world information. Humans naturally categorise and rank the world around them and this impinges on expert information. Lung disease for example can be split into sub classes such as 'cancer' and 'emphysema'. The class of 'cancer' can be split up further into more specific sub classes, and so on. Clearly information higher up the hierarchy is more general and information lower down the hierarchy is more specific. We have described a new approach to uncertain object oriented representation and reasoning in [4] and have implemented these theories in Fril++, the uncertain object oriented logic programming language.

Fril++ enables us to define hierarchies where classes can contain uncertain properties (attributes and methods) and objects can have uncertain memberships in classes. Interval probabilities are used to represent uncertainty in class memberships and property applicability. Intervals across the $[0, 1]$ domain give us a richer representation than point probabilities. We adopt a subsumption partial ordering in place of a fuzzy subset ordering for the sub class relationship. This avoids the problem of a symmetric sub class relation which could generate a network rather than a hierarchy, and thus reduces computational complexity. Membership of an object to a class can be calculated by matching uncertain properties followed by the application of an interval probability form of Jeffrey's rule [5].

3   Fusion in Uncertain Hierarchies

Given our chosen framework of uncertain class hierarchies for the representation of both expert and learnt information we must now consider how the two can be merged, or 'fused'. Any approach to fusion must accept an importance ordering on the information to be fused. Such an importance ordering gives us three base cases; expert knowledge is given more weight than learnt information, expert information has a lower weight than learnt information, or learnt and expert information are equally weighted. We must also consider how expert or learnt information provide prior information that can be used in the construction of the class hierarchy, the transcription of expert information or the way in which learning is performed. Some circumstances may demand that we take expert knowledge to be background (i.e. prior) information which then influences the learning process. Alternatively we might say that learnt information has roots in empirical analysis and results from machine learning should be fed back to experts who can then revise the transcription of their expert knowledge. In this paper we give equal weight to expert and learnt knowledge.

Let us consider the concept T which we are required to model. The expert transcribes his knowledge of T and this is used to construct an uncertain class C_1. At the same time we perform some machine learning from a database of exemplars of T. The learnt knowledge is used to construct a second uncertain class C_2. We now require that C_1 and C_2 be fused. In this work we assume equal weight to expert and learnt information and ensure that C_1 and C_2 are constructed independently. Since, in our example, we know that C_1 and C_2 are related through the common concept T we rank the two classes at the same level in the class hierarchy. In practice this may mean that the majority of the hierarchy concerns the specification of expert knowledge and one class defines learnt information.

Let us now take the example of the two dimensional 'figure eight' shape shown in Figure 1, defined by the parametric equations $x = 2^{-0.5}(\sin(2t) - \sin(t))$ and $y = 2^{-0.5}(\sin(2t) + \sin(t))$. Any point in the shaded area is classified as 'legal' and all other points are classified 'illegal'. An expert might say that this shape resembles the classic 'xor' problem. When pressed the expert might refine this description by saying that the shape resembles a 'figure eight', which is really an 'xor' shape but with small regions at the top left and bottom right corners where no legal points are defined. At the same time we might learn a model of the shape from a database of example legal and illegal points. Figure 2 shows how we might relate learnt and expert knowledge about the figure eight shape. Note that since we have agreed that the concept we are modelling is a figure eight we join the learnt figure eight class with the expert figure eight class through a the common superclass xor. Clearly a more complex modelling problem would result in a more ambiguous choice of where to merge the learnt class.

Having included the learnt class in the expert class hierarchy we can now use the mechanisms of uncertain hierarchical reasoning to test any new data point for legality with respect to the hierarchy. We do this by generating a single object O which is a full member of both the learnt and expert figure eight classes. We can now determine the support for 'legal' and 'illegal' for any data point in the problem space through inheritance of legal and illegal rules defined in each class in the hierarchy.

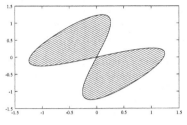

Fig. 1. Figure eight

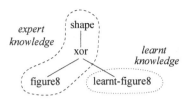

Fig. 2. Figure eight hierarchy

4   Default Reasoning for Inconsistency Resolution

Unfortunately, although the expert knowledge and learnt knowledge could be entirely consistent it is common for there to be some inconsistency between the two. This may be the result of errors or generalisations in expert knowledge, or there may be some problem with the learnt model, either through generalisation or noise. These inconsistencies are especially important in the context of uncertain class hierarchies. Here an object can have a graded membership in a class depending on property matching. It holds that since properties can be uncertain an object may have a finite (although often very small) membership in any or all classes. In this case any reasoning about a property P must take into account *all* definitions for P in the hierarchy. Any reasonably large and diverse hierarchy is likely to incorporate some inconsistent information with respect to P. Of course there are mechanisms for dealing with independent and conflicting information (such as Dempster's rule) but these are often blunt instruments that do not take into account the information contained in the hierarchical structure itself. Another approach is to isolate the most inconsistent information and eliminate it from the reasoning until a consistent conclusion is produced. The problem with this approach is that we would effectively be searching for all possible consistent subsets of contributing evidence and selecting the most consistent. This is an exponential time complexity problem.

A better approach is to return to the original assumption about our uncertain hierarchy: information lower down the hierarchy is more specific. In this regard we might wish to reach a conclusion using this specific knowledge even if it were inconsistent with some distant knowledge higher up the hierarchy. We can define a default behaviour for dealing with inconsistency where we have a structured specificity ranking such as that defined by a class hierarchy. Cao described a default reasoning algorithm for uncertain property inheritance using such a specificity ranking which is polynomial in time complexity [2]. We will now review this algorithm and relate it to the problem of information fusion in uncertain class hierarchies.

4.1   Default Uncertain Inheritance Algorithm

Let us consider the set of all classes C defining an uncertain class hierarchy. We take $C' = \{c_1, .., c_n\}$ to be a unique subset of C that only includes the classes which contain a definition for property ψ. That is, $C' \subseteq C$ and $\forall x \in C/C', \psi \notin x$ and $\forall y \in C', \psi \in y$. We now define an object O which has some membership, expressed as a support interval, in each and every class in C. We wish to work out the support for the property ψ holding for object O using a default reasoning approach. The algorithm is summarised as follows, where $r(x)$ denotes the rank of the class contributing support x, and $r(x) > r(y)$ denotes that y is lower than x in the hierarchy:

1. calculate the support for ψ with respect to each class in C'. This is calculated using an interval form of Jeffrey's rule as described in [1]. This gives us a set of supports for ψ, $\{[l_i, u_i], 1 \leq i \leq n\}$.
2. determine the set of largest consistent subsets from $\{[l_i, u_i], 1 \leq i \leq n\}$. This yields the set $P = \{p_1, ..., p_k\}$ where p_i is a set of consistent subsets, i.e. $\bigcap p_i \neq [\ ]$.
3. we now remove every $p \in P$ from P where there also exists $p^* \in P$ and $p \neq p^*$ and p is preferred to p^*. In the context of an uncertain class hierarchy we say that p is preferred to p^* if there exists $t \in p$ and $t^* \in p^*$ and $r(t) = r(t^*)$ and $t^* \subset t$ and $\forall t' \in p : \forall t'^* \in p^* : r(t') = r(t'^*) \wedge r(t') < r(t) \wedge t' = t'^*$. This gives us the reduced set of consistent subsets P'.
4. finally we aggregate all supports in P' to return the support $S(\psi|O)$ for property ψ in object O using Equation 1.

$$S(\psi|O) = \bigcup_{p_i \in P'} (\bigcap x \mid x \in p_i) \qquad (1)$$

4.2   Practical Reasoning

To illustrate the role of default reasoning in the fusion of learnt and expert knowledge we now reexamine the figure eight problem described above. We define simple rules for the legal and illegal properties in each of the expert classes in Figure 2. These rules map expert linguistic knowledge to data through L, a simple vocabulary of labels, each member of which defines a fuzzy set. The label vocabulary used in this example is defined by the following five peicewise linear fuzzy sets; $\{very\_small = [-1.5 : 1 \ -0.75 : 0], small = [-1.5 : 0 \ -0.75 : 1 \ 0 : 0], medium = [-0.75 : 0 \ 0 : 1 \ 0.75 : 0], large = [0 : 0 \ 0.75 : 1 \ 1.5 : 0], very\_large = [0.75 : 0 \ 1.5 : 1]\}$. The concepts $legal$ and $illegal$ are then modelled as discrete fuzzy sets across these labels and then built into simple rules. For example, the expert rule for 'legal' in class 'xor' can be represented by the following rule:

class is legal if either $f(x)$ is $\{medium : 0.5 \ large : 1 \ very\_large : 1\}$
and $f(y)$ is $\{very\_small : 1 \ small : 1 \ medium : 0.5\}$
or $f(x)$ is $\{very\_small : 1 \ small : 1 \ medium : 0.5\}$
and $f(y)$ is $\{medium : 0.5 \ large : 1 \ very\_large : 1\}$

where $f(i)$ generates the label fuzzy set for value i which is simply the set of $(label : membership)$ pairs taken from matching i to each fuzzy set in L.

Figures 3 and 4 respectively show how the 'xor' and 'figure8' expert classes classify legal points when each is taken in isolation. Note that for the 'shape' class each point is equally likely to be 'legal' as 'illegal'. Figure 5 shows the classification results from our simple machine learning mechanism that defines the 'learnt_figure8' class. Note the decomposition error that results in a horizontally and vertically symmetric shape while the concept we are modelling is clearly *asymmetric* in the horizontal and vertical axes.

Figure 6 shows the result of fusing expert and learnt classes through the hierarchy shown in Figure 2. The fused shape is clearly some combination of learnt and expert information, where each point has been classified using the default mechanism described previously for resolving inconsistent information in uncertain class hierarchies. The key point here is that this approach yields practical results that are meaningful in the general framework of information fusion and have been reached through a formal reasoning process involving uncertain hierarchical information.

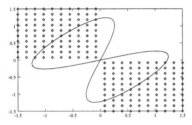

Fig. 3. Expert's xor (60% correct)

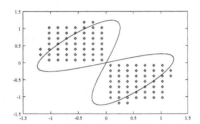

Fig. 4. Expert's figure eight (81.5% correct)

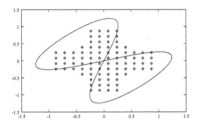

Fig. 5. Learnt figure8 (84% correct)

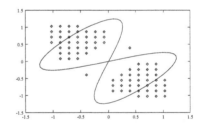

Fig. 6. Fused figure8 (79.5% correct)

5   Conclusions

We have shown how uncertain class hierarchies provide a highly practical and intuitive representation for expert knowledge. We have also shown how learnt information can be merged into the hierarchy of expert knowledge where common concepts are being modelled. A polynomially time complex default reasoning algorithm is implemented and shown to resolve inconsistencies in uncertain class hierarchies involving both expert and learnt information. A simple figure eight example is used to demonstrate the feasibility of fusing expert and learnt information in this uncertain taxonomical structure. We argue that the results show a realistic fusion of information based on formal default reasoning and uncertain inference mechanisms. Future work will test this approach on more complex examples and will consider alternatives to Equation 1 which may yield more intuitive fusion results.

References

1. Cao, T.H., Rossiter, J.M., Martin, T.P., Baldwin. J.F.: Inheritance and Recognition in Uncertain and Fuzzy Object-Oriented Models. Proc. of the 1st Int. Joint Conf. of the Int. Fuzzy Systems Ass. and the North American Fuzzy Information Processing Soc., IFSA/NAFIPS, (2001)
2. Cao, T.H.: Uncertain Inheritance and Reasoning as Probabilistic Default Reasoning, Int. J. of Intelligent Systems, **16** (2001) 781–803
3. Rossiter, J.M., Cao, T.H., Martin, T.P., Baldwin. J.F.: Object-oriented modelling with words. Proc. of the Tenth IEEE Int. Conf. on Fuzzy System, FUZZ-IEEE 2001, (2001)
4. Cao, T.H., Baldwin. J.F., Martin, T.P., Rossiter, J.M.: Towards Soft Computing Object-Oriented Logic Programming. Proc. of the Ninth IEEE Int. Conf. on Fuzzy System, FUZZ-IEEE 2000, (2000), 768–773
5. R.C.Jeffrey "The Logic of Decision" McGraw-Hill, 1965

Organisational Information Management and Knowledge Discovery in Email within Mailing Lists

Emanuela Moreale[1] and Stuart Watt[2]

[1] Knowledge Media Institute (KMi), The Open University,
Walton Hall, Milton Keynes, England. MK7 6AA.
e.moreale@open.ac.uk
[2] School of Computing, The Robert Gordon University,
St. Andrew Street, Aberdeen, Scotland. AB25 1HG
s.n.k.watt@rgu.ac.uk

Abstract. Nowadays, document management is a challenging necessity, especially for businesses. A particularly difficult but essential document management task is that of email management within corporate mailing lists. This paper will show how information extraction, retrieval and integration can be combined to deliver a powerful software tool to extract information from such lists. While they will never replace humans, systems such as the one illustrated in this paper do help alleviate information overload. Moreover, they are important tools in organisational knowledge management, as they enable the discovery of important knowledge within and about an organisation.

1 Introduction

With the increasingly widespread use of computers, the amount of stored documents has risen exponentially, making the task of locating and retrieving useful information rather complex. Today's economy is knowledge-based, so the main asset of companies, and one on which their competitive advantage rests, is their stock of knowledge [1-3]. Document management is thus a must in today's organisations. Most work in this area has focused on web pages. These efforts range from information retrieval (IR) to information extraction (IE) and wrapper generation [4].

One of the most important types of document is email. According to a recent survey commissioned by BT Cellnet [5], UK employees spend up to eight hours per week on email. Most of us feel that there is just too much email to deal with and that better support for this essential working tool is needed. Yet, email is complex: it often contains 'noise' (e.g. parts of earlier emails, signatures) and it displays several different formatting conventions (such as paragraphs and signature layouts).

Within mailing lists, the need for information management for email is even more felt: although the 'noise-to-information' ratio varies across lists, the large number of postings often results in subscribers being unable to keep up. Postings prior to one's subscription can often be found through archives: yet, these are rarely used, perhaps because of the low perceived success rate of this operation, the time needed and unhelpful archiving conventions (e.g. by subject line). Thus, often queries are asked again and again on a list. It is also likely that humans prefer a 'dialectic' discovery

H. Yin et al. (Eds.): IDEAL 2002, LNCS 2412, pp. 87-92, 2002.
© Springer-Verlag Berlin Heidelberg 2002

Table 1. Documents and their Characteristics: Webpages vs. Emails in Mailing Lists

Webpages	Emails & Mailing Lists
• Large volumes	• Smaller volumes
• New documents appear often	• New postings received fairly often
• Document contents change often	• Email: no change; list thread changes
• Most of document:	• Structured "outer envelope" (headers)
• structured or semi-structured	• Text: typically unstructured with noise
• Often contains hyperlinks	• May contain hyperlinks / attachments

approach involving interaction with active entities to mechanical and repetitive searches. What is certain is that humans prefer to ask someone a question to doing the searching themselves [6].

This paper explores the application of IE, IR and a novel information integration (II) technique to mailing lists. Our Sentinel system works with several lists, giving users archiving and retrieval assistance. It provides an intuitive dialectic query method: users can simply email the query and receive a prompt reply day or night. Alternatively, a query can be posted publicly to a forum or a web-like search can be run over the monitored lists. Sentinel automatically links email into a tangled network of stories, and arranges them in a meaningful way (digests, queries asked to date), also providing details of contributors and their postings. Because it allows users to notice relationships between/among pieces of information and people, Sentinel is a useful tool to employ as part of an organisation's knowledge management strategy.

2   Document Analysis and Management: The Case of Email

While considerable effort has taken place in the area of document management (from company document warehouses and intranets to efficient IR on the web), document analysis and management techniques obviously depend on document characteristics. Table 1 gives a taxonomy of two types of documents: web pages and emails in mailing lists. The two types of documents are fairly similar, but mailing lists are characterised by smaller volumes, more complex structure and presence of noise.

Although email is sometimes said to be particularly suitable for knowledge management because "it has a fair amount of metadata attached to it" [6] (e.g. headers and threading information), the latter can give information that is misleading (for instance when people hit 'reply' to send an email on a new subject).

Emails are largely unstructured documents: while headers are structured, the message body – the text written by the sender – is unstructured[1]. This suggests that headers and message body should be treated differently by the text mining operation.

Because of these characteristics of email, it is best not to apply IR to the whole document, but instead minimise noise first. This means totally removing irrelevant

---

[1] For example, an email can be a reply/forward email with different levels of comments from previous emails; paragraphs may be separated by blank lines or not, signatures can have different layouts or be absent; sentences are separated by a full-stop (and optional space).

Table 2. Recommendations from previous work on similar systems

Issue 1: Public vs. Private Interaction
Recommendation: both should be allowed. If all interaction is forced to be public, the total amount of interaction will be reduced. [9]
Issue 2: Anthropomorphism vs Mechanomorphism
Recommendation: these systems are more acceptable to users when mechamorphised, i.e. presented as an "Active Archive" rather than as an anthropomorphic character ("Uncle Derek") [9]. This was overturned (Issue 4).
Issue 3: Closeness vs. Openness / Visibility
Recommendation: it is best to open up the system to users as a series of threads, thus contextualising content to the current discussion. [9]
Issue 4: Fitting into the Company Culture / Groupware sold off-the-shelf is doomed
Groupware needs to be customised [10] and must fit into the company culture [11]. Our target company requested an anthropomorphic character (Fig. 1), thus recommendations to avoid anthropomorphism (Issue 2) were overturned.

emails (e.g. 'out-of-office replies') and then carrying out straightforward IE on header fields and a more sophisticated IE on the body text (e.g. remove salutations and signatures). The 'clean' email text can then be stored in a database, optionally undergoing some kind of information integration. In any case, once in a database, the text is easily searchable and IR techniques can then be successfully used. It is argued that a combination of II, IE, and IR represents the best text mining solution for email.

Email is a dynamic type of document: since changes in employees' interests are reflected in their emails, email gives an up-to-date snapshot of a company's activities and current distribution of expertise within it. Email is also "where coworkers trade stories, ask questions, propose new methods, debate techniques" [7] and where knowledge is created through interaction [8]. Email thus constitutes an ideal target for knowledge discovery once the unstructured nature problems are overcome. The next section illustrates such a project, in which we applied the techniques discussed above.

3   The Sentinel System

We were asked to develop an analysis and management system for email. Our data consisted in files containing several mailing lists arranged as Microsoft Outlook public folders, giving a total of several thousands of complex email messages. Our task was to develop a tool that interacts with mailing lists, extracting information and arranging it in an easily searchable and semantically meaningful way. Sentinel builds on previous work [9]: the key recommendations it implements are listed in Table 2.

The Sentinel system has the following characteristics:

- It extracts and stores important information from emails through text mining;
- It provides a user-friendly and 'dialectic' retrieval mode (e.g. through email);
- It links discussions occurring in different lists; the process of feeding knowledge from one forum to another amounts to knowledge discovery for the latter forum.
- By identifying all contributors to the monitored lists as well as their contributions, it allows people to easily identify each contributor's area of expertise;

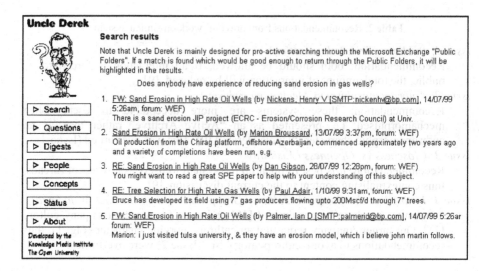

Fig. 1. Screenshot of the Sentinel System showing results of the query "Does anybody have experience of reducing sand erosion in gas wells?" - some text has been omitted.

- It extracts discussion digests and identifies previously-asked questions with re-plies. This low-cost alternative to manually-crafted 'Frequently-Asked Questions' (FAQs) is a partial application of case-based reasoning (CBR) [12]: problems are identified by initial questions (usually starting a new thread), while replies (often containing 'Best Practices') are the source of case solutions and outcomes. Senti-nel can store multiple solution options for each case.
- It is a customised system tailored to the target company and fitting into its culture.

The next section will illustrate the steps we followed in developing the system.

Document Analysis and Text Classification Pre-Filtering. The first step consisted in examining the structure of the public folders and several hundred messages. It was evident that some emails should be ignored (e.g. automated 'out-of-office' replies). Text classification was successfully employed here using pairs or triplets of adjacent terms in a manner similar to [13].

Text Mining: Information Integration and Extraction. First, IE extraction rules were then applied to the 'non-irrelevant' emails to obtain a set of purged email messages. Examples of cleaning rules include: splitting email into simple email chunks and trimming text of main email chunk from both top (to remove salutation) and bottom (to remove signature). The clean text, together with important information about the email (such as threading information), was then stored in a database. Thanks to the hand-crafted rules, the process is remarkably accurate and system recall very high (close to 100% in our system).

An integration step followed: clean email chunks were threaded into 'stories' or coherent sequences of chunks. This story-weaving provides some measure of contex-tualisation and mimics humans' way of organising information [14]. We then identi-

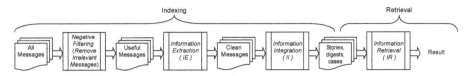

Fig. 2. Text and Information Mining Flow in Sentinel (*operations/techniques*; items)

fied queries asked to date and mapped queries to stories as a means to provide a simple procedure for automated generation of CBR cases.

Information integration is central to Sentinel. Stories are linked by author, by subject, by questions, and by domain concepts. Given a story, a user can use the web interface to find stories by the same author, addressing a similar question, or touching on similar concepts. Stories are woven together using a semantic network index, linking stories to objects through different kinds of relationship ('written by', 'about', and 'asks', are some of the relationships implemented by Sentinel). This low-cost automated hyperlinking technique, simplified from that of [15], turns Sentinel's story-base into a tangled web of related stories, which can be browsed through the web.

Information Retrieval and Knowledge Discovery. The last step was to devise an appropriate method to do text mining out of the database as well as to design a suitable query interface. Unlike typical CBR systems, Sentinel does not try to provide definitive answers but, rather, selects the most relevant cases and likely solutions, leaving the final decision to the user. Any story retrieved by Sentinel forms a starting point for further browsing through the web of stories.

Latent Semantic Analysis (LSA) [16] is used to determine relevance: the success of an LSA-based search does not depend on the natural language query using any of the terms contained in a relevant email. The Sentinel system thus finds matches by searching for those emails that are semantically closest to the query. Only matches with high relevance are shown to the user. The relevance threshold is customisable.

Sentinel offers an interactive way to search the archives: users can query the system via email to the list or private email (to encourage use), or alternatively through a web interface. As well as providing a standard search box, this lists all contributors to the mailing lists, with links to their postings, and allows users to discover knowledge about employees' skills that would otherwise be difficult to gather from the postings.

4 Future Work

Sentinel has been applied with success to internal forums that are part of a corporate intranet. Consideration is being given to expanding its knowledge capture net: being built in a modular fashion, Sentinel can be easily extended to integrate with other document management initiatives to perform more extensive knowledge discovery. It is likely that future versions of the system will make more use of CBR and learning.

5 Conclusion

This paper has illustrated how a combination of shallow text processing techniques (II, IE, and IR) can be successfully used to build a software system that alleviates the problem of information overload and management in mailing lists and helps with a company's overall knowledge management strategy.

The case is made for Sentinel, a software tool that uses II, IE and IR techniques and CBR to manage information in email within several lists. Sentinel is not just an email-mining tool offering a convenient way to archive emails and search over them, but also allows knowledge discovery within mailing lists and organisations.

Acknowledgements. We are grateful to BP for data and support, and to Trevor Collins for valuable input.

References

1. Allee, V.: The Knowledge Evolution: Expanding Organizational Intelligence, Butter-worth-Heinemann (1997)
2. Barchan, M.: How Celemi Ensure Strategic Gains by Measuring Intangible Assets", Knowledge Management Review, September–October 1998 (1998)
3. Uit Beijerse, R.P.: Questions in Knowledge Management: defining and conceptualising a phenomenon, Journal of Knowledge Management, Vol.3, No.2, pp.94–109 (2000)
4. Eikvil, L.: Information Extraction from World Wide Web – A Survey, July 1999 (1999)
5. Sturgeon, W.: Eight hours per week lost to email, Dec 2001, www.silicon.com (2001)
6. Ackerman, M.: Augmenting the Organizational Memory: A Field Study of Answer Garden, Conference on Computer-Supported Cooperative Work, pp. 243-252 (1994)
7. Weinberger, D.: Tacit Knowledge, KMWorld, 22nd Nov 1999 (1999)
8. Nonaka, I. and Konno, N.: The Concept of 'Ba': Building a Foundation for Knowledge Creation, California Management Review, Vol.40, No. 3, Spring 1998 (1998)
9. Masterton, S. and Watt, S.N.K.: Oracles, Bards, and Village Gossips, or Social Roles and Meta Knowledge Management, Information Systems Frontiers 2:3/4, 299-315 (2000)
10. Grudin, J.: Groupware and social dynamics: Eight Challenges for Developers. Communications of the ACM, 37, 1, pp. 92-105 (1994)
11. Beyer, H. and Holzblatt, K.: Contextual Design, Morgan Kaufmann (1998)
12. Watson, I. And Marir F.: Case-Based Reasoning: A Review, Knowledge Engineering Review, Vol. 9, No.4, pp.355–381 (1994)
13. Kushmerick, N., Johnston, E. and McGuinness, S.: Information Extraction by Text Classification, IJCAI-2001 Workshop on Adaptive Text Extraction and Mining (2001)
14. Schank, R.C.: Tell Me a Story: Narrative and Intelligence, Rethinking Theory, Northwestern University Press, Evanston, Illinois, third edition (2000)
15. Cleary, C. and Bareiss, R., Practical Methods for Automatically Generating Typed Links, Seventh ACM Conference on Hypertext (Hypertext '96) (1996)
16. Dumais, S.T., Furnas, G.W., Landauer, T.K., and Deerwester, S. Using Latent Semantic Analysis to Improve Information Retrieval, in Conference on Human Factors in Computing, CHI'98. 281-285 (1988)

Design of Multi-drilling Gear Machines by Knowledge Processing and Machine Simulation

G. Klene[1], A. Grauel[1], H. J. Convey[2], and A. J. Hartley[2]

[1]University of Applied Sciences, Soest Campus, Unit 16, Department Mathematics
Steingraben 21, D-59494 Soest, Germany
Phone: + 49 / (0) 29 21 / 37 81 59, Fax: + 49 / (0) 29 21 / 37 81 80
kleneikv@aol.com
[2]Bolton Institute of Higher Education
Faculty of Technology, Technology Development Unit
Deane Campus, Bolton, BL3 5AB, England
Phone: + 44 / (0) 12 04 / 90 30 64, Fax: + 44 / (0) 10 24 / 37 09 16
h.convey@bolton.ac.uk

Abstract. A software concept for automated design of a multi-spindle drilling gear machine used in furniture production process is proposed. To find an optimised design of the target-machine, this means to find the minimum number of supports and gears as well as the optimised configuration of the multi-spindle drilling gears, an automated system based on pattern identification, knowledge discovery and automated decision process is explained. The transfer of acquired manual design experience from the human expert to a software strategy to solve the multi-criteria optimisation problem will achieve cost reductions during the machine design.

1 Introduction

The target machine for the research work is a large flexible machine consisting of up to eight drill supports and each drill support has one or two drilling gears each having up to 40 individual drill locations called spindles. Each machine has to be specifically designed with regard to the minimum number of drill supports, gears and spindles. The antagonistic goal is to minimise the production time by reducing the number of drilling cycles during production. During one cycle the supports and gears are positioned and a selection or all of the holes of the board are drilled by moving up the spindles for selected drills. In other words there are two antagonistic minimisation goals: the optimisation of the machine design and the optimisation of the board production. Each machine is designed to cover the customer's board specifications that are given by structural component engineering drawings.

The aim of the project is to automate the design of such multi-drilling gear machines that was done previously by a human expert with many years of experience. An automated multi-spindle gear design using database concepts combined with pattern identification and knowledge processing of the expert's design procedure [1-4] is introduced to solve this multi-criteria optimisation problem [5].

H. Yin et al. (Eds.): IDEAL 2002, LNCS 2412, pp. 93–98, 2002.

2 Automated Configuration of Multi-drilling Gears

The automated configuration of multi-drilling gears is based on database concepts combined with pattern identification techniques and algorithms covering the human design procedure. A pattern identification technique similar to the human experts procedure and a fuzzy data representation as techniques for pattern detection and storage are applied [6]. The pattern is a predefined arrangement of holes in a neighbourhood area of one drill. They are stored in project-individual database tables that are created dependent on the identified pattern itself during the program execution. These tables provide better structured data for later design steps.

Following the human expert the problem of automated configuration of the drilling gears can be divided in two major tasks [8]. The first step is to find a generalised pre-placement of drills. The second step is an iterative process, which processes each board by defining the placement of the board in the area of work of the machine, by finding optimised positions for each support and gear and by achieving the possibility to produce each board by defining cycles and suitable drills. A sequence for the consideration of boards is determined using the board complexity (see 2.4) before the iterative configuration process starts. During this configuration process restrictions related to the parameters of the machine have to be observed and each structural component has to be checked to ensure that the production is feasible.

2.1 Board Data and Machine Data

The input data are made up from the set of work pieces W containing each work piece w with $W = \{w_1, \dots, w_n, \dots, w_N\}$ and N the number of work pieces to be manufactured on the machine. Each work piece w_n has M numbers of holes l. The set of holes of a work piece w_n can be written as $L_n = \{l_{n,1}, l_{n,2}, \dots, l_{n,m}, \dots, l_{n,M}\}$. Each hole $l_{n,m} = \{X_{n,m}, Y_{n,m}, \varnothing_{n,m}, \text{Depth}, \text{Mode}_{n,m}\}$ is determined by the x- and y-position, the diameter, the depth of the hole and the drilling-mode. The drilling-mode identifies each hole as a sink-hole or a through-hole.

The machine with its supports, gears and drills (Fig. 1) can be described by the set of supports $S = \{s_1, \dots, s_i, \dots, s_I\}$ with $I = 8$ the maximum number of supports and the set of gears – front and back gears – $G = \{g_{i1}, \dots, g_{ij}, \dots, g_{iJ}\}$ with $J = 2$ the maximal number of gears per support. The set of drills $B = \left\{b_{i,j}^{-\hat{o}-\hat{p}}, \dots, b_{i,j}^{00}, b_{i,j}^{01}, \dots, b_{i,j}^{\hat{o}\hat{p}}\right\}$ is limited by the maximal number of spindle places in positive ($\hat{o}$) and negative x-direction ($-\hat{o}$) and the maximal number of spindle places in positive ($\hat{p}$) and negative y-direction ($-\hat{p}$). A drill is determined by $b_{ij}^{op} = (\Delta x_{i,j}^{op}, \Delta y_{i,j}^{op}, \varnothing_{i,j}^{op}, WK_{i,j}^{op})$ with o the index of spindles in x-direction, p the index of spindles in y-direction.

The $\Delta x_{i,j}^{op}$ and $\Delta y_{i,j}^{op}$ relate to the so-called zero-spindle which is placed above the engine of the gear. This zero-spindle is identified by $(o,p) = (0,0)$. The type of drill-tools is identified by WK whereby WK=60 corresponds to a sink-hole drill, WK=61 to a through-drill and WK=62 to a drill which can be used for both kinds of holes. Using position field notation and the declaration $s_{i,j}^{op} \in \{-1,0,1\}$, whereby 1 denotes a spindle place filled with a drill, 0 a free spindle place and -1 a forbidden spindle place results in a computer friendly notation. A forbidden spindle place occurs if drills in the neighbourhood of this place restrict the mechanical construction, e.g. if the diameter of one drill is bigger then the grid of the spindles. One gear g_{ij} with its drills b_{ij}^{op} can

be written as
$$g_{i,j} = \begin{bmatrix} b_{ij}^{-\hat{o}\hat{p}} & \cdots & b_{ij}^{\hat{o}\hat{p}} \\ \vdots & \cdots & \vdots \\ b_{ij}^{-\hat{o}-\hat{p}} & \cdots & b_{ij}^{\hat{o}-\hat{p}} \end{bmatrix}.$$

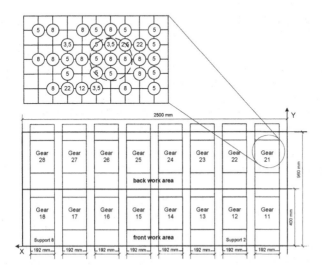

Fig. 1. Schematic of a multi-drilling gear machine and one specific gear.

Additional fields for spindles s_{ij} and the location of the spindles can be written in similar form as Δx_{ij} and Δy_{ij} and the information about the diameters of drills and the kinds of drill tools are written in the fields $\varnothing_{i,j}$ and $WK_{i,j}$ [6].

2.2 Pattern Identification and Storage

The pattern can be separated into the groups of either a known and interpretable pattern or a group of unknown pattern. The pattern identification process works in analogy to the human expert who classifies the boards into structural parts such as cupboard units, side and middle walls, bottom boards and doors. The group of known and interpretable pattern used for the automated drilling system consists of a set of holes in rows, for metal fittings and for construction holes. The holes in rows are later called x-rows because they are a set of holes in x-direction and the construction holes are called y-rows. An x-row pattern can be defined as at least three holes in combination that fulfil the conditions: a.) placed on the same work piece, b.) equal diameter, c.) equal mode, d.) equal y-coordinate, and e.) distance between holes = grid OR 2 times grid. The holes of an identified pattern are stored in a fuzzy way to the generated tables [9]. Further processing can identify that there is the same x-row on different boards. The metal-fitting pattern has a hole with diameter ≥ 12mm and the location is close to the edge of the board and most time they have further holes, e.g. for mounting near the main hole. Algorithms identify these patterns and save them to a fitting-pattern database with the diameter of the main hole, the diameter of the accessory holes for screws, the distances between the accessory holes and the main hole, and the location of the pattern on the board, e.g. the bottom or top surface. With this the pattern is independent from the real x- and y coordinates on the board. The names of the boards where the pattern appear are saved in relation to the pattern. This enables a later check to determine if the same drill-combination planned for one board can be used on a different board.

The group of unknown patterns are an arrangement of at least three holes that are in a grid distance in the x and y direction. They cannot be interpreted as the previous pattern but they can be used to find similar patterns on different boards. They are saved in a database independent from the real coordinates of each hole. Only the number of the first hole – with this it is possible to get all information about the hole like coordinates and other parameters – and the distances between the holes and the parameters of the holes – the diameter and the mode – are saved. Furthermore the gear and the spindle place number of the corresponding drill are saved.

2.3   Initial Number of Supports, Gears, and Spindles

Before the design process can be started an initial configuration defining the number of supports I the number of spindles s_{ij} on each gear is entered by the operator. The operator has to decide if special gears that are mainly used to drill the metal-fitting holes are required. The program supports the operator by giving a visual prompt that shows the number of fitting holes compared to all holes of all boards and the number of required supports to drill the fitting pattern in least number of cycles. The human expert has to decide if he wants the program to include and plan special supports for metal-fittings because this decision is dependant upon a value judgement made by the customer. The customer has to consider the impact of additional process cycles as against the additional costs for special supports. Furthermore the operator is given information if x-row drills are useful. If the amount of x-rows is large and the operator decided to use special rows for x-row drills, the operator has to define the number of spindle places to be planned for x-row drilling on each gear. These values and customer decisions are used to allocate spindle places in the database that are planned in a grid distance in columns and rows for all non-fitting gears. Each spindle place is related to the gears and has the coordinate on the gears as well as a data field for the tool number. The tool number characterises a drill by its diameter and drill mode. The initial tool number is 0 and indicates a free spindle place.

2.4   Generalised Pre-placement and Computation of Board Complexity

The generalised pre-placement is based on the identified pattern. Looking at the work place of the machine a front and back work area is specified (Fig. 1) and with this the x-rows are generalised to a front row and a back row. The drills are placed on suitable spindles using expert's rules [7]. The drills for fitting patterns are placed in such a way that the whole pattern can be drilled in one cycle. For this the spindles are not in a grid distance because these patterns usually have holes out of the grid distance.

During the drilling gear configuration, the knowledge areas about the generalized view of all boards with respect to long drill rows or often seen pattern for fittings, and about each board by itself with its specific holes is considered. When analysing each individual board it is important to start with the most complex because the degree of freedom for the placement of gears decreases with each successive board for which the drills have been positioned. The complexity of each board can be calculated using single-complexities characteristics of each board [8]. In the case that special supports for fitting pattern will be included all boards with these fitting holes will be considered in a special design procedure. In these procedures the focus regarding the board complexity is determined by the diameter of the main hole of the fitting patterns on the boards, the number of additional holes on the boards that do not belong to the fitting pattern and the size of the board.

2.5   Iterative Configuration Process for Multi-drilling Gears

The design of the multi-drilling gears related to each board is an iterative process. After placing the drills for the most important generalised pattern the system has to check if it is feasible to manufacture each board. To find an optimised layout of the drilling gears, rule-based search and positioning algorithms are applied. Additional procedures evaluate the number of supports required for each board and match the supports and gears to regions of each board. The holes in the single regions are analysed to find groups of holes that can be drilled in one cycle. Each hole that is part of one cycle is assigned a cycle number. In further steps only the holes of a particular cycle number are considered. Thus by examining each cycle number the placement of supports and drills is achieved showing that it is feasible to manufacture the board. During optimisation the different constraints of the machine and the gears have to be checked continuously [7]. The boards can be placed in each position of Y-direction as long as the constraints for placement are fulfilled. With regard to the design on the drilling gears an optimised position for each board is used [6].

```
FOR all boards
   DO UNTIL no holes on board
      Get width of non-fitting supports
      Calculate allowed positions of each support
         (first cycle: no restriction for support position
          next cycles: restriction maximal driving distance)
         Partition boards in relation to width of non-fitting supports
            Define holes for actual cycle
            Design gears for actual cycle (use allowed positions)
   LOOP
   Check production possibility for board
Next board
```

3   Conclusion

After briefly introducing the target machine important design goals for multi-spindle drilling gear configuration where shown and a technical concept for automated multi-drilling gear configuration dependent on a generalised pre-placement and an iterative configuration process where proposed. The generalised pre-placement of the automated concept is based on pattern identification to identify characteristic interpretable pattern while the iterative process is based on the complexity of each board and strongly on the non-interpretable pattern. Initial results of the program shows that the automated design is very fast compared to the design of the human expert. A further advantage is the documentation of the expert's design procedure and its verification in this application software tool. The provision of a database providing knowledge as to which drill is used for each single hole provides a simple interface to the CNC-programs that will control the manufacturing machine.

References

1. Berthold, M., Hand, D. J., (eds.): Intelligent data analysis: an introduction. Springer Verlag Berlin Heidelberg New York (1999)
2. Whitelock, P., Kilby, K.; Linguistic and Computational Techniques in Machine Translation System Design, UCL Press (1995), London
3. Karamjit, S. G., (ed.): Human Machine Symbiosis: the foundations of human centred system design, Springer Verlag Berlin Heidelberg New York (1996)
4. Steger, A.: Diskrete Strukturen: Kombinatorik, Graphentheorie, Algebra, Springer Verlag Berlin Heidelberg New York (2001)
4. Zimmermann, H.-J., Gutsche, L.,: Multi-Criteria Analyse: Einführung in die Theorie der Entscheidungen bei Mehrfachzielsetzungen, Springer-Verlag, Berlin (1991)
6. Klene, G., Grauel, A., Convey, H. J., Hartley, A. J.: Intelligent Data Analysis for Design of Multi-Drilling Gear Machines, Proc. European Symposium on Intelligent Techniques, Fotodruck Mainz GmbH, Aachen (2000) 257–262
7. Klene, G., Grauel, A., Convey, H. J., Hartley, A. J.: Cost Oriented Automation by Automated Expert Decision Process, Proc. 6th IFAC Symposium on Cost Oriented Automation, IFAC Publications, Elsevier Science Ltd (2001), 121-126
8. Klene, G., Grauel, A., Convey, H. J., Hartley, A. J.: Automated Experts Decision Process for Customised Design of Multi-Spindle Drilling Machines. Proc. 8th IFAC/IFIP/IFORS/IEA Symposium on Human-Machine Systems, IFAC Preprints, Elsevier Science Ltd. (2001) 683-687
9. Klene, G., Grauel, A., Convey, H. J., Hartley, A. J.: Data Mining and Automation of Experts Decision Process Applied to Machine Design for Furniture Production, Proc. Intern. Conference on Artificial Neural Networks and Genetic Algorithms Springer-Verlag, Wien New York (2001) 453–456

Classification of Email Queries by Topic: Approach Based on Hierarchically Structured Subject Domain

Anna V. Zhdanova[1,2] and Denis V. Shishkin[1,2]

[1] Novosibirsk State University, Novosibirsk 630090, Russia
[2] A.P. Ershov Institute of Informatics Systems, Novosibirsk 630090, Russia
{anna, denis}@sib3.ru

Abstract. We describe a Classifier of email queries, which executes text categorization by topic. The specifics of our Classifier is that it allows accurate categorization of short messages containing only a few words. This advantage is achieved by executing morphological and semantic analyses of an incoming text. Specifically, the Classifier provides an efficient information extraction and takes the meaning of words into consideration. By using the hierarchically structured subject domain and classification rules, the Classifier's engine assigns an email query to the most relevant category or categories.

1 Introduction

The need for implementation of automatic classification or categorization of electronic documents is acute nowadays, due to the increasing flow of data in the World Wide Web and enlarging electronic databases. In particular, classification of electronic queries and information extraction are the key steps towards creating an automatic email answering system. To handle the problem of text categorization, many methods have been proposed. Among these methods are the Naive Bayes technique [1], maximum entropy modeling [2], k-nearest neighbor classification [5], document clustering [3], rule-based method [4], and topic identification via using a hierarchical structure of the subject domain [5]. However, the precision of classification performed by using these approaches is often insufficient for constructing automatic answering systems, because the semantics of words in classified documents is not taken into consideration. Incorporating the word semantics into the classification process by using the external linguistics knowledge-base (WordNet) results in improving the classification precision [5]. The latter approach does however not take into account the word order and special words such as negation words (e.g., the texts consisting of expressions "to be" and "not to be" are assigned to the same category).

In this paper, we describe a Classifier, which makes it possible to categorize email queries of different sizes including those containing only a few words, where identifying the semantics is especially important (questions, addressed to call-centers, are examples of such queries). The software presented contains an

H. Yin et al. (Eds.): IDEAL 2002, LNCS 2412, pp. 99–104, 2002.

information extraction tool with included morphological analysis of words, rule-based engine for assigning an email query to the appropriate category/categories, and a database of hierarchically structured domains with the corresponding dictionaries. A hierarchical domain structure is used by the rule-based engine in order to take into account the semantics of an incoming email query. The semantic analysis implemented in our Classifier is more complete compared to those employed earlier. Combination of these features results in improvement of the precision of classification.

2   Hierarchical Domain Structure

In our approach, the subject domain is represented as a hierarchy (i.e., a tree) of categories, because such domain representation makes it possible to take into consideration the semantics of the words from a query. A hierarchy is built according to the properties of objects belonging to categories. Each category is a generalization of its subcategories, while a subcategory has an "is a" or "part of" relationship with the category it belongs to. Specifically, each category is represented by its mnemonic name, relationships with other categories, and a set of regular expressions. The set of regular expressions attributed to a category should guarantee covering the semantics of all possible queries, which are to be assigned to this category. If a regular expression characterizes all the subcategories, it is replaced to a more general category. Obviously, a set of regular expressions can not be empty.

In the framework of our Classifier, a tree of categories is constructed manually by the experts who are familiar with the corresponding domain. To implement classification, we have constructed category trees for two relatively narrow domains: insurance and banking. We have used English and Russian languages. A part of the hierarchically structured insurance domain is shown in Fig. 1 (the left sub-window).

3   Regular Expressions and Classifier's Dictionary

Information extraction is often based on a dictionary of keywords. Information extraction using a dictionary of regular expressions is however more efficient, because it takes into consideration the morphology and semantics of the words from an email query. Regular expressions include keywords and collocations. In addition, the Classifier's dictionary constructor allows representing a regular expression as a stem of a keyword or collocation and attributed numbers, which correspond to the lengths of the possible endings of this word or collocation. In our Classifier, using regular expressions guarantees extraction of all the relevant words independently of their morphological form and extraction of all the text components, which can be represented as a regular expression (e.g., any email address). The "stem + ending length" approach is especially helpful for inflexional languages (e.g., Russian), because in this way a more complex and unnecessary here morphological analysis is avoided. For English, this approach is also useful, because it allows to differentiate relevant and irrelevant words. For example, creating a regular expression with the meaning of an accident (i.e., crash and/or breakage) and stating that a stem "accident" has a zero or one letter length of ending, we achieve that the words "accident" or "accidents" are matched to this regular expression, but the word "accidental" is not. In addition, the "stem + ending length" approach is more competent in handling the problem of misprints and incorrectly written words in an email query.

The Classifier's dictionary is a list of regular expressions, which corresponds to the chosen domain. Each regular expression has one or several pointers at the related category or categories from the tree. The functional expressions, such as the expressions for negation (e.g., "no", "isn't", "besides"), are marked by special labels. This dictionary structure is independent of a language. To make the Classifier multilingual, it is necessary to add the appropriate regular expressions in different languages to the dictionary.

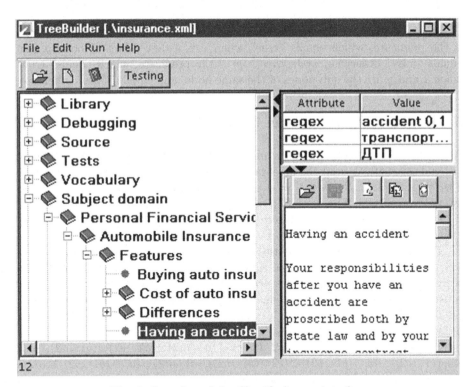

Fig. 1. Snapshot of the Classifier's user interface

4   Classification Rules

After the process of information extraction is completed, we generate a list of pointers at categories (i.e., a set of tree node numbers) and negations in the order of location of the corresponding words (regular expressions or negation expressions). The classifying rules, used to assign a query to the most relevant category/categories associated with the list, are as follows.

Intersection: If a category and its subcategory at any level of the tree are found in the list together, the category, as being more general, is removed from the further processing in order to attain a precise classification.

Negation: The category or categories assigned to the regular expression, which follows a negation expression, are substituted by their nearest-neighbor categories at the same level of a tree.

Union: The categories, which have not been removed, are united in a new list. An email query is assigned to the category or categories of this list, if none of the rules can be executed anymore.

Formally, the rules above can be executed by applying the following operations to the sets of tree nodes (i.e., categories): $A \cap B = \{x : [(x \in A)\&(\exists b \in B : x \leq b)] \vee [(x \in B)\&(\exists a \in A : x \leq a)]\}$, $\neg A = \{x : (x \notin A)\&(\exists a \in A : isBrother(x, a))\}$, $A \cup B = \{x : [(x \in A) \vee (x \in B)]\}$.

Here, A and B are the sets of tree nodes; a, b, and x are the tree nodes; $x \leq y$ is the predicate, which equals "true" when x is a descendant of node y, and equals "false" otherwise; $isBrother(x, y)$ is the predicate, which equals "true" when x and y are the sub-nodes of the same node, and equals "false" otherwise.

5   Implementation of the Classifying Rules

As a reader might have seen in the previous section, we operate with the partially ordered set $< T, \leq >$ and the algebra $\Omega = < A, \cup, \cap, \neg >$, where $A = \{B : (B \subseteq T)\&(\forall a \in T([\exists b \in B : a \leq b] \Rightarrow a \in B))\}$. The operations $\cup, \cap$ are union and intersection of sets. The operation of negation $\neg j = \{x : (x \notin j)\&(\exists a \in j, \exists y \in T : isBrother(y, a)\&x \leq y)\}$, where $j \in A$ and $isBrother(a, b) = \exists c \in T : (a \leq c)\&(b \leq c)\&(\neg\exists d \in T : (a < d < c) \vee (b < d < c))$, where $a, b \in T$.

The definition of algebra Ω uses the existence quantifiers '$\exists$'. For this reason, a straightforward implementation of the operations defined above implies searching through a set of nodes every time a rule is executed, which is time consuming. To avoid this problem, we introduce a new algebra $\Psi = < A^4 = \{< a, b, c, d > : a, b, c, d \in A\}, \cup, \cap, \neg >$ and define its operations (intersection, negation and union) in the following way:

$< a1, b1, c1, d1 > \cap < a2, b2, c2, d2 > = < (a1 \cap a2) \cup (a1 \cap b2) \cup (b1 \cap a2), (b1 \cap b2), (c1 \cap c2) \cup (c1 \cap (b1 \cup b2)) \cup (c2 \cap (b1 \cup b2)), (d1 \cap d2) \cup (d1 \cap (b1 \cup b2)) \cup (d2 \cap (b1 \cup b2)) >$, $\neg < a, b, c, d > = < c, d, a, b >$,

$< a1, b1, c1, d1 > \cup < a2, b2, c2, d2 > = < a1 \cup a2, b1 \cup b2, c1 \cup c2, d1 \cup d2 >$.

Then, we define a mapping $\phi : A \to A^4$. Let $J \in A$, then $\phi(J) = < a1, a2, a3, a4 >$, where $a1 = \{x : \exists a \in J, a \leq x\}$, $a2 = \{x : \exists a \in J, x \leq a\} = J$,

$a3 = \{x : \exists a \in J, \exists b \in T : (b \notin J)\&isBrother(a, b)\&(b \leq x)\}$,

$a4 = \{x : \exists a \in J, \exists b \in T : (b \notin J)\&isBrother(a, b)\&(x \leq b)\}$.

According to the construction above, ϕ is an isomorphism. This enables us to deal with the algebra Ψ instead of the algebra Ω. One can see that the negation operation in the vector space Ψ is global, while the operation of the space Ω is local. In the algebra Ψ, we use the four-dimensional space in order to store the "brothers" (for the operation of negation), "descendants", and "ancestors" (to find the tree nodes corresponding to an element of the algebra Ψ quickly). In the case of the negation operation, the algebra Ψ construction provides a constant execution time of '$\neg$' operation (by using the bit set model). Hence, the model Ψ is more effective then the model Ω.

6   Used Tools

The Classifier's implementation has required construction of a few tools including TreeBuilder, LinguaEngine, and RegExParser. In principle, these tools can be used in solving natural language problems different from classification. Java is employed as a programming language.

The main goal of the program **TreeBuilder** is helping a user to create a tree (a hierarchy of categories in Classifier). The tree nodes and their sub-nodes can be easily created and associated with runnable Java objects or hard disk data (e.g., files). In addition, the TreeBuilder's graphics user interface allows one to edit the source code of rules and dictionaries, create tests, store the hierarchy and its data (the tree is stored in the XML format), and view the debug information. Copy&paste technology can be applied to any hierarchy part that can be edited. A node can be extended on another tree by linking the XML file of a tree to the node. A tree, containing such nodes, may function as a "library" for a user. Thus, the TreeBuilder's features facilitate the process of tree construction.

LinguaEngine is the rule-based engine, used by the Classifier. LinguaEngine takes a list of Java objects (a list of pointers at categories in our case) and rules as an input. The output is the objects left in the input list, when all of the rules have finished their execution. Technically, a rule is presented as a Java method. In the process of execution, a rule replaces a sub-list of objects with another list of objects.

In this paper, we have described only three classification rules. However, the rules might be more numerous after introducing less general rules for more particular cases. The engine makes it possible to unite the rules into groups and to introduce a "group-order". "Group-order" defines the group, containing the rules to be executed earlier than the rules from the other groups. For example, sometimes it is necessary to execute more important rules before the rules of less importance. A group of rules is implemented by the means of a Java class, where every boolean method represents a rule. If a rule is executed, the corresponding method returns "true" (i.e., the engine tries to execute the first rule of this group), else the method returns "false" (i.e., the engine tries to execute the next rule of the same group). When none of the rules from the current group can be executed, the engine switches to the rules of the next group according to the "group-order".

RegExParser is the tool for morphological analysis and information extraction, as described in Sec. 3.

7   Future Work

Performing its main task of text categorization, our Classifier extracts information, which can be used for creating an automatic email answering system. Such a system, for example, may rely on information extraction performed by the Classifier and a template-based natural language generation [6]. Presently, if a query is classified into any category, the Classifier displays a natural language reply proposed by the creators of domain's hierarchical structure. Generation of replies in natural language may result in a higher interactivity with a user and provide an adequate amount of information for different kinds of users [7].

We believe that the performance of an automatic email answering system may also be improved by identifying the genre of an incoming query. After deciding whether the email document is a question, demand, or compliant, the system should act correspondingly. This strategy can be implemented by introducing a multi-dimensional hierarchy of the subject domain.

Finally, it is appropriate to notice that the presently used manual construction of category trees is a time-consuming process that requires special knowledge. For this reason, automation of this step is also desirable.

Acknowledgements. The authors thank F. Dinenberg and I. Kononenko for constructing the hierarchies of categories and useful discussions, and D. Levin and D. Petunin for useful discussions.

References

1. Žižka, J., Bourek, A., Frey, L.: TEA: A Text Analysis Tool for the Intelligent Text Document Filtering. In: Proceedings of the 3-rd International Workshop on Text, Speech and Dialogue (2000).
2. Manning, C.D., Schutze, H.: Foundations of Statistical Natural Language Processing. The MIT Press (2001).
3. Makagonov, P., Sboychakov, K.: Software for Creating Domain-Oriented Dictionaries and Document Clustering in Full-Text Databases. In: Proceedings of the Second International Conference on Intelligent Text Processing and Computational Linguistics (2001).
4. Cohen, W.W.: Fast Effective Rule Induction. In: Proceedings of the Second International Conference on Machine Learning (1995).
5. Tiun, S., Abdullah, R., Kong, T.E.: Automatic Topic Identification Using Ontology Hierarchy. In: Proceedings of the Second International Conference on Intelligent Text Processing and Computational Linguistics (2001).
6. Kosseim, L., Beauregard, S., Lapalme, G.: Using Information Extraction and Natural Language Generation to Answer E-mail. In: Proceedings of the 5-th International Conference on Applications of Natural Language to Information Systems (2000).
7. Bergholtz, M., Johannesson, P.: Validating Conceptual Models - Utilizing Analysis Patterns as an Instrument for Explanation Generation. In: Proceedings of the 5-th International Conference on Applications of Natural Language to Information Systems (2000).

A Knowledge-Based Information Extraction System for Semi-structured Labeled Documents

Jaeyoung Yang, Heekuck Oh, Kyung-Goo Doh, and Joongmin Choi

Department of Computer Science and Engineering
Hanyang University, Ansan, Kyunggi-Do 425-791, Korea
{jyyang, hkoh, doh, jmchoi}@cse.hanyang.ac.kr

Abstract. This paper presents a scheme of knowledge-based wrapper generation for semi-structured and labeled documents. The implementation of an agent-oriented information extraction system, XTROS, is described. In contrast with previous wrapper learning agents, XTROS represents both the domain knowledge and the wrappers by XML documents to increase modularity, flexibility, and interoperability. XTROS shows good performance on several Web sites in the domain of real estate, and it is expected to be easily adaptable to different domains by plugging in appropriate XML-based domain knowledge.

1 Introduction

Information extraction is the task of recognizing and extracting specific data fragments from a collection of documents. The process of information extraction relies on a set of extraction rules, called *a wrapper*, tailored to a particular information source[4].

Since the manual wrapper generation[2] is not scalable, wrapper induction[1, 3] has been suggested to automatically build the wrapper through learning from a set of resource's sample pages. Automatic wrapper induction can be based on either heuristics or domain knowledge. Heuristic wrapper induction has been adopted by most traditional systems such as SHOPBOT[1], STALKER [5], and WHISK[7]. A typical heuristic that has been very useful in most systems is this: a text fragment with a dollar sign followed by a number (e.g., \$250) can be regarded as the *price* information. However, this approach is not effective since the heuristics are mostly simple and naive, and as a result, the systems may extract only a limited number of unambiguous features such as the price or the ISBN number.

Knowledge-based wrapper induction tries to solve these problems by defining and applying the domain knowledge during wrapper generation. The knowledge-based approach is expected to extract more features from the document than the heuristic approach. For example, we might want to extract the number of bedrooms in by describing the meaning and the usage style of BR, Beds, and Bedrooms in the domain knowledge for real estate.

H. Yin et al. (Eds.): IDEAL 2002, LNCS 2412, pp. 105–110, 2002.

This paper proposes a scheme of knowledge-based wrapper generation for semi-structured and labeled documents. The implementation of an knowledge-oriented information extraction system, XTROS, is described. In XTROS, both the domain knowledge and the wrappers are represented by XML documents to increase modularity, flexibility, and interoperability. XTROS shows good performance on several Web sites in the domain of real estate, and it is expected to be easily adaptable to different domains with the plug-in of appropriate XML-based knowledge bases.

This paper is organized as follows. Section 2 presents the XML representation of the domain knowledge specification. Section 3 explains our scheme of knowledge-based wrapper generation algorithm. Section 4 evaluates the system with some experimental results. Finally, Section 5 concludes with the summary and future direction.

2   Domain Knowledge Specification by XML

XTROS is designed to handle *labeled* documents. In a labeled document, each portion of data that needs to be extracted is expressed by a *label-value* pair, where *label* denotes the meaning of its *value* counterpart. Examples in the domain of real estate might be $3195000, 5 BR, Baths:3, and so on. Here, $, BR, and Baths: are the labels, whereas 3195000, 5, and 3 are the values.

Domain knowledge usually describes terms, concepts, and relationships widely used for a particular application domain. It makes up for the weaknesses revealed in lexicon-oriented analysis[6], and plays a crucial role in recognizing the semantic fragments of a document in a given domain. This paper proposes an XML-based scheme for representing the domain knowledge, and an example is shown in Fig. 1 for the domain of real estate.

In our representation, the knowledge for a single domain is represented within the <KNOWLEDGE>..</KNOWLEDGE> structure. The <KNOWLEDGE> construct contains the <OBJECTS>..</OBJECTS> structure that lists the features (called *objects*) whose values are to be extracted. The objects for the real estate domain we have chosen include PRICE(the price of a house), BED(the number of bedrooms), BATH(the number of bathrooms), CITY(the address), MLS(Multiple Listings Service number, specifying a unique ID number to each house for sale), DETAIL(a hyperlink to the detailed information), and IMG(a picture of the house).

An XML construct is maintained for each object. Each XML construct for an object consists of two elements, <ONTOLOGY> and <FORMAT>. <ONTOLOGY> lists the terms that are used to recognize the existence of an object. The PRICE object has PRICE and $ as its <ONTOLOGY> terms so that a fragment can be recognized as PRICE if it contains the string "PRICE" or the symbol $. <FORMAT> describes the data type of the object value and the positional relationship between the ontological terms and the values. For example, the <FORMAT> of PRICE tells that its data type is the digit, and the price value can appear before or after the ontological term.

```
<KNOWLEDGE>
  <OBJECTS>
    <OBJECT>PRICE</OBJECT>              <BATH>
    <OBJECT>BED</OBJECT>                  <ONTOLOGY>
    <OBJECT>BATH</OBJECT>                   <TERM>BATHROOMS</TERM>
    <OBJECT>CITY</OBJECT>                   <TERM>BATHROOM</TERM>
    <OBJECT>MLS</OBJECT>                    <TERM>BATHS</TERM>
    <OBJECT>DETAIL</OBJECT>                 <TERM>BATH</TERM>
    <OBJECT>IMG</OBJECT>                    <TERM>BA</TERM>
  </OBJECTS>                              </ONTOLOGY>
  <PRICE>                                 <FORMAT>
    <ONTOLOGY>                              <FORM>DIGITS [ONTOLOGY]</FORM>
      <TERM>PRICE</TERM>                    <FORM>[ONTOLOGY] DIGITS</FORM>
      <TERM>$</TERM>                      </FORMAT>
    </ONTOLOGY>                           </BATH>
    <FORMAT>                            <MLS>
      <FORM>[ONTOLOGY] DIGITS</FORM>       <ONTOLOGY>
      <FORM>DIGITS [ONTOLOGY]</FORM>         <TERM>MLS ID:#</TERM>
    </FORMAT>                               <TERM>MLS ID</TERM>
  </PRICE>                                  <TERM>MLS#</TERM>
  <BED>                                   </ONTOLOGY>
    <ONTOLOGY>                            <FORMAT>
      <TERM>BEDROOMS</TERM>                 <FORM>[ONTOLOGY] DIGITS</FORM>
      <TERM>BEDROOM</TERM>                </FORMAT>
      <TERM>BEDS</TERM>                  </MLS>
      <TERM>BED</TERM>                   <DETAIL>
      <TERM>BR</TERM>                       -- omitted ----
      <TERM>BD</TERM>                    </DETAIL>
    </ONTOLOGY>                          <IMG>
    <FORMAT>                                -- omitted ----
      <FORM>DIGITS [ONTOLOGY]</FORM>     </IMG>
      <FORM>[ONTOLOGY] DIGITS</FORM>   </KNOWLEDGE>
    </FORMAT>
  </BED>
```

Fig. 1. XML-based domain knowledge for the real estate domain

3   Knowledge-Based Wrapper Induction

One key function of the wrapper generator for the real estate domain is to learn the format of house descriptions from successful search result pages. Our wrapper generation is divided into three phases, i.e., converting HTML sources into logical lines, determining the meaning of logical lines, and finding the most frequent pattern.

In the first phase, the HTML source of the search result page is broken down into a sequence of logical lines. A *logical line* is conceptually similar to a line that the user sees in the browser, and the learner identifies it by detecting some HTML delimiter tags such as <br>, <p>, <li>, <td>, and <tr>. All the HTML tags except <a href=..> and <img src=..> are considered unnecessary and hence removed.

The second phase of the algorithm is to determine the meaning of each logical line by checking the existence of any object in the domain knowledge. A given logical line is recognized as a certain object if it contains any <TERM> in its <ONTOLOGY> specification, and also conforms to any <FORM> in its <FORMAT> definition. For readability and faster pattern matching, each object is assigned a category number. In XTROS, 0 is assigned for PRICE, 1 for BED, 2 for BATH, 3 for CITY, 4 for MLS, 5 for DETAIL, 6 for IMG, and 9 for any general text which cannot be recognized as one of the above 7 cases.

After the categorization phase, the entire page can be expressed by a sequence of category numbers. The third phase of our algorithm finds the most frequent pattern in this sequence. We first obtain all candidate patterns(substrings) from the sequence, and find the longest pattern that has occurred most frequently. For example, consider the following sequence that is obtained from a HOMES(www.homes.com) search result page containing 6 house descriptions. Note that each house description has the sequence of 601245, except for the third one whose sequence is 60125 because of missing MLS number.

$$601245\ 601245\ 60125\ 601245\ 601245\ 601245$$

Eventually, 601245 is selected as the pattern for this site. This pattern implies that this site describes each house by presenting the information in the order of a picture of the house, its price, the number of bedrooms, the number of bathrooms, the MLS ID number, and a hyperlink for the details. An XML-based wrapper is built based on the most frequent pattern. Fig. 2(a) shows the wrapper for the HOMES site.

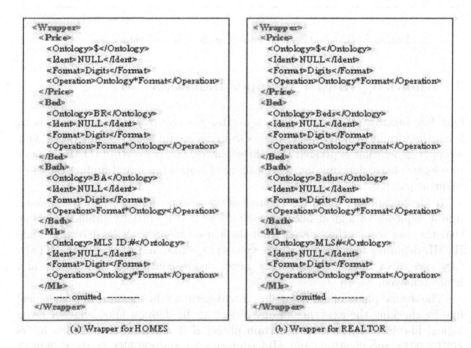

(a) Wrapper for HOMES   (b) Wrapper for REALTOR

Fig. 2. XML-based wrappers for two real estate site

A wrapper is represented by the `<Wrapper>` .. `</Wrapper>` structure that describes the pattern obtained from the previous pattern search module. Each construct consists of `<Ontology>`, `<Ident>`, `<Format>`, and `<Operation>` elements. Here, `<Ontology>` specifies a term that is examined first to determine the existence of the object, `<Ident>` denotes a delimiter that discriminate one object from the other, `<Format>` specifies the data type of the value to be extracted, and `<Operation>` indicates whether the ontological term appears before or after the object value. For example, the `<Bed>` construct in Fig. 2(a) indicates that the interpreter must look for the token BR to get the number of bedrooms from a HOMES page. Also, the `<Operation>` specification tells that the value occurs before the BR token. Note that this wrapper is applicable only to the HOMES site, so a different wrapper must be generated for a different site. For example, the wrapper for the REALTOR site (www.realtor.com) must have Beds as the `<Ontology>` value of the `<Bed>` construct. The wrapper for the REALTOR site is shown in Fig. 2(b).

4   Evaluation

XTROS is completely implemented in Java. For the evaluation of the system, we have done an extensive analysis by examining the precision and recall measures for 9 real estate sites. For each site, we collected approximately 50 Web pages, each of which contains 5 to 10 house descriptions. Table 1 shows the result of this experiment.

Table 1. An experimental result

Sites	# of Web pages tested	# of items tested (**T**)	# of items extracted (**E**)	# of items correctly extracted (**C**)	Precision (**P**) P=C/E	Recall (**R**) R=E/T
HOMES	50	300	300	300	100%	100%
REALTOR	50	250	250	250	100%	100%
ERA	50	464	401	401	100%	86%
IOWN	50	500	424	418	98%	85%
HOMESEEKERS	50	450	321	316	98%	71%
Hawaii Real Estate Central	50	500	492	491	99%	98%
San Francisco Assoc. Realtors	53	472	350	340	97%	74%
San Antonio Board of Realtors	50	500	500	500	100%	100%
Northwest MLS	50	250	250	250	100%	100%

As revealed in the table, XTROS worked perfectly for 4 sites including HOMES and REALTOR. The precision measures are almost perfect for all sites.

However, it achieved low recall ratios for some sites, including 71% for HOME-SEEKERS. This resulted from the fact that the HOMESEEKERS site has two different styles of displaying the information about the number of bathrooms. For example, the value for the label `Baths` can be `6(full) 1(half)` whose format is quite different from the ordinary digit type. Other low-recall sites have similar peculiarities. We are currently working on some of these difficulties, and other than that, we can claim that XTROS behaves very well for most of the semi-structured and labeled documents.

5 Conclusion

We have presented an intelligent Web information extraction system XTROS that represents the domain knowledge and the wrapper by XML documents, and automatically generates wrappers from semi-structured labeled documents. XTROS shows good performance on several Web sites in the domain of real estate, and it is expected to be adaptable to different domains with easy modification of the XML-based domain knowledge.

One of XTROS's current limitations is that it only works for the labeled documents, not functioning with non-labeled ones such as table-type descriptions. We need to work out for resolving this problem, and we are tackling it by investigating a method of building hierarchical trees for the table-type documents and recognize the meaning of table elements by referring their parent nodes. Eventually, we are aiming at building a customized wrapper learning agent that can be applied to a multi-domain environment.

References

1. Doorenbos, R., Etzioni, O., Weld, D.: A scalable comparison-shopping agent for the world wide web. Proceedings of the First International Conference on Autonomous Agents. (1997) 39–48
2. Hammer, J., Garcia-Molina, H., Nestorov, S., Yerneni, R., Breunig, M., Vassalos, V.: Template-based wrappers in the TSIMMIS system. Proceedings of the ACM SIGMOD International Conference on Management of Data. (1997) 532–535
3. Kushmerick, N., Weld, D., Doorenbos, R.: Wrapper induction for information extraction. Proceedings of the International Joint Conference on Artificial Intelligence. (1997) 729–735
4. Kushmerick, N.: Gleaning the web. IEEE Intelligent Systems. **14** (1999) 20–22
5. Muslea, I., Minton, S., Knoblock, C.: A hierarchical approach to wrapper induction. Proceedings of the Third International Conference on Autonomous Agents. (1999) 190–197
6. Soderland, S., Fisher, D., Aseltine, J., Lehnert, W.: CRYSTAL: Inducing a conceptual dictionary. Proceedings of the 15th International Conference on Artificial Intelligence. (1995) 1314–1321
7. Soderland, S.: Learning information extraction rules for semi-structured and free text. Machine Learning. **34** (1999) 233-272

Measuring Semantic Similarity Between Words Using Lexical Knowledge and Neural Networks

Yuhua Li, Zuhair Bandar, and David Mclean

Intelligent System Group, Department of Computing and Mathematics,
Manchester Metropolitan University, Manchester, M1 5GD, England
{y.li, z.bandar, d.mclean}@mmu.ac.uk

Abstract. This paper investigates the determination of semantic similarity by the incorporation of structural semantic knowledge from a lexical database and the learning ability of neural networks. The lexical database is assumed to be organised in a hierarchical structure. The extracted lexical knowledge contains the relative location of the concerned words in the lexical hierarchy. The neural network then processes available lexical knowledge to provide semantic similarity for words. Experimental evaluation against a benchmark set of human similarity ratings demonstrates that the proposed method is effective in measuring semantic similarity between words.

1 Introduction

The study of semantic similarity between words has been a part of natural language processing and information retrieval for many years. Semantic similarity is a generic issue in a variety of applications in the areas of computational linguistics and artificial intelligence. Examples include, word sense disambiguation [10], detection and correction of word spelling errors (malapropisms) [1], multimodal document retrieval [13], and automatic hypertext linking [2]. Similarity between two words is often represented by similarity between concepts associated with the two words. A number of semantic similarity methods have been developed in the previous decade, different similarity methods have proved to be useful in some specific applications of computational intelligence [1, 6]. Generally these methods can be categorised into two groups: edge counting based (or dictionary/thesaurus based) methods [9] and information theory based (or corpus based) methods [10].

The commonly used information sources in previous similarity measures are shortest path length between compared words, depth in the taxonomy hierarchy, semantic density of compared words and information content. Different methods use varying information sources and strategies and thus result in varying levels of performance. Problems with existing similarity measures are: (1) Information sources are directly used as a metric of similarity; (2) A method uses a particular information source without considering the contribution of others; (3) The function from information sources to semantic similarity is assumed to be in a form of specific analytical form (i.e., the function form is in a known formula) which may not be the actual one. Since semantic similarity is influenced by a number of information sources that are interlaced with each other, the information sources should be properly

H. Yin et al. (Eds.): IDEAL 2002, LNCS 2412, pp. 111–116, 2002.

processed to compute a similarity coinciding with human intuition and the function should strongly represent the relationship from information sources to similarity measure. Since neural networks can combine different information and can approximate the function by learning from data, they are used to derive similarity from information sources.

2 Methodology

The proposed method for measuring semantic similarity between words consists of two sub-tasks concerning implementation. Firstly, an extraction of structural semantic knowledge from a lexical database. Secondly, the design of the neural network for mapping lexical knowledge onto semantic similarity of words.

2.1 Semantic Knowledge from WordNet

Thanks to the success of a number of computational linguistic projects, semantic knowledge bases are readily available. The knowledge bases may be constructed in a hierarchy. Fig. 1 shows a portion of such a hierarchical semantic knowledge base.

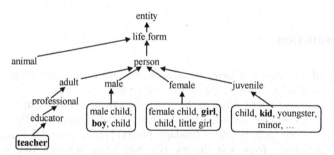

Fig. 1. Hierarchical semantic knowledge base

Given two words: w_1 and w_2, we need to find the semantic similarity of $s(w_1, w_2)$ for them. We can do this by exploration of the knowledge base, as follows. Words are organised into synonym sets (synsets) in the knowledge base [8], with semantics and relation pointers to other synsets. To establish a path between two words, each climbs up the lexical tree until the two climbing paths meet. The synset at the meeting point of the two climbing paths is the subsumer, a path connecting the two words is then found through the subsumer. One direct method for similarity calculation is to find the minimum length of path connecting the two words [9]. For example, the shortest path between *boy* and *girl* in Fig. 1 is *boy-male-**person**-female-girl*, the minimum length of path is 4, the synset of ***person*** is called the subsumer for words of *boy* and *girl*; while the minimum path length between *boy* and *teacher* is 6. Thus we could say *girl* is more similar to *boy* than *teacher* to *boy*. Rada et al [9] demonstrated that this method works well on their much constrained medical semantic nets (with 15000 medical terms). However this method may not be so accurate if it is applied to larger and more general semantic nets such as WordNet [8]. For example, the minimum length from *boy* to *animal* is 4, less than from *boy* to *teacher*, but intuitively we would not say *boy* is more similar to *animal* than to *teacher* (unless you are cursing the boy). To address this weakness, the direct path length method must be modified by utilising more information from the hierarchical semantic nets. It is intuitive that words at upper layers of the hierarchy have more general semantics and less similarity between them, while words at lower layers have more concrete semantics and more similarity. Therefore the depth of word in the hierarchy should be taken into account. On the other hand, for the same shortest path length, words with equal path length to subsumer may have different level of similarity to words with unequal path length to subsumer. As a result, we use two separate path lengths instead of the shortest path length between words.

In summary, similarity between words is determined not only by path lengths but also by depth. We propose that the similarity of $s(w_1, w_2)$ between w_1 and w_2 as a function of path lengths and depth as follows.

$$s(w_1, w_2) = f(l_1, l_2, h) \qquad (1)$$

where, l_i is the path length from w_i (i=1,2) to subsumer.

h is the depth of subsumer in the hierarchy semantic nets.

In this paper, the widely used WordNet [8] is used to extract these semantic features. These semantic features are considered to be well modelled because the lexical database is compiled by a number of lexicographers or linguists and it contains essential common human knowledge.

Synsets in WordNet are designed in a tree-like hierarchical structure going from many specific terms at the lower levels to a few generic terms at the top. The lexical hierarchy is connected by following trails of superordinate terms in "is a" or "is a kind of" (often called ISA) relations. Path lengths are obtained by counting synset links along the path from each of the words to the subsumer. The depth of the subsumer is derived by counting the levels from the subsumer to the top of the lexical hierarchy. If a word is polysemous (i.e., a word having many meanings), multiple paths may exist between the two words. Only the shortest path is then used in calculating semantic similarity between words. The subsumer on the shortest path is considered in deriving the depth of the subsumer.

2.2 Computing Semantic Similarity Using Neural Networks

As discussed above, for each pair of words, we extract three structural semantic features from the lexical database. Similarities between words are encoded in these semantic features, which are source information for any computational methods. Although all previous methods have attempted to improve the performance, they have all built on analytical form. There is no fully satisfactory analytical form of the relationship from semantic features to similarity measure. This is because of the uneven distribution of synonymous sets in the lexical hierarchy. An improvement in some aspects may cause serious side effects elsewhere in the lexical database [11]. It is therefore difficult to capture the whole distribution of the hierarchy in an analytical form. To overcome the weakness of previous methods, a multilayer feedforward neural network with backpropagation algorithm [3] is employed to learn the similarity function.

The neural network has three input nodes, one output node and a hidden layer of six nodes (this figure was empirically derived). The inputs to the network are the path length from w_1 to the subsumer, the path length from w_2 to the subsumer and the depth of the subsumer. The output provides similarity between w_1 and w_2. In computing $s(w_1, w_2)$, we do not consider direction, that is, similarity from w_1 to w_2 has the same similarity from w_2 to w_1, $s(w_1, w_2) = s(w_2, w_1)$. Thus we can form two pairs of training patterns for a pair of words as: $\{l_1 \ l_2 \ d, \ s\}$ and $\{l_2 \ l_1 \ d, \ s\}$, with most likely $l_1 \neq l_2$. This treatment doubles the size of training word set.

3   Experiment

The quality of a computational method for calculating word similarity can only be established by investigating its performance against human common sense. In evaluating our method, we compute word similarity on a benchmark word set with human ratings. A commonly used word set is from an experiment by Miller and Charles [7]. Miller and Charles gave a group of 38 human subjects thirty word pairs and asked the subjects to rate them for similarity in meaning on a scale from 0 (no similarity) to 4 (perfect synonymy). Miller-Charles' 30 word pairs were taken from Rubenstein-Goodenough's (RG) [12] original 65 pairs as 10 from high level, 10 from intermediate level and 10 from low level of semantic similarity. Rubenstein and Goodenough obtained similarity from 51 human subjects. The similarities between words were also rated on the scale of 0.0 to 4.0 for "semantically unrelated" to "highly synonymous". We use RG's original word set but consider the popularity of Miller-Charles' in our experiment.

3.1   Deriving Similarity from Neural Networks

Most researchers have used only 28 word pairs (two pairs not used) of Miller-Charles set, but ignore the remaining pairs in RG set. Since the proposed method derives word similarity from a neural network, it is ideal to use a larger number of word pairs to design the neural network. All 65 word pairs were used in our experiment. To make our results comparable with the work of other researchers, we initially divide RG set into two sub-sets: one contains the commonly used 28 pairs (called Set 0) as in Miller-Charles set, another contains the remaining 37 pairs. The later set is further divided into two sets: one contains 19 pairs (called Set 1), the other contains 18 pairs (called Set 2). We only list the words in Set 1 (in Table 1) due to space limitations. In the table, RG's human ratings are listed in column 3, structural semantic knowledge about the word pairs is extracted from WordNet using ISA relations. Set 1 is used for training the neural network, Set 2 for validating, and Set 0 for testing. Because of the limitation of the word set size, we have only 19 pairs for training. Using the assumption of symmetry for word similarity, we then have 38 training vectors.

Table 1. Word pairs with human ratings and semantic knowledge from lexical database

Word 1	Word 2	Humans	l_1	l_2	d
fruit	furnace	0.05	3	3	2
automobile	wizard	0.11	7	4	0
grin	implement	0.18	15	15	0
asylum	monk	0.39	5	5	0
boy	rooster	0.44	3	8	1
asylum	cemetery	0.79	4	5	1
shore	woodland	0.90	3	2	1
automobile	cushion	0.97	4	3	3
cemetery	woodland	1.18	5	2	1
bird	woodland	1.24	5	2	1
crane	rooster	1.41	3	4	5
cemetery	mound	1.69	5	3	1
magician	oracle	1.82	0	2	4
oracle	sage	2.61	4	3	2
cord	string	3.41	0	1	4
grin	smile	3.46	0	0	7
autograph	signature	3.59	1	0	5
cock	rooster	3.68	0	0	9
cemetery	graveyard	3.88	0	0	6

3.2 Discussion

Ten neural networks were trained using the training word pairs in Set 1. Each of the trained networks was then validated on the word pairs in Set 2. The performance of a trained network was measured by the correlation coefficient between the network outputs and the actual human ratings. The network with the best correlation coefficient on the validation set is selected as the final neural network. This is considered as the best model of the mapping from structural semantic knowledge to semantic similarity between words. As a result, the final neural network computes similarities for test word pairs. This gives a correlation coefficient of 0.8434 against human similarity ratings for test word pairs in Set 0.

As a brief comparison of the proposed method to existing methods, we provide correlation coefficients for some existing methods against RG's human ratings. The existing methods compared are the edge-counting method [9], the information content method [10], the combined method of edge counting and information content [4], and the theoretically derived information content method [5]. The results are listed in Table 2. The results demonstrate that the proposed method provides a higher correlation with human judgements than other methods. This is partly due to the learning ability of the neural network which captures the essential relationship between structural semantic knowledge and similarity rating.

Table 2. Correlation coefficients for computational methods against human ratings

Rada [9]	Resnik [10]	Jiang [4]	Lin [5]	Ours
0.6636	0.7430	0.8236	0.8224	0.8434

4 Conclusion

This paper presented a word similarity algorithm from a new perspective. We first extract structural semantic knowledge from a lexical database. Unlike existing similarity methods, we do not define similarity from directly using this first hand information. Rather all first hand information is properly processed in deriving a similarity measure. A neural network is then used to learn the mapping from structural semantic knowledge to semantic similarity. In a similar manner to other researchers, we carried out experiments on a benchmark set of word pairs with human similarity ratings. The experimental results demonstrate that the proposed method outperforms previous published methods. Since the proposed method derives similarity by supervised learning, it requires a large-enough word set to train the neural network. In this paper, although all 65 word pairs in [12] have been used in validating our method, the word set is still rather small. Constructing a large-enough set of word pairs and obtains human ratings on them remains a very large task.

References

1. Budanitsky, A., Hirst, G., Semantic Distance in WordNet: An Experimental, Application-Oriented Evaluation of Five Measures. Workshop WordNet and other Lexical Resources, North American Chapter of the Assoc. for Computational Linguistics. Pittsburgh, 2001.
2. Green, S.J., Building Hypertext Links by Computing Semantic Similarity. IEEE Trans. Knowledge and Data Engineering 11 pp.713-730, 1999.
3. Haykin, S.S., Neural networks : a Comprehensive Foundation. 2nd edn. Prentice Hall Upper Saddle River, London, 1999.
4. Jiang, J.J., Conrath, D.W., Semantic Similarity Based on Corpus Statistics and Lexical Taxonomy. Proc. ROCLING X. Taiwan, 1997.
5. Lin, D., An Information-Theoretic Definition of Similarity. Proc. Int'l Conf. Machine Learning. Madison, Wisconsin, 1998.
6. McHale, M., A Comparison of WordNet and Roget's Taxonomy for Measuring Semantic Similarity. Proc. COLING/ACL Workshop, 1998.
7. Miller G.A., Charles, W.G., Contextual Correlates of Semantic Similarity. Language and Cognitive Processes 6 pp.1-28, 1991.
8. Miller, G.A., WordNet: A Lexical Database for English. Comm. ACM 38 pp.39-41,1995.
9. Rada, R., Mili, H., Bichnell, E., Blettner M., Development and Application of a Metric on Semantic Nets. IEEE Trans. System, Man, and Cybernetics 9, pp.17-30, 1989.
10. Resnik, P., Semantic Similarity in a Taxonomy: An Information-Based Measure and its Application to Problems of Ambiguity in Natural Language. J. AI Research 11, pp.95-130, 1999.
11. Richardson, R., Smeaton, A.F., Murphy, J., Using WordNet as a Knowledge Base for Measuring Semantic Similarity. Working Paper CA-1294, Dublin City Univ., 1994.
12. Rubenstein, H., Goodenough, J.B., Contextual Correlates of Synonymy. Communications of the ACM 8, pp.627-633, 1965.
13. Srihari, R.K., Zhang, Z.F., Rao, A.B., Intelligent Indexing and Semantic Retrieval of Multimodal Documents. Information Retrieval 2, pp.245-275, 2000.

Extraction of Hidden Semantics from Web Pages

Vincenza Carchiolo, Alessandro Longheu, and Michele Malgeri

Dipartimento di Ingegneria Informatica. e delle Telecomunicazioni
Facoltà di Ingegneria – Università di Catania – V.le A. Doria 6 – Catania – Italy
{car, alongheu, mm}@diit.unict.it

Abstract. One of the main limitation when accessing web is the lack of explicit structure, whose presence may help in understanding data semantics. Here, an approach to extract logical schema from web pages is presented, defining a page model where its contents is divided into "logical" sections, i.e. parts of a page each collecting related information. This model aims to take into account both traditional, static HTML pages, as well as dynamic pages content.

1 Introduction

The World Wide Web is the largest data collection, accessible by anyone from anywhere. Hovever, one of the main limitation is the lack of explicit structure, whose presence helps in understanding data semantics, making it easier and time-saving for users to locate information, in contrast with current browsing/searching, where data comprehension is mainly based on intuition [1].

From an historical point of view, the original goal of WWW was to provide a simple tool to exchange text and file [2]; indeed the initial set of tags included just tags to represent data in a structured way (e.g. using <h1>,...,<h6>). Then, the introduction of larger tag sets improved significantly graphical appearance, though it does not allow to clearly distinguish data structure from its representation; the need of structuring, in this sense, aims to bring web utilization to its initial stage.

Exploiting structure is important both for traditional, static HTML pages, as well as for dynamic pages, which allow to use the web as a front-end for several services based on structured data sources (databases, e-commerce, home banking).

In this paper, we want to focus on existing web pages: indeed, while a good schema can be effectively associated during the design or creation of web pages [3], considerable work must be performed on the great amount of existing web pages [4]. Several attemps have been performed to structure existing web pages [5][6][7][8][9], though these approaches mainly tend to extract specific or partial information from web pages through semiautomatic tools which analyze HTML page source. Our attempt is to provide a schema of the entire page which is also *logical*, i.e. based on "logical" sections, each being a part of the page collecting related information.

In the following, we provide a page model starting to consider static HTML page analysis [10][11], then taking into account that the presence of client/server side programming (Java applets, Active-X technologies, scripting), and style sheets in web pages is increasing significantly, affecting the semantic of that (dynamic) page.

H. Yin et al. (Eds.): IDEAL 2002, LNCS 2412, pp. 117–122, 2002.
© Springer-Verlag Berlin Heidelberg 2002

In section 2 we present logical sections, together with a procedure used to schematize a static web page into such sections; in section 3 we consider dynamic issues, while in section 4 we present conclusions and future work.

2   Modeling Static Web Pages

Information placed inside web pages (e.g. text data, hyperlinks, images), generally do not form a monolithic block, rather it is possible to divide the page into a set of *logical sections* which aim to reflect the logical structure given by the author. The logical sections we define are the following:

- *document information* section, containing metadata (e.g. *<!doctype>*, related DTD, author, etc.). This section, when exists, is enclosed with *<head>* tags.
- *logical heading* section, used to present the page and/or site, e.g. with a title or a logo of the site. This section is generally placed at the beginning of the page.
- *logical footer* section, generally placed at the bottom of page and containing information as e.g. link to webmasters, text with copyright. Header and footer logical sections are generally present in pages belonging to the same site.
- *logical link* section, a set of HTML tags representing a link, and always including a physical one (*<a href...>*). Several properties for logical links can be defined [10].
- *index* section is a group of logical links having similar properties; such links often have similar graphical appearance and are placed closed to each other.
- *logical data* section, where we find main information of the site/page, i.e. where the semantic of the page is mainly placed.
- *interactive* section, i.e. forms for users interaction, as search bar in search engines.

In order to divide a page into such sections, we first model the page as a tree according to the hierarchy of HTML tags, then we locate some specific tags having a primary role for giving a structure to the page.

We define a set of such *primary tags* having the following features: tags used to format text in paragraph, table and any similar graphic presentation, e.g., *<p>*, *<table>* (they are implicitly used by the author to create the logical structure of the document); tags used to divide the page, as *<hr>* (they are also used to separate portion of text usually having different semantics); tags needed to manage frames and forms (the latter are used to detect interactive sections).

Based on these considerations and considering a typical web page, we choose the following html tags as primary nodes: *table, p, map, hr, a, frame, iframe, head, form, select, input, td, tr, option, area.*

We then associate to each primary node a set of properties, used to structure the page: the list of its *attributes*, e.g. *bgcolor* for a *td* element; the *relative depth*, i.e. the number of primary nodes present in the path from root node (the *<html>* tag) to current node (relative depth starts from 0); the *absolute depth*, which is the number of nodes from root node to current node (it is the ordinary depth, starting from 0 as relative depth); the *number of levels*, i.e. the average absolute depth from current node to its leaves; finally, the *number of leaves*, considered just if the primary node *directly* contains leaves (i.e. no other nodes, primary or not, must be present between the primary node and its leaves, otherwise this parameter is set to 0).

After primary nodes and their properties are defined, we introduce the *collection*, defined as *a set of consecutive HTML tags containing repeated similar structures*. For instance, the collection in Tab.1 represents a set of links inside a page; the idea is to detect such repeated structures using their structural *similarity*, in order to further discover logical sections (each made by one or more collections).

Table 1. An example of collection

```
<a href...>...</a><br>
<a href...>...</a><br>
<a href...><img src...>...</a><br>
<a href...>...</a><p>
<a href...>...</a><p>
```

The idea of collections facilitates the structuring of a page: on one hand it avoids to consider each single tag, which is a too detailed level, hence reducing the number of elements (tree nodes) to be analyzed, also making it effective the use of information retrievial techniques [12] applied to the page content; on the other hand, it avoids to consider the page as a whole, dividing it into grainer parts when detecting its semantics.

Collections are built using primary nodes and their properties defined previously. Indeed, we first consider just repeated tags sequences starting with (i.e. embedded into) primary nodes, then using primary nodes properties to evaluate similarity for such sequences, so we group them into a single collection, creating a structural backbone of the page; note that, viewing the page as a tree, these sequences are *subtrees* having primary nodes as *root*.

In particular, we compare subtrees whose roots are primary nodes having the same primary node as ancestor (we refer to these subtrees as *brothers*). Then, we define a *distance* for brothers subtrees using the properties associated to each primary node (root of the subtree): the more the distance is, the less similar subtrees will be.

Distance is evaluated for each brother subtrees pair, establishing if they are similar using a proper threshold. If brother subtrees are similar, they belong to the same collection, and the collection grows until other similar brother subtrees are found. When there are no more similar subtrees, the current collection stops and a new collection is created, while when brother subtrees are all examined, the algorithm continues from the upper level of the tree. This method tends to emulate the schema that intuition suggests. Details about the algorithm, together with a comprehensive example, are shown in [11].

Once collections are built to detect the structural skeleton of the page, they are mapped to logical sections. In particular:

- *document information section* comes directly form the (unique) collection rooted by the *<head>* primary node.
- *header section* is associated to the collection containing the same information present inside the collection rooted by the *<head>* (in particular inside *<title>* and *<meta>* tags) or inside the page URL. To locate header section, all collections must be indexed [12] so their semantics can be analyzed in order to find which collections satisfy the previous criteria. If more collections are candidate, the nearest to the beginning of the page is chosen.

- *footer section*, similarly to header section, semantics has to be analyzed. If more sections are candidate, the nearest to the end of the page is chosen.
- *index sections* is located simply searching collections containing *<a href>* tags, but we could have a data section containing text with some link inside. On the other hand, we could look for *<a href>* tags with no text inside, but we could also have an index section with each link described by some text. In order to distinguish such situations, we compare the number of words contained in text portions with the number of links. An index section can be splitted into different index sections by examining links properties [10].
- *logical data section* can be associated to collection containing text, but as shown before, a more accurate analysis must be performed to check if the collection should be mapped on to a different section [13].
- *interactive sections* comes from collections containing *<form>*, *<input>*, *<select>* tags.

We note that logical section extraction shown so far is actually more complex [13].

3 Dynamic Pages Issues

The use of dynamic web pages is increasing significantly, determining a migration from simple static pages to pages with extended functionalities. In particular, two aspects have to be considered: on one hand, the use of server-side languages, as CGI, PhP, ASP, which provide interactive data entry capabilities and dynamically generated content; on the other, client-side languages, as Active-X controls, Java applets, Javascript, Vbscript, which extend the interaction paradigm by allowing content designers to specify reactive behaviors in web pages in a much more modular and efficient fashion (i.e. reducing the load on the server side when the appearance of the page must be changed in response to some user event). In the following, we introduce some considerations about dynamic issues.

Considering logical sections, both languages categories do not actually determine new sections, rather they empower logical sections functionalities (for instance, for *interactive* sections) or simply their graphical appearance (e.g. Javascript interactive menus), whereas they could make more difficult automatic section recognition.

Starting from considering scripting client-side languages, the code is generally embedded in the page, and it can be identified by searching for the <SCRIPT> tag. This tag has no actually influence during the building of collections, whereas its embedded code can be useful when extracting semantics from collections, in order to map them into logical sections. In particular the semantics can be enriched by analyzing the source code, for instance properly classifying the methods, properties, and events used: if indeed just graphical methods are present, that code probably just improves the appearance and/or user interaction, whereas the presence of forms and/or associated parameters manipulations reveal the presence of additional functionalities.

Note that this approach fail when no source code but just a reference is present, i.e. for Java applets and Active-X controls; in this case, in order to discover some information about methods and events used, the runtime environment should be exploited (for instance, using the Reflection tool in the Java SDK). Both for explicitly present and for just referenced code, it may be difficult to establish precisely what code actually does, so some sort of (possibly simple) code reverse engineering on that code should be anyway performed.

When considering server-side languages, they are used to provide (a) interactive data entry capabilities as well as (b) dynamically generated content; in both cases, the code is not embedded into the page. In the (a) case, the only semantics that can be extracted from that page and that can be used when mapping collections into logical sections, comes from the analysis of type, name and number of parameters exchanged with the server (they for instance can help to better characterize a given interactive section). In the (b) case, the content of a page is dynamically generated, hence the structure of that page is always fixed, making it easier the extraction of collections for instance allowing to build a structure pattern library.

Finally, the use of style sheets is also becoming a frequent choice in designing web pages; their presence can be used to provide useful information during the building of collection and the extraction of logical sections. For instance, the use of a specific statement style for a given tag may reveal a major/minor importance for that tag, and this can be used to refine primary tags definition and/or to refine collections construction; or the use of a given style across a page can also reveal when collections, even different or not consecutive, should be actually intended as a whole, hence causing they will be mapped into a single logical section.

4 Conclusions and Future Work

This paper presents an approach to extract the logical structure of a web page. We start defining some tags having a primary role in representing the structure of the page. We also introduce collections, i.e. sequence of tags (viewed as subtrees in the HTML tree) rooted at some primary tags, which allow to determine a structural schema of the page. Then, the page is divided into collections and finally we use the semantic of each collection to map them into logical sections, achieving a logical schema of the page. Future directions are to extend the model in order to better take into account dynamic aspects, as mentioned in section 3. We are also investigating on how to use full XML capabilities, as defining a set of XML tags to access and locate each section [10], or to put into HTML pages semantics information [14][15][16][17], also considering metadata support as RDF [18][19], XML Namespaces or XML schemas [20]. We are also considering *user profile* (which stores user actions and preferences) to use schema to automatically provide users with filtered pages according to their preferences. Moreover, *page profile* can be defined to create one schema for similar pages, e.g. uniforming different schemas for pages belonging to sites in the same area of interest. Finally, further analysis is needed in order to significantly improve browsing (e.g. developing structure-aware browsers to allow users to exploit page/site schemas [11]) and searching [21][22][23] (e.g. improving it through XML [24]).

References

1. Apers, P.M.G.: Identifying internet-related database reasearch, 2nd Intl. East-West DB Workshop, 1994.
2. WWW Consortium – http://www.w3.org
3. Ceri, S., et al.: Design Principles for Data-intensive Web Sites – Proc. Of ACM SIGMOD, 1999
4. Abiteboul, S.: et al., Data on the Web, Morgan Kaufmann, 2000.
5. Huck, G., et al., Jedi: extracting and synthesizing information form the web, Proc of 3rd IFCIS - CoopIS, 1998.
6. Adelberg, B.: NoDoSe: A tool for semi-automatically extracting structured and semistructured data from text documents, Proc. of ACM SIGMOD, 1998.
7. Hammer, J., et al.: Extracting semistructured information from the web, Workshop on Management of semistr. data, 1997.
8. Smith, D., Lopez, M.: Information Extraction for semi-structured documents, Proc. of Workshop on management of Semistructured data, 1997.
9. Vijjappu, L., et al., Web structure analysis for information mining
10. Longheu, A., Carchiolo, V., Malgeri, M.: Structuring the web, Proc. of DEXA - Takma – London, 2000
11. Longheu, A., Carchiolo, V., Malgeri, M.: Extracting logical schema from the web, Applied Intelligence, Special issue on text and web mining, Kluwer Academic.
12. Baeza-Yates, R. et al.: Modern Information Retrievial, ACM Press, 1999
13. Parisi, C., Longheu, A.: Ristrutturazione dei siti web: un modello semantico per l'accesso alle informazioni, Tech Internal Report No. DIIT00/Ah74, 2000
14. Suciu, D.: On database theory and XML, http://www.cs.washington.edu/ homes/suciu
15. Heflin, J.: Towards the semantic web: knowledge representation in a dynamic, distributed environment, Phd thesis, University of Maryland, College Park. 2001 - http://www.cs.umd.edu/users/heflin/
16. Bry, F., et al.: Towards grouping constructs for semistructured data, technical report PMS-FB-2001-7, Computer Science inst., Munich, Germany
17. Heflin, J., et al: Dynamic ontologies on the web, Proc of the Seventeenth National Conference on Artificial Intelligence - AAAI-2000, 2000
18. RDF Recommendation – http://www.w3.org/TR/REC-rdf-syntax
19. Decker, S., et al.: The semantic web – on the respective roles of XML and RDF, IEEE Internet Computing, 2000
20. Mani, M., et al.: Semantic data modeling using XML schemas, Proc. 20th Intl Conf. on Conceptual Modeling (ER), 2001.
21. Davulcu, H., et al.: A layered architecture for querying dynamic web content, Proc. of ACM Conference on Management of Data (SIGMOD), 1999.
22. Lawrence, S.: Context in web search, IEEE Data engineering bulletin, Vol. 23, no. 3, 2000
23. Suciu, D. et al.: Focusing search in hierarchical structures with directory sets, http://www.cs.washington.edu/homes/suciu
24. Fiebig, T. et al.: Evaluating queries on structure with extended access support relations, Proc. of 3rd International Workshop on Web and Databases - WebDB, 2000

Self-Organising Maps for Hierarchical Tree View Document Clustering Using Contextual Information

Richard Freeman and Hujun Yin

University of Manchester Institute of Science and Technology (UMIST),
Department of Electrical Engineering and Electronics,
PO Box 88, Manchester, M60 1QD,
United Kingdom

rics@swift.ee.umist.ac.uk
h.yin@umist.ac.uk
http://images.ee.umist.ac.uk/rics/
http://images.ee.umist.ac.uk/hujun/

Abstract. In this paper we propose an effective method to cluster documents into a dynamically built taxonomy of topics, directly extracted from the documents. We take into account short contextual information within the text corpus, which is weighted by importance and used as input to a set of independently spun growing Self-Organising Maps (SOM). This work shows an increase in precision and labelling quality in the hierarchy of topics, using these indexing units. The use of the tree structure over sets of conventional two-dimensional maps creates topic hierarchies that are easy to browse and understand, in which the documents are stored based on their content similarity.

1 Introduction

With the tremendous growth of digital content on corporate intranets, organisation and retrieval is becoming more and more problematic. Manual document sorting is difficult and inefficient in a highly competitive and fast moving e-market where the corporations have to keep the leading edge over their competitors. This is why knowledge and content management has recently created so much interest. In this paper we propose a method that greatly enhances automated document management using document clustering which automatically organises documents into a generated hierarchy of topics. This taxonomy is automatically built based on the contents of the documents and without using any prior knowledge or metadata. In the indexing stage all the text corpus for each document is analysed and important features are extracted and formed into vectors. Document clustering is then performed using a set of one-dimensional, independently spun, growing Self-Organising Maps (SOM).

This paper is organised as follows. Section 2 briefly introduces general document clustering procedures. Section 3 describes the related work, which used the SOM for document clustering. Section 4 then presents the proposed method. Section 5 presents and discusses the experiments and finally section 6 concludes and suggests possible future work.

H. Yin et al. (Eds.): IDEAL 2002, LNCS 2412, pp. 123-128, 2002.

2 Document Clustering Overview

Document clustering is an area in Information Retrieval (IR) and deals with grouping similar documents together without any prior knowledge of their organisation. In the first stage, document indexing involves transforming text or strings into commonly a vector or histogram form. In general not all the indexed terms are of interest or useful, so feature selection is performed. Then the remaining terms are usually weighted according to their statistical importance. Finally similarity computations are performed amongst documents using those terms and a clustering algorithm.

2.1 Indexing Methods

The currently most popular method is the Vector Space Model [1], which is claimed to outperform more sophisticated methods, that rely for example on lists of synonyms or tables of term relationships. Single term indexing is one of the most simple and common methods widely used by the IR community. In this method the frequency of each word in each document is recorded in a large documents Vs words matrix. This single term method is also called "bag of words", since a lot of semantics and meaning is lost when ignoring the neighbouring words, which provide some context. Another indexing method that uses a succession of words in a short context partially solves this problem. A comparison for these two indexing methods has shown that more accurate terms and a superior cluster quality for multiple successive words they call "lexical affinities" [2]. Other approaches to indexing also exist such as n-grams, linguistic terms or full sentences.

2.2 Feature Selection and Term Weightings

In most IR systems the indexing phase is then followed by a feature selection and weighting phase. The feature selection involves discarding common words such as "the", "of" or "and" stored in a stop list, which are very frequent and alone do not convey much meaning. Then a suffix-stripping algorithm such as Porter's, is used to stem the words to a common reduced form. The remaining words are then typically weighted using the $tf \times idf$ [1]. This allows the less frequent words to be given more weighting than the more frequent ones. Following Shannon's information theory the less frequent the word, the more information value it conveys.

In IR, feature selection is a phase where the potential relevant features are selected and the less important or irrelevant ones are discarded. For text analysis there are broadly speaking two methods that use thresholds or term co-occurrence analysis methods. Thresholds are generally used to discard all the words that occur in most documents, as these are less likely to help discriminate between different documents. Also words that do not occur in many documents can be discarded, as these might be too specific. The other indexing methods involve term co-occurrence analysis, such as in Latent Semantic Indexing [3], Word Category Maps (WCM) [4] or random projection [5].

2.3 Clustering

Using the terms previously obtained from indexing and feature selection, document clustering can be performed. Many methods from cluster analysis can be applied in IR, such as partitioning methods like k-means or hierarchical methods like compete-linkage. In this paper we focus on using SOM to perform the document clustering. The two reasons for using SOM rather than other clustering methods are that it is topologically preserving and clustering is performed non-linearly on the given input data sets. The topologically preserving property allows the SOM applied to document clustering, to group similar documents together in a cluster and organise similar clusters close together unlike most other clustering methods.

3   Related Work

The SOM and its variants have widely been used to cluster documents such as large two-dimensional map [5], a hierarchical set of maps [6], a growing map [7], a set of growing hierarchical maps [8] and tree view based hierarchical maps [9]. There are also other variants SOM algorithms that could be used for document clustering such as the Neural Gas [10], iSOM [11] or ViSOM [12].

The SOM has also previously been used with contextual information as indexing units rather than using the single term indexing representation. In WEBSOM a two-step approach was used [4]. The first step called WCM was to use a window of three words to create a cluster of categories. Then a second level called Document Map was used to cluster documents using the WCM terms. Note that the three words were only used to cluster terms and not to perform the document clustering. This approach was later abandoned in favour of random projection, which gave superior results [5]. In another SOM based approach, full sentences were used as indexing units [13]. The results using sentences as indexing units and no stemming were similar to using single term approaches in combination with more complicated pre-processing like stemming. However this approach was described as slow and requiring large memory storage even with suggested enhancements.

4   The Proposed Method

Most of the methods using the SOM for documents clustering use the "bag of words" method to represent documents, where only isolated words are indexed. In the proposed method we are extending the work on SOM for tree view based document clustering [9] to make use of short contextual information.

4.1 Document Pre-processing

The document pre-processing includes the indexing, feature selection and term weighting as follows:

1. Discard any words in the stop list of common words (such as pronouns, articles or prepositions) and apply plural stemming to the remaining words.
2. Index the stemmed words using a sliding window over each sentence.
3. Discard words that occur infrequently or too frequently in all documents.
4. Weight the remaining terms using $tf \times idf$ [1] and bias factors depending on feature type (1 word, 2 words or 3 words see **Table 1**).
5. Normalise vectors to give words equal importance in short and longer documents.

For the feature selection we have chosen to use an upper and lower threshold to discard infrequent and too frequent terms that are most unlikely to help discriminate between documents. The flexibility in implementation allows a combination a successive single terms, dual terms and triple terms. This allows a weighting bias for each of these features as shown in **Table 1**. There are more complicated approaches such as performing two levels of clustering: the first selects the suitable terms and second clusters the documents, using those selected terms such as in [4][5][8][13].

Table 1. Preliminary weighting bias for each type of feature

Feature Type	Weighting
1 word	0.25
2 words	0.35
3 words	0.40

4.2 SOM Procedure

Most previous SOM methods for document analysis used a single or a set of two-dimensional maps [4][5][8][13], which we believe makes realistic large-scale documents browsing problematic. Many existing hierarchical organisation systems use one-dimension to effectively sort the documents, files or books. From the Dewey Decimal Classification (DDC), used worldwide to classify books into a hierarchy of predefined topics, up to the tree view file organisations in Graphical User Interface Operating Systems. So in using one-dimensional SOM, we can directly tie the trained maps as a browsable hierarchical tree, without the need of an extra layer of abstraction as shown in **Fig. 1**. In the Tree View SOM [9] growth is done at map and hierarchical levels. The main idea for these growths is not impose a structure on the documents, but to use the underlying structure to create the taxonomy.

5 Experimentation and Discussion

The test data is shown below in **Table 2**. These web documents are variable in both length and content. The content varies greatly from a simple title with one sentence description to table of contents, description of the features, summary, preface and entire articles.

Set A and *Set B* contain documents on sciences, math and economics but *Set C* deals much more with social issues, politics and literature which are more ambiguous to understand and cluster autonomously. From visual inspection it seems that using multiple words has benefits of accurately indexing terms such as "foreign exchange market", "molecular biology" or "corporate finance". However it was also observed that two or three word terms such as "case study", "companion web site" or "real world" also become part of the corpus, which in some cases may not be desirable.

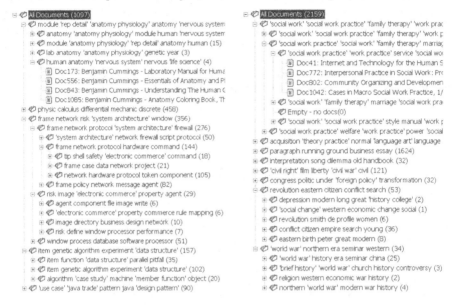

Fig. 1. Shows two trees of topics generated from *Set B* on the left and *Set C* on the Right, using the proposed method. The labels are chosen by ranking the top five terms with the lowest quantization error at each particular node. Multiple terms are marked with single quotes.

Table 2. Test Document Used for Clustering

Set Name	Number of docs	Number of pages	Document source
Set A	618	1 to 16	www.prenhall.com
Set B	1097	1 to 13	www.aw.com
Set C	2159	1 to 28	www.ablongman.com

An advantage of using multiple successive words as indexing units, is that more accurate features such as "document analysis" are taken into account, rather than the isolated words "document" and "analysis". This creates a basic word disambiguation-indexing scheme applicable to most languages. Another advantage is that this creates a larger set of features from which the most interesting and relevant terms can be selected. Labelling is also made clearer, allowing the user to have a better idea of the contents of each folder or sub-folder without viewing their contents. Visual inspection has shown that the weightings given in **Table 1** provides good labels and clusters for the three data sets. When the weightings were all equal, we observed that many two-word terms naturally ranked within the top five for each cluster, showing their importance to the SOM in the clustering process and their relevance to the underlying topics contained in each cluster.

6 Conclusion and Future Work

We have introduced an improved indexing method for the SOM, allowing more precise clustering and more logical labelling. This has been tested on three different realistic data sets of unpredictable content and of greatly variable length. We have also seen that weightings of the short contextual indexing units plays an important role in providing satisfactory results to the overall process of both clustering and labelling. Future work might include looking at the ways to enhance the text processing and feature selection to scale up the number of documents to be clustered. Labelling could also be enhanced with further processing.

References

1. Salton, G., Automatic text processing: the transformation, analysis, and retrieval of information by Computer, Reading, Mass.Wokingham: Addison-Wesley 1988.
2. Maarek, Y.S., Fagin, R., Ben-Shaul, I.Z., Pelleg, D., Ephemeral document clustering for web applications, IBM Research Report RJ 10186, April, 2000.
3. Deerwester, S., Dumais, S.T., Furnas, G.W., Landauer, T.K., and Harshman, R., Indexing by latent semantic analysis. Journal of the American Society for Information Science, 41(6), pp.391-407, 1990.
4. Honkela, T., WEBSOM Self-Organizing Maps of Document Collections, Proceedings of WSOM'97, Workshop on Self-Organizing Maps, Espoo, Finland, June 4-6, 1997.
5. Kohonen, T., Kaski, S., Lagus, K., Salojärvi, J., Paatero, V., Saarela, A., Self Organization of a Massive Document Collection. IEEE Transactions on Neural Networks, Special Issue on Neural Networks for Data Mining and Knowledge Discovery, vol. 11, n. 3, pp.574-585, May, 2000.
6. Miikkulainen, R., Script recognition with hierarchical feature maps. Connection Science, 2(1&2), pp.83-101, 1990.
7. Alahakoon, D., Halgamuge, S.K., Srinivasan, B., Dynamic self organizing maps with controlled growth for knowledge discovery, IEEE Transactions on Neural Networks, vol. 11, pp.601-614, 2000.
8. Dittenbach, M., Merkl, D., Rauber, A., The Growing Hierarchical Self-Organizing Map, Proceedings of the International Joint Conference on Neural Networks (IJCNN 2000), vol. 6, pp.15-19, July 24-27, 2000.
9. Freeman, R., Yin, H., Allinson, N. M., Self-Organising Maps for Tree View Based Hierarchical Document Clustering, Proceedings of the International Joint Conference on Neural Networks (IJCNN'02), vol.2, pp.1906-1911, Honolulu, Hawaii, 12-17 May, 2002.
10. Martinetz, T.M., Berkovich, S.G., Schulten, K.J., "Neural-Gas" Network for Vector Quantization and its Application to Time-Series Prediction, IEEE Transactions on Neural Networks, Vol. 4, No.4, pp.558-569, July, 1993.
11. Yin, H., Allinson, N.M., Interpolating self-organising maps (iSOM), Electronics Letters, Vol. 35, No.19, pp.1649-1650, 1999.
12. Yin, H., ViSOM - A novel method for multivariate data projection and structure visualisation, in IEEE Transactions on Neural Networks, Vol.13, No.1, 2002.
13. Pullwitt, D., Der, R., Integrating Contextual Information into Text Document clustering with Self-Organizing Maps, in Advances in Self-Organising Maps, N. Allinson, H. Yin, L. Allinson, J. Slack (Eds.), Springer, pp.54-60, 2001.

Schema Discovery of the Semi-structured and Hierarchical Data

Jianwen He

Department of Mathematics,Inner Mongolia University,
Inner Mongolia,Huhehot,China, 010021
nddj@imu.edu.cn

Abstract. Web data are typically Semi-structured data and lack explicit external schema information, which makes querying and browsing the web data inefficient. In this paper, we present an approach to discover the inherent schema(s) in semi-structured, hierarchical data sources fast and efficiently, based on OEM model and efficient pruning strategy. The schema discovered by our algorithm is a kind of data path expressions and can be transformed into schema tree easily.

1 Introduction

With the explosive growing of World Wide Web (WWW) and the rapid increase of applications that integrate heterogeneous data sources, semi-structured hierarchical data sources are becoming widely available to users. There are two kinds of semi-structured data: data coming directly from the semi-structured data resources (such as the web pages, electronic documents and E-mails), and data expressed in common data model (such as OEM --- Object Exchange Model, which is needed when integrating heterogeneous data sources). Unlike data stored in typical relational or object oriented databases, semi-structured data does not have fixed schema known in advance and stored separately from the data [1, 6].

The lack of external schema information makes querying and browsing the web data inefficient at best, and impossible at worst [6]. To generate any meaningful query over the semi-structured, hierarchical data, we need first to know how the information in the source is represented, that is to say, we need to know the data schema embedded in the source. So people expect to extract data schema from semi-structured data to make efficient searching by using data structure information [2-5].

There are several ways to deal with the lack of fixed schema [3]. A method is to discover the schema of semi-structured data, that is, to find data structure and relations within data objects. Researchers have done a lot of work in the area [1,2,5,6,8]. S. Nestorov *et al* presented a novel approach in [6] which uses *MFRO* (Minimal Full Representative Objects) to express the schema of hierarchical semi-structured data. The *MFRO* can be used in schema discovery, path queries and query optimization. Their main idea is transforming the OEM graph to the state transforming graph of NFA (Non-deterministic Finite Automation), then determining and minimizing it to get *MFRO*s. To reduce the computational complexity, they

H. Yin et al. (Eds.): IDEAL 2002, LNCS 2412, pp. 129-134, 2002.

present *k-Ro*, which is the approximation of *MFRO*, to replace *MFRO*. Nevertheless, their method produces too large schema and is time-consuming, because all schema information is included in the target schema.

As we know, too large schema may depress the efficiency of querying data, so it is necessary to ignore some infrequent and unimportant structural information. In this paper, we present a novel approach which uses pruning strategy to overcome the shortcomings of Nestorov's algorithm. As a result of using pruning and top-down strategy, our algorithm is of higher efficiency in theory, which has been underpined by experiments.

2 Concepts and Definitions

OEM is a self-describing object model designed specially for expressing semi-structured data [5,6]. It can be regarded as a graph in which a vertex corresponds to a data object and the label attached to an edge between two vertexes represents the hierarchical reference of the two vertexes. Each data object in OEM has two attributes: its identifier and value. Figure 1 is an example of OEM culled from [6] in which circles are elided, for we don't take them into account in the paper.

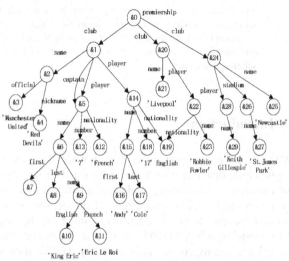

Fig. 1. A example of OEM

Definition 1: *Simple path expression (SPE).*

Let l_i be a label (of object references) for $i = 1...n$, $n \geq 0$. Then $SPE = l_1, l_2, ..., l_n$ is a simple path expression of length *n*. For *i, j* (*i,j*=1,2,...,*n*), if *i≠j*, then $l_i \neq l_j$.

For $SPE1 = l_i, l_{i+1}, ... l_{i+k}$, if $i \geq 1$ and $i+k \leq n$, then *SPE1* is call an ordered subsequence of *SPE* (defined as above), and *k* is the length of *SPE1*. If *SPE* isn't an ordered subsequence of any simple path expression in the OEM, it is called a maximal simple path expression and is noted as *MSPE*.

Definition 2: *Support of SPE.*

It is defined as the value of times that *SPE* occurs in the OEM, and is noted as *SUP(SPE)*.

To prune away simple path expression of lower support, we must assign a minimal support which is noted as *MINSUP*. If the support of a *MSPE* is greater than *MINSUP*, then the *MSPE* is regarded *frequent*, and is noted as *FMSPE*.

Definition 3: *Data path (DP).*

Let O_i be an object for $i = 0...n$, l_i be a label for $i = 1..n$, and $<l_i$, identifier(O_i) $>\in$ value(O_{i-1}) for $i = 1...n$, $n \geq 0$. Then $DP=O_0,l_1,O_1,l_2,...,O_{n-1},l_n,O_n$ is a data path, of length n. It is an instance of the simple path expression $SPE = l_1,l_2,...,l_n$.

Example. To illustrate the above terms, consider the premiership object from Fig. 1.
- Player.Number is a simple path expression of length 2, and is an ordered subsequence of the maximal simple path expression Club.Player.Number.
- It has two instance data paths, i.e. obj(&1).Player.obj(&5).Number.obj(&13) and obj(&1).Player.obj(&14).Number.obj(&18), so its support is 2.
- If the *MINSUP* is 1 or 2, it is *frequnt*, and if the *MINSUP* is equal to or greater than 3, then it is *not frequnt*.

3 Schema Discovery

Schema discovery is used to find the structure embodied in data and relations within data objects. We associate the problem with the discovery of maximal frequent item set in transaction database [7]. The OEM graph can be regarded as the transaction database D and the *FMSPE*s as maximal frequent items. Using the method of association rule mining, we construct the set T including all labels first (T corresponds with transaction item set T), then start at T, create candidate set (*FMSPECS*) from layer down to layer, and produce *FMSPE*s quickly by adopting pruning strategy. So we must construct the sets D and T before discovering the data schema.

3.1 Constructing Set D and T from OEM Graph

As one simple path may correspond to several data path expressions, so we define the set of all data paths as the set D, and design a function spe(dp) to transform a data path to a simple path expression. We also introduce a symbol "$\perp$" to avoid some frequent structures being pruned.

Set T is the set of all labels in D. To improve the efficiency of schema discovery, we sort labels in T according to their layer numbers. For $T=\{l_{11},l_{12},...,l_{21},l_{22},...,l_{n1},l_{n2},...\}$, n is the largest layer number of the OEM graph, and l_{ij} means it is the label of number j in layer i.

Algorithm 1: sup(spe, D)
```
/*Function that calculates the support of spe. */
  { O={};
   for i=1 to |D|  do
        if spe is a ordered subset of spe(D[i])
        then
      { o=last(dp(spe,D[i]);
        if o∈O then
              O=O∪{o} };
   return |O| }
```

Note: The function *dp(spe, D[i])* returns instances of *spe* in *D[i]*, function *last*(dp) returns the last data object in data path *dp*, and '$|O|$' is the degree of *D*, namely the number of elements in set *D*.

3.2 Algorithm for Schema Discovery

Algorithm *schema-discovery*() below use functions *delete*(), *pruning*() and *gen-fmspecs*() to find *FMSPES*, the set of maximal frequent simple path expressions. Here function *delete*(FMSPECS, FMSPECS[i]) deletes element *FMSPECS*[i] from *FMSPECS*, *pruning*() is the pruning function, and *gen-fmspecs*() is function generating *FMSPECS*, the set of candidates of maximal frequent simple path expressions.

In function *gen-fmspecs*(), the *FMSPECS* is generated step by step. The candidate *FMSPEs* in *FMSPECS* of step $k+1$ are generated from *FMSPECS* of step k. As we adopt the top-down method, they are the *MSPEs that* include those *MSPEs* whose lengths are k.

The function pruning() utilizes the hierarchical characteristic of OEM. If a *SPE* isn't frequent, *SPEs* that include it must not be frequent and will be pruned.

Algorithm 2:
```
Schema-discovery(T, D, MINSUP)
{ k=0; FMSPECS={T}; FMSPES={};
  while FMSPECS≠∅ do
  { pruning(FMSPECS, k, MINSUP, D);
    for i=1 to |FMSPECS| do
        if ((|FMSPECS[i]|≤k) .or.
            (sup(FMSPECS[i], D)≥ MINSUP)) then
        { FMSPE=FMSPE∪FMSPECS[i];
                delete(FMSPECS, FMSPECS[i] ) }
    FMSPECS=gen-FMSPECS(FMSPECS, k);
    k=k+1; }
    delete non-MSPE in FMSPES;
    return FMSPES; }
```

Algorithm 3:
```
gen- FMSPECS (FMSPECS, k)
/* to generate the FMSPECS */
{cs={};
for i=1 to |FMSPECS| do
{ mₖ={left(FMSPECS[i],k)};
    /*get anterior k elements of FMSPECS[i]*/
mₖ₊₁={a|a∈FMSPECS[i], level(a)=k+1};
    /*put elements of FMSPECS[i] in layer k+1
    into mₖ₊₁ */
mₕ=FMSPECS[i]- mₖ- mₖ₊₁;
for j=1 to | mₖ₊₁| do
  if mₖ₊₁ [j]="⊥" then cs=cs∪ mₖ₊₁ [j]
  else { m= mₖ ∪ mₖ₊₁ [j] ∪mₕ;
      cs=cs∪{m} }}
return cs }
```

Algorithm 4:
Pruning(FMSPECS, k, MINSUP,D)
{ for i=1 to |FMSPECS| do
 { m_k={left(FMSPECS[i],k)};
    /*get anterior k elements of FMSPECS[i] */
  m_{k+1}={a|a∈FMSPECS[i], level(a)=k+1};
    /*put elements of FMSPECS[i] in layer k+1
    into m_{k+1} */
  m_h=FMSPECS[i]- m_k- m_{k+1};
  for j=1 to | m_{k+1}| do
   if (sup(m_k∪m_{k+1} [j], D)<MINSUP then
 delete(FMSPECS[i], m_{k+1} [j])
  m_{k+1}={a|a∈FMSPECS[i], level(a)=k+1};
  if | m_{k+1}|=0 then FMSPECS[i],=m_k;
  else if (| m_{k+1}|=1 and m_{k+1} [1]="⊥")
     then
       FMSPECS[i],=m_k; ∪ m_{k+1} [j]; } }

4   Transforming the Extracted Schema to the Schema Tree

Using our above algorithms, we extract schema from figure 1. Schema 1 is the result
when MINISUP (mini-support) is 1, and schema 2 is the result when MINISUP is 2.

Schema 1 (MINSUP=1):

{{club.name.official. ⊥}, {club.name.nickname. ⊥},{club.captain.name.first. ⊥}, {club.captain.
name.last. ⊥}, {club.captain.name.nickname.English ⊥}, {club.stadium.sname.⊥}, {club.
captain.member.⊥}, {club.captain.nationality.⊥}, {club.player.member.⊥}, {club.player.nation-
ality.⊥}, {club.player.name.English.⊥}, {club.player.name.French.⊥}, {club.player.name.first.⊥
}, {club.player.name.last.⊥}, {club.captain.name.nickname.French ⊥}}

Schema 2 (MINSUP=2):

{{club.name, ⊥}, { club.player.name.first, ⊥},{ club.player.name.last ⊥}, { club.player.natio-
nality, ⊥},{ club.player.number ⊥}

We can see from schema 1 and schema 2 that the extracted schema includes all the
structure in the original figure when MINISUP is 1, which is the same as Nestorov's
algorithm, but it may be more concise when MINISUP>1, because some *MSPEs* of
lower frequencies are pruned.

5   Experiment

We have tested our algorithm on a Chinese film web site (www. dianying. com) which
have 5328 films. The web site organizes each film as a single HTML page□and
indexes all films on the capital letter of film name. The item of film information
which has single value is set to atomic object, for example, the catalogue or region of
a film, the else is set to complex object. Schema 3 is the extracted result when
MINSUP is 500.

Schema 3 (MINSUP=500):

{{film.year.⊥},{film.catalogue.⊥},{film.theme.⊥},{film.region.⊥},{film.color.⊥},{film.dialog ue.⊥},{film.adaptor.name. ⊥},{film.adaptor. magnum-opus. ⊥},{film.director.name. ⊥}, {film.direcor. magnum-opus. ⊥}, {film.player. name.⊥}, {film.actor. magnum-opus. ⊥}, {film.actress. magnum-opus. ⊥}, {film. Camerist. Name. ⊥}, {film.name.chinese. ⊥},{ film.Camerist. Magnum-opus. ⊥},   {film.name.foreign. ⊥}, {film.producer.name. ⊥}, {film.producer.URL. ⊥}, {film.staffer.art-designer/art-director. ⊥}, {film.staffer.musician. ⊥},{film.staffer.supervisor. ⊥}}

Although our algorithm is of the same time complexity as Nestorov's algorithm, but it usually consumes less time when MINSUP>1. The table 1 is the comparative result of the two algorithms when used to extract the data schema of the above film web site.

Table 1. The contrastive result of the two algorithms

MINSUP	Time comsumed (our algorithm)	Time comsumed (Nestorov's algorithm)
1	4170 seconds	4250 seconds
500	17 seconds	/(absent)
1000	11 seconds	/(absent)

References

1. Buneman, P.: Semi-structured data. In Proc. of PODS (1997).
2. Abiteboul, S.: Querying semi-structured data. In: Foto Afrati, Phokion Kolaities ed. Lecture Notes in Computer Science 1186, Database Thery---ICDT'97. New York: Springer-Verlag(1997) 1-18.
3. Wang N., Chen Y., Yu B.Q., Wang N.B.: Versatile: A scaleable CORBA-based system for integrating distributed data. In: Proceedings of the 1997 IEEE International Conference on Intelligent Processing Systems. Beijing: International Academic Publishers (1997) 1589-1593.
4. Chawathe, S., Garcia-Molina, H., Hammer, J., et al: The TSIMMIS project: integration of heterogeneous information sources. In: Proceedings of the 10th Anniversary Meeting of the Information Processing Society of Japan (1994) 7-18.
5. McHugh, J., Abiteboul, S., Goldman R et al.: Lore: a database management system for semi-structured data. ACM SIGMOD(1997) 26(3)54-66.
6. Nestorov, S., Ullman, J., Wiener, J., et al: Representative objects: concise representations of semi-structured, hierarchical data. ICDE(1997), 79-90.
7. Bayarro, R..: Efficiently mining long patterns from databases. In: Proc. of the 1998 ACMSIGMOD int'l conference on Management of Data(1998) 85-93.
8. Quass, D., et al.: Lore: A lightweight object repository for semi-structured data. In Proceedings of the ACM SIGMOD International Conference on Management of data, page 549, Montreal, Canada, June (1996).

RSTIndex: Indexing and Retrieving Web Document Using Computational and Linguistic Techniques

Farhi Marir and Kamel Houam

School of Informatics & Multimedia Technology, North London University, N7 8DB, UK
{f.marir, k.houam}@unl.ac.uk

Abstract. The amount of information available on the Internet is currently growing at an incredible rate. However, the lack of efficient indexing is still a major barrier to effective information retrieval on the web. This paper presents a new technique for capturing the semantic of the document to be used for indexing and retrieval of relevant document from the Internet. It performs the conventional keyword based indexing and introduces a thematic relationship between parts of text using natural language understanding (NLU) and a linguistics theory called rhetorical structure theory (RST).

1 Introductions and Previous Work

The Internet is currently growing at 300% per annum and if it maintains its high development speed then retrieval of relevant information will become more of a crucial issue than what it is today. A lot of research has gone into developing retrieval systems on the web (Pollitt, 1989; Salton, 1989). Despite all that, using current indexing techniques, it has been reliably estimated that on average only 30% of the returned items are relevant to the user's need, and that 70% of all relevant items in the collection are never returned (Spark-Jones, 1997). Existing indexing techniques, mainly used by search engines, are keyword based. The keywords are assigned some weights depending on factors such as their frequency of occurrence (Kofhage, 1997; Smeaton, 1992). The major drawback to keyword-based methods is that they only use a small amount of the information associated with a document as the basis for relevance decisions. As a consequence, irrelevant information that uses a certain word in a different context might be retrieved or information where different words about the desired content are used might be missed.

The aim of the work presented in this paper is to develop a technique that analyses the document for content based indexing and retrieval using a computational and linguistic technique called rhetorical structure theory (RST) (Mann et al., 1988), which will be later, enhanced with natural language understanding (NLU). The technique will focus on capturing the content of the documents for accurate indexing and retrieval resulting in an enhanced recall. The paper is composed of four sections. The first section is devoted to the introduction and previous work, the second section is devoted to the explanation of the RST and the third section will be devoted to the work which will followed by the conclusion and future work.

H. Yin et al. (Eds.): IDEAL 2002, LNCS 2412, pp. 135-140, 2002.

2   Rhetorical Structure Theory

Efficient document structuring goes back as far as Aristotle (Aristole, 1954), who recognised that in coherent documents, parts of text can be related in a number of ways. A number of authors have pursued this idea and developed theories to relate sentences. Amongst these studies, the theory developed by Mann & Thompson, called Rhetorical Structure Theory (Mann et al., 1988) has a number of interesting characteristics. It postulates the existence of about twenty five relations and is based on the view that these relations can be used in a top down recursive manner to relate parts and sub parts of text. RST determines relationships between sentences and through these relationships the term semantics can be captured. Table 1 illustrates some of the relationships used in RST. Further, these relations can be identified by cue words in the text. This top down nature means that the documents can be decomposed into sub-units containing coherent sub parts with their own rhetorical structure, and therefore opens up the possibility of extracting only relevant information from documents. RST is a descriptive theory of a major aspect of organisation of natural text. It is a linguistically useful method for describing texts and characterising their structure. RST explains a range of possibilities of structure through comparing various sorts of "building blocks" which can be observed to occur in documents. Using RST, two spans of text (virtually always adjacent, but exceptions can be found) are related such that one of them has a specific role relative to the other. A paradigm case is a claim followed by an evidence for the claim. The claims span a *nucleus* and the evidence spans a *satellite*. The order of pans is not constrained, but there are more likely and less likely orders for all of the relations.

Table 1. Some RST common relationships between spans

Relation Name	Nucleus	Satellite
Contrast	One alternative	The other alternative
Elaboration	Basic information	Additional information
Background	Text whose understanding is being facilitated	Text for facilitating understanding
Preparation	Text to be presented	Text, which prepares the reader to expect and interpret the text to be presented.

3   The RSTIndex System

As previously pointed out, conventional indexing techniques suffer from the lack of keyword semantics. We propose to enhance the keyword-based technique with the notion of capturing the relationships between units of texts where keywords occur using RST. RST has previously been used or text generation (Rosener, 1992), we will use it for text indexing. It represents a refinement to our indexing process because it determines the importance of a term occurrence and therefore excludes irrelevant keywords. After this initial filtration, a further refinement is the use of NLU to establish the role of the selected terms in a sentence. With the growing number of the documents available to users and the advance in Internet technology, more robust and reliable document retrieval systems are necessary. There is a need to understand the content of a document, compare it with the meaning of the query and select it only if it is relevant. The intelligent agent presented here is concerned about the semantics, context and the structure of the documents in opposition to single term indexing. It indexes the content of the document through its three phases described below: *keyword extraction, capturing the document linguistic structure* and *capturing the role of the selected keyword* in the sentence where it occurs. For a better understanding of the *RSTindex* System's functionality, an article from The Scientific American will be used throughout the explanation of the different phases of the model.

Title: "Lactose and Lactase".

Abstract: " *Lactose is milk sugar, the enzyme Lactase breaks it down. For want of Lactase, most adults cannot digest milk. In populations that drink milk, the adults have more Lactase, perhaps through natural selection".*

3.1   Keyword Extraction

This technique is a basic keyword extraction technique, based on the term's frequency of occurrence. It operates as follows:

- Eliminate common function words form the document texts by consulting a special dictionary, or stop list, containing a list of high-frequency function words e.g. " *and*", " *or*", " *but*" etc.
- Compute the term frequency (tf) for all the remaining terms T in each document D, specifying the number of occurrences of T in D.
- Choose a threshold frequency Th, and assign to each document D all terms T for which tf > Th.

Let's take the above example consisting of the text entitled *"Lactose and Lactase"*. The result of the initial keyword extraction and the weight calculations would be as shown in Table 2. According to the table, the document entitled *"Lactose and Lactase"* will be retrieved as an answer to a query about *"milk"* because the word *"milk"* appears as one of its most frequent keywords. This is not the case, the document does not discuss the subject of milk instead it discusses topics that are related to milk. Also, this document could be matched against a query about *"adults"* for the same reasons, while it does not discuss a topic specifically related to adult life. This is because single term indexing is not sufficient for representing a document's theme.

Table 2. Term weighting approaches

Keyword	Weight (or occurrence frequency)
milk	0.3
lactase	0.3
adults	0.2
lactose	0.1

3.2 Capturing the Document Linguistic Structure

Applying Mann and Thompson relations (Mann et al., 1988) shown in Table 1, the RST analysis of a text can be illustrated. It recognises that rhetorical relations are often signalled by cue words and phrases (actually, although, but, because, especially, as a consequence, etc...), but emphasize that rhetorical relations can still be discerned even in the absence of such cues. In this work rhetorical relations are identified on the basis of the cohesion. The abstract has been broken into five numbered units for analysis (Vadera et al., 1994) as shown below:

Lactose and Lactase (1), *Lactose is milk sugar* (2), *the enzyme Lactase breaks it down* (3), *For want of Lactase, most adults cannot digest milk* (4), *In populations that drink milk, the adults have more Lactase, perhaps through natural selection* (5).

Based on the above units, the following set of RST relation is produced:

$$
RP = \begin{cases}
RST\_rel(\,Preparation,\ 1,\ 5) \\
RST\_rel(\,Background,\ 2,\ 5) \\
RST\_rel(\,Elaboration,\ 3,\ 2) \\
RST\_rel(\,Contrast,\ 4,\ 5\,)
\end{cases}
$$

These relations hold because the analyst (generally called the observer in RST papers) is saying that the two units that explain the terms lactose and lactase (*"Lactose is milk sugar"* and *"the enzyme Lactase breaks it down"*) are intended to *prepare* and facilitate the understanding of the rest of the text. For the *elaboration* relation, since there is no connective between the two sentences, then that the second sentence *elaborates* on the first. Also, the units (4) (" *For want of Lactase most adults cannot digest milk* ") and (5) (*"In Populations that drink milk the adults have more lactase; Perhaps through natural selection"*) are in the *contrast* relation.

3.3 RST in Document Indexing

Using conventional indexing techniques, documents are represented using keywords. Queries are also represented using keywords. For retrieval, a similarity computation is performed between the two sets of keywords and if they are sufficiently similar then the document is retrieved. These methods are term based, so documents that are not relevant but use a certain term are often retrieved. This is partly due to the lack *of semantic relationships* between different parts of texts. Because RST provides an analysis for any coherent carefully written text, and because such an analysis provides a motivated account of why each element of the text has been included by the author. RST gives an account of textual coherence that is independent of the lexical and grammatical forms of the text. Therefore, it could be used for identifying relationships between the different units where certain keywords appear, stressing the importance of some and disregarding some. This could mean a major refinement to the number of documents retrieved resulting in an enhanced retrieval precision.

Using the RST analysis in Table 3, a preliminary selection excludes the word *"adult"* for the reason that a contrast (and only a contrast) occurs between the sentences where the word appears (units 4 and 5). A preliminary refinement is produced eliminating one keyword 1. However, The word *"milk"* is still identified as a key term because of its frequency of occurrence. The RST analysis reports two relationships between the different occurrences of the word *"milk"*, elaboration and background as shown in Table 3. Also, *"Lactase"* is still not identified as a major part of the text's topic; it has a relatively low weight so we need to process further. Using RST on its own is indeed an improvement but it is not sufficient to prove the document is not about milk. NLU is needed to clarify the role of terms in sentences.

Table 3. Results of applying RST

Keyword	Weight
milk	0.3
lactase	0.3
adult	0
lactose	0.1

3.4 Capturing the Documents Theme

Further investigation landed on Natural Language Understanding techniques (Vadera et al. , 1994). These techniques aim at resolving ambiguity and determining the theme of the text through exploring the roles of certain terms in a text. By applying them to selected pieces of text in opposition to the whole document, considerable processing time is gained. To do this, we have to develop a PARSING using the rules defining a grammar for simple transitive sentences (sentence: noun phrase verb phrase, etc...). Parsing not only verifies that sentences are syntactically well formed but also determines their linguistic structure.

In our example, NLU could be used for the first sentence (*"Lactose is milk sugar"*) to confirm that the subject is indeed Lactose and not milk. Hence, the weight given to the word *"milk"* is decreased by a predetermined value. Furthermore, NLU techniques are performed on the title identifying the term *"lactase"* as a subject term and its weight is increased. The derivation of the second sentence (*"the enzyme lactase breaks it down "*) could be represented as a tree structure:

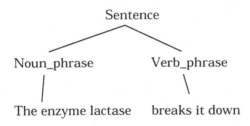

The breakdown of the sentence into noun phrase and a verb phrase specifies the relation between an action and its agent. We confirm the increasing weight of the term "*lactase*". Table 4 which represent the content of the text would be as follows:

Table 4. Results of applying NLU

Keyword	Weight
lactase	0.5
milk	0.2
lactose	0.3
adult	0

4 Conclusions

In this paper, we have presented a computational and linguistic technique for content-based indexing of documents in a large collection of text documents. It introduces an indexing method, which is a combination of traditional keyword based techniques, a text description theory called rhetorical structure theory and natural language understanding. RST was created in the late eighties for text generation primarily; we propose to employ it for text indexing. Using RST, keywords and the weights assigned to them could be refined to produce better retrieval precision. Once RST is applied, NLU techniques are used on selected pieces of text (rather than the whole document) for additional refinement

References

1. Pollitt, A. S, Information Storage and Retrieval Systems. Ellis Horwood Ltd., Chichester, The UK, (1989)
2. Salton Gerard, Automatic Text Processing, Addison-Wesley, USA, (1989)
3. Sparck-Jones, Karen & Willet, Peter, Readings in Information Retrieval. Morgan Kauffman, California, USA, (1997)
4. Korfhage, R. Information Storage and Retrieval. J.Wiley & Sons, (1997)
5. Smeaton, A.F. Progress in the application of natural language processing to information retrieval, The Computer Journal, (1992) 35, 268-278
6. Mann, W.C., & Thompson, S.A. Rhetorical Structure Theory: Towards a functional theory of text organization. Text , (1988) 8 (3), 243-28
7. Rosener,D and Stede, M. Customizing RST for the Automatic Production of Technical Manuals. Lecture Notes in AI, 587, (1992), 199-214
8. Aristotle. The Rhetoric, in W. Rhys Roberts (translator), The Rhetoric and Poetics of Aristotle, Random House, New York, (1954)
9. Vadera, S. and Meziane, F. From English to Formal Specifications. The Computer Journal, 37(9), (1994)

A Case-Based Recognition of Semantic Structures in HTML Documents*
An Automated Transformation from HTML to XML

Masayuki Umehara, Koji Iwanuma, and Hidetomo Nabeshima

Yamanashi University
4-3-11 Takeda, Kofu-shi 400-8511, Japan
{mon,iwanuma,nabesima}@iw.media.yamanashi.ac.jp

Abstract. The recognition and extraction of semantic/logical structures in HTML documents are substantially important and difficult tasks for intelligent document processing. In this paper, we show that *alignment* is appropriate for recognizing characteristic semantic/logical structures of a series of HTML documents, within a framework of case-based reasoning. That is, given a series of HTML documents and a sample transformation from an HTML document into an XML format, then the alignment can identify semantic/logical structures in the remaining HTML documents of the series, by matching the text-block sequence of the remaining document with the one of the sample transformation. Several important properties of texts, such as continuity and sequentiality, can naturally be utilized by the alignment. The alignment technology can significantly improve the ability of the case-based transformation method which transforms a spatial/temporal series of HTML documents into machine-readable XML formats. Throughout experimental evaluations, we show that the case-based method with alignment achieved a highly accurate transformation of HTML documents into XML.

1 Introduction

There are abundant HTML documents in the internet. HTML documents, however, are designed mainly for reading with browsers, and is not suitable for mechanical processing, whereas XML has very nice features for machine processing. Thus, it is absolutely desirable to automatically transform HTML documents into XML formats. A fully automated transformation, however, is extremely difficult, because it essentially needs to understand the contents of HTML documents. On the other hand, there are indeed a large number of temporal/spatial series of HTML pages in actual WEB sites. Typical examples of temporal series are HTML documents provided by news sites, whereas those for sightseeing guides, car catalogs, etc. are examples of spatial series. Every page of a series

* This research was supported partly by Grant-in-Aid from The Ministry of Education, Science and Culture of Japan. and also supported by The Telecommunications Advancement Foundation (TAF).

H. Yin et al. (Eds.): IDEAL 2002, LNCS 2412, pp. 141–147, 2002.

usually has a similar structure with each other. Thus, a *case-based transformation* must be a promising method for such an HTML document series in practice. Umehara and Iwanuma [8] proposed such a case-based transformation method.

In this paper, we address an important problem which remains a substantially difficult problem in intelligent HTML document processing, i.e., an *automated recognition problem of semantic structures* in HTML documents. We show that *alignment* technology is an appropriate tool for treating this difficult problem *when* a transformation example from a similar HTML document to an XML format is given in advance. So far, lots of researches [1,2,3,5,7] have been conducted for the analysis of HTML tags such as H1, ... , H6, P, DIV, UL, OL, TABLE, all of which represent logical structures of HTML documents. However, according to our knowledge, there are no studies on the utilization of text information for understanding HTML documents. The alignment technology can utilize various kinds of text information, which exists as an characteristic property in the given series, and thus significantly improve the capability of the case-based transformation method of HTML series documents. Throughout experiments for 47 HTML pages of 8 series, we show that the case-based method using the alignment achieved a highly accurate transformation into XML formats.

2   A Case-Based Transformation with Recognizing Semantic Structures

Given a series of HTML documents and a transformation sample of an HTML document of the given series into an XML format, then the case-based transformation method first analyses the sample transformation, and next automatically transforms the remaining HTML documents of the series into the XML format with the information extracted from the sample. A given sample HTML (or XML) document is called an *H-document* (or respectively, an *X-document*). The other HTML documents to be transformed automatically are called *T-documents*. Fig.1, 2 and 3 are examples of an H-document, an X-document and a T-document, respectively. The detail of the transformation is as follows:

1. Analyze important features of a given sample transformation. Next generate an XML skeleton (see Fig.4) and a table indicating the correspondence between text blocks[1] of the H-document and XML tags of the X-document (see Table.P1).
2. Analyze T-documents similarly.
3. Transform every remaining T-document of the given series:
   a) Compute the similarity scores to all pairs $\langle s_i, t_j \rangle$ where s_i and t_j are text blocks in the H-document and the T-document, respectively. The similarity measure is based on a term vector model [6,8]. The some details will be shown later.
   b) Extract compound text blocks, i.e., semantic/logical substructures, from the T-document by performing the alignment to the H-documents.

---

[1]   A *text block* is a character string enclosed by arbitrary HTML tags.

```
<HTML><HEAD><TITLE> Spa Guide </TITLE></HEAD>              (s₁)
<BODY> <H1> Nunohiki Spa </H1>                            (s₂)
  <EM> Location </EM>                                     (s₃)
    <P> Kita-Saku district, Nagano pref. Japan </P>      (s₄)
    <P> TEL: 0268-67-3467 </P>                           (s₅)
  <EM> Open Hours </EM>                                   (s₆)
    <P> From 10.15 a.m to 11.30 p.m. </P>                (s₇)
  <EM> Overview </EM>                                     (s₈)
    <P> This facility was established in 1987, and ... <BR>  (s₉)
    The hot spring is located at the front of ...        (s₁₀)
    <B> ''SAWARA'', </B>                                 (s₁₁)
    on the basement floor ... <BR>                       (s₁₂)
    The effects of this hot spring are ... </P>          (s₁₃)
</BODY></HTML>
```

Note: $s_1, \ldots, s_{13}$ are the sequential numbers of text blocks.

Fig. 1. An H-document containing composite semantic structures

```
<spa_guide>
 <name> Nunohiki Spa </name>
 <location> Kita-Saku district, Nagano pref. Japan
     TEL: 0268-67-3467 </location>
 <open_hours> From 10.15 a.m to 11.30 p.m </open_hours>
 <overview> This facility was established in 1987, and ...
     The hot spring is located at the front of ''SAWARA'',
     on the basement floor ...
     The effects of this hot spring are ...
 </overview>
</spa_guide>
```

Fig. 2. An X-document corresponding to the H-document in Fig.1

```
<HTML><HEAD><TITLE>Spa Guide</TITLE></HEAD>               (t₁)
<BODY><H1>Oku-Chichibu Spa</H1>                          (t₂)
  <EM>location</EM>                                       (t₃)
    <P>Chichibu district, Saitama pref. Japan</P>        (t₄)
  <EM> Overview </EM> <BR><BR>                            (t₅)
      The building and bathroom are newly-built ... <BR> (t₆)
      This facility has two resting rooms, which are     (t₇)
      <STRONG> free of charge </STRONG>                  (t₈)
      for any visitors ... <BR>                          (t₉)
</BODY></HTML>
```

Note: $t_1, \ldots, t_9$ are the sequential numbers of text blocks

Fig. 3. A T-document to be transformed automatically

c) Assign each extracted compound block to a field in the XML skeleton.

Now, let us consider the correspondence between two documents in Fig.1 and 3. The sequence $t_5, \ldots, t_9$ in Fig.3 constitutes a compound text block, which is regarded as a semantic substructure of the text, and should correspond with the compound block $s_9, \ldots, s_{13}$ in Fig.1. Notice that each t_i is not similar to any of $s_9, \ldots, s_{13}$, hence a pointwise similarity-based transformation of each block t_j is almost impossible. Moreover the compound block of $t_5 \ldots, t_9$ is formatted only with <BR> tags, whereas $s_9, \ldots, s_{13}$ in Fig.1 are formated with <p> tags. Hence, it is extremely difficult to find out the correspondence between $s_9, \ldots, s_{13}$ and $t_5, \ldots, t_9$, even when a simple HTML-tag-analysis is performed. The semantic analysis of HTML documents is a truly difficult task.

```
<spa_guide>
    <name>              </name>
    <location>          </location>
    <open_hours>        </open_hours>
    <overview>          </overview>
</spa_guide>
```

Fig. 4. An XML skeleton of generated from the X-document in Fig.2

Table 1. Correspondence between text blocks in Fig. 1 and XML tags in Fig. 2

XML tags	<name>	<location>	<open_hours>	<overview>	n.a
Text blocks	s_2	s_4, s_5	s_7	$s_9, s_{10}, s_{11}, s_{12}, s_{13}$	s_1, s_3, s_6, s_8

3   Alignment for Identifying Semantic/Logical Structures

The *pairwise alignment* [4] is the problem of comparing two sequences while allowing certain mismatches between them. *Alignment* of two sequences S and T is obtained by inserting some *gaps* '−' into S and T so that the similarity score between the two resulting sequences becomes maximal as a whole. For example, given two sequences ACGCTTTG and CATGTAT, one possible alignment would be:

$$
\begin{array}{ccccccccc}
A & C & - & - & G & C & T & T & T & G \\
- & C & A & T & G & - & T & A & T & - \\
\end{array}
$$

In this paper, we apply the alignment technology to the extraction problem of semantic/logical structures of HTML documents. As is well known, the alignment can efficiently be computed with dynamic programming technique [4]. Given a sequence $S_1, \ldots, S_m$ of text blocks of an H-document and a sequence $T_1, \ldots, T_n$ of a T-document, we first compute the similarity score for all pairs $\langle S_i, T_j \rangle$. The similarity measure used here is the linear combination [8] of the cosine coefficient of term vectors, whose elements are TF*IDF values [6] of selected important nouns in the documents, and the ratio of the length of text blocks. Next we compute the alignment of two sequences $S_1, \ldots, S_m$ and $T_1, \ldots, T_n$ based on the computed similarity scores. Finally, we extract semantic structures in the T-document, according to the correspondence to the H-document. For example, one possible alignment of two sequences of Fig. 1 and 3 would be:

$$s_1 \ s_2 \ s_3 \ s_4 \ s_5 \ s_6 \ s_7 \ s_8 \ - \ s_9 \ s_{10} \ s_{11} \ s_{12} \ s_{13}$$
$$t_1 \ t_2 \ t_3 \ - \ t_4 \ - \ - \ t_5 \ t_6 \ t_7 \ - \ - \ t_8 \ t_9$$

The semantic/logical structures in $s_1, \ldots, s_{13}$ were already depicted in Table 1. Thus, we can classify each $t_1, \ldots, t_9$ from the correspondence indicated in the above alignment. The result is:

$$\begin{array}{c|c|c|cc|c|c|c|c|cccc} s_1 & s_2 & s_3 & s_4 & s_5 & s_6 & s_7 & s_8 & - & s_9 & s_{10} & s_{11} & s_{12} & s_{13} \\ t_1 & t_2 & t_3 & - & t_4 & - & - & t_5 & t_6 & t_7 & - & - & t_8 & t_9 \end{array}$$

In the above, the block t_6 is assigned to the gap '–' in the sequence $s_1, \ldots, s_{13}$, thus we can not determine the meaning of t_6 directly. In this paper, we join such a uncertain block into its more-similar neighbor block. In this example, t_6 is joined to t_7. That is,

$$\begin{array}{c|c|c|cc|c|c|c|c|cccc} s_1 & s_2 & s_3 & s_4 & s_5 & s_6 & s_7 & s_8 & - & s_9 & s_{10} & s_{11} & s_{12} & s_{13} \\ t_1 & t_2 & t_3 & - & t_4 & - & - & t_5 & t_6 & t_7 & - & - & t_8 & t_9 \end{array}$$

Table 2 shows the final assignment of text blocks in the T-document into XML blocks. Fig. 5 is the XML document finally generated from the one in Fig.3.

Table 2. The final assignment of text blocks in Fig. 3 to XML tags in Fig. 4

XML tags	<name>	<location>	<open_hours>	<overview>
Text blocks	t_2	t_4		t_6, t_7, t_8, t_9

4   Experimental Evaluation

We experimentally evaluated the case-based transformation with alignment. Table 3 describes the features of each series of HTML documents used in experiments. The results are shown in Table 4. Two experiments were conducted for each series: the first is the case where we chose the smallest document D as a sample H-document, i.e. the number of text blocks in D is minimal among other series documents; the second is for the biggest/maximal case. The evaluation measures are *Precision, Recall* and *F-measure*, each of which is:

```
<spa_guide>
  <name>Oku-Chichibu Spa<name>
  <location> Chichibu district, Saitama pref. Japan</location>
  <open_hours> nothing </open_hours>
  <overview> The building and bathroom are newly-built ...
This facility has two resting rooms, which are free of charge
for any visitors, and ...
</spa_guide>
```

Fig. 5. An XML document generated from the T-document in Fig. 3

$$\text{Precision} = \frac{C}{S}, \quad \text{Recall} = \frac{C}{H}, \quad \text{F-measure} = \frac{2 \times \text{Precision} \times \text{Recall}}{\text{Precision} + \text{Recall}},$$

where S is the number of text blocks occurring in generated XML documents, H is the number of text blocks of H-documents to be inserted into XML documents, and C is the number of text blocks correctly inserted into XML documents.

Table 3. HTML document series used in experiments

Series	A	B	C	Site & URL
1	6	12446	7.6	JTB: Guides Separated for Each Prefecture
				http://www.jtb.co.jp/TJsite/library/library_e.html
2	6	5079	5.0	ACM Home page: Calendar of Upcoming Events
				http://www.acm.org/events/coe.html
3	6	22401	22.1	Yahoo! News - Science
				http://story.news.yahoo.com/news?tmpl=index&cid=753
4	6	960	8.1	Yamanashi sightseeing guide (in Japanese)
				http://www.pref.yamanashi.jp/shouko/index-j.html
5	5	5278	12.1	JTB: Guides Separated for Each Prefecture (in Japanese)
				http://www.jtb.co.jp/TJsite/library/library.html
6	6	2276	8.3	Nara National Museum: calligraphy (in Japanese)
				http://www.narahaku.go.jp/meihin/syoseki/
7	6	16638	9.5	goo channel, news channel: society (in Japanese)
				http://channel.goo.ne.jp/news/shakai/
8	6	9641	7.2	excite: Top 10 News (in Japanese)
				http://www.excite.co.jp/News/

A: the number of HTML documents contained by the series.
B: the average size (byte) of HTML document in the series, not including images.
C: the average number of text blocks inserted into a produced XML document.

The experiments shows that the case-based method with alignment achieved more than 90% highly accurate transformation of HTML document series into XML formats. The maximal sample H-documents give better transformation, in general. The alignment succeeded in utilizing several important properties of

Table 4. Experiment results with alignment

Series	Number of blocks[*1]	(Precision/Recall/F-measure)
1	62 (min)	**0.844 / 0.876 / 0.857**
	65 (max)	0.658 / 0.710 / 0.683
2	32 (min)	0.650 / 0.650 / 0.650
	33(max)	**0.920 / 0.920 / 0.920**
3	134 (min)	0.784 / 0.784 / 0.784
	185 (max)	**0.903 / 0.903 / 0.903**
4	13 (min)	**1.000 / 1.000 / 1.000**
	32 (max)	**1.000 / 1.000 / 1.000**
5	20 (min)	0.755 / 1.000 / 0.860
	26 (max)	**0.977** / 0.955 / **0.966**
6	15 (min)	**0.977** / 1.000 / **0.988**
	19 (max)	0.952 / **1.000 / 0.988**
7	113 (min)	0.935 / 0.935 / 0.935
	122 (max)	**0.967 / 0.967 / 0.967**
8	82 (min)	**1.000/ 0.969 / 0.983**
	105 (max)	**1.000/ 0.969 / 0.983**
average	42 (min)	0.864 / 0.899 / 0.880
	54 (max)	**0.922 / 0.928 / 0.926**

*1 The number of text blocks occurring in an H-document used in the series.

texts, such as continuity and sequentiality. Within a case-based reasoning, the alignment is an appropriate method for recognizing semantic/logical structures which are characteristic in a given temporal/spatial series of HTML documents

References

1. N. Ashish and C. A. Knoblock: Wrapper Generation for Semi-Structured Internet Source, *ACM SIGMOD Records*, **26(4)** (1997) 8-15.
2. W. W. Cohen: Recognizing Structure in Web Pages using Similarity Queries, *Proc. of AAAI-99* (1999) 59-66.
3. J. Y. Hsu and W. Yih: Template-Based Information Mining from HTML Documents, *Proc. of AAAI-97* (1997) 256-262.
4. J. B. Kruskal: An Overview of Sequence Comparison: In D. Sankoff and J. B. Kruskal, (ed.), *Time Warps, String Edits and Macromolecules: the Theory and Practice of Sequence Comparison* (Addison Wesley, 1983) 1-44.
5. N. Kushmerick: Regression testing for wrapper maintenance, *Proc. of AAAI-99* (1999) 74-79.
6. G. Salton: *Introduction to Modern Information Retrieval*, (McGraw-Hill, 1983).
7. S-J. Lim, Y-K. Ng: An Automated Change-Detection Algorithm for HTML Documents Based on Semantic Hierarchies, *Proc. of ICDE 2001* (2001) 303-312.
8. M. Umehara and K. Iwanuma: A Case-Based Transformation from HTML to XML, *Proc. of IDEAL 2000 LNAI* **1983** (2000) 410-415.

Expeditious XML Processing

Kelvin Yeow[1], R. Nigel Horspool[1], and Michael R. Levy[2]

[1] Department of Computer Science, University of Victoria, Victoria,
British Columbia, Canada V8P 5C2
{whyeow, nigelh}@csc.uvic.ca
[2] NewHeights Software Corporation, 1006 Government Street, Victoria,
British Columbia, Canada V8W 1X7
mlevy@newheights.com

Abstract. We present a representation for XML documents, derived from Warren's representation of Prolog terms in the Warren Abstract Machine (WAM)*, which permits very efficient access and update operations. Our scheme is implemented in CXMLParser, a non-validating XML processor. We present the results of a performance comparison with two other XML processors, which show that CXMLParser is faster by a factor of 2.2 to 4.3 than its nearest competitor.

1 Introduction

XML is becoming the standard format to exchange information between programs over the Internet. Fast access to information in an XML document is crucial for software performance. An XML processor is a software module that usually exists within a larger system. The efficiency of an XML processor is highly dependent on the representation of the XML document in the computer's memory. We present a representation for XML documents, derived from Warren's representation of Prolog terms in WAM, which permits very efficient access and update operations.

WAM is an abstract machine for the execution of Prolog consisting of an instruction set and a memory architecture that thrives on *terms* [1]. A term is a variable, constant or structure. In Fig. 1, we illustrate a simplified representation for terms consisting of an array of data cells in the form of an addressable heap called HEAP. A heap cell's address is its index in the array HEAP. Of particular interest is the representation of the term structure in the form of $F(t_1, ..., t_n)$ where F is a symbol called a *functor*, and the t's are the *subterms*.

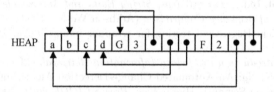

Fig. 1. The heap representation of the functor $F(a, G(b, c, d))$

---

* The parser described in this paper is based on an XML parser called XMLLite which was developed by NewHeights Software Corporation as part of their Helix software environment.

H. Yin et al. (Eds.): IDEAL 2002, LNCS 2412, pp. 148-153, 2002.
© Springer-Verlag Berlin Heidelberg 2002

The heap format for a structure $F(t_1, ..., t_n)$ consists of $n + 2$ contiguous heap cells. The number of subterms for a given functor is its *arity*. The first two of these $n + 2$ cells hold the functor and its arity. The n other cells contain references to the roots of the n subterms in order. If HEAP[k] = F then HEAP[$k + 1$] holds its arity. Hence, HEAP[$k + 2$] will refer to the first subterm t_1 and HEAP[$k + n + 1$] will refer to the n-th (and last) subterm t_n. This representation closely resembles the Postorder With Degrees representation in [2]. The cells that contain the terms need not be contiguous while the references to the terms are strictly contiguous; therein lies the difference.

The arity is assumed to be static; hence, it is particularly inadequate for modification at runtime. We adapted Warren's representation to cater for runtime insertion and deletion. Our scheme is implemented in CXMLParser, a non-validating XML processor written in C++. Informally, an XML document can be abstracted as a directed acyclic ordered tree. Section 2 describes our representation in reference to CXMLParser. Section 3 describes the methodology and the results of the performance comparison. The two other candidate XML processors are Xerces C++ [3] and XML4J (Java) [4]. We provide conclusions and future work in section 4.

2   CXMLParser

CXMLParser is an XML parser and more; it provides facilities to access, modify and create an XML document – collectively, it is an XML processor [5]. Section 2.1 describes the representation of the XML document in CXMLParser. Section 2.2 describes the four operations: insert, delete, parse and traverse.

2.1   The Representation

An XML document contains data and relationships between data. The relationships form the structure of the XML document. The structure of the XML document will be stored in a block of contiguous memory in the form of an oversized integer array. The literals of the XML document are stored in an oversized character array. Throughout the rest of this paper, the integer array and the character array will be known as HEAP and CHAR respectively. For each array, a stack pointer points to the next available cell for consumption. The stack pointers are assumed to point to the next available cell at the end of the used portions of the array. Hence, they will not be shown in the diagrams. There are four types of node: text, attribute, element, and redirection. The type of the node is encoded in the HEAP using an enumeration type constant.

A text node consists of its literals stored in CHAR and its structure stored in HEAP. The heap format used for representing a text node consists of three contiguous heap cells as shown in Fig. 2(a). The contiguous cells store the type of the node denoted by T for text node, a pointer to the first character of its literal in CHAR, and the number of characters (or length).

An attribute has a key and its associated value; both the key and the value are represented as text nodes. An attribute node has two child nodes at any instance. The heap format used for representing an attribute will consist of three contiguous heap cells as shown in Fig. 2(b). The contiguous cells store the type of the node denoted by

A for attribute, a pointer to the key and a pointer to the value. If HEAP[*k*] = *A* then HEAP[*k* + 1] contains the pointer to the key and HEAP[*k* + 2] contains the pointer to the value.

An element is denoted by an open and a close tag. The content of an element node can be other elements, attributes or a text node. The heap format used for representing an element consists of *n* + 3 contiguous heap cells as shown in Fig. 2(c). The first three of these *n* + 3 cells stores the type of node denoted by *E* for element, a pointer to its tag name and arity. The *n* other cells contain references to the roots of the *n* children nodes. If HEAP[*k*] = *E* then HEAP[*k* + 1] contains the pointer to the tag name and HEAP [*k* + 2] contains the arity of the element. Hence, HEAP[*k* + 3] contains the pointer to the first child node and HEAP[*k* + *n* + 2] contains the pointer to the *n*-th (and last) child node.

A redirection node consists of the type of the node denoted by R for redirection and a pointer to the relocated element as shown in Fig. 2(d). The redirection node facilitates insertion; we show (Fig. 3) and describe how it is used in the next section.

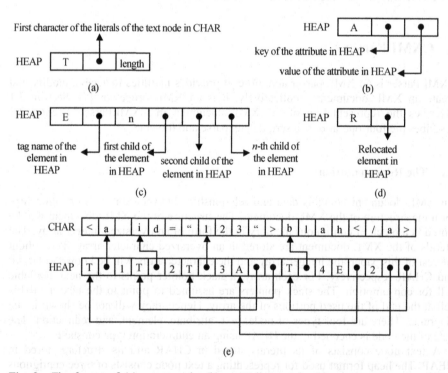

Fig. 2. The format of (a) a text node, (b) an attribute node, (c) an element node, (d) a redirection node, and (e) the representation of *<a id="123">blah</a>* in CXMLParser

2.2   The Operations

If a new child node is added to a parent node at runtime, the changes to HEAP should be (1) the arity of the parent node increases by one and (2) an additional pointer to the new child node is needed. While (1) is a simple increment, (2) requires an additional adjacent cell. Instead of moving all cells to the right by one, our solution is to copy and append the structure of the parent node to HEAP, and place a redirection node at the previous location so that any references to the previous location can be redirected to the new location as shown in Fig. 3. If the parent node is at the end of the HEAP before an insertion, there is no need to copy and append; the next cell is consumed.

A redirection node requires two cells. During a lookup, if a redirection node is encountered, the lookup will proceed through the pointer of the redirection node to the final result. Note that there might be intermediate redirections, i.e. a redirection node pointing to another redirection node (even though, it would be faster if the first redirection node pointed directly to the final result). The immediate failing of this method is that intermediate redirections can be expensive, especially if the parent node is relocated frequently (through insertion). For example, if a parent node is relocated 5000 times, there will be a linked-list of 5000 redirection nodes. However, avoiding multiple redirections would make the updates more expensive. Our compromise strategy is to have fast updates with multiple redirections and delay collapsing the multiple redirections until a lookup is performed.

Deletion is achieved by decrementing the arity of the parent node. Continuing from the insertion example, if the removed child node is not the last child in the list, then move all subsequent child pointers one cell to the left.

A pushdown automaton implements the parse operation with two stacks for the recognition of the nested structures. The XML document is copied into the CHAR array in memory and then annotated. The parse operation is fast because our technique minimises memory allocation calls on two fronts: both HEAP and CHAR are allocated in batches.

The tree traversal operation is controlled by the arity of each parent node. An iteration through the children nodes of an element always starts at HEAP[$k + 3$] through to HEAP[$k + n + 2$] where k is the index of the element in HEAP and n is the arity of the element. Our technique allows random access to any children nodes from the parent node.

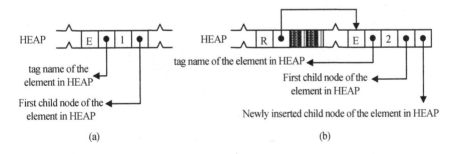

(a)   (b)

Fig. 3. The state of *HEAP* and *CHAR* (a) before and (b) after inserting a node to an element. The shaded cells are the free cells

3   Performance Testing and Comparison

Input. We used three similar but different sized XML documents: 100 KB, 1 MB and 5 MB in size. The XML documents emulate a table with records and fields. The number of records are 500, 5000 and 25000. There are six fields per record. The number of nodes in the XML documents are 3500, 35000 and 175000 respectively.

Methodology. To time the speed of the XML processors, we ran it over the three different sized XML documents using a mixture of four operations: delete, insert, parse and traverse. Each measurement is an average over a set of three measurements taken consecutively. Fig. 4 shows the average throughput of the XML processors.

Environment. The performance test was run on a Pentium III 700 Windows 2000 machine with 128 MB RAM and a virtual memory of 192 MB. No background activity was demanded from the CPU while the tests were conducted. The compilers and interpreters used are packaged as Microsoft Visual C++ version 6.0 Enterprise Edition and Java 2 SDK version 1.3.1.

XML Processors. The version of Xerces-C and XML4J used is 1.4 and 1.1.16 respectively. All of the XML processors were run in non-validating mode with namespace processing disabled. In addition, the XML processors were required to build a tree representation of the XML document. The performance was measured with the _ftime() function available from time.h while, in Java, the System.currentTimeMillis() function was used.

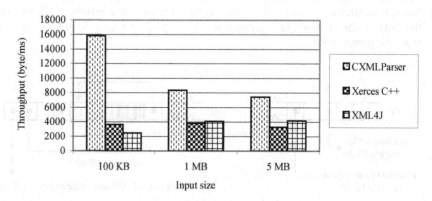

Fig. 4. Average throughput

Results. CXMLParser performs at very competitive speeds. Table 1 shows the throughput of CXMLParser for the operations tested. CXMLParser does not scale well for the delete operation when the file size increases. If the number of children is 5000 and the removed child is the first child, the current implementation moves the other 4999 references one cell left. CXMLParser copes well if insertions to a particular parent node are carried out in batches; otherwise, we know for certain that the current implementation will consume memory at an exorbitant rate. In our test, the children nodes of a parent node are inserted consecutively. We argue that this is a fair trade-off: some extra effort (by the programmer) yields huge savings and thus speed.

Table 1. The throughput for CXMLParser for the operations tested

CXMLParser	Delete byte/ms	Insert byte/ms	Parse byte/ms	Traverse byte/ms
small.xml	33333	10000	10000	10000
medium.xml	5000	8130	6667	13699
big.xml	1108	7485	6812	14409

4 Future Work and Conclusions

One of the highlights of our representation is that a parent node has random access to its children and attributes. It is desirable to treat the attributes as part of the parent node as opposed to proper children, so that a parent node can directly access the i-th child. We believe that this advantage is useful in performing search. We are currently working on optimising search based on this idea.

CXMLParser places a higher premium on speed over memory. The memory consumption can be improved by keeping track of the free cells, i.e. a bookkeeping system consisting of a list of multi-sized free cells. Knuth [2] describes a dynamic storage allocation algorithm for reserving and freeing variable-size blocks of memory.

The experimental timings show that CXMLParser is two to four times faster than its nearest competitor. Depending on the file size, the observed speedup factor ranges from 2.2 to 4.3. The outcome of the performance testing proves that the compact representation of the terms, as first conceived by Warren, can be adapted to represent XML documents while preserving efficient access.

Acknowledgements. Financial support from the Natural Sciences and Engineering Research Council of Canada is gratefully acknowledged.

References

1. Aït-Kaci, Warren's Abstract Machine: A tutorial reconstruction. MIT Press, Cambridge, MA (1991).
2. Knuth, D. E. The art of computer programming: fundamental algorithms. Addison-Wesley, Reading, MA (1997).
3. Apache XML Project. Xerces C++. http://xml.apache.org/xerces-c/index.html (1999).
4. IBM alphaWorks. XML Parser for Java. http://www.alphaworks.ibm.com/ (1999).
5. World Wide Web Consortium. XML version 1.0. http://www.w3.org/xml (1998).

Document Clustering Using the 1 + 1 Dimensional Self-Organising Map

Ben Russell, Hujun Yin, and Nigel M. Allinson

University of Manchester Institute of Science and Technology (UMIST)
Department of Electrical Engineering and Electronics,
Po Box 88, Manchester M60 1QD, United Kingdom
ben.russell@premier-tech.com, {H.Yin, Allinson}@umist.ac.uk

Abstract. Automatic clustering of documents is a task that has become increasingly important with the explosion of online information. The Self-Organising Map (SOM) has been used to cluster documents effectively, but efforts to date have used a single or a series of 2-dimensional maps. Ideally, the output of a document-clustering algorithm should be easy for a user to interpret. This paper describes a method of clustering documents using a series of 1-dimensional SOM arranged hierarchically to provide an intuitive tree structure representing document clusters. Wordnet[1] is used to find the base forms of words and only cluster on words that can be nouns.

1 Introduction

The Information Age is characterized by a wealth of information and the development of techniques that enable the information to be available to anyone who wishes to use it. People have access to more information than ever before with the increased popularity of corporate intranets, the Internet and digital libraries. The sheer volume of information can often be too vast leading to what is commonly referred to as "information overload" [1]. This has lead to the development of a number of techniques for organising, searching and displaying the information.

When an information need is relatively specific, the most common approach at present is to search the information space in order to find information of interest using a query. To successfully achieve this, the user often needs to have knowledge of the subject of interest, in particular the vocabulary of the subject domain. Often the user has the problem of formulating complex queries and typically avoids using the 'advanced' search options. Search engines such as *Google*[2] specialize in locating specific documents in answer to a well-defined information request. Results are displayed in the form of a ranked list. It has been recognised that one limitation of search engine technology is the low precision and high recall of the results returned. Precision is defined as the proportion of the retrieved documents that are relevant while recall is the proportion of relevant documents retrieved [2]. It is not uncommon to get thousands or even millions of matches for a query. It has also recognised that people use a sur

---

[1] For more information on Wordnet see http://www.cogsci.princeton.edu/~wn/
[2] Google can be found at http://www.google.com

H. Yin et al. (Eds.): IDEAL 2002, LNCS 2412, pp. 154–160, 2002.

prisingly vast variety of words to describe the same thing [3]; this has been called the vocabulary problem.

Combined with the precision and vocabulary problems, when the information need is vague or the domain is unknown, obtaining useful information or an overview of a subject can be more difficult. In this case, exploration of taxonomy can be used as an alternative. An example is the *Yahoo! Directory of World Wide Web (WWW) sites*[3]. One benefit of using a hierarchical taxonomy of a document collection is the refinement of your initial query at each level, guiding you to the category that most accurately matches your need. Manually performing the classification of a huge and ever expanding number of documents is clearly an expensive and time-consuming task therefore the use of automatic methods has become necessary. In section II we provide a brief introduction to document clustering. Section III gives a description of previous work in the area of document clustering using the Self-Organising Map (SOM). In section IV the proposed method for document clustering is explained with experimental results. Section V concludes and describes some future directions for this work.

2   Document Clustering

Document clustering methods are 'unsupervised'. The goal is to explore the structure of the data without any assumptions regarding the type and the structure of the model. The dynamic structure provided by an unsupervised method is more appropriate where the domain is fluid (for example documents about news items or current affairs) as there are no fixed or predefined categories. As the document collection grows, the taxonomy can adapt with the labels (text used to describe the major themes contained in a document cluster) reflecting the changes in content.

Hierarchical clustering places documents into a structure that reflects relations between concepts in the domain. The taxonomy is represented using 'isa' and 'superset' relations (and their inverses 'member' and 'subset'). 'isa' links an object to a set of which it is a member, and 'superset' links a set to a superset of it (thus 'member' links a set to one of its members, and 'subset' links a set to one of its subsets). As an example, a 'dogs' category would be a subset of an 'animals' category. Methods such as the *Hierarchical Feature Map* [4] and the *Growing Hierarchical Self-Organising Map* (GHSOM) [5] provide for such an organisation. Non-hierarchical methods or flat partitioning divide documents into a set of flat clusters.

3   Related Work

This section begins with an introduction to the basic SOM algorithm. Two methods of document clustering using the SOM are then described.

---

[3] The Yahoo! Directory of WWW sites can be found at www.yahoo.com

3.1 Introduction to the SOM

The SOM is a popular unsupervised neural network and was first introduced by Kohonen [6]. Data from a high-dimensional input space is mapped onto a low (mainly two) dimensional output space. The SOM has been particularly successful because of its topological preservation i.e. the structure of the input data is preserved as faithfully as possible in the output. In the core SOM algorithm, there are two main steps. These are calculating the winning unit and updating the weights of the winning and neighbouring units. Each node in the SOM has an associated weight vector. For each iteration t, the winning neuron c has the least Euclidian distance to a randomly selected input vector x as shown in equation (1).

$$c : w_c = \arg \min \{ \| x(t) - w_i(t) \| \}$$ (1)

Where $w_i(t)$ is the weight vector of unit i at time t.

The SOM updates the weight of the winning neuron and its neighbouring nodes using:

$$w_i(t+1) = w_i(t) + h_{ci}(t)[x(t) - w_i(t)]$$ (2)

Where $h_{ci}(t)$ is the neighbourhood function at time t. The neighbourhood function is a time decreasing function, which determines to what extent the neighbours of the winning unit are updated. A typical smooth Gaussian neighbourhood kernel is given in equation (3).

$$h_{ci} = \alpha(t) \cdot \exp\left(\frac{\| r_c - r_i \|^2}{2\sigma^2(t)} \right)$$ (3)

Where $\alpha(t)$ is the learning rate function, $\sigma^2(t)$ is the kernel width function and $\| r_c - r_i \|^2$ is the distance of winning unit to unit i. There are a variety of functions used for the learning rate $\alpha(t)$ and kernel width functions $\sigma^2(t)$ but both should decrease monotonically with time to allow convergence. The rate of convergence depends on the shape and width of the kernel function used.

3.2 WEBSOM

The WEBSOM [7] method for document clustering has a two-level information processing architecture. On the first level, a "semantic SOM" [8] is used to categorise the words of the source text into clusters. The aim is to reduce the number of features (the words deemed significant enough to be used in clustering) by clustering the words into meaningful categories. Short segments of text (e.g. three successive words) are used as input. This map is then used to look for features that are useful to represent documents. The second level uses these clusters to create a document map (a 2-dimensional SOM). More recently, randomly projected histograms have replaced the semantic SOM [9]. Experiments on a set of 1 million documents have shown that this method can successfully categorise a huge collection of documents.

3.3   The Growing Hierarchical SOM

The GHSOM [5] was introduced in an attempt to overcome the limitations of the single 2D map. The first limitation is the pre-determined map size, which turns out to be impractical for unknown document collections. A number of different approaches have been suggested to address the problem of defining the size of a SOM in advance, such as *Incremental Grid Growing* [10] or *Growing Grid* [11] where new units are added to map areas where the data, i.e. the topics, are not represented at a particular degree of granularity. The second limitation is the number of documents that can plausibly be displayed on a single map on a screen at once. Methods that use a single flat map tend to produce huge maps limiting their usability for the display and navigation.

GHSOM creates a hierarchy of SOM with a 2x2 SOM at the highest level. This high-level map 'grows' by calculating quantisation error (QE) (calculated as the sum of the distances between the weight vector of a unit and the input vectors mapped onto this unit) and adding additional units until a threshold parameter is reached. Next, a separate SOM is added for each unit of the first level SOM, which is used to represent the documents mapped onto the respective unit in greater detail. Again, this map grows until it has a QE smaller than a fraction of the units QE it derives from. This continues until a particular granularity is achieved.

4   Proposed Methods and Results

The proposed method essentially uses a series of independently trained one-dimensional SOM, organized hierarchically. At each level there are only one-dimensional SOM. We call such a structure the "1+1" dimensional SOM. The advantage of using the hierarchically structured "1+1" SOM is that the resulting maps can be very easily visualised as a hierarchical tree. By providing such a representation, users can rely on their pre-existing "directory-browsing" mental model [12] of information organization as they explore.

For the pre-processing phase, the *Vector Space Model* (VSM) [13] is followed. A clustering algorithm cannot directly interpret text so a compact representation of its contents is used and is uniformly applied through all phases. There are two main phases; these are parsing and indexing. Parsing turns the documents into a succession of words. These words are filtered using a "stop list" of common English words that provide little information such as "the" and "it". We used the Wordnet lexical database to only include words that can be nouns or are not in the dictionary (e.g. names, acronyms etc.).

To reduce the number total number of input dimensions, we only used words that appear in at least 3 documents and in less than 33% of all documents. The *Wordnet Morphy* morphological functions were used to find the base form of each word. In the indexing phase, each document is represented in the VSM. The frequency of occurrence of each word in each document is recorded in a Documents Vs Terms Matrix. The term frequencies are then weighted using equation (4). This equation gives higher weighting to less frequent words, as these possess more information value than frequent words as described in Shannon's *Information Theory* [15].

$$w_{ij} = tf_{ij} \cdot \log\left(\frac{n}{df_i}\right) \tag{4}$$

Where w_{ij} represents the weight of term t_i in document d_j, tf_{ij} is the frequency of term t_i in document d_j, n is total number of documents in collection and df_i is the number of documents containing term t_i

Once the set of document vectors has been created, the clustering algorithm is applied. For the first level SOM we used a fixed number of neurons, usually 8. In future versions we will be starting with a smaller number, and additional neurons will be added by calculating QE as with the GHSOM. We initialised the weights of the neurons using random numbers. A fixed number of training iterations per document are used, so that larger collections have a larger number of training iterations and vice-versa. For each iteration of training, a document vector is chosen at random and the winning unit determined by (1). We also use the same neighbourhood function described earlier (3) with σ set to the number of neurons. When training is complete on the first level, the total QE for each unit determines how many units shall be used in the corresponding lower level SOM. Training of each lower level SOM then begins. This process is repeated until each unit has a sufficiently low QE. The degree of granularity can be altered based on this threshold QE value.

For labelling the clusters we calculate a score for each term based on the Label-SOM [14] technique. We compute the total term frequency divided by the total QE for each element in the document vectors mapped to the cluster. This is shown in equation (5).

$$ts_i = \frac{\sum_{j=1}^{n} tf_{ij}}{\sum_{j=1}^{n} \sqrt{(m_{ij} - x_i)^2}} \tag{5}$$

Where ts_i is the term score for element i, tf_{ij} is the term frequency for element i in document j, m_{ij} is the weight of element i in document j, x_i is the unit weight of element i and n represents total number of documents.

The QE for each term is calculated by summing up the distance for each vector element over all the vectors. We have found the combination of QE and term frequencies more effective than using either on their own. The six terms that score highest are displayed as a label for each topic in the hierarchy. Figure 1 shows the document collection used for training and the generated tree. We used a set of 497 BBC News website[4] documents for testing. The documents covered a variety of recent news and sports topics. Figure 1 shows the generated tree view from this dataset. Looking at the label, we can see the dominant topics in each directory. The major topics discovered by the high level SOM are sport, people, Milosevic, China & science technology, education, public services and bank interest rates.

It can be seen from the titles of the documents in each expanded sub-topic that they have been clustered effectively. The topic expanded contains documents about public services in the UK. The first expanded subtopic contains documents about the UK Government's police pay reforms. The second expanded node contains two docu-

---

[4] The BBC News website can be found at http://www.bbc.co.uk/news

ments about the public's priorities for the health service in the UK and how they will
be funded. The final expanded node contains documents about the latest health service statistics.

5   Conclusion

We have proposed a method, using a series one dimensional SOM that can be used to
generate a tree view of documents. This is an intuitive representation of a set of clustered documents, and one that users will be familiar with. We found the clustering of
the documents into topics and sub-topics to be very effective using this method. We
found that labelling using a combination of term frequency and QE to be most effective, though in future work, we will be looking at extracting key phrases instead of
single words.

In future work, the highest-level SOM will grow dynamically based on QE to allow for more variation in diversity in document collections. We are also working on
an algorithm to break large documents into smaller sections to overcome the problem
of clustering documents which themselves cover a wide range of topic areas.

Fig. 1. The "1+1" SOM results shown in the document tree

References

1. Blair, D.C., Maron M.E.: 1985. An evaluation of retrieval effectiveness for a full-text document-retrieval system. Communications of the ACM, 28 (1985)
2. van Rijsbergen, C., Information Retrieval, (1979)
3. Furnas, G.W., Landauer, T.K., Gomez, L.M., Dumais, S.T.: The vocabulary problem in human-system communication. Communications of the ACM, 30(11):964-971, November (1987).
4. Merkl, D., Exploration of Text Collections with Hierarchical Feature Maps (1997)
5. Rauber, A., Dittenbach, M., and Merkl, D., Automatically Detecting and Organizing Documents into Topic Hierarchies: A Neural Network Based Approach to Bookshelf Creation and Arrangement (2000)
6. Kohonen, T., Self-organized formation of topologically correct feature maps. Biological Cybernetics, 43:-69, 1982.
7. Krista, L., Honkela, T., Kaski, S., and Kohonen, T., WEBSOM - A Status Report (1996)
8. Honkela, T., Pulkki, V., and Kohonen, T. (1995). Contextual relations of words in Grimm tales analyzed by self-organizing map. In Fogelman-Soulié, F. and Gallinari, P., editors, Proceedings of the International Conference on Artificial Neural Networks, ICANN-95, volume 2, pages 3-7, Paris. EC2 et Cie.
9. Kohonen, T., Kasaki., S., Langus., K., Salojärvi, J., Paatero., V. and Saarela, A. Self Organization of a Massive Document Collection. IEEE Transactions on Neural Networks for Data Mining and Knowledge Descovery, Volume 11 (3), pp 574-585. (2000)
10. Blackmore, J., Miikkulainen, R.: Incremental grid growing: Encoding high-dimensional structure into a two-dimensional feature map. In Proc Int'l Conf Neural Networks (ICANN'93), San Francisco, CA, 1993.
11. Fritzke, B.: Growing grid - a self-organizing network with constant neighborhood range and adaption strength. Neural Processing Letters, 2, No. 5:1 - 5, (1995)
12. Chen, H., Houston., A., Sewell, R., Scatz., B., Internet Browsing and Searching: User Evaluations of Category Map and Concept Space Techniques (1998)
13. Salton, G., Wong, A., and Yang, C., Vector space model for automatic indexing, Communications of the ACM 18, pp. 613--620, 1975.
14. Rauber, A., Merkl, D., Automatic Labeling of Self-Organizing Maps: Making a Treasure-Map Reveal its Secrets
15. Freeman, R., Yin, H., Allinson, N., Self-Organising Maps for Tree View Based Hierarchical Document Clustering, Proceedings of the International Joint Conference on Neural Networks (IJCNN'02), Honolulu, Hawaii, vol. 2, pp. 1906-1911, (2002)

Natural Language Processing for Expertise Modelling in E-mail Communication[*]

Sanghee Kim[1], Wendy Hall[1], and Andy Keane[2]

[1]Intelligence, Agents, Multimedia Group, Department of Electronics and Computer Science
University of Southampton, U.K.
{sk98r,wh}@ecs.soton.ac.uk
[2]Computational Engineering and Design Center, School of Engineering Science
University of Southampton, U.K.
ajk@soton.ac.uk

Abstract. One way to find information that may be required, is to approach a person who is believed to possess it or to identify a person who knows where to look for it. Technical support, which automatically compiles individual expertise and makes this accessible, may be centred on an expert finder system. A central component of such a system is a user profile, which describes user expertise level in discussed subjects. Previous works have made attempts to weight user expertise by using content-based methods, which associate the expertise level with the analysis of keyword usage, irrespective of any semantic meanings conveyed. This paper explores the idea of using a natural language processing technique to understand given information from both a structural and semantic perspective in building user profiles. With its improved interpretation capability compared to prior works, it aims to enhance the performance accuracy in ranking the order of names of experts, returned by a system against a help-seeking query. To demonstrate its efficiency, e-mail communication is chosen as an application domain, since its closeness to a spoken dialog, makes it possible to focus on the linguistic attributes of user information in the process of expertise modelling. Experimental results from a case study show a 23% higher performance on average over 77% of the queries tested with the approach presented here.

1 Introduction

A crucial task in the distributed environments that most organizations operate is to effectively manage the useful knowledge held by individuals. Not only does this supplement additional resource, but it also contributes timely and up-to-date procedural and factual knowledge to enterprises. In order to fully maximize individually held resources, it is necessary to encourage people to share such valuable data. As their expertise is accumulated through task achievement, it is also important

---

[*] This work was funded by the University Technology Partnership (UTP) for Design, which is a collaboration between Rolls-Royce, BAE Systems and the Universities of Cambridge, Sheffield and Southampton.

H. Yin et al. (Eds.): IDEAL 2002, LNCS 2412, pp. 161-166, 2002.

to exploit it as it is created. Such an approach allows individuals to work as normal without demanding changes in working environments [6].

An expert finder is a system designed to locate people who have 'sought-after knowledge' to solve a specific problem. It answers with the names of potential helpers against knowledge seeking queries, in order to establish personal contacts which link novices to experts. The ultimate goal of such a system is to create environments where users are aware of each other, maximizing their current resources and actively exchanging up-to-date information. Although the expert finder systems cannot always generate correct answers, bringing the relevant people together provides opportunities for them to become aware of each other, and to have further discussions, which may uncover hidden expertise.

In designing technical support to maximize the use of such personal expertise, two issues have to be addressed; 1) how to simulate the personal contacts found in real environments, and 2) how to capture personal expertise while allowing users to work as they normally do without demanding changes in working environments. The exploitation of e-mail communication, which can be enhanced as a communication-based learning tool, where individual experiences are shared among communicators, is proposed as an enabling technology. E-mail communication has become a major means of exchanging information and acquiring social or organisational relationships, implying that it would be a good source of information about recent and useful cooperative activities among users. It is hypothesized that because of its popularity, information mined from e-mail communication can be considered as information from expertise discovery sources [3; 6]. In addition, as it represents an every day activity, it requires no major changes to working environments, which makes it suitable as a test environment.

A decision about whether an individual is an expert for a given problem may be made by consulting user profiles. Drawn from information retrieval studies, the frequencies of keywords have been extensively used for extracting user information from exchanged e-mail messages. However, there are at least three reasons why such an approach is inadequate when applied to expertise modelling. First, counting keywords is not adequate for determining whether a given document is factual information or contains some level of author expertise. Secondly, without understanding the semantic meanings of keywords, it is possible to assume that different words represent the same concept and vice versa, which triggers the retrieval of non-relevant information. Finally, it is not easy to distinguish question-type texts from potential answer documents, which support retrieval of the relevant documents for the given query. In addition, the argument that user expertise is action-centred and is often distributed in the individual's action-experiences, is the motivation behind work that relies on linguistic-oriented user modelling [2]. With this approach, when we regard given messages as the realization of involved knowledge, user expertise can be verbalized as a direct indication of user views on discussed subjects, and the levels of expertise are distinguished by taking into account the degree of significance of the words employed in the messages.

In this paper, a new expertise model, EMNLP (Expertise Modelling using Natural Language Processing) that captures the different levels of expertise reflected in exchanged e-mail messages, and makes use of such expertise in facilitating a correct ranking of experts, is presented. It examines the application of NLP (Natural

Language Processing) techniques and user modelling to the development of an expert finder system based on e-mail communication. The creation of an expert finder system that can be embedded in a user's working environments enabling a prompt utilisation is one of the two main themes of this paper, and improving its competency values by using NLP for the profiling of users is the second.

2 Related Work

KnowledgeMail from Tacit Corp is the system most related to EMNLP, in that it adds an automatic profiling ability to some of existing commercial e-mail systems, to support information sharing through executing queries about the profiles constructed [6]. User profiles are formulated as a list of weight-valued terms by using one statistical method. A survey focusing on the system's performance reveals that users tend to spend extra time cleaning up their profiles in order to reduce false hits, which erroneously recommend them as experts due to unresolved ambiguous terms [3]. In an effort to reduce such problems, the application of NLP to profiling users is suggested. As a consequence, EMNLP is expected to generate more meaningful terms in user profiles.

The system described by Vivacqua et al. [8] model a user's programming skill by reading Java source code files, and analysing what classes or methods are used and how often. This result is then compared to the overall usage for the remaining users, to determine the levels of expertise for specific methods. Its automatic profiling and mapping of five levels of expertise (i.e., expert-advanced-intermediate-beginner-novice) are similar to those of EMNLP. However, the expertise assignment function is rather too simplified in so far as it disregards various coding patterns that might reveal the different skills of experts and beginners.

3 Descriptions of EMNLP

A design objective of EMNLP is to improve the efficiency of the task search, which ranks peoples' names in decreasing order of expertise against a help-seeking query. Its contribution is to turn once simply archived e-mail messages into knowledge repositories by approaching them from a linguistic perspective, which regards the exchanged messages as the realization of verbal communication among users. Its supporting assumption is that user expertise is best extracted by focusing on the sentence where users' viewpoints are explicitly expressed. NLP is identified as an enabling technology that analyzes e-mail messages with two aims; 1) to classify sentences into syntactical structures (syntactic analysis), and 2) to extract users' expertise levels using the functional roles of given sentences (semantic interpretation). Figure 1 shows the procedure for using EMNLP, i.e. how to create user profiles from the collected messages. Contents are decomposed into a set of paragraphs and heuristics (e.g., locating a full stop) are applied in order to break down each paragraph into sentences.

Syntactical analysis identifies the syntactic roles of words in a sentence by using a corpus annotation [1]. Apple Pie Parser is used and it is a bottom-up probabilistic chart parser [5]. The syntactical analysis supports the location of a main verb in a sentence, by decomposing the sentence into a group of grammatically related phrases.

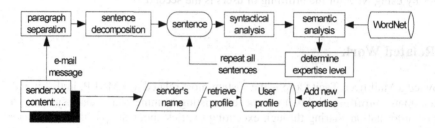

Fig. 1. The procedure for user profiling with the EMNLP

Given the structural information about each sentence, semantic analysis examines sentences with two criteria: 1) whether the employed verb verbalizes the speaker's attitudes, and 2) whether the sentence has a "first person" (e.g., "I", "In my opinion", or "We") subject. This analysis is based on Speech Act Theory (SAT), which proposes that communication involves the speaker's expression of an attitude (i.e. an illocutionary act) towards the contents of the communication [7]. It suggests that information can be delivered with different communication effects on recipients depending on different speaker's attitudes, which are expressed using an appropriate illocutionary act, which represents a particular function of communication. The performance of the speech act is described by a verb, which posits a core element as the central organizer of the sentence. In addition, the fact that working practices are reflected through task achievement implies that personal expertise can be regarded as action-oriented, emphasizing the important role of a "first person" subject in expertise modeling.

EMNLP extracts user expertise from the sentences, which have "first person" subjects, and determines expertise levels based on the identified main verbs. Whereas SAT reasons about how different illocutionary verbs convey the various intentions of speakers, NLP determines the intention by mapping the central verb in the sentence to the pre-defined illocutionary verb. The decision about the level of user expertise is made according to the defined hierarchies of the verbs, initially provided by SAT. SAT provides the categories of illocutionary verbs (i.e. assertive, commissive, directive, declarative, and expressive), each of which contains a set of exemplary verbs. EMNLP further extends the hierarchy in order to increase its coverage for practicability by using the WordNet Database [4]. EMNLP first examines all verbs occurring in the collected messages, and then filters out verbs, which have not been mapped onto the hierarchy. For each verb, it consults the WordNet database in order to assign a value through chaining its synonyms; for example, if the synonym of the given verb is classified into "assertive" value, and then this verb is also assigned into "assertive".

To clarify how two sentences, which may be assumed to contain similar keywords, are mapped onto different profiles, consider two example sentences: 1) "For the 5049 testing, phase analysis on those high frequency results <u>is suggested</u>", and 2) "For the 5049 testing, I <u>know</u> phase analysis on those high frequency results has to be added". The main verb values for both sentences (i.e., suggest and know) are equivalent to "working knowledge", which conveys a modest knowledge for a speaker. However, the difference is that when compared to the first, the second sentence clearly conveys the speaker's intention as it begins with "I know". As a consequence, it is regarded as demonstrating expertise while the first sentence is not. Information extracted from the first sentence is mapped onto a lower-level expertise.

4 Experimental Results

A case study has been developed to test two hypotheses; namely 1) that EMNLP produces comparable or higher accuracy in differentiating expertise from factual information compared to that of the frequency-based statistical model, 2) that differentiating expertise from factual information supports more effective query processing in locating the right experts. As a baseline, a frequency-based statistical model, which builds user profiles by weighting presented terms without considering their meanings or purposes, was used.

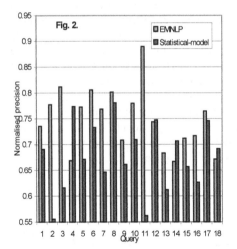
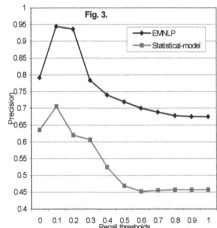

A total of 10 users, who work for the same department in a professional engineering design company, participated in the experiment and a period of three-to-four months duration was spent collecting e-mail messages. A total of 18 queries were created for a testing dataset, and a maximum number of 40 names of predicted experts, i.e. 20 names extracted using EMNLP and 20 names from the statistical model, were shown to a user, who was the group leader of the other users. As a manager, the user was able to evaluate the retrieved names according to the five pre-defined expertise levels: "Expert-Level Knowledge", "Strong Working Knowledge", "Working Knowledge", "Strong Working Interests", and "Working Interests".

Figure 2 summarizes the results measured by normalized precision. For 4 questions (i.e. 4,12,14,18), EMNLP produced lower performance rates than by using the statistical approach. However, for 14 queries, its ranking results were more accurate, and at the highest point, it outperformed the statistical method with a 33% higher precision value. The precision-recall curve, which demonstrates a 23% higher precision value for EMNLP, is shown in Figure 3. The differences of precision values at different recall thresholds are rather small with EMNLP, implying that its precision values are relatively higher than those of the statistical model.

A close examination of the queries used for testing reveals that the statistical model has a better capability in processing general-type queries that search for non-specific factual information, since 1) as we regard user expertise as action-oriented, knowledge is distinguished from such factual information, implying that it is difficult to value factual information as knowledge with EMNLP, and 2) EMNLP is limited to exploring various ways of determining the level of expertise in that it constrains user expertise to be expressed through the first person in a sentence.

5 Future Work

EMNLP was developed to improve the accuracy of ranking the order of expert names by use of the NLP technique to capture explicitly stated user expertise, which otherwise may be ignored. Its improved ranking order, compared to that of a statistical method, was mainly due to the use of an enriched expertise acquisition technique, which successfully distinguished experienced users from novices. We presume that EMNLP would be particularly useful when applied to large organizations where it is vital to improve retrieval performance since typical queries may be answered with a list of a few hundred potential expert names.

Special attention is given to gathering domain specific terminologies possibly collected from technical documents such as task manuals or memos. This is particularly useful for the semantic analysis, which identifies concepts and relationships within the NLP framework, since these terminologies are not retrievable from general-purpose dictionaries (e.g., the WordNet database).

References

1. Allen, J. (1987) Natural Language Understanding, Benjamin/Cummings Publishing
2. Choo, C. W., Detlor, B., Turnbull, D. (2000) WEB WORK Information Seeking and Knowledge Work on the World Wide Web, Kluwer Academic Publishers
3. Forbes (2001) Forbes, You've got expertise, http://www.forbes.com/global/2001/0205/088_print.html
4. Miller, G. A., Beckwith, R., Fellbaum, C., Gross, D., Miller, K. (1993) Introduction to WordNet: An On-Line Lexical Database, University of Princeton, U.S.A.
5. Sekine, S., Grishman, R. (1995) A Corpus-based Probabilistic Grammar with only Two Non-Terminals, In Proceedings of the Fourth International Workshop on Parsing Technology, pp.216-223
6. Tacit (1999) White paper of KnowledgeMail, http://www.tacit.com/knowledgemail
7. Verschueren, J. (1980) On Speech Act Verbs, John Benjamins, Amsterdam
8. Vivacqua, A., Lieberman, H. (2000) Agents to Assist in Finding Help, In Proceedings of the CHI'2000, pp.65-72

A Branch and Bound Algorithm for Minimum Cost Network Flow Problem

Jun Han, Graham McMahon, and Stephen Sugden

School of Information Technology, Bond University
{jhan, gmcmahon, ssugden}@bond.edu.au

Abstract. In this paper we introduce a branch and bound algorithm for finding tree solution of minimum cost network flow problem. We consider different situations such as unit and non-unit traffic demand. The methods used to prune the searching tree in different situations are emphasized respectively but the complete searching process is not interpreted in detail due to limited space. Programming test results show the efficiency of these techniques.

1 Introduction

With the advent of the information age, there has been increased interest in the efficient design of communication networks. Considerable research interest has been shown in problems dealing with the economic synthesis of networks. The aim of this kind of design problem is to satisfy all traffic requirements at minimum cost between a set of nodes. The mathematical formulation of the problem can be as follows:

$$\text{Minimize} \sum_{p=1}^{n} \sum_{q>p}^{n} \sum_{r} h_r^{pq} \sum_{i=1}^{n-1} \sum_{j=i+1}^{n} c_{ij} a_{ij,r}^{pq} \tag{1}$$

S.T.

$$\sum_{r} h_r^{pq} = F^{pq} \qquad \forall p,q \tag{2}$$

$$f_{ij} = \sum_{p=1}^{n} \sum_{q>p}^{n} \sum_{r} a_{ij,r}^{pq} h_r^{pq} \qquad \forall i,j \tag{3}$$

$$0 \le f_{ij} \le f_{ij}^{\max} \qquad \forall i,j \tag{4}$$

$$0 \le h_r^{pq} \qquad \forall p,q,r \tag{5}$$

where
n is the number of nodes,
h_r^{pq} is the amount of traffic on route r between O-D pair $p-q$,

H. Yin et al. (Eds.): IDEAL 2002, LNCS 2412, pp. 167–172, 2002.
© Springer-Verlag Berlin Heidelberg 2002

c_{ij} is the cost per unit flow on arc (i, j),

$a_{ij,r}^{pq}$ is 1 if the arc (i, j) exists on route r between nodes p, q ; 0 otherwise,

F^{pq} is the total flow requirement between O-D pair $p - q$,

f_{ij} is the total flow on arc (i, j),

f_{ij}^{max} is the upper bound of the available capacity on arc (i, j).

There exists a substantial literature dealing with this problem [1]..[8], and many solution techniques have been applied to solve it, such as Genetic Algorithm [2],[3],[5], Simulated Annealing [6], Tabu Search [4], and Integrated GA-LP algorithm [1].

These algorithms are all heuristics. In this paper we present a branch and bound algorithm, which is an exact algorithm. We consider only the case that the cost of building a certain arc is a constant but not a linear function of flow on the arc.

2   The Branch and Bound Algorithm

We consider the solution as a collection of n-1 arcs (for n-node problem) chosen from all candidate arcs, so we will introduce an arc-oriented branch and bound method. We construct a binary searching tree in which each stage corresponds to the decision of either adding a certain arc (ordered in ascendant cost) to the solution arc set or not.

2.1   Pruning the Searching Tree

First we define SMST, the minimum spanning tree under the presupposition that some arcs must be included (suppose these arcs do not make circles), and some arcs must not be included. Since any vertex in our searching tree corresponds to that some certain arcs have been chosen and some arcs have been eliminated, we can use SMST as a bound. At each stage, in addition to the feasibility checking, we find out the current SMST and calculate its total cost. If not desirable (expensive then the cost of a solution already found), we will go backwards on the searching tree. Thus, we prune the sub-tree rooted at the current vertex in the searching tree.

Next, an efficient feasibility check procedure is essential for pruning the searching tree. While the traffic demand between each O-D pair could be equal or not equal, we employ different methods to prune the searching tree quickly in these two situations.

2.1.1   Feasibility Predicting Method for Problem with Unit Traffic Demand
This is the case when the traffic demand between each O-D pair is equal, so we can just consider the traffic demand between each O-D pair to be 1 unit. While there is traffic demand between every pair of nodes, the flow on an arc can be calculated by just multiplying the number of nodes on one side of the arc and the number of nodes on the other side of the arc. Let NL be the number of nodes on the left side of an arc,

NR be the number of nodes on the right side of the arc, then the traffic flow on the arc must be NL times NR units.

Regarding any arc in a feasible solution of an N node problem, $NL + NR$ =N, that is, when NL =1, NR must be N-1; when NL =2, NR must be N-2, and accordingly. Then, depending on the topology of the solution tree, the flow on an arc may be from 1*(N-1)=(N-1) units to (N/2)*(N/2)=N*N/4 units (when N is even) or from (N-1) units to (N/2)*(N-1)/2=N*(N-1)/4 units (when N is odd).

Let N_{max} be the larger number between NL and NR, N_{min} be the smaller one, then the possible combinations of N_{max} and N_{min}, and the value of flow should be as shown in Table 1.

We can see that, if an arc has been used to construct a feasible solution tree, and its N_{min} is m, then its flow capacity must be equal to or greater then m(N-m). Or we can say that, if an arc is to be chosen to construct a feasible solution tree and its flow capacity is T, then, when m(N-m)<= T <(m+1)(N-m-1), the arc's N_{min} must be equal to or smaller than m.

Based on the above feature, we can calculate the flow on an arc quickly, and more significantly, in most cases we are able to foresee that an arc will be overflow.

We add another bound, the N_{min} of an arc, which we call it Link Degree here. Before engaging the searching, we calculate the Link Degree for every arc according to its flow capacity, and at every searching stage, we check if any arc's current NL and NR are both greater than its Link Degree. If so, we should go backwards on the searching tree since it will eventually cause an overflow if we keep going forward and adding more arcs to the solution arc set. This will foretell whether an arc will overflow even if it hasn't yet been connected to some other separated arcs or sub-trees and hasn't yet overflow. Implementing this technique will prune the searching tree far more quickly.

2.1.2   Feasibility Predicting for Problem with Non-unit Traffic Demand

When the traffic demand between each O-D pair is not equal, we use the following method to calculate the possible minimum flow on an arc.

Table 1. Possible flows on an arc for N node problem

N	is	Even	N	is	odd
N_{min}	N_{max}	Flow	N_{min}	N_{max}	Flow
1	N-1	N-1	1	N-1	N-1
2	N-2	2(N-2)	2	N-2	2(N-2)
...	...	...	...	...	...
M	N-m	m(N-m)	m	N-m	m(N-m)
m+1	N-(m+1)	(m+1)(N-(m+1))	M+1	N-(m+1)	(m+1)(N-(m+1))
...	...	...	...	...	...
N/2	N/2	N*N/4	(N-1)/2	(N+1)/2	(N*N-1)/4

At each searching stage, let F_c be the current traffic flow on arc (i, j), set V_l ($|V_l| = L$) be the set of nodes already connected to arc (i, j) and are on the left side of the arc, set V_r ($|V_r| = R$) be the set of nodes already connected to arc (i, j) and are on the right side of the arc, set V_s ($|V_s| = S$) be the set of nodes not having been connected to the arc. Every node m in set V_s will be eventually connected to arc (i, j), either on the left side or on the right side. Let FL_m be the total traffic demand between node m and all nodes in V_l, FR_m be the total traffic demand between node m and all nodes in V_r, that is,

$$FL_m = \sum_{i=1}^{L} Demand(m, Vl(i)) \quad , \quad FR_m = \sum_{i=1}^{R} Demand(m, Vr(i)).$$

Then the minimum flow increased on arc (i, j) after connecting node m to the arc will be either FL_m (when V_l stay unchanged) or FR_m (when V_r stay unchanged). Let F_{min}^m be the smaller value between FL_m and FR_m, then the minimum flow increased on arc (i, j) after connecting all nodes in V_s to the arc is $F_{MIN} = \sum_{j=1}^{S} F_{min}^{V_s(j)}$. Therefore, the minimum total flow on arc (i, j) will be $F_t = F_c + F_{MIN}$. If F_t is greater than the capacity of arc (i, j), we can say that arc (i, j) must encounter over flow later.

At each searching stage we calculate the F_t of every arc, if the F_t of any arc exceed arc capacity, we should go backwards on the searching tree. Here F_t works as a bound of total flow on an arc and it help prune the searching greatly faster.

We can make the bound F_t even tighter. We define V_s' ($|V_s'| = S'$) be the set of separated sub-trees (including separated single nodes), $V_s'^k$ ($|V_s'^k| = S_k'$) be the set of nodes contained in the kth sub-tree of V_s'. Let FL_k' be the total traffic demand between all nodes in $V_s'^k$ and all nodes in V_l, FR_k' be the total traffic demand between all nodes in $V_s'^k$ and all nodes in V_r, that is,

$$FL_k' = \sum_{j=1}^{S_k'} \sum_{l=1}^{L} Demand(V_s'^k(j), V_l(i)),$$

$$FR_k' = \sum_{j=1}^{S_k'} \sum_{l=1}^{L} Demand(V_s'^k(j), V_r(i)).$$

Then the minimum flow increased on arc (i, j) after connecting the kth sub-tree to the arc will be either FL'_k or FR'_k. Let $F'^k_{\min}$ be the smaller value between FL'_k and FR'_k, then the minimum flow increased on arc (i, j) after connecting all sub-trees V'_s to the arc is $F'_{MIN} = \sum_{k=1}^{S'} F'^k_{\min}$.

Regarding each node m in sub-tree V'^k_s, Since $F^m_{\min}$ is the smaller value between FL_m and FR_m, that is, $FL_m >= F^m_{\min}$, $FR_m >= F^m_{\min}$, then for all nodes in sub-tree V'^k_s, we have,

$$FL'_k = \sum_{j=1}^{S'_k} FL_{V'^k_s(j)} >= \sum_{j=1}^{S'_k} F^{V'^k_s(j)}_{\min}, \quad FR'_k = \sum_{j=1}^{S'_k} FR_{V'^k_s(j)} >= \sum_{j=1}^{S'_k} F^{V'^k_s(j)}_{\min}.$$

Since $F'^k_{\min}$ is either FL'_k or FR'_k, we have $F'^k_{\min} >= \sum_{j=1}^{S'_k} F^{V'^k_s(j)}_{\min}$. Therefore, for

all nodes in V_s, $F'_{MIN} = \sum_{k=1}^{S'} F'^k_{\min} >= \sum_{k=1}^{S'} \sum_{j=1}^{S'_k} F^{V'^k_s(j)}_{\min} = \sum_{j=1}^{S} F^{V_s(j)}_{\min} = F_{MIN}$.

After F_{MIN} is replaced by F'_{MIN}, we get a tighter bound $F'_t = F_c + F'_{MIN}$.

3   Computational Experiences

We used a number of sets of instances generated randomly to test our branch and bound algorithm. The computations were performed on a machine with Pentium II 400MHz CPU and 128M RAM.

Table 2 is the results of one set of 20-node problems with unit traffic demand. Method I is our branch and bound algorithm using direct feasibility check (calculating the flow already allocated on each arc). In method II, we use Link Degree to predict the feasibility of a potential solution in unit traffic demand problems. From Table 2 we can see that method II reduced the total searching steps by 99 percent (one "step" corresponds to traveling along one arc in the searching tree). In addition, Method II can solve 50-node problems with an average of 90k searching steps and 8 CPU seconds. It can also solve 100-node problems with an average of 1M searching steps and 100 CPU seconds, while Method I can not solve problems with more than 30 nodes.

We employ F_{MIN} in Method III to predict the flow on each arc for non-unit traffic demand problems, and we use F'_{MIN} instead of F_{MIN} in Method IV. Experiments show that Method IV reduces the searching steps by 10% compared with Method III.

Detailed test data are omitted here due to limited space. All the test problems and solutions can be accessed at: http://www.geocities.com/ilhll/mincostflow.html.

Table 2. Test results of 20-node unit demand problems

Problem file Name	Method I Running Steps	Method II Running Steps	Percentage of Reduced Steps
P20-1.txt	123766	216	99.825%
P20-2.txt	6445	655	89.837%
P20-3.txt	10890072	215	99.998%
P20-4.txt	9598	83	99.135%
P20-5.txt	4865529	423	99.991%
P20-6.txt	25087936	71	99.999%
P20-7.txt	4861602	237	99.995%
P20-8.txt	4364835	69	99.998%
P20-9.txt	10352988	1452	99.986%
P20-10.txt	612423	936	99.847%

4   Conclusion

We have proposed a class of branch and bound algorithm that can solve up to 100-node problem instances (fixed arc costs). Computation experiences show the effectiveness of the algorithms and demonstrate the efficiency of the bounding methods developed.

References

1. Berry, L.T.M.; Murtagh, B.A., McMahon, G.B., Sugden, S.J. and Welling, L.D. An Integrated GA-LP Approach to Communication Network Design. Telecommunication Systems Journal (1999).
2. Berry, L.T.M., Murtagh, B.A.; McMahon, G.B. Sugden, S.J. and Welling, L.D., Genetic Algorithms in the Design of Complex Distribution Networks, *International Journal of Physical Distribution and Logistics Management*, 28, No.5, (1998) 377-381.
3. Berry, L.T.M., Murtagh, B.A., Sugden, S.J. and McMahon, G.B., Application of a Genetic-based Algorithm for Optimal Design of Tree-structured Communication Networks, *Proceedings of the Regional Teletraffic Engineering Conference of the International Teletraffic Congress,* South Africa, September (1995) 361-370.
4. Glover, F., Laguna, M., *Tabu Search*, Kluwer Academic Publishers, Boston MA, (1997).
5. Palmer, C.C., An Approach to a Problem in Network Design Using Genetic Algorithms. *Networks*, 26 (1995) 361-370.
6. Randall, M., McMahon, G. and Sugden, S., *A Simulated Annealing Approach to Communication Network Design*, TR99-04, School of Information Technology, Bond University, (1999).
7. Ahuja, R., Magnanti, T.; Orlin, J.: *Network Flows: Theory, Algorithms and Applications,* Prentice Hall, New Jersey (1993).
8. Minoux, M.: Network Synthesis and Optimal Design Problems: Models, Solution Methods and Applications, *Networks*, 19, (1989) 337-341.

Study of the Regularity of the Users' Internet Accesses

Nicolas Durand and Luigi Lancieri

France Telecom R&D Caen
{nicola.durand, luigi.lancieri}@francetelecom.com

Abstract. The aim of this study is to investigate relationship between past users' behavior (described by access patterns) and future one. The two main ideas are first to explore the possible users' characterization that can be extracted from access pattern. This allows to measure and to have a better understanding of users' behavior. This knowledge allows us to build new services as building interest communities based on a comparative approach and clustering. The second idea is to see if these characterizations can be useful to forecast future access. This could be useful to prefetch web data in proxy-cache. We show that there are some partial mathematical models binding the users' behavior to the repetition of queries.

1 Introduction

Discovery of frequent patterns [1,2] in the past accesses of the web users is a very interesting subject of study if we wish to model their behavior. One of the applications of these studies is to prefetch web information [3]. In our context, the prefetching consists in loading in a local proxy-cache [4] some distant web information having a high probability to be accessed by the users in the future. The aim is to improve the access speed by decreasing the latent period (response time to a query). Thus, the performances of such methods depend on finding regularity or rules on users behavior. The model of user's behavior is also interesting for other purposes including social study [5]. A good model can be used to simulate humans interactions and to have a better understanding of human access to knowledge. A model can also be used to optimize existent services as clustering users in groups of interest having a comparable behavior. So, we made an analysis of users accesses to Web through an operational proxy-cache during a long period of time, in order to determine the level of time regularity and behavioral correlation. Contrary to Web server, proxy-cache allows having a better reflect of users behavior since its trace covers larger information requests (potentially the full Web).

The organization of this document is as follows. In Section 2, we discuss the context of our experiment and the data. Then in Section 3, we describe our method. In Section 4, we detail a batch analysis of the results. In Section 5, we discuss a temporal analysis. In Section 6, we compare the behavior of the users. In Section 7, we discuss previous works on the analysis of the users behavior. We conclude in Section 8.

H. Yin et al. (Eds.): IDEAL 2002, LNCS 2412, pp. 173–178, 2002.

2   Context of the Experimentation

We used the log files of two operational proxies-caches of France Telecom R&D (at Caen), over a period of 17 months (from January 1-st, 1999 to May 31, 2000) concerning 331 users. The total number of queries is 1510358 corresponding to 392853 different objects (a given object can be asked several time).

The log files was purified, we only kept the queries corresponding to an object of mime type: "text". This approach answers the following logic. From a cognitive point of view, the textual pages are strongly linked to the explicit step of the users [5]. In terms of probability, the inclusive objects are primilary textual type accesses. In semantic terms, text is also more easily definable than for example images or video sequences. The remaining data corresponds on average to: 1186 different URLs per user, and approximately 8.6 queries per user and per day.

3   Description of the Regularities Analysis Method

At first, we studied the level of regularity on different sequences of access without worrying about the chronology (see Section 4). Then we made a study to determine the level of time regularity of the users' accesses (see Section 5). The global redundancy is the ratio between the number of queries and the number of unique URLs over the total period of consultation. We computed the percentage of common queries between two different sequences of queries that we noted $CQTS$ (Common Queries in Temporal Sequences). These two variables are calculated per user and on average on all the users. All user queries are sorted chronologically and split into sequences of equal length. This corresponds to a percentage of the total number of user queries and is recorded as T. Figure 1 illustrates the process. For the first sequence noted S_1, we compute the number of common URLs with the following sequence noted Q_2, this corresponds to a space of $\Delta=0$. We repeat this process until all the space of sequence is covered: let (S_i, Q_j) be the pairs of studied sequences, and n the total number of sequences, then $i \in [1, n/2]$ and $j \in [i+1, n/2+i]$. In this way, we have the same number of computed values for each of the chosen sequences S_i.

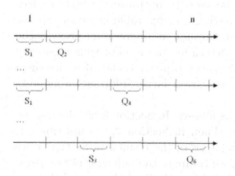

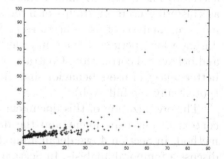

Fig. 1. Method of analysis

Fig. 2. Global redundancy according to $CQTS$

4   Batch Analysis

For every user, we calculated the global redundancy of these accesses and the average of $CQTS$ (with $T=5\%$). We obtained the curve illustrated by the Figure 2, where we have in abscissa, $CQTS$, and in ordinate, the global redundancy. We notice that $CQTS$ and the global redundancy vary in the same direction according to a geometrical law with an increasing dispersal according to the redundancy. In the extreme cases (all URLs identical or all URLs different), the level of $CQTS$ or global redundancy is identical, and in the intermediate cases, the global redundancy grows much slower than $CQTS$.

The redundancy of the queries can be interpreted as illustrating the behavior of the user [5]. For example a monolithic behavior (concentrated accesses on few web sites) will have a strong global redundancy while a more scattered behavior (distributed accesses on a large number of URLs) will have a low redundancy. We observe here the highlighting of the coherence of users' accesses. Indeed, if the accesses were done at random, $CQTS$ would statistically be very close to the global redundancy.

5   Temporal Analysis

In this section, we studied the value of users' $CQTS$ according to the space of time between the sequences of queries (see Figure 1). We made vary the size of the studied sequences ($T=1, 2, 3, 5, 10\%$). The maximal value of $CQTS$ is realized when the space is minimised. The behavior of this curve (except the maximum value of $CQTS$) is independent of the users and shows a strong temporal coherence. The maximal value is not very different according to the size of the studied sequences. It is between 23,6% and 25,3%. We notice that the level of $CQTS$ according to the time separating both compared sequences, follows a sub exponential law. Indeed, after a logarithmic transformation (log X-axis, log A-axis), the increase of the redundancy according to the increase of the time separating sequences is constant (see Figure 3). The slopes of the curves of the Figure 3 have a coefficient of regression of 0.99, that shows an excellent correlation.

The sub exponential law binding these two parameters can be expressed in the following way. Let Δ be the space between the studied sequences, $cqmax$ be the maximal value of $CQTS$, T be the size of studied sequences (expressed in percentage of all the queries), cq be the $CQTS$ value, and k be a constant. We have the following relation: $log(cq) = -kTlog(\Delta) + log(cqmax)$, where $-kT$ is the slope of the straight line. Thus, we have:

$$cq = cqmax.\Delta^{-kT}$$

So, it means that we can determine the value of $CQTS$ knowing the size of the studied sequences and the value of the space of time. We can verify with the Figure 4, that the slope of the straight lines of the Figure 3 evolves linearly according to the size T of the sequences. It brings out that the global behavior of the function cq (derived of the affine function of the Figure 3) is independent of the user whose the behavior intervenes only with the value of $cqmax$.

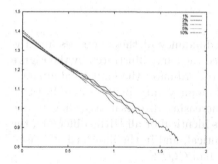

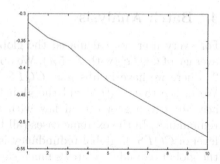

Fig. 3. Logarithm transformation of the temporal analysis

Fig. 4. Evolution of the slope according to T

6   Comparative Analysis of Users

We are interested here in the relations between the behavior of the users, with their maximal $CQTS$ value, and the average of $CQTS$ values. With the Figure 5, we studied the evolution of the maximum $CQTS$ value, $cqmax$, according to the rank of the maximal $CQTS$ value of the user, for $T=5\%$. We notice, by disregarding the extremes, that there is a relatively proportional evolution, what confirms the conclusions of the Section 5.

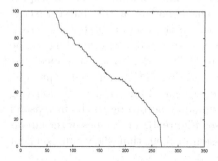

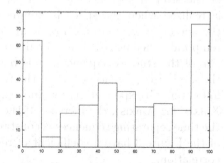

Fig. 5. Maximal $CQTS$ value according to the user rank

Fig. 6. Distribution of the maximal $CQTS$ values among users

The distribution of the values of the maximum $CQTS$ is represented in the Figure 6. We have in ordinate the number of users, and in abscissa the maximum $CQTS$ value. We notice by disregarding the extremes, that the distribution is almost homogeneous. For a $CQTS$ included between 90 and 100%, we have 73 users (22%). This high number explains itself because of a user having a low number of queries and a minimum of regularity, has a $CQTS$ very high for a low space of time (Δ).

Then, we sorted out the users according to their $CQTS$ value (with $T=5\%$). The Figure 7 indicates in abscissa the rank of bigger $CQTS$, and in ordinate the $CQTS$ value. Remember that the more $CQTS$ is high, the more the future

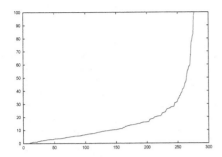

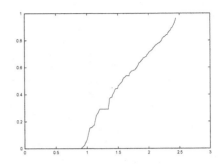

Fig. 7. $CQTS$ according to the users rank

Fig. 8. Hyperbolic tangent transformation of the Y-axis of the logarithm transformation of the Figure 7

accesses will resemble the past ones. We notice clearly that there is a small group of user having a relatively high $CQTS$ (10% of the users with more than 30%). There are very few users with a very high $CQTS$ (2% of the users with more than 70%). Just like the Section 5, we applied some mathematical transformations to try to discover a underlying law to this evolution. We computed the logarithm transformation on the ordinate of the curve of the Figure 7, and we applied the hyperbolic tangent transformation (see Figure 8). The curve of the Figure 8 has a coefficient of linear regression of 0.98 that corresponds to a good correlation. We notice that the increase of the $CQTS$ according to the increase of rank among users classified by increasing $CQTS$, is a constant (in the space of the transformation logarithm / hyperbolic tangent logarithm). It means that if the user A is 3 times as regular as the user B, we can estimate the $CQTS$ of B given the $CQTS$ of A.

7   Related Works

To study the regularity of the accesses, the notion of self similarity is a very interesting tool for the modeling. The self-similarity (heavy tail, Zipf's law) expresses that a series of data shows the same characteristic in different scales (fractals). In the case of a chronological series, the self-similarity implies the dependence between the short term and the long term (spatial and temporal locality [6]). Leland and al [7], and Paxson and al [8], showed respectively in a LAN context and a WAN context, that the forecast of traffic was much more reliable by taking into account a stream distribution of self-similar data rather than a distribution of Poisson. While in the case of Poissonian or Markovian streams, the level of variation or disparity of the queries tends to decrease in the time, the real traffic reveals a stability on various scales of time. Studies [9] tend to show that web tracks do not follow strictly Zipf's law, but which remain nevertheless self-similar. Other works on the variability of the users' behavior of Web were realized by taking into account the semantic aspect underlying the queries [10,5].

8   Conclusion

We studied the regularity of the users' accesses of proxies thanks to the $CQTS$ computation. Except the statistics information on these accesses, we can highlight some natural conclusions on the users' behavior and thus to forecast it better. The users, at least a great majority, are not regular in their accesses. Indeed, the maximal rate of $CQTS$ is low at 25.3%. In spite of this lack of regularity, we brought out the important coherence of the accesses. This internal logic suggests underlying laws, at least by the rational component of the user's behavior. We are far from having discovered a general model of the behavior of the user (assuming that it is possible). However, we showed that there are partial models binding the users' behavior to the repetition of queries. We also showed that the temporal coherence of the accesses was a factor independent from users. We notice the strong diminution of the $CQTS$ value in the time. That means that if we mine the access patterns by using log files at the given moment, then the obtained patterns can really be used only over a short period.

In future works, we will go more to depth: at the level of the keywords of the consulted documents. The $CQTS$ value at the level of the consulted keywords should be higher (a keyword can be common to several URLs). Furthermore, this will allow us to get the centres of interests of the users, which vary less quickly in the time and allow a higher level of description.

References

1. Agrawal, R. and Srikant, R.: Mining Sequential Patterns: Generalizations and Performance Improvements, EDBT'96, Avignon, France (1996)
2. Mannila, H. and Toivonen, H. and Verkamo, A.I.: Discovery of Frequent Episodes in Event Sequences, Helsinki, C-1997-15 (1997)
3. Nanopoulos, A., Katsaros, D., Manolopoulos, Y.: Effective Prediction of Web-User Accesses: A Data Mining Approach, WebKDD'01 Workshop, (2001)
4. Yang, Q. and Zhang, H.H., Li, T.: Mining Web Logs for Prediction Models in WWW Caching and Prefetching, ACM SIGKDD'01, San Francisco, (2001)
5. Lancieri, L., Memory and Forgetfulness: Two Complementary Mechanisms to Characterize the Various Actors of the Internet in their Interactions, University of Caen, France, December, (2000)
6. Almeida, V. and Bestravos, A. and Crovella, M. and de Oliveira, A., Characterizing Reference Locality in the WWW, PDIS'96, Miami Beach, 1996
7. Leland, W. and Taqqu, M. and Willinger, W., Wilson, D., On the Self-Similar Nature of Ethernet Traffic, ACM SIGCOMM93, San Francisco, 183-193 (1993)
8. Paxson, V.: Fast Approximation of Self-Similar Network Traffic, University of California, Berkeley, LBL-36750 (1995)
9. Breslau, L. and Cao, P. and Fan, L. and Phillips, G. and Shenker, S.: On the Implications of Zipf's law for Web Caching, the 3rd Int. WWW Caching Workshop (1998)
10. Legouix, S. and Foucault, J. P. and Lancieri, L.: A Method for Studying the Variability of Users' Thematic Profile, WebNet2000 AACE, San Antonio (2000)

An Intelligent Mobile Commerce System with Dynamic Contents Builder and Mobile Products Browser

Sera Jang and Eunseok Lee

School of Information and Communication Engineering,
Sungkyunkwan Univ. (SKKU)
300 Chunchun Jangahn Suwon Kyunggi South Korea
{lovebiru, eslee}@selab.skku.ac.kr

Abstract. Mobile commerce (MC) is expected to occupy an important part in electronic commerce in spite of a number of problems such as restriction of device, limited contents and expensive charge system. But the functions that can automatically extend the limited contents, which are provided for the MC and efficiently support commercial transaction on the expensive charge system, are essential for the activation of the MC. In this paper we propose a next generation intelligence mobile commerce system, which enables a series of e-commerce activities like searching, ordering and settlement on the mobile device including the functions mentioned above. The proposed system has been actually designed, implemented and confirmed its effectiveness through experiments.

1 Introduction

MC is expected as the next good business in spite of a number of problems as follows: i) Limited contents are provided, which are designed just only for the m-commerce. ii) Mobile call charge increases with the amount used. iii) The small display area and memory size in mobile device. Especially ii) is an important obstacle factor in the South Korea for the activation of M-commerce.

In this paper we propose a solution focused on i) and ii) especially. For i), we build an algorithm for automatic information retrieval about shops, products, and ordering forms of each shop on the Internet. For ii), we made a middlet application that reduce the call charge during the MC, in which the retrieved information from i) is transferred to the mobile device as a file and the connection with network is fired. And a user can search necessary information in various ways on the mobile device without connection with network. After selecting a product, the user can order the product according to the form interface. The order is transferred to server by reestablishing the connection. By this application, a mobile device user can process the transaction only with the minimum connection time.

We have actually designed and implemented the proposed system and confirmed its effectiveness through experiments. In section 2 we discuss the related work. In section 3 we describe the architecture and main functions of the proposed system. Section 4 shows the implementation and evaluation of the system. Section 5 concludes this paper.

H. Yin et al. (Eds.): IDEAL 2002, LNCS 2412, pp. 179-185, 2002.

2 Related Work

Most contents providers for mobile commerce offer strictly limited contents, which can be used for m-commerce only. To solve the problem, that is, to increase the contents, the construction of integrated products information system is necessary. It may be achieved through the seamless connections of data between m-commerce and e-commerce, because conventional e-commerce systems have already abundant contents. There are some instances about the integrated information system such as Bargain Finder, ShopBot and MORPHEUS. Bargain Finder [1] builds a wrapper[1] by analyzing the result from vender by developer's hand. ShopBot [2] creates a wrapper semi-automatically by a wrapper creation module, though it still imposes a big burden to developers.

MORPHEUS [3] also creates a wrapper that analyzes goods search pattern of vender automatically. The all above systems have a common problem that the search speed is very slow because they search products on line. That is one of the reasons that the conventional approaches cannot be applied to the domain of m-commerce directly.

3 Proposed System

3.1 Basic Designs Concepts

The proposed system is intended to support the activation of m-commerce by solving the problems mentioned above. It concretely overcomes the lack of contents by automatic contents generator for m-commerce and offers efficient and economical interaction way to users by providing a middlet application.

3.2 Systems Architecture

Fig. 1 shows the architecture of the proposed system. The system consists of four components as follows: *Shopping Module* gathers and filters product information from shops on the web. It translates product information into XML form and the XML file is transmitted to the mobile device of client.

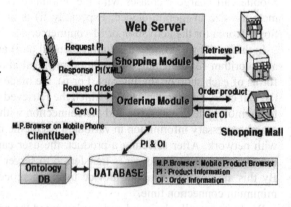

Fig. 1. System Architecture

---

[1] Wrapper is a procedure or a rule for obtaining the contents of information on the source [3].

Ordering Module gathers information related with order form of each shop and orders goods to the corresponding shop by filling in the order form. *M.P.Browser (Mobile Product Browser)* is a middlet application that supports various types of products search on the mobile device. *Database* keeps information of goods that is retrieved by *Shopping Module*, user's personal information and transaction information. *Ontology Server* keeps standard category information about categories. The details of each module are as follows:

Shopping Module. This module consists of *Search Agent, Filtering Agent* and *XML Translator* as shown in Fig 2.

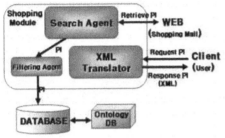

Fig. 2. Architecture of Shopping Module

Search Agent retrieves the URL of shops that exist on the web and extracts products information on each shop. The URL of shops is retrieved by analyzing shopping category of portal sites. And the agent extracts information of goods by visiting the page of each retrieved shop. The function of Search Agent is described in Fig. 3. The algorithm is applicable to the contents, which are built with general web programming languages.

(1) First step is finding the main page of a shop. The first level category of products can be found on the main page in general.

Step1. Visit store
Step2. Search main page
Step3. Search 1 level category
Step4. Now category = 1 level category
Step5. Save information of 1 level category(url, category name)
Step6. For each category do the following:
Step6.1 Visit category page
Step6.2 Search offspring category of current category
Step6.3 If (offspring category)
Step6.3.1 Save offspring category information
Step6.3.2 current category = offspring category
Step6.3.3 Do Step 6
Step6.4 Else
Step6.4.1 display page = current category
Step6.4.2 Search goods information such as URL of the detailed page, goods name and price
Step6.4.3 Visit the detailed page
Step6.4.3.1 Search the detailed goods Information
Step6.4.4 Save goods information

Fig. 3. Algorithm of Search Agent

(2) Second step is searching the first level categories. The category links of shops built with general web programming languages have common characteristics as follows: i)they are close by. ii) they have the same URL. iii) they have different values of variables. If the agent analyzes link tags on the page like this, it can obtain category information. The below shows the detailed algorithm.

   i) Finds link tags. (ex. *<a href = 'test1.asp?cate1=AA'>test</a>*)
   ii) Separates tag and URL
   iii) Extracts the links which have pattern like
       '*filename.extension?{variable=value}+*'
       If the links have the same url of file such as "*filename.extension?*" and they are close by, it assumes that it is the first level(level 1) categories.
   iv) Extracts category names. (Ex. *<a href=..>category names</a>*)

(3) Third step is tracing the links of each category and searching offspring categories of each category repeatedly through the analysis of link patterns. The detailed method is as follows:

    i) Searches links of each category.

    ii) Repeats Third step until reaching to the products display page.

    iii) If the category does not have offspring categories anymore, assume that the page of the link is the products display page.

(4) Fourth step is visiting the products display pages, in where they have links which are linked with product information page with image. Also, it has the same URL of page and variable value that is different. The name and price can be extracted from the products display page. It is more efficient than finding them from the detailed information pages of products. The products price and name can be searched by analyzing the HTML source between image links of products. The information of price can be searched by finding numbers that are located around the words like 'price', 'won', '$', 'dollar' and so on. Detailed information of goods can be obtained from the detailed information page of goods before filtering of items.

Filtering Agent filters goods information that is retrieved by Search Agent. Here the agent removes irrelative information on HTML tag such as table, link, image and so on.

XML Translator searches product information after receiving products search request from client. And it converts the results of search to XML form and transmits to the client. The category of goods is re-categorized by a standard category based on Ontology Server.

Ordering Module. Ordering Module consists of Order Agent and Retrieval Agent as shown in Fig 4. Retrieval Agent gathers information related with order from shops. The retrieved information includes path of order, path of login and necessary filling in item when user orders. The order page has a link pattern like category. It visits the page of links and extracts information of order page by analyzes <form> tag of HTML. The page is an actual

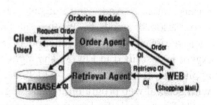

Fig. 4. Structure of Ordering Module

ordering page of shop. It obtains the information about variable transmitted in the actual order page. Usually it can know the role of variables through text in front of <input> tag. The role of variable is decided by Ontology Server.

Order Agent connects and orders the shop, which sells relevant goods if a client requests an order. If the order is completed, the agent transfers the result to the client. Both personal information obtained from user's personal data and delivery information given from user are used for ordering process.

Middlet M.P.Browser (Mobile Product Browser). M.P.Browser is a middlet application that is executed on mobile device. If a user transmits a query for retrieval to the server, the application connects the mobile device with the server. And it makes the device to receive goods information written by XML form, and then closes the connection with the server. The user can search goods on the device with disconnection state. The application offers three types of search methods by parsing the transmitted XML file: directory search, price-based search, and keyword-based search. When the user decides to buy a product, the agent sends order request to the Ordering Module after user's input of the personal information. At this point, the device connects with server again.

4 Implementation and Evaluation

As the implementation environment, we have used IIS web server based on windows 2000 and MS SQL2000 as a server system and J2ME and Wireless Tool Kit as client simulator [6]

4.1 System Implementation

Implementation of Shopping Module. Search Agent analyzes the shopping category page of large-scale portal sites and extracts URL, name and category of each shop. Fig.5 shows the search results. Filtering Agent filters the goods information retrieved by Search Agent. It obtains useful information of the goods by removing HTML tag. This is the detailed information of the products. *XML Translator* searches the detailed information of goods and translates the information into XML form and transmits to client. The categories of goods are reorganized by the standard category defined in Ontology Server.

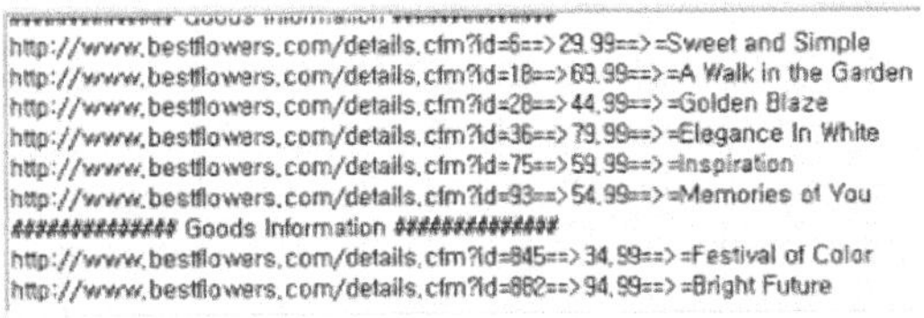

```
************** uuuua iiiuiiiiaiiuii **************
http://www.bestflowers.com/details.cfm?id=6==> 29.99==> =Sweet and Simple
http://www.bestflowers.com/details.cfm?id=18==> 69.99==> =A Walk in the Garden
http://www.bestflowers.com/details.cfm?id=28==> 44.99==> =Golden Blaze
http://www.bestflowers.com/details.cfm?id=36==> 79.99==> =Elegance In White
http://www.bestflowers.com/details.cfm?id=75==> 59.99==> =Inspiration
http://www.bestflowers.com/details.cfm?id=93==> 54.99==> =Memories of You
############# Goods Information #############
http://www.bestflowers.com/details.cfm?id=845==> 34.99==> =Festival of Color
http://www.bestflowers.com/details.cfm?id=882==> 94.99==> =Bright Future
```

Fig. 5. A Retrieval Result.

Implementation of Mobile Product Browser. If a user inputs a keyword on the screen of mobile device and presses search button, the user can connect to our server. After receiving XML file from the server, the network is disconnected. The browser offers various types of search methods by using data based on the transmitted XML file. Directory search can search goods information by category. It displays goods information of relevant category. And it offers searching information of goods by price and keyword. M.P.Browser connects with the server when the user requests an order. The user inputs information such as user's system ID, password and delivery. The browser transmits the information to the server. The browser displays the result of order from the server after the ordering process, and disconnects the connection again.

4.2 System Evaluation

Our experiments have intended to show the followings: one is to show the possibility of automatic and dynamic extensibility of general e-commerce contents for m-commerce. Another is to show the possibility of minimizing of connection time for m-commerce.

Automatic extensibility of contents for MC. We have actually applied our system to 100 shops selected randomly on the Internet. Through the experiment, at 62 shops among 100, we have confirmed that the proposed system could gather, extract the shop's information including category structure, products information, and order form etc.. It can also store the information to our database for m-commerce without any load. The other 38 shops were excluded due to their too individual and poor structure. By this system, users for m-commerce can purchase on the unrestricted contents with the feeling of e-commerce. The mobile service provider can reduce the burden of building the contents. The system offers product information in XML form so that the proposed approach can be applied to various platforms.

Minimizing of connection time for m-commerce. The mobile call charge increases with the amount used. That is, the charge is imposed with connection time to mobile network. That is a big obstacle to activation of m-commerce, particularly in South Korea.

A general work flow for m-commerce is as follows: (1)request products information → (2)browse the provided information → (3)input information for Order → (4)order

The connection time of the general MC is the whole time of (1) to (4). Our system just needs the time for requesting at (1) and ordering at (4). Thus we could largely reduce the time, because users especially spend a lot of time at work (2). Therefore, the application supports efficient m-commerce by offering economic and convenient interaction way.

5 Conclusions

In this paper, we proposed solutions for activation of m-commerce. One was for translation of contents developed for conventional e-commerce to m-commerce automatically and dynamically. By this, we could resolve the problem of restricted contents of m-commerce. Another was for reducing the connection time for m-commerce by providing a middlet application, which works for searching, ordering, and settlement at mobile devices. We have actually designed and implemented the system, and evaluated its effectiveness. Our effort is moving to enhance the ratio of retrieval and personalization in mobile services.

Reference

1. Bailey, J.P. and Y.Bakos, An Exploratory Study of the Emerging Role of Electronic Intermediaries, International Journal of Electronic Commerce, vol. 1, no. 3, 7-20,Sping, 1997.
2. Doorenbos, R.B., O. Etzioni and D.Weld, A Scalable Comparision-Shopping Agent for the World Wide Web, Proceedings of the First International Conference on Autonomous Agent (Agents 97), pp. 39 - 48, 1997.
3. J. Yang, H. Seo, and J. Choi, MORPHEUS: A Customized Comparison Shopping Agent, 5th International Conference on Autonomous Agents (Agents-2001), pp. 63 - 64, Montreal, Canada, 2001.
4. Tveit, A. Peer-to-peer based recommendations for mobile commerce. Proceedings of the first inter-national workshop on Mobile commerce July 2001.
5. Varshney, U., Vetter, R. J., Kalakota, R. Mobile Commerce: A New Frontier. IEEE Computer, 33 (10) : 32 - 38, 2000.
6. Http:// java.sun.com

Focused Crawling Using Fictitious Play

Ville Könönen

Neural Networks Research Centre
Helsinki University of Technology
P.O. Box 5400, 02015 HUT, Finland
ville.kononen@hut.fi

Abstract. A new probabilistic approach for focused crawling in hierarchically ordered information repositories is presented in this paper. The model is suitable for searching the World Wide Web and it is based on the fictitious play model from the theory of learning in games. The leading idea of the play is that players (software agents) are competing of the resources so that the search focuses on areas where relevant information can be found more likely. The model is basically a coordination model of the agent population but it is also possible to plug different features into the model, e.g. features for the user's relevance feedback or semantic links between documents. Additionally, the method is highly scalable and the efficient parallel implementation of the method is possible.

1 Introduction

There are basically three different ways to search the *World Wide Web (Web)*. The first one is to use massive information pre-localization to index a portion of the Web as a full-text database. This approach is used in all large-scale search engines and it is the most used approach at the present moment. The second one is to use pre-organized Web directories from where individual documents can be searched by subject. The third approach is to exploit additional information about links between documents for boosting the search process.

An example of the third approach is the *Google* search engine which uses the *PageRank* algorithm for prioritizing the results for the given query [1]. The algorithm is based on page citation information and the most cited pages are ranked highest by the algorithm. Another way to utilize linkage information of the Web is to try to find areas where the link structure is more dense than in the other areas of the Web and focus the search into these areas (relevance clusters). The idea of utilizing these relevance clusters is not new, although there have not been exact measurements and models of the Web until recently. In the light of these studies, there is strong evidence that there are clear relevance clusters containing pages (sites) of the same topic.

The first algorithms for exploiting the relevance clusters in the Web were dynamic search algorithms that use the current structure of the Web, not the structure stored in the index of the search engine. This approach is too slow for the entire Web but it can be used in a small and dynamic domain specific portion

H. Yin et al. (Eds.): IDEAL 2002, LNCS 2412, pp. 186–192, 2002.

of the Web. An example of these algorithms is the *fish search* [2]. The *Clever* project of the IBM (see [3]) aimed to develop models for the Web and algorithms that make use of hyperlink structure for discovering high-quality information on the Web. The recent studies aim to explain the topology of the Web as a graph with stronger structural properties than those found in the random graph (see [4]).

The model presented in this paper has its roots on the theory of learning in games and it addresses to the problem of utilizing of the relevance clusters in the search of relevant information from hierarchically ordered information repository.

2 Coordination Model

In this section, mathematical theory of the coordination method is discussed in detail. At first we will introduce the basic definitions of multi-agent learning from a game theoretical point of view and then the fictitious play model and its connections to Bayesian inference are presented in briefly.

2.1 Basic Definitions

Let A be the set (possible time varying) of agents $a^i, i = 1, \ldots, N_t$. At a given moment t, each agent a^i has a set of possible actions (strategies) available, i.e. strategies $s_t^i \in S_t^i$. The vector s_t is an N_t-dimensional vector that consists of the strategies selected by different agents. This vector is called a *strategy profile* and it can be denoted as a Cartesian product of the strategy spaces of the individual agents, i.e. $s_t \in S_t = \times_{i=1}^{N_t} S_t^i$.

In the previous definition, it was assumed that an agent selects its strategy according to some deterministic rule. If an agent is doing its decisions using some stochastic rule, we can denote this stochastic (mixed) rule as a $\sigma_t^i \in \Sigma_t^i = \Delta(S_t^i)$, where $\Delta(\cdot)$ is a pdf over the agent's strategy space. Further, mixed strategy profile is denoted as $\sigma_t \in \Sigma_t = \times_{i=1}^{N_t} \Sigma_t^i$.

When agents have selected their strategies, the agent i will get some reward or pay-off according to the function u^i, i.e. $u^i(s_t^i, s_t^{-i})$, where s_t^i is the strategy selected by the agent i and s_t^{-i} is a vector containing strategies selected by other agents. The agent i selects its action according to the following Equation:

$$BR^i(s_t^{-i}) = \arg \max_{s_t^i \in S_t^i} u^i(s_t^i, s_t^{-i}) \tag{1}$$

2.2 Fictitious Play

Fictitious play and its variations are widely used learning models in game theory. Players in fictitious play are facing an unknown distribution of their opponents' strategies. However, each agent observes the strategies their opponents play.

Based on this information each agent can update its beliefs of opponents' strategies and it can choose the best response to the opponents' play. In this study, there is a counter for each agent that keeps track of opponents' strategies:

$$\kappa_t^i(s_t^{-i}) = \kappa_{t-1}^i(s_t^{-i}) + \begin{cases} 1, & s_{t-1}^{-i} = s_t^{-i} \\ 0, & s_{t-1}^{-i} \neq s_t^{-i} \end{cases} \tag{2}$$

When all the players have chosen their current strategies, the list of counters is transformed to the probability distribution using Equation:

$$\gamma_t^i(s_t^{-i}) = \frac{\kappa_t^i(s_t^{-i})}{\sum_{\tilde{s}_t^{-i} \in S_t^{-i}} \kappa_t^i(\tilde{s}_t^{-i})} \tag{3}$$

Fictitious play itself can be defined as any rule ρ that fulfills the condition defined in the following Equation:

$$\rho_t^i(\gamma_t^i) \in BR^i(f(\gamma_t^i)) \tag{4}$$

In (4), f is a function that maps the probability distribution to the set of actions (strategy profile), e.g. MAX- or expectation-operator. The overview of the fictitious play can be found in [5].

2.3   Connections to the Bayesian Inference

Fictitious play can be interpreted as a Bayesian inference method when player a_i believes that his opponent's play constitutes of a sequence of i.i.d. multinomial random variables with fixed but unknown distribution. Moreover, beliefs or a priori knowledge concerning opponents' play must be Dirichlet distributed.

If we denote beliefs over $\Delta(S^{-i})$ as a μ^i, we can write fictitious play as a Bayesian update rule:

$$\gamma_t^i(s_t^{-i}) = \int_{\Sigma_t^{-i}} \sigma_t^{-i}(s_t^{-i}) \mu_t^i d\sigma_t^{-i} \tag{5}$$

2.4   Fictitious Play as a Coordination Method

In this paper, we use the topology of the graph for estimating the performance of agents in different parts of the search space and for transferring energy between agents. The main assumption behind this topology is that relevant nodes have links to other relevant nodes with higher probability than to irrelevant ones. An example picture of the graph with linkage topology and two relevance clusters is in Fig. 1. The key point is that there are more links inside these clusters than elsewhere in the graph.

An agent can produce descendants using the energy it has available; this property is called *replicator dynamics*. The fitness f_i of the agent a_i is the weighted

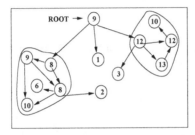

Fig. 1. An example of linkage topology

sum of the number of descendants it can produce (d_i) and the relevance value of these descendants (r_i):

$$f_i = \alpha d_i + \beta r_i, \tag{6}$$

where α and β are constants with values $\alpha = 5$ and $\beta = 0.05$ (heuristically selected). The strategies (S^i) available to the agent a_i are fixed intervals of the fitness values. In this study, 20 intervals are used.

The distribution defined in the equations (3) and (5) is used to predict the fitness value of the opponent agent. In accord with the linkage topology, if this number is big, it is more likely that in this area of the search space relevant information can be found. Prediction can be done e.g. using *Maximum A Posteriori*-estimate (MAP) or expectation estimate.

Energy updating is done so that amount ΔE_i of energy is transferred to the agent a_j. Function ΔE_i is defined as in the following Equation:

$$\Delta E_i = \begin{cases} c_t^i(1 - \theta_t^{ij}) & Exp[\gamma_t^i] < Exp[\gamma_t^j] \\ 0 & Exp[\gamma_t^i] \geq Exp[\gamma_t^j] \end{cases} \tag{7}$$

θ_t^{ij} is defined as the fraction of expected strategies:

$$\theta_t^{ij} = \frac{Exp[\gamma_t^i]}{Exp[\gamma_t^j]}, j = 1, \ldots, N_t, i \neq j \tag{8}$$

In (8), $Exp[\cdot]$ is the expectation operator over opponents' strategy space. In (7), c_t^i is the total amount of energy available to the agent at particular time instant t. Because the overall goal of the system is to visit as many relevant nodes as possible and avoid visiting irrelevant nodes at the same time, this energy transferring scheme can been as the best response to the other agents' play.

The coordination model presented in this paper can be seen as a physical system, in which the total amount of energy is preserved. At first there are many agents in the system and the search is very wide. Gradually, when relevance clusters are found, energy is transferred to the agents in these areas and the crawling is focusing onto these areas.

3 Test Settings

We have tested the method with randomly generated graphs. Topology assumptions set few restrictions on the structure of these graphs.

3.1 Test Graphs

Each test graph contains the unique root node from which the search is started. Also, the number of relevance clusters is known a priori (however, not to agents) and we have tested our algorithm with two and four relevance clusters. The sizes of the relevance clusters and relevance values were normally distributed. The number of nodes in the graphs was 500 nodes in all cases. All simulation runs were repeated 50 times with both number of relevance clusters. The following properties characterize the graphs:

- The total number of nodes in the graph (NG)
- The number of relevance clusters (NRC)
- The mean of the relevance cluster size (MRC)
- The variance of the size of the relevance cluster (VRC)
- The probability of the arc between two nodes in the relevance cluster (PAC)
- The probability of the arc between two nodes outside relevance clusters (PAN)
- The probability of random arcs in the graph (PRA)
- The probability of the arc from root node to some other node (PRN)
- The mean of the relevance values in the relevance clusters (MRVC)
- The variance of the relevance values in the relevance clusters (VRVC)
- The mean of the relevance values not in the relevance clusters (MRVN)
- The variance of the relevance values not in the relevance clusters (VRVN)

The corresponding values of the parameters can be found in Table 1. The initial population of agents consists of one agent located in the root node. The energy for this unique agent was 100 units in all cases and the production of a new descendant required 10 units of energy. So the total number of agents was restricted to 10 agents.

Table 1. Parameter values used in the simulation runs

NG	500	PRA	0.01	NRC	1,2,3	PRN	0.01
MRC	20	MRVC	500	VRC	5		VRVC	10
PAC	0.6	MRVN	100	PAN	0.3		VRVN	50

3.2 Other Compared Methods

The performance of our method is compared with two other methods, breadth-first search and best-first search. The breadth-first search algorithm is a standard tree traversal algorithm which is not using any information about relevance of the nodes or the linkage topology of the graph. The reason for including this method as a test case is to provide an example of a case that does not use any additional information about the problem.

The best-first search is accomplished with a greedy search heuristics. The value of the node i is evaluated using following Equation:

$$f(i) = g(i) + h(i), \tag{9}$$

where $g(i)$ is the averaged relevance value of the path from the root node to the node i and the $h(i)$ is the summed relevance of the child nodes of the node i. The node with the highest f value is selected for expansion. Since the method uses information about child node relevance, it is sensitive for relevance clusters and is therefore eligible for comparison with our method.

4 Results

Test results are shown in Fig. 2. In these figures x-axis shows the total percentage of visited nodes and the y-axis the total amount of relevant visited nodes. Breadth-first search is not using any problem specific information and its progress curve is therefore linear. The heuristic function in the best-first search utilizes some information about relevance values in the graph and it found relevant information more quickly than breadth-first search.

Our focused crawling method converges to the relevance clusters in the test graphs very quickly. In the case of 2 relevance clusters it has found over 90 percent of relevant nodes when only 30 percent of the nodes has been visited. However, when the number of relevance clusters is raised so that very large portion of the nodes are relevant, the progress of our algorithm slows down. The reason for this behavior is that graphs are too homogeneous (the most of the nodes are in relevance clusters) and there are not clear topological properties in the graphs.

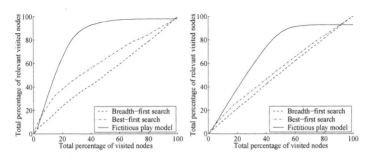

(a) Two relevance clusters   (b) Four relevance clusters

Fig. 2. Results of the simulation runs. The number of the nodes is 500 in each case. In-cluster probability is 0.05 and out-cluster probability is 0.01.

5 Conclusions

In this paper, a new coordination method for the mining of hierarchically ordered information is presented. The method is based on the focusing of search into areas where relevance values are high. Although the test settings were selected to be quite demanding, the results were very promising.

The method presented in this paper is only a coordination method and it is not using any sophisticated relevance judgment or feedback methods. By using some more sophisticated learning method in each agent could lead significantly better results.

References

1. Brin, S. and Page, L.: The anatomy of a large-scale hypertextual Web search engine. In: Proceedings of the 7th International World Wide Web Conference (WWW7), Brisbane, Australia (1998)
2. De Bra, P., Houben, G., Kornatzky, Y., Post, R.: Information Retrieval in Distributed Hypertexts. In: Proceedings of the 4th Recherche d'Information Assistee par Ordinateur Conference (RIAO'94), New York, NY (1994)
3. CLEVER Searching. Network Document. Referenced 8.3.2002. Available: http://www.almaden.ibm.com/cs/k53/clever.html
4. Albert, R.: Statistical Mechanics of Complex Networks. A Dissertation. Notre Dame University (2001)
5. Fudenberg, D. and Levine, D. K.: The Theory of Learning in Games. Economic Learning and Social Evolution Series. The MIT Press (1999)

A User Adaptive Mobile Commerce System with a Middlet Application

Eunseok Lee and Sera Jang

School of Information and Communication Engineering,
Sungkyunkwan Univ.(SKKU)
300 Chunchun Jangahn Suwon Kyunggi South Korea
{eslee, lovebiru}@selab.skku.ac.kr

Abstract. Mobile Commerce (MC) has some common critical problems such as constraints on small mobile device, expensive charge system, limited contents, and so on. In this paper we propose some solutions for solving the problems as follows: 1) *personalized contents providing* to increase the usability of the device by reducing the amount of information transferred to the device with personalization policy. 2) A *middlet application* to support user's purchase activities such as products searching, ordering and settlement on the device with a minimum network connection. The solutions make us to overcome the both problems of the device with small screen and memory and expensive charge system.

1 Introduction

A rapid development in mobile communication technologies leads the diffusion of mobile devices such as cellular phone and PDA. It also leads the movement of general Internet services to mobile ones so that mobile commerce (MC) has drawn big attention as the next generation commerce way. In Korea, although the spread of mobile device is the top of the world, the ratio of mobile Internet including MC is not so high. We can find the reason from the following problems: i) Limited contents are provided, which are built only for MC. ii) Small display area and memory size in mobile device. iii) Mobile call charge increases with the amount used. These problems are commonly discovered from most commercial mobile service such as Wapeye [1], KTF's MagicN [2], SK Telecom's Nate [3] and Itouch [4]. For the above i), we had already developed a solution for automatic contents builder of m-commerce, which can translate general e-commerce contents to m-commerce ones automatically. In this paper we will focus our discussion on ii), iii). First we propose a user adaptive personalized filtering method to reduce the amount of information transferred to mobile device. It is expected to overcome the constraints of mobile device with small display area and memory size. Second we propose a Middlet application to support user's all range of purchase activities like products searching, ordering and settlement on the device. It is free from any kind of charge system and makes us to use m-

H. Yin et al. (Eds.): IDEAL 2002, LNCS 2412, pp. 193-199, 2002.

commerce in the minimum charge. We have actually designed and implemented the proposed system, and confirmed its effectiveness through a number of experiments. In section 2 we describe the architecture and main functions of the proposed system. Section 3 shows the implementation and evaluation of the system. Section 4 concludes this paper and includes future works

2 Proposed System

2.1 Basic Designs Concepts

The proposed system is intended to support the activation of MC by solving the problems mentioned above. It offers efficient and economical interaction way to users by providing a personalization system and a middlet application for searching and ordering of goods and settlement on mobile device.   Therefore, it overcomes the limitations of mobile device in MC.

2.2 Systems Architecture

The system consists of two components as follows: *Recommender System* recommends the products by personalization.

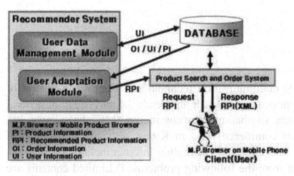

Fig. 1. Architecture of System

M.P.Browser (Mobile Product Browser) is a middlet application which supports various types of products search on the mobile device by parsing the XML file transmitted from *Products Search and Order System (PSOS)* that has already been developed by our research group. PSOS has the functions of retrieval and saving information of shops and products automatically by analyzing page source of internet shops. The proposed system uses the data retrieved by the PSOS. *M.P.Browser* is a middlet application that supports various types of products search on the mobile device (see Fig. 1).

2.2.1 Recommender System
The Recommender System consists of User Data Management Module and User Adaptation Module.

User Data Management Module.   This module manages user's personal data such as user ID, name, age, sex, etc., which are necessary for settlement and login to each shop, and users historical purchase data about ordering and recommendation of goods.

User Adaptation Module. This module recommends goods with user's personal data and purchase data. It consists of two functional components, clustering module and mining module: *Clustering Module* clusters customers based on similarity of personal data of customers. ART2 algorithm is used for clustering users. It is a kind of Neural Net.

The ART algorithm has characteristic that can solve the Stability-Plasticity problem through unsupervised learning. The Stability-Plasticity problem is one of problems of existing Neural Net. The stability means ability that keeps memory stably for patterns which learned before. The plasticity means ability that can process new pattern that has not studied. Therefore it can organize by itself. It can control intensity of classification through vigilance parameter. If value of vigilance parameter set high, specific and minute clustering is available. ART2 algorithm improves ART algorithm and it is possible using the serial data [5]. This algorithm is shown in Fig 2.

Step1 . Begin with one cluster center w1
Step2 . Initiate w1 = x (1) and | N1 | = 1
Step3 . Loop through the data set X pattern-by-pattern
  For each pattern do the following:
Step3.1 Present x (n) to the ANN.
Step3.2 Compute the winner.
Step3.3 Compare $\| wj^*\text{-}x (n) \|$ to the vigilance parameter p .
Step3.3.1 If $\| wj^*\text{-}x (n) \| \cdot p$ then there is a resonance.
  The weight wj* are updated according to
  $wj^* = [| Nj^* | wj^* \cdot x (n)]/[| Nj^* | \cdot 1]$
  And update the clock $| Nj^* | = | Nj^* | \cdot 1$
Step3.3.2 If $\| wj^*\text{-}x (n) \| < p$ then create a new node
  with $wj = x (n)$ and $| Nj | = 1$

Fig. 2. Algorithm of ART2

Mining Module. This Module selects the recommendation products using AprioriAll algorithm. It uses data about purchase information of customers who are in the same cluster. This data is clustered by *Clustering Module*. This algorithm is a kind of association rule and analyzes sequential patterns [6], [7]. The concept of this algorithm is as follow:

i)   there are a history of purchase : A → B → C
ii) someone purchases : A → B
iii) probability that the user of ii) buys C is high

The points of association rule are minimum support and minimum confidence. The main concept of Apriori Algorithm is as follows:

i)   Let $I = \{i1, i2, ..., im\}$ be a set of literals, called items.
ii) Let D be a set of transactions, where each transaction $I \in T$ is a set of items such that $T \in I$.
iii) Let X be a set of items in I. A transaction T is said to contain X, if $X \in T$.

An association rule is an implication of the form X → Y, where $X \in I , Y \in I$.

Minimum confidence (X): Y holds with confidence c in transaction set D, if and only if c% of transactions in D that contain X also contain Y.

Minimum support (X):   Y has support s in transaction set D, if and only if s% of transactions in D contain X → Y.

The AprioriAll algorithm takes a serious view concept of transaction time. Both Transaction (A → B) and Transaction (B → A) include A and B, but it is different transaction. The main step of algorithm is as follow:

i) Create a large item set that satisfy minimum support.

ii) Create rules that satisfy minimum confidence using the large item set.

Step1. L1 = {large 1 - sequence}
Step2. For (k = 2; L_{t-1} != 0 ; K++) do
Step2.1 Ct = New candidates generated from Lt-1
Step2.2 For each customer-sequence c in the database do
Step2.2.2 Increment the count of all candidates in Ct
            that are contained in c
Step2.3 Lt = Candidates in Ct with minimum support
Step3. Answer = Maximal sequence in Ut Lt

Fig. 3. Algorithm of AprioriAll

AprioriAll Algorithm is shown in Fig. 3. The recommended goods information selected by *Recommender System* is translated into XML form by *PSOS*. The information of goods searched by user request is transmitted to the *M.P.Browser*.

2.2.2 Middlet M.P.Browser (Mobile Product Browser)

This Browser is a middlet application that is executed on mobile device. If user transmits query to our server (*PSOS*), the application connects the mobile device with the server through mobile network and makes the device to receive goods information written by XML form. Then the connection is closed and user can search goods on the mobile device without any connection with server. The application offers four types search methods by parsing the transmitted XML file. First, the search of recommendable goods can search recommended goods. Second, directory search method can search goods by category in XML file. Third, price-based search method can search goods by price. Fourth, keyword-based method can search goods by keyword. When a user decides to buy a product, at this moment, the mobile device connects with network server and it sends order request to the server after user's input on personal information such as user ID and password, and delivery information. The connection is temporally cut again until it receives a result of the request from the server.

3   Implementation and Evaluation

We have used IIS Web Server based on Windows2000 and MS SQL2000 for the implementation of server and J2ME and Wireless Tool Kit [9] for the implementation of client respectively.

3.1 Systems Implementation

3.1.1 User Adaptation Module
This Module recommends goods according to both user's personal data and purchase data. The agent first clusters customers into a number of groups by using the personal data. It decides recommendable products with the purchase data of the users within the same cluster. It recommends the products recommendation products using AprioriAll algorithm with purchase data of users within the same cluster. The information is translated into XML file by PSOS. And the system transmits the file to the *M.P.Browser* with other goods information requested.

3.1.2 Implementation of Mobile Product Browser
If a user inputs a keyword on the screen (Fig. 4A) and presses search button, the user can connect to our server (PSOS). After receiving XML file from the server, the network is disconnected. The browser offers various types of search methods (Fig. 4B shows). The recommendable goods can be searched for from the list of recommendation goods as shown in Fig. 4C. Directory search supports category based searching of goods information (shown in Fig. 4D). It displays goods information of relevant. It offers searching information of goods by price and keyword (shown in Fig. 4E, F). If a user decides a product to buy while the user searches products on the *M.P.Browser*, the user selects the item and pushes the button of order (shown in Fig. 4G).

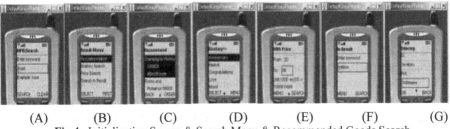

   (A)   (B)   (C)   (D)   (E)   (F)   (G)
Fig.4. Initialization Screen & Search Menu & Recommended Goods Search

3.2 System Evaluation

3.2.1 Efficiency of Personalization
We have evaluated the proposed system to prove the efficiency of the algorithm with real purchasing data. There are information of 240 users, 50 products and 550 purchase transactions. The satisfaction was evaluated with the number of users who satisfy the recommended results among 10 users. The cluster is changed by similarity when a user's purchase pattern is more similar to purchase patterns of users who are not in user's cluster but in other cluster. The satisfaction increased along with the increase of purchase transaction data. When the number of purchase transaction was less, there were many recommended products but user's satisfaction was low because

there were many items that satisfy the minimum confidence among the item sets that satisfy the minimum support. But as increasing in users purchase transactions, the number of recommendation goods decreased but user's satisfaction increased. We recommended products to 10 users and evaluated satisfaction in each point of increasing in purchase transactions data. Through the experiment, we could confirm that the proposed personalization policy was effective and could reduce the amount of information to be transferred to the mobile device. The personalization can be expected as an effective way to overcome the constraints of the mobile device with small display and memory size.

3.2.2 Minimizing of Connection Time for M-commerce

The mobile call charge increases with the amount used. That is, the charge is imposed with connection time to mobile network. A general work flow for m-commerce is shown in below.

(1)Request products information → (2)Browse the provided information → (3)Input information for Order → (4)Order

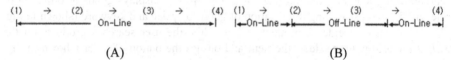

(A)   (B)

Fig. 5. Comparison of a general MC with our system in connection time

The connection time of the general MC is as shown in Fig. 5A. We could largely reduce the time as shown in Fig. 5B, because users especially spend a lot of time at work (2). Also, the personalization in proposed system reduces browsing time (2) by offering personalized information of goods. Therefore the application supports efficient m-commerce by offering economic and convenient interaction way. We could also complement the problems of conventional m-commerce systems in settlement such as vulnerability of security and complication of procedure because our settlement system is coupled with the one of general on-line shops.

4   Conclusion

In this paper we proposed solutions for activation of m-commerce. One was for personalization system developed for offering recommended products. Another was for reducing the connection time for m-commerce by providing a middlet application, which works for searching, ordering, and settlement at mobile devices. The proposed system offers economic and efficient interface to user. We have actually designed and implemented the system, and evaluated its effectiveness. Our effort is moving to enhance the effectiveness of personalization.

References

1. http://www.wapeye.net
2. http://www.nate.com:81/
3. http://www.magicn.com/
4. http://www.itouch017.com
5. Thorsteinn, S., "Lecture Note: Self-Organizing Algorithms", http://www.hh.se/staff/ denni
6. IBM Almaden Research Center, "Mining Sequential Patterns" http://www.cs.duke. edu / ~ geng /
7. Purdom, P., Gucht, D.V., Average Case Performance of the Apriori Algorithm Technica reports from Indiana University Computer Science Department
8. Tveit, A., Peer-to-peer based recommendations for mobile commerce. Proceedings of th first inter-national workshop on Mobile commerce July 2001
9. http://java.sun.com

Weight-Vector Based Approach for Product Recommendation in E-commerce

Bhanu Prasad

School of Computer and Information Sciences
Georgia Southwestern State University, Americus, GA 31709, USA
bhanu@canes.gsw.edu

Abstract. This paper presents a knowledge-based product retrieval and recommendation system for e-commerce. The system is based on the observation that, in Business to Customer (B2C) e-commerce, customers' preferences naturally cluster into groups. Customers belonging to the same cluster have very similar preferences for product selection. The system is primarily based on product classification hierarchy. The hierarchy contains weight vectors. The system learns from experience. The learning is in the form of weight refinement based on customer selections. The learning resembles *radioactive decay* in some situations. Labor profile domain has been taken up for system implementation. The results are at the preliminary stage, and the system is not yet evaluated completely.

1 Introduction

In spite of the significant advances in machine learning and information retrieval, the development of a fully automated system for product retrieval in e-commerce is still an unsolved problem. AI is used in advising the users on the items they want to examine or purchase in e-commerce [2]. There are different types of product selection and recommendation approaches [1, 3, 5]. In this paper, we present a new approach for product retrieval and subsequent learning. Classification hierarchies [6] play an important role in knowledge organization of this system. *Weight vectors* are associated with some elements of the hierarchy. Weight vectors are explained later. They play an important role in product retrieval and subsequent learning from product selection of users. This approach is different from the existing approaches to the best of knowledge. A system has been implemented for *labor profile* domain. The domain is selected due to its practical significance.

Labor profile system is designed to facilitate the recruiting interaction between jobseekers and recruiters. Jobseekers provide concise profiles of themselves, and these are organized in a database. A recruiter enquires the system with the profile of an ideal employee. The system provides a list of top few candidates to the recruiter, and the recruiter selects a candidate from the list.

H. Yin et al. (Eds.): IDEAL 2002, LNCS 2412, pp. 200–205, 2002.

2   System Details

The system is based on the observation that, in B2C e-commerce, customers' preferences/weights naturally cluster into groups. Customers of the same cluster have very similar preferences. As a result, the mean/average preference of a cluster represents individuals in the cluster well enough. The details are provided.

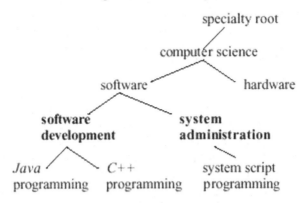

Fig. 1.   Specialty hierarchy

Customers generally have different preferences over different features/attributes of a given product. For example, in labor profile domain, a customer may prefer *C++* programmer than a *Java* programmer. This paper addresses the issues namely, how to represent the preferences, how to identify and group the customers having similar preferences, and how the system learns the preferences from experience, by considering labor profile domain as an example.

Three attributes namely *specialty,* academic *degree,* and *location* are considered here. Specialty represents technical skill of jobseeker. It is represented as a classification hierarchy, as shown in figure 1. Location is the place where the jobseeker prefers to work. The degree attribute is represented as ordered relationships: Ph.D. degree > Masters degree > Bachelors degree > High School Diploma.

2.1   Calculation of Similarities

A similarity metric is defined to find out the similarity between a product and a user query. The similarity between the *specialty* features of two products is defined as: *Similarity (specialty1, specialty2) = (number of common arcs)/(depth of hierarchy).* For example, in figure 1, *Similarity ((Java programming), (C++ programming)) = 3/4.* For *degree* attribute, *Similarity (degree_acquired, degree_required)*
> = 1 (if degree_acquired >= degree_required)
> = 0 (if degree_acquired < degree_required).

For location attribute, *Similarity (State1, State2)*
> = 1 (if State1 equals State2)
> = 0 (if State1 does not equal to State2).

The products have some other attributes and they are not discussed here. If n is the total number of attributes of a product then the similarity between a given query and a product in the database is: *Similarity (product, query)* = $\sum_{(i=1 \text{ to } n)}$ *Similarity (product_attribute$_p$, query-attribute$_i$)* --------> [equation 1].

In real world, a user may have different preferences for different attributes. For example, *specialty* may be given more preference than physical fitness if the job is technical. A weight assigning mechanism is introduced for this purpose.

3 Weight Vectors and Learning

The relative weight of different attributes could be different for each recruiter. Weight vectors are introduced to capture user preferences automatically based on users' product selection patterns. If a product has n features then each weight vector has n weights/components, with each component corresponds to a different feature. In other words, there is a one-to-one mapping between the components and the features. The weight vectors are associated with some critical branching nodes of the classification hierarchy. For example, in figure1, the nodes in bold font are critical nodes. The number of weight vectors is equal to the number of critical branching nodes in the hierarchy. Once the weights are defined, the similarity between a query and a product in the database is calculated as follows:

Similarity (labor_profile, recruiting_profile) =

   $\sum_{(i=1 \text{ to } n)}$ *(Weight$_i$ *Similarity (attr_labor$_p$ attr_rec$_i$))*

   attr_labor$_i$ and *attr_rec$_i$* are the matching i^{th} attributes of *labor_profile* and *recruiting_profile* respectively. Recruiting_profile is the profile of an ideal candidate. *Weight$_i$* is the ith component of the weight vector.

3.1 Learning

Assume that a user supplied a query and the user has not preferred the topmost candidate in the list, and instead selected another candidate, *candidate-O*, from the list. This situation is a potential place for the system to learn, because there is a mismatch between the system and the user in terms of "best suitable" candidate. If the system has sufficient knowledge in understanding the user preference then it would have displayed candidate-O as the topmost element. The learning in this system is in the form of adjusting the weight vectors. It is explained using an example.

   Assume that there are two products P_1 and P_2 with attributes values $Att_{(p1,1)}$, $Att_{(p1,2)}$, $Att_{(p1,3)}$ and $Att_{(p2,1)}$, $Att_{(p2,2)}$, $Att_{(p2,3)}$ respectively. Assume that the user specified a product R, with attributes: $Att_{(R,1)}$, $Att_{(R,2)}$, $Att_{(R,3)}$. Assume also that the weight vector associated with recruiting area, which is the parent node of $Att_{(R,1)}$ in figure 1 is $W = (w_1, w_2, w_3)$. $Att_{(R,1)}$ is the specialty of R. Specialty is organized as leaf-node of the classification hierarchy.

Assume that the system displayed P1 above P2 in the recommendation list. In other words, according to the system, $\sum_{(i=1\ to\ n)} (w_i * Att_{(p1,i)} * Att_{(R,i)}) > \sum_{(i=1\ to\ n)} (w_i * Att_{(p2,i)} * Att_{(R,i)})$. Also assume that the user selected the product P2. This selection implies that there is at least one attribute of P_2 is better than the corresponding attribute of P1 in satisfying the recruiting profile. This is because, if no attribute of P_2 is better than that of P_1 then the user would not have selected P2 over P1 unless he made an unrealistic decision or he specified the recruiting profile wrongly. The situation is discussed below: If all the attributes of P2 are better than the corresponding attributes of P1 then P2 would have been rated first by the system. But P1 is rated first by the system. As a result, there is at least one attribute of P2 that is less than the corresponding attribute of P1. Also, since the user has selected P2, we can assume that: $Att_{(p2,1)}$ is better than $Att_{(p1,1)}$, $Att_{(p2,2)}$ is worse than $Att_{(p1,2)}$, and $Att_{(p2,3)}$ is worse than $Att_{(p1,3)}$.

In order to make the system display P2 first in the list, the weight w1 associated with the first attribute should be increased and the weights w2 and w3 should be decreased. That is, the weights need to be "trained" or adjusted. The training of weights constitutes learning in this system. This training will stabilize the weight vector around a static mean preference of the cluster of users' preferences. The amount/quantity of weight adjustment during training process is the learning factor. Learning factor is explained in the next section.

3.2 Learning Factor and Weight Adjustment

In our system, the learning factor L is defined as $a*10^{(-b*n/h)}$

Here n is the number of times the weight vector is modified due to product selections, a, b and h are constant coefficients, $b=log\ \frac{1}{2}$, h is the *half-life*, and a is the initial learning factor on the interval $(0,1)$. The learning factor is similar to the pattern of radioactive decay [http://isotopes.lbl.gov/]. However, instead of decreasing with respect to time in radioactive materials, L decreases with respect to n. With this exponential decaying learning factor, a weight vector stabilizes around the static cluster mean.

Customers' trend generally changes over time. It is explained in the following section.

4 Trend Change: Detection and Adjustment

Trend change can be explained using a simple example. A construction company may prefer to recruit people having some education qualification, apart from their physical fitness so that they can operate computers.

In general, if a user does not select the first few products of the recommendation list but instead selects another product then it should not be treated as trend change because of the following two reasons: 1). There may not be many qualified products in the database. 2). The weight vector is only a little off with the current recruiter's preference, but it is within a reasonable limit. A threshold value is defined for the purpose of identifying trend change. A trend change is identified if $|Similarity\ (C_1,\ R) - Similarity\ (C_2,\ R)| > S * L * Similarity\ (C_1,\ R)$. Here S is the stabilization factor and it is 5 in our system at present, L is the learning factor, and *similarity* is defined in equation 1. According to the system, C_1 is the product that is best suited to current user query, and it reflects the mean preference of the system. C_2 is the best according to the user, and it reflects the current user preference. If the above inequality is true then the preference vector has to be adjusted by a quantity of at least $5*L^1$ to rank C_2 above C_1 in the list. That is, the above inequality signals that the current user preference deviates $5*L$ from mean preference.

If trend change is detected, the learning factor is adjusted quickly by adjusting the value of n as: $n = n - 2 * h$. Here h is the half-life and n does not reflect the number of training cases, instead it is changed as specified.

5   Comparisons and Conclusions

In this paper we presented a system for product retrieval and recommendation in e-commerce. The system is implemented for labor profiles domain. To the best of knowledge, this is the first system in which the learning factor is similar to radioactive decay in some situations. The implementation details of the system are available in [9].

When compared to the static preference models [7], the system is more dynamic and can also cope more precisely with varied preference patterns.

Both the *generalized vector-space model* [8] and this system address pair-wise orthogonal problem of index terms in retrieval. Generalized vector-space model allows vectors to be pair-wise non-orthogonal. This system approaches it by organizing index terms in knowledge structures.

We are in the process of investigating a general formula for identifying "critical branching nodes" to associate the weight vectors. Right now only one attribute is organized as a classification hierarchy, and we are investigating the nature and organization of weight vectors for the following three cases: 1). Zero or more attributes are organized as classification hierarchies. 2). Zero or more attributes are organized as hierarchies other than classification type. 3). Combination of previous cases. We are also in the process of evaluating the system for its flexibility to trend change and stabilization.

We hope that incorporation of principles of natural phenomena such as radioactive decay into AI research help the systems behave more natural.

Acknowledgement. My sincere thanks to Mr. Kundi for his help in publishing this paper.

---

[1] The adjustment value is 5*L if and only if $|Similarity\ (C_1,\ R) - Similarity\ (C_2,\ R)| = 5 * L * Similarity\ (C_1,\ R)$. The recruiter ranks C_1 and C_2 almost the same in this case.

References

1. Burke, R.: The Wasabi Personal Shopper: A Case-Based Recommender system. In Proceedings of the 11th National Conference on Innovative Applications of Artificial Intelligence. AAAI (1999).

2. Driskill, R., Riedl, J.: Recommender Systems for ECommerce: Challenges and Opportunities. In proceedings of the AAAI-99 Workshop on AI for Electronic Commerce, USA (1998).

3. Shardanand, U., Maes, P.: Social Information Filtering Algorithms for Automating "word of mouth". In Proceedings of the Conference on Human Factors in Computing Systems. ACM press, USA (1995).

4. Burke, R.: Knowledge-Based Recommender Systems. Encyclopedia of Library and Information Science (2000).

5. Tran, T., Cohen, R.: Hybrid Recommender Systems for Electronic Commerce. In Proceedings of the AAAI-00 Workshop on Knowledge-Based Electronic Markets, USA (1999).

6. Bhanu Prasad: Hybrid Hierarchical Knowledge Organization for Planning. In Progress in Artificial Intelligence, Springer LNAI 2258 (2001).

7. Branting, K.L.: Acquiring Customer Preferences from Return-Set Selections. In Proceedings of the 4th International Conference on Case-Based Reasoning, ICCBR (2001).

8. Wong, S.K.M., Ziarko, W., Wong, P.C.N.: Generalized Vector Space Model in Information Retrieval. In Proceedings of the 8th ACM SIGIR Conference on Research and Development in Information Retrieval, USA (1985).

9. Xue, K.: Knowledge Hierarchies and Weight Vectors-Based Approaches for E-Commerce. M.S. Thesis, Georgia Southwestern State University, USA (2001).

The Development of an XML-Based
Data Warehouse System

Shi-Ming Huang and Chun-Hao Su

Department of Information Management, National Chung Cheng University
160 San-Hsing, Min-Hsiung, Chia-I 621, Taiwan, R.O.C.
Phone: 886-5-272-0411 ext: 16810
Fax: 886-5-272-3943
smhuang@mis.ccu.edu.tw

Abstract. Along with the enterprise globalization and Internet popularization, the Internet-based Data Warehouse System (DWS) has gradually replaced the traditional DWS and becomes its mainstream structure. The manager can easily obtain and share the data on the distribution system using the Internet. Through the multiple data source collections, the quality and broad base of DWS can be increased and thus help managers to make more decisive policies. However, utilizing the basic client/server structure of DWS can increase many tolerances and cost based problems. This paper uses the XML to establish the Internet-based DWS and utilize the advantage of its flexibility, self-definition, self-description and low cost to improve the unavoidable defect of the client/server DWS. We also use pull and push method approaches to determine what information can be shared on the Internet or delivered through e-mail. In this work, we show that the DWS architecture can not only improve the scalability and speed but also enhance the system security. In addition, it can be applied for both traditional client/server DWS and web-based DWS. We present a case study to prove the validity of this system architecture and create a prototype system to show the feasibility of this system architecture.

1 Introduction

The DWS is the concept of database system developed mainly for the demand to assist the decision making. The background of this development is due to the long time accumulative sources of various exchange data of many companies with the hope using those data to analyze the results for supporting the decision making. In order to observation of various angles of data and make quick changes of analysis, the DWS uses the multi-dimensional data type called Data Cube (DC) [1]. The traditional DWS is built mainly in the closed type network structure of Client/Server system. This kind of structure has the following disadvantages [2].

(1) The two-tier client/server infrastructure makes the system establishment and maintenance difficult and costly. It can only show up the multiple data information by using a special type of the front-end software.

(2) The Information in organization is no longer sufficient for the coming stage of e-commerce, the enterprise Supply Chain Management (SCM) and Customer

H. Yin et al. (Eds.): IDEAL 2002, LNCS 2412, pp. 206-212, 2002.
© Springer-Verlag Berlin Heidelberg 2002

Relationship Management (CRM) in one organization must be invested heavily on the related enterprises to make mutual cooperation and to win the customer's confidence.

In today's circumstance, the web-based DWS delivers all of the same kinds of applications that the data warehousing solutions deliver. Nevertheless, a number of challenges still exist in implementing web-based DWS due to immaturity of this technology and to some management concerns. These challenges are Scalability, Speed and Security [3].

In order to solve the challenges of the web-based DWS, this study uses XML structure and adds push and pull technology to form a novel Internet-based DWS. Because XML has more durability and flexibility, self-defined and self-description, highly literary structure and easy usage, we consider that the future Internet-based DWS will be based on XML. With a combination of "pull" and "push" technology, users are presented only with information directly related to their functions, while they still have the option to receive additional information on demand.

2 Related work

2.1 Traditional Client/Server Data Warehouse

Traditionally, the format of the client/server DWS is using the Online Analytical Processing (OLAP) tools to extract the data and to store it temporarily in the data mart. Those data have been reviewed through the procedure of the analysis. The usage data will then show up in many interfaces through the Executive Information System (EIS) [4].

2.2 Web-Based Data Warehouse

The web-based DWS includes client, web server and application server, it allows end users to use web browsers as a user interface in order to access and manipulate data. The server side offers the web page service and controls the flow of information between server and client. The end side of the server side connects to the application side which includes the DWS and the web application format for controlling the storage and extracting the information [2].

2.3 Data Cube and Star Schema

A DC is a multi-dimensional database. It includes a collection of at least one fact table and a set of dimension tables. The purpose of the DWS is to design analytically for answering various queries. Using the method of the DC, the system can quickly respond and satisfy the user's demand.

Due to the fact that the data is stored in the relational DWS, the original data after analysis, conversion and filtering will be stored in the star schema and becomes the data cube. Therefore each DC has its own characteristics. One can often inquire and analyze the data from every respective angle in DC such as: Roll-Up, Drill-Down, Slice and Dice [5].

3   The XML-Based Data Warehouse System Architecture

3.1   The System Architecture

The architecture combines push and pull technology to enable the users to receive the DWS data through web browser or e-mail. With a combination of "pull" and "push" approaches, users are presented only with information directly related to their functions, while they still have the option to receive additional information on demand. Users can still use the traditional OLAP tools to browse the Data in the DWS. In this architecture, it can be used to prioritize the security needs for different users. Security is intended to allow users access to those resources necessary for performing their job functions while restricting them from access privileges that do not fall under their job scope [6]. It uses the different methods to deliver cube data for different priority users. Table 1 lists the three types of the priority for users.

Table 1. The three types of priorities.

	Low Priority	**Middle Priority**	**High Priority**
Security	Low Security	Medium Security	High Security
OLAP Method	Through E-mail	Web Browser	Traditional Client/Server OLAP

Fig. 1. illustrates our architecture. The architecture includes client, web server, and DWS server. On the client side, all users have to connect to the Internet. Users can use web browser or e-mail to get the information. On the data server side, a DWS designer generates the data cubes according to the different requirements. Then, it transfers the data cubes to the XML OLAP cubes by the XML wrapper. The results are displayed on web pages or delivered to the users though the e-mail server.

In this architecture, it provides a platform independent environment. We can also implement to limit users' privileges of accessing data in DWS. It can determine what information can be shared on the Internet or delivered through e-mail. Therefore, the security control on the Internet can provide the level of security. This technique is also used to reduce too many users to access the data in DWS on the same time, so it can improve the system scalability and speed.

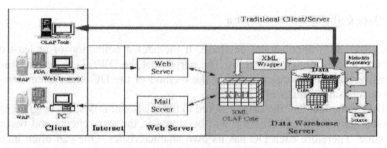

Fig. 1. System Architecture

3.2   The Methodology to Develop an XML Data Cube

In order to build an Internet-based DWS, one needs to design the possible storage place to store the Metadata schema. In this system, we design a Metadata schema to store the Metadata in the XML cube and then convert the Metadata to DTD format for XML data usage. To establish the XML star schema, the star schema Metadata must be first stored to the inside of XML star schema Metadata repository by mapping the Metadata in the existing DWS and then make XML star schema according to the Metadata. Fig 2 shows the star schema model.

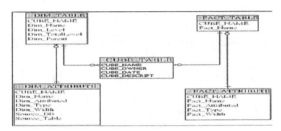

Fig. 2. Meta-Data Schema

This system operation flow can be divided into the following steps:

Step1: Build XML Star Schema. We can get the metadata from the data cube in the existing DWS. Then, the metadata can be transformed into the XML star schema by mapping the XML star schema DTD metadata. This is done by converting the metadata presented in the Dimension table, Dimension Attribute table, Fact table, and Fact Attribute table into XML format. Since it is a one-to-one mapping, the process is very straightforward.

Step2: Build XML Data Cube. The existing cube data is stored in the fact table of the star schema. The process will retrieve the data from the fact table by mapping with the XML star schema to build the XML cube data.

Step3: XML OLAP Wrapper. After the above steps, the XML cube data can let users browse data by the web browser or deliver the data through e-mail. By the web browser, the users can easily access, analyze, and refresh data from the proper web authorization. Through the e-mail, the mail software such as Microsoft Outlook Express will attach the documents including an XML file and an XSLT file to an outgoing e-mail message. Our Wrapper has two main parts: XSLT Processor Object and XSLT Templates/Controls. The main purpose of XSLT Templates/Controls module is to store format syntax to display the XML document and some controls in OLAP. The XSLT Processor module is responsible for reading the XML Cube data and parsing it; after parsing, the processor will convert the XML Cube data into the document according to the rules in the XSLT Templates/Controls module.

(1)   XML OLAP Control Operations.
In our XML wrapper, there are OLAP control operations. The data cube is constructed mainly to provide users the flexibility to view data from different perspectives as long as some dimensions of the cube contain multiple levels of abstraction. The main goals for OLAP are fast access, fast calculations, user-friendly

interfaces, and flexible viewing, given the challenges of lots of data with many levels of detailed and multiple factors in a decentralized multi-user environment.

(2)   XSLT Processor Object.

The XSLT processor object is responsible for reading the XML cube data and for parsing it. The processor is according to the different rules and algorithms we defined in the XSLT Templates and XML OLAP Control Operations to convert the XML cube data into the output interface. The XSLT Processor has four main objects: Drill-Down Object, Roll-Up Object, Slice Object and Dice Object. Fig. 4 shows the XSLT processor object architecture. Fig. 3 shows the steps methodology to develop the XML Internet-based DWS.

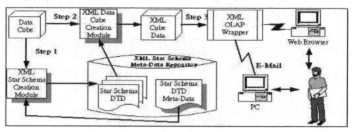

Fig. 3. The Methodology

4   The Prototype System and System Evaluation

This paper uses Microsoft Visual Basic and XML structure to establish one Internet-based DWS according to the previous descriptive structure and methods. This prototype system shows feasibility of our Internet-based DWS architecture. We also transfer the XML data cube into the XML OLAP interface by XML OLAP Wrapper. The results are shown in Fig 5. The established cube is shown in Fig. 6.

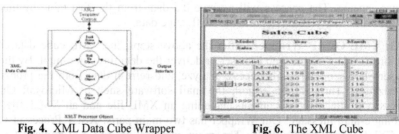

Fig. 4. XML Data Cube Wrapper   **Fig. 6.** The XML Cube

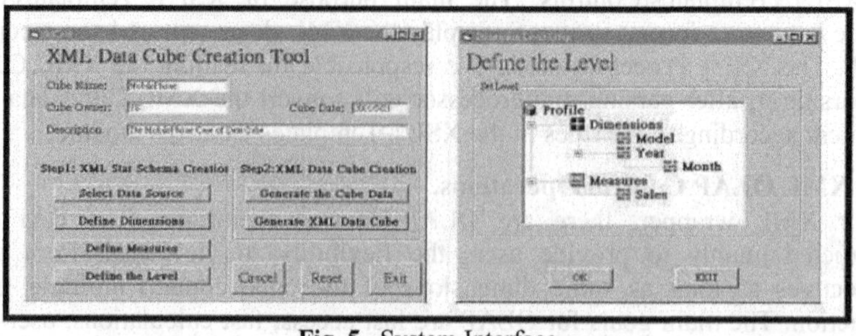

Fig. 5. System Interface

In our system uses XML structure and adds push technology to improve the functionality of the traditional web-based DWS. It can implement a combination of "pull" and "push" approaches when delivering information to users. The effect evaluation of our Internet-based DWS needs to be shown better than the conventional data warehouse system in using aspect. We will discuss three issues as the following:

- **Scalability Issue:**
  We can use pull and push approaches to determine what information can be shared on the client/server, Internet or delivery through e-mail. It can avoid the users to access the data concurrently and then improve the scalability.
- **Security Issue:**
  We can set the users' privileges of accessing the data in a different way. The highest priority users can use the client/server and the next priority users can use the web browser to access the data. The lowest priority users just receive the data that send from the system. Therefore, we can improve the system security.
- **Speed Issue:**
  We classify the different levels to access the data in different ways. Therefore, we can reduce the amount of data that are required to manipulate at the same time and then the speed will be improved.

However, there have some problems in this prototype system as discussed below.

(1) In order to resolve problem in data cube duplicated, we provide different levels of users based on their needs, can select the different ways to generate the XML data cube. Therefore, the system will reduce the amount of the cube data for different users.
(2) When the legacy system modifies the cube data, the data inconsistency may occur. Our system can provide the existence OLAP commands that generate the XML data cube before. Therefore, it can reduce the problem of data consistency.

5 Conclusions and Future Development

In this paper, we provide a new structure to build Internet-based DWS by using XML. In this new structure, the cube data in the DWS will be in the XML format. Therefore one can browse by the general browser and does not need the special interface to perform the job. This in turn solves the limitation in the traditional client/server DWS. Using this system, the users not only can browse directly to see the contents of the data information through the Internet but also can reduce the cost of network and user's interface. Besides, using XML data one can also deliver the formulation of the diversified information through e-mail to other users. In this way, it can enhance the safety and overcome the over usage problem in the whole Internet-based DWS. In the future research, we hope that we can enhance the effectiveness and interface to strengthen this prototyped system and offer more data types service, and also provide the new concept and method to other researchers to develop the new and more efficient system.

Acknowledgements. The National Science Council, Taiwan, under Grant No. NSC 89-2213-E-194-041 has supported the work presented in this paper. We greatly appreciate their financial support and encouragement.

Reference

1. Gupta, A., et. al, "Aggregate-Query Processing in Data Warehousing Environments", Proceedings of the 21st International VLDB Conference, (1995)
2. Chen, L., and Frolick, M., "Web-Based Data Warehousing: Fundamentals, Challenges, and Solutions", Information Systems Management, (2000)
3. Ceponkus, A., and Hoodbhoy, F., Applied XML: A Toolkit for Programmers, Wiley (pub.), (2000)
4. Chaudhuri, S., and Dayal, U., "An Overview of Data Warehousing and OLAP Technology", ACM SIGMOD Record, Vol.26, No. 1, 1997.
5. Han, J., and Nishio, S., "Generalization-based data mining in OODB using an object cube model", Data and Knowledge Engineering, vol.25 1998.
6. Stamper, D., Business Data Communications, The Benjamin/Cummings Publishing Company, Inc., 1991.
7. Huang, S., and Lin, Y., "Actual Application Examples for Building Data Warehouse", The Fifth Seminar on Information Research Management, 1999.
8. Huang, S., et. al, "Developing an XML Gateway for Business-to-Business Commerce", Proceedings of The 1st International Conference on Web Information Systems Engineering, Hong Kong, China, Vol. 2, 2000, pp.67-74.
9. Moeller, R., Distributed Data Warehousing Using Web Technology, AMACOM, 2001.
10. Roy, J. and Ramanujun, A., "Building an XML application: key management issues", Proceedings of XML Europe 2000 Conference, 2000.

Identifying Data Sources for Data Warehouses

Christian Koncilia[1] and Heinz Pozewaunig[2]

[1] University of Klagenfurt
Dep. of Informatics-Systems, Austria
koncilia@isys.uni-klu.ac.at
[2] SEZ AG, Villach, Austria
hpozewaunig@sez.at

Abstract. In order to establish a useful data warehouse, it must be correct and consistent. Hence, when selecting the data sources for building the data warehouse, it is essential know exactly about the concept and structure of all possible data sources and the dependencies between them. In a perfect world, this knowledge stems from an integrated, enterprize-wide data model. However, the reality is different and often an explicit model is not available.

This paper proposes an approach for identifying data sources for a data warehouse, even without having detailed knowledge about interdependencies of data sources. Furthermore, we are able to confine the number of potential data sources. Hence, our approach reduces the time needed to build and maintain a data warehouse and it increases the data quality of the data warehouse.

Keywords: Data Warehouses, Data Source Identification, Multiple Sequence Analysis

1 Introduction and Motivation

A data warehouse is an integrated, materialized view of several data sources [1]. Data can be maintained in a full structured or semi-structured form. Building a useful data warehouse is a challenging task. The first step is to elicit user-needs, usually performed by two tasks: 1) Identify *what* the user wants, which leads to the facts stored in the data warehouse. 2) Identify *how* the user wants the data, which determines the needed dimensions and granularity of the data materialized in the data ware house. The next step is to identify the correct data sources. This activity is very costly and consumes between 50% and 70% of the overall project resources [2,3]. Ideally, this step is based on an integrated enterprize-wide data model. The bad news is, that we don't live in such a perfect world and many companies do not have an explicit enterprize-wide model. Even worse, if it is available, in most cases it is not up-to-date. Hence, the designer of the data warehouse has to have deep knowledge about all potentially data sources and about the relationships between those sources. However, what must be done, if such an expert is not available?

Imagine the following situation: the users want to analyze facts along several dimensions. One dimension is the concept of "Cost Center". The data ware-house designer identified several tables in different databases containing information about the cost center structure. On the one hand, some of these data sources provide only with a partial view

H. Yin et al. (Eds.): IDEAL 2002, LNCS 2412, pp. 213–218, 2002.

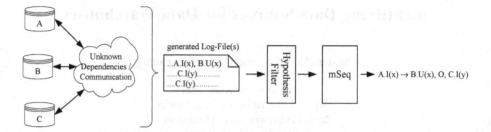

Fig. 1. An overview to the Source Identification Process

to the enterprize-wide concept of a cost center. On the other hand, the information about cost centers stored in one specific table depends computationally on the information stored in different table. Even worse, the attribute name "cost center" is denominated differently in the sources, e.g., CostCenter, CostC or CC. The problem now is to identify the table(s) and attributes whose data must be imported into the data warehouse in order to ensure a complete and consistent materialized view.

Closely related is the problem of detecting changes in dependencies for data warehouse maintenance. Quite often, modifications are not communicated. In the best case, the data extraction tools used to import data terminate with an error. In the worst case, they import erroneous data, thus corrupting the integrity of the data warehouse.

Contribution. Our approach helps to identify semi-automatically data sources for data warehouses, even without having detailed knowledge about existing dependencies. Furthermore, it allows to detect dependency changes. It provides with a concept to support the data warehouse designer to understand dependencies between databases. Furthermore, it helps to confine the number of sources that have to be analyzed when building and maintaining a data ware house.

Outline. This paper is organized as follows: The main idea of our approach is presented in section 2. A analysis algorithm for inferring descriptions of regularities will be explained in section 3 and in section 4 the application it is demonstrated. In section 5 we will discuss how to interpret the results and we conclude in section 6.

2   Data Warehouse Source Identification Process

The starting point is information hidden in sequences of "events". Some examples of events are messages generated by an active database system [4], or operations executed to access a passive database system. The approach is characterized by four steps, depicted in figure 1:

1. Select a set of log-files containing data base events.
2. Build a hypothesis about important central data elements. In the introductory example this is the Cost_Center.
3. Analyze the assumed dependencies using the multiple sequence analysis algorithm MSEQ [5].
4. Interpret the results of the analysis.

The first step is to identify on a general level the data sources which may contain interesting dependencies. We assume that operations of business cases accessing a variety of databases are contained in a log. Irrelevant information, such as time stamps, user information and other meta data is filtered out.

Forming an interesting hypothesis is a more challenging task which is performed manually or semi-automatically. Here, the central data element of a concept has to be stated. This task demands detailed knowledge about the involved business cases as well as the requirements to the data warehouse. However, due to the overwhelming amount of data, sometimes this knowledge is not sufficient to detect anchors for data dependencies. Then, data mining techniques for gathering dependencies automatically help [6]. They are able to detect frequent subsequences in logs and to identify dependencies between them. Such subsequences then may render helpful when forming hypotheses, which subsequently determine log entries containing interesting data elements.

In the third step the MSEQ algorithm processes the selected log entries. MSEQ detects structural regularities expressed as formal, context free grammars which describe the correct order of events passed between the databases. Since the log has been collected from all data sources relevant to a business case, the language represents a global view onto the whole system (with respect to the focussed business cases). Due to the fact that regularities of events provide with one dimension of the problem domain only, in the last step the inferred languages must be interpreted.

3   The MSEQ Inference Algorithm

The process of inferring regularities from sequences belongs to the field of sequence learning [7]. In the current problem domain an important restriction must be considered: only *positive* examples are available, since no given input sequence can be excluded from the event log. Therefore, the problem class is called *positive grammar inference* in literature [7]. MSEQ originates from the SEQUITUR algorithm [8] constructed to encode regularities in a sequence of tokens. As a by-product a structural explanation in the form of a finite regular language is produced. For short, SEQUITUR substitutes a repetition r in the input sequence by a non-terminal variable A which is the left hand side of a grammar rule $A \rightarrow r$. A repetition is given if a subsequence of tokens occurs more than once in the input sequence. In that way the input sequence finally is described by a set of rules, which are a context free grammar. Due to fact that these grammars describe finite languages only, the resulting languages are regular .

SEQUITUR is able to analyze one sequence only, hence, regularities dispersed in multiple sequences can not be detected. Suppose, there are two sequences, a b c and b c a. From that SEQUITUR produces two independent grammars and the fact that the sequence b c is indeed a pattern occurring multiply is not evident in the grammar. However, if it is assumed that the sequences are output of different executions of the same business transaction type, this result is not satisfying.

To adhere to the requirements we extended SEQUITUR to handle multiple sequences. The MSEQ [5] (multiple sequence analyzer) detects patterns spread between different sequences and produces a generalized grammar based on the individual grammars obtained by SEQUITUR. An example is presented in section 4. The algorithm merges each individual grammar into the generalized one by mapping their rule structures and adding not yet included (sub)rules into the general one. Since rule names are not considered during merging, the general grammar describes all input sequences.

A further improvement is the introduction of iteration heuristics. Since subsequently occurring tokens may indicate to some kind of loop in the underlying business case, the analyst may incorporate this knowledge during the analysis step. E.g., a sequence a a a may be produced by a loop. The analyst then can enable MSEQ to introduce a rule $\mathbf{A} \rightarrow (a)+$. The construct (a)+ indicates a repetition of the token a. In that way the accuracy of the result may suffer, since the production of this rule is based on heuristics, however, the domain may demand such a representation. The reader interested in more details is referred to [5].

In contrast to SEQUITUR the MSEQ algorithm is more flexible for analysis. However, there is domain knowledge necessary to get the optimal grammar representation. At least the algorithm allows to "play" with its parameters. Such fiddling is sometimes very helpful in situations, where the domain structure is not clear at the first sight.

4   A Simple Dependency Analysis Example

The problem of sequence analysis for the given data warehouse domain may be restated as follows: Given is a set of databases which holds mutually dependent data. A possible dependency may be that on each update of an attribute x of database A an insertion of an attribute y into database C must follow. All operations are recorded in a log file, which stores a sequence of operations for each transaction.

The starting point of the analysis step is a hypothesis concerning a *data element*,e.g. an attribute. From the log of all transactions those entries are selected containing that data element. Consider the following extract from a transaction log where an entry DB.*op*(*elem*) describes an operation *op* issued for a database DB which operates on the parameter *elem*. For readability we condensed the representation in the way that data bases represent an unique access to a relation. Hence, the denominator *data base* is a unique access path to a certain table within.

As we are interested in write operations only, the log holds insert (I), update (U) and deletion (D) operations solely. Each line contains one business transaction. In that way the first line of the example is interpreted as: In database B data element x is deleted, followed by insertion of y into database A and the update of x in B. The business transaction finally performs an update of data element y in database C.

```
1. B.D(x)  A.I(y)  B.U(x)  C.U(y)
2. A.I(y)  B.U(x)  C.D(x)  B.I(y)  B.U(z)  D.U(y)
3. B.I(y)  B.U(z)  C.D(z)  B.I(y)  B.U(z)
4. B.U(x)  C.D(x)  B.I(y)  B.U(z)  D.U(y)
```

Now we want to know, what regularities and dependencies exists in the collaboration of the federated databases A, B, C and D. The (arbitrary) hypothesis is, that element x plays an important role in the transactions. Therefore, the log of transaction 3 is not considered, since it contains no operation on the data element x. Next, MSEQ [5] is applied to the filtered log. The result is the following grammar explaining the regularities contained in the log:

```
S  →  B.D(x) A C.U(y) | A C.D(x) B | B.U(x) C.D(x) B
A  →  A.I(y) B.U(x)
B  →  B.I(y) B.U(z) D.U(y)
```

This grammar describes some regularities with respect to data element x. E.g., from the start rule it is recognizable that the deletion of x is a recurring operation in each transaction; in most cases it is even the central operation. Rule **B** conceptually seems to do some cleaning. Furthermore, we infer that there is a tight connection between the operations B.I(y), B.U(z), and D.U(y), since each insertion of y in database and table B is followed by a corresponding update of z in B and a final update of z in D. The second and third alternative of the start rule hints to a transaction pattern of *preparation*, *central operation* (the deletion of x), and *tidy*. Additionally, the preparation operation is not specialized, because **A** appears before the central operation as well as afterwards. These structural observations are present in the initial log as well, however, the condensed form of the grammar eases the task of identifying them.

5   Interpreting the MSEQ Results with Dependency Graphs

After applying MSEQ to the logs we have to analyze the results with respect to the task of data warehouse source selection. This source should deliver all needed information, which means it must be complete. Data sources must be accurate (and in the granularity required) and the result should be consistent with respect to redundant sources [9].

When analyzing potential data sources, objective and subjective quality factors must be considered [10,3]. At the moment the interpretation of the results of MSEQ is not supported by tools. However, our approach helps the designer of the data warehouse to select where to start from.

We support interpretation by identifying all *I-Sinks$_H$*. An *I-Sink$_H$* (*Input Only Sink*) is a data element which is target of a data dependency with respect to the hypothesis H and it must not be the source of any data dependency (with respect to H). Since we can not determine the real nature of the dependencies, we assume a dependency from each terminal symbol in a grammar rule to all terminal symbols on its right (which were issued in the log later on). Due to the such implied temporal order of a rule $D \rightarrow$ A.I(y) B.U(x) we define a data dependency from A.I(y) to B.U(x) but not vice versa. When building a *data dependency graph* on the basis of a grammar, an *I-Sink* is a vertice of a dependency graph with no outgoing arcs. The dependency graph for the previously presented example is given in figure 2. Database D is not source of any data dependency, hence, it is a *I-Sink$_{\{x\}}$* with respect to the data element x.

An I-Sink indicates that the corresponding data element is potentially a high quality data source, since after a finishing business transaction it reflects a consistent final state. Therefore, we analyze all identified I-Sinks with respect to predefined quality dimensions such as data coherence, data completeness and data freshness [10]. To our experience, this step covers in almost all cases the needed data source. Nevertheless, if no I-Sink exists, the designer has to analyze all data elements. At least in that case our approach helps to confine the number of data elements that have to be analyzed.

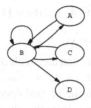

Fig. 2. The data dependency graph of the example

6   Conclusion

The method proposed in this paper is a first step towards an automatic process to identify high quality data sources for a warehouse project, even without having detailed knowledge about all databases and legacy systems available. The knowledge required stems from the underlying systems directly and is given in the form of transaction logs. Based on this information structural dependencies can be inferred automatically by analyzing the given event sequences. In that way, our approach supports the understanding of dependencies between several heterogeneous databases. As a by-product, it confines the number of data elements that have to be analyzed when selecting data sources. We expect that our approach reduces the time needed to build and maintain a data warehouse (and therefore it helps to minimizing costs), but it also increases the quality of the data stored in a data warehouse.

References

1. Eder, J., Koncilia, C.: Changes of Dimension Data in Temporal Data Warehouses, Proc. of the DaWak 2001 Conference, Munich, Germany (2001)
2. Kurz, A.: Data Warehousing - Enabling Technology, MITP-Verlag, Bonn (1999)
3. Kachur, R.: The Data Warehouse Diary: Source System Assessment for Data Warehouse, DM Review Online, http://www.dmreview.com/ (2000)
4. Paton, N., Diaz, O.: Active Database Systems, ACM Computing, Survey, vol. 31, No 1 (1999)
5. Pozewaunig, H.: Mining Component Behavior to Support Reuse, University Klagenfurt, Austria (2001)
6. Pinto, H., Han, J., Pei, J., Wang, K., Chen, Q. Dayal, U.: Multi-Dimensional Sequential Pattern Mining, Proc. of the 2001 Int. Conf. on Information and Knowledge Management (CIKM'01), Atlanta, GA, (2001)
7. Sun, R., Giles, C.L.: Sequence Learning – Paradigms, Algorithms, and Applications, Lecture Notes in Computer Science 1828, Springer Verlag, (2001)
8. Nevill-Manning, C.G.: Inferring Sequential Structure, University of Waikato (1996)
9. Williams, J.: Tools for Traveling Data, DBMS Magazine, http://www.dbmsmag.com/, Miller Freeman Inc. (1997)
10. Vassiliadis, P. Bouzeghoub, M., Quix, C.: Towards Quality-Oriented Data Warehouse Usage and Evolution, Proc. of the 11th Conference on Advanced Information Systems Engineering (CAiSE '99), Heidelberg (1999)

Coordinating Learning Agents via Utility Assignment

Steven Lynden and Omer F. Rana

Department of Computer Science, University of Wales, Cardiff, UK.
{s.j.lynden, o.f.rana}@cs.cf.ac.uk

Abstract. In this paper, a coordination technique is described for fully cooperative learning based multiagent systems, based on the Collective Intelligence work by Wolpert et al. Our work focuses on a practical implementation of these approaches within a FIPA compliant agent system, using the FIPA-OS agent development toolkit. The functionality of this system is illustrated with a simple buyer/seller agent application, where it is shown that the buyer agents are capable of self-organising behaviour in order to maximise their contribution to the global utility of the system.

1 Introduction

Various approaches to multiagent system (MAS) coordination exist, many of which are based on off-line techniques, in which predefined cooperation protocols [7] and social laws [9] are engineered, and agent behaviour is specified using rule based decision making processes. We believe that such approaches limit the potential for useful emergent, self-organising behaviour, and are less adaptable than MAS consisting of agents that use machine learning techniques such as reinforcement learning (RL) [3]. Learning agents require some form of payoff function in order to guide their learning process. In many approaches, the agent's payoff function is determined by its local utility function, which rates the performance of the agent according to various desirable characteristics. Utility functions are designed to give an indication of the degree of success with which an agent is achieving the goals it was designed to perform. In this work, the focus is on engineering fully cooperative MAS, where agents work towards common goals; an additional aim of this work is that agents are not restricted by explicit centralised control. A global utility function rates the performance of the MAS as a whole, based on various aspects of the collective performance of the agents. Agents learn to adapt their behaviour in order to maximise their local utility, so the challenging issue here is to assign local utility functions that reflect the contribution of each agent towards the global utility, also known as the credit-assignment problem [6]. The obvious approach is to use team-game utility functions, which simply assign the global utility function to each agent as the local utility function. This does not scale well in large MAS, due to the fact that it becomes increasingly difficult for an agent to determine the effect of its actions on its utility value as the number of agents increases. More promising results are achieved using the Collective Intelligence (COIN) [1] framework,

H. Yin et al. (Eds.): IDEAL 2002, LNCS 2412, pp. 219–224, 2002.

in which various utility function assignment techniques are investigated that overcome this signal-to-noise problem.

The focus of this paper is to illustrate the application of LEAF (the Learning Agent based FIPA compliant agent toolkit), a toolkit for developing coordinated learning based multiagent systems. The motivation for the development of LEAF is to provide a generic toolkit that can be used to develop agent based systems applicable to a diverse range of domains. Coordination in LEAF is based on the utility function assignment techniques of COIN, and support for this is incorporated into the LEAF infrastructure. It is intended that the LEAF toolkit be used to design, implement and monitor the performance of learning based MAS, and support is provided for each of these three key areas. The importance of interoperability with other agent systems and the role of standards is recognised, and for this reason LEAF builds on the FIPA-OS [4] agent development toolkit. FIPA-OS is an open source agent platform supporting the development of agents implementing the standards that must be met in order to develop FIPA compliant [5] agent systems. The use of FIPA-OS therefore enables interaction between LEAF agents and other FIPA compliant agents via FIPA ACL (FIPA agent communication language).

2 Utility Assignment

The essential concept on which the LEAF toolkit is based is that machine learning based agents can learn to maximise their personal local utility functions, which are assigned to agents with the aim of engineering a system in which improvements made to local utility are beneficial to the system globally. In the LEAF system, we endeavour to provide a toolkit for the rapid development of coordinated, FIPA compliant, learning based MAS utilising the utility function assignment ideas of COIN.

Collective Intelligence (COIN) [1] is a framework for designing large-scale learning based MAS, where centralised control of individual agents is extremely difficult or impossible due to scale. The COIN framework assumes a defined world utility function that rates the functional performance of the MAS as a whole. In order to engineer coordinated MAS where agents should not exhibit behaviour that is detrimental to world utility, COIN introduces a technique where local utility functions are assigned to agents, which are then maximised by the agent's internal learning processes. The framework investigated here, based on COIN, lies between centralised control and complete autonomy, where utility functions can be assigned to agents, and the functions parameterised by group/world dynamics, which necessitates some form of centralised communication to transfer parameters to the agent's local utility functions. Agents are autonomous in the sense that they are able to make their own decisions concerning how to maximise their utility function. Unlike centralised control, these utility assignment techniques do not involve a centralised entity with detailed models of agents, and no explicit instructions are given to agents.

(a) The development process

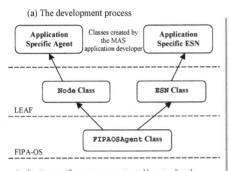

Application specific agents are constructed by extending the Node class, which in turn extends the FIPAOSAgent class. An application specific ESN is created by extending the ESN class, which also extends the FIPAOSAgent class. The ESN and Node classes provide access to an API supporting the development of LEAF MAS.

(b) Deployment of agents and the ESN

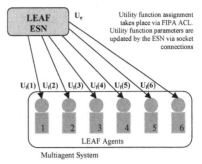

$U_l(i)$ is the local utility function of agent i. U_g is the global utility function

Fig. 1. The LEAF System

Among the various utility functions assigned to agents in COIN, some require centralised communication, whereas others can be computed by information available locally to an agent [2]. It is therefore clear that any practical implementation of the COIN techniques requires some means of dynamically providing information (that is not available locally) to agents concerning MAS state. In the LEAF system, this task is performed by an environment service node (ESN), which is responsible for maintaining the system information necessary for updating local and global utility functions. Multiple ESN's can co-exist in the system, each of which can specialise in a particular aspect of utility. We therefore foresee the existence of multiple environments (or markets – as described in section 3), with ESN's being federated across these environments. The LEAF toolkit has been developed in Java, utilising the FIPA-OS agent development toolkit. A basic knowledge of Java programming is required to develop agents using our framework as agent behaviour, comprised of various learning algorithms, must be programmed in Java. The LEAF system is illustrated in figure 1.

3   Marketplace Application

In order to demonstrate an application of the LEAF system, we outline an example application based on a buyer/seller marketplace. It is not the intention here to present an environment simulating realistic market behaviour; the aim is to illustrate a simple market based application to which the LEAF system can be applied. In this application, the learning based MAS consists of a set of buyer agents, which aim to maximise their local utility by making certain purchases from seller agents within a number or markets. Agents exist within a variety of markets, each of which contains a number of buyer agents and a number of seller agents. Seller agents offer a number of items, which can be purchased by buyer agents within the same market only. Buyer agents are given one credit each day, with which one purchase can be made from a seller agent, from a number of different categories of items which can be purchased. The buyer agents are placed in markets with the purpose of making purchases that will achieve the global objective of making as many purchases as possible, with the constraint that at least some quantity of each type of item is purchased each day. Each buyer agent's learning process is defined by simple RL algorithms.

3.1   Agent Behaviour

Seller agents existing within a market sell items to buyer agents within the same market. Each seller agent maintains a price list which determines the quantity of items it will sell for one credit, however this information is not made public and buyer agents must "gamble" by giving the seller agent one credit (specifying the desired item) before knowing the quantity of that item the seller agent will return. The price list of a seller agent is generated randomly when the seller agent is created, where the quantity of an item returned for one credit is a random integer between 0 and 100. Seller agents are assumed to have a large number of items to sell, the quantity of items they offer do not vary over time, and they never refuse to sell items. All seller agents sell items categorised as food, textiles, luxuries, computers, machinery and alloys. There is no difference in the quality of the items sold by the agents. Seller agents do not receive local utility functions as they are considered to be part of the environment in which the buyer agents exist, and not part of the MAS that is being coordinated.

Buyer agents purchase items from seller agents with the aim of maximising their local utility functions, which are distributed by the ESN. Each buyer agent attempts to maximise its local utility function using a simple RL algorithm, which weighs purchases according to the effect they have on local utility. Buyer agents make the assumption that it is desirable to obtain the greatest quantity of an item from each purchase (they aim for the maximum value-for-money in each purchase); making this assumption allows a buyer agent to maintain a set of gating weights, related to the number of items received from seller agents in previous interactions. The local utility function of each buyer agent therefore influences the type of item that the buyer is likely to purchase.

The Agent Learning Process. The actions that a buyer agent can perform are determined by the items it can buy - food, textiles, machinery, computers, luxuries or alloys. Once the decision is made to buy an item, the gating network is used to decide the agent from which to purchase. A simple RL technique is used to select which item to buy at the start of each day. A set of action-values are used, which record the average change in local utility that occurs after an action is selected - these values are then used to select an action each day using a simple Softmax action selection technique [3].

A set of weights (referred to here as gating weights) are used by buyer agents to determine which seller agents to purchase specific items from (in order to get the greatest number of items from the purchase), while the RL algorithm allows the buyer agent to determine which items to purchase (in order to benefit the system globally). The gating weights simply record the number of items returned by the seller agents when a purchase is made. $Gat(s, i)$ gives the quantity of item i received from agent s in a purchase. The following steps are repeatedly performed, with one iteration executed each day, where a day is an arbitrary system wide standard unit of time: (1) An item i is selected to be purchased based on the action-values held. (2) A seller agent s is selected to purchase from based on the gating weights held, which give an indication of the value of previous interactions with sellers. (3) The purchase of the item i is made from seller s. (4) The agent computes its local utility function, and rewards the action (purchasing item i) by the change in utility, which is determined by comparison with the result of the previous utility computation.

3.2   Utility Functions

The overall objective of the MAS is to achieve a situation in which each agent makes the best purchases it possibly can given the characteristics of its market, and the daily global utility of the system is computed each day as $U_g(d) = \sum_{\forall i \in I} Max(N_d^i)$ where I is the set of item types, and $Max(N_d^i)$ is the maximum quantity of item i purchased in any individual purchase made on day d by any of the buyer agents.

The global utility of the system is calculated as the sum of daily global utility values, hence $U_g = \sum_{d=1}^{n} U_g(d)$, where the system has existed for n days. The following local utility functions are assigned to the buyer agents: $U_l(a) = \sum_{d=1}^{n} U_g(Purchased_{a,d} = 0) - U_g$, where $Purchased_{a,d}$ is the number of items purchased on day d by agent a. $U_g(Purchased_{a,d} = 0)$ is the global utility function for day d computed without considering any of the purchased made by agent a, where the system has existed for n days. In order to compute local utility functions, agents are dynamically supplied with the following parameters: $U_g(Purchased_{a,d} = 0)$ and U_g. The ESN performs the tasks involved in maintaining and updating these values.

3.3   Results and Observations

Experiments were performed with 6 buyer agents, 6 markets (one buyer agent per market), 2 seller agents in each market, and 6 categories of items. The experiments were allowed to run for 250 days in each case. In all cases, the buyer agents experimented with different purchases initially, and then learned to concentrate on one specific purchase. This behaviour was a common feature of all buyer agents in all simulations. The results are illustrated in figure 2, which shows the value (sum of the maximum quantities of each item purchased) of the purchases settled on by the LEAF agents, and compares this to the best possible combinations of purchases that could have been achieved. It can be

	LEAF	Optimal
1	469	540
2	453	535
3	530	530
4	509	529
5	480	522
6	532	540
7	538	549
8	513	521
9	470	508
10	483	517

The results from 10 experiments are displayed.

The column labelled "LEAF" contains the value of the combination of purchases settled on by the buyer agents in each experiment.

The column labelled "Optimal" shows the best possible combination that could have been achieved with a centralised controller with complete knowledge of the states of all markets.

Fig. 2. Results

seen that only in experiment number 3 do the buyer agents learn to select the optimal combination of purchases, but all other experiments achieve at least 84% of the value of their optimal combinations. The benefit of the suboptimal combinations is that they are achieved without complete centralised control, via the individual learning processes of agents, combined with local utility function assignment. More complex, realistic applications will be the focus of future work.

References

1. D. Wolpert & K. Tumer: *An Introduction to Collective Intelligence*, In Handbook of Agent Technology. AAAI Press/MIT.
2. David Wolpert and Kagan Tumer *Optimal Payoff Functions for Members of Collectives* In Advances in Complex Systems, 2001 (in press).
3. R. S. Sutton & A. G. Barto: *Reinforcement Learning: An introduction*, MIT Press, Cambridge, MA, 1998. Press, 1999.
4. S.J. Poslad, P. Buckle & R. Hadingham: *The FIPA-OS Agent Platform: Open Source for Open Standards*,Proceedings of PAAM 2000, Manchester, UK, (April 2000).
5. FIPA (Foundation of Intelligent Physical Agents) homepage: http://www.fipa.org
6. S. Sen & G. Weiss: *Learning in Multiagent Systems*, In Multiagent Systems: A Modern Approach to Distributed Artificial Intelligence The MIT Press (1999).
7. G. Zlotkin & J.S. Rosenschein: *Negotiation and Task Sharing Among Autonomous Agents in Cooperative Domains*, Proceedings of the International Joint Conference on Artificial Intelligence 1989.
8. Michael L. Littman. *Markov games as a framework for multi-agent reinforcement learning* In 11th International Conference on Machine Learning, pages 157–163, 1994.
9. D. Fitoussi & M. Tennenholtz *Choosing social laws for multi-agent systems: Minimality and simplicity* Artificial Intelligence 119 (2000) 61-102

AGILE: An Agent-Assisted Infrastructure to Support Learning Environments

Nicoletta Dessì

Università di Cagliari, Dipartimento di Matematica, Via Ospedale 72
09100 Cagliari, Italy
dessi@unica.it

Abstract. This paper describes AGILE, an agent-assisted infrastructure with the aim of structuring information and processes in a distributed learning environment. AGILE is based on a generalized producer-consumer schema: agents are providers of educational resources consumed by users (learners). The model assumes that agents support learning tasks and facilitate delivery and the collaborative share of learning resources. User agents are responsible for the student representation, tutorial agents facilitate the access to educational material and supervisor agents route and distribute information. Agent interactions are modelled as asynchronous occurrences of internal events triggered by user requests. Meta-knowledge expresses user roles in defining groups and user competence levels.

1 Introduction

Recent years have witnessed extraordinary advances in multimedia information systems and network technologies. Thereby, a wide variety of educational institutions are increasingly finding novel and innovative uses for these technologies, uses that encompass and include various learning fields. This results in many systems whose main benefit comes from the ability to provide some educational facilities enabling the integration of multimedia resources over the Internet.The relative weakness of these systems derives from their incapacity in recognizing the collaborative feature inherent distributed learning environments [1] whose requirements are difficult to be determined by formal descriptions. It has been argued [1] that learning is a process not sufficiently understood and supported and core activity of learning environments must be accompanied by tasks supporting group interaction. Learning environments introduce new requirements for data engineering, which cannot be met by using existing models, developed for well structured tasks and well-understood domains. In addition, replacing the traditional classroom with a virtual environment will require significant additional research because network technology is dramatically changing the elements of "time", "place" and "space where the learning occurs: the distance is not the magnitude of geographical separation but the lack of interaction between teachers and students. Space is eliminated from the knowledge distribution role

H. Yin et al. (Eds.): IDEAL 2002, LNCS 2412, pp. 225–230, 2002.

and the major challenge is to maintain the sense of "the classroom" despite geographical separation. The scenario is large and it is has been studied before [7] and several conceptual model and frameworks [2][3][4][5] have been proposed for studying various issues in distance learning. Despite these advances, the design and the implementation of distributed learning environments is a key challenge [2] and top priority [4] must be given to the design of an infrastructure supporting distributed learning and encouraging the accommodation of different levels of knowledge as well as various styles of learning. The virtual and collaborative environment, free from constraints of time and space that characterize distributed learning applications for wide-area networks suggests multi-agent systems [6] as a promising approach in education [7] .

Based on the above reflections, this paper aims to provide AGILE a comprehensive agent-assisted infrastructure to support distributed learning environments.This paper is organized as follows: in the next section the characteristics of AGILE are outlined focusing on the representation of educational domain. Section 3 e 4 introduces, respectively, user representation and agent interactions. In Section 4, first validation experiments performed in a simplified learning environment are briefly presented.

2   Educational Resources

The proposed infrastructure is outlined in Fig.1.

It is centered on a set of objects, generally named as educational resources, and a number of specialized agents with different expertise. The distributed learning environment is modelled according to a producer-consumer schema: agents are providers of educational resources consumed by users (learners).

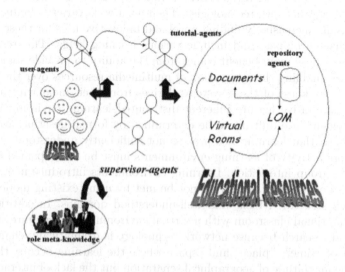

Fig. 1. AGILE: The Agent-assisted Infrastructure

Agents are able to discover the educational resources and to select the appropriate ones. The selection is performed within different criteria, such as the user's privileges or the styles of learning. AGILE is completely object-oriented and maps both users and educational resources into objects, whose interaction takes place via events. This interaction is essentially based on generating, manipulating and exchanging a set of objects, formally referred to educational resources, that consist, in turn, of documents, LOMs and virtual rooms.

Documents are learning objects characterized by a content stored in a datafile. As stated in the specification of IEEE's [8] a learning object (LO) is defined as "an entity, digital or non digital, which can be used, reused or referenced during technology-supported learning". Documents model the static knowledge within a didactic domain and are usually taken as the complement of conventional teaching methods in a classroom (i.e. word-processing documents, graphics, Web documents).

In order to facilitate the search, the acquisition and the use of documents, Learning Objects Metadata (LOM) [8] defines the attributes to describe learning objects. LOM allows to group appropriate metadata fields of a specific aspect of a learning object. Relevant aspects include [8] general metadata (e.g. title, language, structure or description), life cycle (e.g. status, version and role), meta-metadata (e.g. cataloguer, cataloguer entry), technical (e.g. format, browser requirements), educational (e.g. difficulty, learning context), rights (e.g. commercial use), relations (e.g. links to be able to refer to other LOs), classification and annotation. By LOM we are able to customize the LO content to the user's needs.

A virtual room is a shared space that provides a context-dependent access to learning objects as well as a persistent data space to support the construction of new learning resources. It is used for logical encapsulation of learning objects and groups documents, graphics and tools. For example, a virtual room may enable a tutorial where all the participants can be assembled to evaluate together a set of documents distributed through the network and located in various virtual rooms. To avoid interferences, each room has its own identifier and different users in the same room may have different privileges as explained as follows.

3   Users and Roles

In a distributed learning environment, there is the need to represent all the individual users as well as an arbitrary number of users, which can vary over time. In AGILE this meta-knowledge on the users pertains to roles that define user privileges. A role denotes specific concerns and activity associated with individuals involved in distributed learning environment. Examples of privileges can be the capability to access educational resources or to carry out a set of educational tasks. A role allows users to share a group of learning objects and to access a defined set of rooms. Users are assigned to the roles depending on their educational positions as well as on educational tasks they perform.

In AGILE, role meta-knowledge is exploited by the role graph model [9]with the following properties : there exists one group containing all users and one group for each individual user, group membership lists are unique. Different privileges may be accorded in managing educational resources. For example, one user may be allowed to read and write a document, while another may only have read permission. Roles are associated with individuals and a group denotes all users in the same room at the same time. Depending on particular learning needs and educational context, a user can temporarily switch into another role denoting a higher/lower level of competence occurring in qualitative competence levels (i.e. initial, low, medium, high).

4   Learning Agents

Agents support learning tasks and facilitate delivery and collaborative share of learning resources.

User agents represent the students. Each student is assigned a unique personal user-agent that helps the student by viewing, gathering and exchanging educational resources. It is in charge of being notified of all actions done by the student.As described in follows, the user-agent talks with the supervisor agent to be notified of the events about actions done by others students.

Tutorial agents are responsible for managing delivering, processing and presenting educational material. They are meta-information agents that manage the learner profiles, which characterize students and their knowledge. Tutorial agents assemble dynamically the educational material, collect performance data and are responsible for updating learner profiles. They decide which document is shown at a given time and enable navigation through educational resources. Both LOMs and learner's profiles support the tutorial agent activity in showing different learning resources through different paths tailored to users involved in the same course.

To facilitate the accessibility of educational resource, repository agents cooperate to provide storage for the educational material as well as for documents generated by learners.

Supervisor agents are responsible for delivering information to user and for handling all kinds of request. They route and distribute information to user agents and suggest meta-information to help other agents in performing their own tasks.

According to an event-based approach [10], the agent interactions are modelled as asynchronous occurrences of internal events triggered by user requests. Examples of internal events are the best location needed for storing a learning object , the access to cooperative area on which a group edit texts or deposit documents. Each agent informs other agents about the occurrence of an internal event by the emission of a notification [10], a small information object about the event. Upon receiving notifications, agents react performing actions that, in turn, may trigger the occurrence of other events and the delivery of additional notifications. In addition, supervisor agents receive support from meta-knowledge expressed by roles to define groups as well as the user competence level within a specific learning environment.

5   Experimental Implementation

A major component in experimentation was the availability of learning resources for students enrolled in the first course in Computer Science at University of Cagliari. In distance learning situation, the 2001 course had 140 students at 4 sites (classes) in Sardinia. A distance of over 200 kilometers separates the two furthest sites. In Cagliari, the main local class (80 students) attend live lectures. A video and audio-conference system enables the remote groups of students to attend lessons at their sites. Both local and remote students are enrolled in lab courses and conduct the lab exercises on an equal footing : each laboratory room is equipped with a LAN connection to each student workstation that access to an intranet networking local and remote laboratories. The intranet is based on a client server architecture enabled by ISDN lines and TCP/IP and consists of 4 class servers , an external web server connected with each class server and student clients.

A first experimental implementation has been performed to support lab activities in a simplified learning environment where only two kinds of virtual rooms are supported : a class room grouping all local and remote users and a private room for each individual user. Each virtual room contains a set of available services (audio, video, presenter, annotation and sharing tools).

Students are allowed to interact with a tutor by pressing a button on their desktop where a view enables their private rooms.

The class virtual room is implemented by a shared view of any received service and all changes to this view are propagated to all students.In the main local class, the current tutor controls the layout of the shared view.

The ability to move between rooms is supported by two software agents namely, SVA(Supervisor Agent, one per class) running on the class server and SA (Student Agent, one per desktop) running on the student workstations. They are implemented by two processes whose connection is maintained by TCP/IP for the lifetime of lab activities. Session participants are allowed to access the set of shared services by the GUI of each agent.

SVA is a server supporting login and initial configuration of private rooms before any SA can join a session. It maintains the class room as well as the current room (IP address, port, time) for each individual user involved in the same session and acts as session manager and supervisor between all SAs.

SA has in charge the notification of the startup of a service required by a student in his current room. The notification is scheduled by SVA whose GUI allows the current tutor to refuse or to accept the request. When a request is accepted, SVA and SA share a view that may be dynamically updated and the set of major services (video, audio, sharing tools). Information on SA room may be returned by SVA to each SA in order to make the view simultaneously visible to all session participants.

Software components are built on top of RFB (Remote Frame Buffer)[11], a standard TCP/IP application level protocol. Virtual rooms and agents are enabled by VNC [12], a freely available interface subject to GNU Public Licence (GPL) and Visual C++. Because of the component's small size (SVA 176KB and SA 659KB),the initial configuration is easily performed through the network and requires only a few minutes.

6   Conclusions

The outlined implementation attempts to bridge the gap between the theoretical ideas expressed by AGILE focusing on the practical implementation in a real learning environment. An important challenge in the near term will be the organization of educational materials in XML documents whose logical structure expressed by LOM may be specified by a DTD in order to allow the encapsulation of learning objects as well as the implementation of tutorial agents supporting learning tasks.

Acknowledgments. I would like to thank Francesco Aymerich for his contribution in discussing many of the ideas presented in this paper.

References

1. Stahl,G., :A Model for Collaborative Knowledge Building. Proceedings of ICLS, Mahwah, NJ(2000) 70-77
2. Shang,Y.,Shi,H.,and Chen,S..: An Intelligent Distributed Environment for Active Learning . ACM Journal of Educational Resources in Computing, Vol.1, (2001)
3. English,,S.,Yazdani M.: Computer Supported Cooperative Learning in a Virtual University. Journal of Computer Assisted Learning, Vol. 15 (1999) 282-292
4. Hampel ,T. and Keil-Slawik,R.: Steam - Design an Integrative Infrastructure for Web-Based Computer-Supported Cooperative Learning. Proceedings of WWW10,Hong Kong (2001) 76-85
5. Marquès, J.,M. and Navarro L.: WWG: A Wide-Area Infrastructure to Support Groups.Proceeding of GROUP'01,Boulder,Colorado,USA (2001), 179-186
6. Weiss,G.(ed.): Multiagent Systems : a Modern Approach to Distributed Artificial Intelligence. MIT Press, Cambridge, MA (1999)
7. Barnett,L.,Kent,J.F.,Casp,J.,and Green,D.: Design and Implementation of an Interactive tutorial framework. SIGSE Bulletin (1998) 30,1,87-91
8. IEEE Learning Technology Standards Committee(LTSCE) IEEE P1484.12 ,Learning Objects Metadata Working Group, http://ltsc.ieee.org./wg12/
9. Nyanchama,M., and Osborn,S.,L. :The Role Graph Model and Conflict of Interest.ACM TISSEC(1999) 2 (1):3-33
10. Wray ,M. and Hawkes : Distributed Virtual Environment and VRML : an Event based Architecture. Proceedings of WWW7 (1998), Brisbane,Australia
11. http://www.uk.research.att.com/vnc/rfbproto.pdf
12. http://www.uk.research.att.com/vnc/

Multi-agent Fuzzy Logic Resource Manager

Dr. James F. Smith III

Naval Research Laboratory, Code 5741
Washington, D.C., 20375-5000
Telephone: 202.767.5358
jfsmith@drsews.nrl.navy.mil

Abstract. A fuzzy logic expert system has been developed that automatically allocates resources in real-time over a collection of autonomous agents. Genetic algorithm based optimization is conducted to determine the form of the membership functions for the fuzzy root concepts. The resource manager is made up of four trees, the isolated platform tree, the multi-platform tree, the fuzzy parameter selection tree and the fuzzy strategy tree. The isolated platform tree provides a fuzzy decision tree that allows an individual platform to respond to a threat. The multi-platform tree allows a group of platforms to respond to a threat in a collaborative self-organizing fashion. The fuzzy parameter selection tree is designed to make optimal selections of root concept parameters. The strategy tree is a fuzzy tree that an agent uses to try to predict the behavior of an enemy. Finally, the five approaches to validating the expert system are discussed.

1 Introduction

Modern naval battleforces generally include many different platforms, e.g., ships, planes, helicopters, etc. Each platform has its own sensors, e.g., radar, electronic support measures (ESM), and communications. The sharing of information measured by local sensors via communication links across the battlegroup should allow for optimal or near optimal decisions. The survival of the battlegroup or members of the group depends on the automatic real-time allocation of various resources.

A fuzzy logic algorithm has been developed that automatically allocates electronic attack (EA) resources in real-time. In this paper EA refers to the active use of electronic techniques to neutralize enemy equipment such as radar [1]. The particular approach to fuzzy logic that will be used is the fuzzy decision tree, a generalization of the standard artificial intelligence technique of decision trees [2].

The controller must be able to make decisions based on rules provided by experts. The fuzzy logic approach allows the direct codification of expertise forming a fuzzy linguistic description [3], i.e., a formal representation of the system in terms of fuzzy if-then rules. This will prove to be a flexible structure that can be extended or otherwise altered as doctrine sets, i.e., the expert rule sets change.

The fuzzy linguistic description will build composite concepts from simple logical building blocks known as root concepts through various logical connectives: "or", "and", etc. Optimization has been conducted to determine the form of the membership functions for the fuzzy root concepts.

H. Yin et al. (Eds.): IDEAL 2002, LNCS 2412, pp. 231–236, 2002.

The algorithm is designed so that when the scenario databases change as a function of time, then the algorithm can automatically re-optimize allowing it to discover new relationships in the data. Alternatively, the resource manager (RM) can be embedded in a computer game that EA experts can play. The software records the result of the RM and expert's interaction, automatically assembling a database of scenarios. After the end of the interaction, the game makes a determination of whether or not to re-optimize the RM using the newly extended database.

To be consistent with terminology used in artificial intelligence and complexity theory [4], the term "agent" will sometimes be used to mean platform, also a group of allied platforms will be referred to as a "meta-agent." Finally, the terms "blue" and "red" will refer to "agents" or "meta-agents" on opposite sides of a conflict, i.e., the blue side and the red side.

Section 2 briefly introduces the ideas of fuzzy logic and discusses data mining with genetic algorithms and genetic programs. Section 3 discusses the RM's five major components. Section 4 discusses the five approaches to validating the RM. Finally, section 5 provides a summary.

2 Fuzzy Logic, Genetic Algorithms, Genetic Programs and the RM

The RM must be able to deal with linguistically imprecise information provided by an expert. Also, the RM must control a number of assets and be flexible enough to rapidly adapt to change. The above requirements suggest an approach based on fuzzy logic. Fuzzy logic is a mathematical formalism that attempts to imitate the way humans make decisions. Through the concept of the grade of membership, fuzzy set theory and fuzzy logic allow a simple mathematical expression of uncertainty [5,6]. The RM requires a mathematical representation of domain expertise. The decision tree of classical artificial intelligence provides a graphical representation of expertise that is easily adapted by adding or pruning limbs. The fuzzy decision tree, a fuzzy logic extension of this concept, allows easy incorporation of uncertainty as well as a graphical codification of expertise [2]. Finally, a detailed discussion of the particular approach to fuzzy logic and fuzzy decision trees used in the RM is given in reference [6].

Each root concept on the fuzzy decision tree has a membership function with parameters to be determined. The parameters of the root concept membership function are obtained by optimizing the RM over a database of scenarios using a genetic algorithm (GA) [7]. Once the root concept membership functions are known, those for the composite concepts [6] follow immediately. At this point the necessary fuzzy if-then rules for the RM have been fully determined. A detailed discussion of the GA for data mining as well as the construction of the chromosomes and fitness functions are given in reference [6].

The GA based procedures used above determine the parameters that in turn control the form of fuzzy membership functions. The GA does not determine the structure of the fuzzy decision trees, i.e., how the vertices and edges are connected. This is done by converting rules obtained by interviewing human experts into fuzzy if-then rules and then fuzzy decision trees. In instances where no human expertise exists or validation of rules is sought, a genetic program (GP) is used to data mine fuzzy decision tree structure. A genetic program is a computer program that evolves other computer programs using a survival of the fittest approach [8].

3 Subtrees of the RM

The resource manager is made up of four decision trees, the isolated platform decision tree (IPDT), the multi-platform decision tree (MPDT), the fuzzy parameter selection tree and the fuzzy strategy tree. The EA decision algorithm, which can be called by the IPDT or the MPDT, is an expert system for assigning electronic attack techniques. The IPDT provides a fuzzy decision tree that allows an individual platform to respond to a threat [6]. The MPDT allows a group of platforms connected by communication links to respond to a threat in a collaborative fashion [9]. The communications model used for simulation purposes is described elsewhere [9]. The fuzzy parameter selection tree is designed to make optimal or near optimal selections of root concept parameters from the parameter database assembled during previous optimization with the genetic algorithm. Finally, the strategy tree is a fuzzy tree that an agent uses to try to predict the behavior of an enemy.

This section discusses the four major decision trees that make up the RM, the fuzzy EA decision algorithm and how they make efficient use of the Network-Centric paradigm. The Network-Centric paradigm refers to strategies that make optimal use of multiple allied platforms linked by communication, resources distributed over different platforms, and decentralized command.

3.1 The Isolated Platform Decision Tree

The IPDT allows a blue platform that is alone or isolated to determine the intent of a detected platform. It does this by processing data measured by the sensors, e.g., ESM, radar, IFF, etc. Even when an incoming platform's ID is very uncertain, the IPDT can still establish intent based on kinematics. When faced with multiple incoming platforms the IPDT can establish a queue of which platforms to attack first. Various subtrees of the IPDT have been discussed extensively in the past [9].

3.2 The Multi-platform Decision Tree

The IPDT made limited use of the Network-Centric paradigm, using the other networked platforms for surveillance and electronic intelligence. However, it is the purpose of the Network-Centric paradigm to use the multiple platforms to gain geometric, physical and tactical advantage to employ multi-platform techniques that are more effective than standard techniques. Such techniques require coordination and communication from platform to platform, as well as some command and control structure.

As it stands, the IPDT can not take full advantage of the Network-Centric paradigm. To do this another decision tree, the MPDT is required. Using sensor output, the MPDT allows a group of platforms, connected by a communications network to work together in an optimal fashion to take advantage of the full potential of the Network-Centric paradigm.

3.3 The Fuzzy EA Decision Algorithm

Once the IPDT or the MPDT determines an action is required, the fuzzy EA decision algorithm becomes active. This fuzzy algorithm allows the RM to pick the best EA technique(s) to use against the incoming emitters. The RM's decision is based on the emitters' ID, uncertainty in ID, available assets within the blue group, blue asset reliability, logistics for re-supplying blue assets, battlespace geometry, intelligence reports related to red assets, red asset reliability, logistics for re-supplying the red forces, weather and atmospheric conditions, etc.

The fuzzy EA decision algorithm is an expert system based partially on military doctrine obtained by interviewing experts, preferred techniques found in the literature, and entirely new classes of techniques invented that exploit the Network-Centric paradigm.

As well as making use of fuzzy rules, it can make use of fuzzy linear or fuzzy non-linear programming techniques for optimal real-time power allocation in the face of uncertainty. Both the linear and nonlinear programming approaches use fuzzy number theory to quantify uncertainty in parameters [5].

3.4 The Fuzzy Parameter Selection Tree

The fuzzy parameter selection tree can be called by the IPDT, MPDT, the fuzzy strategy tree, and the fuzzy EA algorithm. It allows each tree to select the best parameters determined off-line using genetic optimization. The selections are a function of emitter ID, uncertainty in ID, intelligence reports, battlespace geometry, geography, weather, etc. These parameters can include probabilities for the best strategy calculated using game theory.

By selecting specialized parameters sets for different situations the RM can use the same decision trees and functional forms for the fuzzy membership functions. This also allows the RM to be employed on many different types of blue platforms and deal with very general red threats.

3.5 The Fuzzy Strategy Tree

A strategy tree is an agent's concept of an opposing agent's decision tree. If an agent has sufficient knowledge of the enemy's past behavior the strategy tree can be very useful for predicting future behavior.

4 Validation of the RM Expert System

There have been to date four different approaches to the validation of the RM conducted. These approaches are the evaluation of the RM within a digital war game environment [9]; the development of measures of effectiveness (MOE), one of which is described below; testing the RM using a hardware simulator, and using genetic programs to evolve fuzzy decision tree structure from a random starting point using constraints based on expertise.

The scenario generator (SG) and the related activity of co-evolutionary data mining is described in detail elsewhere [9]. So only a quick summary will be given here. The SG allows the creation of a very general battlespace that may have a battle map with desert, forest, jungle, urban areas, and water. Very general blue agents, i.e., the defending platforms each one of which runs its own copy of the RM can be placed within the battlespace. The agents can be ships, planes, helicopters, soldiers, decoys, etc. The SG allows the agents to be equipped with very general sensors, weapons, etc. Likewise, the SG allows very general red agents to be created and well equipped. The SG has two modes of operation, computer vs. computer (CVC) mode, and human vs. computer mode (HVC). In both modes each blue agent has its own copy of the RM. The blue agent's RM exercises all control functions over that agent and only that agent. In CVC mode each red agent is controlled by its own computerized logic different from the RM. In HVC mode, a human expert controls one red agent per time step through a GUI with a PPI radar display, the controls for firing red missiles and motion controls. The human player can select a different red agent each time step to control: those red agents not under human control run under computer logic as in CVC mode. Many different battles can be fought using the SG, the results are stored in a database and also a computer movie. Human experts have evaluated many of the computer movies and agreed on the RM's excellent decisions.

Another approach to validation that has been pursued is to write down, based on expertise, measures of effectiveness (MOE). These are typically fuzzy decision trees. The MOE's allows quantification of the value of the RM's responses. The RM has been very successful when evaluated in this way.

A third validation effort involves the use of a hardware simulator referred to as the search radar electronic warfare simulator (SRES). This type of evaluation is similar to the work done with the SG, but in this case the digitally simulated radars, electronic warfare equipment, communication systems, and sensor displays of the SG are replaced with real hardware systems. In this application the RM is used as a controller on SRES, allowing evaluation of the RM and electronic warfare techniques. As in the previous two approaches to validation, the RM has also passed its test at this level.

The fourth contribution to the validation effort consists of using a genetic program to mine military data bases for fuzzy decision tree structure and along with them, fuzzy rules [5,8]. The original approach to rule determination was to consult domain experts or existing doctrine. In the GP based approach using a minimum of constraints imposed by domain experts and random starting points, fuzzy decision tree structures and also fuzzy rules are evolved. In many cases the same rules and fuzzy decision trees written down based on experts rules or pre-existing doctrine are re-obtained. The GP's rediscovery of rules and fuzzy decision trees already in use provides support and hence a kind of validation. Of course, the GP's are also being used to data mine new rules and fuzzy decision tree structures.

Finally, even though the RM has been very successful when subjected to the test described above, field test are planned. Experiments in the field, i.e., on the ocean and other demanding terrain will expose the RM to conditions difficult to simulate digitally or in hardware.

5 Summary

A fuzzy logic based algorithm for optimal allocation and scheduling of electronic attack resources distributed over many platforms is under development. Optimization of the resource manager is conducted by using a genetic algorithm as a component of a data mining process. Construction of the database, which is used for optimization was summarized. The four decision trees making up the resource manager are discussed. These trees include the isolated and multi-platform decision trees that allow a lone platform or a collection of platforms to respond to a threat. The strategy tree allows the resource manager to make effective use of a threat's past history. The fuzzy parameter selection tree allows threat and scenario specific parametrization of fuzzy membership functions. The fuzzy EA model is also discussed. This is an expert system that allows the isolated and multi-plaform trees to select the best EA techniques for a given scenario. Finally, five procedures for validating the resource manager are discussed.

Acknowledgements. The Office of Naval Research sponsored this project.

References

1. Schleher, D. C.: Electronic Warfare in the Information Age, Artech House, Boston (1999)
2. Blackman, S., Popoli, R.: Design and Analysis of Modern Tracking Systems, Artech House, Boston (1999) Chapter 11
3. Tsoukalas, L.H., Uhrig, R.E.: Fuzzy and Neural Approaches in Engineering, John Wiley and Sons, New York (1997) Chapter 5
4. Holland, J. H.: Hidden Order How Adaptation Builds Complexity , Perseus Books, Reading (1995) 1-15
5. Zimmerman, H. J.: Fuzzy Set Theory and its Applications, Kluwer Academic Publishers Group, Boston (1991) Chapter 1
6. Smith III, J.F., Rhyne II, R.: A Resource Manager for Distributed Resources: Fuzzy Decision Trees and Genetic Optimization in Proceedings of the International Conference on Artificial Intelligence, IC-AI'99, Vol. II. CSREA Press, Las Vegas, (1999) 669-675
7. Goldberg, D.E.: Genetic Algorithms in Search, Optimization and Machine Learning, Addison-Wesley, Reading (1989)
8. Koza, J.R., Bennett III, F.H., Andre, D., Keane, M.A.: Genetic Programming III: Darwinian Invention and Problem Solving, Morgan Kaufmann Publishers, San Francisco (1999) Chapter 2
9. Smith III, J.F., Rhyne II, R.: Optimal Allocation of Distributed Resources Using Fuzzy Logic and a Genetic Algorithm, NRL Formal Report NRL/FR/5741-00-9970, Naval Research Laboratory, Washington D.C. 20375-5000, September 29, 2000.

Transactional Multiple Agents

Xinfeng Ye[1], John Keane[2], and Guoqing Zhang[3]

[1] Department of Computer Science, University of Auckland, Auckland, New Zealand
[2] Department of Computation, UMIST, Manchester, UK
[3] Institute of Computing Technology, Chinese Academy of Sciences, P.R. China

Abstract. In a Multi-agent system (MAS), agents work to achieve common goals. This paper gives a flexible model for writing agents and a mechanism to guarantee correctness of the MAS when agents operate on multiple databases.

1 Introduction

In a multi database systems (DBSs), agents operate concurrently at different sites. To be useful in such applications, agent technology must support transaction properties, such as atomicity and isolation [4]. Approaches that ensure these properties in a multi-DB environment (by preventing access to data used by an un-committed transaction) are inefficient for long-lived applications, like mobile agents [3, 5].

This paper presents a transaction model for writing MAS application and a scheme to manage the model. The approach provides a flexible model for writing agents, and guarantees correctness of the MAS when agents operate on multiple DBSs.

2 Multi Transactional Agents

A multi-agent application is termed a *multi transactional agent* (MTA). Each MTA consists of several (stationary or mobile) agents. An MTA commits if all its agents commit. If one agent aborts, an MTA aborts all its other agents. An agent contains code for making decisions and generating SQL statements to interact with a DB.

Some agent operations are compensatable, e.g. book/cancel a seat, while others are not, e.g. issue cash. An agent whose operations are compensatable is called a *compensatable agent*, otherwise, it is called a *pivot agent*. As its effects can be undone, a compensatable agent can commit its operations when they finish without waiting for its MTA to commit. This is used to improve efficiency, e.g. [1], as the data used by a compensatable agent is immediately made available to other agents. Generally, compensating operations are application-dependent, thus, programmers must code such operations. As operations of pivot agents cannot be undone easily, such operations can only be committed when all other agents in that MTA commit.

All DBSs are assumed to be autonomous, i.e. they do not reveal internal states. The scheme here can only use SQL statements to interact with the DBSs. Once the scheme requests a DBS to commit, the DBS may fail to commit due to system error. Thus, if an MTA has several pivot agents, some might be committed, while others are not, and

H. Yin et al. (Eds.): IDEAL 2002, LNCS 2412, pp. 237–242, 2002.

hence, MTA atomicity is compromised. As a DBS is autonomous, there are no known solutions to this issue, and manual operations must be done to remove inconsistency.

Many MTAs can exist in the system. Their agents may access several DBSs concurrently. To ensure correctness of concurrent access, global serializability must be satisfied [2], i.e., MTA agents should access the DBSs in the same relative order. The access order is called *serialization order* which is denoted as $x \rightarrow y$. x is called the *predecessor* of y, and $\rightarrow$ is transitive. The *ticket scheme* [2] is used to impose serialization order on a DBS. By combining the serialization orders on all sites, a global serialization graph can be formed. Global serializability is violated if there is a cycle in the graph [2]. The scheme here detects cycles in the serialization graph.

3   The Scheme

A system consists of DBs running on different sites. A multi transactional agent manager (MTAM) is set up on each site. An MTAM acts as the *coordinator* of the MTAs submitted on that site. An MTA coordinator manages the commit/abort of the agents of an MTA running on various sites. The MTAMs on different sites cooperate with each other to ensure global serializability. An MTA can be submitted to any of the MTAMs. The MTA coordinator dispatches the agents of an MTA to their relevant sites. When an MTAM receives an agent, it creates an *execution engine* (EE). An EE is a process, assigned to an agent at a site, that accepts SQL commands from the agent and interacts with the DBS on the agent's behalf. The MTAM at the site where the EE resides is called the *local MTAM* of the EE. The local MTAM of the EE controls the communications between the EE and the coordinator of the EE's corresponding agent.

A mobile agent may travel to several sites before it terminates. An EE is created for the agent on each site visited. As, according to the agent's coordinator, the EEs interact with the DBSs to commit/abort the operations carried out by the agent, a mobile agent can move before its operations are committed/aborted on the current site. Before a compensatable agent moves it must pass the compensating operation code to the EE. Thus, the EE can carry out the compensating operations if needed.

The principles of the scheme are:

1. To use the ticket scheme to force serialization order, a data item *ticket* is stored on each DBS. An update operation on *ticket*, *w(ticket)*, is imposed on each agent. Each EE must request the DBS to perform *w(ticket)* on *ticket* first. After the DBS completes *w(ticket)*, the EE submits operations of its agent to the DBS. On a DBS, only one EE is allowed to submit *w(ticket)* at any time. The order of committing agent operations must be the same as the order of submitting *w(ticket)* to the DBS. Consequently, this is the serialization order amongst the agents on the DBS.
2. The coordinator of an MTA is informed of the serialization order concerning the MTA on the sites where the MTA's agents visit. The coordinator constructs the serialization graph dynamically to check whether the MTA is in a cycle in the graph. If the MTA is in a cycle, the MTA is aborted.
3. When an agent terminates, its coordinator is informed. When all agents of an MTA have terminated successfully, the coordinator commits the MTA. If one agent of an MTA aborts at a site, the coordinator aborts all agents of the MTA.

1. **when** changed to *register* state: submit *w(ticket)* to DBS;
2. **when** *w(ticket)* is completed by the DBS:
3.   sends *finish-register* message to local MTAM and becomes *active*;
4.   submit operations of the agent to the DBS;
5. **when** submitted operations are completed by the DBS:
6.   **if** the agent is compensatable **then**
7.   submit commit request to the DBS;
8.   send *request-to-clean* message to local MTAM and becomes *idle*;
9.   **else** send *request-to-commit* message to local MTAM;
10.   **endif**
11.   **if** the agent terminates **then**
12.   send *finish* message to local MTAM
13.   **endif**;
14. **when** received *commit* message:
15.   submit commit request to the DBS
16.   **if** the DBS carries out the commit successfully
          then send *success* message to local MTAM;
17.   **else** send *fail* message to the local MTAM;
18.   **endif**;
19. **when** received a failure message from DBS or DBS fails to execute a submitted operation:
20.   send *abort* message to local MTAM;
21. **when** received an *all-abort* message:
22.   **if** (engine's state is *idle*) **and** (the agent is compensatable) **then**
23.   submit compensating operations of the agent to DBS;
24.   **else** request DBS to abort all the operations /* i.e. EE state is *active* */
25.   **endif**
26.   terminate itself;
27. **when** received a *clean-up* message: terminate itself;

An EE is in one of several states. An MTAM creates an EE when the MTAM receives the agent of an MTA. The created EE is in *dormant* state. An MTAM activates an EE by changing its state to *register* when no other EE are in *register* state. When an EE enters the *register* state, it submits *w(ticket)* to the DBS (line 1). When *w(ticket)* is completed by the DBS, the EE informs its local MTAM and enters *active* state (line 3). An EE in *active* state submits the operations of its associated agent to the DBS (line 4). When all agent operations are completed by the DBS, the EE sends to its MTAM either (a) a *request-to-commit* message, if the agent is a pivot (line 9), or (b) a *request-to-clean* message and enters *idle* state, if the agent is compensatable (line 8). Operations of a compensatable agent are committed by the DBS immediately (line 7), for a pivot agent, the EE has to wait until the coordinator of the agent has decided to commit the agent to ask the DBS to commit (lines 14-18). When an agent terminates, the EE sends a *finish* message to its MTAM (lines 11-13). A DBS may abort the operations of an agent due to the DBS's internal reasons. If so, the EE sends an *abort* message to the coordinator through its local MTAM (lines 19-20). When the MTA coordinator instructs its agents to abort (i.e. an *all-abort* message is received), if the agent's operations have not been committed by the DBS, the EE requests the DBS to abort all the agent's operations (line 24). Otherwise, the compensating operations are carried out (lines 22-23). As the agent is aborted, its EE terminates (line 26). The EE of a compensatable agent terminates when the MTA to which the agent belongs terminates (i.e. a *clean-up* message is received) (line 27).

An MTAM only activates an EE when no other EEs are in *register* state (i.e. when no *w(ticket)* is waiting to be completed) (lines 30 and 35). Thus, only one EE can submit *w(ticket)* to the DBS. As a result, *ticket* is accessed in the same order as the agents are activated; and this is the agent's serialisation order. For cycle detection purposes, a *request-to-check* message is sent to the agent coordinator, say *at*, after the *w(ticket)* operation has been carried out on behalf of *at* (line 34). The *request-to-check* message contains all the uncommitted/unaborted MTAs that precede *at* on the site (i.e. the MTAs whose agents carried out the *w(ticket)* operation before *at*).

28. **when** received an agent *at*:
29.   create an execution engine for *at*;
30.   **if** there are no engines in *register* state **then** set the engine to *register* state;
31.   **else** set *at* to *dormant*;
32.   **endif**
33. **when** received *finish-register* message from the execution engine of agent *at*:
34.   send *request-to-check* message to *at*'s coordinator;
35.   activate an execution engine that is *dormant* (if any);
36. **when** received a *request-to-commit/request-to-clean* message from agent *at*'s exec engine:
37.   **if** all the agents which precede *at* have committed or aborted **then**
38.   forward the message to the coordinator of *at*;
39.   **else** hold the message;
40.   **endif**
41. **when** received a *clean-up/all-abort* message from an agent's, say *at*'s, coordinator:
42.   pass the message to *at*'s execution engine;
43.   check if received an *request-to-commit/request-to-clean* message
            from another agent, say *at'*, which follows *at*;
44.   **if** such a message has been received **then** forward the message to coordinator of *at'*

To achieve global serializability, an MTAM only allows the *request-to-commit/request-to-clean* message of an agent, say *a*, to be sent to *a*'s coordinator when all agents that precede *a* have committed/aborted (lines 36-40). This ensures that, if the agents of some MTAs have different serialisation orders on various sites, the MTAs will not be committed. When an agent is committed/aborted (i.e. when a *clean-up/all-abort* message is received from the agent's coordinator), the agent's EE is informed (line 42). The MTAM also checks to see if the committed/aborted agent's successor is ready to commit (lines 43-44). As the EEs do not have direct contact with the MTAMs on other sites, the EEs' local MTAM forwards the messages to/from the engines. The rules below only list the messages whose receipt trigger a local MTAM to carry out control operations. Apart from these, an MTAM also receives messages like *abort, finish, success* and *commit* that are sent between an EE and its coordinator.

When an MTA is submitted to an MTAM, the MTAM starts execution of the MTA by dispatching its agents to appropriate sites (line 45). The MTAM also creates data structures to hold information about the MTA. For each MTA, a set, *predecessors*, is kept by the MTAM to record known predecessors of the MTA. When a *request-to-check* message is received, *predecessors* is updated accordingly (line 47). *predecessors(m)* denotes the predecessors of the agent on whose behalf message *m* is sent (line 47). Probes are then sent to check for cycles (line 48). *visited* is a set, kept by the MTA coordinator, that records the sites visited by the MTA's agents. *visited* is updated to include the sender of a *request-to-check* message (line 49). Agents may move amongst sites, and so, the predecessors of an agent may change, and thus the serialization graph of an MTA may also change. A new set of probes is sent when a *request-to-check* message is received to discover changes to the serialization graph.

need-commit is a set that records those sites that have been visited by an MTA's pivot agents. *ready* is a set that records the sites visited by the MTA's compensatable agents. *finished* is a set containing the MTA's agents that have terminated. These three sets are updated as the relevant messages are received (lines 50-52). *agent(m)* denotes the identity of the agent on whose behalf message *m* is sent.

45. **when** received an MTA: send MTA's agents to their corresponding sites
46. **when** received a *request-to-check* message *m*:
47. $predecessors = predecessors \cup predecessors(m)$;
48.   send a *check-cycle-probe* to each site in set *predecessors*;
49. $visited = visited \cup \{m$'s sender$\}$;
50. **when** received a *request-to-commit* message *m*: $need\text{-}commit = need\text{-}commit \cup \{m$'s sender$\}$;
51. **when** received a *request-to-clean* message *m*: $ready = ready \cup \{m$'s sender$\}$;
52. **when** received a *finish* message *m*: $finished = finished \cup agent(m)$;
53. **when** received an *abort* message: send *all-abort* message to all the sites in *visited*;
54. **when** (*finished contains all MTA's agents*) $\land$ (*visited* = (*need-commit* $\cup$ *ready*)):
55.   send a *commit* message to each site in set *need-commit*;
56.   **if** receives an *abort* message from one of the sites in *need-commit* **then**
57.   send *all-abort* message to each site in *ready* and
            raise alert with *need-commit* as a parameter;
58.   **endif**
59.   send a *clean-up* message to each site in set *visited* and remove MTA records;
60. **when** received a *check-cycle-probe* *m*:
61.   **if** there is no record about *mta(m)*
        then send an *agent-terminate* message to *m*'s sender;
62.   **else**
63. $path(m) = path(m) \cup mta(m)$;
64.   **if** (*mta(m)* does not have any predecessor) **then** drop *m*;
65.   **else if** ($path(m) \cap (predecessors\ of\ mta(m))) \neq \emptyset$ **then**
66.   send a *cycle-found* message to the coordinator of each of the *MTAs* in *path(m)*
67.   **else**
68.   duplicate *m* & send *m* to coordinator of each MTA in *mta(m)*'s *predecessors* set;
69.   **endif**
70.   **endif**
71. **when** received a *cycle-found* message *m*: send *all-abort* message to each site in *visited*;
72. **when** received *agent-terminate* message *m*: $predecessors = predecessors - \{m$'s MTA$\}$;

An MTA is aborted when one of its agents is aborted. To abort the MTA, an *all-abort* message is sent to each site visited by the MTA's agents (line 53). *agent* is a set recording all the agents of an MTA. The MTA is ready to commit (line 54), when (a) all its agents have terminated (i.e. (*finished contains all MTA's agents*) holds) and (b) the sites visited have all permitted the agents' operations to be committed (i.e. *visited* = (*need-commit* $\cup$ *ready*)). Firstly, operations carried out by pivot agents need to be committed (line 55). If any of these fail, the MTA has to be aborted (lines 56-58). However, despite failure on some DBSs, it is possible that, on other DBSs, the operations of the pivot agents are committed successfully. As a result inconsistency may arise and an alert is generated to ask users to manually restore consistency as necessary (line 57). After an MTA is committed/aborted, *clean-up* messages are sent to all sites visited by the MTA's agents to terminate the EE of these agents (line 59).

Lines 60-70 describe the cycle-detection algorithm. *check-cycle-probe* are sent from an MTA to its predecessors, i.e., if $x \rightarrow y$, a probe is sent from y to x. *mta(m)* (line 61) denotes the MTA who is the predecessor of probe m's sender. *check-cycle-probe* is propagated through the predecessors. When an MTA is committed/aborted, its coordinator removes all the records on the MTA, thus, if no record about an MTA can be found, the MTA must have terminated. Hence, it is impossible for the MTA to be involved in a cycle, thus, the MTA needs not to be considered. Hence, an *agent-terminate* message is sent to the probe's sender to remove the MTA from the sender's *predecessors* set (lines 61 and 72). This avoids probes being sent to a terminated MTA in the future. *path(m)* (line 63) records the MTAs that have been reached by the probe. If *mta(m)* does not have a predecessor, the probe cannot be sent further and is dropped (line 64). If a predecessor of *mta(m)* is already in *path(m)*, there is a cycle in the serialization graph. Hence, relevant coordinators are informed (lines 65-66); in turn, the coordinators will abort the corresponding MTAs (line 71). If no cycles are found, the probe are replicated and sent to each predecessor of *mta(m)* (line 68).

4   Conclusions

Transaction management used in multi-DBSs abort transactions to prevent deadlocks, and are thus inefficient when applied in an MTA environment as mobile agents tend to be long lived. As a result, agents tend to be aborted prematurely in an MTA environment using traditional schemes. In this paper a scheme for managing access to DBSs by MTAs is proposed. The scheme only aborts agents after a deadlock occurs, thus avoiding unnecessary abortion. The use of EEs allows agents to move without waiting for operations to be committed on their current sites. Compared with traditional multi-DBSs schemes, the scheme here is both more efficient and flexible.

References

1. Garcia-Molina, H, Salem, K.: Sagas. Proc. ACM SIGMOD, ACM Press, 1987
2. Georgakopoulos, D., Rusinkiewicz, Sheth, A.: On Serializability of Multi-Database Transaction Through Forced Local Conflicts. Proc. 7th ICDE, IEEE Press, 1991
3. Nagi, K.: Transactional Agents, LNCS 2249, Springer-Verlag, 2001
4. Sher, R., Aridor, Y., Etzioni, O.: Mobile Transactional Agents, Proc. 21st Intl. Conf. On Distributed Computing Systems, IEEE Press, 2001
5. Batra, R.K., Rusinkiewicz, M.: A decentralized deadlock-free concurrency control method for multidatabase transactions, Proc. 12th Int. Conf. On Distributed Computing Systems, IEEE Press, 1992

An Information Model for a Merchant Trust Agent in Electronic Commerce

Mohd Khairudin Kasiran and Farid Meziane

School of Sciences, Computer Science, University of Salford
Salford M5 4WT, UK
mkasiran@aol.com, f.meziane@salford.ac.uk

Abstract. eCommerce is a faceless business arrangement where the process of creating trust towards merchants, hereby referred to as "merchant trust", is still a big challenge. Merchant trust framework can be created by using factors such as existence, affiliation, performance and policy. In this paper, we present an information model for a merchant trust based on the previously cited factors. We then provide a framework for the implementation of the model using intelligent agents. Gathering the required information on the merchant is the first step in helping consumers to evaluate merchant trust in an eCommerce setting.

Keywords: eCommerce, Trust, Intelligent Agent

1 Introduction

Electronic Commerce (eCommerce) is a faceless business arrangement, where merchants are placing their business images in the cyber world using web technology. These images can travel around the world in a few seconds and be viewed by consumers anywhere at the comfort of their own places. However, it was argued that eCommerce could only become a success if the general public can put their trust in this virtual business channel [13]. Lack of trust from both sides has been identified as one of the major obstacles to the success of eCommerce. A recent survey by the US Congress of major US corporations has shown that 75% of eCommerce companies executives indicated that they lacked confidence in the Internet as a vehicle of eCommerce because of its vulnerability from trust related issues [11]. It has also been reported that in 1999, consumers lost to Internet fraud was over US$3.2 millions and this is increasing every year [1]. This has affected consumers' trust towards online business. Since consumers are the initiators of the transactions in the business to consumer (B2C) segment, creating trust toward merchants, hereby referred to as "merchant trust", will be important especially for non-digital goods where the transaction cannot be completed instantaneously. Due to the scope of Internet coverage and the nature of eCommerce operations, the creation of merchant trust mostly depends on the information provided by the merchants web sites. In this paper we propose an information model for creating a merchant trust. In the next sections, we describe the model and the proposed initial architecture for its implementation.

H. Yin et al. (Eds.): IDEAL 2002, LNCS 2412, pp. 243–248, 2002.

2   Related Work

Trust has been identified as an important subject in many domains and has been studied in many areas for different reasons as a consequence, many definitions were given. For the purpose of this paper, we adopt the definition that has been frequently cited in the trust literature when related to eCommerce [9]. Trust has been defined as:

> "the willingness of a party to be vulnerable to the action of another party based on the expectation that the other will perform a particular action important to the trustor, irrespective of the ability to monitor or control that other party."

Several trust models have been proposed in the literature [2,7,8,9,12,13]. [12] suggested that there are generally three types of trust: calculated based trust, stable knowledge-based trust and stable identification based-trust. [7,6] extended the work of [12] by looking at the development of trust from one type to another. While these two models are for understanding trust in general, the others are closely related to eCommerce. For example, [2] has developed a model of trust development in eCommerce from the consumer buying behaviour point of view. [13] proposed a generic model of trust requirements for Internet transactions, and they have identified two trust determinants: trust in the other party and trust in electronic mechanism. [8,9] gave more specific requirements for trust creation. Both of them agreed that benevolence, ability and integrity are key requirements for creating trust towards the other parties involved in a trust relationship.

3   The Proposed Model

The proposed model is based on the relationship between trust and risk as well as control. According to [9], one of the important aspects of trust in eCommerce that needs to be addressed is its association with the element of risk. By definition, the need of trust appears when the perceived risk in a relationship is present [5]. As trust declines, people become increasingly unwilling to take risks and demand a greater protection against the probability of betrayal [11]. The relationship between trust and risk can be described as a positive correlation [13]. In other words, the higher the risk, the higher the level of trust is needed. However, trust has a negative correlation with control. Therefore, trust creation can be enhanced by giving more control to the trustor [13]. By having more control, the trustor can reduce the perceived risk, which in turn will reduce the level of trust needed in the relationship. Meanwhile, the model proposed by [8,9] shows that benevolence, ability and integrity are key requirements for creating trust towards other parties involved in the trust relationship.

Our model, is proposing to convey the above mentioned factors to consumers while they are shopping at a merchant's web site. Information such as merchant existence, affiliation, policy and performance can generate merchant trust by factor of benevolence, ability and integrity. However, the importance level of each information will be based on individual trust propensity [8,9]. Based on the above arguments, the proposed model is shown in Figure 1

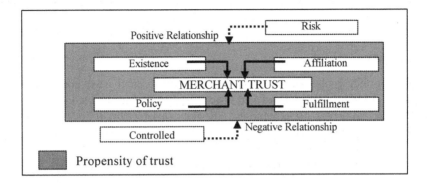

Fig. 1. A proposed information framework for merchant trust in eCommerce

3.1   Existence

Trust is a relationship between two or more parties. Therefore, in a trust relationship the existence of the parties involved need to be first established before trust can be developed between them. Since consumers are the initiators of eCommerce transactions, merchants need to communicate that they really exist behind their website. Providing information about the company's physical existence such as address and telephone number can convey the message that the company is reachable from outside cyber world which in turn will give more control and alternatives to the user to initiate communication when needed. In addition, providing information regarding registration with certain governmental bodies increase the trust. Information such as the company's registration number and the registering body help the consumer to verify the merchant validity.

3.2   Affiliation

A strong trust relationship can be established between two parties if it is being developed through direct experience. As stated in [2], "trustworthiness is about experience over time where the process of creating trust between two parties is dynamic and continuous". A series of successful trust relationships will deepen the relationship but it can also be easily destroyed by one unsuccessful trust relationship. For the new users, recommended trust can be used to establish initial trust relationship [2,10]. Several possible methods of affiliation that can be looked at closely in eCommerce environment are third party endorsement, membership registration and portal linkages. The influences of third party endorsement for example will become more significant to unknown merchants where the perceived risk is higher than well-known merchant like Amazon.com. Membership registration to certain bodies and organisations can be used to create recommended trust in areas where skill and expertise is important. Merchant trust can also be sparked through the digital entrance affiliation or portal. Well-trusted portals usually gather trusted merchants in their digital supermarket.

3.3   Policy

Merchant policy is also important in creating merchant trust in consumers since it sets the guidelines for method and procedure in running the business. In eCommerce, policies such as privacy policy, customer satisfaction policy and guarantee policy can help consumers to evaluate the trustworthiness of a merchant. Consumer satisfaction policies and guarantee policies are very important since they can influence the level of risk involved in the transaction. Policy such as money back guarantee can lower the consumers' risk by giving more control to the user towards the output of the transaction since they can return the product without total loss if they are not satisfied with their quality. As stated in many researches, one of the main factors that hindered consumer from being involved actively in the digital market is related to consumer privacy [2,3]. Consumers are afraid that their personal data will be sold to other parties or being used in marketing databases. It is important for eCommerce websites to specify their privacy policy or privacy statement.

3.4   Fulfillment

It is important for merchant websites to communicate their ability to fulfill their duties with regards to delivery and payment methods to consumers. Since the consumers have fulfilled or partially fulfilled their duty to pay for the goods in the transaction instantly when completing the online transaction by providing credit card details for example, merchants need to tell the consumers how and when they will deliver the product. The information that needs to be included for example is the delivery method, the company's name and order tracking method.

Tracking the merchant's reputation is considered to be an antecedent toward establishing trust environment towards the merchant [4]. Reputation conveys some information about the merchants' performance as well as behaviour in the past. A positive reputation can create basic building block of merchant trust and carry some assumption that the merchant will perform and behave in the same manner in the future.

4   The Model

Searching and evaluating information on the Web can be a tedious and frustrating task. Asking consumers to find information for establishing merchant trust based on the suggested model can create a negative shopping experience.

Therefore, the proposed model should be accompanied by tools that can help the consumer to find and evaluate the required information in a transparent manner. A personal software agent is suggested as the implementation tool to help consumers perform this task. The agent's overall objective is to find and establish trust toward merchants while they are shopping on-line. The proposed agent will be running at the back of a shopping session as a semi-autonomous agent requiring minimal intervention from the user to start its operation. The agent is only using the information provided by the merchant's website and other sites that have direct linkages to it. The overall development will be based on the architecture given in Figure 2.

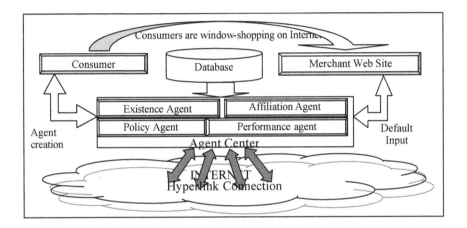

Fig. 2. Overall Architecture of the Trust Framework

The process of evaluating information for merchant trust is initiated by a consumer's request. When a consumer is online and wish to know more about the merchant he is currently visiting, he can initiate the agent at any stage during a shopping session.

A typical scenario would start with the initiation of the agent by the consumer for a specific merchant. The agent will first check if there is any previous evaluation of the merchant. If there is one then the consumer will have the choice between using the existing information or launch a new search. Because different consumers may give different importance to the various factors of the trust model, the consumer may provide different weights to the different factors. A new search request to the agent centre will involve in general the launch of 4 "sub-agents". These are the existence agent, affiliation agent, performance agent and policy agent. These sub-agents are designed to find and evaluate related information as specified in the framework in order to establish merchant trust score. The agent centre will distribute the information from the consumer request to relevant sub-agents. For example, sub agent existence will try to find information about merchant existence in the main page such as address, telephone number and others as specified in the information trust model. If the information is not available in the main page, the existence agent will look at the linkages provided by agent center to be explored. Linkage to the section such as "company background", "contact information" or "about us" will be explored by the existence agent in order to find the information required to establish the score. Other sub-agents will perform similar processes.

Each information extracted from the web site that has been identified as a merchant trust information factor will score certain points. The summation of all four sub-agents scores will establish merchant which will be reported back to the consumers.

5 Conclusion

In this paper we presented a model for eCommerce trust for the business to consumer segment. This model is based on four main type of information, existence, affiliation, policy and performance. A software agent is suggested as a possible implementation of this model to facilitate its use by consumers.

References

1. S. Ba. Establishing online trust through a community responsibility system. *Decision Support Systems*, (13):323–336, 2001.
2. Cheskin Research and Studio Archtype/sapient. ecommerce study trust. WWW, http://www.studioarchetype.com/cheskin/assets/images/etrust.pdf, 1999.
3. D. L. Hoffman, T.P. Novak, and M. Peralta. Building consumer trust online. *CACM*, 42(4), 1999.
4. S. Jarvenpaa, N. Tractinsky, and M. Vitale. Consumer trust in an internet store. *Information Technology and Management Journal*, 1(1-2):45–47, 2000.
5. K. Konrad, G. Fuchs, and J. Barthel. Trust and electronic commerce - more than a technical problem. In *Proceeding of the 18th IEEE Symposium on Reliable Distributed Systems*, pages 360–365, Lausanne, Switzerland, 1999.
6. R. M. Kramer and T. R. Tyler, editors. *Trust in Organization: Frontiers of Theory and Research*. Sage Publication, Thousand Oaks, CA, 1996.
7. R. J. Lewicki and B. B. Bunker. *Developing and maintaining trust in work relationship*, pages 114–139. In Kramer and Tyler [6], 1996.
8. K. O. Matthew and E. Turban. A trust model for consumer internet shopping. *International Journal of Electronic Commerce*, 6(1):75–91, 2001.
9. R.C. Mayer, J.H. Davis, and F.D. Schoorman. An integrative model of organizational trust. *Academy of Management Review*, 20(3):709–734, 1995.
10. A. Noteberg, E. Christiaanse, and P. Wallage. The role of trust and assurance service in electronic channels: An exploratory study. In *Proceeding of the Information Industry Outlook Conference*, pages 472–478, Charlotte, North Carolina, 1999.
11. P. Ratnasingham. The importance of trust in electronic commerce. *Internet Research: Electronic Networking Applications and Policy*, 8(4):313–321, 1998.
12. D. Shapiro, B. H. Sheppard, and L. Cheraskin. Business on a handshake. *The Negotiation Journal*, pages 365–378, October 1992.
13. T. Tao-Huan and W. Theon. Towards a generic model of trust in electronic commerce. *International Journal of Electronic Commerce*, 5(2):61–74, 2001.

MASIVE: A Case Study in Multiagent Systems

Goran Trajkovski

Towson University, 8000 York Road, Towson, MD 21252, USA
GoranTrajkovski@cs.com

Abstract. The project MASIVE (Multi-Agent Systems Interactive Virtual Environments) is the multi-agent extension of our Interactivist-Expectative Theory on Agency and Learning (IETAL). The agents in the environment learn expectations from their interactions with the environment. In addition to that, they are equipped with special sensors for sensing akin agents, and interchange their knowledge of the environment (their intrinsic representations) during their imitation conventions. In this paper we discuss the basics of the theory, and the social consequences of such an environment from the perspective of learning, knowledge dissemination, and emergence of language.

1 Introduction

Our work in the domain of the IETAL theory during the past years, [7], we have focused on exploring the concept of learning the environment by the autonomous agent, and the problems that it encounters during its stay there. The key concepts of IETAL are those of expectancy and learning through interactions with the environment, while building an intrinsic model of it. Depending on the set of active drives, the agent uses the appropriate projection of its intrinsic model in order to navigate within the environment on its quest to satisfy the set of active drives. Every row of the contingency table is attributed an emotional context, depending on the combination of the active drives in a given moment in time.

In this paper we outline our MASIVE theory, which is the multi-agent, [3], version of IETAL. The agents are homogenous, and posses a sensor for other agents of the same kind in the environment. While sensing each other, the agents exchange their contingency tables, and continue exploring the environment they are in. This approach is inspired by results from both neurophysiology and psychology on the phenomenon of imitation [2], [4].

The paper is organized as follows. In Section 2, we briefly overview the basics of the IETAL theory. Section 3 reviews the process of building the intrinsic representation in the agents. Section 4 discusses MASIVE and various aspects of it, such as social structures, and emergence of language in the multiagent society. The last section overviews the paper and gives directions for further research.

H. Yin et al. (Eds.): IDEAL 2002, LNCS 2412, pp. 249–254, 2002.

2 IETAL Preliminaries

The notion of expectancy has a central role in IETAL, in which we bring attention to the notion of being in a world and define it as a faculty of an agent to anticipate the effects of its own actions in the world. This means that, given some current percept p the agent can generate expectancies about the resulting percepts p_1, p_2,... if it applies actions a_1, a_2,... After inhabiting some environment for certain time, an agent builds a network of such expectancy triplets p_i-a_j-p_k, which brings us to the second key concept in the theory - agent environment interaction. Given an agent with its sensors and actuators and the environment it inhabits, a structure emerges because of their interaction, [8].

Due to the fact that two locally distinct places in the environment can be perceived the same due to the sensory limitations of the agents, the notion of perceptual aliasing, [1], is also taken into consideration.

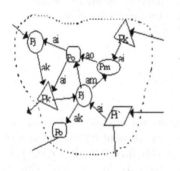

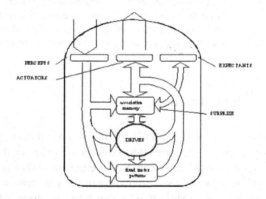

Fig. 1. Agent-environment interaction represented as polychromatic oriented graph, [7],[10]. The labels of the vertices are the percepts, and the edges are the actions from the agent's repertoire. By applying an action, the agent gets to a place that is perceived as the label of the endpoint of the corresponding edge.

Fig. 2. Architecture of the autonomous agent Petitagé, an instantiation of IETAL, [7]. All the agents that inhabit the multi-agent environment discussed in Section 4 comply to this architecture. Unlike the agents that inhabit uniagent environments, the agents in the multi-agent environments have a sensor that senses other akin agents, and the drive to sense them is the top of the lattice of their drives. Note that the drives have a central role in the architecture.

The main problems in this setting therefore are: first, to learn the environment (or at least a partition of it) and second, to know how to use it, so there is no more need to spoon-feed the agent with the needed partitioning. We don't believe that it is crucial for the agent to build the model of the whole graph, which is a biologically implausible task. What an agent could have at best is some partial model of its environment, which is constantly being revised according to the environmental changes. The agent assimilates the environment and then accommodate to it. So, the success of the agent is not measured in terms of how well it has "learned" the graph but rather how well it uses its expectancy network to satisfy currently active drives.

3 Intrinsic Representations

In this section, we propose an algorithm for building the intrinsic representation (IR) of the agent, [10]. The IR's contingency table, where every row is attributed an emotional context, dependant on the active drive and the actuality/usability of the actual entry in the table, which is evaluated against the expectancies.

```
Generate_Intrinsic_Representation (G: Interaction_Graph,
            ξ: Schema; GIR: Assotiative_Memory)
BEGIN_PROCEDURE
        Initialize (RΔ=∅); Initialize_Position (G; Position);
        Try (Position, ξ; (B1, S1));
        Add ( [(λ, λ), (B1,S1)]; RΔ);
        WHILE (Active_Drive_Not_Satisfied) DO
                Try (Position, ξ; (B2, S2));
                Add ([(B1, S1), (B2, S2)]; RΔ);
                (B1, S1):=(B2, S2);
        END_WHILE
        Propagate_Context ( (B1, S1), drive; GIR).
END_PROCEDURE
Try (Position: Location_In_Interaction_Graph, ξ: Schema;
    (B, S): Percepts_Actions_Pair)
BEGIN_PROCEDURE
        S:=λ;
        TryIn (Position, ξ; (Add (S, Current_Percept), B));
        REPEAT
                TryIn (Position, B; (Add (S, Current_Percept), B)
        UNTIL NOT enabled (B)
END_PROCEDURE
Propagate_Context (d: drive; GIR: Assotiative_Memory)
BEGIN_PROCEDURE
        N:=0;
        WHILE (B1, S1) ∈ Projection2 (GIR) DO
                Context/Projection3(GIR) := exp(-N);
                INC (N)
        END_WHILE
END_PROCEDURE
```

Fig. 3. The IR algorithm

Apart from the drives, every agent is equipped with an inborn schema ξ (sequence of actions from the agent's actions repertoire) that it is trying to execute in full, which is sometimes impossible, due to the topology of the environment, so only subschemas of ξ execute. Depending on the percepts and the actions that "fired" out of the schema, new rows are added to the contingency table for the active drive RΔ. Initially, at the moment when the agent enters the new environment, the table is empty. The symbol λ in Fig 3 is used as a token for no action.

4 MASIVE: The World of Petitagés

With the increasing complexity of the artificial agents within the embodied mind paradigm, more effective ways of learning (better than direct programming) in those artifacts are needed. This status of the affairs renewed the interest in learning by imitation (or learning by watching; teaching by showing). Thorndike [9] defines it as "[imitation is] learning to do an act from seeing it done, whereas Piaget [5] mentioned as a major part when offering his theory for development of the ability to imitate going through six stages. Rizzolatti et al, [6], discover the so called "mirror neurons" - neurons that fire while one is performing some motor actions or look at somebody else doing the same action.

In MASIVE, the individual agents-Petitagés (Fig 2) are equipped with a special sensor that is sensing other Petitagé-like agents. While in the imitating mode, the agents exchange their contingency tables. The tables (of both, or selected agents, according to social hierarchies discussed later) are being updated by new rows.

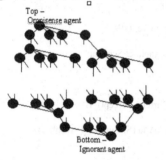
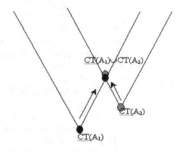

Fig. 4. All possible states of the agents in the multiagent environment, ordered by knowledge (in terms of rows in the contingency tables).

Fig. 5. After the imitation, both of the agents are being propagated upwards towards their union in the lattice in Figure 4. CT stands for Contingency Table, A₁ and A₂ are agents.

4.1 Social Hierarchies

The social hierarchies that may define the direction of the information interchange, in case of limitation to the imitation conventions and information interchange can range over a plethora of measures that would define those hierarchies. One of those measures is the age (time spent in the environment). The question that arises is if an "older" agent carries more information on the environment in its IR. Depending on the place in the environment it was initially put at, the agent could have learned well a very limited portion of the environment, where it has been able to satisfy all the drives that become active. Therefore the contents of its contingency tables could be very limited, as compared to younger agents who "experienced" a bigger portion of the environment.

The size of the contingency table (CT) could be another measure that can define a hierarchy in the multi-agent world. However, we would have the same problems as in the case of age-based hierarchies, discussed above.

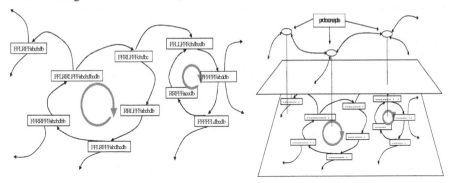

Fig. 6. The agent's conceptualization of the environment depicted via the rows of the contingency tables.

Fig. 7. The rows of the tables as protoconcepts are exchanged between the agents.

The age, and CT-size are ordering relations that define a linear ordering in the agents. However, if we observe the CT ordering by set-inclusion, there might be agents that are incomparable. The hierarchy ordering is not linear any more, and could be a vary general relational structure, a substructure of the Boolean lattice presented in Fig. 4.

The problem of inability to exchange the whole contingency tables due to hardware or time constraints is a practical constraint that needs to be taken into serious considerations while simulating a multiagent environment inhabited by Petitagé-like agents. These tendencies are also biologically justifiable.

4.2 The Protolanguage in MASIVE

The rows of the contingency tables are interpreted as protoconcepts in MASIVE. By exchanging rows of the tables, the agents are exchanging concepts. Any convention on tagging the concepts (rows) is considered a protolexeme. And that is where the protolanguage in MASIVE emerges. The process of emergence of the concepts is depicted in Fig. 6 and 7. Figure 6 shows how the agent conceptualizes the environment while building its IR of it. Figure 7, on the upper level, has the contingency table of the agent. The contingency table is the relation whose graph is depicted on the upper level. Its vertices are the protoconcepts in the theory.

5 Conclusions and Further Work

Expectancy, interaction, and imitation are central concepts in our theory. In MASIVE, the drive to imitate is the highest on the hierarchy of drives of all agents. After the convention of two agents, they interchange their contingency tables, and continue to explore the rest of the environment. The problems associated with the imitation stages and the changes in the agents have been observed from different angles.

The abundance of approaches towards multiagent systems that are not necessarily compliant with the mainstream AI, give us the motivation to explore further the theory. In an upcoming stage of our research, we will simulate the World of Petitagés, and explore the problems that such a simulation will reveal, for, eventually, a successful robot implementation of the approach.

We have already started investigating human uniagent and multiagent collaborative systems in our POPSICLE (Patterns in Orientation: Pattern-Aided Simulated Interaction Context Learning Experiment) experiment, [11], form the perspective of IETAL and MASIVE theories.

References

1.   Bozinovski, S., Stojanov, G., Bozinovska L., "Emotion, Embodiment, and Consequence Driven Systems", 1996 AAAI Fall Symposium, **FS-96-02** (1996) 12-17.
2.   Byrne R.W.,, Russon, A.E. " Learning by Imitation", Behavioral and Brain Sciences (2001).
3.   Ferber, J: Multi-Agent Systems: An Introduction to Distributed Artificial Intelligence, Addison-Wesley, 1999.
4.   Nehaniv, C., Dautenhahn, K. Mapping between dissimilar bodies: Affordances and the algebraic foundations of imitation. Proceedings of the Seventh European Workshop on Learning Robots Edinburgh , UK (1998) pp. 64--72.
5.   Piaget, J Play, Dreams, and Imitation in Childhood. New York: Norton, .1945.
6.   Rizzolatti G, Fadiga L, Gallese V, Fogassi L, Premotor cortex and the recognition of motor actions. Cognitive Brain Research, **3**(2) (1996) 131-141
7.   Stojanov, G., Bozinovski S., Trajkovski, G "Interactionist-Expectative View on Agency and Learning", IMACS Journal for Mathematics and Computers in Simulation, North-Holland Publishers, Amsterdam, Vol. **44** (1997).
8.   Stojanov, G., Trajkovski, G., Bozinovski, S. "The Status of Representation in Behavior Based Robotic Systems: The Problem and A Solution", IEEE Conference Systems, Man, and Cybernetics, Orlando (1997).
9.   Thorndike, E.L. "Animal intelligence: an experimental study of the associative process in animals" Psychological Review Monograph **2**(8) (1898) 551-553.
10.   Trajkovski, G., Stojanov, G., "Algebraic Formalization of Environment Representation", in (Tatai, G., Gulyas, L. (eds)) Agents Everywhere, Springer, Budapest, HU (1998) 59-65.
11.   Trajkovski, G., Goode, M., Chapman, J., Swearingen, W., "Investigating Learning in Human Agents: The POPSICLE experiment", KES 2002, Crema, IT (to appear).

Learning Multi-agent Strategies in Multi-stage Collaborative Games

W. Andy Wright

BAE SYSTEMS (ATC)* Sowerby Building, PO Box 5, Bristol, UK.
Andy.Wright@bris.ac.uk

Abstract. An alternative approach to learning decision strategies in multi-state multiple agent systems is presented here. The method, which uses a game theoretic construction which is model free and does not rely on direct communication between the agents in the system. Limited experiments show that the method can find Nash equilibrium point for 3 player multi-stage game and converges more quickly than a comparable co-evolution method.

1 Introduction

The use of machine learning to determine appropriate decision strategies for multi-agent systems is becoming increasingly important within a number of fields. These include:

- *multiple robotics/UAVs* the coordinated use of multiple platforms potentially provides both computational and performance advantages for navigation and map building [2], and in the performance of manipulative tasks [8].
- *software systems* where the use of coordinated software agents provide an alternative approach to the construction of programs for large involved problems [5].

These examples provide an illustration of the problems that are common in many multi-agent systems. Often the environment that these agents will be placed in is unstructured and uncertain. Furthermore, the system may be complex involving many states and possible actions, this is particularly the case in robotics. The design of a control strategy for such systems, therefore, is expensive since it is often the case that hand crafted b-spoke solutions have to be produced.

An alternative approach is to *learn* appropriate strategies for the individual agents such that they learn to function as a coherent whole. For sequential decision processes reinforcement learning has been shown to provide both a robust and general approach to this problem for *single* decision agents [11]. For multi-agent systems this is not the case. The reward to any agent is not controlled by any single agent but is a function of strategies adopted by all the agents. That is the future expected reward (Q value) for any agent is a function not only of

---

* Currently visiting Fellow in Department of Mathematics University of Bristol.

H. Yin et al. (Eds.): IDEAL 2002, LNCS 2412, pp. 255–260, 2002.

its current and future actions but also those of the other agents. Any learning system, therefore, that attempts to learn an appropriate strategy for a single agent by maximising its expected reward must take into consideration (directly or indirectly) the strategy adopted by the other agents. The difficulty in doing this is ensuring that the process adopted converges since the strategy adopted by the other agents, has also be adapted and so is non-stationary.

It can be shown that the desired fixed points of such a process is a Nash equilibrium [3]. This is the point where that agents adopt a set of strategies where deviation by any agent from their strategy results in an decrease in the expected reward to that agent. Unfortunately, although Nash proved that any game has at least one Nash equilibrium point [9] it has not been possible to produce a learning method that is guaranteed, firstly to converge, and secondly if it does converge find the Nash equilibrium strategies.

One approach to this problem is to treat the agents as coupled reinforcement learners (RL) [10,1,12]. In the Joint Action Learner (JAL), agents derive a belief about the actions of other agents based on sufficient statistics derived from messages passed between the agents about the actions taken in previous states [1]. Unfortunately this method scales like $O(||\mathcal{A}||^N)$, where $||\mathcal{A}||$ is the size of an individuals action space and N is the number of collaborating agents. For large systems involving large numbers of agents, and more importantly systems with multiple states, this approach rapidly becomes impracticable. Consequently, research addressing the problem of learning collaborative strategies for multi-agent systems has been limited to *single stage* repeated 2 player games.

Recent theoretical work [6] has proposed a multi-agent learning method which, for certain restricted games, if it converges, is guaranteed to find the Nash equilibrium. Here the agents act as independent reinforcement learners [1], but importantly evolve their decision strategy at a different rate compared to their estimate of their future expected reward, or Q value.

This paper presents an instantiation of this differential learning (DL) approach. Here the agent learners are "model free" and so do not require explicit knowledge of other agent actions. A limited empirical study shows this approach is able to converge to a set of *mixed* strategies that form the Nash equilibrium for a 3 player multi-stage zero sum game that cannot be found by a comparable Independent Learner (IL) method.

2   Sequential Reinforcement Learning for Multiple Agent

To understand the method it is necessary to extend the usual formalism used for reinforcement learning. Consider a collection $\mathcal{C}$ of n (heterogenous) RL agents, where each agent $i \in \mathcal{C}$ has a finite set of possible actions $a^i \in \mathcal{A}^i(s)$ in each state $s \in \mathcal{S}$ of the system. The vector of actions from all the agents forms a *joint action* $\mathbf{a} = \{a^1, \ldots, a^n\} \in \mathcal{A}$. The decision system is modelled as a series of Markov transitions, with transition probability $P_{s,s'}^{\mathbf{a}} \in P_t : \mathcal{S} \times \mathcal{A} \times \mathcal{S} \rightarrow [0,1]$, where the system moves from one state $s \in \mathcal{S}$ to another $s' \in \mathcal{S}$ under the influence of some policy, $\sigma(s, \mathbf{a})$. The value of an the ith agent's action in state

s is given by the expected reward $Q^i(s, \mathbf{a}) = \sum_{s'} P^{\mathbf{a}}_{s,s'} \left[r^i_{s,s'} + \gamma V^i(s') \right]$, which is also a function of the joint action $\mathbf{a}$. Here $\gamma \in [0, 1]$ is a discount function, $r^i_{s,s'} \in \mathcal{R} : \mathcal{S} \rightarrow \Re$ is the reward given to agent i when the system moves from state s to s' and $V^i(s) = \max_{a^i \in \mathcal{A}^i} Q(s, \mathbf{a})$. The whole system, therefore, is described by the N tuple $\langle \mathcal{S}, \mathcal{A}, P_t, \mathcal{R} \rangle$. If a model free assumption is imposed such that the agents cannot observe each other the learning system can be seen as a set of independent learners [1], coupled by a common reward structure. An agent's Q value now is only a function of its own action a^i and this dramatically eases the scaling problem encountered by the JAL scheme. Unfortunately, the decision process is now *partially observed*. However, this can be overcome if learning process is treated as a process with a *non-stationary* reward structure and a form of Q learning that can track these rewards adopted.

Here an on policy temporal difference learning TD(0) (Sarsa) approach was used and the Q values (which are now only a function of the agent's own action a^i) are updated to give

$$Q_{t+1}(s, a^i) = Q_t(s, a^i) + \alpha_t \left[r + \lambda Q_t(s', a^{i'}) - Q_t(s, a^i) \right] \tag{1}$$

where r is the observed reward, s' is the state observed by the agent by taking action a^i at state s, actions a^i and $a^{i'}$ are obtained by sampling from the Boltzmann distribution

$$\pi(s', a^{i'}) = \frac{\exp(Q_t(s', a^{i'})/T)}{\sum_{b^i \in \mathcal{A}^i} \exp(Q_t(s', b^i)/T)}, \tag{2}$$

$\alpha_t = 1/t$ is a time varying *learning parameter*[1]. To ensure convergence the temperature T in equation 2 was reduced exponentially per iteration t of the Sarsa algorithm [4].

The multi-agent component of this reinforcement learning approach is constructed as follows. Rather than updating all the agents Q values simultaneously the algorithm iteratively selects an agent i and updates Q^i while the other agents' Q values, Q^{-i}, are fixed. However, to adhere DL framework this is only undertaken for few iterations (for the results presented here $N = 5$) ensuring that the estimate $\hat{Q}^i$ does not converge faster than the policy. To overcome any cycles in the learning process the agents play what is termed "best response with error" [7] by adopting a strategy based on the Boltzmann distribution (equation 2). The Q^i is then updated such that

$$Q^i_{\tau+1}(s, a^i) = \delta \hat{Q}^i(s, a^i) + (1 - \delta) Q^i_\tau(s, a^i), \tag{3}$$

where $0 < \delta < 1$ is a constant. This process is then repeated for all $i \in \mathcal{C}$ this gives one epoch enumerated by τ. The whole procedure then repeated until the value functions for all the agents has converged.

---

[1] Note that $\sum_t^\infty \alpha_t = \infty$ and $\sum_t^\infty (\alpha_t)^2 < \infty$ ensuring convergence.

3   Results

The utility of this method is demonstrated on a simple predator pray game introduced here. The game although simple in conception involves a number of agents together with a variable number of states and stages. Furthermore, the solution to this game can only be obtained if the agents adopt a cooperative but randomised *mixed* strategy [13]. That is the optimal policy for a given agent requires it to select an action with a probability $Pr = \sigma(s, a^i) < 1$ for certain states. Previous research [1,10] has only looked at repeated single stage games where it is only necessary for the agents to adopt a *pure* strategy in a given state (i.e. $Pr = \sigma(s, a^i) = \delta_{ik}(s)$). Consequently this problem provides a radical departure from the usual single stage multi-agent test problems.

Specifically the game involves two distinct types of player: two *Monsters* whose only aim is to catch the second type, a single *Princess*. The players are placed on a ring of positions. Each player is able to move around the ring or stay still by taking one of three possible actions *move clockwise, move anti-clockwise, stay still*. The players are placed randomly, using a uniform distribution, on the ring at the start of the game at time $t = 0$. At each time step all the players act simultaneously. It is also assumed that the players have no memory. The aim of the Monster is to catch the Princess by placing itself, at the same time on the same ring position as the Princess. If either Monster catches the Princess both Monsters receive a reward of +1 while the Princess gets a reward of -2. At any other time step, where the Princess is not caught, the Monsters receive a reward of -1 and the Princess a reward of +2. At any time the Monsters are able to pass over each other, as they are the Princess, and further are able to occupy the same position as each other. Thus if the Monsters are taken as a collaborative pair then this game is zero sum.

In addition to the restrictions on the players actions the range of their perception is also restricted. That is all the players can only see a limited number of positions to either side of itself. Specifically, a Monsters/Princess is only able to detect the relative position of the Princess/Monster to itself when the Princess/Monster is within a range of one position either side of it. The Monsters are unable to detect the relative position of each other. Where both Monsters are within the perceptual range of the Princess but are equi-distant from the Princess then it is assumed that the Princess can only see one of the Monsters with probability 0.5. These restrictions were introduced for two reasons. The limitation on the perceptual range of the of the players is to approximate the finite range of any sensory system of the predator or prey. The rather artificial restrictions on the Princess only being able to see one Monster and that neither Monster is able to see the each other were introduced to reduce the size of the state space for the two player types consequently simplify the game theoretic analysis of the game making it tractable.

Analysis of this game [13] is very involved and so cannot be presented within the confides of this paper. However, the analysis shows that the Nash strategy for both players is to adopt a *mixed* strategy. Specifically there is no *fixed* action that provides the best strategy for either the Monsters or Princess in those positions where the Monsters can detect the Princess. This follows if one considers possible strategies that the Monster may adopt. If it adopts a strategy of always attacking the Princess when it detects her then the Princess by simultaneously moving toward the Monster can jump over the Monster preventing capture. Similarly if the Monster does not attack anticipating the Princess jumping toward it then the Princess can stay still in anticipation of this. Significantly, there is *always* a strategy that the Princess can adopt to avoid capture if the Monsters adopt a pure strategies. Analysis shows that the Nash strategy for the Monster is to attack with probability $p_a(D)$, where D is the size of the ring, and stay still with probability $p_s(D) = 1 - p_a(D)$ when next to the Princess. Likewise the Princess takes up a strategy that is in equilibrium with the Monster. Here the Princess moves away from the Monster with probability $q_a(D)$ and remains static with probability $q_s(D) = 1 - q_a(D)$. In all other states the Monsters always moves toward the Princess and the Princess stays still until she detects on of the Monsters.

The DL method was used to determine the equilibrium strategies for the Monsters and Princess in this game. Here the method was run to convergence. To ensure that no bias was introduced during the learning process the positions of the agents were randomised every time the game was restarted during the learning process. The results were then compared with those obtained for an IL approach on the same problem. The results[2] for different sizes (D) of ring are shown in table 1. These show that the learning algorithm, at least for this game, were able to find strategies that mirrored the Nash strategies derived theoretically. Importantly, these results differ significantly from those obtained for the IL method which converges to pure strategies. Consequently the IL Monsters are *unable* to catch the Princess.

Table 1. Table comparing theoretical results with those obtained using the learning method.

	D	$1-q$	q	p	$1-p$
Theory	12	0.11	0.89	0.25	0.75
DL	12	0.15	0.85	0.30	0.67
IL	12	0.0	1.0	0.0	1.0
Theory	20	0.12	0.88	0.43	0.57
DL	20	0.16	0.83	0.45	0.52
IL	12	0.0	1.0	0.1	0.9
Theory	30	0.12	0.88	0.55	0.45
DL	30	0.14	0.85	0.52	0.46
IL	12	0.0	1.0	0.0	0.9

---

[2] Note the probabilities obtained from the simulation do not add to unity. This is because player has another action (e.g. for the Monster moving away from the Princess) which the learning method can give a positive, but small, probability.

4   Conclusions

This paper presents a reinforcement learning approach for multiple agents based on sequential learning using a game theoretic best response with errors approach. The method is demonstrated on a three player multi-stage zero-sum cooperative game which has a known theoretical result. The convergence of the method is compared empirically against the co-evolution independent learner (IL) is significantly different. The IL method is unable to find the optimal *mixed* strategy that defines the Nash equilibrium of this game. Specifically the IL method is only able to learn pure strategies which are sub-optimal.

Acknowledgments. This work was supported by Royal Society Industrial Fellowship together with the University of Bristol. The author would like to thank Sean Collins and David Leslie of the Bristol Universities Statistics Group for the help and direction relating to this work.

References

1. C. Claus and C. Boutiler. The dynamics of reinforcement learning in cooperative multi-agent systems. In *AAAI-98*, volume 1, 1998.
2. R.H. Deaves, D. Nicholson, D. Gough, and L. Binns. Multiple robot systems for decentralised SLAM investigations. In *SPIE*, volume 4196, page 360, 2000.
3. D. Fudenberg and D.K. Levine. *The Theory of Learning in Games*. Economic Learning and Social Evolution. MIT Press, 1998.
4. T. Jaakkola, M.I. Jordan, and S.P. Singh. On the convergence of stochastic iterative dynamic programming algorithms. *Neural Computation*, 6:1185–1201, 1994.
5. M. Kearns, Y. Mansour, and S. In UAI 2000 Singh. Fast planning in stochastic games. In *UAI*, 2000.
6. D. Leslie and S. Collins. Convergent multiple-timescales reinforcement learning algorithms in normal form games. Submitted to Annals of Applied Probability, 2002.
7. J.M. MacNamara, J.N. Webb, T. Collins, E.J. Slzekely, and A. Houstton. A general technique for computing evolutionary stable strategies based on errors in decision making. *Theoretical Biology*, 189:211–225, 1997.
8. J. M. Maja. Behavior-based robotics as a tool for synthesis of artificial behavior and analysis of natural behavior. *Trends in Cognitive Science*, 2(3):82–87, 1998.
9. J.F. Nash. Non-cooperative games. *Annals of Mathematics*, 54:286–295, 1951.
10. M. Tan. Multi-agent reinforcement learning: Independent vs cooperative agents. In *Proceedings of the tenth international conference on machine learning*, pages 330–337, 1993.
11. C.J.C.H. Watkins and P. Dyan. Q-learning. *Machine Learning*, 8:279–292, 1992.
12. W.A. Wright. Sequential strategy for learning multi-stage multi-agent collaborative games. In Georg Dorffner, Horst Bischof, and Kurt Hornik, editors, *ICANN*, volume 2130 of *Lecture Notes in Computer Science*, pages 874–884. Springer, 2001.
13. W.A. Wright. Solution to two predator single prey game: The two monster single princess game. In preparation, 2002.

Emergent Specialization in Swarm Systems

Ling Li, Alcherio Martinoli, and Yaser S. Abu-Mostafa

California Institute of Technology, Pasadena, CA 91125, USA

Abstract. Distributed learning is the learning process of multiple autonomous agents in a varying environment, where each agent has only partial information about the global task. In this paper, we investigate the influence of different reinforcement signals (local and global) and team diversity (homogeneous and heterogeneous agents) on the learned solutions. We compare the learned solutions with those obtained by systematic search in a simple case study in which pairs of agents have to collaborate in order to solve the task without any explicit communication. The results show that policies which allow teammates to specialize find an adequate diversity of the team and, in general, achieve similar or better performances than policies which force homogeneity. However, in this specific case study, the achieved team performances appear to be independent of the locality or globality of the reinforcement signal.

1 Introduction

Swarms of relatively simple autonomous agents can exhibit complex behavior which appears to transcend the individual ability of the agents. Perhaps the most striking examples are from nature: social insect colonies are able to build sophisticated structures and regulate the activities of millions of individuals by endowing each individual with simple rules based on local perception. Swarm intelligence is an innovative computational and behavioral metaphor for solving distributed problems that takes its inspiration from the behavior of social insects [1] and swarming, flocking, herding, and shoaling phenomena in vertebrates [2].

Artificial swarm systems based on swarm intelligence are truly distributed, self-organized, and inherently scalable since there is no global control or communication. The agents are designed to be simple and interchangeable, and may be dynamically added or removed without explicit reorganization, making the collective system highly flexible and fault tolerant. One of the domains in which the swarm intelligence approach has been successfully applied is collective mobile robotics. In this paper, we will present a specific case study in this domain previously investigated using hand-coded solutions only. We will show that distributed learning represents an effective method for automatically selecting individual control parameters, which in turn influence the team performance.

Martinoli and Mondada [3] and successively Ijspeert et al. [4] investigated collaboration in groups of reactive, non-communicating robots engaged in a stick pulling experiment (see Fig. 1). In this experiment, a team of robots search a circular arena and pull sticks out of holes in the ground. The length of a stick

H. Yin et al. (Eds.): IDEAL 2002, LNCS 2412, pp. 261–266, 2002.

Fig. 1. Physical set-up for the stick pulling experiment.

has been chosen so that a single robot is not capable of pulling a stick out on its own. Collaboration between two robots is necessary for solving this task. Each robot is characterized by a gripping time parameter (GTP), which is the length of time that a robot waits for the help of another robot while holding a stick. Two cases can occur: either a second robot helps the first one (we define this as a successful collaboration) or the GTP expires before any other robot can help and the first robot resumes the search for sticks in the arena. The specific values of GTPs play a crucial role in the overall collaboration rate (defined as the number of successful collaborations per unit time), which is the metric adopted in both previous papers as well as in this one for measuring the team performance.

In addition to experiments performed using real robots and sensor-based, embodied simulations, Ijspeert et al. proposed a microscopic model which delivered both qualitatively and quantitatively accurate predictions. In this paper, we exploit this result by integrating our distributed learning algorithms into their microscopic model. As a consequence, although we have not tested our learning algorithms using real robots or realistic simulations, we believe that their validity is not limited to abstract agents.

Alternatively, optimal control parameters of a swarm system can be computed with the help of macroscopic models [5]. However, macroscopic models have two major drawbacks in comparison with a machine learning method. First, quantitatively correct macroscopic models based uniquely on features of the individual agents are not always trivial to devise, in particular when agent-to-agent and agent-to-environment interactions are more complicated than simple elastic bounces. Second, these models intrinsically assume that a certain number of agents can be clustered in a caste which in turn is represented by a set of differential or difference equations. In our machine learning approach, we do not assume the existence of any caste (each agent in principle can be different from any other agent) and, if clusters of specialists arise, these are due to the learning process rather than to a priori established categories.

Finally, depending on the size of the search space and the number of agents, a systematic investigation of the optimal individual control parameters (such as that conducted in [4]) could be prohibitively time consuming even allowing for the fact that in this particular case study, microscopic models have been proven to be four or five orders of magnitude faster than real robot experiments.

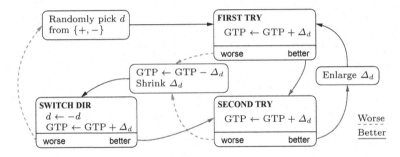

Fig. 2. State graph of the learning algorithm. GTP is adjusted according to the current state and performance change (better or worse). Δ_d is the search step in direction d.

2   Learning Algorithm

The major challenge in designing a distributed learning algorithm able to tune individual parameters so that the team performance is optimized is to solve the credit assignment problem [6] in a system where the information available locally is incomplete and noisy. In our specific case study, the optimal GTPs depend on the number of other robots working together, the environmental characteristics (e.g., number of sticks), and other robots' GTPs. Without global communication and perception, all these conditions can only be estimated by an individual agent.

The learning principle we propose in this paper is intuitively similar to what a human being would do in a partially (locally) known environment (see Fig. 2). The agent first tries to change its GTP in a randomly chosen direction. After the change, the agent maintains that GTP for a small period of time and monitors the performance improvement. If the improvement is positive, the agent will continue in that direction; if negative, the agent will undo the last change and try the other direction. The search step Δ_d can vary between $[\Delta_{\min}, \Delta_{\max}]$ and is adjusted according to the success of the previous try.

Note that in this diagram the change of GTP is linear, meaning that in k periods of time, the maximal change is $k\Delta_{\max}$. We call this linear way of adjusting the GTP the "Δ-method." However, since the collaboration rate is much less sensitive to changes in the GTP when the GTP is large, a more effective search method for large GTPs is to use a search step proportional to the absolute value of the GTP. We call this alternative way of tuning the GTP the "%-method." Since a specific method is more effective than the other in a given part of the search space, in the following we use a hybrid learning algorithm which alternates sequentially both methods.

3   Experimental Results

We ran stick pulling experiments using two to six robots and four sticks. Each run, characterized by different initial GTPs, was repeated 100 times. For each experiment, we first conducted a 1600 min learning phase, during which robots

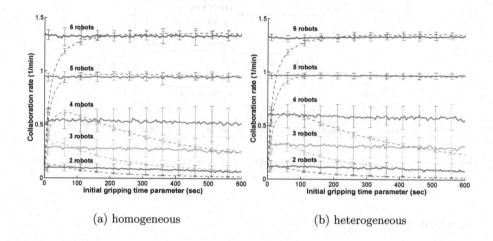

(a) homogeneous   (b) heterogeneous

Fig. 3. The collaboration rates with and without learning for varying number of robots. Robots were initialized with the same GTP. The dashed curves in both plots represent the collaboration rates obtained by systematic search and homogeneous teams while the solid lines show those after learning with (a) global reinforcement and homogeneous teams; or (b) local reinforcement and heterogeneous teams.

could iteratively adapt their GTPs. Then a 1600 min test phase was conducted to measure the performance of the learned solutions. In all of the following plots, the error bars represent the standard deviation over different repetitions.

3.1 Homogeneous Teams

We first investigated homogeneous teams, meaning that all the robots were characterized by the same GTP. We compared systematic hand-coded results with learned solutions using global reinforcement[1].

Figure 3(a) and Fig. 4(b) compare the collaboration rates obtained with and without learning. The collaboration rate consistently achieves the same level, independent of the initial GTP and is above the average collaboration rate obtained with fixed GTPs. With teams of five or six robots, the learning algorithm achieves the optimal average collaboration rate (as obtained in the systematic search) for each initial GTP. This is not the case for teams of two to four robots, although the maximal collaboration rate obtained in the systematic study is within one standard deviation of that reached with learning.

Further studies are needed to understand the limitations of the proposed learning algorithm. In particular we will closely investigate the role of noise affecting the reinforcement on the convergence towards a global optimum.

---

[1] While local reinforcement is more realistic for a swarm system, global reinforcement, which usually implies physically a supervisor that measures and broadcasts the team performance to the individual agents, provides an interesting term of comparison.

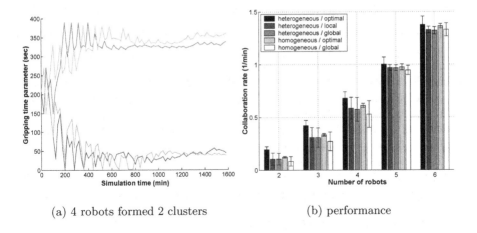

(a) 4 robots formed 2 clusters   (b) performance

Fig. 4. Specialization and performance. (a) 4 robots using the Δ-method had 210 sec as the initial GTP. At the end of the simulation, they formed two clusters, one characterized by a large GTP and the other by a small GTP. (b) Performances obtained with a systematic search and after learning under different reinforcement and team diversity.

3.2 Heterogeneous Teams

For each robot, the local reinforcement is the rate of successful collaborations (regardless of whether a robot was the first or the second in gripping the stick). Figure 3(b) shows the performance after learning outperforms that in the homogeneous teams. In most cases the robots became specialized after learning. Figure 4(a) shows the GTP curves of four robots in a single run. All robots started with the same initial GTP. As the experiment progressed, their GTPs diversified and formed two clusters. Our results are consistent with the results of systematic experiments reported in [4] which showed that, when the number of robots is less than or equal to the number of sticks, specialization is helpful.

The increase in the performance lies essentially in the heterogeneity of the solution, rather than in the learned values themselves. Indeed, a systematic study of all possible GTP combinations (see Fig. 4(b)) has shown that similar problems of noise and convergence found in homogeneous team also exist in this case—learned solutions perform slightly worse than those found by systematic search[2].

For the sake of completeness, following [7] we investigated heterogeneous teams combined with global reinforcement. Once again, probably due to the high alignment of individual and team performances, we did not obtain any significant difference in the quality of the learned solution as a function of the reinforcement type (see Fig. 4(b)).

---

[2] For heterogeneous teams, we tested all GTP combinations where GTP (in seconds) is from the set $\{5k\}_{k=1}^{20} \cup \{10k\}_{k=11}^{15} \cup \{175, 200, 250, 300, 400, 500, 750, 1000\}$.

4   Conclusions

In this paper, we investigated several distributed learning policies based on different reinforcement signals (global and local) and different team diversity (homogeneous and heterogeneous). The discussion was based on a faithful microscopic probabilistic model previously developed for investigating the team performance in a concrete case study in collective robotics (the stick pulling experiment). The results show that policies which allow teammates to specialize find an adequate diversity of the team as a function of the task constraints and, in general, achieve similar or better performances than policies which force homogeneity.

The obtained specialization is an interesting result, since we never explicitly rewarded diversity nor there was any explicit communication between agents. In this specific case study, the achieved team performances appear to be independent of the locality or globality of the reinforcement signal, probably due to the high alignment between both forms of reinforcement.

Acknowledgements. We would like to acknowledge Lavanya Reddy and Eric Tuttle for having implemented a first version of the Δ-method we are using in this paper.

This work was supported by the Caltech Center for Neuromorphic Systems Engineering under NSF Cooperative Agreement EEC-9402726.

References

1. Bonabeau, E., Dorigo, M., Théraulaz, G.: Swarm Intelligence: From Natural to Artificial Systems. Oxford University Press, New York (1999)
2. Parrish, J.K., Hamner, W.M., eds.: Animal Groups in Three Dimensions. Cambridge University Press, New York (1997)
3. Martinoli, A., Mondada, F.: Collective and cooperative group behaviours: Biologically inspired experiments in robotics. In Khatib, O., Salisbury, J.K., eds.: Proceedings of the Fourth International Symposium on Experimental Robotics (1995). Lecture Notes in Control and Information Sciences, Vol. 223. Springer-Verlag, Berlin (1997) 3–10
4. Ijspeert, A.J., Martinoli, A., Billard, A., Gambardella, L.M.: Collaboration through the exploitation of local interactions in autonomous collective robotics: The stick pulling experiment. Autonomous Robots 11 (2001) 149–171
5. Lerman, K., Galstyan, A., Martinoli, A., Ijspeert, A.J.: A macroscopic analytical model of collaboration in distributed robotic systems. Artificial Life 7 (2001) 375–393
6. Versino, C., Gambardella, L.M.: Learning real team solutions. In Weiß, G., ed.: Distributed Artificial Intelligence Meets Machine Learning: Learning in Multi-Agent Environments. Lecture Notes in Artificial Intelligence, Vol. 1221. Springer-Verlag, Berlin (1997) 40–61
7. Murciano, A., del R. Millán, J., Zamora, J.: Specialization in multi-agent systems through learning. Biological Cybernetics 76 (1997) 375–382

Distributed Mobile Communication Base Station Diagnosis and Monitoring Using Multi-agents

J.Q. Feng[1], D.P. Buse[1], Q.H. Wu[1], and J. Fitch[2]

[1] Department of Electrical Engineering and Electronics,
The University of Liverpool, Liverpool L69 3GJ, U.K.
q.h.wu@liv.ac.uk
[2] Network Engineering, The National Grid Company plc,
Leatherhead KT22 7ST, U.K.

Abstract. Most inherently distributed systems require self diagnosis and on-line monitoring. This is especially true in the domains of power transmission and mobile communication. Much effort has been expended in developing on-site monitoring systems for distributed power transformers and mobile communication base stations. In this paper, a new approach has been employed to implement the autonomous self diagnosis and on-site monitoring using multi-agents on mobile communication base stations.

1 Introduction

The world has seen phenomenal growth in the deployment of cellular wireless equipment, with close to 200,000 wireless base stations by the end of 1998. Mobile communication service providers endeavor to offer their customers a stable, high quality communication service. The base transceiver system(BTS) is the most important item of equipment in the base station. The performance of a BTS not only depends on the quality of the BTS equipment itself, but also relates to the base station power supply system and environmental factors.

Base stations are inherently distributed, and many approaches have been tried to implement distributed remote diagnosis and monitoring. Almost all of these attempt to transmit all the real-time monitoring information from the base stations to a central site. However, these approaches are significantly limited, primarily by the long distance and limited bandwidth between the monitoring center and base stations. A secondary limitation is the fragility of the personal computer architecture.

A mobile communication base station includes, among other devices, a BTS and base station controller (BSC). The details of autonomous monitoring and diagnosis of the whole base station are too complex to permit discussion here. Therefore, this paper will focus on the implementation of diagnosis of the power supply system and environmental factors, and on-site monitoring of the base stations.

H. Yin et al. (Eds.): IDEAL 2002, LNCS 2412, pp. 267–272, 2002.

The approach taken to autonomous diagnosis and on-site monitoring is based on multi-agent systems and embedded micro-processors. For the detection of environmental factors, the system utilises autonomous agents, encapsulated as Java entities and embedded within a micro-processor system. These agents interact with the base station power supply's "intelligent self-check" system.

2   The Need for a Multi-agent System

Base stations in a mobile communication system are vital to the radio transmissions. Some complicated diagnosis modules have therefore been embedded into the base transceiver system to monitor the condition of the hardware.

The base transceiver system (BTS) is the main item of equipment for data transmission at the base station, which is controlled by a Base Station Controller (BSC) and transmits and receives signals between the Base Station System (BSS) and mobile terminals between cells. The main functions of the BTS are to encode/decode, modulate/demodulate, interlace/deinterlace, and encrypt/decrypt data carried on different channels using the channel identifications from the BSC. With the introduction of strict quality control procedures, BTS equipment is becoming more and more reliable. However, the power supply modules, which are vital to the system, remain unpredictable, as do faults due to environmental factors. These are therefore the two main priorities for base station diagnosis and monitoring.

2.1   Power Supply Modules and Environmental Factors

With the mobile communication network covering more and more cells, most base stations are located on the top of buildings, along major roads, and even on hills and mountains. In order to provide a reliable communication service, the provision of a small-sized, reliable and efficient power supply at the base station is extremely important. Therefore, more and more base station power supply modules contain embedded self diagnosis and monitoring micro units. Usually, these units offer RS232, RS485 and RS422 industrial communication interfaces for remote monitoring, management and control. Figure 1 shows the basic self diagnosis functions provided by power supply modules. The self diag-

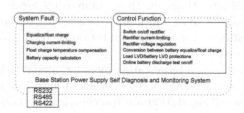

Fig. 1. The power supply module's self diagnosis and monitoring functions

nosis and monitoring micro system can detect many important factors relating to the power supply modules, including float charge system faults, charging current-limiting system faults, etc. Furthermore, the system can perform some routine control operations, such as switching rectifier on or off, rectifier voltage regulation, etc.

Environmental factors include base station temperature and humidity, along with inputs from detectors of motion, water, smoke and broken glass. Because of the large number of microchips contained in the BTS, the temperature and humidity are the most important factors in determining whether the BTS is working under appropriate conditions. The temperature detector is intended to assist in preventing faults which result from unacceptably high temperatures. Smoke and water detectors provide warning of fires and water hazards, while motion and broken glass detectors are intended to prevent theft.

2.2 Why Should a Multi-agent System Be Used?

Base stations are distributed over a wide area. Traditional diagnosis and monitoring systems for base station attempt to centralize the monitoring of all base stations. In these kind of centralize monitoring system, fixed communication channels are set for real-time data transmission. Information from base stations will be lost when these communication channels break up. It will take time to manually reboot the system and to set up the communication channels manually once the sub-monitoring system at the base stations broke down or communication broke up. This means that irreversible damage might occur within the duration of a sub-monitoring system or communication breakdown.

Multi-agent systems are a natural model for the solution of distributed problems [1]. Monitoring and fault diagnosis has been identified as one application area for agent-based systems [2]. The autonomous, self-motivated, intelligent and mobile characteristics of agents made an agent-based system an appropriate solution to meet this application's needs for reliability and flexibility.

3 The Multi-agent System Infrastructure

A diagnosing agent should be able to perform self-testing of its own status and cooperate for system diagnosis with other diagnosing agents[3]. Since more complex devices provide self-checking, this provides an opportunity to reduce the task of diagnosing the system as a whole to the diagnosis of parts of the system and integrate these results on a more complex level [4] [5].

The objective of diagnosis and monitoring system in the base station is to detect the communication power supply system faults events and environmental factors, provides series autonomous reactions to cope with the emergency. There are three major roles in this distributed diagnosis and monitoring system: base station monitoring agent (BMA), mediation agent (mediator) and personal assistant agent (PAA). Figure 2 shows the infrastructure of multi-agents in base station diagnosis and monitoring system.

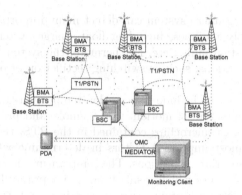

Fig. 2. The multi-agent infrastructure for distributed diagnosis and monitoring

3.1   The Base Station Monitoring Agent

The base station monitoring agent (BMA) performs the major role in this system. The agent is designed as a small Java program embedded in a micro process unit. This unit includes basic analog and digital input/output interfaces along with RS232,RS485, RS422 and T1/modem communication interfaces. Fig. 3 gives a block diagram of the BMA.

More and more power supply modules at base station are now providing a "self-check" micro unit. The BMA communicates with this unit and controls the behavior of the power supply module. In order to do this it monitors the real-time measurements from the analog/digital input interface module to determine whether the temperature of the base station exceeds its upper limit. Fig. 2 shows the cooperation block diagram of the BMA.

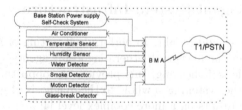

Fig. 3. Block diagram of the base station monitoring agent

3.2   The Mediation Agent

The mediation agent ("mediator") is an agent that mediates between the BMA and the PAA. The mediator is hosted in a server at the mobile communication Operation and Maintenance Center (OMC).

The routine duties of the mediator are to transfer system fault messages and to assist engineers in the maintenance of the base station. For example, if smoke is detected, an alarm will be sent to the BSC via a transparent 64-kbps timeslot of the Abis interface (T1) or a PSTN network. The BSC will then forward the information to the OMC and the mediator agent will deal with the event immediately. The mediator will send a personal assistant agent (PAA) to the personal digital assistant (PDA) or portable monitoring client nearest to the base station at which the fault occurred. Fig. 4 shows the cooperation between the various agents involved in on-site monitoring.

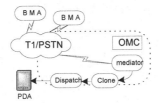

Fig. 4. Block diagram of the mediator

3.3   The Personal Assistant Agent

When a technical support engineer logs into the OMC agent service, a personal assistant agent (PAA) will be dispatched by the mediator to his/her PDA or portable monitoring client. The PAA will then become the engineer's delegate for routine communication and negotiation with the mediator. Furthermore, the PAA can be a be a private secretary to assist the engineer with tasks such as time scheduling, base station maintenance scheduling, etc.

4   Design of Multi-agent System

One of the great benefits of agent-based systems is their ability to generate complex system-level performance from relatively simple individual agents[6]. In the distributed diagnosis and monitoring system, agents provide information access, control and autonomous diagnosis, and adjust the power supply and air conditions in the base station. Information access involves finding, retrieving, and fusing information from a number of heterogeneous sources[7].

In a distributed system, the failure of a network link is indistinguishable from the failure of a processor on the other side of that link[8]. Therefore the system should have the ability to detect the network environment. In this case, base station monitoring agents will connect to the T1 or PSTN network only to transfer information between base stations or when a PAA requests access to an information resource. Upon completion of the transmission, the connection should be terminated to release the communication resource.

The PAA is designed to assist engineers in retrieving information from the distributed base stations. Furthermore, it will monitor the interests of system users in order to improve the quality of service for users.

5   Conclusion and Future Work

Autonomous diagnosis and on-site monitoring of base station power supply and environmental factors using multi-agents achieves highly encouraging results: reduced investment, simplified system maintenance and higher efficiency.

During trials, some issues were encountered that require further investigation, particularly relating to the embedded Java and microchip technology used for the base station monitoring agent. Of these, the most important is the optimization of the learning algorithm and decision model on chip. Resource sharing among base stations and cooperation with the "self-checking" modules of the BTS should also be investigated to fulfil the needs of information retrieval.

References

1. T. J. Norman and N. R. Jennings. "Constructing a Virtual Training Laboratory using Intelligent Agents", *Continuous Engineering and Life-Long Learning*, vol. 12, 2002.
2. Nicholas R. Jennings and Katia Sycara and Michael Wooldridge. "A roadmap of multi-agent research", *Autonomous Agents and Multi-Agent Systems*, 1998, pages 7-38.
3. Michael Schroeder and Gerd Wagner, "Distributed Diagnosis by Vivid Agents". In *Proceedings of the First International Conference on Autonomous Agents (Agents'97)*, 1997, ACM Press.
4. James M. Crawford, Daniel Dvorak et al. "Device Representation and Reasoning with Affective Relations", *IJCAI 1995*, pages 1814-1820.
5. N. R. Jennings, J. M. Corera et al. "Using ARCHON to develop real-world DAI applications for electricity transportation management and particle accelerator control", *IEEE Expert*, vol. 11 no. 6, December 1996, pages 60-88.
6. H. Van Dyke Parunak. "Industrial and Practical Applications of DAI", In Gerhard Weisss, editor, *Multiagent Systems: A Modern Approach to Distributed Artificial Intelligence*, 2000, MIT Press.
7. Matthias Klusch. "Intelligent Information Agents:Agent-based Information Discovery and Management on the Internet", Springer-Verlag Berlin Heidelberg, 1999.
8. Jim Waldo, Geoff Wyant, Ann Wollrath and Sam Kendall. "A Note on Distributed Computing", Sun Microsystems Laboratories Technical Report TR-94-29, 1994.

ABBA – Agent Based Beaver Application – Busy Beaver in Swarm

Alessandro Perrone and Gianluigi Ferraris

1 Introduction

In this paper we follow an "evolutionary approach" to solve the "Busy Beaver Game" using agent based techniques.

In 1962 Tibor Rado proposed one function based on what is known today as the "Busy Beaver Game or Problem".

The question Rado asked was: Suppose a Touring Machine (TM) with a two ways infinite tape and a tape alphabet ={0,1}. What is the maximum number of 1's that can be written by an N-State (N does not include the final state) halting TM when started on a blank tape? This number, which is function of the number of states, is denoted by Σ (N). A machine that produces Σ (N) non-blank cells is called a Busy Beaver (BB).

The problem with Σ (N) is that it grows faster than any computable function, i.e., Σ (N) is non computable. Some values for Σ (N), and the corresponding TM's are known today for small values of N, as described in the following table. As the number of states increases the problem becomes harder, and, for n >= 5, there are some "theoretical" candidates (or contenders) which set lower bounds on the value of Σ (N).

Table 1. The State of the Busy Beaver World

States	BB(n)	Σ (N)
2	4	6
3	6	13
4	13	96
5	4098	47.176.870

Due to these difficulties, the Busy Beaver problem has attracted the attention of many researchers and several contests were organised trying to produce the best candidates.

In this paper we address the problem of finding promising candidates for 2 to 4 state Busy Beaver, following alternative ways for codifying and interpreting Touring Machine, using Agent Based Techniques, and in particular we use the Swarm simulation toolkit to write the "Busy Beaver" game.

Our approach uses a variety of learning techniques such as Genetic Algorithms (GA), Classifier Systems, Multiple GA, Random search to find the "best solution" to the Game.

H. Yin et al. (Eds.): IDEAL 2002, LNCS 2412, pp. 273–278, 2002.

2   The Problem

Busy Beaver (BB) is one of a series of sets of Turing Machine programs. The BBs in the Nth set are programs of N states that produce a larger finite number of ones on an initially blank tape than any other program of N states. Some work has been done to figure out productivities of bigger Busy Beavers - the 7th is in the thousands (22961).

A Touring Machine consists of an infinitely long "tape" with symbols (chosen from some finite set[1]) written at regular intervals. A pointer marks the current position and the machine is in one of a finite set of "internal states". At each step the machine reads the symbol at the current position on the tape. For each combination of current state and symbol read, a program specifies the new state and either a symbol to write to the tape or a direction to move the pointer (left or right) or to halt.

The tape may be infinite in one direction only, with the understanding that the machine will halt if it tries to move off the other end.

BB can be viewed as a tournament of Touring Machines. For each machine that halts, we count the number of 1s on the tape when it halts (we are not interested in machines that do not halt, even though they may produce an infinite number of 1s, as they are not useful for any practical purpose).

Since a machine with more states ought to be able to write more 1s, a fair comparison would be among machines with the same number of states, which leads us to the Busy Beaver Problem.

3   The Model

We build a BB Game based on various competing TM's. Agents are completely independent. Each agent is a TM and exploits independent pseudo-random number generators. Every similar learning Agents are divided in groups. The communication among agents is allowed only within the same group, while there's not any kind of communication among agents of different groups. Each agent looks for transition rules, among the TM states, that will increase by one its production without breaking the game's rules.

There are three kinds of Agent Beavers:

- full-knowledge Beavers, which is composed of agents endowed with a complete set of rules, so that optimal behaviour is granted. We use these agents to guarantee that the model computation is correct. Since their behavior is given, only one "instance" is needed;
- lucky-Based Beavers, which act upon utterly random rules. They do not entertain cost-benefit analysis on their behaviour: they simply "randomize" their strategy each time;
- learning Beavers: they employ three variations of the GA paradigm;

---

[1] The symbol set can be limited to just "0" and "1"

1. Simple GA: Each individual in the population contains the entire set of TM rules
2. Multi-GA: each Beaver employs as many populations as there are admissible TM states. This procedure will evolve those sub-rules that best interact synergetically.
3. Classifier System The search is bounding each experiment conditions (character scanned, number of visited states etc.) to an appropriate action. The rules are choosen accordingly to a good direction.

Each Beaver inherits characteristics and variables of a TM that it will manage by moving the scanner: reading and writing on the tape. Decisions are dictated by the ruleManager related to the Beaver using a specific set of rules.

Agents' independence is guaranteed by the use of separate stocks of norms recorded in special objects: dataWarehouse. The latter contain also information on pseudo-random number distributions specific to each agent.

DataWarehouse contains the complete representation of the agent's knowledge as expressed by the metrics of inference engine adopted. An object in the class Interface will translate the metrics for the agent.

The use of the pair DWh-Interface makes it possible to insert, in a very simple way, new methods of rule management: this can be achieved by codifying for each RuleMaster the relevant objects DataWarehouse and Interface.

A ruleMaster acts upon each dataWarehouse, its role is to select a rule given the problem representation that has reached the agent. RuleMaker will generate new rules departing from those currently contained in the pool available to the agent. "Non-learning" methods do not require a ruleMaker.

To summarize, each Beaver is characterized as an instance of the class Beaver. It encompasses a TM and has the ability to record rules elaborated in past experiences, a DataWarehouse, an Interface, and pseudo-random number generators both in the integer and in the floating point domain.

DWh can create all "accessories": rules, lists, etc, including objects specific to the AI approach adopted.

RuleMaster and RuleMaker are generated in a single instance. They work by loading rules contained in the client's DWh and by employing the specific client's pseudo random number generators.

4   The Environment

Swarm Simulation Toolkit. The model is implemented in Objective-C using the Swarm Simulation Toolkit. In a paper written by the original Swarm Development team, the authors define Swarm as a "multi-agent platform for the simulation of complex adaptive systems". Swarm is a programming library that facilitates both research and teaching in the field of complex systems and agent-based modelling. It is used and supported by a worldwide network of researchers of all fields, from economics to financial ones.

The ERA Scheme The ERA is a proposal to develop ABM distinguishing the environment, the agents and their behavioural rule as different kind of objects. [2] It is a general scheme that can be employed in building agent-based simulations. The scheme dictates the structure of the swarm: the environment is encompassed by ModelSwarm, agents are objects called Beaver and exploit the services provided by rule Managers and Producers. Each of these specializes in a particular production method. The main value of the Environment-Rules-Agents (ERA) scheme, introduced in Gilbert and Terna (2000) is that it keeps both the environment, which models the context by means of rules and general data, and the agents, with their private data, at different conceptual levels.

5   Learning Techniques

Genetic algorithms are probably the most widely known type of EA. Introduced by Holland (1975), they have been developed keeping in mind the goal of a general theory of adaptive systems that communicate with their environment via a set of binary detectors.

Classifiers systems According to Goldberg, *"Genetic Algorithms"*, a classifier system is a machine learning that learns sintactically simple string rules (called *classifiers*) to guide its performance in an arbitrary environment. A classifier system consists of three main components: (1) Rule and message system, (2) Apportionment of credit system and (3) A Genetic algorithm.

6   The Simulation

In order to run a simulation, we need to set a few "initial conditions" which are

1. numberofStati: it represent the number of Busy Beaver's state;
2. maxtran: number of transactions of each beaver;
3. stBeaver: number of Static beaver of the simulation;
4. gmRules: the real GA population, which contain the basic rules evolving every step;
5. cwRules: act on specific rule of CW which handle two types of learning: in the first-run period handle in selecting more fitted and more adapted rles in the settings. In the long-run period it use random values to decide Rulemaler calls. the Rulemaker evolves the rules for next steps It starts with current population whose fitness has been modified during first-step runnings, and obtain a new set of rules;
6. cwGeneLength: define the lengh of the each part of the CW Genoma;
7. gmTurnOverRate: it calcules the number of new "children rules" which will replace the old ones;
8. gmCrossOverRate it is the probability of having a crossover. i.e. mixing the parent-genomas to obtain children-ones;

---

[2] For further info see http://web.econ.unito.it/terna/ct-era/ct-era.html

9. gmMutationRateit is the probability of Genetic Mutation, the probability of each character of childres-rule can nutate.

Once the simulaton runs, on the screen appear 5 windows in which in the first 4 there are 3 graphs representing the reached "learning level" drawing the best solution of TM each type of agent has done, comparing to the average result and the best a priori solution the system knows since the beginning of the simulation, and in last one there's one window in which there are all the graphs.

7   Results

In all the cases the optimal score is known (number of states < 4), the package has found easily a Touring machine that achieve it. We have not still attempted runs for State =5 due to large number of simulation steps it is apparently necessary to run machines for an order to find a new "champion"[3]. Now we'll run an experiment of number of STates = 4.

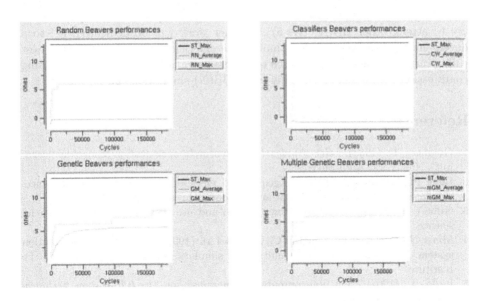

Fig. 1. Result of the simulation

AS we can see from the figure 1[4], the simple AG (GMBeaver) have been best even if he has not caught up the maximum expected. Also the multiplesGenetic

---

[3] The source code of the model along with the results of various experiments with differet TM-States, can be downloaded from the following URL: http://www.alessandroperrone.it, in IDEAL02 link.

[4] The parameters of the simulations are: NumberOfStati=4; MaxTran=150; gmMode=3; stBeaver=mBeaver=gmBeaver=mGmBeaver=cwBeaver=1; gmRules=100; cwRules=16; cwGeneLength=5; gmTurnoverRate=gmCrossoverRate=0.7 and gmMutaion=0.005

(MGMBeaver) have exhibited a good degree of learning. The CW (classifier system) have uncovered some good machines but the average has not conserved them (the average is always under the Zero line): this could depend on the fact that the length of 5 for the rule is not enough. The CW store in the "condition part" a piece of tape and, probably, 5 bytes taken in the middle of the same one, stretch to remain the same after processing, so the condition is always the same and only one rules is taken, while the other "die". The model, even if it has not caught the performance desired, is correct. Infact the STatic beaver go to the result expected (so the TM works well). The randomBeaver, even if achieve good results, exhibits a constant average. The "not so good results" of the other learning techniques can be explained by a "premature convergence" (if GeneticBEaver finds a mean TM, it tends to that one), so we have to work more to choose the right parameters for the GeneticBeaver and the CWBeaver[5].

8   Future Works

In near future, once the authors have access to a multiprocessor computer, we'll try to attack other BB(N) (N>5) . Further work will be dedicated: (1) to a development of the cooperation among different Beavers, by sharing of the best rules every step and (2) to a search of a better representation of the tape, using compression technique, so virtually every BB(N) simulation can be run.

References

1. Goldberg, D. (1989), "*Genetic algorithms* in search, optimization & machine learning", New York, Addison-Wesley
2. Luna F., Perrone A. (2001), "Agent based methods in Economics and Finance: simulations in Swarm", Dordrecht and London, Kluwer Academic Press
3. Gilbert N., Terna P., (2000) "How to build and use agent-based models in social science.", in *Mind and Society*
4. Minar N., Burkhart R., Langton C., Askenazi M. (1996), "The SWARM simulation system: a tool-kit for building multi-agent simulations", working paper Santa Fe Institute
5. Rado, T. (1962), "On non-computable functions", in *The bell System Technical Journal*, vol. 41, no 3, pp 877-884
6. Perreira, Machado, Costa and Cardoso, (1999) "Busy Beaver, an evolutionary approach", *CIMAF-99*, Cuba

---

[5] The result of the simulation is a variety of Touring Machine. In the showed one, the result is the following 4-State TM 00000000010111111111111100 and the system says that the best Beaver was the number 400 of type: 4 (the Multiple Genetic Beaver) who has written 13 one's with 107 transaction

Centralised and Distributed Organisational Control

J.M.E. Gabbai[1], W.A. Wright[2], and N.M. Allinson[1]

UMIST, Manchester M60 1QD, England[1]
BAE SYSTEMS, ATC PO Box 5, FPC 267, Bristol BS34 7QW, England[2]

Abstract. As many systems and organisations are migrating from centralised control to a distributed one, there is a need for a better understanding of organisational behaviour. The implications of such a trend are discussed with reference to current agent technology. A custom simulation, together with some preliminary results, for the investigation of organisational scenarios is presented. Finally, the development of suitable metrics to quantify the efficiency and effectiveness of differing control mechanisms is considered.

1 Background and Motivation

We are living in an intricate world; man-made systems, products and the organisations for their creation and maintenance are becoming increasingly complex, and often exhibit behaviour that is not easily predictable when considering the individual components of the system (*for a vivid example see* [1]). Exhibited behaviours are often unintended and detrimental [2]. Conversely, benefits can be gained when simple systems interact to produce desired complex behaviours where the whole is greater than the sum of its parts [3-6]. Quoting Sir Richard Evans, chairman of the defence company BAE SYSTEMS, "Systems capability has become more important than individual technologies and products. Obviously it's easier to make a single item, however sophisticated, than to integrate it into a large environment of complex devices and understand how it will perform" [7]. This critical issue can be applied not only to products but to entire systems and even organisations that exhibit high levels of interactivity and complexity.

As well as increasing complexity, there is a broad decentralisation trend that is sweeping through many different domains. Organisations are increasing the autonomy of business units and empowering employees aiming to be more flexible and responsive to the needs of rapidly changing environments [8, 9]. National defence is focusing on distributed (*i.e.* spatially and/or temporally separated) systems on the battlefield to increase autonomy and robustness; by reducing centralised top-down control, the sense → act loop is shortened, so allowing faster responses to emerging threats.

The level of autonomy is directly related to the level of centralisation, or *control*, imposed upon a system. With this in mind, control in systems can be characterised along a 'continuum', shown in **Table 1**. At the 'loose' end of the continuum, elements in any system have complete autonomy, there is no control and relationships are random. At the 'tight' end of the continuum, there is no autonomy for individual elements as relationships are fixed or rigid, as in traditional mechanical systems.

H. Yin et al. (Eds.): IDEAL 2002, LNCS 2412, pp. 279-284, 2002.
© Springer-Verlag Berlin Heidelberg 2002

Table 1: Continuum of control and order in systems

Loose end				Tight end	
Description of Control	**No Control**	**Strange Attractors**	**Control without Controlling**	**Command/ Control**	**Total Control**
System Type	Random	Chaotic	Coherent	Top down Command	Mechanistic or Rigid
Relationships	Independent random relationship; anarchy	Random relationships with underlying regularities	Highly ordered interdependent relationships in which the costs of achieving order minimised, i.e. "order for free"	Predominantly dependent relationships. Order is controlled from above with significant added costs	Fully dependent, fixed and immutable relationships

What is not explicit in the table is the change that occurs in two key attributes that vary across the autonomy spectrum, namely the *distribution of control* and *asynchrony of control*. As a system's autonomy becomes less mechanical and more localised, the distribution of the control changes from a top-down command structure to a more individual autonomy. Similarly, the relationship between members moves away from a prescribed, structural nature, to a localised one. This move can be described as an increase in the asynchrony of control.

The middle ground, 'Control without Controlling' is of particular interest as this is where flocking behavioural models apply, where there are prescribed rules but only in a local context. This is also where some organisations and products/systems are moving. It is, therefore, important to explore the mechanisms of this continuum; which position on the continuum is most appropriate to which application and why; how do the properties of the organisational structure, such as hierarchy, hierarchical level, control and specialisation change along this continuum and ultimately, how can an appropriate organisational structure be created and even self-organise to align itself with a changing environment.

Multi Agent Systems (MAS) can be seen as a collection of autonomous entities which interact with each other locally, affecting the global behaviour of a system. Therefore agents are an appropriate way of exploring the questions raised above [10]. Unfortunately the MAS field (e.g. load balancing [11]), while advancing research in the architecture for individual agents and agent communications has placed the exploration of agent society and organisation as a peripheral theme, "primarily a specific coordination technique – not really one of the central intellectual issues of the field" [12]. However, by emphasising the plurality of agents and the organisational structure that binds them, the focus is shifted from designing ((*intelligent agent*) *systems*) to (*intelligent* (*agent systems*)). As agents get smarter, their functionality reduces [13]. For this reason, the following simulation explores external agent interactions in an organisational context.

2 Initial Concept Demonstrator Overview

The Java-based Initial Concept Demonstrator (ICD) creates a multi-agent scenario to examine emergent organisational behaviour of homogenous and heterogeneous agents, as well as centralised and distributed control. The scenario is based on a two-dimensional grid operating a generic "seek, identify and destroy" objective. The agents move randomly around the grid searching for one 'target' amongst 'decoys'. Agents have sensing capabilities, which determine the *sensor range* – the distance an agent can sense a target/decoy but not differentiate between them, and the *threshold range* – the distance an agent can differentiate between targets and decoys.

When a target/decoy is within the sensor range, the agent communicates that a potential target has been found by placing a communication 'sink' around the target/decoy. Agents that can differentiate between targets and decoys and are inside a 'sink' region will travel down this attractor basin. This is a form on non-explicit communication that relies on stigmergy. Sinks can overlap, implying that agents will move down the steepest possible slope. Each simulation scenario is repeated with random start positions of agents, targets and decoys until the average time taken to find the target converges

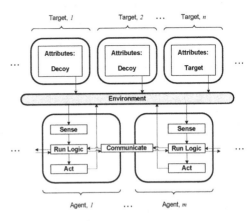

Fig. 1. Agent, target and environment

[14]. The interaction between agents and target/decoys is show in *Figure 1*. A typical heterogeneous agent scenario screen shot is provided in *Figure 2* with explanations.

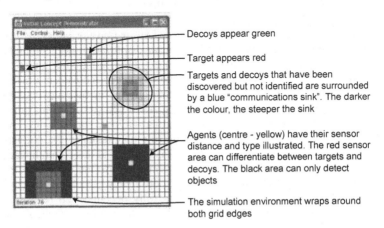

Decoys appear green

Target appears red

Targets and decoys that have been discovered but not identified are surrounded by a blue "communications sink". The darker the colour, the steeper the sink

Agents (centre - yellow) have their sensor distance and type illustrated. The red sensor area can differentiate between targets and decoys. The black area can only detect objects

The simulation environment wraps around both grid edges

Fig. 2. A typical ICD scenario display

3 Simulation Scenarios and Results

The first scenario examines the relationship of centralised, non-explicit (*i.e.* via stigmergy) control over homogenous agents. Centralised control is defined as the ability to impact on agent behaviour. To achieve this, at the start of each simulation, all decoys and targets are initialised with a sink surrounding them. This is the metaphorical equivalent of using a radar-like image of an environment as the basis for coordinating local agent movement. The environment grid size and the agents' sensor range are kept constant, but the number of decoys and sink communication radii are varied. The simulation is illustrated for four and eight homogenous agents. The converged average number of iterations (time) taken to discover the target is shown in Figure 3.

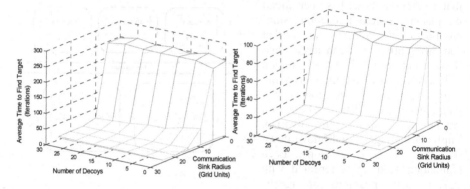

Fig. 3. 4 (left) and 8 (right) homogenous agents, with a sensor range radius of 5 grid units in a 50 by 50 sized grid under centralised control; number of decoys and communication sink radius varied

For both cases, at a communications sink radius between zero and 5 grid units (the agents' sensor range is also 5 grid units), there occurs the equivalent of fully decentralised control, as there is no means of communicating to the agents. There is then a dramatic decrease in the average time taken to find the target, as centralised control takes effect. There is an unexpected result displayed in both simulation runs; as the number of decoys is increased between communication sink radius 10 to 15, there is a *decrease* in the time taken to find the target. An increase in time would be expected, but as the number of decoys is increased, the agents' movement changes from random to ordered, as they are travelling down the sinks. In this small search area, the agents therefore have a greater probability of encountering the target. However at a sink radius of 20 to 25 grid units, the time taken to find the target does in fact increase with the number of decoys. This is because the communication is no longer at a local level, but at a global level - agents perform the same task, increasing redundancy in the organisation and reducing efficiency. Doubling the number of agents from four to eight when the system is fully decentralised reduces the time taken by an average of 162 iterations. Doubling the number of agents when the system is under fully centralised control reduces the time taken by an average of 6 iterations.

The second scenario explores heterogeneous agent combinations under distributed control; there are several agents that can only sense targets/decoys but not differentiate between them ('threshold agents'), and several that can tell the difference ('range agents'). The combination is altered, as indicated in *Figure 4*, which also includes the results and a comparison with the fully centralised scenario for 4 agents with 15 decoys. The grid size is the same as before, and the number of decoys is kept constant at 15.

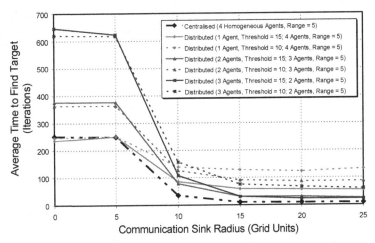

Fig. 4. Various heterogeneous agent combinations, in a 50 by 50 sized grid; number of decoys kept at 15 and communication sink radius varied

Scenarios with 'threshold agents' that have a radius of 10 grid units perform worse than ones with 15. In both cases increasing the number 'threshold agents' at the expense of 'range agents' increases performance once the simulation moves out of the fully decentralised region, but there is a limit to the performance. In most cases, at a communication sink radius of 25, the time to find the target increases for reasons explained earlier. Compared to these scenarios, the equivalent fully centralised scenario exhibits superior performance. The results indicate the trade off between efficiency and robustness. If centralised control is disrupted, the time taken increases from around 9 iterations to 250. However, in systems with two or more 'threshold agents' disruption to one such agent results in a much smaller performance penalty.

4   Discussion and Future Work

We have shown that the ICD, despite some initially unintuitive results, is a valid model to explore, understand and therefore exploit organisational behaviour – an often overlooked, yet very important aspect, in MAS. The next stage is to develop measurement systems to extract organisational behaviour information from different scenarios. Such metrics need to include specialisation, hierarchy, hierarchical levels and centralisation. These are tailored adaptations based on research carried out in the social sciences. It is also necessary to implement a cost function that describes the system, and can be used to monitor tradeoffs, such as robustness versus efficiency; something alluded to in the previous section. The final stage is to implement organisational adaptation based on reinforcement learning, where the cost function will act as a feedback mechanism. The aim is to develop a clear picture of how an organisation should be built based on preset requirements, and how it can self-organise to a changing environment.

Acknowledgements. This work is supported by an EPSRC studentship and BAE SYSTEMS, for an Engineering Doctorate (EngD) based at UMIST. JG would like to thank Les Gasser, H. Van Parunak and the participants of the last two Agent Summer Schools for their insight and discussions.

References

1. Neumann, P.G.: Cause of AT&T network failure, in The Risks Digest, vol. 9, 1990.
2. Meek, J.: Things Falling Apart (interview with J. Cohen), in The Guardian. London, 2001, pp. 2 - 3.
3. Cohen, J., Stewart, I.: The collapse of chaos: discovering simplicity in a complex world. New York: Viking, 1994.
4. Ashby, R.: Principles of the self-organizing dynamic system, Journal of General Psychology, vol. 37, pp. 125 - 128, 1947.
5. Kauffman, S.A.: The origins of order: self-organization and selection in evolution. New York; Oxford: Oxford University Press, 1993.
6. Prigogine, I., Stengers, I.: Order out of chaos: man's new dialogue with nature. London: Fontana Paperbacks, 1985.
7. Evans, S.R.: Hard Choices, in Aerospace International, May 2001.
8. Resnick, M.: Changing the Centralized Mind, in Technology Review, 1994.
9. Resnick, M.: Beyond the Centralized Mindset, Journal of the Learning Sciences, vol. 5, 1994.
10. Wooldridge, M.: Multiagent systems: a modern approach to distributed artificial intelligence. Cambridge, Mass.: London: MIT Press, 1999.
11. Heusse, M., Snyers, D., Guérin, S., Kuntz, P.: Adaptive Agent-Driven Routing and Load Balancing in Communication Network', presented at Ants '98, Brussels, 1998.
12. Gasser, L.: Perspectives on Organizations in Multi-agent Systems, presented at Multi-Agent Systems and Applications, Prague, Czech Republic, 2001.
13. Parunak, V.: Industrial Applications of Agents, presented at 2nd European Agent Summer School, Saarbrucken, 2000.
14. Chan, T.F., Golub, G.H.: Algorithms for computing the sample variance: analysis and recommendations, The American Statistician, vol. 37, pp. 242-247, 1983.

Mining Dependence Structures from Statistical Learning Perspective

Lei Xu*

Department of Computer Science and Engineering, Chinese University of Hong Kong,
Shatin, NT, Hong Kong, P.R. China
lxu@cse.cuhk.edu.hk

Abstract. Mining various dependence structures from data are important to many data mining applications. In this paper, several major dependence structure mining tasks are overviewed from statistical learning perspective, with a number of major results on unsupervised learning models that range from a single-object world to a multi-object world. Moreover, efforts towards a key challenge to learning have been discussed in three typical streams, based on generalization error bounds, Ockham principle, and BYY harmony learning, respectively.

1 Basic Issues of Statistical Learning

Statistical learning is a process that an intelligent machine or system $\mathcal{M}$ either estimates/learns the underlying distribution together with dependence structures among what to be learned (i.e., among the world $\mathbf{X}$ that $\mathcal{M}$ observes). Specifically, learning is made via certain media that is usually a set of samples from the world $\mathbf{X}$. Statistical learning takes an essential role in the literature of neural networks. It also acts as a major part in the field of intelligent data processing, or called *data mining* with an ever increasing popularity.

According to how learning media is used, studies on learning can be further classified into two quite different domains. One is the so called active learning, with the feature that the strategy of getting samples varies according to the current status of $\mathcal{M}$. The other is the conventional statistical learning, during which samples come from the world according to its underlying distribution in a given sampling strategy that is independent of the status of $\mathcal{M}$. This paper focuses on the latter one only. In this case, learning is featured by the following basic issues or called ingredients:

- A world $\mathbf{X}$ in the form of a underlying distribution of the world with certain dependence structures.
- A machine $\mathcal{M}$ in an appropriate architecture that is able to accommodate/model/represent the underlying distribution.
- A finite size set $\mathcal{X} = \{x_t\}_{t=1}^{N}$ of random samples that comes from the underlying distribution.

* The work described in this paper was fully supported by a grant from the Research Grant Council of the Hong Kong SAR (project No: CUHK4383/99E).

H. Yin et al. (Eds.): IDEAL 2002, LNCS 2412, pp. 285–306, 2002.
© Springer-Verlag Berlin Heidelberg 2002

- A learning principle or theory that coordinates the above three issues in order to get a best estimate of the underlying distribution by $\mathcal{M}$ based on $\mathcal{X}$.
- An efficient algorithm that implements the above learning theory.

Though the entire world faced by $\mathcal{M}$ usually very complicated, we can conduct studies by decomposing a complicated task into a number of learning tasks on much simplified small worlds, as to be discussed in two subsequent sections.

2   Dependence among Samples from a One-Object World

We start at considering a simple world $\mathbf{X}$ of only single object that is observed via a set $\mathcal{X}$ of samples with each sample $x = [x^{(1)}, \cdots, x^{(d)}]^T$ from a same underlying probability distribution or density $p(x)$. Typically, we can use one or more of the following five ways to describe the dependence structures among $\mathbf{X}$.

(a) Nonparametric joint density. In general, dependence among variables $x^{(1)}, \cdots, x^{(d)}$ can always be described by a nonstructural or nonparametric joint density. A typical example is either simply the empirical density:

$$p_0(x) = \frac{1}{N} \sum_{t=1}^{N} \delta(x - x_t), \text{ where } \delta(x) \text{ is a } \delta\text{-function}, \qquad (1)$$

or a non-parametric Parzen window density estimate (Devroye, 1996):

$$p_h(x) = \frac{1}{N} \sum_{t=1}^{N} K_h(x, x_t), \qquad (2)$$

where $K_h(x, x_t)$ is a kernel function located at x_t. One typical example is that $K_h(x, x_t)$ is a hyper cubic of volume h^d with its center located at x_t. In this case, $p_h(x)$ becomes the widely used histogram estimate, which is a smoothed version of eq.(1). The smoothness is controlled by a given parameter $h > 0$ that is called *smoothing parameter*. Another more smoothed example is $K_h(x, x_t) = G(x|x_t, h^2 I)$, where $G(x|m, \Sigma_x)$ denotes a Gaussian density with mean vector m and covariance matrix Σ_x.

Such a nonparametric and non-structural joint density estimate, though conceptually implying all the dependence relations among variables, have three major weak points. One is that it is usually a bad estimate when the size N of samples is finite, especially when the dimension d of x is high. The second is that dependence relations are not given directly. The other is the expensive computing cost for each calculation on $p(x)$ at any point $x = x'$. To improve the weak points, efforts are made along two directions.

(b) Sample statistics. The first direction is to describe dependences among variables $x^{(1)}, \cdots, x^{(d)}$ collectively by sample statistics up to certain orders, instead of a joint density that conceptually implies statistics of all the possible orders. The most widely encountered case is to use statistics up to the 2nd order only, representing in the covariance matrix $\Sigma_x = E(x - m_x)(x - m_x)^T, m_x = Ex$

that captures the linear dependence structures among all the variables, where and throughout this paper the notations $E(u) = Eu = E[u]$ denotes the expectation of random variable u. Equivalently, this case is actually to assume that the underlying distribution is a parametric Gaussian density with parameters m_x, Σ_x. Of course, we can also similarly further consider higher order statistics. However, the number of such statistics increases exponentially, e.g., in the order of d^m for the m-th order statistics, which brings us to the weak points similar to that for estimating a nonparametric density.

(c) Co-occurrence and associations. The second direction is to focus on the pair-wise dependences between u, v that denote two or two subsets of variables $x^{(1)}, \cdots, x^{(d)}$. The simplest one is co-occurrence or association. That is, we are interested in finding those events $u = U, v = V$ that will co-occur with high probability, e.g., with the corresponding probability $P(u = U, v = V)$ higher than a pre-specified threshold. We are also interested in getting an association rule $(u = U) => (v = V)$ that describes how we can infer the occurrence of the event $v = V$ from the occurrence of the event $u = U$, which is measured by its support $P(u = U, v = V)$ and confidence $P(v = V|u = U)$, as called in the literature of *data mining* for the market basket analysis (Ch.7, Han & Kamber, 2001).

We can see that the task of association rule mining is actually a simplified task of estimating the joint density $p(x)$. It is not necessary and too expensive in cost to estimate $p(x)$. What we are interested in are only those events $u = U$ and $v = V$ with $P(u = U, v = V) > s$ and $P(v = V|u = U) > c$ for the pre-specified thresholds $s > 0, c > 0$. In addition to those approaches given in (Ch.7, Han & Kamber, 2001), here we suggest a stochastic approach with its key idea as follows:

- Find a way such that all the possible values of V, U can be sampled with an equal probability, which is referred as random sampling;
- Make n_s/s times of such random sampling, if a specific pair $\bar{V}, \bar{U}$ appears more than $s \times n_s/s = n_s$ times, we get $(u = \bar{U}) => (v = \bar{V})$ as a candidate association rule;
- Conditioning on $u = \bar{U}$, make n_c/c times of random sampling on V, if the specific value $\bar{V}$ appears more than $c \times n_c/c = n_c$ times, we take $(u = \bar{U}) => (v = \bar{V})$ as an association rule with its support larger than s and its a confidence larger than c.

(d) Linear and nonlinear generative structures. On the second direction, we further explore the pair-wise dependences in more sophisticated structures. One typical structure is the following explicit stochastic linear function:

$$x = Ay + e, \quad E(e) = 0, \quad e \text{ is independent from } y. \tag{3}$$

The earliest effort on this linear model can be traced back to the beginning of the 20th century by (Spearman, 1904), and had been followed by various studies in the literature of statistics. In this model, a random sample x of observation is generated via a linear mapping matrix A from k hidden factors in the form $y = [y^{(1)}, \cdots, y^{(k)}]^T$ from a parametric density $q(y)$, disturbed by a noise e. Generally, samples of e are independently and identically distributed (i.i.d.) from a parametric density $q(e)$, and the function forms of $q(y)$ and $q(e)$ are given. What to be learned are the matrix A and the statistics of y_t and e_t.

The problem is usually not well defined because there are an infinite number of solutions. To reduce the indeterminacy, we consider that samples of x and e are i.i.d. and correspondingly samples of y are also i.i.d. such that dependence among variables of x is equivalently modeled by the following parametric density

$$q(x) = \int q(x - Ay)q(y)dy, \tag{4}$$

which implies a parametric density of x, described via the matrix A, these statistics of y and e subject to the constraint eq.(3) and the given density forms of $q(y)$ and $q(e)$. Also, eq.(3) implies that all the statistics of x are subject to the constraints, e.g., with $\Sigma_x, \Sigma_y, \Sigma_e$ being covariance matrices of x, y and e respectively, we have

$$\Sigma_x = A^T \Sigma_y A + \Sigma_e. \tag{5}$$

Particularly, when y is Gaussian $G(y|0, I)$ as well as uncorrelated to e, and e is also uncorrelated among its components with a diagonal covariance matrix Σ_e. The model eq.(3) is called factor analysis (McDonald, 1985; Rubi, 1976), which is firstly formulated by Anderson and Rubin (1956). In this case, the integral $q(x)$ is analytically solvable and becomes simply Gaussian. Also eq.(5) is simplified into

$$\Sigma_x = A^T A + \Sigma_e. \tag{6}$$

As discussed in (Xu, 2001a), this constraint alone is not enough to uniquely specify A and Σ_e. If we further impose the constraint

$$A = \phi D, \phi^T \phi = I, \quad \Sigma_e = \sigma_e^2 I, \tag{7}$$

it follows (Anderson & Rubin, 1956; Xu, 1998b) that the maximum likelihood learning on $q(x)$ results in that ϕ consists of the k principle eigenvectors of Σ_x with D^2 consisting of the corresponding principle eigenvalues, i.e., it becomes equivalent to the so called principal component analysis (PCA). In recent years, such a special case of factor analysis has also been reiterated in the literature of neural networks under a new name called probabilistic PCA (Tipping & Bishop, 1999).

When y is nonGaussian, the model eq.(3) implies not only the constraint eq.(6) but also constraints on higher order statistics such that the indeterminacy on A and Σ_e is removed. However, the integral $p(x)$ becomes analytically unsolvable when y is real and nonGaussian because it usually incurs a lot of computation cost.

Generally, eq.(3) can also be either a nonlinear structure

$$x = g(y, A) + e, \quad q(x) = \int q(x - g(y, A))q(y)dy, \tag{8}$$

or even a general probabilistic structure

$$q(x) = \int q(x|y)q(y)dy. \tag{9}$$

Actually, the above two cases are regarded being equivalent via the link

$$g(y, A) = E(x|y) - Ee, \quad e = x - g(y, A), \tag{10}$$

where e generally relates to y instead of being independent of y.

(e) Linear and nonlinear transform structures. Another typical structure for describing dependence among variables is a forward transform or mapping $y = f(x, W)$.

The simplest case is $y = Wx$ when $Ex = 0$ (otherwise its mean can subtracted in a preprocessing). It specifies a relation $Eyy^T = \Sigma_y = W^T \Sigma_x W$ between the 2nd order statistics of y and of x such that dependence among variables of x are implicitly specified via W as well as the statistics of y. When Σ_y becomes diagonal, the mapping $y = Wx$ is said to de-correlate the components of x. Moreover, $\max_{W^T W=I} E\|y\|^2$, $E\|y\|^2 = Tr[\Sigma_y]$ leads to the well known principle component analysis (PCA) with y being the principle components, which can be backtracked to as early as by Hotelling (1936), and has been also widely studied in the literatures of statistics, pattern recognition and neural networks (Oja,1983). Equivalently, PCA is also reached by maximizing the entropy below,

$$\max_{W^T W=I} J(W), \quad J(W) = -\int p(y) \ln p(y)dy, \tag{11}$$

when x comes from Gaussian and $y = Wx$ is still Gaussian.

Moreover, when $y = Wx$ satisfies

$$q(y) = \prod_{j=1}^{k} q(y^{(j)}) \tag{12}$$

with at most one component being Gaussian, the mapping $y = Wx$ is said to implement the independent component analysis (ICA) (Jutten & Herault, 1988; Tong, et al, 1993; Comon,1994). Moreover, when each component of y_t is interpreted as a sample of a time series at the moment t, the ICA solution $\hat{y}_t = Wx_t$ recovers y_t from $x_t = Ay_t$ up to a scaling indeterminacy. That is, the waveform of each component series can be recovered by $\hat{y}_t = Wx_t$, which is also called blind source separation (BSS) that blindly separates the mixed signal $x_t = Ay_t$ with scaling indeterminacy (Tong, et al, 1993). In the case that W is invertible, the target eq.(12) has been explored from different perspectives (Gaeta & Lacounme, 1990; Bell & Sejnowski, 1995; Amari, et al, 1996). All these studies meet at maximizing the following cost

$$L = \ln |W| + \frac{1}{N} \sum_{t=1}^{N} \sum_{j=1}^{k} \ln q(y_t^{(j)})|_{y_t=Wx_t}. \tag{13}$$

With $q(y^{(j)})$ being a pre-fixed estimate for $y^{(j)}$.

However, an ICA algorithm with $q(y^{(j)})$ pre-fixed works well only on the cases that either all components of y are super-Gaussians or all components of y are sub-Gaussians (Amari, et al, 1996; Bell & Sejnowski, 1995), but not on the cases that components of y are partly super-Gaussians and sub-Gaussians. This problem can be solved by learning $q(y^{(j)})$ via a mixture of parametric densities or equivalently learning the cumulated distribution function (cdf) of $q(y^{(j)})$ by a mixture of parametric cdfs (Xu, Yang, & Amari, 1996; Xu, Cheung, & Amari, 1998), in which requiring that W is invertible is relaxed to be a full rank $k \times d, k \le d$ matrix.

Efforts have also been made on using a non-linear mapping $y = f(x, \theta)$ to implement a nonlinear ICA (Taleb & Jutten, 1997; Xu, 1998b). However, the satisfaction of eq.(12) will keep unchanged after any component-wise nonlinear transformation on y. Thus, a nonlinear ICA mapping $y = f(x, \theta)$ usually does not retain the feature of performing BBS since it is no longer able to recover the original y with only scaling indeterminacy, unless in a specific situation with extra constraints imposed.

Instead of considering nonlinear ICA, we suggest to consider a non-linear mapping $y = f(x, \theta)$ from the perspective of modeling the cumulated distribution function (cdf) of input data x. If a non-linear mapping $y = f(x, W)$ can successfully map x into y that uniformly distributes on $[0, 1]^k,$, $f(x, \theta)$ actually acts as a parametric estimate of the cdf of x or equivalently $\hat{p}(x) = |W(x)W^T(x)|^{0.5}$ is a density estimate of x, where $W(x) = \frac{\partial f(x, \theta)}{\partial x^T}$. A specific three layer architecture for a mixture of cdfs has been used in (King & Xu, 1995) for histogram equalization and in (Xu, Yang, & Amari, 1996) for ICA.

More generally, we can consider a non-linear mapping $y = f(x, \theta)$ to map x into y with its underlying distribution is approximately in a parametric form $q(y)$ by eq.(12). Imagining that y is further mapped into the uniform distribution on $[0, 1]^k$ by $g(y^{(j)}) = \int_{-\infty}^{y^{(j)}} q(r)dr$, we see that the composite function $g(f(x, \theta))$ maps x into the uniform distribution on $[0, 1]^k$. This is, $g(f(x, \theta))$ approximates the cumulated distribution function (cdf) of x, or equivalently we get a density estimate of x as follows:

$$\hat{p}(x) = |U(x)U^T(x)|^{0.5}, U(x) = \frac{\partial g(y)}{\partial y^T} \frac{\partial f(x, \theta)}{\partial x^T} = diag[q(y^{(j)}), \cdots, g(y^{(k)})]W(x),$$

$$\hat{p}(x) = |W(x)W^T(x)|^{0.5} \prod_{j=1}^{k} q(y^{(j)}). \tag{14}$$

Considering the maximum likelihood learning $\max L$ with

$$L = \sum_{t=1}^{N} \ln \hat{p}(x_t), \ \ln \hat{p}(x_t) = 0.5 \ln |W^T(x)W(x)| + \sum_{j=1}^{k} \ln q(y^{(j)}). \tag{15}$$

When $y = Wx$ we have $W(x) = W$ and thus L returns to eq.(13) when $d = k$. That is, the above equation implements either an ICA when $y = Wx$ for $k \le d$ or a nonlinear ICA when $y = f(x, \theta)$ in general.

Particularly, given a sigmoid scalar function $0 \leq s(r) \leq 1$ and a notation $s(y) = [s(y^{(1)}), \cdots, s(y^{(k)})]^T$ for $y = [y^{(1)}, \cdots, y^{(k)}]^T$, when $\bar{y} = s(y), y = Wx$ and $q(y^{(j)}) = q_j^{y^{(j)}}(1 - q_j)^{1-y^{(j)}}$, we have $W(x) = |WW^T|^{0.5} \prod_{j=1}^{k} q_s(y^{(j)})$ with $q_s(r) = ds(r)/dr$. Then, it follow from eq.(15) that

$$L = 0.5N \ln |WW^T| + \sum_{t=1}^{N}\sum_{j=1}^{k}[\ln q_s(y^{(j)}) + \bar{y}^{(j)} \ln q_j + (1 - \bar{y}^{(j)}) \ln (1 - q_j)] \quad (16)$$

Let $q_j = 1/(1 + e^{c_j})$, we make max L with respect to c_j by the gradient ascent and with respect to W by the natural gradient ascent, resulting in the following adaptive algorithm:

$$c_j^{new} = c_j^{new} + \gamma_t q_j(\bar{y}^{(j)} - q_j), \quad q_j^{new} = 1/(1 + e^{c_j^{new}}), \quad \bar{y} = s(y), \quad y = W^{old}x,$$

$$W^{new} = W^{old} + \gamma_t(I + \phi^y y^T)W^{old}, \quad q_s'(r) = \frac{dq_s(r)}{dr},$$

$$\phi^y = [q_s'(y^{(1)}) + q_s(y^{(1)}) \ln \frac{q_1^{new}}{1 - q_1^{new}}, \cdots, q_s'(y^{(k)}) + q_s(y^{(k)}) \ln \frac{q_k^{new}}{1 - q_k^{new}}]. \quad (17)$$

Being different from the ICA algorithm by (Bell & Sejnowski, 1995; Amari, et al, 1996), the probability q_j is updated during the learning.

Interestingly, this q_j can be used as an identifier on whether this source is super-gaussian or subgaussian. Since $E\bar{y}^{(j)} = q_j$ and

$$\kappa_j = E(\bar{y}^{(j)} - q_j)^4 - 3[E(\bar{y}^{(j)} - q_j)^2]^2 = (1 - q_j)q_j(6q_j^2 - 6q_j + 1) =$$

$$(1 - q_j)q_j[q_j - \frac{3 + \sqrt{3}}{6}][q_j - \frac{3 - \sqrt{3}}{6}] \begin{cases} > 0, & \text{if } q_j > \frac{3 + \sqrt{3}}{6} \text{ or } q_j < \frac{3 - \sqrt{3}}{6} \\ < 0, & \text{if } \frac{3 + \sqrt{3}}{6} \geq q_j \geq \frac{3 - \sqrt{3}}{6} \end{cases} \quad (18)$$

Moreover, this q_j also adjusts the function ϕ^y to improve the updating on W accordingly in eq.(17). As a result, similar to the the the so called learned-parametric-model (LPM)-ICA algorithm in (Xu, Yang, & Amari, 1996; Xu, Cheung, & Amari, 1998), eq.(17) will work well on sources partly from super-Gaussians and partly from sub-Gaussians (Amari, et al, 1996). Moreover, we can initially set k large enough and then after learning we remove those sources with its corresponding q_j becoming either near 0 or 1. This provides a way to determine an appropriate dimension k for y.

In the LPM-ICA algorithm, we have $y = Wx$ and thus $W(x) = W$. Moreover, $q(y^{(j)})$ is a parametric model of finite mixture with each component being either a Gaussian or $ds(r)/dr$ for a sigmoid function $0 \leq s(r) \leq 1$. However, a number of parameters need to learned to adapt either a super-gaussian source or a sub-guassian source. As guessed in (Xu, Cheung, & Amari, 1998), there may be plenty of room to simplify. E.g., for each source we may need a mixture of two Gaussians $p(y^{(j)}) = 0.5G(y^{(j)}|m_1^{(j)}, 1) + 0.5G(y^{(j)}|m_2^{(j)}, 1)$, with only two mean parameters updated per source. While in the algorithm eq.(17), only one parameter per source is updated. This may be the simplest choice. For $q(y^{(j)})$ being a uniform density, we always have $\kappa_j < 0$. For $q(y^{(j)})$ being a Gaussian, we have $\kappa_j = 0$. Even for $q(y^{(j)}) = D_j^{-1}e^{-|x|^{\alpha_j}}$, we need to update α_j at least under the constraint $D_j = \int e^{-|x|^{\alpha_j}} dx, \alpha_j > 0$.

All the above discussions can also be extended to a noisy mapping $y = f(x, \theta) + \varepsilon$ and thus $W(x) = \frac{\partial f(x,\theta)}{\partial x^T} + \frac{\partial \varepsilon}{\partial x^T}$. When ε is independent of x, we have $\frac{\varepsilon}{\partial x^T} = 0$ and thus $W(x)$ returns to the same as in eq.(15). However, ε will affect the learning on $q(y^{(j)})$. When ε comes from a Gaussian $G(\varepsilon|0, \sigma_\varepsilon^2 I)$ with an appropriate σ_ε^2, a regularization will be imposed on learning, which is helpful in the case of a small size of samples.

For implementing ICA, both maximum information transfer and minimum mutual information lead to eq.(13) and thus are equivalent, which actually perform the well known redundancy reduction principle that was suggested for unsupervised learning in a neuro-perception system (Barlow, 1989). However, the role of maximum information transfer is more than implementing ICA, it also results in estimating the above discussed $\hat{p}(x)$.

3   Dependence among Samples from a Multi-object World

3.1   Dependence among Samples from a Multi-object World

We observe a world $\mathbf{X}$ with multiple objects that are either visible or invisible. We start at considering the cases that all the objects are visible, with each label ℓ in a set L denoting a specific object observed via a sample vector $x_\ell = [x_\ell^{(1)}, \cdots, x_\ell^{(d)}]^T$.

We can simply discover dependence structures within each object $\ell \in L$ individually in the same ways as introduced in the previous subsection. Moreover, dependence structures exist across different objects. They are described both qualitatively by the topology of L and quantitatively by the dependence structures among variables of x_ℓ across objects.

In the most complicated cases that there will be dependence structures between any pair of objects, the topology of L is a complete graph with every pair of nodes connected. Specifically, if there is no dependence between a pair of objects, the connection between the corresponding two nodes is broken and thus can be removed. Usually, three types of simplified topology are often encountered, described as follows.

(a) A linear or serial chain   The simplest case is that the topology is a simple chain $1, 2, \cdots, \ell-1, \ell, \ell+1, \cdots$ with the object ℓ directly connecting to only the object $\ell-1$ and the object $\ell+1$. In this case, $x_1, x_2, \cdots, x_{\ell-1}, x_\ell, x_{\ell+1}, \cdots$ form a sequence or called a time series when ℓ denotes the time. The task of learning is to estimate quantitatively the dependence structures by the joint distribution of the whole sequence in certain serial/temporal dependence structure. The task is often encountered in signal processing and stochastic process modeling, such as time series prediction, speech, audio and text processing via AR, ARMA models and especially Hidden Markov model (Rabiner & Juang, 1993).

(b) An image and a d-dimensional lattice topology   We further consider the cases where labels in L are organized in a regular lattice topology with each object ℓ denoted by a coordinate $[\ell_1, \ell_2, \ldots, \ell_d]$. It degenerates back to the above chain and time series modeling when $d = 1$. Moreover, $\{x_\ell : \ell \in L\}$ denotes an image when $d = 2$ and a 3D array or video when $d = 3$, etc, with x_ℓ being a pixel. Similarly, the task of learning is to estimate the dependence structures by the joint distribution of all the pixels (usually in help of certain dependence structures between a pixel and pixels in its neighborhood), which actually leads to a stochastic field or even a stochastic field process. Such tasks are often encountered in image processing, computer vision and video processing.

(c) A tree topology   Another typical case is that L has a tree topology with each object ℓ being a node on the tree, i.e., each node has direct dependence only on its father or children. The task of learning is to estimate the dependence structures by the joint distribution $\{x_\ell : \ell \in L\}$ subject to this tree dependence structure. This is a typical task that has been studied under the popular topic called probabilistic graphical model or Belief networks in the recent literatures of AI, statistics and neural networks, readers are referred to the books (Pearl, 1988; Jensen, 1996).

3.2   Mining Dependence Structure across Invisible Multi-objects

Next, we further observe a world of invisible multiple objects with each sample vector x coming from one object $\ell \in L$ but with its label ℓ missing.

Given a set of such samples, we want to discover the dependence structures among the objects, which are again described both qualitatively by the topology of L and quantitatively by the dependence structures among variables of x within and across objects. Still, the tasks of learning can be classified according to what types of topology of L being taken into our consideration.

(a) Finite Mixture   The simplest case is that we ignore the topology of L and only consider the dependence structures among variables of x, which depends on the dependence structure between each sample x and each label ℓ. The general form of the dependence is described by an joint distribution $q(x, \ell)$ that describes the joint occurrence of the event that a sample is valued by x and the event that the sample comes from the object ℓ.

Specifically, $q(x, \ell)$ can be represented via the decomposition $q(x|\ell)q(\ell)$, which describes $q(x, \ell)$ in a casual view on where x comes from. Each of $q(x|\ell), \ell = 1, \cdots, k$ describes the dependence structures within the ℓ-th object, and

$$q(\ell) = \sum_{j=1}^{k} \alpha_j \delta(\ell - j), \quad \text{with the constraint} \quad \alpha_\ell \geq 0, \sum_{\ell=1}^{k} \alpha_\ell = 1, \quad (19)$$

where α_ℓ denotes a priori probability that x comes from the ℓ-th object.

The task of learning is to estimate α_ℓ and to discover dependence structures within each $q(x|\ell)$, which is equivalent to learning the dependence structures in the format of

$$q(x) = \sum_{\ell \in L} \alpha_\ell q(x|\ell). \quad (20)$$

It is usually called finite mixture model in the literature (Dempster et al, 1977; Redner & Walker, 1984; McLachlan, & Krishnan, 1997). As a byproduct, we also have the so called Bayesian rule

$$q(\ell|x) = \alpha_\ell q(x|\ell)/q(x), \tag{21}$$

and thus another decomposition $p(x, \ell) = p(\ell|x)p(x)$ with $p(\ell|x)$ describing an inference view on which object the observation x may come. It results in a partition of a set of samples into different objects, and thus is usually called pattern recognition or clustering analysis (Devijver & Kittler, 1982). Particularly, when the dependence structure of $q(x|\ell)$ is simply a Gaussian $q(x|\ell) = G(x|c_\ell, \Sigma_\ell)$, eq.(20) becomes the widely used Gaussian mixture (Dempster, et al, 1977; Redner & Walker, 1984; McLachlan & Krishnan, 1997) and eq.(21) is called Bayesian classifier (Duda & Hart 1973). Moreover, when $\Sigma_\ell = \sigma^2 I$, a hard-cut version of eq.(21) leads to the conventional least square clustering (Xu, 1997).

(b) *Self-organizing map*   We further consider the cases that L has a given regular d-dimensional lattice topology. Since the label ℓ associated with x is invisible, we are not able to recover the dependence structures of among variables of x across different objects. Alternatively, we re-establish dependence structures according to *a general belief that objects locating topologically in a small neighborhood N_ℓ should be same or similar to each other*, where a small neighborhood N_ℓ of a knot ℓ usually consists of 2^d knots that are directly connected to ℓ.

A direct placement of all the objects on such a lattice, according to a criterion or measure to judge whether two objects are same or similar, is computationally a NP hard problem. Instead, this placement can be implemented approximately. Interestingly, a good approximate solution for this problem is provided by biological brain dynamics of self-organization (von der Malsburg, 1973), featured by a Mexican hat type interaction, namely, neurons in near neighborhood excite each other with learning, while neurons far away inhibit each other with de-learning. Computationally, such a dynamic process can be simplified by certain heuristic strategies. Here, we consider two typical ones.

(1) *One member wins, a family gains*   That is, as long as one member wins in the WTA competition, all the members of a family gain regardless whether other members are strong or not. This direction is initialized by a simple and clever technique, i.e., the well known Kohonen self-organizing map (Kohonen, 1982&95), In the literatures, a great number of studies have been made on extending the Kohonen map. Recently, a general formulation of this strategy has also been proposed (Xu, 2002a).

(2) *Strongers gain and then teaming together*   That is, a number of strongers are picked as winners who not only gain learning but also are teamed together such that they become the neighbors to each other (Xu, 2002a). It can speed up self-organization, especially in the early stage of learning. Also, we can combine the first and the second strategies by using the second in the early stage and subsequently switching to the first.

(c) *Self-organizing graphical topology*   Following a similar line, we can also extend the above studies to a more complicated topology of either a tree or even a general graph. The only difference is that a small neighborhood N_ℓ of a specific ℓ consists of all the knots that are directly connected to ℓ and that the number of elements in N_ℓ is usually not 2^d but equal to the degree of the node ℓ.

4   A Key Challenge and Existing Solutions

4.1   A Key Challenge and Existing Solutions

A key challenge to all the learning tasks is that learning is made on a finite size set $\mathcal{X}$ of samples from the world $\mathbf{X}$ but our ambition is to get the underlying distribution such that we can apply it to all or as many as possible new coming samples from $\mathbf{X}$.

In help of certain pre-knowledge about $\mathbf{X}$ (e.g., certain dependence structures discussed in the previous two subsections), the learner $\mathcal{M}$ is usually designed via a parametric family $p(x|\theta)$ with its density function form covering or being as close as possible to the function form of the true density $p_*(x|\cdot)$. Then, we obtain an estimator $\hat{\theta}(\mathcal{X})$ with a specific value for θ such that the correspondingly specified density $p(x|\hat{\theta}(\mathcal{X}))$ is as close as possible to the true density $p_*(x|\theta^*)$ with the true value θ^*. This is usually obtained by determining a specific value of $\hat{\theta}$ that minimizes a cost functional

$$\mathcal{F}(p(x|\theta), \mathcal{X}) \text{ or } \mathcal{F}(p(x|\theta), q_{\mathcal{X}}(x)), \tag{22}$$

which results in an estimator $\hat{\theta}(\mathcal{X})$. $q_{\mathcal{X}}$ is an estimated density of x, that is rather easily obtained from $\mathcal{X}$, e.g., given by either eq.(1) or eq.(2).

When $p(x|\theta) = p_0(x)$ given by eq.(1), a special case of eq.(22), i.e.,

$$\min_{\theta} -\mathcal{F}(p(x|\theta), \mathcal{X}) = -\int p_0(x) \ln p(x|\theta) dx \tag{23}$$

leads to the maximum likelihood (ML) estimator $\hat{\theta}(\mathcal{X})$. For a fixed N, we usually have $\hat{\theta}(\mathcal{X}) \neq \theta_o$ and $p(x|\hat{\theta}(\mathcal{X})) \neq p_*(x|\theta_o)$. Thus, though $p(x|\hat{\theta}(\mathcal{X}))$ best matches the sample set $\mathcal{X}$ in the sense of eq.(22) or eq.(23), $p(x|\hat{\theta}(\mathcal{X}))$ may not well apply to new samples from the same world $\mathbf{X}$.

However, if there is an oracle who tells us the function form of $p_*(x|\cdot)$, we can simply use it to be the function form of $p(x|\cdot)$. In this case, it follows from the well known large number law in probability theory that the ML estimator $\hat{\theta}(\mathcal{X}) \to \theta_o$ and $p_*(x|\theta) \to p_*(x|\theta_o)$ as $N \to \infty$. Shortly, the estimator $\hat{\theta}(\mathcal{X})$ is said to be statistically consistent. Actually, this large number law can be regarded as the mathematical formularization of a fundamental philosophy or principle of modern science that a truth about the world exists independent of our perception and we will tend to and finally approach the truth as long as the evidences we collected about the truth become infinite many.

Unfortunately, this ML-type principle is challenged by two facts. First, the purpose of learning is to guide a learner $\mathcal{M}$ to interact with the world that is usually not only random but also in dynamic changing. Thus, there are usually not a plenty time as well as plenty resources for collecting enough samples before $\mathcal{M}$ has to make certain actions. Therefore, what $\mathcal{M}$ encounters is usually a finite number N of samples and thus the large number law does not apply. Second, assuming knowing the true density form of $p_*(x|\cdot)$ implies actually a knowledge on a major structure of the world $\mathbf{X}$ and what remain to be precisely discovered are relatively details. Unfortunately, in many realistic problems we have no such an oracle to tell us the knowledge on the true function form of $p_*(x|\cdot)$, and thus in these cases the large number law may fail even as $N \to \infty$.

In past decades, many efforts have been made towards this critical challenge, roughly forming two main streams.

4.2   Efforts in the First Stream

Insisting in that there is a true underlying density $p_*(x|\theta_o)$, we desire a best estimate by minimizing $\mathcal{F}(p(x|\theta), p_*(x|\theta_o))$. Unfortunately, this is not directly workable since $p_*(x|\theta_o)$ is not known. Alternatively, a classic idea is to quantitatively estimate the discrepancy between $\mathcal{F}(p(x|\theta), p_*(x|\theta_o))$ and $\mathcal{F}(p(x|\theta), \mathcal{X})$ such that we have

$$\mathcal{F}(p(x|\theta), p_*(x|\theta_o)) = \mathcal{F}(p(x|\theta), \mathcal{X}) + \Delta(p(x|\theta), p_*(x|\theta_o), \mathcal{X}), \qquad (24)$$

where $\Delta(p(x|\theta), p_*(x|\theta_o), \mathcal{X})$ is an estimate of $\mathcal{F}(p(x|\theta), p_*(x|\theta_o)) - \mathcal{F}(p(x|\theta), \mathcal{X})$. It is usually difficult to be accurately estimated since we still need to know $p_*(x|\theta_o)$. In literatures, what have been made are usually let Δ to be the estimates on certain bounds of this discrepancy, which may be obtainable based on $\mathcal{X}$ and the structural features of $p(x|\theta)$ in help of some structural knowledge about $p_*(x|\theta_o)$. Using the bounds, we implement either or both of the following two types of correcting on estimates from eq.(22):

(a) *Regularization*   Assume that we are able to estimate a bound of Δ that varies with θ, i.e., $\Delta(\theta)$, we correct the estimate from eq.(22) by minimizing $\Delta(\theta) + \mathcal{F}(p(x|\theta), \mathcal{X})$ with respect θ. If we are able to design the function form of $p(x|\cdot)$ to be the true function form of $p_*(x|\cdot)$, it can be observed that this idea does improve the problem of a finite number N of samples. Also, the estimated bound Δ will tend to 0 as $N \to \infty$ according to the large number law. In the existing literature, such types of efforts are usually referred as *regularization* since it regularizes certain singularity caused by a finite set of samples.

(b) *Model Selection*   We consider a number of candidate models $M_j, j = 1, \cdots, k$ with each having its own density function forms $p(x|\theta_j, M_j)$. We estimate each bound Δ_j for the discrepancy between $\mathcal{F}(p(x|\theta_j, M_j), p_*(x|\theta_o))$ and $\mathcal{F}(p(x|\theta_j, M_j), \mathcal{X})$. Over all candidate models, we select the j^*-th model by minimizing $\mathcal{F}(p(x|\theta_j, M_j), \mathcal{X}) + \Delta_j$, which is referred as *Model Selection*. We usually encounter two typical situations. One is that the obtained bound Δ_j depends only on the structure of M_j either without the appearance of θ_j or with θ_j being setting at a ML estimate. The other is that the bound Δ_j depends on both the structure of M_j and the value of θ_j. In the latter case, an implementation of model selection is companioned by the above discussed regularization.

Several approaches have been developed in this stream. One typical example is the VC dimension based learning theory (Vapnik, 1995), which considers $\mathcal{F}$ as the error or loss of making a discrete-nature task on a set $\mathcal{X}$ of samples, such as classification or decision, with Δ_j estimated based on a complexity measure of the structure of M_j. The second type of examples are AIC (Akaike, 1974) as well as its extensions AICB, CAIC, etc (Akaike, 1981 & 87; Sugiura, 1978; Bozdogan, 1987&88; Hurvich & Tsai, 1989&93; Cavanaugh, 1997), which usually consider a regression or modeling task, with Δ_j estimated as a bias of the likelihood $- \int p_0(x) \ln p(x|\theta) dx$ to the information measure $- \int p_*(x) \ln p(x|\theta) dx$. Another typical example is the so called cross validation (Stone, 1974&78; Rivals & Personnaz, 1999). Instead of estimating a bound of Δ_j, it targets on estimating $\mathcal{F}(p(x|\theta_j, M_j), p_*(x|\theta_o))$ via splitting $\mathcal{X}$ into a training subset $\mathcal{X}_t$ and a validation subset $\mathcal{X}_v$. First, one gets an estimate $\hat{\theta}_j$ by minimizing $\mathcal{F}(p(x|\theta_j, M_j), \mathcal{X}_t)$ and then estimates $\mathcal{F}(p(x|\theta_j, M_j), p_*(x|\theta_o))$ via jointly considering $\mathcal{F}(p(x|\hat{\theta}_j, M_j), \mathcal{X}_t)$ and $\mathcal{F}(p(x|\hat{\theta}_j, M_j), \mathcal{X}_v)$. Moreover, studies on cross validation relate closely to Jackknife and bootstrap techniques (Efron, 1983; Efron& Tibshirani, 1993). In the existing literatures, most of studies on these typical approaches focus on making model selection only, since the problem of obtaining a bound of Δ requires more knowledge on the true $p_*(x|\theta_o)$, which is usually difficult.

4.3   Efforts in the Second Stream

Instead of taking a true underlying density $p_*(x|\theta_o)$ as the target of considerations, the well known Ockham's principle of economy is used as the learning principle. Namely, if there are a number of choices for getting a model to fit a set $\mathcal{X}$ of samples, we use the one such that $p(x|\theta)$ not only matches $\mathcal{X}$ well but also has a minimum complexity. This principle can be intuitively well understood. When $\mathcal{X}$ consists of a finite number N of samples, we can have an infinite choices on $p(x|\theta)$ that describe or accommodate $\mathcal{X}$ well or even better and better as the complexity of $p(x|\theta)$ increases from satisfying a minimum requirement. That is, learning is a typical ill-posed problem with intrinsic indeterminacy on its solution. The indeterminacy depends on how large the complexity of $p(x|\theta)$ is. The larger is it, the lower is the chance of getting the true underlying density $p_*(x|\theta_o)$, and thus the more likely the learned choice generalizes poorly beyond the N samples in $\mathcal{X}$. Therefore, we choose the choice with the minimum complexity among all those that are able to describe $\mathcal{X}$ sufficiently well.

Based on this Ockham's principle, approaches have been developed for both regularization and model selection.

(a) One type of examples consists of various efforts either under the name 'regularization' or via certain equivalent techniques. One of most popular one is the well known Tikhonov regularization theory (Girosi, 1995; Tikhonov & Arsenin, 1977), which minimizes $\mathcal{F}(p(x|\theta), \mathcal{X})$ plus a so called stabilizer that describes the irregularity or non-smoothness of $p(x|\theta)$. In the literatures of both statistics and neural networks, there are also many efforts that minimize

$\mathcal{F}(p(x|\theta), \mathcal{X})$ plus a penalty term in various forms. These heuristics take a role similar to the Tikhonov stabilizer (Sclove, 1987; Devroye, et al, 1996). One critical weak point of these efforts is lacking a systematic or quantitative way to guide how to choose the added term and to control the strength of the term in minimization. For this reason, this type of efforts is usually used for regularization only. In the literature of statistics, the role of the added term is alternatively interpreted as controlling a trade-off between bias and variance for an estimator (Geman, Bienenstock, & Doursat, 1992; Wolpert, 1997; Jacobs, 1997).

(b) The second type of efforts for implementing the Ockham's principle consists of those studies based on Bayesian approach. There are three major versions (Kontkanen, 1998). One is called maximum a posteriori probability (MAP) since it maximizes the posteriori probability

$$p(M_j, \theta_j|\mathcal{X}) = p(\mathcal{X}|\theta_j, M_j)p(\theta_j|M_j)p(M_j)/p(\mathcal{X}). \tag{25}$$

Specifically, its maximization with respect to θ_j is equivalent to maximizing $\ln[p(\mathcal{X}|\theta_j, M_j)p(\theta_j|M_j)] = \ln p(\mathcal{X}|\theta_j, M_j) + \ln p(\theta_j|M_j)$ with the first term being a special case of $\mathcal{F}(p(x|\theta_j), \mathcal{X})$ and $\ln p(\theta_j|M_j)$ acting as a regularization term. That is, it provides a perspective that determines the Tikhonov stabilizer via a priori density $p(\theta_j|M_j)$. Moreover, model selection can be made by selecting j^* with the corresponding $p(\mathcal{X}|\hat{\theta}_j, M_j)p(\hat{\theta}_j|M_j)p(M_j)$ being the largest, where each a priori $p(M_j)$ is usually setting uniformly and thus ignored, and $\hat{\theta}_j$ is given by either the above MAP regularization or simply by a ML estimator which is equivalent to simply using a non-informative uniform prior as $p(\theta_j|M_j)$.

Instead of basing on a special value $\hat{\theta}_j$ of θ_j, the other version of Bayesian approach makes model selection by selecting j^* of the largest one of

$$p(M_j|\mathcal{X}) = p(\mathcal{X}|M_j)p(M_j)/p(\mathcal{X}), \ \ p(\mathcal{X}|M_j) = \int p(\mathcal{X}|\theta_j, M_j)p(\theta_j|M_j)d\theta_j, \tag{26}$$

or simply the largest one of $p(\mathcal{X}|M_j)$ with $p(M_j)$ being regarded as uniform and thus ignored. The term $p(\mathcal{X}|M_j)$ is called the evidence (EV) or marginal likelihood, and thus it is also shortly referred by the EV approach. Typical studies include not only the so called BIC and variants (Schwarz, 1978; Kashyap, 1982; Neath & Cavanaugh, 1997) that were proposed as a competitor of AIC and variants in the literature of statistics since the late 70's, but also those renewed interests in the literature of neural networks in the last decade, exemplified by the study of (Mackey, 1992a&b; Cooper & Herskovitz, 1992).

Another version of Bayesian approach is to use the Bayesian factor (BF),

$$BF_{ij} = p(\mathcal{X}|M_i)/p(\mathcal{X}|M_j) \tag{27}$$

i.e., the ratio of evidences, for making model comparison via hypothesis testing (Gelfand & Dey, 1994; O'Hagan, 1995; Kass & Raftery, 1995).

A common key problem in all three versions of Bayesian studies is how to get a priori density $p(\theta|M_j)$. Its choice reflects how much a priori knowledge is used. One widely used example is the Jeffery priori (Jeffreys, 1939; Berger, 1985). The other one is simply using the non-informative uniform priori (Mackey, 1992 a&b;

Neath & Cavanaugh, 1997; Kontkanen, 1998). Also, other choices for this priori are discussed in (Kass & Wasserman, 1996). Moreover, the EV approach and the BF approach have the problem of how to compute the evidence accurately and efficiently since it involves an integral. Stochastic simulation techniques such as importance sampling approach and MCMC are usually used for implementations (Neal, 1996; Newton&Raftery, 1994; Chib, 1995). Certain comparisons are referred to (Neal, 1996; DiCiccio, et al, 1997). Recently, the Variational Bayes (VB) method has been also proposed in the literature of neural networks as an alternative way for efficient implementation (Waterhouse, et al, 1996; Ghahramani & Beal 2000; Sato, 2001).

The third type of efforts is made towards to implement the Ockham's principle directly. One typical example is called the minimum message length (MML) theory (Wallace & Boulton, 1968; Wallace & Freeman, 1987; Wallace & Dowe, 1999), which was firstly proposed in the late 60s' as an information measure for classification. The message length is defined via a two-part message coding way. First, one needs a length for coding a hypnosis H, described by $\log_2 P(H)$. Second, one needs a length for coding the residuals of using H to fit or interpret the observed set $\mathcal{X}$, described by $\log_2 P(\mathcal{X}|H)$. The two-part message length

$$M_L = -\log_2 P(H) - \log_2 P(\mathcal{X}|H) \tag{28}$$

is minimized, which is conceptually equivalent to the posterior probability $P(H)P(\mathcal{X}|H)$, where H denotes either a specific parameter θ with a known probability function or generally a model M. The MML theory closely relates to the MAP approach eq.(25) but actually has a difference. The MML theory considers the coding length of probability instead of considering density in the MAP approach. E.g., for the case of densities $p(\theta)$ and $p(\mathcal{X}|\theta)$, the MML results in an additional term $\log|I(\theta)|^{0.5}$ added to the MAP approach, where $I(\theta)$ is the Hessian matrix of $\log p(x|\theta)$. If one insists to regard the MML as the MAP, then it actually uses an improper prior $p(\theta)|I(\theta)|^{0.5}$ (Wallace & Dowe, 1999).

The other typical example is the Minimum Description Length (MDL) theory (Hinton & Zemel, 1994; Rissanen, 1986&89&99). The basic idea is to represent a family of densities with a unknown parameter set θ but a given density form via a universal model that is able to imitate any particular density in the family. Such a universal model is described by a single probability distribution. Via the fundamental Kraft inequality, one constructs a code, e.g., a prefix code, for such a probability distribution, and conversely, such a code defines a probability distribution. In this way, we can compare and select among different families by the code length of each family, which explains the name 'MDL' principle.

A specific implementation of the MDL theory depends how the code length is described. In the early stage, this length is actually specified via a two-part coding way similar to the MML, and thus the corresponding implementation of the MDL is basically the same as the MML. Later, the mixture $p(\mathcal{X}|M_j)$ in eq.(26) is used as the universal model for the family of M_j, and thus $\ln p(\mathcal{X}|M_j)$ is used as the code length. In this case, the corresponding implementation of the MDL is basically equivalent to the EV or BIC approach as in eq.(26). However, by selecting a non-informative uniform prior $p(\theta|M_j)$ and approximating the integral in getting the mixture $p(\mathcal{X}|M_j)$ via simplification, a MML code length and an average of all the MML code lengths for all distributions in a family become no different. Thus, this MDL implementation usually becomes identical to the MML still. In the latest implementation of the MDL, a so called normalized maximum likelihood (NML) model is used as the universal model, which leads an improved code length and becomes different from both the MML and the EV/BIC approach (Rissanen, 1999). Such a NML is also used to get a new estimation on the BF factor for making model comparison.

Both the MML and MDL can be regarded as specific implementations of the more general algorithmic complexity, featured by the celebrated Kolmogorov complexity. The above discussed connections between MML/MDL and MAP/EV actually reveal the deep relations between the fields of statistics, information theory, and computational complexity theory. Moreover, relations between the first two main types of efforts have also explored in the past two decades, particularly on typical examples of the 1st type such as AIC and cross validation versus typical examples of the 2nd type such as MAP, EV/BIC, and BF, etc (Stone, 1977a&77b&79; Atkinson, 1981; Chow, 1981). Furthermore, various applications of all the above discussed studies can be found in literatures, ranging from linear regression, time series modeling, Markov chain (Katz, 1981), as well as complicated neural network modeling problems.

5   Bayesian Ying-Yang Harmony Learning

Alternatively, the Bayesian Ying-Yang (BYY) harmony learning was proposed as a new general framework of the third stream. Firstly proposed in 1995 (Xu, 95&96) and systematically developed in past years (Xu, 2001a & 01b & 02 a & 02b), this BYY harmony learning acts as a general statistical learning framework not only for understanding various generative structures, transform or mapping structures, finite mixture structure, and topological map structure, but also for tackling the previously discussed key challenge with a new learning mechanism that makes model selection implemented either *automatically* during parameter learning or *subsequently after* parameter learning via a new class of model selection criteria obtained from this mechanism. Also, this BYY harmony learning has motivated three types of regularization, namely a data smoothing technique that provides a new solution on the hyper-parameter in a Tikinov-like regularization (Tikhonov & Arsenin, 1977), a normalization with a new conscience de-learning mechanism that has a nature similar to the rival penalized competitive learning (RPCL) (Xu, Krzyzak, & Oja, 1993), and a structural regularization by imposing certain structural constraints via designing a specific forward structure in a BYY system.

Specifically, the BYY harmony learning in different specific cases results in various specific learning algorithms as well as the detailed forms for implementing regularization and model selection, covering three main statistical learning paradigms.

First, new results are obtained on several major unsupervised learning tasks, including

- criteria obtained from the BYY harmony principle for selecting the number of clusters in the mean-square-error clustering (e.g., by the K-means algorithm) and the number of Gaussians in a Gaussian mixture (e.g., by the EM algorithm), with adaptive EM-like algorithms (Xu, 1997);
- elliptic RPCL-type algorithms that performs elliptic clustering and local PCA based clustering, with both the number of clusters and the dimensions of subspaces selected either automatically during learning or alternatively by the corresponding criteria obtained from the BYY harmony principle (Xu, 2001b&02a);
- a RPCL-type adaptive algorithm for Gaussian factor analysis and its local extensions, with the number of local models and the dimension of principal subspace of each model selected either automatically during learning or alternatively by the BYY criteria (Xu, 1995 & 98b&01a&02a);
- extensions of the learned parametric model (LPM) ICA algorithm (Xu, Cheung, & Amari, 1998) to the so called competitive LPM-ICA for implementing ICA on a set of local models (Xu, 2001a & 02a);
- adaptive algorithms for independent binary factor analysis, independent non-Gaussian factor analysis or called noisy ICA, as well as their local extensions, with the number of independent factors and the number of local models determined either automatically during learning or alternatively by the corresponding BYY criteria (Xu, 1998b&01a&02a);
- Not only a new adaptive algorithm has been obtained for implementing LMSER learning (Xu, 1991&93) such that the number of hidden units can be selected either automatically during learning or alternatively by the BYY criteria, but also several extensions of LMSER have been developed, including a local extension of LMSER (Xu, 1991&93) is obtained for not only acting as a fast implementation that implements competitive principal ICA a set of local models (Xu, 2000&01&02a).

Second, we can not only get a unified insight on the following major supervised learning models

- three layer forward net with back-propagation learning (Rumelhart, Hinton & Williams, 1986),
- mixture expert (ME) model (Jacobs, et al, 1991; Jordan & Jacobs, 1994; Jordan & Xu, 1995) and its alternative model (Xu, Jordan, & Hinton, 1995; Xu, 1998a),
- normalized radial basis function (RBF) nets (Moody& Darken, 1989; Nowlan, 1990; Xu, Krzyzak, & Yuille, 1994) and its extensions (Xu, 1998a),
- kernel regression (Devroye, et al, 1996);

but also adaptive EM-like algorithms for learning with the number of hidden units, the number of experts, and the number of basis functions determined either automatically during learning or after learning by the corresponding criteria obtained from the BYY harmony principle (Xu, 1998a& 01b &02a & 02b).

Moreover, based on the Parzen window estimate and kernel regression (Devroye, et al, 1996), a new learning algorithm has been developed for support vector machine (Xu, 2002a).

Third, BYY harmony learning has also been extended to act as a general state space approach for modeling data that has temporal relationship among samples, which provides not only a unified point of view on Kalman filter, Hidden Markov model (HMM), ICA and blind source separation (BSS) with extensions, but also several new results such as higher order HMM, independent HMM for binary BSS, temporal ICA (TICA), competitive TICA, temporal factor analysis (TFA) for noisy real BSS, competitive TFA, temporal LMSER (TLMSER), and competitive TLMSER with adaptive algorithms for learning with the number of states or sources determined either automatically during learning or after learning by the corresponding BYY criteria (Xu, 2000&01a).

References

1. Akaike, H. (1974), "A new look at the statistical model identification", *IEEE Tr. Automatic Control*, **19**, 714-723.
2. Akaike, H., (1981), "Likelihood of a model and information criteria", *Journal of Econometrics*, **16**, 3-14.
3. Akaike, H., (1987), "Factor analysis and AIC", *Psychometrika*, **52**, 317-332.
4. Amari, S.-I., Cichocki, A., & Yang, H.H., (1996), "A new learning algorithm for blind separation of sources", in D. S. Touretzky, et al, eds, *Advances in Neural Information Processing 8*, MIT Press, 757-763.
5. Anderson, T.W., & Rubin, H., (1956), "Statistical inference in factor analysis", *Proc. Berkeley Symp. Math. Statist. Prob. 3rd 5*, UC Berkeley, 111-150.
6. Atkinson, A. C., (1981), "Likelihood ratios, posterior odds and information criteria", *Journal of Econometrics*, **16**, 15-20.
7. Barlow, H.B., (1989), "Unsupervised learning", *Neural Computation, 1*, 295-311.
8. Bell, A.J. & Sejnowski, T.J., (1995), "An information-maximization approach to blind separation and blind de-convolution", *Neural Computation 7*, 1129-1159.
9. Berger, J., (1985), *Statistical Decision Theory and Bayesian Analyses*, Springer-Verlag, New York.
10. Bozdogan, H. (1987) "Model Selection and Akaike's Information Criterion: The general theory and its analytical extension", *Psychometrika*, **52**, 345-370.
11. Bozdogan, H. & Ramirez, D. E., (1988), "FACAIC: Model selection algorithm for the orthogonal factor model using AIC and FACAIC", *Psychometrika*, **53** (3), 407-415.
12. Cavanaugh, J.E. (1997), "Unifying the derivations for the Akaike and corrected Akaike information criteria", *Statistics & Probability Letters* , **33**, 201-208.
13. Chib, S. (1995), "Marginal likelihood from the Gibbs output", *Journal of the American Statistical Association*, **90** (432), 1313-1321.
14. Chow, G. C., (1981), "A comparison of the information and posterior probability criteria for model selection", *Journal of Econometrics*, **16**, 21-33.
15. Cooper, G. & Herskovitz, E., (1992), "A Bayesian method for the induction of probabilistic networks from data", *Machine Learning*, **9**, 309-347.
16. Comon, P. (1994), "Independent component analysis - a new concept?", *Signal Processing 36*, 287-314.

17. Dempster, A.P., et al, (1977), "Maximum- likelihood from incomplete data via the EM algorithm", *J. of Royal Statistical Society*, **B39**, 1-38.
18. Devijver, P.A., & Kittler, J., (1982), *Pattern Recognition: A Statistical Approach*, Prentice-Hall.
19. Devroye, L., et al (1996), *A Probability Theory of Pattern Recognition*, Springer.
20. DiCiccio, T. J., et al, (1997), " Computing Bayes factors by combining simulations and asymptotic Approximations", *Journal of the American Statistical Association*, **92** (439), 903-915.
21. R.O.Duda and P.E.Hart, *Pattern classification and Scene analysis*, Wiley (1973).
22. Efron, B. (1983) "Estimating the error rate of a prediction rule: Improvement on cross-validation", *Journal of the American Statistical Association*, **78**, 316-331.
23. Efron, B. & Tibshirani, R., (1993), *An Introduction to the Bootstrap*, Chaoman and Hall, New York .
24. Fyfe, C.,et al, ed. (1998), Special issue on *Independence and artificial neural networks*, Neurocomputing, Vol.22, No.1-3.
25. Gaeta, M., & Lacounme, J.-L, (1990), "Source Separation without a priori knowledge: the maximum likelihood solution", in *Proc. EUSIPCO90*, 621-624.
26. Gelfand, A. E. & Dey, D. K. (1994), " Bayesian model choice: Asymptotics and exact calculations", *Journal of the Royal Statistical Society B*, **56** (3), 501-514.
27. Geman, S., Bienenstock, E., & Doursat, R., (1992), "Neural Networks and the bias-variance dilemma", *Neural Computation*, **4**, 1-58.
28. Ghahramani, Z. & Beal, M.J., (2000), "Variational inference for Bayesian mixture of factor analysis", S.A. Solla, T.K. Leen & K.-R. Muller, eds, *Advances in Neural Information Processing Systems 12*, Cambridge, MA: MIT Press, 449-455.
29. Girosi, F., et al, (1995) "Regularization theory and neural architectures", *Neural Computation*, **7**, 219-269.
30. Han, J. and Kamber, M., (2001), *Data Mining: Concepts and Techniques*, Morgan Kaufmann, 2001.
31. Hinton, G.E. & Zemel, R.S., (1994), "Autoencoders, minimum description length and Helmholtz free energy", *Advances in NIPS*, **6**, 3-10.
32. Hotelling, H., (1936), "Simplified calculation of principal components", *Psychometrika 1*, 27-35.
33. Hurvich, C.M., & Tsai, C.L. (1989), "Regression and time series model in samll samples", *Biometrika*, **76**, 297-307.
34. Hurvich, C.M., & Tsai, C.L. (1993), "A corrected Akaike information criterion for vector autoregressive model selection", *J. of Time Series Analysis*, **14**, 271-279.
35. Jacobs, R.A., et al, (1991), "Adaptive mixtures of local experts", *Neural Computation*, **3**, 79-87.
36. Jacobs, R. A., (1997) "Bias/Variance Analyses of Mixtures-of-Experts Architectures", *Neural Computation*, **9**.
37. Jeffreys, H., (1939), *Theory of Probability*, Clarendon Press, Oxford.
38. Jensen, F.V., (1996), *An introduction to Bayesian networks*, University of Collage London Press.
39. Jordan, M. I., & Jacobs, R.A., (1994), "Hierarchical mixtures of experts and the EM algorithm", *Neural Computation*, **6**, 181-214.
40. Jordan, M. I., & Xu, L., (1995), "Convergence results for the EM approach to mixtures of experts", *Neural Networks*, **8**, 1409–1431.
41. Jutten, C. & Herault, J., (1988), "Independent Component Analysis versus Principal Component Analysis", *Proc. EUSIPCO88*, 643-646.
42. Kashyap, R.L., (1982), "Optimal choice of AR and MA parts in autoregressive and moving-average models", *IEEE Trans. PAMI*, **4**, 99-104.

43. Kass, R. E. & Raftery, A. E., (1995), " Bayes factors", *Journal of the American Statistical Association*, **90** (430), 773-795.
44. Kass, R. E. & Wasserman, L., (1996), "The selection of prior distributions by formal rules", *Journal of the American Statistical Association*, **91** (435), 1343-1370.
45. Katz, R. W., (1981), "On some criteria for estimating the order of a Markov chain", *Technometrics*, **23**(3), 243-249.
46. King, I. & Xu, L., (1995), "Adaptive contrast enhancement by entropy maximization with a 1-K-1 constrained network", *Proc. ICONIP'95*, pp703–706.
47. Kohonen, T, (1995), *Self-Organizing Maps* , Springer-Verlag, Berlin.
48. Kohonen, T., (1982), "Self-organized formation of topologically correct feature maps", *Biological Cybernetics 43*, 59-69.
49. Kontkanen, P., et al, (1998), "Bayesian and Information-Theoretic priors for Bayeisan network parameters", *Machine Learning: ECML-98*, Lecture Notes in Artificial Intelligence, Vol.1398, 89-94, Springer-Verlag.
50. Mackey, D. (1992a) "A practical Bayesian framework for backpropagation", *Neural Computation*, **4**, 448-472.
51. Mackey, D. (1992b) "Bayesian Interpolation", *Neural Computation*, **4**, 405-447.
52. von der Malsburg, Ch. (1973), Self-organization of orientation sensitive cells in the striate cortex, Kybernetik **14**, 85-100.
53. McDonald, R, (1985), *Factor Analysis and Related Techniques*, Lawrence Erlbaum.
54. McLachlan, G.J. & Krishnan, T. (1997) *The EM Algorithm and Extensions*, John Wiley & Son, INC.
55. Moody, J. & Darken, J., (1989) "Fast learning in networks of locally-tuned processing units", *Neural Computation*, **1**, 281-294.
56. Neath, A.A., & Cavanaugh, J.E., (1997), "Regression and Time Series model selection using variants of the Schwarz information criterion", *Communications in Statistics A*, **26**, 559-580.
57. Neal, R.M., (1996), *Bayesian learning for neural networks*, New York: Springer-Verlag.
58. Newton, M. A. & Raftery, A. E., (1994), "Approximate Bayesian inference with the weighted likelihood Bootstrap", *J. Royal Statistical Society B*, **56**(1), 3-48.
59. Nowlan, S.J., (1990), "Max likelihood competition in RBF networks", *Tech. Rep. CRG-Tr-90-2, Dept. of Computer Sci., U. of Toronto*.
60. O'Hagan, A., (1995), "Fractional Bayes factors for model comparison", *J. Royal Statistical Society B*, **57** (1), 99-138.
61. Oja, E., (1983), *Subspace Methods of Pattern Recognition*, Research Studies Press, UK.
62. Pearl, J, (1988), *Probabilistic reasoning in intelligent systems: networks of plausible inference*, San Fransisca, CA: Morgan Kaufman.
63. Rabiner, L. & Juang, B.H., (1993), *Fundamentals of Speech Recognition*, Prentice Hall, Inc..
64. Wolpert, D. H., (1997), "On Bias Plus Variance ", *Neural Computation*, **9**.
65. Vapnik, V.N., (1995), *The Nature Of Statistical Learning Theory*, Springer-Verlag.
66. Redner, R.A. & Walker, H.F., (1984), "Mixture densities, maximum likelihood, and the EM algorithm", *SIAM Review*, **26**, 195-239.
67. Rissanen, J. (1986), "Stochastic complexity and modeling", *Annals of Statistics*, **14**(3), 1080-1100.
68. Rissanen, J. (1989), *Stochastic Complexity in Statistical Inquiry*, World Scientific: Singapore.

69. Rissanen, J. (1999), "Hypothesis selection and testing by the MDL principle", *Computer Journal*, **42** (4), 260-269.
70. Rivals, I. & Personnaz, L., (1999) "On Cross Validation for Model Selection", *Neural Computation*, **11**, 863-870.
71. Rubi, D & Thayer, D., (1976), "EM algorithm for ML factor analysis", *Psychometrika 57*, 69-76.
72. Rumelhart, D.E., Hinton, G.E., & Williams, R.J., (1986), "Learning internal representations by error propagation", *Parallel Distributed Processing*, **1**, MIT press.
73. Sato, M., (2001), "Online model selection based on the vairational Bayes", *Neural Computation*, **13**, 1649-1681.
74. Schwarz, G., (1978), "Estimating the dimension of a model", *Annals of Statistics*, **6**, 461-464.
75. Sclove, S. L., (1987), " Application of model-selection criteria to some problems in multivariate analysis", *Psychometrika*, **52** (3), 333-343.
76. Spearman, C., (1904), "General intelligence domainively determined and measured", *Am. J. Psychol. 15*, 201-293.
77. Stone, M. (1974), "Cross-validatory choice and assessment of statistical prediction", *J. Royal Statistical Society B*, **36**, 111-147.
78. Stone, M. (1977a), "Asymptotics for and against cross-validation", *Biometrika*, **64**(1), 29-35.
79. Stone, M. (1977b), "An asymptotic equivalence of choice of model by cross-validation and Akaike's criterion", *J. Royal Statistical Society B*, **39** (1), 44-47.
80. Stone, M. (1978), "Cross-validation: A review", *Math. Operat. Statist.* , 9, 127-140.
81. Stone, M. (1979), "Comments on model selection criteria of Akaike and Schwartz. *J. Royal Statistical Society B*, **41** (2), 276-278.
82. Sugiura, N. (1978), "Further analysis of data by Akaike's infprmation criterion and the finite corrections", *Communications in Statistics A* , **7**, 12-26.
83. Tikhonov, A.N. & Arsenin, V.Y., (1977), *Solutions of Ill-posed Problems*, V.H. Winston and Sons.
84. Tipping, M.E., and Bishop, C.M., (1999), "Mixtures of probabilistic principal component analysis", *Neural Computation*, **11**, 443-482.
85. Tong, L., Inouye, Y., & Liu, R., (1993) "Waveform-preserving blind estimation of multiple independent sources", *IEEE Trans. on Signal Processing 41*, 2461-2470.
86. Wallace, C.S. & Boulton, D.M., (1968), "An information measure for classification", *Computer Journal*, **11**, 185-194.
87. Wallace, C.S. & Freeman, P.R., (1987), "Estimation and inference by compact coding", *J. of the Royal Statistical Society*, **49**(3), 240-265.
88. Wallace, C.S. & Dowe, D.R., (1999), "Minimum message length and Kolmogorov complexity", *Computer Journal*, **42** (4), 270-280.
89. Waterhouse, S., et al, (1996), "Bayesian method for mixture of experts", D.S. Touretzky, et al, eds, *Advances in NIPS 8*, 351-357.
90. Xu, L., (2002a), " BYY Harmony Learning, Structural RPCL, and Topological Self-Organizing on Mixture Models ", to appear on *Neural Networks*, 2002.
91. Xu, L., (2002b), " BYY Learning, Regularized Implementation, and Model Selection on Modular Networks with One Hidden Layer of Binary Units ", to appear on a special issue, *Neurocomputing* , 2002.
92. Xu, L., (2001a), "BYY Harmony Learning, Independent State Space and Generalized APT Financial Analyses ", *IEEE Trans on Neural Networks*, **12** (4), 822-849.

93. Xu, L., (2001b), "Best Harmony, Unified RPCL and Automated Model Selection for Unsupervised and Supervised Learning on Gaussian Mixtures, Three-Layer Nets and ME-RBF-SVM Models", *Intl J. of Neural Systems* **11** (1), 43-69.

94. Xu, L., (2000), "Temporal BYY Learning for State Space Approach, Hidden Markov Model and Blind Source Separation", *IEEE Trans on Signal Processing* *48*, 2132-2144.

95. Xu, L., (1998a), "RBF Nets, Mixture Experts, and Bayesian Ying-Yang Learning", *Neurocomputing*, Vol. 19, No.1-3, 223-257.

96. Xu, L., (1998b), "Bayesian Kullback Ying-Yang Dependence Reduction Theory", *Neurocomputing* *22*, No.1-3, 81-112, 1998.

97. Xu, L., Cheung, C.C., & Amari, S.-I., (1998) "Learned Parametric Mixture Based ICA Algorithm", *Neurocomputing* *22*, No.1-3, 69-80. A part of its preliminary version on *Proc. ESANN97*, 291-296.

98. Xu, L., (1997), "Bayesian Ying-Yang Machine, Clustering and Number of Clusters", *Pattern Recognition Letters 18*, No.11-13, 1167-1178.

99. Xu, L. Yang, H.H., & Amari,S.-I., (1996), "Signal Source Separation by Mixtures Accumulative Distribution Functions or Mixture of Bell-Shape Density Distribution Functions ", Research Proposal, presented at *FRONTIER FORUM (speakers: D. Sherrington, S. Tanaka, L.Xu & J. F. Cardoso)*, organized by S.Amari, S.Tanaka & A.Cichocki, RIKEN, Japan, April 10, 1996.

100. Xu, L., (1996&95), "A Unified Learning Scheme: Bayesian-Kullback YING-YANG Machine", *Advances in Neural Information Processing Systems*, **8**, 444-450 (1996). A part of its preliminary version on *Proc. ICONIP95-Peking*, 977-988(1995).

101. Xu, L., (1995), "A unified learning framework: multisets modeling learning," *Proceedings of 1995 World Congress on Neural Networks*, vol.1, pp. 35-42.

102. Xu, L., Jordan, M.I., & Hinton, G.E., (1995), "An Alternative Model for Mixtures of Experts", *Advances in Neural Information Processing Systems 7*, eds., Cowan, J.D., et al, MIT Press, 633-640, 1995.

103. Xu, L., Krzyzak, A., & Yuille, A.L., (1994), "On Radial Basis Function Nets and Kernel Regression: Statistical Consistency, Convergence Rates and Receptive Field Size", *Neural Networks*, **7**, 609-628.

104. Xu, L., Krzyzak, A. & Oja, E. (1993), "Rival Penalized Competitive Learning for Clustering Analysis, RBF net and Curve Detection", *IEEE Tr. on Neural Networks 4*, 636-649.

105. Xu, L., (1991&93) "Least mean square error reconstruction for self-organizing neural-nets", *Neural Networks 6*, 627-648, 1993. Its early version on *Proc. IJCNN91'Singapore*, 2363-2373, 1991.

k^*-Means — A Generalized k-Means Clustering Algorithm with Unknown Cluster Number

Yiu-ming Cheung

Department of Computer Science
Hong Kong Baptist University, Hong Kong
ymc@comp.hkbu.edu.hk

Abstract. This paper presents a new clustering technique named *STepwise Automatic Rival-penalized (STAR) k-means algorithm* (denoted as k^*-means), which is actually a generalized version of the conventional k-means (MacQueen 1967). Not only is this new algorithm applicable to ellipse-shaped data clusters rather than just to ball-shaped ones like the k-means algorithm, but also it can perform appropriate clustering without knowing cluster number by gradually penalizing the winning chance of those extra seed points during learning competition. Although the existing RPCL (Xu et al. 1993) can automatically select the cluster number as well by driving extra seed points far away from the input data set, its performance is much sensitive to the selection of the de-learning rate. To our best knowledge, there is still no theoretical result to guide its selection as yet. In contrast, the proposed k^*-means algorithm need not determine this rate. We have qualitatively analyzed its rival-penalized mechanism with the results well-justified by the experiments.

1 Introduction

Clustering analysis is a fundamental but important tool in statistical data analysis. In the past, the clustering techniques have been widely applied in the interdisciplinary scientific areas such as pattern recognition, information retrieval, clinical diagnosis, and micro biology analysis.

In the literature, the k-means is a typical clustering algorithm, which partitions the input data set $\{\mathbf{x}_t\}_{t=1}^N$ that generally forms k^* true clusters into k categories (also simply called *clusters* without further distinction) with each represented by its center. Although the k-means has been widely used due to its easy implementation, it has two major drawbacks:

(1) It implies that the data clusters are ball-shaped because it performs clustering based on the Euclidean distance only;

(2) It needs to pre-assign the number k of clusters. Many experiments have shown that the k-means algorithm can work well when k is equal to k^*. However, in many practical cases, it is impossible to know the exact cluster number in advance. Under the circumstances, the k-means algorithm often leads to a poor clustering performance.

H. Yin et al. (Eds.): IDEAL 2002, LNCS 2412, pp. 307–317, 2002.

The former can be circumvented by considering the data correlations like in [9]. As for the latter, some works have been done along two directions. The first one is to formulate the cluster number selection as the choice of component number in a finite mixture model. In the past, there have been some criteria proposed for model selection, such as AIC [2,3], CAIC [4] and SIC [6]. Often, these existing criteria may overestimate or underestimate the cluster number due to the difficulty of choosing an appropriate penalty function. In recent years, a number selection criterion developed from Ying-Yang Machine has been proposed and experimentally verified in [7,8], whose computing however is laborious. The other direction invokes some heuristic approaches. For example, the typical incremental clustering gradually increases the number k of clusters under the control of a threshold value, which unfortunately is hard to be decided. Another typical example is the RPCL algorithm [9] that for each input, not only the winner of the seed points is updated to adapt to the input, but also its rival is de-learned by a smaller learning rate (also called *de-learning rate* hereafter). Many experiments have shown that the RPCL can select the correct cluster number by driving extra seed points far away from the input data set, but its performance is much sensitive to the selection of the de-learning rate. To our best knowledge, there is still no theoretical result to guide this rate selection so far.

In this paper, we will present a new clustering technique named **ST**ep-wise **A**utomatic **R**ival-penalized (STAR) k-means algorithm (denoted as k^*-*means* hereafter), which consists of two separate steps. The first step is a pre-processing procedure, which assigns each true cluster at least a seed point. Then, the next step is to update the seed points based on a winner-take-all learning rule while each input is dynamically assigned to a cluster under the maximum-a-posteriori (MAP) principle. The k^*-means is actually a generalized version of the conventional k-means [5] with the major improvements on two fold. On the one hand, the k^*-means generally works on ellipse-shaped clusters, but not just on ball-shaped ones like the k-means algorithm. On the other hand, this new clustering algorithm has a similar mechanism to RPCL [9] that penalizes the winning chance of those rival seed points in the competition for learning to adapt to the inputs, but this proposed new one need not determine the de-learning rate. The experiments have successfully shown its outstanding clustering performance.

2   A Metric for Data Clustering

Suppose N inputs (also called *data points*) $\mathbf{x}_1, \mathbf{x}_2, \ldots, \mathbf{x}_N$ are independently and identically distributed from a mixture-density-of-Gaussian population:

$$p^*(\mathbf{x}; \boldsymbol{\Theta}^*) = \sum_{j=1}^{k^*} \alpha_j^* G(\mathbf{x}|\mathbf{m}_j^*, \boldsymbol{\Sigma}_j^*), \tag{1}$$

with

$$\sum_{j=1}^{k^*} \alpha_j^* = 1, \quad \text{and} \quad \alpha_j^* \geq 0 \quad \text{for} \quad 1 \leq j \leq k, \tag{2}$$

where k^* is the mixture number, $\boldsymbol{\Theta}^* = \{(\alpha_j^*, \mathbf{m}_j^*, \boldsymbol{\Sigma}_j^*)|1 \leq j \leq k^*\}$ is the true parameter set, and $G(\mathbf{x}|\mathbf{m}, \boldsymbol{\Sigma})$ denotes a multivariate Gaussian density of $\mathbf{x}$ with mean $\mathbf{m}$ and covariance $\boldsymbol{\Sigma}$. We consider the following Kullback-Leibler divergence function:

$$Q(\mathbf{x}; \boldsymbol{\Theta}) = \int p^*(\mathbf{x}; \boldsymbol{\Theta}^*) \ln \frac{p^*(\mathbf{x}; \boldsymbol{\Theta}^*)}{p(\mathbf{x}; \boldsymbol{\Theta})} d\mathbf{x}$$

$$= \int p(j|\mathbf{x}) p^*(\mathbf{x}; \boldsymbol{\Theta}^*) \ln \frac{p^*(\mathbf{x}; \boldsymbol{\Theta}^*)}{p(\mathbf{x}; \boldsymbol{\Theta})} dj d\mathbf{x}$$

$$= \int p(j|\mathbf{x}) p^*(\mathbf{x}; \boldsymbol{\Theta}^*) \ln \frac{p(j|\mathbf{x}) p^*(\mathbf{x}; \boldsymbol{\Theta}^*)}{\alpha_j G(\mathbf{x}|\mathbf{m}_j, \boldsymbol{\Sigma}_j)} dj d\mathbf{x} \qquad (3)$$

with

$$p(j|\mathbf{x}) = \frac{\alpha_j G(\mathbf{x}|\mathbf{m}_j, \boldsymbol{\Sigma}_j)}{p(\mathbf{x}_t; \boldsymbol{\Theta})}, \qquad 1 \leq j \leq k, \qquad (4)$$

where k is an assumed mixture number, $\boldsymbol{\Theta} = \{(\alpha_j, \mathbf{m}_j, \boldsymbol{\Sigma}_j)|1 \leq j \leq k\}$ is an estimator of $\boldsymbol{\Theta}^*$ with $\mathbf{m}_j$'s called the seed points in consistency with the names in the k-means algorithm, and $p(j|\mathbf{x})$ is the posterior probability of an input $\mathbf{x}$ from Cluster j as given $\mathbf{x}$. It is clear that $Q(\mathbf{x}; \boldsymbol{\Theta})$ reaches the minimum at $\bar{\boldsymbol{\Theta}} = \boldsymbol{\Theta}^*$, where $\bar{\boldsymbol{\Theta}} = \boldsymbol{\Theta} - \Lambda(\boldsymbol{\Theta})$ with $\Lambda(\boldsymbol{\Theta}) = \{(\alpha_j, \mathbf{m}_j, \boldsymbol{\Sigma}_j)|\alpha_j = 0, 1 \leq j \leq k\}$. Hence, Eq.(3) is an appropriate metric for data clustering by means of $p(j|\mathbf{x})$. Here, we prefer to perform clustering based on MAP principle. That is, we assign an input $\mathbf{x}$ into Cluster j if

$$I_j = \begin{cases} 1, \text{ if } j = \arg\max_{1 \leq r \leq k} p(r|\mathbf{x}); \\ 0, \text{ otherwise,} \end{cases} \qquad (5)$$

which can be further specified as

$$I_j = \begin{cases} 1, \text{ if } j = \arg\min_r \rho_r; \\ 0, \text{ otherwise} \end{cases} \qquad (6)$$

with

$$\rho_r = [(\mathbf{x}_t - \mathbf{m}_r)^T \boldsymbol{\Sigma}_r^{-1}(\mathbf{x}_t - \mathbf{m}_r) - \ln(|\boldsymbol{\Sigma}_r^{-1}|) - 2\ln(\alpha_r)]. \qquad (7)$$

Consequently, minimizing Eq.(3) is approximate to minimize

$$R(\mathbf{x}; \boldsymbol{\Theta}) = \int I(j|\mathbf{x}) p^*(\mathbf{x}; \boldsymbol{\Theta}^*) \ln \frac{I(j|\mathbf{x}) p^*(\mathbf{x}; \boldsymbol{\Theta}^*)}{\alpha_j G(\mathbf{x}|\mathbf{m}_j, \boldsymbol{\Sigma}_j)} dj d\mathbf{x}, \qquad (8)$$

which can be further simplified as

$$R(\mathbf{x}_1, \mathbf{x}_2, \dots, \mathbf{x}_N; \boldsymbol{\Theta}) = H - \frac{1}{N} \sum_{t=1}^{N} \sum_{j=1}^{k} I(j|\mathbf{x}_t) \ln[\alpha_j G(\mathbf{x}|\mathbf{m}_j, \boldsymbol{\Sigma}_j)] \qquad (9)$$

as N is large enough, where H is a constant term irrelevant to Θ. Hence, we can perform clustering on line by Eq.(6) while adaptively learning Θ via minimizing Eq.(9). Before closing this section, two things should be noted. The first one is that Eq.(9) can be degenerated to mean-square-error (MSE) function if α_j's are all forced to $1/k$, and Σ_j's are all the same. Under the circumstances, the clustering based on Eq.(6) is actually the conventional k-means algorithm. The other thing is that the term $\ln(\alpha_r)$ with $r \neq j$ in Eq.(6) is automatically decreased because of the summation constraints among α_r's in Eq.(2) when α_j is adjusted to adapt the winning of Cluster j for an input $\mathbf{x}_t$. Consequently, all rival seed points (i.e., except for the winning one) are automatically penalized while the winner is modified to adapt to the input $\mathbf{x}_t$. In the next section, we will show that such a penalization can drive the winning chance of extra seed points in one true cluster to zero.

3   Qualitative Analysis of MAP-Based Data Clustering Assignment

For simplicity, we consider one cluster with two seed points denoted as $\mathbf{m}_1$ and $\mathbf{m}_2$, respectively. In the beginning, we assume that $\alpha_1^{(\tau)} = \alpha_2^{(\tau)}$ with $\tau = 0$, where the superscript $\tau \geq 0$ denotes the number of times that the data have been repeatedly scanned. Hence, based on the data assignment condition in Eq.(6), $\mathbf{m}_1^{(0)}$ and $\mathbf{m}_2^{(0)}$ divide the true cluster into two regions: Region 1 and Region 2 by a separating line $L^{(0)}$ as shown in Fig. 1(a). In general, the number $n_1^{(0)}$ of the inputs falling in Region 1 is different from $n_2^{(0)}$ in Region 2. Without loss of generality, we further suppose $n_1^{(0)} > n_2^{(0)}$. During data scanning, if $\mathbf{m}_j^{(0)}$ wins given an input $\mathbf{x}_t$, $\alpha_j^{(0)}$ will be increased by a unit $\Delta\alpha$ while $\mathbf{m}^{(j)}$ is modified to adapt to the input $\mathbf{x}_t$. Since $n_1^{(0)} > n_2^{(0)}$, after scanning all the data points in the cluster, the net increase of $\alpha_1^{(0)}$ will be about $n_d^{(0)}\Delta\alpha$ with $n_d^{(0)} = n_1^{(0)} - n_2^{(0)}$, and the net decrease of $\alpha_2^{(0)}$ will be in the same amount due to the constraint that $\alpha_1^{(0)} + \alpha_2^{(0)} = 1$. Consequently, the separating line between Region 1 and Region 2 is moved towards the right direction as shown in Fig. 1(b). That is, the area of Region 1 is being expanded towards the right meanwhile Region 2 is being shrunk. This scenario will be always kept along with τ's increase until the seed point $\mathbf{m}_2$ is stabilized at the boundary of the cluster with its associated $\alpha_2 = 0$. From Eq.(6), we know that $\mathbf{m}_2$ has actually been dead because it has no chance to win again. Although $\mathbf{m}_2$ still stays in the cluster, it cannot interfere with the learning of $\mathbf{m}_1$ any more. Consequently, $\mathbf{m}_1$ will gradually converge to the true cluster center.

In the above, we just investigate a simple one-cluster case. In general, the analysis of multiple clusters is more complex, but the results are similar. The experiments in Section 5 will further justify this.

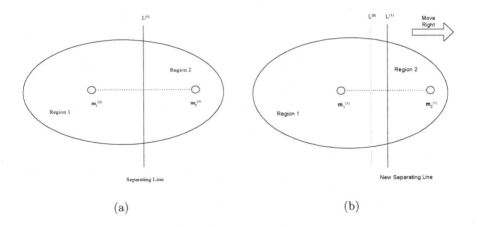

Fig. 1. The domain of the seed points $\mathbf{m}_1$ and $\mathbf{m}_2$ that divide the true cluster into two regions: Region 1 and Region 2 by a separating line L with (a) the initial region boundary, and (b) the boundary after all data points in the cluster have been scanned once.

4 k^*-Means Algorithm

From the results of Section 3, we know that the data assignment based on the condition in Eq.(6) can automatically penalize the extra seed points without requiring any other efforts. Hence, the k^*-means algorithm consists of two steps. The first step is to let each cluster acquires at least one seed point, and the other step is to adjust the parameter set Θ via minimizing Eq.(9) while assigning the data points based on Eq.(6). The detailed k^*-means algorithm is given out as follows:

Step 1   We implement this step by using Frequency Sensitive Competitive Learning [1] because they can achieve the goal as long as the number of seed points is not less than the exact number k^* of clusters. Here, we suppose the number of clusters is $k \geq k^*$, and randomly initialize the k seed points $\mathbf{m}_1, \mathbf{m}_2, \ldots, \mathbf{m}_k$ in the input data set.

Stage 1.1   For a data point $\mathbf{x}_t$, and for $j = 1, 2, \ldots, k$, let

$$u_j = \begin{cases} 1, & \text{if } j = \arg\min_r \lambda_r d_r \\ 0, & \text{otherwise,} \end{cases} \qquad (10)$$

with the Euclidean distance

$$d_r = \|\mathbf{x}_t - \mathbf{m}_r\|, \qquad r = 1, 2, \ldots, k, \qquad (11)$$

where $\lambda_j = n_j / \sum_{r=1}^{k} n_r$, and n_r is the cumulative number of the occurrences of $u_r = 1$.

Stage 1.2   Update the seed points $\mathbf{m}_w$ with $u_w = 1$ only by

$$\mathbf{m}_w^{\text{new}} = \mathbf{m}_w^{\text{old}} + \Delta\mathbf{m}_w \qquad (12)$$

with $\Delta\mathbf{m}_w = \eta(\mathbf{x}_t - \mathbf{m}_w)$, where η is a small positive learning rate.

Stage 1.1 and **Stage 1.2** are repeated for each input until the k series of u_j, $j = 1, 2, \ldots, k$ remain unchanged for all $\mathbf{x}_t$'s. Then go to **Step 2**.

Step 2   Initialize $\alpha_j = 1/k$ for $j = 1, 2, ..., k$, and let $\boldsymbol{\Sigma}_j$ be the covariance matrix of those data points with $u_j = 1$.

Stage 2.1   For a data point $\mathbf{x}_t$, and for $j = 1, 2, ..., k$, let I_j be given by Eq.(6).

Stage 2.2   Update the seed point $\mathbf{m}_w$ with $I_w = 1$ only (that is so-called *winner-take-all* learning rule) by Eq.(12), but $\Delta\mathbf{m}_w$ becomes

$$\Delta\mathbf{m}_w = \eta\boldsymbol{\Sigma}_w^{-1}(\mathbf{x}_t - \mathbf{m}_w). \qquad (13)$$

Also, update the parameters α_j's and $\boldsymbol{\Sigma}_w$. The updates of the former can be obtained by minimizing Eq.(9) through a constrained optimization algorithm in view of the constraints on α_j's in Eq.(2). Alternatively, we here let

$$\alpha_j = \frac{\exp(\beta_j)}{\sum_{r=1}^{k} \exp(\beta_r)}, \qquad 1 \le j \le k, \qquad (14)$$

where the constraints of α_j's are automatically satisfied, but the new variables β_j's are totally free. Consequently, instead of α_j's, we can learn β_w^{new} only by

$$\beta_w^{\text{new}} = \beta_w^{\text{old}} + \eta[exp(-0.5\rho_w - \ln\xi) - \alpha_w], \qquad (15)$$

with $\xi = \sum_{j=1}^{k} exp(-0.5\rho_j)$, where ρ_j's are given by Eq.(7). As for the latter, since Eq.(6) and Eq.(13) only involve $\boldsymbol{\Sigma}_j^{-1}$'s rather than $\boldsymbol{\Sigma}_j$'s. To save computing costs and calculation stability, we therefore directly update $\boldsymbol{\Sigma}_j^{-1}$'s by

$$\boldsymbol{\Sigma}_w^{-1\,\text{new}} = \frac{\boldsymbol{\Sigma}_w^{-1\,\text{old}}}{1 - \eta_s}[\mathbf{I} - \frac{\eta_s \mathbf{z}\mathbf{z}^T \boldsymbol{\Sigma}_w^{-1\,\text{old}}}{1 - \eta_s + \eta_s \mathbf{z}^T \boldsymbol{\Sigma}_w^{-1\,\text{old}} \mathbf{z}}], \qquad (16)$$

where $\mathbf{I}$ is an identity matrix, $\mathbf{z} = \mathbf{x}_t - \mathbf{m}_w$, and η_s is a small positive learning rate. To make the covariance learned smoothly, by rule of thumb, η_s should be chosen much smaller than η, e.g., $\eta_s = 0.1\eta$.

Stage 2.1 and **Stage 2.2** are repeated for each input until k series of I_j, $j = 1, 2, \ldots, k$ remain unchanged for all $\mathbf{x}_t$'s.

5   Experimental Results

We perform two experiments to demonstrate the performance of k^*-means algorithm. Experiment 1 used the $1,000$ data points from a mixture of three Gaussian distributions:

$$p(\mathbf{x}) = 0.3G[\mathbf{x}| \begin{pmatrix} 1 \\ 1 \end{pmatrix}, \begin{pmatrix} 0.1, & 0.05 \\ 0.05, & 0.2 \end{pmatrix}] + 0.4G[\mathbf{x}| \begin{pmatrix} 1 \\ 5 \end{pmatrix}, \begin{pmatrix} 0.1, & 0 \\ 0, & 0.1 \end{pmatrix}]$$

$$+ 0.3G[\mathbf{x}| \begin{pmatrix} 5 \\ 5 \end{pmatrix}, \begin{pmatrix} 0.1, & -0.05 \\ -0.05, & 0.1 \end{pmatrix}]. \tag{17}$$

As shown in Fig. 2(a), the data form three well-separated clusters. We randomly initialized six seed points in the input data space, and set the learning rates $\eta = 0.001$ and $\eta_s = 0.0001$. After **Step 1** of k^*-means algorithm, each cluster has acquired at least one seed point as shown in Fig. 2(b). We then performed **Step 2**, resulting in α_1, α_5 and α_6 converging to 0.2960, 0.3987 and 0.3053 respectively, while the others converged to zero. That is, the seed points $\mathbf{m}_2$, $\mathbf{m}_3$ and $\mathbf{m}_4$ are the extra ones whose winning chance in competition has been penalized to zero. Consequently, as shown in Fig. 2(c), the three true clusters have been well recognized with

$$\mathbf{m}_1 = \begin{pmatrix} 1.0087 \\ 0.9738 \end{pmatrix}, \ \boldsymbol{\Sigma}_1 = \begin{pmatrix} 0.0970, 0.0471 \\ 0.0471, 0.1984 \end{pmatrix}$$

$$\mathbf{m}_5 = \begin{pmatrix} 0.9756 \\ 4.9761 \end{pmatrix}, \ \boldsymbol{\Sigma}_5 = \begin{pmatrix} 0.0870, 0.0019 \\ 0.0019, 0.0919 \end{pmatrix}$$

$$\mathbf{m}_6 = \begin{pmatrix} 5.0158 \\ 5.0065 \end{pmatrix}, \ \boldsymbol{\Sigma}_6 = \begin{pmatrix} 0.1045, & -0.0520 \\ -0.0520, & 0.1062 \end{pmatrix}, \tag{18}$$

while the extra seed points $\mathbf{m}_2$, $\mathbf{m}_3$ and $\mathbf{m}_4$ have been pushed to stay at the boundary of their corresponding clusters. It can be seen that this result is in accordance with the analysis in Section 3.

In Experiment 2, we used $2,000$ data points that are also from a mixture of three Gaussians:

$$p(\mathbf{x}) = 0.3G[\mathbf{x}| \begin{pmatrix} 1 \\ 1 \end{pmatrix}, \begin{pmatrix} 0.15, 0.05 \\ 0.05, 0.25 \end{pmatrix}] + 0.4G[\mathbf{x}| \begin{pmatrix} 1 \\ 2.5 \end{pmatrix}, \begin{pmatrix} 0.15, 0 \\ 0, & 0.15 \end{pmatrix}]$$

$$+ 0.3G[\mathbf{x}| \begin{pmatrix} 2.5 \\ 2.5 \end{pmatrix}, \begin{pmatrix} 0.15, & -0.1 \\ -0.1, & 0.15 \end{pmatrix}], \tag{19}$$

which lead to have a seriously overlapping area among clusters as shown in Fig. 3(a). Under the same experimental environment, we first performed **Step 1**, resulting in the six seed points distributed in the three clusters as shown in Fig. 3(b). Then we performed **Step 2**, which led to $\alpha_1 = 0.2705$, $\alpha_2 = 0.4244$, and $\alpha_6 = 0.3051$ while the others became to zero. Consequently, the corresponding

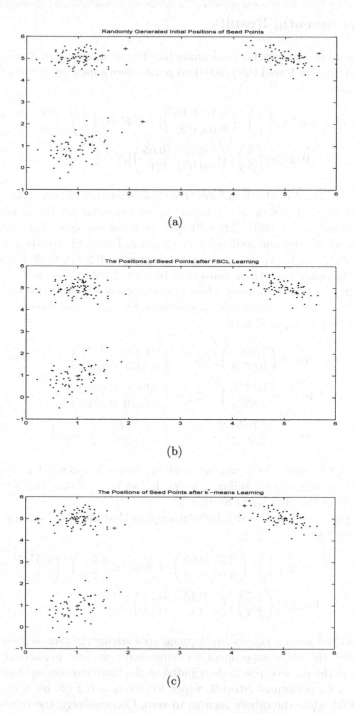

Fig. 2. The positions of six seed points marked by '+' in the input data space at different steps in Experiment 1: (a) the initial positions, (b) the positions after **Step 1** of the k^*-means algorithm, and (c) the final position after **Step 2**.

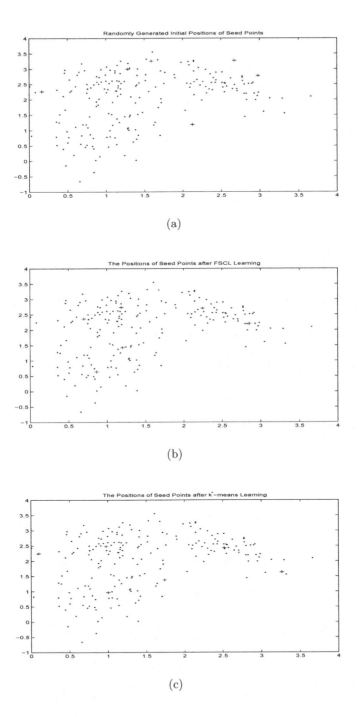

Fig. 3. The positions of six seed points marked by '+' in the input data space at different steps in Experiment 2: (a) the initial positions, (b) the positions after **Step 1** of the k^*-means algorithm, and (c) the final position after **Step 2**.

converged $\mathbf{m}_j$'s and $\boldsymbol{\Sigma}_j$'s are:

$$\mathbf{m}_1 = \begin{pmatrix} 1.0026 \\ 0.9691 \end{pmatrix}, \quad \boldsymbol{\Sigma}_1 = \begin{pmatrix} 0.1462, 0.0433 \\ 0.0433, 0.2105 \end{pmatrix}$$

$$\mathbf{m}_2 = \begin{pmatrix} 0.9769 \\ 2.4844 \end{pmatrix}, \quad \boldsymbol{\Sigma}_2 = \begin{pmatrix} 0.1255, 0.0057 \\ 0.0057, 0.1411 \end{pmatrix}$$

$$\mathbf{m}_6 = \begin{pmatrix} 2.5172 \\ 2.4317 \end{pmatrix}, \quad \boldsymbol{\Sigma}_6 = \begin{pmatrix} 0.1587, -0.1027 \\ -0.1027, 0.1529 \end{pmatrix}, \tag{20}$$

and the extra seed points $\mathbf{m}_3$, $\mathbf{m}_4$ and $\mathbf{m}_5$ are pushed to stay at the boundary of their corresponding clusters as shown in Fig. 3(c). Once again, the analysis results in Section 3 have been verified.

6   Conclusion

We have presented a new clustering algorithm, which is a generalization of conventional k-means one with two major improvements: (1) it is applicable to ellipse-shaped data clustering as well as ball-shaped ones; (2) it can automatically determine the number of clusters by penalizing the winning chance of those extra seed points to zero without any other extra efforts. We have qualitatively analyzed its rival-penalized mechanism. The conducted experiments have shown the algorithm's outstanding performance in data clustering.

Acknowledgment. This work was supported by a Faculty Research Grant of Hong Kong Baptist University.

References

1. S.C. Ahalt, A.K. Krishnamurty, P. Chen, and D.E. Melton, "Competitive Learning Algorithms for Vector Quantization", *Neural Networks*, Vol. 3, pp. 277–291, 1990.
2. H. Akaike, "Information Theory and An Extension of the Maximum Likelihood Principle", *Proceedings of Second International Symposium on Information Theory*, pp. 267–281, 1973.
3. H. Akaike, "A New Look at the Statistical Model Identfication", *IEEE Transactions on Automatic Control AC-19*, pp. 716–723, 1974.
4. H. Bozdogan, "Model Selection and Akaike's Information Criterion: The General Theory and its Analytical Extensions", *Psychometrika*, Vol. 52, No. 3, pp. 345–370, 1987.
5. J.B. MacQueen, "Some Methods for Classification and Analysis of Multivariate Observations", *Proceedings of 5nd Berkeley Symposium on Mathematical Statistics and Probability*, 1, Berkeley, Calif.: University of California Press, pp. 281–297, 1967.
6. G. Schwarz, "Estimating the Dimension of a Model", *The Annals of Statistics*, Vol. 6, No. 2, pp. 461–464, 1978.

7. L. Xu, "How Many Clusters?: A Ying-Yang Machine Based Theory for A Classical Open Problem in Pattern Recognition", *Proceedings of IEEE International Conference on Neural Networks*, Vol. 3, pp. 1546–1551, 1996.

8. L. Xu, "Bayesian Ying-Yang Machine, Clustering and Number of Clusters", *Pattern Recognition Letters*, Vol. 18, No. 11-13, pp. 1167–1178, 1997.

9. L. Xu, A. Krzyżak and E. Oja, "Rival Penalized Competitive Learning for Clustering Analysis, RBF Net, and Curve Detection", *IEEE Transaction on Neural Networks*, Vol. 4, pp. 636–648, 1993. Its preliminary version was appeared in *Proceedings of 1992 International Joint Conference on Neural Networks*, Vol. 2, pp. 665–670, 1992.

Multiagent SAT (MASSAT): Autonomous Pattern Search in Constrained Domains

Xiaolong Jin and Jiming Liu

Department of Computer Science,
Hong Kong Baptist University
Kowloon Tong, Hong Kong
{jxl, jiming}@comp.hkbu.edu.hk

Abstract. In this paper, we present an autonomous pattern search approach to solving Satisfiability Problems (SATs). Our approach is essentially a multiagent system. To solve a SAT problem, we first divide variables into groups, and represent each variable group with an agent. Then, we randomly place each agent onto a position in the correspoding local space which is composed of the domains of the variables that are represented by this agent. Thereafter, all agents will autonomously make search decisions guided by some reactive rules in their local spaces until a special pattern (i.e., solution) is found or a time step threshold is reached. Experimental results on some benchmark SAT test-sets have shown that by employing the MASSAT approach, we can obtain performances comparable to those of other popular algorithms.

Keywords: Autonomous Pattern Search, Satisfiability Problem (SAT), Multiagent System, MASSAT

1 Introduction

Many problems, both practical and theoretical, can be viewed as *Constraint Satisfaction Problems* (CSPs) where some constraints among a group of variables are given. The goal is to find the values for all variables that will satisfy the given constraints. Actually, to solve a constraint satisfaction problem is to search one or some special patterns (i.e., solutions) of the variable value combinations in the solution space which is specified by the given problem, and the patterns should satisfy all constraints. In this paper, we will describe a novel autonomous pattern search approach to solving *Satisfiability Problems*, a special class of Constraint Satisfaction Problems.

1.1 Satisfiability Problems

A *satisfiability problem* is a problem of determining whether or not there exists a solution for a propositional formula. The following is the formal definition of *satisfiability problem*:

H. Yin et al. (Eds.): IDEAL 2002, LNCS 2412, pp. 318–328, 2002.

Definition 1. A *satisfiability problem* (SAT), P, consists of:

1. A finite set of propositional variables, $\mathbf{X} = \{X_1, X_2,..., X_n\}$.
2. A domain set, $\mathbf{D} = \{D_1, D_2,..., D_n\}$, for all $i \in [1, n]$, $X_i \in D_i$ and $D_i = \{True, False\}$.
3. A clause set, $\mathbf{CL} = \{Cl(R_1), Cl(R_2), ..., Cl(R_m)\}$, where each R_i is an subset of X, and each clause $Cl(R_i)$ is a conjunction or disjunction of the literals corresponding to the variables in set R_i.

It is well known that any SAT problem P can be transformed into a Conjunctive Normal Form (CNF), i.e., $P = \wedge_{i=1}^{m} Cl_i$, where each clause Cl_i is a disjunction of variables or their negations. If l_i denotes the length of clause Cl_i, and $\forall i \in [1, m], l_i \leq k$, then we call this propositional formula a k-SAT problem. It has been proven that 2-SAT is solvable in linear time, and $\forall k \geq 3$, k-SAT is NP-Complete. So far, the SAT community has primarily focused on 3-SAT problems, and has found that in 3-SAT problems there is a phase transition phenomenon around $m/n = 4.3$. The really hard 3-SAT problems exist in this region. In this paper, we will consider only those really hard problems.

Generally speaking, the methods for solving SAT problems fall into two categories: *complete* methods and *incomplete* methods. Complete methods systematically examine an entire search space. For a satisfiable formula, they can guarantee to find a solution. At the same time, for an unsatisfiable formula, they can prove its unsatisfiability. On the contrary, incomplete methods cannot guarantee to check the entire search space. Therefore, they cannot guarantee to find a solution for a formula even though it is satisfiable.

Complete Methods. Complete methods assign values to partial variables and then check if there exist some unsatisfied clauses. If this is the case, they will backtrack to one of the previous variables to assign it with another value, and then repeat this process. Or else, they will select a new variable to branch until a solution is found or the unsatisfiability of the problem is proven. The following are some typical complete methods: REL_SAT [1],TABLEAU [2], SATZ [7], and GRASP [10].

Incomplete Methods. Many incomplete methods for solving SAT problems are based on *local search*. Local search is a recent method, which was proposed in [4][15]. A local search procedure starts with a complete and randomly initialized assignment, then checks if it satisfies all clauses. If not, it will randomly or heuristically select a variable to flip (i.e., change its value). It repeats this process until a solution is found or a certain threshold (e.g., a maximum number of steps) is reached. There are two main streams in local search studies, namely, GSAT [15] and WalkSAT [12][14]. They both have many variations, for example, GWSAT [14], GSAT/Tabu [11] of GSAT, and Novelty, R-Novelty [12], Novelty+, and R-Novelty+ [6] of WalkSAT.

Recently, two more effective local search methods have been proposed, they are: SDF [13] and UnitWalk [5]. Generally speaking, SDF makes a greedy descent on its objective function similar to other local search methods. But a special feature of SDF is that it not only counts the number of unsatisfied clauses, but also considers how strongly a clause is satisfied. In addition, SDF makes the use of a weighting technique to continue its search process, if a local optimum is encountered. Another latest method is UnitWalk, a special form of local search. In the UnitWalk method, Hirsch and Kojevnikov employ *unit clause elimination* to guide the local search process. At each step, the UnitWalk algorithm checks if there are unit clauses in the current formula. If so, unit clauses will be eliminated first. Or else, the UnitWalk algorithm selects a variable and substitutes its value. As compared to other local search Methods, both SDF and UnitWalk exhibit good performance.

We will see that our new approach belongs to the category of incomplete methods. We will also compare our approach with other incomplete methods mentioned above.

1.2   Multiagent Systems

A *Multiagent System* is a cooperative system in which several agents interact and work together in order to achieve certain goals. Agents in such a system may be homogeneous or heterogeneous, and may have common or distinct goals. Interested readers are refered to [8] for more details. Our new approach is essentially to build a multiagent system that solves SAT problems.

Here, we want to highlight a special example of multiagent system, *Swarm*. Swarm is a software platform for simulating distributed multiagent systems. It has three main components: *agents*, *environment* where agents live, and *actions schedule*. In the Swarm system, swarm is the basic unit, which is a collection of agents living in a certain environment and executing a schedule of actions. As a Swarm-based computing paradigm, Liu et. al. in [9] proposed an approach called *ERA* to solving *constraint satisfaction problems*. In the ERA approach, each agent represents a variable. All agents select values in a common environment that corresponds to the domains of all variables. In order to solve a given CSP problem, the agents will make a series of search decisions, governed by their own reactive rules, until a solution state is reached. Using this approach, they can achieve promising results on some benchmark CSPs, e.g., *n-Queen Problems* and *Coloring Problems*.

2   The MASSAT Approach

In the section, we will describe the MASSAT approach in detail. The basic idea of our approach is to create a multiagent system where a group of agents are placed in an environment that is composed of the domains of all vairables. Combining all agents' positions, we can obtain an assignment to the given SAT problem. In order to solve the problem, all agents will autonomously make search decision guided by their reactive rules in their environment until all of them find an appropriate position.

For the ease of description, first of all, we assume that we can divide n variables into u groups. Without lose of generality, we further assume that $G_i = \{X_{i1}, X_{i2}, ..., X_{ik}\}$ is the ith variable group, and the domain set corresponding to G_i is $\{D_{i1}, D_{i2}, ...D_{ik}\}$.

2.1   An Environment

In the MASSAT approach, the environment consists of local spaces. One local space belongs only to a unique agent. Other agents cannot enter it. Each variable group corresponds to a local space.

Definition 2. A *local space*, s_i, corresponding to variable group G_i is a row vector $< p_1, p_2, ..., p_{|D_{i1} \times D_{i2} \times ... \times D_{ik}|} >$, where $\forall j \in [1, |D_{i1} \times D_{i2} \times ... \times D_{ik}|]$, p_j is a cell called a *position*.

In local space s_i, there are $|D_{i1} \times D_{i2} \times ... \times D_{ik}|$ positions. p_j^i can index the jth position in the ith local space s_i.

Definition 3. An *environment*, E, is a column vector composed of all local spaces, i.e.,$E = < s_1, s_2, ..., s_u >^T = \begin{pmatrix} s_1 \\ s_2 \\ ... \\ s_u \end{pmatrix}$.

Generally speaking, environment E is a regular (if all local spaces s_i have the same number of positions) or irregular (if not all local spaces s_i have the same number of positions) grid board. In environment E, we use $e(j, i)$ to index the jth position in local space s_i. It means $e(j, i) \equiv p_j^i$. For convenience, we also call s_i the ith row, i.e., row_i of E. The positions in environment E are not only used to serve for an agent to stay, but also used for information: *domain values*.

Definition 4. The *domain value* recorded in position $e(j, i)$, i.e., $e(j, i).value$ is the jth element in Cartesian product $D_{i1} \times D_{i2} \times ... \times D_{ik}$.

If agent a_i stays at $e(j, i)$, and $e(j, i).value =< x_{i1}, x_{i2}, ..., x_{ik} >$ (where $\forall x_{iq}, q \in [1, k], x_{iq} \in D_{iq}$), it means $X_{i1} = x_{i1}$, $X_{i2} = x_{i2}, ...,$ and $X_{ik} = x_{ik}$.

2.2   An Agent

Definition 5. An *agent, a,* is an entity with a special tuple, i.e., $a = (Var, Act, Eval)$, where Var is a group of variables that agent a represents; Act is a set of actions that agent a can take; $Eval$ is a function that is used by agent a to evaluate the positions in its local space.

Definition 6. The   *evaluation   value*   related   to   a   position $e(j, i)$,   i.e., $e(j, i).evalua$
tion is a number that reflects the goodness if agent a_i stays at position $e(j, i)$.

The *evaluation value* of a position evaluated by an agent dynamically changes with the positions of other agents, namely, for a position in s_i, if the positions of other agents are changed, the evaluation value of this position will possibly be changed.

Now, let us introduce some important details on agents' actions.

Moving strategies. We use function Ψ to define an agent's movement.

Definition 7. The movement function for agent a_i:

$$\Psi : \; [1, |D_{i1} \times D_{i2} \times ... \times D_{ik}|] \to [1, |D_{i1} \times D_{i2} \times ... \times D_{ik}|]$$

$\Psi(x)$ gives the new position of agent a_i, after it moves from position $e(x, i)$. So, the new position can be represented as $e(\Psi(x), i)$.

In our approach, we design three basic move strategies: *best-move*, *better-move*, and *random-move*. At each time step, agent can probabilitically choose one to perform.

– *Best-move*

   Definition 8. *best-move*: An agent moves to a best-position with a probability of *best-p*.

   Definition 9. A position $e(j, i)$ in local space s_i is called a *best-position*, if $\forall x \in [1, |D_{i1} \times D_{i2} \times ... \times D_{ik}|], e(j, i).evaluation \succ e(x, i).evaluation$.

   where $e(j, i).evaluation \succ e(x, i).evaluation$ means $e(j, i).evaluation$ is better than or at least equal to $e(x, i).evaluation$. We will see that the specific meaning of '$\succ$' is dependent on that of 'evaluation value'.
   If there exists more than one best-position, we let the agent randomly choose one. Assume there are b_n best-positions, the best-move strategy can be expressed as: $\Psi_{best}(j) = AbsPos(Random(b_n))$, where function $Random(k)$ can uniformly generate a random number between 1 and k. $AbsPos(k)$ is a function that returns get the kth best-position in local space s_i. In the best-move function, the number of computational operations to find the best position for each i is $|D_{i1} \times D_{i2} \times ... \times D_{ik}|$. This strategy is instinctive to all agents.
– *Better-move*

   Definition 10. *better-move*: An agent moves to a better-position with a probability of *better-p*.

   Definition 11. A position $e(j, i)$ in local space s_i is called a *better-position*, if $e(x, i)$ is agent a_i's current position, and $e(j, i).evaluation \succ e(x, i).evaluation$.

To perform a better-move, an agent will randomly select a position and then compare its evaluation value with that of its current position to decide whether or not to move to this position. This movement can be defined by Ψ_{better}:

$$\Psi_{better}(j) = \begin{cases} j & if \quad e(r,i).evaluation \succ e(j,i).evaluation \\ r & if \quad e(r,i).evaluation \prec e(j,i).evaluation \end{cases}$$

where $r = Random(|D_{i1} \times D_{i2} \times ... \times D_{ik}|)$. Although a better-move may not be the best choice for an agent, the computational cost required for this strategy is less than that of best-move. Only two operations are involved for deciding this movement, i.e., producing a random number and performing a comparison.

– *Random-move*

Definition 12. *random-move*: An agent randomly moves to a position in its local space with a probability of *random-p*.

Random-p will be relatively smaller than the probabilities of selecting best-move and better-move strategies. It is somewhat like a random-walk in local search. For the same reason as in local search, the random-move strategy is necessary, because without randomized movements the system will get stuck in some local optima, that is, all the agents are at best-positions, but it is not a solution state. In the state of local optima, no agent will move to a new position if using the strategies of best-move and better-move alone. Thus, the agents will lose their chances for finding a solution if without any techniques to avoid getting stuck in local optima.

Random-move can be defined as Ψ_{random}:

$$\Psi_{random}(j) = Random(|D_{i1} \times D_{i2} \times ... \times D_{ik}|)$$

Evaluation. After an agent selects a best-move or a better-move, it will evaluate all or some positions in its local space before it actually move. We define the evaluation function Φ of the agent as follows:

$$\Phi : \; [1, |D_{i1} \times D_{i2} \times ... \times D_{ik}|] \rightarrow R$$

where R is the set of real numbers.

In local search, the most important issue is how to select the next variable to flip. To do so, an appropriate function is needed to evaluate the current state. Similarly, in the MASSAT approach, how to select the next position in solution space to move is also important. A good evaluation function Φ is crucial, which can make a pattern search process clever and more efficient.

A commonly used evaluation function in the SAT-related local search methos is based on the number of satisfied clauses. The number of un-satisfied clauses can also be defined as an evaluation function. In the former case, if $e(x,i).evaluation \succ e(y,i).evaluation$, it means that if agent a_i stays at position $e(x, i)$, more clauses will be satisfied than if it stays at position $e(y, i)$. In the latter case, $e(x, i).evaluat$ $ion \succ e(y, i).evaluation$ means that if agent a_i stays at $e(x, i)$, fewer clauses will be unsatisfied than at $e(y, i)$.

In this paper, we will use two different evaluation functions as two different cases, and compare their results in performance. The first one is the number of satisfied clauses, that is, $\Phi = \sum_{i=1}^{m} T(Cl_i)$, where $T()$ is a function that returns the truth value of a clause, m is the number of clauses. We have found that, by employing this evaluation function, the approach is easy to get stuck in local optima, and cannot efficiently escape from them. So, as a common local optimum escaping technique, we introduce weighting into our MASSAT approach. General speaking, a weighting technique adds a weight to each clause. The higher a clause's weight, the more chance it will be satisfied. Intuitively, given an assignment, an unsatisfied clause is hard to satisfy. Hence, if we increase its weight, it will get more chance to be satisfied. Adding a weight to each clause, the evaluation function will be changed to $\Phi = \sum_{i=1}^{m} W_i \cdot T(Cl_i)$, where $T()$ and m are the same as in the previous formula, and W_i is the weight of clause Cl_i which is updated according to the following function:

$$W_i^{t'+1} = \begin{cases} W_i^{t'} & if \quad T(W_i^{t'}) = True \\ W_i^{t'} + \delta & if \quad T(W_i^{t'}) = False \end{cases}$$

where t' records the weights updating steps. δ expresses certain learning from the past failure assignments. So we call it *learning rate*. The higher δ is, the faster the learning will be. Initially, we set the weights of all clauses to 1, i.e., $W_i^0 = 1$. Generally speaking, in our MASSAT approach, we can update the weights of the clauses with two different strategies, i.e., to update weights after a time step is over, and to update weights after a local optimum occurs. The first one is easy to implement, but we found it is inefficient to improve the performance. Different from the first one that updates the weights of the clauses unconditionally, the second one only updates the weights of the clauses when a local optimum occurs. In the MASSAT approach, after a time step, if there is no agent that moves to a new position, obviously, it indicates the algorithm has gotten stuck in a local optimum. The second strategy updates the weights of the clauses in this situation. We can readily see that in both evaluation functions, all agents will instinctively try to move to a position with a higher evaluation value.

To differentiate the above two MASSAT mechanisms, we refer to the one that adopts formula $\Phi = \sum_{i=1}^{m} T(Cl_i)$ as evaluation function as MASSAT1, and the one that employs formula $\Phi = \sum_{i=1}^{m} W_i \cdot T(Cl_i)$ as MASSAT2.

2.3   The System Schedule

At each time step, all agents are given a chance to take a certain movement. If an agent selects a best-move or a better-move, it must evaluate all or some positions in its local space, and then decides to move to a certain new position or stay.

Because in the MASSAT approach, the configuration of the distributed agents represents an assignment to the current SAT problem, an agent must consider the positions of all other agents if it evaluates the positions in its local space. But, because all agents have a chance to move, the question becomes which positions of other agents should be considered in this situation. If the new positions of other agents are considered, the system can only be implemented in a sequential way. Therefore, to make all agents move asynchronously, we employ a common blackboard to record the positions of all agents before each time step. At a time step, an agent gets the positions of other agents from the blackboard, no matter the corresponding agents have moved to a new position or not. After a time step, the system will update the new positions of all agents in the blackboard.

3 Experimental Results

In the preceding section, we have provided a detail description of the MASSAT approach. In this section, we will present some experimental results on some benchmark SAT problems.

To evaluate the MASSAT approach in solving SAT problems, we have conducted experiments on two commonly used benchmark problem packages from SATLIB [16]: uf100 of *Uniform Random-3-SAT* and flat50 of *Flat Graph Coloring*. All instances in uf100 and flat50 are 3-SAT problems, and the ratio m/n is 4.3. In an instance of Uniform Random-3-SAT problems, each clause has exactly 3 literals which are randomly selected from n variables and randomly decide whether add them or their negations to this clause. In an instance of flat100, clauses may have different number of literals, but at most 3.

In [5], the authors presented their experimental results on benchmark SAT problem packages, include the above two packages. To compare with those of other algorithms, we conducted the same experiments on each package using the MASSAT approach. In Table 1, we list the mean and median numbers of movements that our MASSAT approach takes to get a solution. We also list some related data extracted from [5], i.e., the mean and median numbers of flips other algorithms take to get solutions of the same problem packages.

From the results, we can see that MASSAT2 is much better than MASSAT1. In addition, although the performance of MASSAT2 is not as good as SDF and UnitWalk. But it outperforms the other algorithms.

Here, one important issue we should clarify is the rationale behind the comparison between the movements in the MASSAT algorithm and the flips in other algorithms. In general local search algorithms, such as those listed in Table 1, the number of *flips* is a commonly used index to evaluate the performance. In the MASSAT approach, because each agent represents a group of variables, a movement of an agent will cause, in an extreme case, n/u variables change their values. If we just consider the value changes occur on the variables, the comparison in Table 1 is unfair to other algorithms. But, in essence, what those algorithms should count is how many time clicks they take to get a solution rather than values changed. Here, 'time click' means the minimum time unit. In

Table 1. Results on uf100 and flat50. Both uf100 and flat50 have 1000 instances. The parameter setting is: Variable group size 5; Ratio of probability between best-move and random-move 80:1; Learning rate 1.

Algorithm	uf100		flat50	
	Mean Flips/Moves	Median Flips/Moves	Mean Flips/Moves	Median Flips/Moves
GWSAT	6,532	3,398	7,023	4,846
WalkSAT	3,652	1,981	3,896	3,078
WalkSAT/Tabu	2,485	1,041	61,393	1,265
Novelty	15,699	962	24,421	934
R-Novelty	1,536	581	7,109	739
SDF	876	515	773	537
UnitWalk	2,547	1,862	261	200
MASSAT1	2,950	2,563	3,548	3,111
MASSAT2	1,462	1,198	982	780

this sense, time click is the same as time step in the MASSAT approach. In those local search algorithms, because of their sequential nature, the number of time clicks is equal to the number of flips. So, the correct way to compare the MASSAT approach and other algorithms is to compare their time clicks. But, because the MASSAT algorithm as implemented in this paper is a sequential simulation of the actual MASSAT algorithm, we recorded the movements of all agents and compared them with those of other algorithms in Table 1. Although one movement may possibly cause multiple flips, all these flips happen *simultaneously*. So, we think comparing movements with flips in this way is fair.

4   Conclusion and Future Work

In this paper, we have described an autonomous pattern (i.e., solution) search approach to solving SAT Problems, namely, MASSAT. In solving a SAT problem with this approach, we first divide variables into groups, and then represent each group with an agent. The environment for the whole multiagent system contains all possible domain values for the problem. All agents can move within their own local spaces, which represent their domain, to search a special pattern. We have introduced three elementary moving strategies: *random-move*, *best-move* and *better-move*. The movement of an agent will affect the evaluation values of positions in the environment. After being randomly initialized, the MASSAT-based system will keep on dispatching agents, according to a certain order, to choose their movements until a solution is found or a time step threshold is reached.

We also presented experimental results on two commonly used benchmark SAT problem packages: uf100 and flat50. Our experimental results have shown that by employing the MASSAT approach, we can obtain comparable results to some other popular algorithms. But, the results presented in the paper is based on a non-optimal implementation of the MASSAT approach in solving SAT problems. In addition, we use a sequential way to simulate the MASSAT approach. This limits its parallel nature.

From our experiments, we have noticed that, there are some further aspects we should study. One appears to be very promising in improving our MASSAT approach is how to divide variables into groups. In the experiments provided in this paper, we equally partition all variables. We have found that different sizes of variable groups may lead to different results. It indicates that the performance of the MASSAT approach is relative to variable group. Intuitively, if we could partition the variables with some identical or similar 'properties' into a group, in this case, all variables in the same group can 'synchronizely' move, then the performance of the MASSAT approach will possibly be better.

References

1. B. J. Bayardo Jr. and R. C. Schrag, Using CSP Look-back Techniques to Solve Real-world SAT Instances, in *Proceedings of the 14th National Conference on Artificial Intelligence*, pp. 203-208, 1997.
2. J. M. Crawford and L. D. Auton, Experimental Results on the Crossover Point in Random 3SAT, *Artificial Intelligence*, Vol. 81, No. 1-2, pp. 31-57, 1996.
3. S.A. Cook, The Complexity of theorem proving procedures, in *Proceedings of the 3rd Annual ACM Symposium on the Theory of Computation*, pp. 151-158, 1971.
4. J. Gu, Efficient local search for very large-scale satisfiability problem, *SIGART Bulletin*, vol. 3, pp. 8-12, 1992.
5. E. A. Hirsch and A. Kojevnikov, UnitWalk: A new SAT solver that uses local search guided by unit clause elimination, in *Proceedings of the 5th International Symposium on the Theory and Applications of Satisfiability Testing (SAT 2002)*, pp. 35-42, 2002.
6. H. H. Hoos, On the run-time behavior of stochastic local search algorithms for SAT, in *Proceedings of the 16th National Conference on Artificial Intelligence*, AAAI'99, pp. 661-666, 1999.
7. C. M. Li and Anbulagan, Look-ahead Versus Look-back for Satisfiability Problems, in *Proceedings of CP'97*, pp. 341-345, 1997.
8. J. Liu, *Autonomous Agents And Multi-Agent Systems: Explorations in Learning, Self-Organization and Adaptive Computation*, World Scientific, 2001.
9. J. Liu, H. Jing and Y. Y. Tang, Multi-agent oriented constraint satisfaction *Artificial Intelligence*, vol. 136, pp. 101-144, 2002.
10. J. P. Marques-Silva and K. A. Sakallah, GRASP - A New Search Algorithm for Satisfiability, in *Proceedings of IEEE/ACM International Conference on Computer-Aided Design*, 1996.
11. B. Mazure, L. Sais, and É. Grégoire, Tabu Search for SAT, in *Proceedings of AAAI'97*, pp. 281-285, 1997.
12. D. McAllester, B. Selman, and H. Levesque, Evidence for Invariants in Local Search, in *Proceedings of AAAI'97*, pp. 321-326, 1997.
13. D. Schuurmans and F. Southey, Local search characteristics of incomplete SAT procedures, *Artificial Intelligence*, vol. 132, no. 2, pp. 121-150, 2001.

14. B. Selman, H. A. Kautz, and B. Cohen, Noise Strategies for Improving Local Search, in *Proceedings of AAAI'94*, pp. 337-343, 1994.
15. B. Selman, H. Levesque, and D. Mitchell, A New Method for Solving Hard Satisfiability Problems, in *Proceedings of AAAI'92*, pp. 440-446, 1992.
16. http://www.intellektik.informatick.tu-darmstadt.de/SATLIB/.

A Text Mining Agents Based Architecture for Personal E-mail Filtering and Management

Ning Zhong[1], Takahisa Matsunaga[1], and Chunnian Liu[2]

[1] Dept. of Information Eng., Maebashi Institute of Technology
460-1 Kamisadori-Cho, Maebashi-City, 371-0816, Japan
`zhong@maebashi-it.ac.jp`
[2] School of Computer Science, Beijing Polytechnic University
Beijing 100022, P.R. China
`cslcn@bjpu.edu.cn`

Abstract. E-mail messages can be modeled as semi-structured documents that consist of a set of classes and a number of variable length free-text. Thus, many text mining techniques can be used to develop a personal e-mail filtering and management system. This paper addresses a text mining agents based architecture, in which two kinds of text mining agents: USPC (uncertainty sampling based probabilistic classifier) and R2L (rough relation learning) are used cooperatively, for personal e-mail filtering and management.

1 Introduction

E-mail is becoming a frequently used and accepted means of communication in the school, businesses environment. Some of this communication is personal. Some of it is confidential. But most of it is essential to keeping your school, businesses running efficiently. In particular, the e-mail system has been integrated with World-Wide Web browser such as Netscape and Microsoft Internet Explorer as a useful function of Web-based electronic commerce to make it overused by enterprise to promote products and spread information. The mailbox of a user may often be crammed with e-mail messages some or even a large portion of which are not of interest to her/him. Such flood of e-mail messages has created a need for developing an intelligent agent that automate the selection, sorting, storage, reply, and retrieval of e-mails [2,5]. It will also be an important function for Web and Internet intelligence [19].

E-mail messages can be modeled as semi-structured documents that consist of a set of classes and a number of variable length free-text. Thus, many text mining techniques can be used to develop a personal e-mail filtering and management system. Text mining is to mine knowledge (regularities) from semi-structured or unstructured text. Text mining is a multidisciplinary field, involving various techniques such as data mining, information retrieval, natural-language understanding, case-based reasoning, statistics, and intelligent agent technology [21]. This paper addresses a text mining agents based architecture, in which two kinds of text mining agents: USPC (uncertainty sampling based probabilistic

H. Yin et al. (Eds.): IDEAL 2002, LNCS 2412, pp. 329–336, 2002.

classifier) and R2L (rough relation learning) are used cooperatively, for personal e-mail filtering and management.

The rest of the paper is organized as follows. Section 2 gives the proposed system architecture of e-mail filtering and management system. Sections 3 and 4 discuss two mining agents: USPC and R2L, respectively. Section 5 discusses the related work. Finally, Section 6 gives conclusions.

2   System Architecture

Figure 1 shows a multi-agent based architecture of e-mail filtering system, which is capable of performing intelligent e-mail management in a dynamic, personal environment by incorporating the characteristics such as autonomous, adaptive, collaborative and communicative into text mining methods.

The task of e-mail filtering and management is a long-term learning cycle in which two text mining agents are used cooperatively. At the earlier stage, the USPC (uncertainty sampling based probabilistic classifier) agent is used to produce classifiers (i.e. e-mails with class labels). In the USPC agent, selecting examples (terms) as an initial classifier by a user is an important feature because of the need for personalization. By using this way, the requirements and biases of a user are represented and a Bayesian classifier is carried out based on such requirements and biases.

On the other hand, the R2L (rough relation learning) agent is activated to produce first-order (relational) rules from e-mails with class labels as samples once such samples are available. In our application, a first order (relation) learning rather than a propositional one is indeed needed for representing the order of words in an e-mail. The e-mail filtering system attempts to classify new e-mails by using the rules generated by the R2L agent. The USPC agent may be activated again if the generated rules are not good enough to classify some new e-mails.

A personal-specific ontology forms the heart of the personal e-mail filtering system for the user. It is used to guide the relational induction and the use of relational rules. The ontologies can be constructed semi-automatically with human intervention [21]. Furthermore, a user can also modify and add rules and ontologies according to his/her preference and structured features of e-mails. Here the structured features are features represented by structured fields in the header part of an e-mail document such as sender domain, sender address, recipient (single, in a group, via a mailing list), subject, date, mailtype, and content type.

3   USPC Agent

USPC agent is used to produce classifiers (i.e. e-mails with class labels). In order to produce such classifiers, we first need to annotate the e-mails with class labels. This annotation task is that of e-mail classification. However, it is expensive that

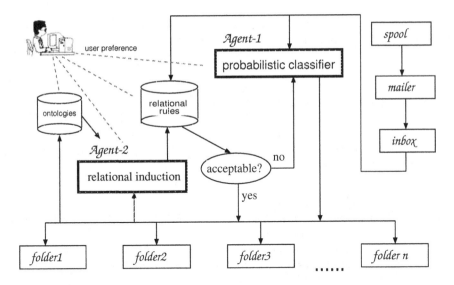

Fig. 1. Architecture of e-mail filtering system

the large amounts of e-mails are manually labeled. The USPC agent is a semi-automatic approach to classify e-mails, which is based on uncertainty sampling and probabilistic classifier. The main contribution of ours is to extend the method proposed by Lewis et al. [9] for multiple classes classification.

We use a variant of the Bayes' rule below:

$$P(C|w) = \frac{\exp(\log\frac{P(C)}{1-P(C)} + \sum_{i=1}^{d}\log(P(w_i|C)/P(w_i|\overline{C})))}{1 + \exp(\log\frac{P(C)}{1-P(C)} + \sum_{i=1}^{d}\log(P(w_i|C)/P(w_i|\overline{C})))} \tag{1}$$

where $w = \{w_1, \ldots, w_d\}$ is a set of the terms in an e-mail, and C is a class. Although we treat, in this equation, only two classes $C_1 = C$ and $C_2 = \overline{C}$ with $P(\overline{C}) = 1 - P(C)$, it can be extended to deal with multiple classes classification by using the method to be stated in the end of this section.

However, Eq. (1) is rarely used directly in e-mail classification, probably because its estimates of $P(C|w)$ are systematically inaccurate. Hence we use Logistic regression, which is a general technique for combining multiple predictor values to estimate a posterior probability, in Eq. (1). Thus, we obtain the following equation:

$$P(C|w) = \frac{\exp(a + b\sum_{i=1}^{d}\log(P(w_i|C)/P(w_i|\overline{C})))}{1 + \exp(a + b\sum_{i=1}^{d}\log(P(w_i|C)/P(w_i|\overline{C})))}. \tag{2}$$

Intuitively, we could hope that the logistic parameter a would substitute for the hard-to-estimate prior log odds in Eq. (1), while b would serve to dampen extreme log likelihood ratios resulting from independence violations.

Furthermore, we use the following equation to estimate the values $P(w_i|C)/P(w_i|\overline{C})$ as the first step in using Eq. (2),

$$\frac{P(w_i|C)}{P(w_i|\overline{C})} = \frac{\frac{c_{pi}+(N_p+0.5)/(N_p+N_n+1)}{N_p+d(N_p+0.5)/(N_p+N_n+1)}}{\frac{c_{ni}+(N_n+0.5)/(N_p+N_n+1)}{N_n+d(N_n+0.5)/(N_p+N_n+1)}} \tag{3}$$

where N_p and N_n are the numbers of terms in the positive and negative training sets, respectively, c_{pi} and c_{ni} are correspondingly the numbers of examples of w_i in the positive and negative training sets, respectively, and d is the number of different terms in an e-mail.

Based on the preparation stated above, we briefly describe the main steps of e-mail classification below:

Step 1. Select examples (terms) as an initial classifier for N classes by a user and all the N classes are regarded as a set of the negative classes.

Step 2. Select a class from the set of the negative classes as a positive class, and the remaining ones are regarded as a set of the negative classes.

Step 3. While a user is willing to label e-mails.

> *Step 3.1* Apply the current classifier to each unlabeled e-mail.
> *Step 3.2* Find the k e-mails for which the classifier is least certain of class membership by computing their posterior probabilities in Eq (2).
> *Step 3.3* Have the user label the subsample of k e-mails.
> *Step 3.4* Train a new classifier on all labeled e-mails.

Step 4. Repeat *Step 2* to *Step 3* until all classes were selected as a positive class.

We emphasize that selecting examples (terms) as an initial classifier by a user is an important step because of the need for personalization. Thus, the requirements and biases of a user are represented in the classifier.

4   R2L Agent

R2L (rough relation learning) agent is activated to produce first-order rules from e-mails with class labels as samples once such samples are available. In our application, a rough first-order (relation) learning rather than a propositional one is indeed needed for representing the order of words in an e-mail.

In our experiments, the development of the R2L agent is based on incorporating the agent characteristics such as autonomous, adaptive, collaborative and communicative into the RS-ILP system that is developed by incorporating characteristics of rough set theory into the existing well-known ILP systems: FOIL and PROGOL [6,11,13,17].

4.1   RS-ILP

Relation learning or called Inductive Logic Programming (ILP) is a relatively new method in machine learning. ILP is concerned with learning from examples within the framework of predicate logic [6,13]. ILP is relevant to text mining, and compared with the attribute-value learning methods, it possesses the following advantages:

- ILP can learn knowledge which is more expressive than that by the attribute-value learning methods, because the former is in predicate logic while the latter is usually in propositional logic.
- ILP can utilize background knowledge more naturally and effectively, because in ILP the examples, the background knowledge, as well as the learned knowledge are all expressed within the same logic framework.

An ILP problem can be briefly stated as follows:

Given the positive examples E^+ and the negative examples E^- (both are sets of clauses) and the background knowledge B (a finite set of clauses), ILP is to find a theory H (a finite set of clauses) which is correct with respect to E^+ and E^-. That demands:

1. $\forall_{e \in E^+} H \cup B| = e$ *(completeness wrt. E^+);*
2. $H \cup B \cup \overline{E^-}$ *is satisfiable (consistency wrt. E^-).*

However, when applying ILP to text mining from e-mails, we can identify one of weak points compared with the attribute-value learning methods, that is, the theory, techniques and experiences are much less mature for ILP to deal with imperfect data (uncertainty and incompleteness). A solution is to combine rough set theory with ILP, that is, RS-ILP, to deal with imperfect data which occur in e-mails. We have developed several rough settings in ILP to deal with different kinds of imperfect data [10]. For example, a useful RS-ILP approach can deal with indiscernible examples (same keywords from different e-mails and belonging to different classes) by using the following rough setting in ILP.

Given:

- The target predicate p (the set of all ground atoms of p is U).
- $E^+ \subseteq U$ and $E^- \subseteq U$. where $E^+ \cap E^- \neq \emptyset$.
- Background knowledge B.

The rough sets to consider and the hypotheses to find:

- Taking the identity relation I as a special equivalence relation R, the remaining description is the same as in the above rough setting.

We can define the learning quality in the rough setting as the percentage of examples with respect to that the induced hypotheses should be correct. That is:

$$\gamma_R(H^+) = 1 - (|E^{-+}|/|E^+ \cup E^-|)$$
$$\gamma_R(H^-) = 1 - (|E^{+-}|/|E^+ \cup E^-|)$$

where $|S|$ denotes the cardinality of S.

Another useful RS-ILP approach can deal with unclassified e-mails. If $E^+ \cup E^-$ is a small set, we cannot expect that the induced hypothesis H will have high prediction accuracy. Sometimes we may have an additional set of e-mails (examples) $E^?$ that are unclassified (i.e. just received new e-mails in *inbox*). Can we utilize $E^?$ to increase the prediction accuracy? The following rough setting in ILP is for this purpose:

Given:

- The target predicate p (the set of all ground atoms of p is U).
- An equivalence relation R on U (we have the approximation space $A = (U, R)$).
- A set of positive examples $E^+ \subseteq U$ and A set of negative examples $E^- \subseteq U$.
- A set of unclassified examples $E^? \subseteq U$.
- Background knowledge B.

Considering the following rough sets:

1. $E^{+?} = E^+ \cup \{e^? \in E^? | \exists_{e \in E^+} eRe^?\}$;
2. $E^{-?} = E^- \cup \{e^? \in E^? | \exists_{e \in E^-} eRe^?\}$.

To find:

- Hypothesis $H^?$ (the defining clauses of p) which is correct with respect to $E^{+?}$ and $E^{-?}$. That is,
    1. $H^? \cup B$ covers all examples of $E^{+?}$;
    2. $H^? \cup B$ rejects all examples of $E^{-?}$.

In such rough problem setting, we use equivalence relation R to "enlarge" the training set (by distributing some examples from $E^?$ to E^+ and E^-). Different R will produce different hypothesis $H^?$. It is reasonable to expect that the more unclassified examples are added to E^+, the more general hypothesis will be induced; the more unclassified examples are added to E^-, the more specific hypothesis will be induced.

4.2   Learning Process in R2L

Based on the preparation stated above, we briefly describe the main steps of learning process in R2L for producing first-order (relational) rules from e-mails with class labels below:

Step 1. Select keywords by using the following equations.

$$recall = \frac{a}{a + b} \tag{4}$$

$$precision = \frac{a}{a + d} \tag{5}$$

where a denotes the number of e-mails in which the term occurs, in all e-mails belonging to class +; b denotes the number of e-mails in which the term does not occur, in all e-mails belonging to class +; d denotes the number of e-mails in which the term occurs, in all e-mails belonging to class -.
In our experiments, we select the terms with ($recall > 0.5$) and ($precision > average$) as keywords.

Step 2. Represent keywords in the first-order format.

That is, $kw_i(c, p)$ is true when kw_i is a keyword occurring in the class c, and p is the position at which the kw_i occurs.

Step 3. Define meta/background knowledge (or ontologies) that is used to represent the relation between keywords. The following are examples of such meta knowledge:

$link(p_1, p_2)$ is true when $p_2 = p_1 + 1$.

$near(p_1, p_2)$ is true when $|p_1 - p_2 \leq 2$.

Step 4. Learn relations among the keywords by using the RS-ILP approach stated above.

5   Related Work

An important issue in the application of machine learning techniques to information management tasks is the nature of features extracted from textual information. Boone has created an intelligent e-mail agent that can learn actions such as filtering, prioritizing, downloading to palmtops, and forwarding e-mail to voice-mail using automatic feature extraction [2]. Their feature extraction approach is based on first-order learning concepts to present within the e-mail, then using these concepts as features for learning actions to perform on the messages.

Cohen compared two methods for learning text classifiers that might arise in filtering and filing personal e-mail messages: a traditional IR method based on TF-IDF weighting, and a new method for learning sets of keyword-spotting rules based on the RIPPER rule learning algorithm [4]. The experimental results demonstrated that both methods obtain significant generalizations from a small number of examples; that both methods are comparable in generalization performance on problems of this type; and that both methods are reasonably efficient, even with fairly large training sets.

Diao et al. addressed personal e-mail filtering by casting it in the framework of text classification [5]. They compared a naive Bayesian classifier and a decision tree based classifier for e-mail filtering and discussed different features of the two classifiers.

6   Conclusions

The paper investigated the architectural aspects of a multi-agent based e-mail filtering system, in which two text mining agents, namely USPC and R2L, are used cooperatively. A personal-specific ontology forms the heart of the personal e-mail filtering system for the user. It is used to guide the relational induction and the use of relational rules. Based on the proposed architecture, a multi-agent based e-mail filtering system is under construction.

Acknowledgments. This work was partially supported by Telecommunications Advancement Foundation (TAF).

References

1. Aggarwal, C.C. and Yu, P.S. "On Text Mining Techniques for Personalization", Zhong, N., Skowron, A., and Ohsuga, S. (eds.) *New Directions in Rough Sets, Data Mining, and Granular-Soft Computing*, LNAI 1711, Springer-Verlag (1999) 12-18.
2. Boone, G. "Concept Features in Re:Agent, an Intelligent Email Agent", *Proc. the 2nd International Conference on Autonomous Agents (Agents'98)* ACM Press (1998) 141-148.
3. Cohen, W.W. "Text Categorization and Relational Learning", *Proc. ML-95* (1995) 124-132.
4. Cohen, W.W. "Learning Rules that Classify E-Mail", *Proc. AAAI Spring Symposium on Machine Learning in Information Access*, AAAI Press (1996) 18-25.
5. Diao, Y., Lu, H., Wu, D. "A Comparative Study of Classification Based Personal E-mail Filtering", *Proc. PAKDD-2000* (2000) 408-419.
6. Dzeroski, S. and Lavrac, N. "Relational Data Mining", Springer (2001).
7. Fensel, D. *Ontologies: A Silver Bullet for Knowledge Management and Electronic Commerce*, Springer-Verlag (2001).
8. Ishikawa, Y. and Zhong, N. "On Classification of Very large Text Databases" *Proc. the 11th Annual Conference of JSAI* (1997) 300-301.
9. Lewis, D.D. and Catlett, J. "Heterogeneous Uncertainty Sampling for Supervised Learning", *Proc. Eleventh Inter. Conf. on Machind Learning* (1994) 148-156.
10. Liu, C. and Zhong, N. "Rough Problem Settings for ILP Dealing with Imperfect Data", in Special Issue on "Rough Sets, Data Mining, and Granular Computing", *Computational Intelligence, An International Journal*, Vol.17, No.3, Blackwell Publishers (2001) 446-459.
11. Mitchell, T.M. *Machine Learning*, McGraw-Hill, 1997.
12. Mizoguchi, R. "Ontological Engineering: Foundation of the Next Generation Knowledge Processing", Zhong, N., Yao, Y.Y., Liu, J., and Ohsuga, S. (eds.) Web Intelligence: Research and Development, LNAI 2198, Springer-Verlag (2001) 44-57.
13. Muggleton, S. "Inductive Logic Programming", New Generation Computing, Vol. 8, No 4 (1991) 295-317.
14. Z. Pawlak, "Rough Sets", *International Journal of Computer and Information Science*, Vol.11, 341-356, 1982.
15. Z. Pawlak, *Rough Sets: Theoretical Aspects of Reasoning about Data*, Kluwer Academic Publishers, Boston, 1991.
16. Quinlan, J.R. *C4.5: Programs for Machine Learning*, Morgan Kaufmann (1993).
17. Quinlan, J.R. "Induction of Logic Program: FOIL and Related Systems", New Generation Computing, Vol.13 (1995) 287-312.
18. Zhong, N. *Knowledge Discovery and Data Mining*, in the Encyclopedia of Microcomputers, Volume 27 (Supplement 6) Marcel Dekker (2001) 93-122.
19. Zhong, N., Yao, Y.Y., Liu, J., and Ohsuga, S. (eds.) *Web Intelligence: Research and Development*, LNAI 2198, Springer-Verlag (2001).
20. Zhong, N., Liu, J., Ohsuga, S., and Bradshaw, J. (eds.) *Intelligent Agent Technology: Research and Development*, World Scientific (2001).
21. Zhong, N. "Ontologies in Web Intelligence", L.C. Jain, Z. Chen, N. Ichalkaranje (eds.) *Intelligent Agents and Their Applications*, Physica-Verlag (2002) 83-100.

Framework of a Multi-agent KDD System

Ning Zhong[1], Yasuaki Matsui[1], Tomohiro Okuno[1], and Chunnian Liu[2]

[1] Dept. of Information Eng., Maebashi Institute of Technology
460-1 Kamisadori-Cho, Maebashi-City, 371-0816, Japan
`zhong@maebashi-it.ac.jp`
[2] School of Computer Science, Beijing Polytechnic University
Beijing 100022, P.R. China
`cslcn@bjpu.edu.cn`

Abstract. How to increase both *autonomy* and *versatility* of a knowledge discovery system is a core problem and a crucial aspect of KDD (Knowledge Discovery and Data Mining). We have been developing a multi-agent based KDD methodology/system called GLS (Global Learning Scheme) for performing multi-aspect intelligent data analysis as well as multi-level conceptual abstraction and learning. With multi-level and multi-phase process, GLS increases versatility and autonomy. This paper presents our recent development on the GLS methodology/system.

1 Introduction

The KDD (Knowledge Discovery and Data Mining) process is usually a *multi-phase* process involving numerous steps like data preparation, preprocessing, search for hypothesis generation, pattern formation, knowledge evaluation, representation, refinement, and management. Furthermore, the process may be repeated at different stages when database is updated [3,13]. Although the process-centric view has recently been widely accepted by researchers in the KDD community as important methodology for knowledge discovery from real-life data [20], a key shortcoming of the existing KDD process is that they rely on human beings to plan and control the exact steps in a KDD process for solving the problem, and to carefully distribute the task to individual KDD systems [5]. In order to increase both *autonomy* and *versatility* of a KDD system, we are confronted with the following issues:

- How to plan, organize, control, and manage the KDD process dynamically for different KDD tasks;
- How to get the system to know it knows and impart the knowledge to decide what tools are appropriate for what problems and when.

Solving of such issues needs to develop *meta levels* of the KDD process by modeling such a process. We argue that modeling of the KDD process constitutes an important and new research area of KDD, including formal specification of the process, its planning, scheduling, controlling, management, evolution, and reuse.

Our methodology is to create an organized society of KDD agents. This means

H. Yin et al. (Eds.): IDEAL 2002, LNCS 2412, pp. 337–346, 2002.

- To develop many kinds of KDD agents for different tasks;
- To use the KDD agents in multiple learning phases in a distributed cooperative mode;
- To manage the society of KDD agents by multiple meta-control levels.

That is, the society of KDD agents is made of many smaller components that are called *agents*. Each agent by itself can only do some simple thing. Yet when we join these agents in an *organized* society, this leads to implement more complex KDD tasks. Based on this methodology, we have also designed a multi-strategy and multi-agent KDD system called GLS (Global Learning Scheme). This paper presents our recent development on the GLS methodology/system. Section 2 gives a brief summary of the architecture of the GLS system. Sections 3 and 4 describes how to define an ontology of KDD agents for implementing a KDD process planner (i.e. planning meta-agent (PMA)). Section 5 discusses how to develop the controlling meta-agent (CMA) and communicate with KDD agents. Finally, Section 6 gives concluding remarks.

2   Architecture of the GLS System

KDD process is a multi-step process centered on data mining agents to identify what is deemed knowledge from databases. In [16], we model the KDD process as an organized society of autonomous knowledge discovery agents (KDD agents, for short). Based on this model we have been developing a multi-strategy and multi-agent KDD system called GLS which increases both autonomy and versatility. Here we give a brief summary of the architecture of the GLS system [16,17].

The system is divided into three levels: two meta-levels and one object level as shown in Figure 1. On the first meta-level, the *planning meta-agent* (PMA, for short) sets the discovery process plan that will achieve the discovery goals when executed. On the second meta-level, the KDD agents are dynamically generated, executed, and controlled by the *controlling meta-agent* (CMA, for short). Planning and controlling dynamically the discovery process is a key component to increase both autonomy and versatility of our system. On the object level, the KDD agents are grouped into three learning phases:

Pre-processing agents include: agents to collect information from global information sources to generate a central large database; agents to clean the data; and agents to decompose the large database into several local information sources (sub-databases), such as *RSH* (rough sets with heuristics for feature selection), *CBK* (attribute oriented clustering using background knowledge), *DDR* (discretization by the division of ranges), *RSBR* (rough sets with Boolean reasoning for discretization of continuous valued attributes), *C4.5dis* (C4.5 agent for discretization of continuous valued attributes), *FSN* (forming scopes/clusters by nominal or symbolic attributes), and *SCT* (stepwise Chow test for discovering structure changes in time-series data) [23,8].

Knowledge-elicitation agents include: agents such as *KOSI* (knowledge oriented statistic inference for discovering structural characteristics – regression models), *DBI* (decomposition based induction for discovering concept clusters),

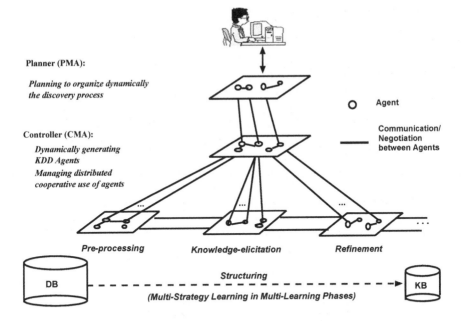

Planner (PMA):

*Planning to organize dynamically
the discovery process*

Controller (CMA):

*Dynamically generating
KDD Agents*
*Managing distributed
cooperative use of agents*

○   **Agent**

───   **Communication/
Negotiation
between Agents**

Pre-processing   **Knowledge-elicitation**   **Refinement**

DB

Structuring
(Multi-Strategy Learning in Multi-Learning Phases)

KB

Fig. 1. The architecture of the GLS system

GDT-RS (generalization-distribution-table and rough sets based induction for discovering classification rules), *C4.5tree* (C4.5 agent for decision tree induction), *C4.5rule* (C4.5 agent for rule generation), *PRM* (peculiarity rule miner), and *RS-ILP* (rough first-order rule miner) [23,20].

Knowledge-refinement agents acquire more accurate knowledge (hypothesis) from coarse knowledge (hypothesis) according to the domain knowledge and data change. KDD agents such as *IIBR* (inheritance-inference based refinement) and *HML* (hierarchical model learning) are commonly used for this purpose [15,14].

Note that the GLS system, as a multi-strategy and multi-agent KDD system, must provide alternative KDD agents for each learning phase. On the other hand, because of the complexity of databases and the diversification of discovery tasks, it is impossible to include all known/forthcoming KDD techniques. The KDD agents listed above are by no means exhaustive: they are included here because they have been developed previously by us. More agents will enter the system when the involved techniques become mature.

In terms of AI planning, no matter how many KDD agents we have, each of them is an *operator*. Each operator by itself can only do some simple thing, only when they are organized into a society, we can accomplish more complex discovery tasks. The KDD planner reasons on these operators to build KDD process plans – networks of KDD agents that will achieve the overall discovery goals when executed. But to apply AI planning techniques, we must be able to formally describe the KDD agents as operators. This is the subject of the next section.

3   Ontology of KDD Agents

The KDD planner, as any AI planner, needs a World State Description (WSD) and a pool of Operators (Ops). We use an ontology, which is represented as an OOER (Object-Oriented Entity Relationship) data model, to describe them. The traditional ER model has concepts of entity/relation, type/instance, instance-level attributes, and so on. The ontology further incorporates object-oriented concepts such as sub-typing, multiple inheritance, procedures, and type-level attributes/procedures, and so on. There are two kinds of types, *D&K* types and *Agent* types, for passive and active objects respectively. Figure 2 shows the (simplified) ontology used in the GLS system.

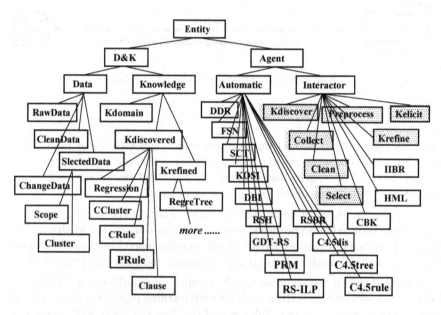

Fig. 2. The ontology of the GLS system

The *D&K* types describe various data and knowledge presented in a KDD system. On the data part, we have *RawData* from the global information source, *CleanData* from the central large database, *SelectedData* (*Scope* or *Cluster*) from the sub-databases, and so on. On the knowledge part, we first distinguish among *Kdomain* (the background knowledge), *Kdiscovered* (the discovered knowledge), and *Krefined* (the refined knowledge). The type *Kdiscovered* has sub-types: *Regression* (structural characteristics), *CCluster* (conceptual clusters), *CRule* (classification rules), *FRule* (peculiarity rules) *Clause* (first-order rules), and so on. *Krefined* has sub-types *RegreTree* (family of regression models) and so on.

The *Agent* types describe various KDD techniques used in the GLS system. We distinguish Automatic (KDD algorithms) from Interactor (KDD techniques that need human assistance). *Kdiscover* means the overall KDD task, while *Preprocess, Kelicit* and *Krefine* stand for the three learning phases: preprocessing, knowledge-elicitation, and knowledge-refinement, respectively. *Collect, Clean* and *Select* are activities in *Preprocess*. Most agent types take the same technical names as mentioned in Section 2, such as *RSH, CBK, DDR, RSBR, FSN, SCT, KOSI, DBI, GDT-RS, PRM, RS-ILP, IIBR, HML, C4.5dis, C4.5tree, C4.5rule*.

Note that in Figure 2, we show only the sub-type relations among KDD objects (a sub-type *is-a* special case of the supertype). For instance, all of *Kdiscover, Preprocess, Kelicit, Krefine* are sub-types of Interactor. We will see below how to express the sub-agent relation, for instance, *Preprocess, Kelicit, Krefine* are three sub-agents of *Kdiscover*.

Types have the ordinary instance-level attributes. For instance, *D&K* has the attribute status describing the current processing status of the data/knowledge (created, cleaned, reviewed, stored, etc.), and this attribute is inherited by all sub-types of *D&K*. *Kdiscovered* has the attribute timestamps recording the time when the knowledge is discovered, and this attribute is inherited by all sub-types of *Kdiscovered (Regression, CCluster, Rule,* and *Clause)*.

As for Agent types, there are additional properties defined. For instance, we may have type/instance-level procedures expressing operations on the types or instances (creation, deletion, modification, etc.). However, the most interesting properties of Agent types are the following type-level attributes with information that is used by the planning meta-agent (PMC):

- In/Out: specifying the types of the input/output of an agent type. The specified types are some sub-types of *D&K,* and the types of the actual input/output of any instance of the agent type must be sub-types of the specified types. For instance, the In/Out for agent type *CBK* is:

  CleanData and *Kdomain* → *$Scope* ($ means unspecified number of)

- Precond/Effect: specifying the preconditions for an agent (an instance of the agent type) to execute, and the effects when executed. Precond/Effect are logic formulas with the restrictions as in the classical STRIPS (see [10], for instance). However, we allow more readable specifications for them. In next section we will see that the PMA has a (KDD) domain-specific layer, and part of this layer will transform the high-level specifications into low-level logic formulas. As matter of the fact, a large part of the Precond/Effect, concerning constraints on input/output of the agent type, has been specified implicitly by the In/Out attribute. This is more declarative, and also because the detailed form (as conjunctions of literals) may not be able to write down at the type level. At planning time, the In/Out specification will be transformed into conjunctions of literals, then added to the Precond/Effect on which the planner reasons.

- Action: a sequential program performing real KDD actions upon agent execution (e.g. to call the underlying KDD algorithms). It is empty for high-level agents (see below).
- Decomp: describing possible sub-tasking. Instances of high-level agents (marked by shadowed boxes in Figure 2 should be decomposed into a network of sub-agents. Decomp specifies the candidate agent types for the sub-agents. For instance, the Decomp for agent type *Kdiscover* is: {*Preprocess, Kelicit, Krefine*}. This specifies that a *Kdiscover* agent should be decomposed into a sub-plan built from *Preprocess, Kelicit* and *Krefine* agents. The exact shape of this sub-plan is the result of planning (in this case, the sub-plan happens to be a sequence of the three learning phases). When the CMA meets a high-level agent HA in the plan, it calls the PMA to make a sub-plan to achieve the effect of HA. Then the PMA searches the pool of the (sub)agent types listed in Decomp of HA, rather than Ops - the entire set of operators.

4   Planning Mate Agent (PMA)

The planning meta-agent (PMA) has three layers as shown in Figure 3. The inner layer is a domain-independent non-linear planner, the middle layer deals with KDD-specific issues, and the out layer interacts with the controlling meta-agent (CMA), to realize hierarchical planning.

Because the core of the planner is domain-independent, we provide a middle layer as shown in Figure 3 to deal with all KDD specific issues:

- To transform the KDD goals into STRIPS goals (logic formulas in the style of STRIPS, that is, conjunctions of literals), especially to translate the input/output constraints specified in the In/Out attribute into Precond/Effect.
- To search the pool of operators (or more exactly, to search the types of sub-agents specified in the DECOMP attribute of a high level agent HA in the decomposition process) to introduce suitable KDD agents into the plan.
- To consult the world state description (WSD) to see if a precondition is already satisfied by the WSD, and/or help to transform the In/Out specification into conjunction of literals as part of Precond/Effect.
- To represent the resulting plan as a network of KDD agents, so the controller can dynamically generate and execute the KDD agents according to the network. The network can be also used by the user of the GLS system as a visualization tool.

5   Controlling Mate Agent (CMA) and KDD Agents

The controlling meta-agent (CMA) has the capability and responsibility of process planning (globally or locally). First, by means of the planning meta-agent

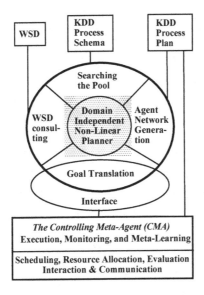

Fig. 3. Architecture of PMA and coupling of PMA and CMA

(PMA) as shown in Figure 1, a KDD process is planned and organized by communicating with a user or learning from environment according to different discovery tasks. Then the CMA dynamically creates, executes, and controls the KDD agents in the object level according to the process plan.

Figure 4 shows the protocol for communication between CMA and KDD agents. CMA sends firstly a port number and a job processing request to a KDD agent when it receives a request for a job processing from PMA. After that CMA will receive responses and results of the job processing from the KDD agent.

A KDD agent is implemented by adding the function of communicating with CMA to an existing KDD technique (algorithm). For example, C4.5, a well-known data mining technique [12], can be decomposed into three components: C4.5dis, C4.5tree, and C4.5rule, and then they are used as KDD agents, respectively, by adding the function of communicating with CMA in our GLS system. Another example is that a rough set based knowledge discovery system developed by us [21] can decomposed into three KDD agents: GDT-RS for discovering classification rules from databases with uncertain and incomplete data, RSH for attribute selection, and RSBR for discretization of real valued attributes, respectively.

One of main reasons for developing a multi-agent KDD system is that we cannot expect to develop a single data mining algorithm that can be used to solve all problems since diversification and complexity of real-world applications. Hence, various KDD agents need to be cooperatively used in multiple learning phases for performing multi-aspect intelligent data analysis as well as multi-level conceptual abstraction and learning. Furthermore, *meta-learning* as a function

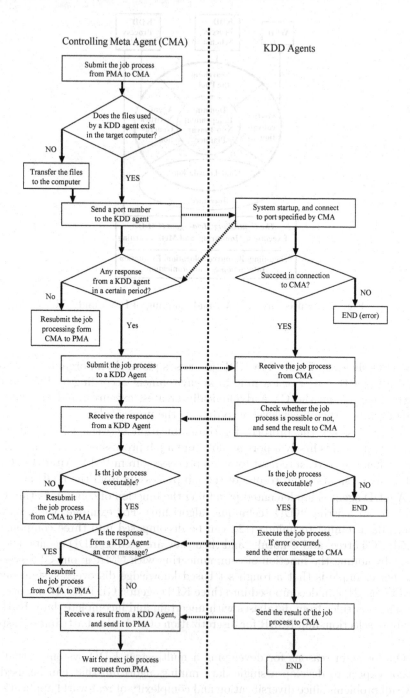

Fig. 4. Protocol for communication between CMA and KDD agents

of CMA is required to evaluate a number of results learned by multiple and distributed KDD agents so that an optimal (sub-optimal) result can be achieved. For example, a meta-learning algorithm in CMA is used to learn how to integrate or select the results of discretization of real valued attributes by using different agents for discretization such as RSBR and C4.5dis.

Another reason for developing a multi-agent KDD system is that when a database is very large and complex, a KDD task needs to be decomposed into sub-tasks. Thus these sub-tasks can be solved by using one or more KDD agents that are distributed over different computers. Thus the decomposition problem leads us to the problem of distributed cooperative system design.

6   Conclusions

We presented the framework of a multi-agent KDD system called GLS for increasing both *autonomy* and *versatility* of a discovery system. In comparison, GLS is mostly similar to INLEN in related systems [7]. In INLEN, a database, a knowledge-base, and several existing methods of machine learning are integrated as several operators. These operators can generate diverse kinds of knowledge about the properties and regularities existing in the data. INLEN was implemented as a multi-strategy KDD system like GLS. However, GLS can dynamically plan and organize the discovery process performed in a distributed cooperative mode for different discovery tasks. Moreover, the refinement for knowledge is one of important capabilities of GLS that was not developed in INLEN.

Since the GLS system to be finished by us is very large and complex, however, we have only finished several parts of the system and have undertaken to extend it for creating a more integrated, organized society of autonomous knowledge discovery agents. That is, the work that we are doing takes but one step toward a multi-strategy and multi-agent KDD system.

References

1. Brachman, R.J. and Anand, T. "The Process of Knowledge Discovery in Databases: A Human-Centred Approach", In *Advances in Knowledge Discovery and Data Mining*, MIT Press (1996) 37-58.
2. Engels, R. "Planning Tasks for Knowledge Discovery in Databases - Performing Task-Oriented User-Guidance", *Proc. Second International Conference on Knowledge Discovery and Data Mining (KDD-96)*, AAAI Press (1996) 170-175.
3. Fayyad, U.M., Piatetsky-Shapiro, G, and Smyth, P. "From Data Mining to Knowledge Discovery: an Overview", In *Advances in Knowledge Discovery and Data Mining*, MIT Press (1996) 1-36.
4. Fayyad, U.M., Piatetsky-Shapiro, G., Smyth, P., and Uthurusamy, R. (eds.) "Advances in Knowledge Discovery and Data Mining", AAAI Press (1996).
5. Kargupta, H. and Chan, P. (eds.) "Advances in Distributed and Parallel Knowledge Discovery", AAAI Press (2000).

6. Liu, C. and Zhong, N. "Rough Problem Settings for Inductive Logic Programming", Zhong, N., Skowron, A., and Ohsuga, S. (eds.) *New Directions in Rough Sets, Data Mining, and Granular-Soft Computing*, LNAI 1711, Springer-Verlag (1999) 168-177.

7. Michalski, R.S., Kerschberg, L., Kaufman, K.A., and Ribeiro, J.S. "Mining for Knowledge in Databases: The INLEN Architecture, Initial Implementation and First Results", *Journal of Intell. Infor. Sys.*, Kluwer Academic Publishers, Vol.1, No.1 (1992) 85-113.

8. Nguyen, S.H. and Nguyen, H.S. "Quantization of Real Value Attributes for Control Problems", *Proc. Forth European Congress on Intelligent Techniques and Soft Computing EUFIT'96* (1996) 188-191.

9. Ohsuga, S. and Yamauchi, H. "Multi-Layer Logic - A Predicate Logic Including Data Structure as Knowledge Representation Language", *New Generation Computing*, Vol.3, No.4 (1985) 403-439.

10. Russell, S.J. and Norvig, P. *Artificial Intelligence - A Modern Approach* Prentice Hall, Inc. (1995).

11. Piatetsky-Shapiro, G. and Frawley, W.J. (eds.), *Knowledge Discovery in Databases*, AAAI Press and The MIT Press (1991).

12. Quinlan, J.R. *C4.5: Programs for Machine Learning*, Morgan Kaufmann (1993).

13. Zhong, N. and Ohsuga, S. "Toward A Multi-Strategy and Cooperative Discovery System", *Proc. First International Conference on Knowledge Discovery and Data Mining (KDD-95)*, AAAI Press (1995) 337-342.

14. Zhong, N. and Ohsuga, S. "A Hierarchical Model Learning Approach for Refining and Managing Concept Clusters Discovered from Databases", *Data & Knowledge Engineering*, Vol.20, No.2, Elsevier Science Publishers (1996) 227-252.

15. Zhong, N. and Ohsuga, S. "System for Managing and Refining Structural Characteristics Discovered from Databases", *Knowledge Based Systems*, Vol.9, No.4, Elsevier Science Publishers (1996) 267-279.

16. Zhong, N., Kakemoto, Y., and Ohsuga, S. "An Organized Society of Autonomous Knowledge Discovery Agents", Peter Kandzia and Matthias Klusch (eds.) *Cooperative Information Agents*. LNAI 1202, Springer-Verlag (1997) 183-194.

17. Zhong, N., Liu,C., and Ohsuga, S. "A Way of Increasing both Autonomy and Versatility of a KDD System", Z.W. Ras and A. Skowron (eds.) *Foundations of Intelligent Systems*. LNAI 1325, Springer-Verlag (1997) 94-105.

18. Zhong, N., Liu, C., Kakemoto, Y., and Ohsuga, S. "KDD Process Planning", *Proc. Third International Conference on Knowledge Discovery and Data Mining (KDD-97)*, AAAI Press (1997) 291-294.

19. Zhong, N., Liu, C., and Ohsuga, S. "Handling KDD Process Changes by Incremental Replanning", J. Zytkow and M. Quafafou (eds.) *Principles of Data Mining and Knowledge Discovery*. LNAI 1510, Springer-Verlag (1998) 111-120.

20. Zhong, N. *Knowledge Discovery and Data Mining*, in the Encyclopedia of Microcomputers, Volume 27 (Supplement 6) Marcel Dekker (2001) 93-122.

21. Zhong, N. and Skowron, A. "A Rough Sets Based Knowledge Discovery Process", *International Journal of Applied Mathematics and Computer Science*, Vol. 11, No. 3, Technical University Press, Poland (2001) 101-117.

22. Zhong, N., Liu, J., Ohsuga, S., and Bradshaw, J. (eds.) *Intelligent Agent Technology: Research and Development*, World Scientific (2001).

23. Zhong, N. and Ohsuga, S. *Automatic Knowledge Discovery in Larger Scale Knowledge-Data Bases*, in C. Leondes (ed.) The Handbook of Expert Systems, Vol. 4, Academic Press (2001) 1015-1070.

Intraday FX Trading: An Evolutionary Reinforcement Learning Approach

M.A.H. Dempster and Y.S. Romahi

Centre for Financial Research
Judge Institute of Management
University of Cambridge
{mahd2, yr206}@cam.ac.uk

Abstract. We have previously described trading systems based on unsupervised learning approaches such as reinforcement learning and genetic algorithms which take as input a collection of commonly used technical indicators and generate profitable trading decisions from them. This article demonstrates the advantages of applying evolutionary algorithms to the reinforcement learning problem using a hybrid credit assignment approach. In earlier work, the temporal difference reinforcement learning approach suffered from problems with overfitting the in-sample data. This motivated the present approach.

Technical analysis has been shown previously to have predictive value regarding future movements of foreign exchange prices and this article presents methods for automated high-frequency FX trading based on evolutionary reinforcement learning about signals from a variety of technical indicators. These methods are applied to GBPUSD, USDCHF and USDJPY exchange rates at various frequencies. Statistically significant profits are made consistently at transaction costs of up to 4bp for the hybrid system while the standard RL is only able to trade profitably up to about 1bp slippage per trade.

1 Introduction

Kaelbling *et al.* [10] illustrate the challenges facing reinforcement learning in scaling up to realistic tasks. Of relevance to building a financial trading system is the issue of rarely occurring states. Previous work by the authors [7] examined the issue of searching value function space (through an RL based approach) vs searching the policy space (using an evolutionary algorithm). The two approaches were shown to provide complementary strengths though the RL showed classic signs of overfitting as a result of the rarely occurring states. This led to the currently proposed system that combines a *genetic algorithm* (GA) with a *reinforcement learning* (RL) framework to bring about a *hybrid credit assignment* approach. This paper examines the hybrid approach and contrasts it with standard RL.

In Section 2 we give a brief literature review of relevant earlier work. The *stochastic optimization* problem to be solved by all the compared methods is

H. Yin et al. (Eds.): IDEAL 2002, LNCS 2412, pp. 347–358, 2002.

defined in Section 3, while the following sections, 4 and 5, briefly describe how each approach can be applied to solve this optimization problem approximately. In Section 6, computational experiments are outlined and their results given. Section 7 concludes with a discussion of these results and some potential further avenues of research.

Reinforcement learning has to date received limited attention in the financial literature and this paper demonstrates that RL methods show significant promise. The results for the hybrid approach developed indicate that generalization and incorporation of constraints limiting the ability of computational learning algorithms to overfit improves out-of-sample performance.

2   Literature Review

Despite a century long history amongst investment professionals the technical analysis methods introduced by Dow at the turn of the last century initially met a high degree of academic scepticism culminating in a belief in the *efficient markets* or *random walk* hypothesis. As evidence has increased that markets are less efficient than was originally believed academics have only recently begun to make serious attempts to study the assumptions behind technical analysis [12, 13].

A number of researchers have examined net returns due to various trading rules in the foreign exchange markets [11,20,16,18,4,3,6]. The general conclusion is that trading rules are able to earn significant returns net of transaction costs and that this cannot be easily explained as compensation for bearing risk.

The application of *computational learning* techniques to technical trading and finance has experienced significant growth in recent years. *Neural networks* have received the most attention in the past and have shown varying degrees of success. However recently there has been a shift in favour of user-transparent, non-black box evolutionary methods like genetic algorithms and genetic programming. An increasing amount of attention in the last several years has been spent on these genetic approaches which have found financial applications in option pricing [2] and as an optimization tool in technical trading applications [18,9,5].

Pictet *et al.* [21] employ a GA to optimize a class of exponentially weighted moving average rules, but run into serious overfitting and poor out-of-sample performance. They report 3.6% to 9.6% annual returns net of transaction costs. Neely and Weller [16] report that for their GA approach, although strong evidence of predictability in the data is measured out-of-sample when transaction costs are set to zero, no evidence of profitable trading opportunities arise when transaction costs are applied and trading is restricted to times of high market activity.

Reinforcement learning has to date received only limited attention in financial applications.

As fundamental research in reinforcement learning advances, applications to finance have started to emerge. Neuneier [19] has demonstrated Q-Learning in an asset allocation framework applying it to the German DAX stock index. Moody *et al.* [15] examine a *recurrent* reinforcement learning algorithm that seeks to optimize an online estimate of the Sharpe ratio. They also compare the *recurrent RL* approach to that of *Q*-learning. Dempster *et al.* [6] similarly explore GAs and RLs, as well as the exact solution of an appropriate Markov decision problem and a simple heuristic, in an asset allocation framework.

The main shortcoming of this previous work however is that most technical analysts active in the foreign exchange market are *traders* and also operate at the high frequency level. In fact even technical traders who look for patterns in daily data alone often use tick data for confirmatory entry signals. In subsequent work [7] the authors contrast evolutionary methods with reinforcement learning within such a *trading* framework [5] and this framework will also be used in the sequel.

3   The Problem Defined

3.1   Modelling Trading

This paper considers agents that trade fixed position sizes in a single exchange rate. This setting can be generalized to more sophisticated agents that trade varying quantities of a currency, several currencies or indeed manage multiple portfolios.

Traditionally, trading strategies have been evaluated as *asset allocation* strategies in the academic literature (eg. in [18]). The agent has a current lump sum of money and must choose at each timestep whether to allocate this money to be held in the home currency or the foreign currency (possibly earning the overnight interest rate in the chosen currency). Any profit or loss made is added to or subtracted from the lump sum to be allocated in the next timestep, *i.e.* *reinvested*.

High frequency traders, however, typically are able to draw on a fixed credit line from which they may borrow in either the home or the foreign currency. The money borrowed is then converted to the other currency at the current market rate to hold cash in one currency and a debt in the other. When the trader wishes to close his position he converts his cash at the new (hopefully advantageous) exchange rate and pays any profit into or shortfall from his account. Thus he places a series of fix-sized bets.

More formally, a trade with proportional transaction cost c, exchange rates (expressed per unit of home currency) of F_t at trade entry and $F_{t'}$ at trade exit, drawing on a credit line of C units of home currency and taking a long position in the foreign currency (and a corresponding short position in the home currency) will yield a profit of

$$C \left[\frac{F_t}{F_{t'}} (1 - c)^2 - 1 \right]. \tag{1}$$

If a short position is taken in the foreign currency (and correspondingly long in the home) then C/F_t units of foreign currency are drawn from the credit line and the profit is

$$C\left[(1-c) - \frac{F_{t'}}{F_t}\frac{1}{(1-c)}\right]. \tag{2}$$

The asymmetry of these equations is apparent and results from the profit or loss on a short position in the foreign currency being credited in the home currency. Both formulae involve transaction costs being paid per unit on two currency conversions (see [5] for a discussion of the *slippage* c).

In this paper, we examine two approaches. The first system is continuously forced to be in the market while the second system is able to maintain a neutral out-of-market position. These are termed the *2 state* and *3 state* systems respectively.

3.2   Technical Indicators

We consider a set of technical indicators, to be used as input for our trading strategies and employ eight commonly used indicators with parameters suggested by [1] as in [5,6]. These are Price Channel Breakout, Adaptive Moving Average, Relative Strength Index, Stochastics, Moving Average Convergence/Divergence, Moving Average Crossover, Momentum Oscillator and Commodity Channel Index. Each indicator produces two signals: buy (long) or not buy, and sell (short) or not sell. These sixteen binary signals together define the *market state* $\mathbf{s}_t \in \mathcal{S} = \{0,1\}^{16}$.

3.3   Trading Strategies

We can consider the market state **s** represented by the indicator signals to be a *stochastic process* driven by the *exchange rate* process **F** and make the required trading decisions by solving the *stochastic optimization problem* defined by the maximization of expected return over the *trading horizon T* net of transactions costs, *viz.*

$$\mathbb{E}\sum_{i=1}^{\mathbf{N}_T} r_i(\mathbf{F}_{t_i}, \mathbf{F}'_{t_i}), \tag{3}$$

where $\mathbf{N}_T$ denotes the random number of trades to the horizon each with return $r(\mathbf{F}_t, \mathbf{F}_{t'})$ in the home currency.

The systems we consider attempt to find approximate solutions to this problem. They attempt to discover a *trading strategy* $\phi : \mathcal{S} \times \{l, s\} \to \{l, s\}$ that maps the current market state $\mathbf{s}_t$ and current position (long, short or neutral) to a new position (long, short or neutral). It should be noted that although our trading strategies ϕ are formally *Markovian* (feedback rules), the technical indicators require a number of periods of previous values of $\mathbf{F}$ to compute the corresponding $0 - 1$ entries in $\mathbf{s}_t$.

The objective of the trading strategies developed in this paper is thus to maximize the expected home currency (dollar) return (after transaction costs) using the model of § 3.1.

3.4 Evaluation

Since we do not have an explicit probabilistic model of how exchange rates evolve, we adopt the familiar approach of dividing our data series into an *in-sample* region, over which we optimize the performance of a candidate trading strategy, and an *out-of-sample* region, where the strategy is ultimately tested.

4 Applying RL to the Technical Trading Problem

The ultimate goal of reinforcement learning based trading systems is to optimize some relevant measure of trading system performance such as profit, economic utility or risk-adjusted return. This paper follows the approach of [6] which is summarised here.

Reinforcement learning systems consist of an *agent* interacting with an *environment*. At each time step t the agent *perceives* the state of the environment $s_t \in \mathcal{S}$ and chooses an *action* $a_t \in \mathcal{A}$ from the set of available actions in state s_t. As a consequence of this action the agent observes the new state of the environment s_{t+1} and receives a *reward* r_t. This can be defined as a *dynamic programming* problem where the objective is to find the *policy* π (state to action mapping) that maximises the *optimal value function* V^* given by

$$V^*(s) = \max_a \mathbb{E}\left\{r_{t+1} + \gamma V^*(s_{t+1}) | s_t = s\right\}, \qquad (4)$$

where γ is the *discount factor* representing the preference given to immediate over future rewards.

The value of state s can be considered in terms of the values of each action a that can be taken from that state assuming that policy π is followed subsequently. This value Q^* is referred to as the *Q-value* and is given by

$$Q^*(s, a) = \mathbb{E}\{r_{t+1} + \gamma \max_{a'} Q^*(s_{t+1}, a') | s_t = s, a_t = a\}. \qquad (5)$$

The optimal value function expresses the obvious fact that the value of a state under an optimal policy must equal the expected return for the best action from that state, *i.e.*

$$V^*(s) = \max_a Q^*(s, a).$$

The functions Q^* and V^* provide the basis for learning algorithms expressed as solutions of Markov decision problems.

We use Watkins's *Q-learning algorithm* [23] that estimates the *Q-value function* using data from the previous learning episode. The *Q*-learning *update* is the backward recursion

$$Q(s_t, a_t) \leftarrow Q(s_{t_c}, a_{t_c}) + \alpha[r_{t+1} + \gamma \max_a Q(s_{t+1}, a) - Q(s_{t_c}, a_{t_c})], \qquad (6)$$

where the current *state-action pair* $(s_t, a_t) := (s_{t_c}, a_{t_c})$, that from the previous learning episode. At each *iteration* (episode) of the learning algorithm, the action-value pairs associated with all the states are updated and over a large number of iterations their values converge to those optimal for (5) [22].

For our trader the state s_t is the market state as defined by the technical indicators and the set of actions $\mathcal{A}$ in the *2-state system* is whether to take a long or short position in the foreign currency (and is not state dependent). In the *3-state system* a neutral position is also a possible action in all states. Following Maes and Brookes' [14] suggestion that immediate rewards are most effective the reward function r_{t+1} is the differential change in value of the agent's portfolio from time t to $t + 1$.

5   Evolutionary Reinforcement Learning Approach

In [7], it was demonstrated that a *Q*-Learning based system suffers from overfitting the in-sample dataset. Its in-sample performance was significantly superior to that of the genetic algorithm while its performance out-of-sample tended to be inferior. It was therefore clear that the inputs to the RL system needed to be constrained and the notion of a hybrid evolutionary reinforcement learning system was thus introduced. The role of the GA here is to choose some optimal subset of the underlying indicators that the RL system will then use.

The form of GA utilised is the binary string form due to Holland [8]. Each bit in the bitstring represents whether or not the corresponding indicator is being fed into the RL. An initial population of 50 was used and the GA was allowed to evolve for 100 generations. Selection is based on the *roulette wheel* approach. However across every generation we also introduce *elitism*. Thus a number of the top individuals in each population are allowed to survive into the next generation.

With regards to fitness evaluation, the in-sample period was broken down into 8 months of true in-sample data with a further 4 months of data in the *evaluation* period which is used to evaluate individuals within the GA's population of potential solutions. The return over this second period is used as the fitness function of the GA. Once the optimal bitstring is found, the subset of indicators that the bitstring represents is fed into the RL system described earlier (see Figure 1).

6   Numerical Experiments

The results reported here were obtained by applying the approaches described above to GBPUSD, USDCHF and USDJPY midpoint exchange rate data of 1

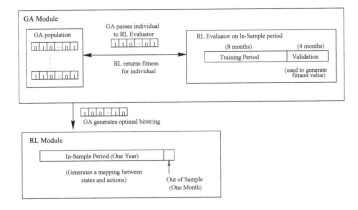

Fig. 1. Hybrid System

minute frequency from January 1994 to January 1998 using a moving window of 1 year for training (fitting) followed by 1 month out-of-sample testing (cf. [6]).

There are several issues that we wish to highlight in these results. Primarily, we try to answer the question as to whether or not using evolutionary learning as part of the credit assignment approach in the reinforcement learning framework improves performance of the system. The resolution of this question is important both in shedding light on the development of successful trading systems and in highlighting basic research issues of interest to the RL community.

Previous work by the authors [7] showed that although the RL consistently outperformed the GA at no slippage; once slippage was introduced the RL system showed classic signs of overfitting. We therefore felt that we could improve upon the original results by constraining the inputs fed into the RL system and this led to the introduction of the hybrid approach discussed above.

At no slippage all four systems tested are able to trade profitably consistently at a 15 minute trading frequency (as shown in Figure 2). However it can be seen that the hybrid approach consistently did as well or better than the basic RL. It is important to note that typical transactions costs in the foreign exchange markets faced by traders for market makers are of the order of 2bp. Considering Figure 2 the performance of the two methods start to diverge at 2bp. It is immediately clear that once we introduce slippage the ability of the system to take neutral positions becomes important. Figure 3 also demonstrates that at lower frequencies this is also a desirable property.

More importantly however we consider the performance of the hybrid systems compared to their respective standard RL systems. At 2bp slippage at both the 15 minute frequency (Figure 2) and the 1 hour frequency (Figure 3) it is clear that the hybrid systems consistently outperform the standard RL. Furthermore at lower frequency trading (consider Figure 4) performance of these systems is attenuated. Our previous results [7] demonstrated that frequency selection is best left to the learning algorithm which adapts the trading frequency to the

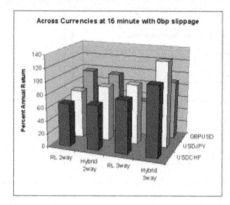
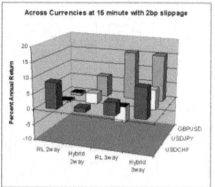

Fig. 2. 15 minute trading frequency at 0bp & 2bp across methods and currencies

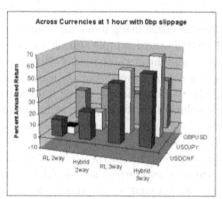
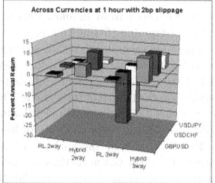

Fig. 3. 1 hour trading frequency at 0bp & 2bp across methods and currencies

slippage rather than forcing a user-constrained choice. The algorithms studied in [7] in fact adapt remarkably well as slippage increases. In general, the results hold across all three currency pairs examined.

The Sharpe ratio is a measure commonly used to evaluate portfolio models given by

$$\frac{\hat{\mu}_{R_\mathrm{month}}}{\hat{\sigma}_{R_\mathrm{month}}}, \tag{7}$$

where $\hat{\mu}_{R_{month}}$ and $\hat{\sigma}_{R_{month}}$ denote the mean and standard deviation of monthly out-of-sample returns over the test period of 36 months. The Sharpe ratios shown in Table 1 demonstrate that on the dataset used we are able to gain substantial risk-adjusted returns up to and including a slippage value of 2bp. At 4bp the

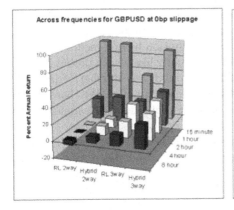
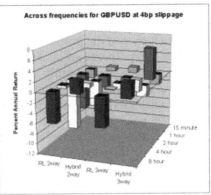

Fig. 4. Across frequencies: GBPUSD at 0bp & 4bp

results were mixed and by 10bp a trend was no longer visible - although there remained pockets of profitability.

Table 1. Out-of-sample annualized Sharpe ratios - 15 minute trading

	GBPUSD	USDCHF	USDJPY
RL 2 state - 0bp	2.82	1.28	0.82
RL 3 state - 0bp	1.62	2.08	1.36
Hybrid 2 state - 0bp	2.26	1.32	1.24
Hybrid 3 state - 0bp	**2.21**	**2.22**	**1.82**
RL 2 state - 2bp	-0.04	0.24	0
RL 3 state - 2bp	0.76	0.07	-0.07
Hybrid 2 state - 2bp	0.45	0.15	0.12
Hybrid 3 state - 2bp	**0.7**	**0.25**	**0.13**
RL 2 state - 4bp	-0.21	-0.22	-0.01
RL 3 state - 4bp	0.05	0.18	0.09
Hybrid 2 state - 4bp	0.2	0.11	0
Hybrid 3 state - 4bp	**-0.04**	**0.16**	**0.12**
RL 2 state - 10bp	0	-0.17	-0.17
RL 3 state - 10bp	0.06	0.07	0.08
Hybrid 2 state - 10bp	-0.02	-0.39	-0.07
Hybrid 3 state - 10bp	**-0.01**	**0.23**	**0**

Having motivated the hybrid (evolutionary RL) approach and demonstrated that it is indeed able to outperform the RL, we now examine the statistical significance of these results. To this end we utilize the following simple nonparametric binomial test [5]. We take as the null hypothesis that out-of-sample cumulative trading profits and losses are periodically sampled from a continuous time stationary ergodic process with state distribution having median zero. Under this null hypothesis, profits and losses are equally likely with probability $1/2$. It follows that over n monthly out-of-sample periods the number of profitable months n_+ is binomially distributed with parameters n and $\frac{1}{2}$. We therefore test the two-tailed alternative hypothesis that median profit and loss is non-zero with the statistic n_+.

The significance of our results is given in Table 2. (Note that significance levels were not included for the 10bp case as these results were uniformly not significant.) Considering the significance levels given for the 15 minute trading frequency in Table 2, we can see that the hybrid approach shows significant promise. When we consider lower frequencies we find returns are more volatile and the results are no longer as consistently significant. These values have not been included for lack of space. The significant profitability of the hybrid 3 state system at 4 basis points in spite of a negative (cumulative) return shows the importance of risk management to stop a small number of large drawdowns. (It also suggests the use of more powerful nonparametric tests for profitability which we are currently developing that take account of signed return *magnitudes*.)

Table 2. Significance level of the 15 minute trading results (N/S=Not Significant)

	GBPUSD	USDCHF	USDJPY
RL 2 state - 0bp	0.01%	0.01%	0.01%
Hybrid 2 state - 0bp	0.01%	0.01%	0.01%
RL 3 state - 0bp	0.01%	0.01%	0.01%
Hybrid 3 state - 0bp	**0.01%**	**0.01%**	**0.01%**
RL 2 state - 2bp	N/S	N/S	N/S
Hybrid 2 state - 2bp	5%	N/S	25%
RL 3 state - 2bp	0.1%	10%	25%
Hybrid 3 state - 2bp	**0.01%**	**1%**	**5%**
RL 2 state - 4bp	N/S	N/S	N/S
Hybrid 2 state - 4bp	N/S	N/S	25%
RL 3 state - 4bp	N/S	20%	15%
Hybrid 3 state - 4bp	**10%**	**10%**	**5%**

7   Discussion and Future Work

We have shown that the use of computational learning techniques in high frequency foreign exchange trading shows significant promise. The fact that the techniques investigated here return positive results both in-sample and out-of-sample implies that there is useful information in the technical indicators that can be exploited. This is consistent with the tenets of technical analysis and contradictory to the Efficient Market Hypothesis. Furthermore, the evolutionary RL's relatively good out-of-sample performance demonstrates that using a combination of technical indicators leads to better performance than using the individual indicators themselves. In fact, Dempster and Jones [5,9] demonstrate that these indicators are largely unprofitable on a different data set when considered in isolation. At low slippage values, annual returns of 10-20% are not uncommon. However, these slippage values are only typically available to market makers. Investment managers for example, who more typically face slippage of up to 10bp, would be unable to utilize the methods outlined here in the manner described. In general, we have shown that by constraining the inputs to the RL system using a GA, we have improved the performance of the underlying system. Results were furthermore statistically significant and similar across currencies.

The next step is to consider different optimization functions, in particular, exploring risk adjusted rather than raw return and overlaying the system with cash management such as stop losses. Another current avenue of research is the use of alternative reinforcement learning approaches such as the *recurrent* reinforcement learning approach described by Moody [15]. We are also exploring the incorporation of trade volume data into the learning algorithms. Generalizing the work to more sophisticated agents that trade several currencies simultaneously is currently being considered as well.

References

1. S. ACHELIS, *Technical Analysis from A to Z*, McGraw-Hill, New York, 2001.
2. N. CHIDAMBARAN, C. JEVONS LEE, AND J. TRIGUEROS, *An adaptive evolutionary approach to option pricing via genetic programming*, Proceedings of the 6th International Conference on Computational Finance, (1999).
3. M. A. H. DEMPSTER AND C. M. JONES, *Can technical pattern trading be profitably automated: 2. The head and shoulders.* Working Paper No. 12/99, Judge Institute of Management, University of Cambridge, 1999.
4. ———, *The profitability of intra-day FX trading using technical indicators.* Working Paper No. 35/00, Judge Institute of Management, University of Cambridge, 2000.
5. ———, *A real-time adaptive trading system using genetic programming*, Quantitative Finance, 1 (2001), pp. 397–413.
6. M. A. H. DEMPSTER, T. W. PAYNE, Y. ROMAHI, AND G. THOMPSON, *Computational learning techniques for intraday fx trading using popular technical indicators*, IEEE Transactions on Neural Networks, Special Issue on Computational Finance, 12 (2001), pp. 744–754.
7. M. A. H. DEMPSTER, T. W. PAYNE, AND Y. S. ROMAHI, *Intraday FX trading: Reinforcement learning vs evolutionary learning.* Working Paper No. 23/01, Judge Institute of Management, University of Cambridge, 2001, December 2001.
8. J. H. HOLLAND, *Adaptation in natural and artificial systems*, University of Michigan Press, Ann Arbour, MI, 1975.
9. C. M. JONES, *Automated technical foreign exchange trading with high frequency data*, PhD thesis, Centre for Financial Research, Judge Institute of Management Studies, University of Cambridge, June 1999.

10. L. P. KAELBLING, M. L. LITTMAN, AND A. W. MOORE, *Reinforcement learning: A survey*, Journal of Artificial Intelligence Research, 4 (1996), pp. 237–285.

11. R. LEVICH AND L. THOMAS, *The significance of technical trading rule profits in the foreign exchange market: A bootstrap approach*, Journal of International Money and Finance, 12 (1993), pp. 451–474.

12. A. W. LO AND A. C. MACKINLAY, *Stock market prices do not follow random walks: Evidence from a simple specification test*, Review of Financial Studies, 1 (1988), pp. 41–66.

13. A. W. LO AND A. C. MACKINLAY, *A Non-Random Walk Down Wall Street*, Princeton University Press, Princeton, NJ, 1999.

14. P. MAES AND R. BROOKS, *Learning to coordinate behaviors*, Proceedings of the 8th National Conference on Artificial Intelligence, (1990), pp. 796–802.

15. J. MOODY, L. WU, Y. LIAO, AND M. SAFFELL, *Performance functions and reinforcement learning for trading systems and portfolios*, The Journal of Forecasting, 17 (1998), pp. 441–470.

16. C. NEELY AND P. WELLER, *Intraday technical trading in the foreign exchange market*. Working Paper 99-016A, Federal Reserve Bank of St. Louis, November 1999.

17. C. J. NEELY, *Technical analysis in the foreign exchange market: a layman's guide*, in Federal Reserve Bank of St. Louis Review, September/October 1997, pp. 23–38.

18. C. J. NEELY, P. A. WELLER, AND R. DITTMAR, *Is technical analysis in the foreign exchange market profitable? a genetic programming approach*, Journal of Financial and Quantitative Analysis, 32 (1997), pp. 405–426. Also available as Federal Reserve Bank of St. Louis Working Paper 96-006C.

19. R. NEUNEIER, *Enhancing Q-learning for optimal asset allocation*, in Advances in Neural Information Processing Systems, M. I. Jordan, M. J. Kearns, and S. A. Solla, eds., vol. 10, The MIT Press, 1998.

20. C. L. OSLER AND P. H. K. CHANG, *Methodical madness: Technical analysis and the irrationality of exchange-rate forecasts*, Economic Journal, 109 (1999), pp. 636–661.

21. O. V. PICTET, M. M. DACOROGNA, B. CHOPARD, M. OUDSAIDENE, R. SCHIRRU, AND M. TOMASSINI, *Using genetic algorithm for robust optimization in financial applications*, Neural Network World, 5 (1995), pp. 573–587.

22. R. S. SUTTON AND A. G. BARTO, *Reinforcement learning: An introduction*, The MIT Press, 1998.

23. C. WATKINS, *Learning from Delayed Reward*, PhD thesis, Kings College, University of Cambridge, 1989.

An Up-Trend Detection Using an Auto-Associative Neural Network : KOSPI 200 Futures

Jinwoo Baek and Sungzoon Cho

Department of Industrial Engineering
Seoul National University
San 56-1, Shillim-Dong, Kwanak-Gu, 151-744, Seoul, Korea
baekhana@snu.ac.kr , zoon@snu.ac.kr

Abstract. We propose a neural network based up-trend detector. An auto-associative neural network was trained with "up-trend" data obtained from the KOSPI 200 future price. It was then used to predict an up-trend. Simple investment strategies based on the detector achieved a two year return of 19.8 % with no leverage.

1 Introduction

Technical analysis uses certain stock chart patterns and shapes as signals for profitable trading opportunities [12]. The general goal of technical analysis is to identify regularities in the time series of prices by extracting nonlinear patterns from noisy data. Technical analysts concentrate on the formation of a specific pattern. The human eyes can perform this signal extraction.

Recent breakthroughs in computer technology and numerical algorithms give rise to many methods in financial engineering. Nevertheless, technical analysis has survived through the years, because pattern recognition is one of the few repetitive activities for which computer do not have an absolute advantage yet [7]. Efforts to automate the pattern recognition process have been reported but their monetary performance left a lot to be desired [3]. We report yet another effort in that direction.

In this paper, we propose a neural network based up-trend detector using an auto-associative neural network. An auto-associative neural network (AANN) is basically a neural network whose input and target vectors are the same. The proposed detection process is as follow. First, the up-trend data is identified in historical database. Second, they are used to train AANN. Third, the trained AANN is used as an up-trend detector. A positive signal recommends to take a long position (see Fig. 1).

In section 2, our definition of "up-trend" is given. In section 3, it is shown how to detect up-trend using auto-associative neural network. Experimental methods and results are given in sections 4 and 5. Concluding remarks are given in section 6.

H. Yin et al. (Eds.): IDEAL 2002, LNCS 2412, pp. 359–365, 2002.

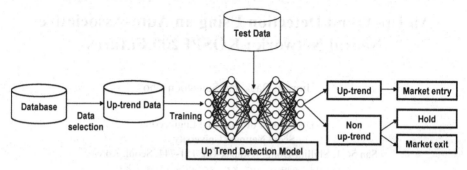

Fig. 1. Detection Process framework

2 Definition of Up-Trend

The definition of an up-trend in financial market is ambiguous and subjective. In order to obtain a training data set, we have to define an up-trend pattern. Before defining an up-trend, we introduce FK and FD variables, which reveal the trend of the price movement.

The value of traditional $\%K_n^k$ of the stochastic process invented by Lane[10] reveals where the closing price of the current trading day stands relative to the retrospective fluctuation range of prices in the last k trading days. To represent where the closing price of the current trading day will stand in relation to the fluctuation range of price for the consecutive k trading days, FK_n^k, the forward version of $\%K_n^k$, is defined by the following equation [9]:

$$FK_n^k = 2 \times \frac{Max_{i=n}^{n+k}(H_i) - C_n}{Max_{i=n}^{n+k}(H_i) - Min_{i=n}^{n+k}(L_i)} - 1.$$

And its moving average FD_n^j is defined as follows:

$$FD_n^j = \sum_{i=n}^{n+j-1} FK_i^k.$$

Now, the up-trend is defined as follows:

1. Identify up-trend beginning day(i_{begin}) or ending day(i_{end}) as follows.

    If (FD_{i-1}^j < Upper Threshold)&(FD_i^j >Upper Threshold)

        then $i_{begin} = i$;

        else {if (FD_{n-1}^j > Lower Threshold) & (FD_n^j <Lower Threshold)

            then $i_{end} = i$;}

2. Choose a larger i_{begin} and a smaller i_{end}.

3. Select the subinterval [i_{begin} , i_{end}].

3   Auto-Associative Neural Network as an Up-Trend Detector

A pattern classification method such as a neural network is an ideal candidate in an up-trend detection problem. The detection problem can now be formulated as a 2-class problem. A neural network is trained with up-trend data and non-up-trend data. Then given a new input data, or a current situation, the network tries to classify it as an up-trend or a non-up-trend. A problem with this approach is the inability to collect a sufficient case of non-up-trend data. This is a well known problem of partially-exposed environments in pattern classification where training data from on class are very few or non-existent. Related Problems include counterfeit bank note detection and typing pattern identity verification [1].

Auto-Associative Neural Network (AANN) has been used in many partially-exposed environments [1]. AANN is basically a neural network whose input and target vectors are the same [6]. AANN should reproduce an input vector at the output with a least error [4]. Let F denote an auto-associative mapping function, x_i an input vector and y_i an output vector. Then network F is usually trained to minimize the mean square error given by the equation:

$$E = \sum_{i=1}^{N} \left\| x_i - y_i \right\|^2 = \sum_{i=1}^{N} \left\| x_i - F(x_i) \right\|^2$$

Historical financial data have particular trends and characteristics. They tend to repeat themselves. The financial situations that correspond to up-trend are assumed to have unique characteristics. If the core information can be incorporated into the network input variables, the unique characteristics can be captured by the subspace of AANN embodied by the transformation at the hidden layers. Once AANN is trained with up-trend data, any up-trend data that shares common characteristic will result in a small error at the output layer while non-up-trend data will result in a large error at the output layer. With an appropriate threshold, the AANN can be used to detect the occurrence of the up-trend.

4   Data Collection and Neural Network Training

We used Korea Composite Stock Price Index 200 (KOSPI 200) future price data from Jan 1997 to Dec 2001 for the experiment. The KOSPI 200 is a kind of a market-value weighted index, similar to S&P 500 future [13]. The base date is May 1, 1996 with the base index of 100. And KOSPI 200 future is based on KOSPI 200.

For neural network training, such technical indicators as VR, RSI and MACD were used as input variables (for more details about technical indicators, see reference [11]). Using technical indicators can reduce the number of input variables effectively, while maintaining historical information. Reducing the number of input variables helps to prevent overfitting [8].

Figure 3 displays KOSPI 200 future data used in the training of this experiment. Only 208 days were found to fit the definition of the "up-trend" out of 883 days. The

AANN used has a 4-layer structure whose hidden layers have a nonlinear transfer function (tangent sigmoid used). To reduce the variation, bagging approach was used [5]. The Levenberg-Marquardt algorithm was employed to minimize the sum of square error function. The experiment was performed on Matlab 5.3.

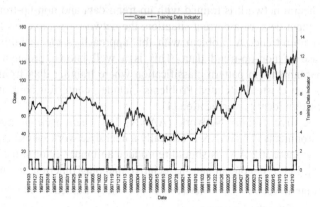

Fig. 3. KOSPI 200 future price from Jan 1997 to Dec 1999

5 Results

Table 1 shows the mean and the standard deviation of distances between input vectors and output vectors. The distance of up-trend is generally smaller than that of non-up-trend.

Table 1. The means and standard deviations of the distance between input and output

Measurements	Up-trend	Non Up-trend
Mean	1.67	2.73
Standard Deviation	0.35	0.73

Fig. 4 shows the KOSPI200 Future price during the test period 2001 as well as the network's detection results of up-trend. Up-trend score is a reciprocal of the distance between input and output.

Two thresholds were employed. Up-trend score is a reciprocal of the distance between inputs and outputs. θ_{EER} makes False Acceptance Rate(FAR) and False Rejection Rate(FRR) equal, namely Equal Error Rate(EER), in training set. $\theta_{FAR10\%}$ makes FAR about 10%.

The classification performance of AANN in test set (Jan 2000-Dec 2000) is given in Table 2. There is a trade-off between FRR and FAR. If the threshold of up-trend score increases, FAR becomes smaller and FRR becomes lager. Otherwise, vice versa.

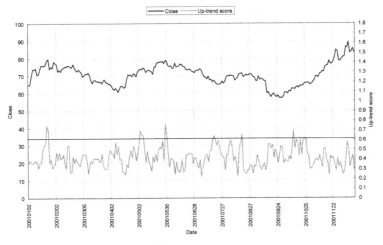

Fig. 4. The results of test set

Table 2. Classification performance of AANN in test set

Measurement		Training	Test
EER Threshold(θ_{EER})	FRR	16.4%	87.8%
	FAR	17.4%	8.0%
FAR 10 % Threshold($\theta_{FAR10\%}$)	FRR	28.8%	93.9%
	FAR	10.1%	5.1%

The large FRR in test set did not result in poor trading performance since one correct signal in the early stage of up-trend in sufficient to generate profit (see the strategy later).The proposed approach is also evaluated based on a financial measure of return rate. $S(i)$, based on hypothetical investment strategy based on up-trend signals, can be used as trading signals. $S(i)$ is as follows :

$$S(i) = \begin{cases} 1 & \text{if the distance between input and output is below entry threshold}(\theta_{entry}) \text{ at i - th day} \\ -1 & \text{if the distance between input and output is above exit threshold}(\theta_{exit}) \text{ at i - th day} \\ 0 & \text{other wise} \end{cases}$$

For example, when $S(i)$ changes from 0 to 1, we can take a long position (see Table 3).

Table 3. Simple trading strategy based on an LR signal

Current Position $S(i)$	Long position	No position
1	Hold long position	Take a long position
0	Hold long position	Hold no position
-1	Close long Position	Hold no position

Stop loss is employed with threshold θ_{stop} to manage the risk of investment. Threshold θ_{entry}, θ_{exit} and θ_{stop} were determined in training set. In this paper, threshold θ_{EER} and $\theta_{FAR10\%}$ were used as θ_{entry}. Threshold θ_{exit} was set such that the FFR equals to 1 % in training data set.

For comparison, the buy and hold strategy was also evaluated. We assumed that one buys or sells at the next day's opening price and that the market is perfectly liquid.

Table 4. The trading performance of tested strategies (Jan 2000 ~ Dec 2001)

Strategy	Total point earned (A)	Number of trades	Maximum Drawdown (B)	Stirling Ratio (A/B)
EER Threshold	25.12	33	14.2	1.77
FAR 10% Threshold	21.17	21	12.3	1.72
Buy and Hold	-47.3	1	68.45	-0.69

The trading performance of AANN in test set 2000-2001 is given in Table 4. For 2001 test, the AANN was retrained with additional 241 data from year 2000. We assumed that only 1 contract was bought and sold no matter how the system performs. The total point earned (TPE) is the total point that was accrued following the proposed system. A 0.01% transaction cost, charged by most Korean brokerage firms, was included. The maximum equity drawdown is the biggest drop in terms of TPE during the course of 2 year simulation trading. The TPE of detection with EER threshold is better than that of detection with FAR 10% threshold.

6　Conclusions

In this paper, we proposed a neural network based up-trend detector. For the experiment, a definition of "up-trend" is given and the up-trend data were selected from the Korea Composite Stock Price Index 200 future price of 36 months (Jan 1997 – Dec 1999). The auto associative neural network was trained with the obtained data. It was then tested on out-of-sample period of Jan 2000 – Dec 2001 with a retraining. A simple investment strategy based on the detector achieved a two year profits of 25.75 points or 19.8 % in return (no leverage) in comparison with -47.3 points or -36.4% in return from a buy and hold strategy.

There are several limitations in this work. First, up-trend detection leads to market entry signal. Even more important is to find a way to give market exit signal. Detection of down-trend may help. Second, the parameter k in FK_n^k was simply set to 10 since short-term trend indicators usually use 10. We need to investigate ways to find the "optimal" value of k. But, of course, we are always in a danger of overfitting.

Acknowledgement. This research was supported by Brain Science and Engineering Research Program sponsored by Korean Ministry of Science and Technology and by the Brain Korea 21 Project.

References

1. Cho, S., Han, C., Han, D., Kim, H.: Web Based Keystroke Dynamics Identity Verification using Neural Network. Journal of Organizational Computing and Electronic Commerce. Vol. 10, No. 4, December, 2000.
2. Baek, J., Cho, S.: Time to Jump in?: Long Rising Pattern Detection in KOSPI 200 Future Using an Auto-Associative Neural Network , ICONIP, pp. 160~165, Shanghai, China, Nov. 14-17, 2001.
3. Dempster, M.A.H., Jones, C.M.: Can technical pattern trading be profitably automated? 1. The channel & 2. Head and shoulders, Working Paper, Judge Institute of Management, University of Cambridge, 1999 (revised as: 2001 Can channel pattern trading be automated? Euro. J. Finance at press)
4. Bishop, C.: Neural Networks for Pattern Recognition. Oxford: Clarendon press,1994.
5. Breiman, L.: Bagging Predictors, Machine Learning, Vol. 24, No. 2, pp. 123-140, 1994.
6. Kramer, M.A.: Nonlinear Principal Components Analysis Using Auto Associative Neural Networks, AIChe J., Vol 37, No. 2, pp. 233-243, 1991
7. Lo, A.W., Mamaysky, H., Wang, J.: Foundation of Technical Analysis: Computational Algorithms, Statistical Inference and Empirical Implementation. Journal of Finance, Vol LV, NO4, pp1705-1765, 2000
8. Deboeck, G.S., Cader, M.: Pre- and Postprocessing of Financial Data, Trading on The Edge, John Wiley & Sons, Inc, pp 27- 44, 1994
9. Jang, G.S., Lai, F.: Intelligent Trading of an Emerging Market, Trading on The Edge, John Wiley & Sons, Inc, pp 80-101, 1994
10. Lane, G.C.: Trading Strategies, Future Symposium International, 1984
11. Murphy, J. J.: Technical Analysis of The Financial Markets: A Comprehension Guide to Trading Methods and Applications, New York Institute of Finance. 1999
12. Borsanaliz.com company, Tools for technical analysis stock exchange, http://www.geocities.com/ wallstreet/floor/ 1035/formations.htm, 2000
13. Korea Stock Exchange, KOSPI & KOSPI 200, http://www.kse.or.kr, 2000

Stock Price and Index Forecasting by Arbitrage Pricing Theory-Based Gaussian TFA Learning

Kai Chun Chiu and Lei Xu

Department of Computer Science and Engineering
The Chinese University of Hong Kong, Shatin, N.T., Hong Kong, P.R. China
{kcchiu,lxu}@cse.cuhk.edu.hk

Abstract. Viewed as a promising application of neural networks, financial time series forecasting was studied in the literature of neural nets and machine learning. The recently developed Temporal Factor Analysis (TFA) model mainly targeted at further study of the Arbitrage Pricing Theory (APT) is found to have potential application in the prediction of stock price and index. In this paper, we aim to illustrate the superiority of using the APT-based Gaussian TFA model as compared to three conventional approaches which are not financial model-based.

1   Introduction

The application of backpropagation networks in the prediction of stock prices was initiated by White [1] in 1988. Subsequent fruitful application of feedforward neural networks in stock price prediction was shown in [2,3,4,5]. The better performance of neural networks as compared to conventional statistical approaches in financial forecasting can be attributed to neural networks' capability to learn, adapt and generalize. Nonetheless, a typical weakness of feedforward neural networks is the inability to model existing temporal relations in financial time series. To overcome this limitation, recurrent neural networks with feedback were adopted in [4,6].

From the perspective of statistical learning, stock price prediction was implemented via a special case of the alternative models for mixture of experts, called Extended Normalized Radial Basis Function (ENRBF), via the well-known Expectation-Maximization (EM) algorithm [7]. Furthermore, the concept of mixture of experts was further integrated with economic time series modelling, leading to the inception of the so-called mixture of Autoregressive Moving Average (ARMA) Models [8].

Still, all the above efforts failed to consider some well-known finance models which not only has established their foundation in the literature of economics and finance, but also has undergone rigorous statistical test concerning their explanatory power on certain empirically observed phenomena. Therefore it would be desirable that learning algorithms designed for financial forecasting also take advantage of those models. In literature, forecasting of stock prices within the framework of the Arbitrage Pricing Theory (APT) was discussed in [3]. Although it was a good initiative to adopt finance model in training neural networks for prediction, a major drawback is that the factors had to be assumed heuristically to be some items on the balance sheets of companies in the universe of U.K. stocks.

H. Yin et al. (Eds.): IDEAL 2002, LNCS 2412, pp. 366–371, 2002.

Recently, a new technique aiming at the classical financial APT model and termed Temporal Factor Analysis (TFA) was proposed in [9] . In this paper, we consider how the APT-based Gaussian TFA model can be used for stock price and index prediction. Comparisons with some similar, previously adopted techniques are shown.

The rest of the paper is organized in the following way. Sections 2 and 3 briefly review the APT and the Gaussian TFA model respectively. Section 4 illustrates, via experimental comparisons, how Gaussian TFA can be applied to stock index forecasting. Section 5 concludes the paper.

2   Review on Arbitrage Pricing Theory

APT begins with the assumption that the $n \times 1$ vector of asset returns, R_t, is generated by a linear stochastic process with k factors [10]:

$$R_t = \bar{R} + A f_t + e_t \tag{1}$$

where f_t is the $k \times 1$ vector of realizations of k common factors, A is the $n \times k$ matrix of factor weights or loadings, and e_t is a $n \times 1$ vector of asset-specific risks. It is assumed that f_t and e_t have zero expected values so that $\bar{R}$ is the $n \times 1$ vector of mean returns.

3   Overview of Temporal Factor Analysis

Suppose the relationship between a state $y_t \in \mathbb{R}^k$ and an observation $x_t \in \mathbb{R}^d$ are described by the first-order state-space equations as follows:

$$y_t = B y_{t-1} + \varepsilon_t, \tag{2}$$
$$x_t = A y_t + e_t, \qquad t = 1, 2, \ldots, N. \tag{3}$$

where ε_t and e_t are mutually independent zero-mean white noises with $E(\varepsilon_i \varepsilon_j) = \Sigma_\varepsilon \delta_{ij}$, $E(e_i e_j) = \Sigma_e \delta_{ij}$, $E(\varepsilon_i e_j) = 0$, Σ_ε and Σ_e are diagonal matrices, and δ_{ij} is the Kronecker delta function. Specifically, it is assumed that ε_t is Gaussian distributed. The above model is generally referred to as the Gaussian TFA model. In the context of APT analysis, (1) can be obtained from (3) by substituting $(\tilde{R}_t - \bar{R})$ for x_t and f_t for y_t. The only difference between the APT model and the TFA model is the added (2) for modelling temporal relation of each factor. The added equation represents the factor series $y = \{y_t\}_{t=1}^T$ in a multi-channel auto-regressive process, driven by an i.i.d. noise series $\{\varepsilon_t\}_{t=1}^T$ that are independent of both y_{t-1} and e_t. Details about the TFA model and adaptive algorithms for its implementation can be found in [11].

4   Using Gaussian TFA for Stock Index Prediction

In this section, we aim to compare the relative performance of four similar approaches in financial prediction of stock prices and indices. Based on the input source, they fall into two categories. Category I consists of the N-ENRBF and S-ENRBF approaches for which only time series of the respective stock/index data is supplied. Category II consists of the ICA-ENRBF and APT-based TFA-ENRBF approaches for which not only time series of the stock/index itself, but also data of the corresponding constituent stocks are involved. Since the constituent stock returns are used to recover market factors, approaches belonging to category II may be generally referred to as market-based approaches whereas those belonging to category I time series approaches. The following is a brief description of each approach.

- **N-ENRBF Approach**   The adaptive ENRBF algorithm in [7] is used. The input vector consists of nonstationary raw index prices and is set as $\mathbf{x_t} = [p_{t-1}, p_{t-2}, p_{t-3}]^T$ at time t.
- **S-ENRBF Approach**   Quite similar to the previous approach, the adaptive ENRBF algorithm is adopted. The input vector at time t is $\mathbf{x_t} = [\tilde{R}_{t-1}, \tilde{R}_{t-2}, \tilde{R}_{t-3}]^T$, where stationary index returns $\tilde{R}_t$ are used instead of nonstationary index prices p_t. The index price at time t can be recovered from the predicted returns via $p_t = p_{t-1}(1 + \tilde{R}_t + \bar{R})$. Refer to section 4.2 for the definition of $\tilde{R}$ and $\bar{R}$.
- **ICA-ENRBF Approach**   This approach consists of two steps. First, the inverse mapping $\mathbf{y}_t = W\mathbf{x}_t$ is effected via the technique called Independent Component Analysis (ICA) for higher-than-second order dependence reduction. For this step the stock returns of the corresponding index constituents at time $t-1$ are used as input to recover independent components $\mathbf{y}_{t-1}$. Then, the adaptive ENRBF algorithm is adopted for establishing the relationship between $\mathbf{y}_{t-1}, x(t-1)$ and $x(t)$. In implementation, the Learned Parametric Mixture based ICA (LPM-ICA) algorithm [12] is used in view of its ability to separate any combination of sub-Gaussian and super-Gaussian source signals.
- **APT-Based TFA-ENRBF Approach**   This approach differs from the preceding approach only in the first step. Here the Gaussian TFA algorithm instead of the LPM-ICA algorithm is used to recover independent hidden factors $\mathbf{y}_{t-1}$ at time $t-1$ from cross sectional stock returns $\mathbf{x_{t-1}}$. According to our previous work [13], the number of factors determined via the model selection ability of TFA is found to be 4 for HSI constituents and 3 for HSCCI constituents.

Account of experiments related to the first three approaches can be found in [7,11]. Here we focus on using the fourth approach where the classical financial APT model is taken into account and prediction is effected via utilizing the hidden factors extracted from stationary time series of returns.

4.1   Data Considerations

The analysis are based on past Hong Kong stock and index data. Daily closing prices of three major stock indices as well as 86 actively trading stocks covering the period from January 1, 1998 to December 31, 1999 are used. The number of trading days throughout this period is 522. Of the 86 equities, 30 of them are Hang Seng Index (HSI) constituents, 32 are Hang Seng China-Affiliated Corporations Index (HSCCI) constituents, and the remaining 24 are Hang Seng China Enterprises Index (HSCEI) constituents.

4.2   Data Preprocessing

Except for the first approach, both stock and index prices should be converted to stationary returns. The required transformation can be described in four steps as shown below.

Step 1 Transform the raw prices to returns by $R_t = \frac{p_t - p_{t-1}}{p_{t-1}}$.

Step 2 Calculate the mean return $\bar{R}$ by $\frac{1}{N}\sum_{t=1}^{N} R_t$.

Step 3 Subtract $\bar{R}$ from R_t to get the zero-mean return.

Step 4 Let the result of above transformation be the adjusted return $\tilde{R}_t$.

4.3   Experimental Results

Experimental investigation is based on the performance of prediction of the three stock indices, the HSI, HSCCI and HSCEI, as well as one of the stocks, the HSBC Holding, which is also a HSI constituent. We use the first 400 data for training and the remaining 120 data for test. Both training and test are carried out in an adaptive fashion. The number of optimum hidden units is determined by the automatic model selection of Rival Penalized Competitive Learning (RPCL) algorithm [14]. Typical results of HSI, HSCCI, HSBC prices using the N-ENRBF, S-ENRBF, ICA-ENRBF and APT-based TFA-ENRBF approach are shown in Fig. 1(a)-(d), 2(a)-(d) and 3(a)-(d) respectively.

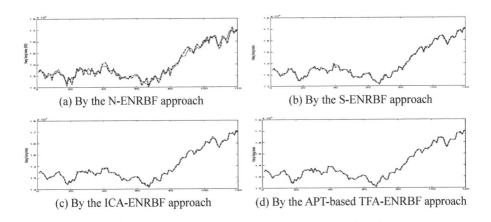

(a) By the N-ENRBF approach   (b) By the S-ENRBF approach

(c) By the ICA-ENRBF approach   (d) By the APT-based TFA-ENRBF approach

Fig. 1. Result of prediction on HSI prices. "–" represents the desired signal while "-." represents the predicted signal.

The performance of each method can be compared quantitatively by their respective Root Mean Square Errors (RMSE) between the predicted prices $\hat{p}_t$ and the desired prices p_t. As shown in Table 1, the APT-based TFA-ENRBF approach consistently outperforms the other three approaches by having the least RMSE for all three indices and the stock HSBC Holding. The ICA-ENRBF approach comes second and and the N-ENRBF approach the worst.

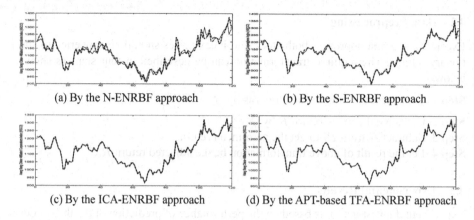

(a) By the N-ENRBF approach

(b) By the S-ENRBF approach

(c) By the ICA-ENRBF approach

(d) By the APT-based TFA-ENRBF approach

Fig. 2. Results of prediction on HSCCI prices. "–" represents the desired signal while "-." represents the predicted signal.

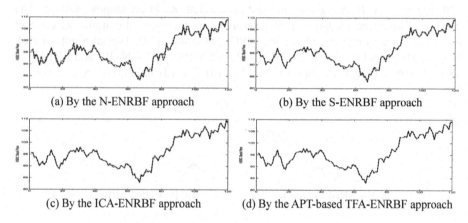

(a) By the N-ENRBF approach

(b) By the S-ENRBF approach

(c) By the ICA-ENRBF approach

(d) By the APT-based TFA-ENRBF approach

Fig. 3. Results of prediction on the HSBC Holding stock prices. "–" represents the desired signal while "-." represents the predicted signal.

Table 1. Root Mean Square Error (RMSE) for different approaches

Approach Type	HSI	HSCCI	HSCEI	HSBC
N-Adaptive ENRBF	232.9625	25.8021	9.9819	0.7957
S-Adaptive ENRBF	80.8164	8.7290	4.2516	0.4347
ICA-ENRBF	63.9681	6.0765	3.4340	0.3147
APT-based TFA-ENRBF	47.6031	4.5202	2.2187	0.2346

4.4 Performance Evaluation

Theoretically, the APT-based TFA-ENRBF approach is superior to the ICA-ENRBF approach because it takes into account the observation noise e_t ignored by the LPM-ICA algorithm. The term e_t in (3) of the TFA model speaks for itself. On the other hand, the ICA-ENRBF approach performs better than both the N-ENRBF approach and S-

ENRBF approach because signals preprocessed by the ICA technique in general contain less redundancy. When viewed from an information perspective, both the S-ENRBF approach and N-ENRBF approach is lacking in information owing to the fact that no constituent stock returns are provided during parameter learning. Consequently, less precise parameters are estimated. It should be noted that in the N-ENRBF approach, nonstationary raw prices are used while in the other three approaches, stationary stock returns are used instead. Since nonstationary signals, such as the those referred to as random walks in finance, are in general more difficult to anticipate, this unfavorable condition makes the N-ENRBF approach the worst of all.

5   Conclusion

In this paper, we suggest how the Gaussian TFA model can be applied to stock price and index forecasting. We find that the APT-based TFA-ENRBF approach has demonstrated consistently superior performance over three other conventional approaches.

References

1. White, H.: Economic prediction using neural networks: The case of ibm daily stock returns. IEEE Int. Conf. on Neural Networks (1988)
2. Schoneburg, E.: Stock prediction using neural networks. Neurocomputing 2 (1990) 17–27
3. Refenes, A.N., Azema-Barac, M., Zapranis, A.D.: Stock ranking: Neural networks vs multiple linear regression. IEEE Int. Conf. on Neural Networks 3 (1993) 1419–1426
4. Giles, C.L., Lawrence, S., Tsoi, A.C.: Rule inference for financial prediction using recurrent neural networks. Proc. of IEEE/IAFE Conf. of Comput. Intell. for Fin. Eng. (1997) 253–259
5. Sagar, V.K., Lee, C.K.: A neural stock price predictor using qualitative and quantitative data. Proc. of 6th Int. Conf. on Neural Information Processing (ICONIP'99) 2 (1999) 831–835
6. Pantazopoulos, K.N., et al.: Financial prediction and trading strageqies using neurofuzzy approaches. IEEE Trans. on Systems, Man and Cybernetics 28 (1998) 520–531
7. Xu, L.: RBF nets, mixture experts, and Bayesian Ying-Yang learning. Neurocomputing 19 (1998) 223–257
8. Kwok, H.Y., Chen, C.M., Xu, L.: Comparison between mixture of ARMA and mixture of AR model with application to time series forecasting. Proc. of 5th Int. Conf. on Neural Information Processing (1998) 1049–1052
9. Xu, L.: Temporal BYY learning for state space approach, hidden markov model and blind source separation. IEEE Trans. on Signal Processing 48 (2000) 2132–2144
10. Ross, S.: The arbitrage theory of capital asset pricing. Journal of Economic Theory 13 (1976) 341–360
11. Xu, L.: BYY harmony learning, independent state space and generalized APT financial analyses. IEEE Transactions on Neural Networks 12 (2001) 822–849
12. Xu, L., Cheung, C.C., Amari, S.I.: Learning parametric mixture based ICA algorithm. Neurocomputing 22 (1997) 69–80
13. Chiu, K.C., Xu, L.: A comparative study of Gaussian TFA learning and statistical tests on the factor number in APT. to appear in Proc. of International Joint Conference on Neural Networks (IJCNN'02) (2002)
14. Xu, L., Krzyzak, A., Oja, E.: Rival penalized competitive learning for clustering analysis, RBF net, and curve detection. IEEE Trans. on Neural Networks 4 (1993) 636–649

A Comparative Study on Three MAP Factor Estimate Approaches for NFA

Zhiyong Liu and Lei Xu

Department of Computer Science and Engineering
The Chinese University of Hong Kong, Shatin, N.T. Hong Kong, P.R. China

Abstract. In this paper we comparatively study three MAP factor estimate approaches, i.e., *iterative fixed posteriori approximation*, *gradient descent approach*, and *conjugate gradient algorithm*, for the non-Gaussian factor analysis (NFA). With the so-called *Gaussian approximation* as initialization, the *iterative fixed posteriori approximation* is empirically found to be the best one among them.

1 Introduction

Independent component analysis (ICA)

$$\mathbf{x}(t) = \mathbf{A}\mathbf{s}(t), \ \mathbf{x}(t) \in \mathbb{R}^n, \mathbf{s}(t) \in \mathbb{R}^m, \mathbf{A} \in \mathbb{R}^{n \times m} \tag{1}$$

concerns the task of recovering some unknown sources $\mathbf{s}(t)$ from the observations $\mathbf{x}(t)$ as $\mathbf{y}(t) = \mathbf{W}\mathbf{x}(t)$. Recently, ICA has found wide application in many cases. However, evidence has revealed that the above ideal *noise-free* model can hardly satisfy the assumption embedded in some real-world applications.

In view of this, non-Gaussian factor analysis (NFA) firstly proposed in [1] and subsequently developed in [2] considers the following model with additive noise:

$$\mathbf{x}(t) = \mathbf{A}\mathbf{s}(t) + \mathbf{e}(t) \tag{2}$$

In NFA, each source component is assumed component-wise independent and whose density can be modelled by a Gaussian mixture (non-Gaussian) in the following form:

$$p(\mathbf{y}) = \prod_j p(y_j), p(y_j) = \sum_r \alpha_{j,r} G(y_j | m_{j,r}, \sigma_{j,r}^2) \tag{3}$$

where $G(y_j | m_{j,r}, \sigma_{j,r}^2)$ denotes a Gaussian pdf with mean $m_{j,r}$ and variance $\sigma_{j,r}^2$. Based on BYY harmony learning, a four-step iterative algorithm was proposed in [2] to estimate the NFA model. The first step of the algorithm solves the maximum a posteriori (MAP) problem as $\hat{\mathbf{y}}(t) = \arg\max_{\mathbf{y}} \ln[p(\mathbf{x}(t)|\mathbf{y}(t))p(\mathbf{y}(t))]$, where $p(\mathbf{x}(t)|\mathbf{y}(t)) = G(\mathbf{x}(t)|A\mathbf{y}(t), \mathbf{\Sigma_e})$ and $\mathbf{\Sigma_e}$ denotes the covariance matrix of noise e_t.

H. Yin et al. (Eds.): IDEAL 2002, LNCS 2412, pp. 372–377, 2002.

Although the MAP problem is important for performing learning on NFA, it is analytically intractable. In this paper, we empirically compare three suggested typical numerical algorithms. This paper is organized as follows. Section 2 briefly describes the MAP problem and the three approaches. An experiment is then given in section 3, based on which some comments are made in section 4.

2   Approaches for MAP Estimate Problem in NFA

The MAP factor estimate problem for the NFA model is as follows:

$$\hat{\mathbf{y}} = \arg\max_{\mathbf{y}} \ln[p(\mathbf{x}|\mathbf{y})p(\mathbf{y})]$$

$$= \arg\max_{\mathbf{y}}[\sum_j \ln \sum_r \alpha_{j,r} G(y_j|m_{j,r},\sigma_{j,r}^2) + \ln G(\mathbf{x}|\mathbf{Ay}, \boldsymbol{\Sigma_e})] \qquad (4)$$

Here, we consider three numerical approaches suggested for this analytically intractable problem.

2.1   Iterative FPA

The first is the so-called *fixed posteriori approximation* (FPA) approach proposed in Tab. 2 of [2] as

$$\hat{\mathbf{y}} = (\mathbf{A}^T \boldsymbol{\Sigma_e}^{-1} \mathbf{A} + diag[b_1, ..., b_k])^{-1}[\mathbf{A}^T \boldsymbol{\Sigma_e}^{-1}\mathbf{x} + \mathbf{d}] \qquad (5)$$

where $b_j = \sum_r \frac{h_{j,r}}{\sigma_{j,r}^2}$, $d_j = \sum_r \frac{h_{j,r}m_{j,r}}{\sigma_{j,r}^2}$, and the posteriori $h_{j,r} = \frac{\alpha_{j,r}G(y_j|m_{j,r},\sigma_{j,r}^2)}{\sum_r \alpha_{j,r}G(y_j|m_{j,r},\sigma_{j,r}^2)}$ is approximated irrelevant to $\mathbf{y}$.

Based on it, we use the following iterative algorithm:

step 1: calculate $\mathbf{h} = [h_{j,r}]$ based on a properly initialized $\mathbf{y}$.
step 2: fix $\mathbf{h}$, update $\mathbf{y}$ according to eq 5.
step 3: fix $\mathbf{y}$, update $\mathbf{h}$. If converged, stop; otherwise, go to step (2).

The *Iterative FPA* has been proved to be exactly the EM-algorithm for (4) in a sister paper [3], and thus its convergence can be guaranteed.

2.2   Gradient Descent Approach

The derivative of $f(\mathbf{y}) = \ln[p(\mathbf{x}(t)|\mathbf{y}(t))p(\mathbf{y}(t))]$ with respect to $\mathbf{y}$ takes the following form:

$$\nabla_{\mathbf{y}}(f) = \mathbf{A}^T \boldsymbol{\Sigma_e}^{-1}(\mathbf{x} - \mathbf{Ay}) + \mathbf{g} \qquad (6)$$

where $\mathbf{g} = [g_1, ..., g_m]^T$, $g_j = \sum_r h_{j,r}\frac{m_{j,r}-y}{\sigma_{j,r}^2}$, and $h_{j,r}$ is the same as in the above *iterative FPA*.

(6) can be directly used as gradient to implement the *gradient descent approach (gradient DA)*. However, learning will be slow due to its linear convergence speed.

2.3   Conjugate Gradient Method

Since the Quasi-Newton method is not suitable here due to the difficulty of finding the Hessian matrix, we choose the *conjugate gradient method* because of its superior convergence property (see, for instance, [4]). Its learning rate is calculated according to the approach in [5]. For brevity, we do not present the detailed algorithm here, which is based on the gradient in (6).

2.4   Gaussian Approximation Initialization

Proper initialization is necessary for all the three numerical approaches above. In this paper, they are initialized according to the so-called *Gaussian approximation* proposed in Tab. 2 in [2]:

$$\hat{\mathbf{y}} = \mathbf{A}_{\mathbf{y}}^{-1}(\mathbf{x_A} + \mathbf{\Lambda}^{-1}\mathbf{d}) \tag{7}$$

where $\mathbf{d} = [d_1, ..., d_k]^T$, $\mathbf{\Lambda} = diag[\lambda_1, ..., \lambda_k]$, with $d_j = \Sigma_r \alpha_{j,r} m_{j,r}$, $\lambda_j = \Sigma_r \alpha_{j,r}[\sigma_{j,r}^2 + (m_{j,r} - d_j)^2]$, $\mathbf{x_A} = \mathbf{A}^T \mathbf{\Sigma_e}^{-1}\mathbf{x}$, and $\mathbf{A_y} = \mathbf{A}^T \mathbf{\Sigma_e}^{-1}\mathbf{A} + \mathbf{\Lambda}^{-1}$. The essence is that a Gaussian density was used to approximate the Gaussian mixture in (4) such that an analytic solution can be obtained by (7).

3   Experimental Demonstration of NFA

For simplicity and without loss of generality, we choose to compare the three MAP factor estimate approaches using only two source signals.

3.1   Data Description

We consider 100 observations, of which only the first 50 are shown in Fig 1 for clarity. The data are generated according to (2) with the parameters preset as follows: $\mathbf{A} = \begin{pmatrix} 1.2 & -1.0 \\ 0.6 & 1.4 \end{pmatrix}$, $\mathbf{y}(t) = (s_1(t) \; s_2(t))^T$, and $\mathbf{e}(t)$ is randomly generated from the pdf $G(\mathbf{e}|0, \mathbf{\Sigma})$, where $s_1(t)$ is from an uniform distribution between [-0.5 0.5], $s_2(t)$ from bimodal symmetric $\beta(2, 2)$ distribution with mean removed, and $\mathbf{\Sigma}$ is a 2×2 matrix with diagonal elements $\sigma_{ii} = 0.01$ and off-diagonal elements $\sigma_{ij} = 0$. The source signals are shown in Fig 2.

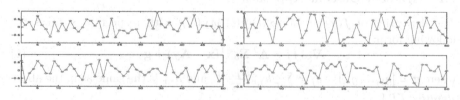

Fig. 1. The two observed samples   **Fig. 2.** The two sources signals

3.2   Experimental Results

The same experiment is repeated 20 times with random initializations. Experimental results are presented below according to the estimate accuracy and efficiency respectively.

Results on Estimate Accuracy. Two typical recovered signals via the NFA are shown in fig 3,4, and 5, where the source signals are denoted by "o", and recovered by "∗", and all of their mean and variance are normalized to be 0 and 1 respectively. The Mean Square Error (MSE) (average over 20 repetitions) between the normalized estimated state y_j and the true state s_j, and three typical estimated noise covariances $\hat{\Sigma}_e$ are shown in Tab. 1(col. 2 and 3).

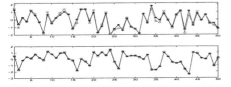

Fig. 3. Two restored sources with *iterative FPA* for MAP estimate.

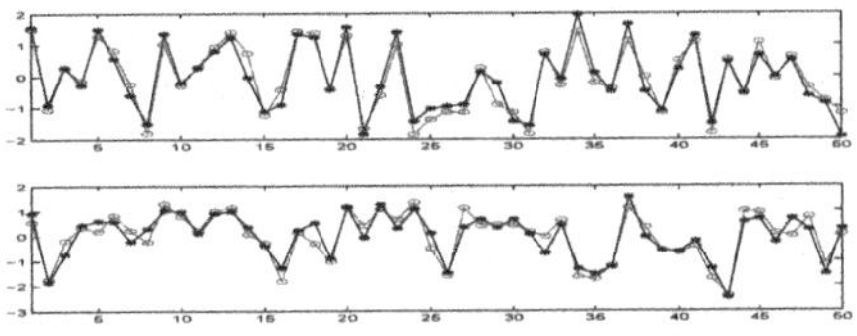

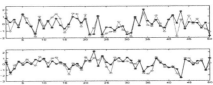

Fig. 4. Two restored sources with *gradient DA* for MAP estimate.

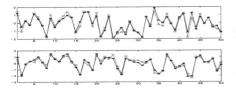

Fig. 5. Two restored sources with *conjugate GA* for MAP estimate.

Fig. 6. Two restored sources with *Gaussian approximation* for MAP estimate

Results on Estimate Efficiency. The cost-time (average over 20 repetitions) of the three MAP approaches based NFA models are listed in Tab. 1 (col. 4).

4   Discussion on the MAP Factor Estimate Process

As witnessed by the experiment results, NFA not only can recover the source signals, but also is capable of estimating the noise model. Although *gradient DA* is the worst on **estimate accuracy**, its performance does not differ significantly

Table 1. Comparative experiments results on three MAP approaches based NFA

	Mean Square Error		noise covariance	time-cost of	time-cost of a
	signal 1	singal2	$\hat{\boldsymbol{\Sigma}}_e$	NFA	MAP
iterative FPA	0.0687	0.0086	$\begin{pmatrix} 0.0172 & -0.0023 \\ -0.0023 & 0.0196 \end{pmatrix}$	17.36s	3ms
gradient DA	0.1397	0.1667	$\begin{pmatrix} 0.0212 & 0.0014 \\ 0.0014 & 0.0183 \end{pmatrix}$	232.49s	61ms
conjugate GA	0.1004	0.0865	$\begin{pmatrix} 0.0122 & -0.0033 \\ -0.0033 & 0.0264 \end{pmatrix}$	62.43s	13ms

from the other two. Yet the story can be considered quite different for **estimate efficiency**. Below we try to explain the results via a typical MAP estimate process shown in fig 7.

4.1   A Typical MAP Factor Estimate Process

Fig 7 illustrates a typical MAP problem, where the maximum and initial points obtained via *Gaussian approximation* are represented by two arrows. The value of ln $[p(\mathbf{x}|\mathbf{y})p(\mathbf{y})]$ are -5.4412 and -5.4603, and the corresponding "factors" are $\mathbf{y}$ are $[0.1860, 0.3072]^T$ and $[0.4857, 0.6668]^T$ respectively. The three MAP estimating processes are shown in fig 8, and the corresponding time-cost are shown in Tab. 1 (col. 5).

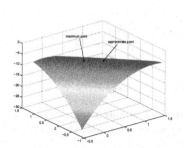

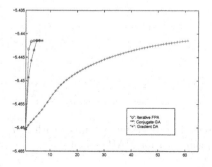

Fig. 7. the MAP problem, where coordinates making up the horizontal plane are y_1 and y_2, and the erected one is ln$[p(\mathbf{x}|\mathbf{y})p(\mathbf{y})]$

Fig. 8. Convergence process of the three MAP approaches

4.2   Discussion on Estimate Accuracy

As shown in fig 8, all the three approaches can approximately arrive at the optimal point with the same initialization. This explains why the estimate accuracy of the three approaches does not differ greatly from each other. However, for *gradient DA* sometimes the process may be too long to get to the optimal solution due to its linear convergence speed. For instance, in this typical example there is still a little error for *gradient DA* after 62 iterations. Thus the *gradient DA* being the worst one on estimate accuracy is as expected.

To demonstrate the essentiality of the estimate accuracy, we directly use the *Gaussian approximation* as the MAP factor estimate result. The two recovered signals are shown in fig 6, and the MSE for signal 1 and 2 are 0.4782 and 0.3347 respectively, which implies the failure of the direct adoption of the *Gaussian approximation* as the factor.

4.3   Discussion on Estimate Efficiency

As shown in Fig 8, *gradient DA* is much slower than the other two. This is reasonable since *gradient DA* has at best a linear convergence rate [6]. Generally speaking, the convergence rate of *iterative FPA* (EM algorithm) is linear [7], and *conjugate GA* enjoys at least a linear rate [4]. But fig 8 surprises us in that *iterative FPA* converged as quickly as the *conjugate GA*. Specific to this problem where the *Gaussian approximation* usually makes the initialization close to the true result, and according to the conclusions in [8] that state "for gaussian mixtures locally around the true solution...and when the overlap in the mixture is small...the convergence rate for the EM algorithm tends to be asymptotically superlinear", we guess that the *iterative FPA* here enjoys this merit. Although the convergence rates of the two approaches are close, the process for finding a proper learning rate in *conjugate GA* is time-consuming. This accounts for the significant divergence on estimate efficiency in Tab. 1 (col. 4 and 5).

4.4   Concluding Remarks

Based on the discussions above we can conclude that with the *Gaussian approximation* as initialization the *iterative FPA* is the best one among the three MAP factor estimate approaches for the NFA.

References

1. Xu, L.: Bayesian kullback ying-yang dependence reduction theory. Neurocomputing **19** (1998) 223–257
2. Xu, L.: Byy harmony learning, independent state space and generalized apt financial analysis. IEEE Transaction on Neural Network **12** (2001) 822–849
3. Liu, Z.Y., Xu, L.: On convergence of an iterative factor estimate algorithm for the nfa model. ICANN'02 (2002)
4. McCormick, G.P., Ritter, K.: Alternative proof of the convergence properties of the conjugate gradient method. J. of Opti. Theo. and Appl. **13** (1974) 497–518
5. Fletcher, R.: Practical Methods of Optimization. John Wiley and Sons. (1987)
6. Kelley, C.T.: Iterative Methods for Optimization. SIAM, PA, USA (1999)
7. Wu, C.: On the convergence properties of the em algorithm. The Annals of Statistics **11** (1983) 95–103
8. Ma, J., Xu, L., Jordan, M.I.: Asymptotic convergence rate of the em algorithm for gaussian mixtures. Neural Computation **12** (2000) 2881–2907

A Neural Classifier with Fraud Density Map for Effective Credit Card Fraud Detection

Min-Jung Kim and Taek-Soo Kim

Information Technology Lab. LG Electronics Institute of Technology,
Seoul, 137-724, Korea
{lafwing, tskim}@ lge.com

Abstract. In this paper, we propose a way of effective fraud detection to improve the detection efficiency. We focus on the bias of the training dataset, which is typically caused by the skewed distribution and highly overlapped classes of credit card transaction data and leads to lots of mis-detections[1]. To reduce mis-detections, we take the fraud density of real transaction data as a confidence value and generate the weighted fraud score in the proposed scheme. The effectiveness of our proposed scheme is examined with experimental results on real data.

1   Introduction

Even using salient features and advanced classification techniques, the detection of credit card frauds is a very complicated problem. Two major characteristics in the credit card transaction data may explain this difficulty. The one is the skewed distribution of data. Fraudulent transactions happen very rarely as compared with legitimate transactions and the percentage of fraudulent transaction is usually considered to be 0.1% or less [1]. And the other is that a large part of fraudulent transactions are overlapped with the legitimate ones. It is not easy to extract frauds from non-frauds efficiently. So achieving high fraud detection rate always inevitably accompanies lots of mis-detections.

In the development process of the fraud detection system, we have experienced some technical problems caused by peculiar characteristics of data, such as large volume of data, skewed distribution, irregular cost of transaction, and highly overlapped classes [2][3]. Most serious one is the construction of training data set for the classifier. Especially for the classifier based on an unstable learning algorithm such as neural networks, decision tree or decision rule, its learning result undergoes significant changes in response to small changes in the training data set [4]. For these reasons, generation of the unbiased data set for training the classifier is essential in the first stage of modeling fraudulent behaviors. But, it is also not so easy because of extremely skewed distribution of data as well as their huge size. In most cases, training data set is susceptible to have a dissimilar distribution from the real data as

---

[1] A 'mis-detected' transaction means a transaction classified into the fraud-class although it is not a fraud actually. That is, it is a false positive detection. A 'detected' transaction means a transaction classified into the fraud-class whatever it is a fraud or not actually.

H. Yin et al. (Eds.): IDEAL 2002, LNCS 2412, pp. 378-383, 2002.

shown in Fig. 1. Fig. 1 (a) shows the distribution of training data set. The circled area 'A' and 'B' are considered to have same distribution in the space of training data set. But for the same areas in the space of real data set, more legitimate transactions could be seen in area 'A' than in area 'B'. That is, transactions in area 'A' should be considered to have a lower probability to be a fraud in real world than those in area 'B'. But, transactions in both areas may be treated identically by a classifier. Such an overemphasis of fraudulent transactions in training data is apt to lead the classifier to over-fit strongly to fraud-class and it can cause superfluous mis-detections.

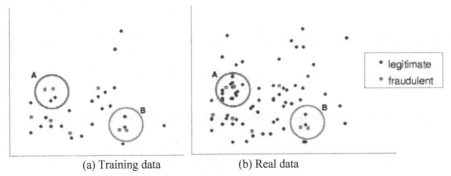

(a) Training data   (b) Real data

Fig. 1. Inconsistent distributions between the training data and real data

Therefore, we need to regulate the decision of the classifier inclined to fraud-class with real data to reflect legitimate transaction data, of which a major part are excluded in the training data. Unfortunately, such technical problems have not been widely studied in the domain of credit card fraud detection.

2   Fraud Detection Scheme with Fraud Density Map

The basic objective of this paper is to improve the performance of the neural classifier which is constructed with training data set that contains only a small part of real transaction data and is very extremely biased to fraudulent transactions. As the bias of training data set is inevitable in constructing the neural classifier for the detection of fraudulent transactions, we designed the classification scheme with fraud density map using analyzed information over the real data.

The key idea in the proposed scheme is to use the fraud density at a point in input space corresponding to an issued[2] transaction to adjust the output of the classifier. From the intuitions that the input transaction can be regarded suspicious if it is on the fraud-ridden area in the input space and the fraud density represents the probability of fraud occurrence, we take the fraud ratio of neighborhood around the point represented by a input vector in the input data space as a confidence value, with which we adjust the fraud score of the neural classifier.

---

[2] An 'issued' transaction means a transaction requested on the company to get the usage admission and pass through the fraud detection system for the investigation.

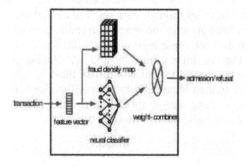

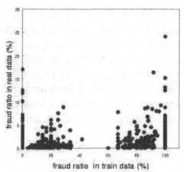

Fig. 2. Schematic of fraud detection system with fraud density map

Fig. 3. The X-Y plot of cells in the fraud density map with fraud ratios in training data and real data

There are two major issues in designing the system to reflect the fraud density of some transaction to the final decision. The first one is how to get the fraud density of a random input vector. In order to refer the fraud density corresponding to an input vector immediately, we construct the map of fraud density and fetch instantly the fraud density from it for the requested transaction. Fraud density map is a simple but effective approach to provide the fraud density considering the situation that the system should be operated in a real time and the fraud ratio seldom undergo a sudden change for a long term. The other one is how to determine the neighborhood of an issued transaction. In our scheme, we partition the input space into a large number of areas applying the main idea of decision tree algorithm.

2.1   Fraud Detection System

Fig. 2 shows the schematic of our fraud detection system. In this system, an input transaction is transformed into a feature vector on the input space. As for the neighborhood of an input transaction, we divide the input space multidimensionally into a set of areas and define it as the partitioned input space, that is, a partition of the input space. And we also define an area of the partitioned input space as a cell.

In our system, the neural classifier generates the fraud score from the feature vector, which is transformed from the transaction requested by a cardholder. Simultaneously, its fraud density is generated from the feature vector by the fraud density map. Finally, the weight-combiner produces the weighted fraud score combining the fraud score by the neural classifier and the fraud ratio by the fraud density map and generates the final decision of admission or refusal for the requested transaction.

2.2   Fraud Density Map

Fraud density map is a component for the reflection of the distribution of the real data, which contains the sparseness of frauds in each areas and links its own fraud density on input space to each transaction. Each cell of the fraud density map contains the number of fraudulent or legitimate transactions belonging to its own area in the whole partitioned input space, which are used to get the fraud density defined as the fraud ratio of each cell. The definition of the fraud density of transaction i, which is located in the cell j as follows.

$$\text{Fraud Density}(i) \ (\%) = \frac{\text{number of fraudulent transactions in the cell}(j)}{\text{number of total transactions in the cell}(j)} \times 100 \qquad (1)$$

The fraud ratio of the cell selected by an input feature vector can be immediately calculated by the fraud density map. Because of operational constraints of the real on-line system, it should be constructed in advance with the real data in a sufficient period and be designed to produce the fraud density for any transaction in a real time.

In our fraud detection system, we used the decision tree algorithm to partition the input space. The data structure is an extended decision tree, of which each leaf nodes have two additional fields for the numbers of fraudulent transactions and legitimate transactions.

Two stages with each training data are needed for constructing the fraud density map. The first one is partitioning the input space with the training data, which is partially selected from real transaction data. It is accomplished by ID3 algorithm developed by J.R. Quinlan [5]. Then, using the other training data, which has natural distribution, two fields at each leaf node of the decision tree are filled with the values of counting its contained transactions. It can be easily obtained by increasing either of two fields at leaf node for each data. Consequently, the fraud density map is made up completely by calculating the distribution with the partitioned input space using the real data. Because the process in the second stage is just analyzing the real data, which is not used in the stage of training the classifier, it can be simply obtained by just one data scanning in a reasonable time even for the huge size of data.

2.3   Combining the Fraud Score and the Fraud Density

Many combining methods have been explored in the ensemble model of multiple classifiers [4]. Unfortunately, we could not apply them to our system since they assume that their individual classifiers are independent and their outputs represent a class as a discrete value, not a continuous value such as numeric score.

We regarded a fraud density as a weighting value for adjusting the fraud score by biased neural classifier. For this reason, the weight-combiner is designed to generate the weighted fraud score based on the fraud score with the fraud density.

$$\text{Weighted Fraud Score} = \alpha \times \text{W(fraud density)} \times \text{fraud score} \qquad (2)$$

The regulated fraud density applied with a weighting function is designed to get the weighted fraud score instead of a raw fraud density. In our experiments, the range of fraud ratios in the fraud density map is from 0% to about 25%, but approximately 24% cells in the fraud density map have the fraud ratio of less than 0.1% and fraud ratios of about 42% cells are concentrated in the range of from 0.1% to 1%. So, we use some monotonic increasing functions such as atan, tanh, log as a weighting function.

3   Experimental Results

As stated in [1], evaluation based on classification accuracy, a standard performance measure in machine learning is not appropriate in credit card fraud detection. In this experiment, the number of fraudulent transactions that are detected is considered for the evaluation criteria when the number of detected transactions is fixed.

Let nDF and rDT defined as follows.

- nDF : the number of detected frauds, that is, the number of frauds classified into fraud-class.

- rDT : the ratio of detected transactions to total issued transactions

The training data used for the neural classifier are chosen from records of transactions in 1995, which were provided by some credit company in Korea. The sample size of the training data is 47,000 and fraudulent-to-legitimate transaction ratio is 1:4. Testing was done six million transactions issued over three months with 1:1288. We made up another training data for constructing the fraud density map with all the transaction data issued during six months before the period of transaction data for testing the classifier.

Backpropagation method is used to train neural networks with sigmoidal activation functions in the hidden layer. Its structure is 8-40-1. We used 898 cells for fraud density map. Each partitioned areas in the fraud density map has a diverse fraud ratio form 0% to 24.07%. Fig. 3 presents a discrepancy in fraud ratio distributions with training data and real data by plotting cells in the fraud density map.

In our experiments, generally as rDT increases, nDF also increases. Our proposed schemes perform better than the neural classifier even though there is a degree of variation according to applied weighting functions for the weight-combiner. In the range of over 0.7% linear function performs slightly better and in the range of under 0.5%, curves using tanh and atan for a weighting function are a little more effective. Fig. 4(a) shows experimental curves of nDF versus rDT for the neural classifier-only and our proposed scheme with the fraud density map using tanh function. In overall ranges of rDT, more frauds are detected by the proposed scheme than by the neural classifier-only. Note that when rDT is larger than 0.5%, our scheme achieves very higher detection efficiency. But, when rDT is smaller than 0.3%, the effects of the fraud density map are not outstanding compared to those in the range of larger rDT. Hence, we expect that our proposed scheme is remarkably effective in an aggressive detection system.

Considering that only a part of issued transactions are actually investigated, the proposed method with a step function and the neural classifier with expert-designed filter[3] are very similar in their approaches. But the selection of transactions to be examined based on fraud density is more effective than based on the knowledge of domain experts as shown in Fig. 4(b).

---

[3] It is an approach that only some portions of issued transactions selected by some predefined rules pass through the classifier.

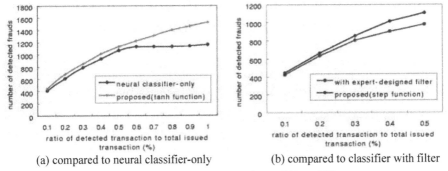

(a) compared to neural classifier-only   (b) compared to classifier with filter

Fig. 4. Performance comparison: *rDT* vs *nDF*

4   Conclusions

We have proposed a neural fraud detection system with the fraud density map to improve the detection efficiency. In particular, we have motivated from the problem of biased train data due to extremely skewed distribution of real data and have suggested the scheme to adjust the biased result by reflecting the distribution of the real data. Our approach provides more general and flexible method to reduce mis-detections. In the experiments, our scheme was seen remarkably effective to increase the number of detected frauds.

References

1. R. Brause, T. Langsdorf, M. Hepp.: Neural Data Mining for Credit Card Fraud Detection, Proc. 11th Int'l Conf. Tools with Artificial Intelligence (1999) 103-106.
2. Jose R. Dorronsoro, at el.: Neural Fraud Detection in Credit Card Operations, IEEE Trans. on Neural Networks, vol.8, no.4 (1997) 827-834.
3. Philip K. Chan, Wei Fan.: Distributed Data Mining in Credit Card Fraud Detection, IEEE Intelligent System, vol.14 issue 6 (1999) 67-74.
4. Tomas G. Dietterich.: Machine Learning Research: Four Current Directions, AI Magazine, vol.18 no 4 (1997) 97-136.
5. J. R. Quinlan: Induction of Decision Trees, Machine Learning, v1 (1986) 81-106.
6. Philip K. Chan, Salvatore J. Stolfo: Toward Scalable Learning with Non-uniform Class and Cost Distributions: A Case Study in Credit Card Fraud Detection, Proc. Fourth Int'l Conf. KDDM, AAAI Press, Menlo Park, California (1998) 164-168.
7. Emin Aleskerov, Bernd Freisleben, Bharat Rao: CARDWATCH: A Neural Network Based Database Mining System for Credit Card Fraud Detection, Proc. of Int'l Conf. Computational Intelligence for Financial Engineering, (1997) 220-226.
8. Sushimito Ghosh, Douglas L.Reilly: Credit Card Fraud Detection with a Neural-Network, Proc. 7th Hawaii Int'l Conf. Syst. Sci., (1994) 621-630.
9. Sholom M.Weiss, Nitin Indurkhya: Predictive Data Mining: A Practical Guide, Morgan Kaufmann (1998)
10. J. R. Quinlan: C4.5: Programs For Machine Learning, Morgan Kaufamn (1993)

A Comparison of Two Techniques for Next-Day Electricity Price Forecasting

Alicia Troncoso Lora[1], Jesús Riquelme Santos[1], José Riquelme Santos[2],
Antonio Gómez Expósito[1], and José Luís Martínez Ramos[1]

[1] Department of Electrical Engineering, University of Sevilla, Sevilla, Spain
[2] Department of Languages and Systems, University of Sevilla, Sevilla, Spain
ali@esi.us.es, jesus@us.es riquelme@lsi.us.es, {age, camel}@us.es

Abstract. In the framework of competitive markets, the market's participants need energy price forecasts in order to determine their optimal bidding strategies and maximize their benefits. Therefore, if generation companies have a good accuracy in forecasting hourly prices they can reduce the risk of over/underestimating the income obtained by selling energy. This paper presents and compares two energy price forecasting tools for day-ahead electricity market: a k Weighted Nearest Neighbours (kWNN) the weights being estimated by a genetic algorithm and a Dynamic Regression (DR). Results from realistic cases based on Spanish electricity market energy price forecasting are reported.

1 Introduction

The Spanish electric industry is moving from a centralized operational approach to a competitive one since 1998, and it is mainly based on two separated day-ahead markets [1]: the energy market, managed by the Market Operator and the market for regulation reserves.

Forecasting energy prices has become an essential tool in competitive electricity markets. In the short term, expected price profiles, both in terms of energy and reserve prices, help market participants to determine their optimal bidding strategies and, consequently, maximize their benefits. Therefore, if generation companies have a good accuracy in forecasting hourly prices they can reduce the risk of over/underestimating the income obtained by selling energy.

In a non-perfect oligopolistic market, the energy prices time series presents a high percentage of unusual prices. Due to this fact, nowadays, no approaches based on time series analysis that successfully forecast next-day Spanish electricity prices exist.

This paper presents and compares two energy price forecasting effective tools for day-ahead electricity market: a k Weighted Nearest Neighbours (kWNN), in which the weights are estimated by a genetic algorithm and a Dynamic Regression (DR). First, a k Weighted Nearest Neighbours algorithm is proposed using a Weighted-Euclidean distance. Second, two Dynamic Regression models are developed and applied to the 24-hour energy price forecasting problem, and the expected errors are quantified.

H. Yin et al. (Eds.): IDEAL 2002, LNCS 2412, pp. 384–390, 2002.

2   Structure of the Spanish Electricity Market

The study reported in this paper is based on the hourly Spanish spot market prices recorded from January 2001 to August 2001. As weekends and holidays constitute separate cases, only data corresponding to working days have been retained and analyzed.

Figure 1a shows the hourly averages and standard deviations of prices for the working days of March 2001, in cents of Euro per kWh.

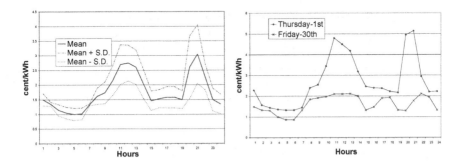

Fig. 1. a) Hourly average of spot market prices for March 2001. **b)** Evolution of energy prices for two days of March 2001.

Average spot prices larger than 2 cent/kWh take place during the morning and evening peak hours (10am-2pm and 8-10pm respectively). Except for a few valley hours, the s.d. of this price exceeds 20% of the mean value, reaching even 40% at 8pm and 9pm.

Figure 1b represents the energy prices for two selected days of March 2001. The significant differences in the prices of the peak hours can not be explained by a change in the demand profile, probably revealing market power mechanisms.

3   k Weighted Nearest Neighbours

In this section, a combined kWNN [2] and GA [3] for hourly market energy prices forecasting is described. The kWNN finds the daily market energy prices that are "similar to" the prices of previous days. GA are computational techniques based on the mechanics of natural selection in which each individual in the population represents a possible solution to the problem, and a fitness factor is assigned to each individual, with the best ones receiving higher fitness factors. A particular GA is characterized by issues such as population size, mutation rates, and selection and new population creation mechanisms. In this paper, the GA (with float codification) is used to compute the optimal weights to outweight the most significant hours.

The prediction aims at estimating the prices for a certain day from a linear combination of the energy prices of the days that follow the nearest neighbours days.

The prediction of a time series requires the knowledge of some parameters: the time delay, the embedding dimension and the value of k. The optimal determination of these parameters has been studied in the last years [4].

Energy prices are collected every hour and, in consequence, the time delay is an hour. For short-term forecasting, it has been decided to organize the temporal data with a shifting window of prices comprising 24 hours and, consequently, the embedding dimension is 24.

As far as the number of steps to predict is concerned, only one possibility has been evaluated: twenty four hours corresponding to the prices of a whole day, whose values are determined by those of the previous day. This possibility implies that the window is shifted 24 hours each time.

In this case, the time series is the electricity market energy prices, and the Weighted-Euclidean distance is preferred because not all the hours of a day have the same influence on the prices of the following day. This distance is defined by

$$d_w^2(q, z) = \sum_{i=1}^{r} w_i \cdot (q_i - z_i)^2 \tag{1}$$

where $r = \text{length}(q)$ and $w_i \in [0, 1]$.

The prediction of stock energy prices for one day $d + 1$ is computed through two steps taking into account the weights of all the hours of a day:

1. Calculate the distances between the prices of the day d, P_d, and the preceding points $\{P_{d-1}, P_{d-2}, ...\}$ using (1). Let be $v_1,...,v_k$ the k nearest days to the day d, sorted by closeness.
2. The prediction is:

$$\widehat{P}_{d+1} = \frac{1}{\alpha_1 + ... + \alpha_k} \sum_{l=1}^{k} \alpha_l \cdot P_{v_l+1} \tag{2}$$

where

$$\alpha_i = \frac{d_w(P_d, P_{v_k}) - d_w(P_d, P_{v_i})}{d_w(P_d, P_{v_k}) - d_w(P_d, P_{v_1})} \tag{3}$$

Notice that if the k nearest neighbours of a vector P_d are $[P_{v_1}, ..., P_{v_k}]$, where v_i is the ith nearest neighbour, the set of points $[P_{v_1+1}, ..., P_{v_k+1}]$ will usually be the nearest to P_{d+1}, at least if the dynamic system is stable.

3.1 Test Results

The kNN+GA has been applied in several experiments to obtain the forecast of Spanish electricity market energy prices. February 2001 has been used to determine the weight for every hour of the day, using a GA whose main parameters have been: the population size 100, the probability of crossover and mutation 1 and 0.1 respectively and the maximum number of generations 5000. The available period of March-August 2001 has been chosen as a test set to check the forecasting errors. The number of neighbours has been considered equal to one in all experiments due to the low influence on the forecasted errors.

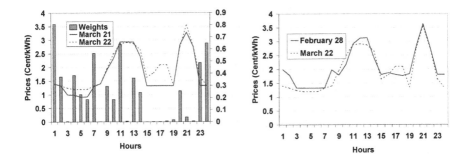

Fig. 2. Nearest neighbour using: **a)** the Weighted-Euclidean, **b)** the Euclidean distance.

Figure 2a represents the relative weights for every hour, along with the energy prices for a selected day, March 22, and its nearest neighbour, calculated using the Weighted-Euclidean distance (1). The nearest neighbour corresponds to March 21.

It can be noticed that the hours whit greater weights, (1am, 7am, 11am, 11pm and 12pm), have almost the same energy prices. However, at 3pm, 4pm, 5pm, 6pm and 7pm, when the differences in prices are larger, the weights are approximately equal to zero.

Figure 2b represents the energy prices of March 22, along with its nearest neighbour calculated using the Euclidean distance. In this case, the nearest neighbour corresponds to February 28. Notice the influence of the chosen distance in the calculation of the nearest neighbour.

4   Dynamic Regression

In this section, several models based on DR approach are described and tested [5,6]. Basically, this approach aims at estimating the price at hour t from the values of past prices at hours $t-1$, $t-2$,..., etc. A study of the correlation between the variables P_t, P_{t-1}... has been first made to determine the underlying model of the price time series.

Figure 3a shows the average correlation coefficient between the past prices and the present price for the period March-August 2001. Notice that this coefficient presents a periodicity corresponding to a day. Moreover, the correlation decreases as the number of past hours increases.

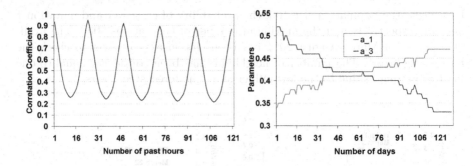

Fig. 3. a) Correlation Coefficient. **b)**Evolution of the parameters a_1 and a_3

The two proposed models based on the former correlation study are the following:

$$\widehat{P}_t = a_0 P_{t-1} + a_1 P_{t-23} + a_2 P_{t-24} + a_3 P_{t-25} + a_4 P_{t-48} \qquad (4)$$
$$\widehat{P}_t = a_0 P_{t-23} + a_1 P_{t-24} + a_2 P_{t-25} + a_3 P_{t-48} \qquad (5)$$

The difference lies in the presence of P_{t-1} which, except for the first time, is also an estimated quantity. Experience has shown that, including other terms in (4) and (5), like P_{t-47}, P_{t-49}, makes no difference as far as accuracy is concerned. In turn, the parameters a_i are estimated by minimizing the least-squares objective function that follows:

$$\sum_t (P_t - \widehat{P}_t)^2 \text{ where } \widehat{P}_t \text{ is defined by (4) or (5)} \qquad (6)$$

These parameters can be calculated at once on a given training set or updated every day of the selected period to forecast and validate the performance of both models.

4.1   Results

The two models described in the previous section have been applied to predict the energy prices of the Spanish electricity market. January-February 2001 has been used to determine the parameters of the models, by the least-squares method, providing: $a_0 = 0.6760$, $a_1 = -0.4815$, $a_2 = 0.5213$, $a_3 = 0.077$ and $a_4 = 0.2072$ for the first model, and $a_0 = 0.0848$, $a_1 = 0.3369$, $a_2 = 0.0416$ and $a_3 = 0.5236$ for the second model. Table 1 presents the s.d. of actual prices, the average absolute value of forecasting errors and the maximum errors for Spring and Summer seasons for every model with the previous parameters. It can be concluded that the presence of P_{t-1} in (4) has a negative influence on the forecasting errors, because errors get accumulated during the last hours

Table 1. Comparison of predicted prices for two models.

	Model 1		Model 2	
	March-May	June-August	March-May	June-August
s.d.	0.184	0.242	0.173	0.209
Average absolute errors	0.275	0.332	0.239	0.288
Maximum errors	2.22	2.81	2.28	2.55
Average Relative errors (%)	12.2	9.4	10.6	8.1

of the prediction horizon. Figure 3b shows the evolution of the parameters corresponding to the second model when they are calculated for every day of the period March-August 2001 (excluding weekends).

Table 2. Comparison of predicted daily prices for both methods.

	Daily Prices			
	March-May		June-August	
	kWNN	DR	kWNN	DR
s.d.	0.2186	0.170	0.26	0.210
Average absolute errors	0.256	0.228	0.33	0.265
Maximum errors	2.13	2.11	2.36	2.41
Average Relative errors (%)	11.4	10.1	9.3	7.5

Finally, table 2 presents the s.d. of actual prices, the average absolute value of forecasting errors and the maximum errors for Spring and Summer seasons. Note that, the average error, when using the second DR model with daily parameter updating, ranges from 7.5% (Summer) to 10% (Spring) of the hourly average price, while the obtained average error, using a kNN combined with a GA ranges from 9% (Summer) to 11% (Spring).

5   Conclusions

Optimal bidding strategies are relevant in a competitive market, the computation of a good forecasted price profiles being crucial for the generation companies. In this sense, this paper presents two energy price forecasting tools for day-ahead electricity market: a k Weighted Nearest Neighbours and a Dynamic Regression. Both algorithms have been applied to the 24-hour energy price forecasting problems, using real data of the Spanish energy markets and their performance have been compared.

Acknowledgments. The authors would like to acknowledge the financial support of the Spanish Government under grants PB97-0719, DPI2001-2612 and TIC2001-1143-C03-02.

References

1. A. Canoyra, C. Illán, A. Landa, J.M. Moreno, J.I. Pérez Arriaga, C. Sallé and C. Solé: The Hierarchical Market Approach to the Economic and Secure Operation of the Spanish Power System. Bulk Power System Dynamic and Control IV, August 24-28, Santorini, Greece.
2. B.V. Dasarathy (Ed): Nearest neighbour (NN) Norms: NN pattern classification techniques. IEEE Computer Society Press, 1991.
3. D. E. Goldberg: Genetic Algorithms in Search, Optimization and Machine Learning. Addison-Wesley, 1989.
4. A. W. Jayawardena, W. K. Li and P. Xu: Neighbourhood selection for local modelling and prediction of hydrological time series. Journal of Hydrology 258, 40-57.
5. A. D. Papalexopoulos and T. C. Hesterberg: A Regression-Based Approach to Short-Term System Load Forecasting. IEEE Trans. on Power System, Vol. 5, pp. 1535-1547. 1990.
6. F. J. Nogales, J. Contreras, A. J. Conejo and R. Spínola: Forecasting Next-Day Electricity Prices by Time Series Models. IEEE Trans. on Power System, to appear in 2002.

Support Vector Machine Regression for Volatile Stock Market Prediction

Haiqin Yang, Laiwan Chan, and Irwin King

Department of Computer Science and Engineering
The Chinese University of Hong Kong
Shatin, N.T. Hong Kong
{hqyang,lwchan,king}@cse.cuhk.edu.hk

Abstract. Recently, Support Vector Regression (SVR) has been introduced to solve regression and prediction problems. In this paper, we apply SVR to financial prediction tasks. In particular, the financial data are usually noisy and the associated risk is time-varying. Therefore, our SVR model is an extension of the standard SVR which incorporates margins adaptation. By varying the margins of the SVR, we could reflect the change in volatility of the financial data. Furthermore, we have analyzed the effect of asymmetrical margins so as to allow for the reduction of the downside risk. Our experimental results show that the use of standard deviation to calculate a variable margin gives a good predictive result in the prediction of Hang Seng Index.

1 Introduction

Support Vector Machine (SVM), based on Statistical Learning Theory, was first developed by Vapnik [4,6]. It has become a hot topic of intensive study due to its successful application in classification tasks [7,8] and regression tasks [5,3], specially on time series prediction [1] and financial related applications [2].

When using SVM in regression tasks, the Support Vector Regressor must use a cost function to measure the empirical risk in order to minimize the regression error. Although there are many choices of the loss functions to calculate the cost, e.g., least modulus loss function, quadratic loss function, etc., the ε-insensitive loss function is such a function that exhibits the sparsity of the solution [4]. Typically, this ε-insensitive loss function contains a fixed and symmetrical margin(FASM)term. When the margin is zero or very small, one runs into the risk of overfitting the data with poor generalization while when the margin is large, one obtains a better generalization at the risk of having higher testing error. For financial data, due to the embedded noise, one must set a suitable margin in order to obtain a good prediction. This paper focuses on two ways to set the margins in SVR.

When applying SVR to time series prediction, the practitioners usually overlook the choices of the margin setting. For example, in [2], they simply set the margin to 0. This amounts to the least modulus loss function. Others have just set the margin to a very small value [5,9,10]. In [1], they applied additional calculations, e.g., validation techniques, to determine a suitable margin empirically.

H. Yin et al. (Eds.): IDEAL 2002, LNCS 2412, pp. 391–396, 2002.

One of the shortcomings of the above methods is that the margin is symmetrical and fixed. Consequently, this technique is insensitive and non-adaptive to the input data. This may result in less-than-optimal performance in the testing data while it obtains a good result on the training data.

In this paper, we propose to use an adaptive margin in SVR for financial prediction to minimize the downside risk, which is an essential part in financial prediction with volatile financial data. More specifically, we present two approaches: one uses the fixed and asymmetrical margins(FAAM), whereas the other uses non-fixed and symmetrical margins(NASM).

A key difference between FAAM and FASM is that there exist an up and a down margin that are asymmetrical. In the case of FAAM when the up margin is greater than the down margin, the predictive results tend to be smaller than the predictive results which are produced by using FASM.

In NASM, the margin is adaptive to the input data. There are many possible choices to set the margin. For example, one may use the n-th order statistics to calculate the margin. More specifically, we choose the second order statistics, the standard deviation, as our method to calculate the adaptive margin. This is because that the standard deviation is frequently used as a measure of the volatility of stock prices in financial data. When the stock price is highly volatile, it has a high standard deviation. In financial time series the noise is often very large, and we try to tolerate our prediction by having a larger margin when the stock price is highly volatile. On the other hand, a smaller margin may be more suitable for less volatile stock activities. Hence, our approach avoids the fixed margin in order to obtain a better prediction result.

The paper is organized as follows. We introduce a general type of ε-insensitive loss function and give the inferential result in Section 2. We report experiments and results in Section 3. Lastly, we conclude the paper with a brief discussion and final remarks in Section 4.

2   Support Vector Regression

Given a training data set, $(x_1, y_1), \ldots, (x_N, y_N)$, where $x_i \in X, y_i \in R$, N is the size of training data, and X denotes the space of the input samples–for instance, R^n. The aim is to find a function which can estimate all these data well. SVR is one of the methods to perform the above regression task [4,3].

In general, the estimation function in SVR takes the following form,

$$f(x) = (w \cdot \phi(x)) + b, \tag{1}$$

where $(\cdot)$ denotes the inner product in Ω, a feature space of possibly different dimensionality such that $\phi : X \to \Omega$ and $b \in R$.

Now the question is to determine w and b from the training data by minimizing the regression risk, $R_{reg}(f)$, based on the empirical risk,

$$R_{reg}(f) = C \sum_{i=1}^{N} \Gamma(f(x_i) - y_i) + \frac{1}{2}(w \cdot w), \tag{2}$$

where C is a pre-specified value, $\Gamma(\cdot)$ is a cost function that measures the empirical risk. In general, the ε-insensitive loss function is used as the cost function [4]. For this function, when the data points are in the range of $\pm\varepsilon$, they do not contribute to the output error. The function is defined as,

$$\Gamma(f(x) - y) = \begin{cases} 0, & \text{if } |y - f(x)| < \varepsilon \\ |y - f(x)| - \varepsilon, & \text{otherwise} \end{cases}. \tag{3}$$

In this paper, we introduce a general type of ε-insensitive loss function, which is given as,

$$\Gamma'(f(x_i) - y_i) = \begin{cases} 0, & \text{if } -\varepsilon_i^{down} < y_i - f(x_i) < \varepsilon_i^{up} \\ y_i - f(x_i) - \varepsilon_i^{up}, & \text{if } y_i - f(x_i) \geq \varepsilon_i^{up} \\ f(x_i) - y_i - \varepsilon_i^{down}, & \text{if } f(x_i) - y_i \geq \varepsilon_i^{down} \end{cases}, \tag{4}$$

where ε_i^{up} and ε_i^{down} correspond to the i-th up margin and down margin respectively. When ε_i^{up} and ε_i^{down} are both equal to a constant, for all $i, i = 1, \ldots, N$, Eq. (4) amounts to the ε-insensitive loss function in Eq. (3) and it is labeled as FASM (Fixed and Symmetrical Margin). When $\varepsilon_i^{up} = \varepsilon^{up}$, for all $i = 1, \ldots, N$ and $\varepsilon_j^{down} = \varepsilon^{down}$, for all $j = 1, \ldots, N$ with $\varepsilon^{up} \neq \varepsilon^{down}$, this case is labeled as FAAM (Fixed and Asymmetrical Margin). In the case of NASM (Non-fixed and Symmetrical Margin), we use an adaptive margin for which the up margin equals to the down margin. The last case is with an adaptive and asymmetrical margin. In this paper, we just consider the first three cases, i.e., FASM, FAAM, and NASM.

Using the Lagrange function method to find the solution which minimizes the regression risk of Eq. (2) with the cost function in Eq. (4), we obtain the following Quadratic Programming (QP) problem:

$$\arg\min_{\alpha,\alpha^*} \frac{1}{2} \sum_{i=1}^{N} \sum_{j=1}^{N} (\alpha_i - \alpha_i^*)(\alpha_j - \alpha_j^*)(\phi(x_i) \cdot \phi(x_j)) + \sum_{i=1}^{N} (\varepsilon_i^{up} - y_i)\alpha_i$$
$$+ \sum_{i=1}^{N} (\varepsilon_i^{down} + y_i)\alpha_i^* \tag{5}$$

subject to

$$\sum_{i=1}^{N} (\alpha_i - \alpha_i^*) = 0, \alpha_i, \alpha_i^* \in [0, C], \tag{6}$$

where α and α^* are corresponding Lagrange multipliers used to push and pull $f(x_i)$ towards the outcome of y_i respectively.

Solving the above QP problem of Eq. (5) with constraints of Eq. (6), we determine the Lagrange multipliers α and α^* and obtain $w = \sum_{i=1}^{N} (\alpha_i - \alpha_i^*)\phi(x_i)$. Therefore the estimation function in Eq. (1) becomes

$$f(x) = \sum_{i=1}^{N} (\alpha_i - \alpha_i^*)(\phi(x) \cdot \phi(x_i)) + b. \tag{7}$$

So far, we have not considered the computation of b. In fact, this can be solved by exploiting the Karush-Kuhn-Tucker(KKT) conditions. These conditions state that at the optimal solution, the product between the Lagrange multipliers and the constraints has to equal to zero. In this case, it means that

$$\alpha_i(\varepsilon_i^{up} + \xi_i - y_i + (w \cdot \phi(x_i)) + b) = 0 \qquad (8)$$
$$\alpha_i^*(\varepsilon_i^{down} + \xi_i^* + y_i - (w \cdot \phi(x_i)) - b) = 0$$

and

$$(C - \alpha_i)\xi_i = 0$$
$$(C - \alpha_i^*)\xi_i^* = 0.$$

where ξ_i and ξ_i^* are slack variables used to measure the error of up side and down side. Since $\alpha_i \cdot \alpha_i^* = 0$ and $\xi_i^{(*)} = 0$ for $\alpha_i^{(*)} \in (0, C)$, b can be computed as follows:

$$b = \begin{cases} y_i - (w \cdot \phi(x_i)) - \varepsilon_i^{up}, & \text{for } \alpha_i \in (0, C) \\ y_i - (w \cdot \phi(x_i)) + \varepsilon_i^{down}, & \text{for } \alpha_i^* \in (0, C) \end{cases}. \qquad (9)$$

Using the trick of kernel function, Eq. (7) can be written as, $f(x) = \sum_{i=1}^{N}(\alpha_i - \alpha_i^*)K(x, x_i) + b$, where the kernel function, $K(x, x_i) = (\phi(x) \cdot \phi(x_i))$, which is a symmetric function and satisfies the Mercer's condition. In this paper, we select a common kernel function, e.g., RBF function, $K(x, x_i) = \exp(-\beta|x - x_i|^2)$, as the kernel function.

In the next section, we apply our inferential result of SVR based on the general type of ε-insensitive loss function to the regression of financial data, for example, indices and stock prices. By applying regression to the data, we can build a dynamic system to model the data and hence use the system for predicting future prices.

3   Experiments

In this section, we conduct two experiments to illustrate the effect of FASM, FAAM, and NASM. The first experiment illustrates the SVM financial prediction with fixed margin, including FASM and FAAM. The second experiment tests the SVM financial prediction with NASM under shift windows.

In our experiment, we use the daily closing price of Hong Kong's Hang Seng Index (HSI) from January 15, 2001 to June 19, 2001, a total of 104 days' of data points, out of which 100 data points for training and testing. We set the length of the shift window to 80. The dynamic system is modeled as $\widehat{I}_t = f(I_{t-4}, I_{t-3}, I_{t-2}, I_{t-1})$, where I_t is the real stock price at time t, and $\widehat{I}_t$ is the predictive value at time t. Therefore, the first training data set is from January 15, 2001 to May 22, 2001, a total of 84 days' of HSI. We use them to predict the next day's HSI. This window is then shifted and an entire training is performed again to predict the following day's HSI for the remaining testing data.

The SVR algorithm used in our experiment is modified from LibSVM [10]. Before running the algorithm, we need to determine some parameters. They are C, the cost of error; β, parameter of kernel function, and the margins. After performing a cross-validation in the first training data, we set $C = 6000$, $\beta = 2^{-24}$. Since different margins will affect the results of prediction, we use different values in our tests. Furthermore, we use the following three error definitions to measure the testing errors, $error \equiv \frac{1}{M}\sum_{t=1}^{M}|I_t - \widehat{I}_t|$, $error_{pos} \equiv \frac{1}{M}\sum_{t=1, I_t \geq \widehat{I}_t}^{M}(I_t - \widehat{I}_t)$, $error_{neg} \equiv \frac{1}{M}\sum_{t=1, I_t < \widehat{I}_t}^{M}(\widehat{I}_t - I_t)$, where M is the size of the testing data and $error$ reflects the total risk, $error_{pos}$ reflects the upside risk and $error_{neg}$ reflects the downside risk respectively.

The experiments are conducted on a Pentium 4, with 1.4 GHZ, 512M RAM and Windows2000. With these configurations, the predictive results are obtained within seconds.

In the first experiment we use different values for up margin and down margin to test the effect of FASM and FAAM. We show the setting of the margin in the second and third columns of Table 1, and report the corresponding errors in the last three columns. In all but the first and the last margin setting, their overall margin widths are the same, i.e., $\varepsilon^{up} + \varepsilon^{down} = 150$. This allows us to have a fair comparison of the four cases. From the Table 1, we can see that the $error_{pos}$ gradually increases with the increase of ε^{up}. At the same time, with the increase of ε^{up}, we allow for more errors above the predictive values. Thus the $error_{neg}$ decreases. In terms of the overall error, it increases and then decreases again. This indicates that neither a narrow margin for the upside nor the downside would be desirable in terms of the overall error.

In the second experiment, after considering the volatility of the financial data, we set the up margin and down margin both equal to the standard deviation of the input vector x to perform the prediction. The predictive error of the experiment with the NASM is reported in the last row of Table 1 and the result shows that the total error is significantly decreased comparing with the fixed ones.

Table 1. Experiment Results

Case	ε^{up}	ε^{down}	$error$	$error_{pos}$	$error_{neg}$
1	0	0	134.59	56.46	78.13
2	50	100	131.96	49.44	82.52
3	75	75	129.03	60.47	68.56
4	100	50	129.96	73.44	56.52
5	150	0	135.64	101.28	34.36
6	σ	σ	116.19	53.29	62.90

4   Discussion and Conclusion

In this paper, we present a general type of ε-insensitive loss function in SVR and outline the various margins used, i.e., FASM, FAAM and NASM. Using Hong Kong's HSI as the data set for SVR with different types of margins, we have the following conclusions:

1. One interesting observation is that neither the up margin nor the down margin would affect the *error* unilaterally. This can be seen from the results of Case 2 to Case 5 in Table 1.
2. Another interesting observation is that from the point of view of the downside risk, Case 5 in Table 1 is a good result since its $error_{neg}$, which is related to the downside risk, is minimum. In practice, we can reduce the downside risk by increasing the up margin while decreasing the down margin.
3. In the NASM case, we find that using standard deviation to calculate the margin, which can reflect the change in volatility of the financial data, results in the best prediction in our experiment since this result has a minimal *error*.

Acknowledgement. The work described in this paper was partially supported by a grant from the Research Grants Council of the Hong Kong Special Administration Region, China. The authors thank Lin, Chih-Jen for helpful suggestions on using the LibSVM.

References

1. K. R. Müller, A. Smola, G. Rätsch, B. Schölkopf, J. Kohlmorgen and V. N. Vapnik. Predicting time series with support vector machines. ICANN, 999-1004, 1997.
2. T. B. Trafalis and H. Ince. Support vector machine for regression and applications to financial forecasting. IJCNN2000, 348-353.
3. A. Smola and B. Schölkopf. A Tutorial on Support Vector Regression. 1998, Technical Report NeuroCOLT NC-TR-98-030.
4. V. N. Vapnik. The Nature of Statistical Learning Theory. Springer, New York, 1995.
5. V. N. Vapnik, S. Golowich and A. Smola. Support vector method for function approximation, regression estimation and signal processing.
6. V. N. Vapnik. Statistical Learning Theory. Wiley, New York, 1998.
7. Edgar Osuna and Robert Freund and Federico Girosi. Support Vector Machines: Training and Applications. AIM-1602, MIT, 38, 1997.
8. Christopher J. C. Burges. A Tutorial on Support Vector Machines for Pattern Recognition. Data Mining and Knowledge Discovery, 2(2):121-167, 1998.
9. S. Mukherjee, E. Osuna and F. Girosi. Nonlinear prediction of chaotic time series using support vector machines. IEEE Workshop on Neural Networks for Signal Processing VII, IEEE Press, J. Principe and L. Giles and N. Morgan and E. Wilson, 511, 1997.
10. Chih-Chung, Chang and Chih-Jen, Lin. LIBSVM: a Library for Support Vector Machines (Version 2.31), 2001.
11. Frank A. Sortino and Stephen E. Satchell. Managing downside risk in financial markets : theory, practice, and implementation. Oxford, Boston:Butterworth-Heinemann, 2001.

Complexity Pursuit for Financial Prediction

Ying Han and Colin Fyfe

Applied Computational Intelligence Research Unit
The University of Paisley
Scotland.
PA1 2BE
{ying.han, colin.fyfe}@paisley.ac.uk

Abstract. We compare pre-processing time series data using Complexity Pursuit (CP) 2 and Logarithm Complexity Pursuit (LCP) [2] with a view to subsequently using a multi-layer perceptron (MLP) to forecast on the data set. Our rationale [1] is that forecasting the underlying factors will be easier than forecasting the original time series which is a combination of these factors. The projections of the data onto the filters found by the pre-processing method were fed into the MLP and it was trained to find Least Mean Square Error (LMSE). Both methods find interesting structure in the time series but LCP is more robust and achieves the best (in terms of least mean square error) performance.

1 Complexity Pursuit

Complexity Pursuit 2 is a new method for finding the underlying factors in a time series, specifically using the fact that a time series typically contains structure across time i.e. the value at time t to some extent determines the value at time $t+1$. It is so-called because of its relation to Kolmogoroff Complexity [3].

One way to compactly code a time series is to encode the differences between the value at time t and the value at time $t+1$. This gives a more compact representation than coding the values alone. Kolmogoroff Complexity can be used to measure how short a code for a time series is.

The method of Complexity Pursuit can be thought of as an extension of the method of Exploratory Projection Pursuit: Exploratory Projection Pursuit (EPP) looks for a projection which gives interesting low dimensional projections in which a human observer can look for structure in the data set. Complexity Pursuit looks for the projection which minimises the length of the code for a time series and, in many cases, it's cheaper to code the residual than the original value y(t).

We may describe a general formulation of forecasting by predictive coding as:

$$\hat{y}(t) = f(y(t-1), y(t-2), \dots y(1))$$

In practice, Hyvärinen 2 uses autoregressive (AR) linear models for prediction:

$$\hat{y}(t) = \sum_{\tau>0} \alpha_\tau y(t-\tau)$$

We are looking for a coding of the dataset which minimises the Kolmogoroff Complexity of the residual, $\delta y(t) = y(t) - \hat{y}(t)$.

H. Yin et al. (Eds.): IDEAL 2002, LNCS 2412, pp. 397–402, 2002.

Assuming these residuals are independent of each other, [3] shows that the coding complexity can be approximated by the sum of the entropies of the residuals:

$$\hat{K}(y) = \sum_t H(\delta y(t))$$

which, on the assumption of stationarity in the data set, is equivalent to

$$\hat{K}(y) = TH(\delta y)$$

where T is the number of data points. As with EPP, we standardise the residuals to have unit variance which means that

$$H(\delta y) = H(\frac{\delta y}{\sigma_\delta}) + \log \sigma_\delta$$

Now it is an often repeated fact in the ICA community that, in many algorithms, the actual form of the nonlinearity used in the algorithms does not matter too much: a general nonlinearity appropriate for the extraction of super-Gaussian signals will be successful in extracting all super-Gaussian signals. Hyvärinen thus approximates the entropy of residual with

$$H(\delta y) \approx E\{G(\frac{\delta y}{\sigma_\delta})\} + \log \sigma_\delta$$

where E() is the expectation operator and G is some suitable function. For example, if we postulate that $\delta y(t) = y(t) - \hat{y}(t)$ is drawn from $p(\delta y) = \frac{1}{\sqrt{2}}\exp(-\frac{1}{\sqrt{2}}|\delta y|)$, we may take G() to be $-\log\exp(-|\delta y|) = |\delta y|$.

We can therefore formulate the criterion:

$$\hat{K}(w^T x(t)) = E\{G(\frac{1}{\sigma_\delta(w)} w^T (x(t) - \sum_{\tau>0}\alpha_\tau(w)x(t-\tau)))\} + \log \sigma_\delta(w)$$

which we wish to minimise with respect to the weights , **w**, and parameters σ and α . We have followed 2, in using the notation $\sigma_\delta(w)$ etc to emphasise the dependency that these parameters have on **w**. Hyvärinen derives an algorithm by gradient descent on this criterion with respect to **w**.

$$\nabla\hat{K}(w^T x(t)) \approx \frac{1}{\sigma_\delta(w)} E\{(x(t) - \sum_{\tau>0}\alpha_\tau(w)x(t-\tau))g(\frac{1}{\sigma_\delta(w)} w^T (x(t) - \sum_{\tau>0}\alpha_\tau(w)x(t-\tau)))\}$$

where g( ) is the elementwise derivative of G() with respect to its argument. If G( ) is taken as above, we would use g( )=sign( ) or its softened version tanh( ).

The algorithm may be simplified by whitening the data using

$$z(t) = Vx(t) = (E\{x(t)x(t)^T\})^{-\frac{1}{2}} x(t)$$

We can thus ignore the effect of the variance of the data and the algorithm becomes

$$w \leftarrow w - \mu E\{(z(t) - \sum_{\tau>0}\alpha_\tau(w)z(t-\tau))g(w^T (z(t) - \sum_{\tau>0}\alpha_\tau(w)z(t-\tau)))\}$$

followed by an explicit normalisation: $w \leftarrow w/\|w\|$

Since α and σ are functions of *w*, they must be recalculated at each iteration i.e. each time a new value of *w* is calculated.

Hyvärinen uses an AR(1) process as a forecast tool in the algorithm. This has the advantage that the parameter α_1 in the algorithm can be estimated very simply by a least-squares method as:

$$\hat{\alpha}_1 = \mathbf{w}^T E\{\mathbf{z}(t)\mathbf{z}(t-1)^T\}\mathbf{w}$$

Now Hyvärinen reports results on mixtures of first order AR signals using this method and so it might be argued that the method is only applicable to AR(1) processes. In [2], we show that, even when an AR(1) model is inaccurate for the data, the above method can still be used to accurately and robustly identify the underlying factors in time series, when the series is stationary

2 Logarithmic Differences

An alternative method of calculating the AR parameters is suggested by the standard random walk model often used in economic modeling. Consider the model $x_t = (1 + p_t)x_{t-1} + \omega_t$. Typically, p_t is taken to be a small percentage value and so each day's value is a small increment on the previous day's value. Econometricians often pre-process such time series by taking logs and differencing; their motivation is to equalize variances across data sets. If we do the same we have

$$\nabla(\ln(x_t)) = \ln((1 + p_t)x_{t-1} + \omega_t) - \ln(x_{t-1} + \omega_{t-1})$$

whose expected value is $\ln(1 + p_t)$. Now for small value values of p_t,

$$\ln(1 + p_t) \approx p_t$$

and so we may use $\nabla(\ln(x_t))$ to calculate the autoregressive parameter.

Consider a model with $\qquad\qquad \delta y(t) = \alpha \delta y(t-1) + \varepsilon(t-1)$

We have $\qquad\qquad y(t) - y(t-1) = \alpha(y(t-1) - y(t-2)) + \varepsilon(t-1)$

or $\qquad\qquad\qquad y(t) = (1 + \alpha)y(t-1) - \alpha y(t-2) + \varepsilon(t-1)$

which yields a non-stationary time series, similar to the above model. The estimate of the AR parameter is then

$$\hat{\alpha} = E\{\ln(w^T z_t) - \ln(w^T z_{t-1})\}$$

We continue to use this estimate in exactly the same way when we are forecasting (and hence calculating the new value of the weights, w). In practice, then, our algorithm alternates between finding the new AR parameter using the current value of the weights

$$\alpha = E(\ln(w.z_t) - \ln(w.z_{t-1}))$$

and then using this value in the weight update equation

$$w \leftarrow w - \mu E\{(z(t) - z(t-1) - \alpha(z(t-1) - z(t-2))g(w^T(z(t) - z(t-1) - \alpha(z(t-1) - z(t-2)))\}$$

A typical financial data set has a trend component, a component which exhibits cyclical behaviour on a short timescale, a component which exhibits cyclical behaviour on a long timescale and a noise component.

Therefore we have created [2] artificial datasets containing fast cycle data, slow cycle data, nonstationary data and AR(2) data.

- *Fast cycle data* $\Rightarrow$ $S_1(t+1) = 0.5\,S_1(t) + \cos(t\,/100) + \mu_t$
- *Slow cycle data* $\Rightarrow$ $S_2(t+1) = 0.8\,S_2(t) + \sin(t\,/\,10) + \mu_t$
- *Non stationary data* $\Rightarrow$ $S_3(t+1) = 1.25\,S_3(t) - 0.25\,S_3(t-1) + \omega_t$
- *AR(2) data* $\Rightarrow$ $S_4(t+1) = 0.4\,S_4(t) + 0.1\,S_4(t-1) + \omega_t$

where μ_t is drawn from a two sided exponential distribution while ω_t is drawn from a Gaussian distribution.

The first two data sets show cyclic behaviour because of the trigonometric functions while the third data set is non-stationary because the absolute value of the sum of the autoregressive components is not less than 1.

Results on our pseudo-financial data set are given in [2] and show that both the LCP and the CP method are effective at identifying the underlying factors in a time series and that the LCP is somewhat more robust. The WVA matrix product is shown in Table 1. It clearly approximates a permutation matrix and shows that the individual factors have been found.

Table 1. The absolute product WVA matrix by logarithmic differencing a data set composed of some ARIMA factors, some seasonal factors and some stationary ARMA data.

0.0000	0.0223	**1.0005**	0.0007
0.0164	**0.9996**	0.0106	0.0001
1.0010	0.0504	0.0407	0.0167
0.0301	0.0064	0.0037	**1.0000**

3   Comparing the Methods on Real Data

We were supplied with a data set comprising a financial time series and a series called indicators with no further details supplied. Both methods were trained on half of the data and the MLP was subsequently trained on the projections space found by the unsupervised network. The MLP also was only trained on half of the data and then forecasts and actual values were compared on the other half of the data set.

The data set comprises a bivariate time series but, as is standard practice in this area, we convert this to a multivariate time series by creating a vector of consecutive values.

$$\mathbf{x}(t) = (x(t), x(t-1), x(t-2), \ldots, x(t-9), i(t), i(t-1), \ldots, i(t-9))^{T}$$

where x(k) is the value of the time series we wish to predict at time k and i(k) is the indicator's value at time k.

In all experiments on which we report, we use an embedding length of 10. To facilitate comparisons, we used 5 projections from each of the projection methods, CP and LCP.

The experiments were repeated with different parameter sets (embedding length, number of projections etc) and the results were found to be qualitatively similar.

3.1 Results

The CP filters were highly structured; examples are shown in Figure 1. The first filter identifies the indicators for the previous week and has an associated AR parameter of -0.933. The second identifies this week's price series and has an AR parameter of 0.978.

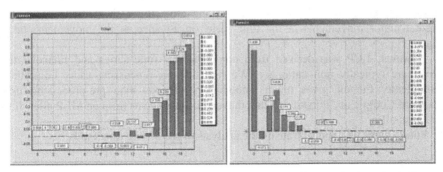

Fig. 1. The first two filters found by Complexity Pursuit. The first emphasizes the indicators for the previous week and has an associated AR parameter of -0.933. The second emphasizes this week's price series and has an AR parameter of 0.978.

The MSE using an MLP was 0.0146 and the predictions and the actual values are shown in the left half of Figure 2. We see that the MLP often correctly predicts a rise or fall in the time series but its estimates show rather a large variance. The filters found by the LCP method were somewhat similar, the MSE was 0.0076, and the predictions and actual outputs are shown in the right half of Figure 2. The predictions are much smoother after LPC pre-processing.

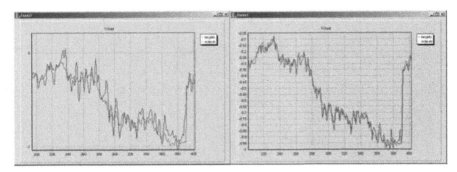

Fig. 2. Left: prediction by MLP after CP pre-processing, MSE=0.0146. Right: prediction by MLP after LCP pre-processing, MSE=0.0076.

The above results show that the CP method is effective even although it is using a wrong model for the data. Experiments on simple AR(2) data with AR(1) models estimating the autoregressive parameter have shown that it is possible to achieve reasonably accurate estimates of the AR parameters though the accuracy is not as high as with the AR(1) model on AR(1) data. This leads us to suggest that using an AR(1) model for all stationary data sets is probably an effective strategy.

4 Conclusion

We have compared two methods based on Complexity Pursuit as means of pre-processing time series. Both methods converge on similar though not identical filters of the data set. Fortunately, the type of filters which we found corroborated the prior beliefs of the analysists who provided us with the data. Both methods outperform pre-processing using other linear methods [1] and crucially, both methods allow us to predict major movements in the time series in advance of the movements taking place.

However, LCP was derived from non-stationary time series and financial time series are typically non-stationary. We find that pre-processing using Logarithmic Complexity Pursuit gives much smoother predictions than pre-processing using standard Complexity Pursuit and that the mean square error from an MLP after this is much smaller.

Future work will concentrate on the analysis of the different methods.

References

1.   Han, Y. and Fyfe, C. A Comparative Study of Mixtures of Principal Component Analysis Forecasts and Factor Analysis Forecasts. The Third ICSC Conference on Soft Computing, SOCO2001.
2.   Han, Y. and Fyfe, C. Finding Underlying factors in Time Series, Cybernetics and Systems, March 2002
3.   Hyvärinen, A. 2001. Complexity Pursuit: Separating interesting components from time series. Neural Computation, 13: 883-898

Artificial Intelligence in Portfolio Management

Man-Chung Chan[1], Chi-Cheong Wong[1], W.F. Tse[1],
Bernard K.-S. Cheung[2], and Gordon Y.-N. Tang[3]

[1]Department of Computing, The Hong Kong Polytechnic University, Hong Kong
[2]GERAD and Ecole Polytechique de Montreal, Canada
[3]Dept of Finance and Decision Sciences, Hong Kong Baptist University, Hong Kong
csccwong@comp.polyu.edu.hk

Abstract. Artificial intelligence supports decision by analyzing enormous information. This paper introduces an intelligent portfolio management system (IPMS) that applies artificial intelligence to assist investors in planning their investments. A prototype is developed based on the portfolio management process, involving stock selection and asset allocation optimization. A genetically optimised fuzzy rule-base is developed for stock selection. Genetic algorithm is used to optimize asset allocation according to investor's risk aversion.

1 Introduction

Investors always find it difficult to analyze enormous financial information from numerous financial instruments. With artificial intelligence, enormous financial data can be analyzed for the investment decision support. In this paper, we introduce an intelligent portfolio management system (IPMS) that applies artificial intelligence to assist investors in planning their investments. A prototype is developed for stock selection and asset allocation optimization. A genetically optimized fuzzy rule-base is developed for stock selection. Genetic algorithm is used to optimize asset allocation.

In the next section, artificial intelligence technologies are described. Section 3 outlines the intelligent portfolio management system. Experiments and results are described in Section 4. Conclusion and discussion are remarked in Section 5.

2 Artificial Intelligence Technologies

2.1 Genetic Algorithm

Genetic algorithms (GA) are search algorithms to find the optimal solution. They bases on the survival-of-the-fittest fashion by manipulating the potential problem solutions to obtain the more superior solutions. The skeleton of μGA is depicted as,
1. Initialize a small population randomly
2. Evaluate each chromosome.
3. Applying elitist selection, carry the best individual to the next generation.

H. Yin et al. (Eds.): IDEAL 2002, LNCS 2412, pp. 403-409, 2002.

4. Select chromosomes for reproduction.
5. Apply crossover and mutation to reproduce the next generation.
6. Evaluate the new chromosomes.
7. If the termination condition is satisfied, return the best solution; if not, carry the elite to the next generation.
8. If the reshuffling condition is reached, randomly generate the remaining individuals go to 6; if not, go to 4.

2.2 Fuzzy Network

Fuzzy logic systems extend classical logic based on Zadeh's Fuzzy Set Theory [9]. A *fuzzy network*[3] is a mapping from fuzzy domain space $X = \{x_1,..,x_n\}$ to fuzzy range space $Y = \{y_1,..,y_p\}$. The network encodes a set of rules that associate the output fuzzy set B with the input fuzzy set A. The rules are evaluated in parallel and the outputs are calculated based on a weighted average of the activated rules. The antecedent and consequence clauses of a rule compose of variables in conjunction paired with the respective fuzzy set term. A rule is denoted by $(A_1,..,A_n ; B_1,..,B_p)$. Both clauses may have null values (∅) to make a variable not related in a rule. If all variables are null, the rule is eliminated. The null value offers GA a greater flexibility in searching best relationships between the output and input variables. The weight w_{jk} is the *relative strength* (or *credibility)* of the connection from rule R_j to output y_k. and is adjusted by a learning algorithm. The *activation level* s_j of the rule R_j, is dependent on the *fuzzification* of the input with respect to the fuzzy sets A_j is $s_j = \min\{\mu_{A_{ij}}(x_i)\}$ for $1 \leq i \leq n$. Output y_k is calculated by a *center-of-mass* procedure that defuzzifies the rules' activation levels s_j with respect to the fuzzy sets B_{jk} and the weights w_{jk}, $1 \leq j \leq m$. The mass M_{jk} is computed by multiplying the weight w_{jk} with the area under the membership function $\mu_{Bjk}(v_{jk})=s_j$. The output y_k is the *centroid* of the masses

$$y_k = \sum_{j=1}^{m} v_{jk} M_{jk} / \sum_{j=1}^{m} M_{jk}.$$

2.3 Fuzzy Network Synthesized with Genetic Algorithm

Genetic Algorithm is used to optimize the rule base and the connection weights which are packed end-to-end to form the chromosome. An arbitrarily large number of rules are set prior to training. The number of rules can be decreased if the network is under saturated due to disconnected rules. In training a fuzzy network for pattern recognition, the fitness of the chromosome is defined as reciprocal of *root mean square error (RMSE) between the target training data and the fuzzy network output.*

3 Intelligent Portfolio Management System

In portfolio management, stock selection and asset allocation are two core processes. An investor has to select good investment instruments for investment and then determines how much he or she should allocate to each investment instrument. A prototype is developed based on the portfolio management. A fuzzy rule-based system optimized by genetic algorithm is used to rate stocks for stock selection. Genetic algorithm is used to optimize asset allocation according to investor's risk aversion.

3.1 Stock Rating Subsystem

Stock rating system is to distinguish good stocks for investment. Financial ratios are popular to analyze the quality of stocks. Different financial ratios may draw different conclusions on stock quality. A set of fuzzy rules, each of which takes some financial ratios as *antecedents* and an estimated stock rating as *consequences*, would be helpful to give a whole picture of stock quality. Throughout the study, financial ratios of *return on capital employed (ROCE)*, *current ratio* and *yield* are used as antecedent part of a rule. The consequence part of a rule consists of an output variable is *company rating*.

GA optimizes the fuzzy network adaptively to uncover the relationship between financial ratios and stock rating of the company. The chromosomal representation of a fuzzy network is shown in Figure 1.

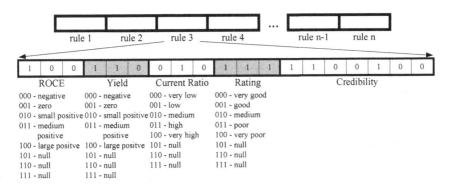

Fig. 1. Chromosomal Representation of Fuzzy Network for Stock Rating

To evaluate a chromosome, a target is set for GA learning. The stock rating target can be estimated by ranking stocks according to the *annual price return*. N stocks can be assigned a ranking r from 1 to N, whereas 1 is the highest while N is the lowest. Then the ranking r is mapped linearly into the stock rating ranged from 0 to 5 by $t\arg et\ \ rating = 5 \times (N - r)/(N - 1)$. The chromosomal fitness is defined as reciprocal of root mean square error between the rating from fuzzy network and the target rating.

3.2   Asset Allocation Optimization Subsystem

Asset allocation optimization is to decide the percentage of the overall portfolio value allocated to each asset. The multi-stage stochastic model [8] manages portfolio in constantly changing financial markets by periodically rebalancing the asset portfolio to achieve return maximization and/or risk minimization. The stochastic nature incorporates scenario analysis into the model. Each scenario depicts a single path over a time step in the multi-stage planning horizon, sharing the same history. In our system, a scenario of a time stage is determined by the percentage changes on market index. It can be denoted by $s=\{1, \dots ,n_s\}$, where 1 represents that market index is decreased mostly while n_s represents that the index is increased mostly.

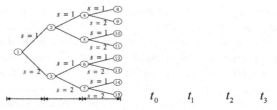

Fig. 2. A scenario tree with two scenarios and three time periods

Suppose we have to optimize A assets, with 1 denoting cash and the others represent any assets. The entire planning horizon T is divided into t time stages. Investment decisions are made at each of the time stage. Each time stage may have different scenarios s. The mathematical formulation is described as follows:

$r_{i,t}^{s}=1+\rho_{i,t}^{s}$, where $\rho_{i,t}^{s}$ is the return percentage of asset i at time t under scenario s

π_s is probability that scenario s occurs, thus $\sum_s \pi_s =1$

w_0 is the wealth at the beginning of time 0

w_t^{s} is the wealth at the beginning of time t under scenario s

$v_{i,t}^{s}$ is the amount of money in asset i at the beginning of time t under scenario s before rebalancing

T is the total number of time stages considered in investment decision-making

Decision variables:

$x_{i,t}^{s}$ is the amount of money allocated to asset i at time t under scenario s after rebalancing

$p_{i,t}^{s}$ is the amount of asset i purchased for rebalancing at time t under scenario s

$d_{i,t}^{s}$ is the amount of asset i sold for rebalancing at time t under scenario s

$$\text{Max } Z= \sum_s \pi_s Measure_T^{s} \tag{1}$$

subject to $\displaystyle\sum_i x_{i,0}^s = w_0 \quad \forall s$ (2)

$\displaystyle\sum_i x_{i,t}^s = w_t^s \quad \forall s, \ t=1,...,T$ (3)

$v_{i,t}^s = r_{i,t-1}^s x_{i,t-1}^s \quad \forall s, \ \forall i \in A, \ t=1,...,T$ (4)

$x_{1,t}^s = v_{1,t}^s + \displaystyle\sum_{i\neq 1} d_{i,t}^s - \displaystyle\sum_{i\neq 1} p_{i,t}^s \quad \forall s, \ t=1,...,T$ (5)

$x_{i,t}^s = v_{i,t}^s + p_{i,t}^s - d_{i,t}^s \quad \forall s, \ t=1,...,T, \ i \neq 1$ (6)

$x_{i,t}^s = x_{i,t}^{s'}$ for all scenarios s and s' with identical past up to time t (7)

where $Measure_T^s$ is performance measure value under scenario s at time stage T.

Chromosome. Our decision variables are the allocation of various selected assets under

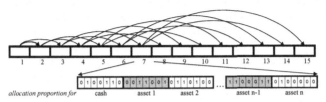

Fig. 3. Chromosome for the scenario tree shown in figure 2.

different scenarios over the planning horizon. These variables are in tree structure and encoded as a chromosome in the form of sequential array. Each node of the array contains the percentage of the overall portfolio value allocated to all assets under a particular scenario. For each scenario s at time t, the total asset allocation proportion must be 100%. Each asset allocation proportion a_{it}^s under the same scenario is normalized by $a_{it}^{s'} = a_{it}^s / \displaystyle\sum_{i=1} a_{it}^s$.

Fitness Function. Although mean-variance model is popular in evaluating a portfolio, it has unrealistic properties [1,2]. Economic utility is a more realistic one. The power law utility function or called von Neumann-Morgenstern utility function [7] is used since it has constant relative risk aversion for any value of risk-aversion value γ. The performance measure function is $Measure = \begin{cases} ln(w) & if \ \gamma = 0 \\ (w)^\gamma / \gamma & elsewhere \end{cases}$.

So the fitness function is $Z = \begin{cases} \displaystyle\sum_s \pi_s ln(w_T^s) & if \ \gamma = 0 \\ \displaystyle\sum_s \pi_s (w_T^s)^\gamma / \gamma & elsewhere \end{cases}$.

4 Experiments

To test the stock rating subsystem, the maximum number of fuzzy rules in the fuzzy network and the number of chromosomes are varied. Root mean square error between the rating derived from fuzzy network and the historical rating in the next year is used to measure the quality of the solution. The result is recorded in Table 1.

Table 1. Testing Result for Stock Rating Subsystem

RMSE	Test set			
	Rule = 10 Chromosome=10	Rule = 10 Chromosome=20	Rule = 20 Chromosome=10	Rule = 20 Chromosome=20
Year 1	1.112479	1.126551	1.113354	1.137180
Year 2	1.270862	1.242321	1.196350	1.298048
Year 3	1.242451	1.199691	1.161928	1.233259

Generally, RMSE is very small. The stock rating system can rate stocks accurately.

The top 10 stocks given by the stock rating system and cash were fed into the asset allocation optimization system. The entire planning horizon was divided into three periods. Each period lasts a month and has two scenarios: rise and drop. The performance of portfolio optimization system was tested in terms of expected return, variance and utility value weighted by the probability of scenario occurrence. The performance of market index, equally weighted portfolio and GA-optimize portfolio with risk aversion parameter = 0 in the testing phase are shown in figures 4.

Compared with equally weighted portfolio, GA-optimized portfolio has a higher expected return and utility value but a lower variance. Compared with market index, GA-optimized portfolio has a higher expected return and utility value but a larger variance. Investors may select their investment between them based on their attitudes towards expected return and risk. Since the optimizer optimizes the portfolio in terms of utility value, not variance, the variance of the GA-optimized portfolio is greater than that of market index. This is acceptable by risk-seeking and risk-neutral investors. For risk-averse investors, since the expected return of GA-optimized portfolio is nearly twice as that of the market index, GA-optimized portfolio is also attractive.

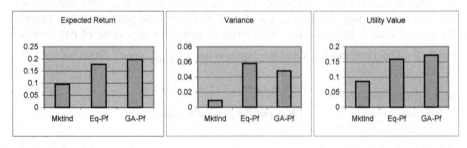

Fig. 4. Performance of market index, equally weighted portfolio and GA-optimized portfolio with $\gamma = 0$.

5 Conclusion and Discussion

In this paper, a prototype is developed to assist investors in stock selection and asset allocations. The experiments show that the stock rating subsystem can rate stocks accurately and generally speaking, the asset allocation optimizer can generate a multi-stage portfolio with the highest expected return and utility value. Future research can be focused on developing a hybrid form of algorithms in order to improve performance. Time can be saved from parallel or distributed processing. Rating system should be further developed for investment instrument.

References

1. Dahl Henrik, Meeraus Alexander and Zenios Stavros A. Some Financial Optimization Models: I Risk Management. Financial Optimization. Stavros A. Zenios. Cambridge University Press, 1993.
2. Elton Edwin J. Modern Portfolio Theory and Investment Analysis. Wiley, 1995.
3. Feldman, D.S. Fuzzy Network Synthesis with Genetic Algorithm. Proceedings of the Fifth International Conference on Genetic Algorithm and their Applications. pp. 312-317. July (1993)
4. Goldberg D E. Genetic Algorithms in Search, Optimization, and Machine Learning, Addison-Wesley, (1989).
5. Krishnakumar, K. Micro-Genetic Algorithms for Stationary and Non-Stationary Function Optimization. SPIE Proceedings: Intelligent Control and Adaptive Systems, pp 289-296, (1989).
6. Markowitz H. Portfolio Selection. Journal of Finance, Vol 7, pp77-91, 1952.
7. Mulvey J.M. Incorporating transaction costs in models for asset allocation. Financial Optimization. Stavros A. Zenios. Cambridge University Press, 1993.
8. Mulvey J.M., Rosenbaum D.P., Shetty Bala. Strategic Financial Risk Management and Operations Research. European Journal of Operational Research, pp 1-16 (1997).
9. Zadeh, L.A. Fuzzy Set. Information and Control. Vol 8, pp. 338-353 (1965).

The Multilevel Classification Problem and a Monotonicity Hint

Malik Magdon-Ismail[1], Hung-Ching (Justin) Chen[1], and
Yaser S. Abu-Mostafa[2]

[1] Dept. of Computer Science, RPI, Lally 207,
110 8th Street, Troy, NY, USA 12180
{magdon, chenh3}@rpi.edu
[2] Learning Systems Group,136-93,Caltech, Pasadena, CA, USA, 91125
yaser@cs.caltech.edu

Abstract. We introduce and formalize the multilevel classification problem, in which each category can be subdivided into different levels. We analyze the framework in a Bayesian setting using Normal class conditional densities. Within this framework, a natural monotonicity hint converts the problem into a nonlinear programming task, with non-linear constraints. We present Monte Carlo and gradient based techniques for addressing this task, and show the results of simulations. Incorporation of monotonicity yields a systematic improvement in performance.

1 Introduction

In most disease handbooks, not only are unrelated diseases listed, but versions (or severities) of a given disease are also provided. An example is the heart condition. A suggested categorization is (in order of increasing severity), essential hypertension, hypertension with complications and secondary hypertension, acute myocardial infarction, coronary atherosclerosis (see for example [2]). A grouping of diseases might look something like

⋮

•Diseases of the Circulatory System
  •Diseases Affecting the Heart
    –Hypertension ...

⋮

While the categories (diseases) may be unrelated, within a category, the various levels are related by some form of a severity criterion. Some additional examples can be found in [2,4,5]. The motivation for such a categorization in handbooks is the need to be able to distinguish between these cases. Different categories (diseases) will have essentially different treatments, and different severities within the same category will usually have different levels of treatment. Similar observations also apply in numerous other areas, for example fault diagnosis in machinery (categories correspond to faults, and levels correspond to the seriousness of the fault), weather prediction (categories correspond to weather patterns,

H. Yin et al. (Eds.): IDEAL 2002, LNCS 2412, pp. 410–415, 2002.

and levels to the magnitude of the expression, for example tornado versus mild winds, rain versus thunderstorm versus hurricane). In all cases, the goal is to predict the category, and the level within the category, given some observed feature vector (in the case of disease prediction, the symptom). Similar issues also exist in multistage image analysis, [6], where larger parts of the image are categorized first and finer detail added later, and data mining, [7], where the mining occurs at increased levels of generality.

Suppose that there are K categories, and l levels within each category. When $l = 1$ we have the usual K-class pattern recognition problem. When $l > 1$, we have a (K, l)-multiclass-multilevel pattern recognition problem. The simplest approach might be to treat this as a $K \times l$ multiclass problem (with independent classes), but to do so would be ignoring valuable information available about the structure of the learning problem - one expects that the nature of mild heart attack symptoms might convey quite a bit of information about the nature of severe heart attack symptoms. For example, if we know the cholesterol level of mild heart attack victims, it is reasonable to guess that the cholesterol level of severe heart attack victims should be higher. Ignoring this additional information could be a severe handicap, especially if the data set is small and noisy. The purpose of this paper is to develop a mathematical framework for exploiting this added structure in the (K, l)-multilevel-multiclass problem.

2   Problem Setup

Assume the classification problem has K categories, $c_1, \ldots, c_K$. Within each category c_i, there are l_{c_i} levels (which can be viewed as severities). As with most fault classification problems, there is usually a special category, c_0, the normal class (for example, a healthy patient). We will represent this (common) normal class by level 0 in each category. Thus, the classification problem has a total of $1 + \sum_{i=1}^{K} l_{c_i}$ classes. The data set consists of N d-dimensional feature vectors $\mathbf{x}_i$, with $N_{c,l}$ features in each category-level combination. We assume that each feature vector was generated using a Normal class conditional density

$$P[\mathbf{x}|\boldsymbol{\mu}, \boldsymbol{\Sigma}] = \mathcal{N}(\mathbf{x} - \boldsymbol{\mu}, \boldsymbol{\Sigma}) = \frac{1}{(2\pi)^{d/2}|\boldsymbol{\Sigma}|^{1/2}} e^{-\frac{1}{2}(\mathbf{x}-\boldsymbol{\mu})' \boldsymbol{\Sigma}^{-1}(\mathbf{x}-\boldsymbol{\mu})} \tag{1}$$

where $(\cdot)'$ represents the transpose operation. In order to keep track of the numerous parameters, we introduce definitions that will be used throughout.

$\mathcal{Q}_{c,l}$: The set of $N_{c,l}$ feature vectors in category c, level l.

$p_{c,l}$: The a priori probability of category c, level l. $p_{c,l} \approx N_{c,l}/N$.

$\boldsymbol{\mu}_{c,l}$: The true class conditional mean for each class: $E[\mathbf{x}|c, l]$.

$\boldsymbol{\Sigma}_{c,l}$: The true covariance matrix for each class: $E\left[(\mathbf{x} - \boldsymbol{\mu}_{c,l})(\mathbf{x} - \boldsymbol{\mu}_{c,l})'|c, l\right]$.

$\boldsymbol{m}_{c,l}$: The sample mean: $\sum \mathbf{x}/N_{c,l}$, $\mathbf{x} \in \mathcal{Q}_{c,l}$.

$\boldsymbol{S}_{c,l}$: The sample covariance matrix: $\sum(\mathbf{x} - \boldsymbol{m}_{c,l})(\mathbf{x} - \boldsymbol{m}_{c,l})'/N_{c,l}$, $\mathbf{x} \in \mathcal{Q}_{c,l}$.

$\hat{\boldsymbol{m}}_{c,l}$: The estimated mean.

$\hat{\boldsymbol{S}}_{c,l}$: The estimated covariance matrix: $\sum(\mathbf{x} - \hat{\boldsymbol{m}}_{c,l})(\mathbf{x} - \hat{\boldsymbol{m}}_{c,l})'/N_{c,l}$, $\mathbf{x} \in \mathcal{Q}_{c,l}$.

$\mathcal{R}_{c_1,l_1}^{c_2,l_2}$: The risk matrix: cost of classifying (c_2, l_2) when the true class is (c_1, l_1).

We assume that the data is generated independently, according to $p_{c,l}$ and (1), and $\mathcal{R}$ is given. An intuitive example of an asymmetric periodic risk matrix could be as shown to the right, where between category errors are penalized more

	$(c,0)$	$(c_1,1)$	$(c_1,2)$	$(c_1,3)$	$(c_2,1)$	$(c_2,2)$	$(c_2,3)$
$(c,0)$	0	3	7	9	3	7	9
$(c_1,1)$	3	0	2	4	1	3	5
$(c_1,2)$	3	2	0	2	3	1	3
$(c_1,3)$	7	4	2	0	5	3	1
$(c_2,1)$	3	1	3	5	0	2	4
$(c_2,2)$	3	3	1	3	2	0	2
$(c_2,3)$	7	5	3	1	4	2	0

than within category errors. The periodicity arises because c_1 and c_2 may be any two different categories. The goal is to estimate $p_{c,l}, \boldsymbol{\mu}_{c,l}, \boldsymbol{\Sigma}_{c,l}$, which can be used to implement a Bayes minimal risk classifier [3].

We are now ready to introduce the *monotonicity hint* – it is well known that hints can considerably aid the learning process [1]. The interpretation of the different levels as severities will help motivate the monotonicity hint. Consider a given feature dimension, and a given category c. If the value of that feature increases in going from (say) level 0 (normal) to level 1, then

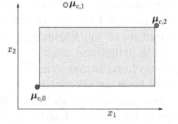

it is reasonable to expect that the value should increase from level 1 to level 2. The situation is illustrated in the figure above where the shaded area represents the allowed region for $\boldsymbol{\mu}_{c,1}$. Monotonicity should hold for every feature dimension, every category c, and for every ordered triple of levels $(i < j < k)$ within that category. Using $\mathbf{a}.^*\mathbf{b}$ to denote component by component multiplication of two vectors, we formalize the monotonicity constraint by

$$(\boldsymbol{\mu}_{c,j} - \boldsymbol{\mu}_{c,i}).^*(\boldsymbol{\mu}_{c,k} - \boldsymbol{\mu}_{c,j}) \geq \mathbf{0}, \qquad \begin{array}{l} \forall\, c \text{ such that } 1 \leq c \leq K \\ \forall\, i,j,k \text{ such that } 0 \leq i < j < k \leq l_c \end{array} \tag{2}$$

It is important that all triples within a category be included in the constraint, and equality with 0 allows for the possibility of irrelevant features.

If the sample means satisfy the monotonicity constraint (2), then there is not much else to do other than estimate the $\boldsymbol{\Sigma}$'s. On the other hand, due to the randomness in the data, the sample means may not satisfy (2), in which case, one ought to be able to improve the risk of the classifier by updating the sample means, taking into account (2). This is the focus of this paper.

2.1   Incorporating the Monotonicity Hint

The likelihood of the sample means, given estimates for the class means and covariance matrices will be Normal with the same mean and a covariance matrix decreased by a factor of $N_{c,l}$, i.e., $P[\mathbf{m}_{c,l}|\hat{\mathbf{m}}_{c,l}, \hat{\mathbf{S}}_{c,l}, N_{c,l}] = \mathcal{N}(\mathbf{m}_{c,l} - \hat{\mathbf{m}}_{c,l}, \hat{\mathbf{S}}_{c,l}/N_{c,l})$. The joint distribution of the sample means is independent given the estimated means, hence

$$P[\{\mathbf{m}_{c,l}\}|\{\hat{\mathbf{m}}_{c,l}, \hat{\mathbf{S}}_{c,l}, N_{c,l}\}] = \prod_{c,l} \mathcal{N}(\mathbf{m}_{c,l} - \hat{\mathbf{m}}_{c,l}, \hat{\mathbf{S}}_{c,l}/N_{c,l}) \tag{3}$$

To convert this likelihood into a posterior, we use the monotonicity constraint to guide the choice of a prior. The only implication of (2) is that the support of the prior be for assignments to the means that satisfy (2). There are many ways to assign such a prior, and we pick the simplest, namely a prior that assigns a uniform probability density to means that satisfy (2) and a 0 probability density otherwise. We thus conclude that the posterior density for the means is given by

$$P[\{\hat{\mathbf{m}}_{c,l}\}|\{\mathbf{m}_{c,l}, \hat{\mathbf{S}}_{c,l}, N_{c,l}\}] \propto P[\{\hat{\mathbf{m}}_{c,l}\}] \prod_{c,l} \mathcal{N}(\hat{\mathbf{m}}_{c,l} - \mathbf{m}_{c,l}, \hat{\mathbf{S}}_{c,l}/N_{c,l}) \quad (4)$$

where the prior $P[\{\hat{\mathbf{m}}_{c,l}\}]$ is some constant when the set of means satisfies (2) and zero otherwise. This posterior could be used in a Bayesian formalism to obtain expectations. However, we are presently after a specific estimate of the μ's, namely the maximum a *posteriori* probability (MAP) estimate. Taking the logarithm and discarding constant terms, we get the following optimization problem. *Minimize with respect to* $\{\hat{\mathbf{m}}_{c,l}\}$

$$\frac{1}{2} \sum_{l,c} N_{c,l}(\hat{\mathbf{m}}_{c,l} - \mathbf{m}_{c,l})' \hat{\mathbf{S}}_{c,l}^{-1}(\hat{\mathbf{m}}_{c,l} - \mathbf{m}_{c,l}) + \frac{1}{2}\log|\hat{\mathbf{S}}_{c,l}| \quad (5)$$

subject to the non-linear inequality constraints given in (2).
Notice that $\hat{\mathbf{S}}_{c,l}$ depends on $\hat{\mathbf{m}}_{c,l}$. Without the constraints, the solution is given by the sample means, $\hat{\mathbf{m}}_{c,l} = \mathbf{m}_{c,l}$. The objective function encourages the estimates to be close to the sample means, favoring low variance directions of $\hat{\mathbf{S}}$ and classes in which more data are available. However, aside from such intuitive observations, the analytical solution of this problem is elusive. We thus resort to numerical techniques. It is tempting to treat each category independently, but the means interact with each other due to the monotonicity constraint (through the normal class). Two approaches immediately suggest themselves. The first is essentially a global search for the solution, which is feasible in low dimensional problems with few classes. The second is a gradient based technique that is considerably trickier to implement, but more efficient.

Monte Carlo approach: First generate an estimate for the normal mean from $\mathcal{N}(\hat{\mathbf{m}}_{c,0} - \mathbf{m}_{c,0}, \mathbf{S}_{c,0}/N_{c,0})$. Given the normal mean, we generate means in each category independently, according to $\mathcal{N}(\hat{\mathbf{m}}_{c,l} - \mathbf{m}_{c,l}, \mathbf{S}_{c,l}/N_{c,l})$, and accept if they satisfy the monotonicity constraint (2). After generating the monotonic means for every category, we compute the objective (5) and repeat, keeping the set of monotonic means that attains the minimum for (5). It can be shown that with probability approaching 1, for any $\epsilon > 0$, the resulting set of monotonic means will have an objective value at most ϵ greater than the optimal value, as long as the number of Monte Carlo events is allowed to be arbitrarily large.

Gradient based approach: At the expense of introducing a regularization parameter Ω, we convert the optimization problem to one of minimizing an unconstrained objective function $E = E_{prob} + \Omega E_{mon}$. E_{prob} is given in (5), and E_{mon} is designed to have a minimal value when (2) is satisfied. We will use

$$E_{mon} = -\sum_{c=0}^{N} \sum_{0 \le i < j < k \le l_c} \sum_{\alpha=1}^{d} \left[(\hat{m}_{c,j}(\alpha) - \hat{m}_{c,i}(\alpha))(\hat{m}_{c,k}(\alpha) - \hat{m}_{c,j}(\alpha)) \right]^{-} \quad (6)$$

where $[x]^{-} = x$ if $x < 0$ and 0 otherwise, and $\hat{m}(\alpha)$ is the αth component of $\hat{m}$. The value of Ω determines the tradeoff between E_{prob} and E_{mon}, and it is only in the limit of large Ω that this solution can approach a solution to the original problem, (5). Among the challenges are the facts that E_{mon} is quite non-linear and non-differentiable. This means that gradient based approaches need to be careful at the non-differentiable points. Nevertheless, we can compute the gradient when it is defined. A complication arises due to the fact the $\hat{S}$ depends on $\hat{m}$. Ignoring this dependence, by approximating $\hat{S} \approx S$, we get

$$\frac{\partial E_{prob}}{\partial \hat{m}_{c,l}} = N_{c,l} S_{c,l}^{-1} (\hat{m}_{c,l} - m_{c,l}) \quad (7)$$

To compute the gradient of the monotonicity error with respect to $\hat{m}_{c,l}(\alpha)$, there are three types of terms that we need to consider – in the summation over triples, l could be the lowest, middle or highest level. The result is

$$\frac{\partial E_{mon}}{\partial \hat{m}_{c,l}(\alpha)} = \sum_{\substack{l<j<k \\ or \\ k<j<l}} \hat{m}_{c,k}(\alpha) - \hat{m}_{c,j}(\alpha) + \sum_{j<l<k} 2\hat{m}_{c,l(\alpha)} - \hat{m}_{c,j}(\alpha) - \hat{m}_{c,k}(\alpha) \quad (8)$$

where contributions to the gradient occur only when a term contributes to E_{mon}. This gradient can now be used to descend on the objective function.

3   Experimental Simulations and Further Study

Since we focus on the update of the means, we show results for a 2-dimensional learning problem in which the covariance matrices of each class were equal, and the means satisfied the monotonicity constraint (2). Since each class had the same covariance matrix, we estimated the covariance matrix using the data from every class. This is the covariance matrix that was used for the classifier using the monotonic means as well as the sample means. We also chose a risk matrix that is 0 along the diagonal and 1 everywhere else, hence the risk is the probability of error. The general problem presents no additional difficulties.

We consider both a 1 category and a 3 category problem, with 4 levels per category (including normal). An example of how the means get updated due to the monotonicity constraint is shown to the right (for 1 category). The total number of data points generated varied from 30 to 300, and for each data set size, we ran 5000 simulations. A simulation entailed generating the data, and computing the risk of the Bayes minimal risk classifier that uses the sample means, compared to the one

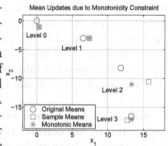

that uses the monotonic means (obtained using the Monte Carlo and gradient

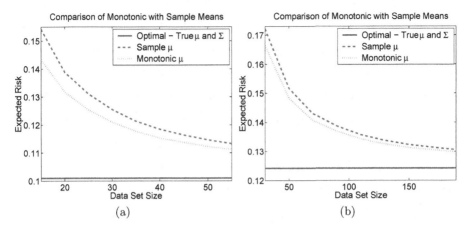

Fig. 1. Risk for the (a) single category and (b) three category learning problems.

based approaches). These risks were computed using a test set of size 10000. Results of the simulations are shown in Figure 1. The monotonicity hint clearly gives a systematic improvement.

Work in progress includes further study of the optimization problem (2), the extension to more complicated learning models such as neural networks, and the application to real world problems.

Acknowledgments. Many have contributed to the progress of this work. In particular, we single out Honeywell Corporation for alerting us to the problem and providing initial motivation, James Psota and Amir Atiya for useful discussion.

References

1. Y. Abu-Mostafa. Hints. *Neural Computation*, 4(7):639–671, 1995.
2. Agency for Healthcare Research and Quality. Clinical classifications software. fact sheet. *http://www.ahrq.gov/data/hcup/ccsfact.htm*, Internet Citation.
3. C. Bishop. *Neural Networks for Pattern Recognition*. Clarendon Pr., Oxford, 1995.
4. D. Rixen, J. H. Siegel, and H. P. Friedman. "Sepsis/SIRS" physiologic classification, severity stratification, relation to cytokine elaboration and outcome prediction in posttrauma critical illness. *Journal of Trauma*, 41:581–598, 1996.
5. J. H. Siegel, D. Rixen, and H. P. Friedman. Physiological classification and stratification of illness severity of posttrauma 'sepsis' patients as a basis for randomization of clinical trials. *Journal of Endotoxin Research*, 2(17):177–188, 1995.
6. J. Smith and S. Chang. Multi-stage classification of images from features and related text. *In 4th Europe EDLOS Workshop*, Aug 1997.
7. M. Taylor. Discovering multi-level classification rules in platelet transfusion databases. *Ph.D. Dissertation Proposal, University of Maryland*, December 1996.

Adaptive Filtering for GARCH Models

Paul E. Lynch and Nigel M. Allinson

University of Manchester Institute of Science and Technology, Department of
Electrical and Electronic Engineering, Manchester M60 PO Box 88.
lyh@swift.ee.umist.ac.uk

Abstract. The volatility of a speculative asset is a fundamental ingredient of many financial pricing algorithms, therefore, accurate forecasts
of volatility are essential to financial practioners. Autoregressive Conditional Heteroscekdastic models and their generalisations (GARCH) have
been shown to provide reasonable forecasts of volatility with relatively
few parameters. Recent evidence suggests, however, that financial volatility is a multiplicative process whereby dominant time frames can be located by the derivative of volatility [14]. Using the Widrow Hoff learning
rule, this paper shows how the GARCH(1,1) forecast can be improved
by filtering the volatility derivative against the residual forecast error
from a GARCH(1,1) model. Information criterion is used to evaluate the
contribution of the new adaptive parameter.

1 Introduction

The volatility of a speculative asset, the second moment of a time series, provides
potential investors with a measurement of risk exposure to that asset; if an asset
displays high volatility investors will seek high returns to invest in that asset. For
this reason, volatility has become the fundamental ingredient of many celebrated
financial theory's [11] [1]. As volatility is central to any trading strategy, an accurate model of speculative price movement is required to employ theses strategies
effectively. Furthermore, volatility is known to cluster and display seasonality at
various time horizons [8] [5]. Autoregressive conditional hetrosecasdicity models
(ARCH) and their generalized variations have dominated academic literature
for almost twenty years as they provide a good estimate of the volatility process
with relatively few parameters [7] [2] [3]. Variations of these model are currently
being used by financial institutions that are exposed to risk [10]. Recently, the
mechanics of the volatility derivative, the rate of change of volatility, has been
shown to contain information about the future magnitude of volatility [14]. This
article shows how the volatility derivative can be filtered against the residual
error from a GARCH(1,1) model leading to an improvement in forecasting performance. The paper proceeds as follows, section two describes and defines the
data and statistical operators followed by an introduction to the GARCH(1,1)
model in section three. Sections four explains the adaptive filtering technique and
the results are presented in section five. Concluding remarks follow thereafter.

H. Yin et al. (Eds.): IDEAL 2002, LNCS 2412, pp. 416–422, 2002.

2   Volatility Definitions

Financial time series produce inhomogeneous data, meaning that price information arrives at irregular times in the form of current market bid and offer quotes. This raw financial data is converted into a matrix of time, T, and logarithmic middle price, x

$$\mathbf{A} = [T(t)\ x(t)] \tag{1}$$

where

$$x = (\ln p_{bid} + \ln p_{ask})\ /\ 2 \tag{2}$$

Global financial markets display seasonality over many time horizons. This problem is particually acute when working in the intra day time range (i.e. European financial markets witness an increase in volatility at the opening of the US financial markets). To remove this seasonality, $\mathbf{A}$ is computed in a dynamical ϑ-time to yield a new matrix [1]

$$\mathbf{B} = [\vartheta(t)\ x(t)] \tag{3}$$

The volatility of $x(t)$ can be computed over a time frame, τ, through the application of an operator $\Omega[x(t)]$. However, there is no universally accepted volatility operator and we have to choose either a *hard* or *smooth* volatility measurement. Although a smooth volatility measurement, such as the exponential moving average volatility, has the desirable property of a smooth decaying kernel (a hard volatility measurement has been shown to generate noise due to the discrete cut off in its rectangular window), an overlapping bias is created in bi-variate analysis. For this reason we define volatility using a traditional hard volatility measurement based on a point wise price difference.

$$\sigma[\tau](t) = \left(\frac{1}{n-1} \sum r^2[\tau']\right)^{\frac{1}{2}} \tag{4}$$

$$r[\tau'; x](t) = \frac{x(t) - x(t - \tau')}{\sqrt{\tau'/1y}} \tag{5}$$

The denominator in equation 5 annualizes the return so that the expectation $E[r^2[\tau]]$ is independent of τ with a typical value of 10% for forien exchange rates. To enable consistency over many time frames, the number of returns use to compute the volatility over a time frame τ is chosen to be

$$\tau' = \tau/24 \tag{6}$$

Therefore, $n = 24$. We define the volatility derivative as

$$\dot{\sigma}[\tau] = \sigma[\tau](t) - \sigma[\tau](t - \tau) \tag{7}$$

---

[1] In a basic diffusion process, $\Delta x(t) \propto \sqrt{t}$, therefore $\Delta x(t)^2 \propto t$. Hence, the justification of a time scale transformation based on volatility. For exact details, the interested reader should refer to [4].

However, this definition is conditional on the level of volatility. An unconditional definition of the volatility derivative is

$$\dot{\sigma}_{\ln}[\tau] = \ln \frac{\sigma[\tau](t)}{\sigma[\tau](t - \tau)} \tag{8}$$

The statistical properties of the conditional and unconditional derivative are very similar. However, for brevity, only the unconditional derivative is studied in this paper. Realized volatility is defined as

$$\sigma_r[\tau](t) = \sigma_h[\tau](t + \tau) \tag{9}$$

The residual error is defined as

$$\Delta\tilde{\sigma}[\tau] = \sigma_{r[\tau]} - \tilde{\sigma}_{r[\tau]} \tag{10}$$

where $\tilde{\sigma}_r[\tau]$ is the forecast implied by the GARCH(1,1) model. These equations were applied to USD / CHF for the period 1990-2000 with volatility being calculated over many time frames ranging from 4 hours to 28 days. The years 1990 / 91 are used as a training set for the filter with 1992 - 2000 being used for out of sample performance evaluation.

3   The GARCH(1,1) Process

The Generalized Autoregressive Conditional Hetroscedasticity process which is known by the mercifully short abbreviation, GARCH, was introduced by Tim Bollerslov in 1986, [2], and it incorporates the volatility clustering phenomena that exists in financial markets.

$$r_i = \sigma_i \epsilon_t \tag{11}$$
$$\sigma_i^2 = \alpha_0 + \alpha_1 r_{i-1}^2 + \beta_1 \sigma_{i-1}^2 \tag{12}$$

Equation 12 is the GARCH(1,1) where, i is an arbitrary index, $E[\epsilon_i] = 0$ and $E[\epsilon_i^2] = 1$. The GARCH(1,1) process is stationary if $\alpha_1 + \beta_1 < 1$. The properties of the process can be re-writing equation 12 as,

$$\sigma_i^2 = \sigma^2(1 - \mu_{\text{corr}}) + \mu_{\text{corr}} \left(\mu_{\text{ema}}\sigma_{i-1}^2 + (1 - \mu_{\text{ema}})r_{i-1}^2 \right) \tag{13}$$
$$= \sigma^2 + \mu_{\text{corr}} \left(\mu_{\text{ema}}\sigma_{i-1}^2 + (1 - \mu_{\text{ema}})r_{i-1}^2 - \sigma^2 \right)$$

where

$$\sigma^2 = \frac{\alpha_0}{1 - \alpha_1 - \beta_1} \tag{14}$$

$$\mu_{\text{corr}} = \alpha_1 + \beta_1 \tag{15}$$

$$\mu_{\text{ema}} = \frac{\beta_1}{\alpha_1 + \beta_1} \tag{16}$$

The parameter μ_{corr} corresponds to the exponential decay of the conditional mean volatility. The parameter μ_{ema} is acting similar to an exponential moving average. These parameters are estimated using the *Broyden-Fletcher-Goldfarb-Shanno* quasi-Newton optimization technique [12] and updated on a rolling basis throughout the dataset.

3.1   GARCH(1,1) Volatility Forecast

Figure 3.1 shows the linear correlation between the volatility derivative and the residual forecast error form the GARCH(1,1) model over thirty two time frames ranging from four hours to twenty eight days. Clearly significant forecasting information is contained in the volatility derivative. Some of this signal can be explained the fact that the parameters were optimized the eight hour time frame horizon, these parameters have been shown to be inadequate at explaining the volatility process at different time horizons [6]. For computational reasons, however, it is not practical to optimize GARCH models for every possible time horizon. By applying an adaptive filter, the forecasting signal contained in the volatility derivative can be encapsulated into the GARCH(1,1) forecast.

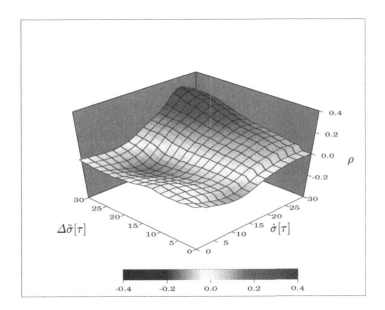

Fig. 1. Correlation matrix of $\dot{\sigma}[\tau]$ vs $\Delta\tilde{\sigma}[\tau]$ for USD/CHF for GARCH(1,1)

4   Adaptive Filtering

The contamination of a time series of interest by unwanted signals or noise is a problem encounter in many applications throughout science and engineering. Common examples are biomedical engineering and digital communication networks. Adaptive filtering presents a solution to this problem by attempting to filter out the unwanted noise. The main objective in noise filtering is to produce an optimum estimate of the noise in the contaminated signal and therefore, an optimum estimate of the desired signal. Common algorithms that have found widespread application are the least mean square (LMS), the recursive least squares, and the Kalman filter algorithms [9]. Computationally, the LMS filter is the most efficient. Furthermore, it has been shown to be more stable than the other two filters [13]. For these reasons this paper concentrates on the LMS algorithm.

4.1   Adaptive LMS Filter

The adaptive LMS filter consists of adjusting the weight from sample to sample in such a way as to minimize the mean square error. The weights obtained from the LMS filter are only estimates , but these estimates improve with time as the weights are adjusted and the filter *learns* the characteristics of the signal.

4.2   Applying $\dot{\sigma}[\tau]$

Section 3.1 showed the linear correlation between $\dot{\sigma}[\tau]$ and $\Delta\tilde{\sigma}[\tau]$. Making an optimal estimate of the noise would obviously lead to an enhancement of the actual forecast. However, this correlation value is unlikely to be stationary. Applying the adaptive LMS-filter $\dot{\sigma}[\tau]$ can be used as a reference signal to produce an estimate of $\Delta\tilde{\sigma}[\tau]$, which is the desired signal. $w[\tau]$ is a non-stationary unknown weight which relates the reference signal to the desired signal. The equations for the filter are as follows,

$$\hat{f}_{\text{lms}}[\tau] = w[\tau]\dot{\sigma}[\tau] \tag{17}$$

$$\varepsilon[\tau] = \Delta\tilde{\sigma}[\tau] - \hat{f}_{\text{lms}}[\tau] \tag{18}$$

$$w[t+\tau] = w[\tau] + 2\mu\varepsilon[\tau]\dot{\sigma}[\tau] \tag{19}$$

Where

$$\hat{f}_{\text{lms}}[\tau] = \text{filter estimate} \tag{20}$$

$$\varepsilon[\tau] = \text{filter error} \tag{21}$$

$$\mu = \text{learning parameter} \tag{22}$$

Essentially, the adaptive LMS-filter is giving a dynamic measurement of the LMS estimate $w[\tau]$ which adapts to the non-stationary environment. LMS from the training set is used to provide an initial estimate of the filter weight, $\hat{w}[\tau]$, and the learning rate, μ, is set to 0.05.

5   Results

Table one column three shows the percentage improvement by incorporating the volatility derivative with each time frame showing an enhancement in forecast. Obviously, by using an additional parameter we should improve the forecast error.To evaluate the actual contribution of the adaptive parameter to the

Table 1. Initial $\hat{\beta}[\tau]$, root mean square error reduction percentage and information criteria for GARCH(1,1) and Adaptive GARCH models

Index value	Initial $\hat{w}[\tau]$	% gain	AIC_G	$AIC_{A\ G}$	BIC_G	$BIC_{A\ G}$
0	0.210	46.28	-51438	-62422	-51416	-62394
1	0.173	45.38	-51436	-62126	-51414	-62098
2	0.148	44.61	-51434	-61874	-51413	-61846
3	0.021	41.12	-53696	-63058	-53675	-63029
4	-0.012	37.92	-53691	-62117	-53669	-62089
5	-0.041	35.61	-53685	-61464	-53663	-61435
6	-0.061	36.19	-54267	-62208	-54246	-62180
7	-0.074	34.00	-54257	-61599	-54235	-61571
8	-0.058	32.16	-55530	-62388	-55509	-62360
9	-0.053	33.16	-55970	-63090	-55949	-63062
10	-0.007	34.58	-56071	-63570	-56050	-63542
11	-0.072	32.88	-56656	-63702	-56635	-63674
12	-0.151	30.46	-57174	-63592	-57152	-63564
13	-0.196	30.78	-57220	-63723	-57199	-63694
14	-0.159	29.95	-57142	-63433	-57121	-63404
15	-0.204	29.44	-57233	-63396	-57212	-63367
16	-0.199	27.64	-57789	-63507	-57768	-63479
17	-0.211	28.41	-57481	-63387	-57460	-63358
18	-0.190	29.06	-58064	-64131	-58042	-64103
19	-0.133	30.89	-57965	-64495	-57944	-64466
20	-0.072	31.50	-58559	-65245	-58538	-65217
21	-0.011	30.62	-58985	-65444	-58963	-65416
22	0.013	31.45	-58976	-65650	-58954	-65621
23	0.098	31.23	-59219	-65836	-59198	-65808
24	0.178	32.31	-59519	-66416	-59498	-66387
25	0.315	30.49	-59783	-66211	-59762	-66183
26	0.433	29.40	-59768	-65920	-59747	-65892
27	0.543	27.23	-59756	-65373	-59735	-65345
28	0.473	29.28	-59835	-65956	-59813	-65928
29	0.367	30.89	-60063	-66593	-60041	-66564
30	0.208	34.54	-59866	-67356	-59845	-67328
31	0.085	33.90	-60087	-67404	-60066	-67375

performance of the model find we can use information criterion whereby the model which minimizes the information criterion is considered optimal. Table one columns four and five show the Akaike information criterion (AIC) the GARCH(1,1) and the Adaptive GARCH(1,1). In all cases the adaptive model has a lower AIC value and is therefore a superior forecasting model. This is reinforced through the Bayesian (Schwarz) information criterion in columns six and seven.. Clearly, the additional adaptive parameter provides a superior model over all the time frames.

6   Conclusion

This paper has shown how GARCH models can be improved by filtering the residual error of the model against the derivative of the volatility. This adaptive technique has been shown to be superior over all time horizons through the reduction of information criterion. It may be possible to enhance this filter by considering the predictability of the volatility derivative conditional on its sign or magnitude to see if there are threshold effects in the signal. This could perhaps lead to a dual regime adaptive filter based on a threshold autoregressive model for the volatility derivative. Future work is focused on this task.

References

1. F. Black and M. Scholes. The pricing of option and corporate liabilities. *Journal of Political Economy*, 81:637–659, 5 1973.
2. T. Bollerslev. Generalized autoregressive conditional heteroskedasticity. *Journal of Econometrics*, 31:307–327, 1 1986.
3. T. Bollerslev, R. Y. Chou, and K. F. Kroner. ARCH modeling in finance. *Journal of Econometrics*, 52:5–59, 1 1992.
4. W. Breymann, G. Zumbach, M. M. Dacorogna, and U. A. Müller. Dynamical deseasonalization in otc and localized exchange-traded markets. Internal document WAB.2000-01-31, Olsen & Associates, Seefeldstrasse 233, 8008 Zürich, Switzerland, January 31 2000.
5. M. M. Dacorogna, U. A. Müller, R. J. Nagler, R. B. Olsen, and O. V. Pictet. A geographical model for the daily and weekly seasonal volatility in the FX market. *Journal of International Money and Finance*, 12(4):413–438, 8 1993.
6. F. Drost and T. Nijman. Temporal aggregation of GARCH processes. *Econometrica*, 61:909–927, 1 1993.
7. R. F. Engle. Autoregressive conditional heteroskedasticity with estimates of the variance of U. K. inflation. *Econometrica*, 50:987–1008, 1 1982.
8. R. F. Engle, T. Ito, and W.-L. Lin. Meteor showers or heat waves? Heteroskedastic intra-daily volatility in the foreign exchange market. *Econometrica*, 58:525–542, 6 1990.
9. A. C. Harvey. *Forecasting, Structural Time Series Models, and the Kalman Filter*. Cambridge University Press, Cambridge, 1989.
10. J. P. Morgan. RiskMetrics – technical document. Technical report, J. P. Morgan and International marketing – Reuters Ltd., 12 1996.
11. H. M. Markowitz. *Portfolio Selection: Efficient Diversification of Investments*. Wiley, Yale University Press (1970), New York, 1959.
12. W. H. Press, B. P. Flannery, S. A. Teukolsky, and W. T. Vetterling. *Numerical recipes. The art of scientific computing*. Cambridge University Press, Cambridge, 1 1986.
13. B. Widrow and S. D. Stearns. *Adaptive Signal Processing*. Prentice-Hall, Englewood Cliffs, N.J., 1985.
14. G. Zumbach and P. Lynch. Heterogeneous volatility cascade in financial markets. *Physica A*, 298(3-4):521–529, 2001.

Application of Self-Organising Maps in Automated Chemical Shift Correction of In Vivo ^{1}H MR Spectra

Juhani Pulkkinen[1], Mika Lappalainen[2], Anna-Maija Häkkinen[3],Nina Lundbom[4], Risto A. Kauppinen[1], and Yrjö Hiltunen[2]

[1]NMR Research Group, A. I. Virtanen Institute, University of Kuopio, Finland
{juhani.pulkkinen, risto.kauppinen}@uku.fi
http://www.uku.fi
[2] Pehr Brahe Software Laboratory, University of Oulu, Rantakatu 8,
FIN-92100 RAAHE, Finland
{yrjo.hiltunen, mika.lappalainen}@ratol.fi
http://www.pbol.org
[3]Department of Oncology, Helsinki University Hospital, Finland
Anna-Maija.Hakkinen@hus.fi
http://www.hus.fi
[4]Department of Radiology, Helsinki University Hospital, Finland,
Nina.Lundbom@hus.fi
http://www.hus.fi

Abstract. Frequency shift differences in ^{1}H MRSI spectra due to magnetic field inhomogeneities pose a problem, if automated lineshape fitting routines (LF) or artificial neural network (ANN) methods are used for spectral quantification. Use of self-organizing map (SOM) analysis for automated shift correction of long echo time (TE=270 ms) *in vivo* ^{1}H NMR spectra of human brain is demonstrated. The map is obtained by training a SOM with proton spectra and the chemical shifts of the reference vectors were calibrated. The maps were then used for classification of spectroscopic imaging data and the calibration information for corrections of chemical shifts.

1 Introduction

Magnetic resonance spectroscopy (MRS) offers a non-invasive, multi-metabolic approach *in vivo* to obtain valuable biochemical information [1]. MR spectroscopy is expected to have an important role in clinical neuroscience [2-4]. However, biological systems are inherently complex, which augment the problems associated with MRS data analysis. The multitude of information causes difficulties in the analysis of biomedical MRS data. Automated transformation of spectroscopic information is crucial for the method to become clinically useful.

Each ^{1}H magnetic resonance spectroscopic imaging (^{1}H MRSI) study of the human brain produces as much as hundred spectra, which makes the manual analysis time-consuming. Recent applications have demonstrated that an artificial neural network can provide an efficient and highly automated alternative MRS data analysis [5-8]. The ANN and LF methods require correct chemical shifts of spectra to be quantified,

H. Yin et al. (Eds.): IDEAL 2002, LNCS 2412, pp. 423-428, 2002.
© Springer-Verlag Berlin Heidelberg 2002

and therefore, the inputs for ANN and the initial parameters for LF analysis should be sufficiently correct. In clinical ^{1}H MRSI spectra significant shift of frequency can arise i.e. from the boundaries between air, bone, fluid, and tissue. In particular, brain tumour spectra may have large intensity variations of individual metabolites making it difficult to create *a prior* values for correction of chemical shift errors. Also several other automated spectral analysis methods have been proposed, only a few reports demonstrating automated correction of frequency shift differences in MRSI data have been presented [9-10].

Here, we have applied the self-organizing maps (SOM) [11] in chemical shift correction of *in vivo* [1]H MR tumour spectra. The results indicate that the unsupervised neural network analysis is successful in the automation of the chemical shift calibration *in vivo* MRS data.

2   Methods

2.1   *In vivo* ^{1}H NMR Spectroscopy

^{1}H MRSI data set consisted of 191 spectroscopic images from 14 healthy controls and 71 glioma patients. ^{1}H MRSI measurements were performed in a 1.5 T MR scanner (Magnetom Vision, Siemens, Erlangen, Germany) using a standard circularly polarized head coil. For MRSI localization, 2D FLASH images in 3 orientations were acquired. A double spin echo sequence with 16 x 16 phase encoding steps was used with TR = 2600 ms and TE = 270 ms with 2 scans per phase encode with water suppression and a rectangular field of view of 160 mm^2. Volume pre-selection of 80/100x80/100x15 mm^3 with nominal voxel size 1.5 cm^3, was used including the tumour area. Spectral data were collected from one or two 15 mm thick slices covering the tumour volume as judged from the localizer MR images.

In order to remove the residual water signal from the experimental spectra, the Hankel Lanczos singular value decomposition (HLSVD) [12] method was applied. Both real and imaginary parts were used for conversion of spectroscopic data into the magnitude mode. Fig. 1 shows some examples of different kinds of experimental human brain spectra, which visualize the intensity and chemical shift variations of the spectra.

2.2   SOM Analysis

The experimental human brain ^{1}H NMR spectra (n=14816) were divided into two subsets. The first subset (8488 of the spectra) was the training set, which was used for computing the reference vectors of the map. The second subset (6328 of the spectra) was the test set. The 241 data points of the spectra were used as an input for the SOM. The spectrum included the choline-containing compounds (Cho), creatines (Cr), N-acetyl aspartate (NAA), lactate, and lipid resonances. The intensity of each frequency point of each spectrum was first divided by the maximum intensity of each spectrum. One SOM was performed for the chemical shift correction consisting of 225 neurons in a 15x15 hexagonal arrangement. A Gaussian function was used as the neighbourhood function. The learning rate was chosen to decrease linearly as a function of time. The map was taught with 500 epochs and the initial neighbourhood had the value of 3. The SOM Toolbox program (Version 2.0beta) was used in the training of the map. The actual chemical shift correction program is a part of the automated analysis software (MRSTools Ltd, Kuopio, Finland) under a Matlab-software platform (Mathworks, Natick, MA, USA).

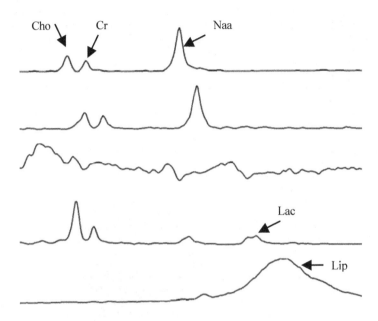

Fig. 1. Some *in vivo* ^{1}H MR spectra of human brain. (Cho) the choline-containing compounds, (Cr) creatines, (Naa) N-acetyl aspartate, (Lac) lactate and (Lip) lipids.

3 Results and Discussion

SOM analysis was applied for the chemical shift correction of *in vivo* ^{1}H MR spectra of human brain. Fig. 2 shows some reference vectors of the map, which were obtained by training a self-organizing network with 8488 ^{1}H MR spectra. The spectral clusters calculated by the k-means method are also shown in Fig. 2. The reference vectors formed five main clusters as follows: spectra from normal brain (1) and (2), spectra with poor resolution i.e. from volumes in the vicinity of compartment boundaries (3), spectra with decreased NAA (4) and spectra with large lipid resonances (5). The chemical shift scales of the reference vectors were calibrated using two rules. Firstly, the chemical shift correction was made by referencing frequencies to the NAA resonance and secondly, in the absence of NAA, the Cho resonance was used as a reference.

The method was tested using the remaining 6328 spectra analysed independently with the SOM method. The automated corrections were checked manually. 94% of the test samples were calibrated correctly by the SOM analysis (±0.03 ppm variations accepted). The remaining cases were either calibrated incorrectly or the correction was incomplete due to poor spectral quality. These results illustrate that the calibration information is recognized by the SOM analysis and the chemical shift errors can be corrected automatically. Although the number of spectra used in this work was large, the data included spectra from tumours and normal brain only. Further analysis of other diseases would be needed to clarify if this model is aimed for wide range of applications. However, tumour spectra show inherently large variations in metabolites, and it is likely that this model will analyse spectra from other diseases without a difficulty.

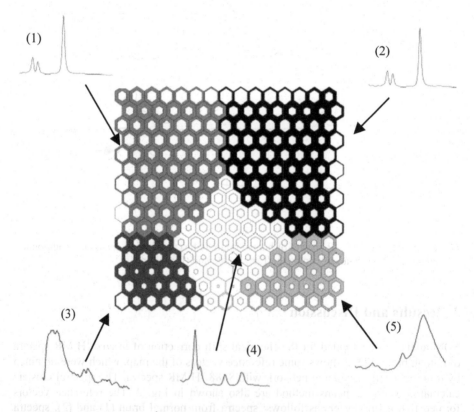

Fig. 2. SOM using the *in vivo* ^{1}H MR spectra of human brain showing the number of the hits on the size of the depicted neuron. The reference vectors related to some example neurons are shown. The background colours show the main clusters of the map: (1) and (2) spectra from normal brain, (3) poor quality spectra, (4) spectra with decreased NAA and (5) spectra with large lipid resonances.

Some automated correction methods of frequency shift differences in MRSI data have been proposed, which are based on cross-correlation with an ideal spectrum generated from the spectral database information [9] or a multiscale approach [10]. However, these techniques have also difficulties in regions of poor SNR or extreme lineshape distortion. Our SOM-based method provides a new tool for chemical shift corrections. It could be routinely utilized in the analysis of MRSI data and requires no extensive knowledge of neural nets. It is also easy to be included in any kind of analysis software. Furthermore, the SOM can be retrained, if new types of spectra would be under analysis.

4   Conclusion

These results suggest that the SOM analysis makes it possible to extend the automation procedure for the chemical shift calibration. The present study shows that SOM analysis may play a significant role in biomedical MRS data analysis. We anticipate that clinical MRSI studies producing large quantity of data will most likely benefit from the automated ANN analysis methods.

Acknowledgments. This study was supported by the Academy of Finland, The Special Federal Grant no. TYH8224 of Helsinki University Central Hospital, the Magnus Ehrnrooth Foundation, the Alfred Kordelin Foundation and the Jenny and Antti Wihuri Foundation.

References

1. Pfeuffer, J., Tkac, I., Provencher, S. W., Gruetter, R.: Toward an *in vivo* neurochemical profile: quantification of 18 metabolites in short-echo-time ^{1}H NMR spectra of the rat brain, J. Magn. Reson. **141** (1999) 104-120
2. Hakumäki, J.M., Ala-Korpela, M., Kauppinen, R.A.: [1]H nuclear magnetic resonance spectroscopy: noninvasive neurochemistry for basic research and clinical applications, Curr. Top. Neurochem. **1** (1997) 59-85
3. Ross, B., Michaelis, T.: Clinical applications of magnetic resonance spectroscopy, Magn Reson Q **10** (1994) 191-247
4. Barker, P.B., Glickson, J.D., Bryan, R.N.: *In vivo* magnetic resonance spectroscopy of human brain tumors, Top Magn Reson Imaging **5** (1993) 32-45
5. Usenius, J.-P., Tuohimetsä, S., Vainio, P., Ala-Korpela, M., Hiltunen, Y., and Kauppinen, R.: Automatic Classification of Human Brain Tumours by Neural Network Analysis Using In Vivo [1]H Magnetic Resonance Spectroscopic Metabolite Phenotypes NeuroReport **7** (1996) 1597–1600
6. Kaartinen, J.; Hiltunen, Y.; Kovanen, P. T., Ala-Korpela, M: Classification of Human Blood Plasma Lipid Abnormalities by [1]H Magnetic Resonance Spectroscopy and Self-Organizing Maps. NMR Biomed. **11** (1998) 168-176
7. Kaartinen, J., Mierisova, S., Oja, J. M., Usenius, J.-P., Kauppinen, R. A., Hiltunen, Y.: Automated quantification of human brain metabolites by artificial neural network analysis from in vivo single-voxel ^{1}H NMR spectra, J. Magn. Reson. **134** (1998) 176-179

8. Hiltunen, Y., Kaartinen, J., Pulkkinen, J., Häkkinen, A.M., Lundbom, N., Kauppinen, R.: Quantification of Human Brain Metabolites from In vivo 1H NMR Magnitude Spectra Using Automated Artificial Neural Network Analysis. J. Magn. Reson. **154** (2002), 1–5
9. Soher, B. J., Young, K., Govindaraju, V., Maudsley, A. A..: Automated spectral analysis. III. Application to in vivo proton MR spectroscopy and spectroscopic. Magn. Reson. Med. **40** (1998) 822-831
10. Zang, X., Heberlein, K., Sarkar, S., Hu, X.: A multiscale approach for analyzing in vivo spectroscopic imaging data. Magn. Reson. Med. **43** (2000) 331-334
11. Kohonen, T.: *Self-organizing Maps*; Springer-Verlag, Berlin Heidelberg New York, (2001)
12. Pijnappel, W.W.F., van den Boogaart, A., de Beer, R., van Ormondt, D.: SVD-based quantification of magnetic resonance signals, J. Magn. Reson. **97** (1992) 122-134

Supervised Learning of Term Similarities

Irena Spasić, Goran Nenadić, Kostas Manios, and Sophia Ananiadou

School of Sciences, University of Salford, UK
{I.Spasic, G.Nenadic, K.Manios, S.Ananiadou}@salford.ac.uk

Abstract. In this paper we present a method for the automatic discovery and tuning of term similarities. The method is based on the automatic extraction of significant patterns in which terms tend to appear. Beside that, we use lexical and functional similarities between terms to define a hybrid similarity measure as a linear combination of the three similarities. We then present a genetic algorithm approach to supervised learning of parameters that are used in this linear combination. We used a domain specific ontology to evaluate the generated similarity measures and set the direction of their convergence. The approach has been tested and evaluated in the domain of molecular biology.

1 Introduction

The automatic discovery of new knowledge encoded in text documents relies heavily on the identification of concepts, linguistically represented by domain specific terms [3]. New terms representing newly identified or created concepts appear rapidly due to a continuously increasing amount of new knowledge and textual data describing it. This makes the automatic term extraction tools essential assets for efficient knowledge discovery. However, automatic term extraction itself is not our ultimate goal: extracted terms need to be associated with other terms already stored in the existing knowledge-bases. This means that terms should be classified and/or clustered so that semantically similar terms are grouped together. Classification and/or clustering of terms are indispensable for improving information extraction, knowledge acquisition, and document categorisation. Classification can also be used for the efficient term management and update of exisiting ontologies in a consistent manner.

In this paper, we present an approach to the automatic discovery of term similarities, which serves as a basis for both classification and clustering of domain-specific concepts represented by terms. The method is based on the automatic extraction of significant patterns in which terms tend to appear. Beside the features that represent patterns, we also use lexical and functional similarities between terms in order to define a hybrid similarity measure as a linear combination of the three similarities. We also present a genetic algorithm approach to the supervised learning of parameters that are used in this linear combination. Thus, the method for the discovery of term similarities is fully automated.

The paper is organised as follows. In Section 2, we describe term similarity measures in detail. Section 3 presents a method for tuning similarity measure with a genetic algorithm. Finally, we give the preliminary results in Section 4.

H. Yin et al. (Eds.): IDEAL 2002, LNCS 2412, pp. 429–434, 2002.

2   Term Similarity Measure

Our approach to measuring term similarities is based on a hybrid method that incorporates three types of term similarity: contextual, functional and lexical.

2.1   Contextual Similarity

Our approach to contextual similarity is based on automatic pattern mining. The aim is to identify the most relevant lexico-syntactic context patterns in which terms appear. *Context pattern* (CP) is a lexicalised regular expression that corresponds to either the left or right context of a term. In order to construct CPs we first collect concordances for all terms recognised automatically by applying the term recognition algorithm based on the C/NC-value measure [1]. This is a hybrid, fully automatic approach to term recognition combining linguistic knowledge and statistics. The context normalisation process starts with the mapping of constituents into syntactic categories. However, other grammatical and lexical information attached to the context constituents can also be used to construct CPs. For instance, the lemmatised form of a simple or compound word may be attached to its syntactic category. CP constituents regarded as irrelevant for discriminating terms (e.g. adverbs, linking words) may be removed. In our approach, a user has the choice which categories to instantiate/remove.

Once CPs have been normalised, we calculate the values of a measure called *CP-value* in order to statistically estimate their relevance. CP-value provides the ranking of CPs according to three criteria: total frequency of a CP ($f(p)$), its length ($|p|$, as the number of constituents) and the frequency of its occurrence within other CPs ($|T_p|$, where T_p is a set of all CPs that contain p). The following formula provides details of how the CP-value is calculated:

$$CP(p) = \begin{cases} \ln |p| \cdot f(p) & , \text{ if } p \text{ is not nested} \\ \ln |p| \cdot \left(f(p) - \frac{1}{|T_p|} \sum_{b \in T_p} f(b) \right) & , \text{ otherwise} \end{cases}$$

The CPs whose CP-value is higher than a chosen threshold are regarded as relevant. These patterns are domain-specific as they rely solely on the information found in a domain specific corpus. However, they are not manually defined, but rather are extracted from a domain specific corpus in a fully automated manner.

At this point, each term is associated with a set of the resulting CPs with which it occurs. We treat these CPs as term features, and we use a feature contrast model [7] to calculate similarities between terms as a function of both common and distinctive features. Let us now formally define the context similarity measure. Let C_1 and C_2 be two sets of CPs associated with terms t_1 and t_2 respectively. Then, the contextual similarity between t_1 and t_2 is defined as follows:

$$CS(t_1, t_2) = \frac{2|C_1 \cap C_2|}{2|C_1 \cap C_2| + |C_1 \backslash C_2| + |C_2 \backslash C_1|}$$

2.2   Functional Similarity

By analysing the distribution of similar terms in corpora, we observed that some lexical patterns indicate a high degree of correlation between terms. Some of these patterns have been previously used to discover hyponym relations between terms [2]. In our approach, however, we do not discriminate between different types of similarity relationships among terms, but instead, we consider terms appearing in the same syntactical roles as highly correlated. We have defined several types of lexical patterns (see Table 1)[1], including co-ordination patterns, which describe a specific type of co-occurrence in which terms are used *concurrently* within the same context. We hypothesise that the concurrent usage of terms within the same context denotes similarities in syntactic function, thus indicating a high degree of correlation between terms.

Table 1. Sample of lexical patterns used to discover functional similarities.

`<Term> (,<Term>)* [,] <&> other <Term>`
`both <Term> and <Term>`
`(<Noun>|<Adj>) (,<Noun>|<Adj>)* [,] <&> (<Noun>|<Adj>) <Term>`
`(<Noun>|<Adj>) <Term>/<Term>`

Currently, we set functional similarity between two terms to 1, if the two terms appear together in any one of the patterns, and to 0 otherwise. Our experiments show that functional similarity provides high precision, but low recall when used on its own. In future work, we plan to experiment with assigning different values according to: **a)** the type of patterns and **b)** the frequency of co-occurrence of terms in these patterns.

2.3   Lexical Similarity

The last type of similarity we use is the similarity between words that make up terms. If two terms share the same head, we assume that they share the same concept as an (in)direct hypernym (e.g. progesterone receptor and estrogen receptor). Furthermore, if one of such terms has additional modifiers, this may indicate concept specialisation (e.g. nuclear receptor and orphan nuclear receptor). Bearing this in mind, we base the definition of lexical similarity on sharing a head and/or modifier(s). Formally, if t_1 and t_2 are terms, then their similarity is calculated according to the following formula:

$$LS(t_1, t_2) = a \cdot \text{shared\_head}(t_1, t_2) + b \cdot \text{shared\_modifiers}(t_1, t_2)$$

where $\text{shared\_head}(t_1, t_2)$ and $\text{shared\_modifiers}(t_1, t_2)$ represent the number of shared term constituents, while a and b $(a > b)$ are weights.

---

[1]   Non-terminal symbols are given in angle brackets. The symbol `<&>` denotes a conjunctive word sequence, i.e. the following regular expression: `(as well as) | (and[/or]) | (or[/and])`. Other non-terminals have obvious interpretations.

3   Tuning a Similarity Measure with a Genetic Algorithm

The combined term similarity is defined as a linear combination of the three similarity measures described in the previous section:

$$S_{\alpha\beta\gamma}(t_1, t_2) = \alpha \cdot CS(t_1, t_2) + \beta \cdot FS(t_1, t_2) + \gamma \cdot LS(t_1, t_2) \tag{1}$$

We tested this measure with the values 0.3, 0.4 and 0.3 for the weights α, β and γ respectively in the domain of molecular biology. Random samples of results have been evaluated by a domain expert, and the combined measure proved to be a good indicator of semantic similarity (see Section 4).

As the parameters can be adjusted, the results may be further improved. However, the choice of the weights α, β and γ in formula (1) is not a trivial problem. Therefore, we fine-tuned the above measure automatically rather then experimenting with manually determined weights. In particular, we aim at automatic learning of weights as opposed to manual tuning. We have implemented a supervised learning method using an existing ontology. Our learning algorithm is based on term similarities that are calculated using both the vertical position of terms and their horizontal distance in an ontology [3]. Namely, we use a *commonality measure* as the number of shared ancestors between two terms in the ontology, and a *positional measure* as a sum of their distances from the root. Similarity between two terms corresponds to a ratio between commonality and positional measure. This similarity measure is used as the 'golden standard'.

In order to determine appropriate values for the weights, we chose a genetic algorithm approach. *Genetic algorithms* (GAs) are meta-heuristics incorporating the principles of natural evolution and the idea of 'survival of the fittest' [6]. A solution is encoded as a sequence of genes, referred to as an *individual*. In our case, an individual is represented as a triple of genes (α, β, γ), where $\alpha+\beta+\gamma = 1$. In the initial phase of the GA we generate in a random manner a number of triples (α, β, γ) such that $\alpha, \beta, \gamma \geq 0$ and $\alpha + \beta + \gamma = 1$.

Operators typical of GAs, namely selection, crossover, mutation, and replacement, are applied, in that order, in each iteration of the GA. *Selection* is defined probabilistically: the better the solution, the higher the probability for that solution to be selected as a parent. We applied *tournament selection*, a technique where a group of individuals is singled out randomly, and after that the fittest ones are selected for crossover.

Crossover is applied to a pair of parents resulting in their recombination, called children. We used a *uniform crossover* in which each gene position is chosen with 50% probability for the genes at that position to be swapped. Note that the crossover operator defined in this way is likely to affect the feasibility of the resulting solution, i.e. the constraint $\alpha + \beta + \gamma = 1$, which every individual needs to satisfy. We, therefore, apply a simple repair approach in order to transform an infeasible solution into a feasible one.

The *mutation* operator introduces diversity into a population by modifying a small portion of newly formed solutions in a random manner. A triple (α, β, γ), chosen with a small probability, is changed in the following manner: one of the genes α, β and γ is randomly chosen and its value is changed randomly. However, this operator may also lead to the violation of the constraint $\alpha + \beta + \gamma = 1$, in which case the resulting triple is repaired in the same way it is done after performing crossover.

Once a sufficient number of new solutions have been created by applying the three genetic operators, they are evaluated according to a predefined quality criterion, called *fitness*. In our problem, we estimate the fitness of a triple (α, β, γ) through the Euclidean distance:

$$f(\alpha, \beta, \gamma) = \sum_{\substack{t_i, t_j \in T \\ t_i \neq t_j}} (S_{\alpha\beta\gamma}(t_i, t_j) - O(t_i, t_j))^2 \qquad (2)$$

In formula (2), set T is an intersection between two sets of terms, one derived from the ontology and other containing all automatically recognised terms; $S_{\alpha\beta\gamma}(t_i, t_j)$ is the hybrid similarity measure calculated for the given weights α, β, γ, and $O(t_i, t_j)$ is the similarity measure derived from the ontology. The goal is to find a triple that minimises the value of the evaluation function. In other words, we want to minimise the deviation from the similarity values derived from the ontology.

Once all the new individuals have been evaluated, the fittest ones *replace* the appropriate number of the less fit old solutions, thus forming a new population. Each population formed in this way is referred to as a *generation*. This process is repeated from generation to generation until a stopping condition is fulfilled. The stopping condition is satisfied if the current generation contains an individual for which the value of the evaluation function is smaller than a given threshold. If there is more than one such individual, the one with the smallest value is chosen. However, it is possible that such an individual does not exist at all, therefore, we limit the number of iterations in order to avoid an infinite loop.

4   Experiments and Evaluation

The hybrid similarity measure has been incorporated into the ATRACT workbench [5] and tested in the domain of molecular biology. Term similarities have been calculated based on a corpus of 2082 abstracts retrieved from the MEDLINE database [4], and as the 'golden standard' we have used the similarity measure derived from an existing ontology.

We have used part of the ontology as the training set for learning weights. In Table 2 we present a sample from the testing set (terms that exist in the ontology, but are not used for learning weights). It shows the similarities of term `retinoic acid receptor` to a number of terms. The first column represents the similarity values calculated for manually chosen weights, the second shows the corresponding values for automatically learned weights using the proposed GA, while the third column stands for similarity values derived from the ontology. Note that the functional similarity appears not to be important ($\beta = 0.06$). This similarity is corpus-dependent: the size of the corpus and the frequency with which the lexical patterns are realised in it affect the functional similarity. In

Table 2. Comparison of similarity values for `retinoic acid receptor`.

Term	$S_{.30,.40,.30}$	$S_{.13,.06,.81}$	O
`nuclear receptor`	0.75	0.55	0.80
`progesterone receptor`	0.37	0.53	0.67
`estrogen receptor`	0.29	0.49	0.67
`glucocorticoid receptor`	0.29	0.49	0.67
`human estrogen receptor`	0.28	0.37	0.57

the training corpus, such patterns occurred infrequently relative to the number of terms, which indicates that a bigger corpus is needed in the training phase.

The hybrid measure proved to be consistent as similar terms shared most of their "friends". However, the measure with automatically determined weights showed a higher degree of stability relative to ontology-based similarity measure. For example, the ratio between the values in the first and third column ranged from 1.06 to 2.31, whilst the same ratio for the second and third column ranged from 1.26 to 1.54. The results are promising, as terms were grouped reliably according to their contextual, functional and lexical similarities.

5   Conclusion

In this paper we have presented a method for the automatic discovery and tuning of term similarities. The preliminary results in the domain of molecular biology have shown that the measure proves to be a good and consistent indicator of semantic similarity between terms. The approach is fully automatic, domain independent, and knowledge-poor for the part concerned with the generation of the three similarity measures: context, functional, and lexical similarity. However, in order to learn domain-appropriate term similarity parameters, we need a knowledge-intensive approach. In our approach we have used an ontology as way of representing domain-specific knowledge.

References

1. Frantzi, K., Ananiadou, S., Mima, H.: Automatic Recognition of Multi-Word Terms. Int. J. on Digital Libraries 3/2 (2000) 117-132
2. Hearst, M.: Automatic Acquisition of Hyponyms From Large Text Corpora. Proceedings of COLING 92, Nantes, France (1992)
3. Maynard, D., Ananiadou, S.: Identifying Terms by Their Family and Friends. Proceedings of COLING 2000, Luxembourg (2000) 530-536
4. MEDLINE: National Library of Medicine. www.ncbi.nlm.nih.gov/PubMed/ (2002)
5. Mima, H., Ananiadou, S., Nenadić, G.: ATRACT Workbench: An Automatic Term Recognition and Clustering of Terms. In: Matoušek, V. et al. (eds.): Text, Speech and Dialogue – TSD 2001. LNAI 2166. Springer Verlag (2001) 126-133
6. Reeves, C.: Modern Heuristic Techniques. In: Rayward-Smith, V. et. al (eds.) Modern Heuristic Search Methods. John Wiley & Sons Ltd., New York (1996) 1-25
7. Santini, S., Jain, R.: Similarity Measures. IEEE Transactions on Pattern Analysis and Machine Intelligence 21/9 (1999) 871-883

BIKMAS: A Knowledge Engineering System for Bioinformatics

Victoria López-Alonso[1], Lucia Moreno[2], Guillermo López-Campos[1], Victor Maojo[2], and Fernando Martín-Sanchez[1]

[1]Department of Bioinformatics. Health Informatics Coordination Unit. Institute of Health "Carlos III". Ministry of Health and Consumer Affairs Ctra. Majadahonda a Pozuelo Km. 2. 28220 Majadahonda, Madrid. Spain
{victorialopez, glopez, fmartin}@isciii.es
[2]Artificial Intelligence Lab. Polytechnical University of Madrid. Spain

Abstract. We present the functional and architectural specification of BIKMAS, a Bioinformatics Knowledge Management System. BIKMAS contains an interactive user interface, a database in which several sources of knowledge are registered and a nucleus of knowledge management implemented with an algorithm that filters scientific information and assists the user in the task of using knowledge. BIKMAS is an active information system capable of retrieving, processing and filtering scientific information, checking for consistency and structuring the relevant information for its efficient distribution and convenient use. Two of the most important aspects of BIKMAS are that the system is based on an object-oriented database and it has been developed in JAVA tightly integrated in Internet.

1 Introduction

A Bioinformatics research unit receives massive amounts of scientific information that should be transformed into a useful resource to generate knowledge. Knowledge management provides the methodological and technological framework to: "capture both the experimental knowledge intrinsic to what we are doing, the empirical knowledge derived from the outcomes of what we have done and the operational knowledge to serve as a strategic decision-making resource and ensemble of rules, trend predicting insights, workflow analysis, analytic outcomes, procedural guidelines and so on" [1].

There are powerful systems to store information in scientific research units, however in many cases there is a gap between information storage and user's ability to analyse it and to reorganise the structure of the information into operative knowledge [2]. The process of distributing information is usually made manually, this causes delays, errors and multitude of consultations due to doubts and differences of criteria according to the person who made the process. Group members differ in the expertise, knowledge and information that they bring to the group [3] and group performance not only depends on the information resources available to the group, but also on the process of structuring the information to be used [4].

Users of a scientific research unit should have adequate access to information that might impact their routine work. For this reason we have developed BIKMAS a

H. Yin et al. (Eds.): IDEAL 2002, LNCS 2412, pp. 435–440, 2002.

semiautomatic system that could assist members of a Bioinformatics Unit in the process of knowledge management. BIKMAS is capable of retrieving scientific information from different sources (e.g. Internet, journals, books). It evaluates and filters the relevant information according to several established criteria to store and to use it as needed by the scientific research unit tasks (e.g. web pages, research unit mailing list, working files).

The basic idea of BIKMAS is to structure the process of deciding what to do with new information assets implemented into the system. To achieve this goal, it is necessary to establish and define Bioinformatics terms and concepts (e.g. data describing author, date, theme, subtheme). The process by which information is given a meaning and a use is related to the structure of these defined terms and makes knowledge acquisition possible. A conceptual analysis of terms and an ontology of Bioinformatics themes and subthemes supports the re-use of terminology in BIKMAS.

2 Methodology

In a Bioinformatics unit a variety of users with different scientific and cultural backgrounds (e.g. biologists, chemists, physicians and computer scientists interested in biological discovery) supply large amount of information. BIKMAS provides the means to create, store and manage scientific information, stimulating users to share their knowledge and creating the mechanism to formalize existing information.

In the design of BIKMAS we thought in an architectural model as generic as possible since technologies and configurations are highly susceptible to change. The system uses an object-oriented database and Java technology; this Internet-based architecture allows users to remotely access BIKMAS.

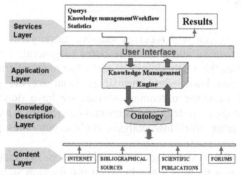

Fig. 1. BIKMAS tool architectural layout.

The system is structured in the following layers (Fig. 1):
- The content layer is associated with the set of information assets that could be used in BIKMAS. A large amount of information coming from diverse origins is received in a Bioinformatics Unit in different formats. Information can be obtained by Internet (e.g. electronic mail, web cast, distribution lists, debate forums, online journals) or by paper (scientific journals, scientific press,

bibliographical sources and forums). The user interface presents diverse information with great flexibility and comfortable viewing. The user manually assigns descriptors (author, data, origin, theme and subtheme) to each information asset.
- The knowledge description layer captures the terms by which users search information. The idea is to connect the terms by which the system structures the knowledge with the terms employed by the user.
BIKMAS is a system in which one of the main goals is the formalization of the Bioinformatics knowledge. Themes and subthemes are structured like a semantic network: the meaning of a node should be entailed by the links it has with other nodes, determining which concepts are a consensus among users.
- The application layer is implemented with a filter that establishes the system specifications and provides the capability for capturing, storing, processing and distributing data. The system will discard some type of information, however, based on diverse criteria the system will consider that other information assets must be stored and in some cases published. Criteria to manage information by the system have been defined (e.g. date, theme of interest and origin of information). These criteria are weighted by their ability to execute different strategies in the system according to the priorities of the Unit. So during a specific period of time we would like a much more restrictive knowledge management system that only stores high quality information that is both recent and related to a certain theme of interest.

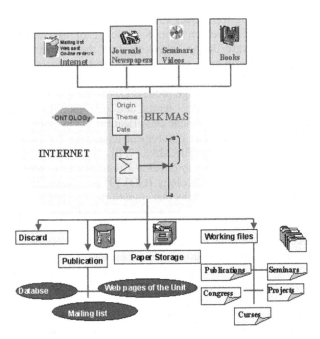

Fig. 2. BIKMAS structure: sources of information and distribution of knowledge.

The status associated with an information asset could be discarded, published or stored (Fig. 2). Each scientific unit will also define where to store and publish its information to gain knowledge in a particular area. When a paper asset is stored, the system will distribute it in files utilising layer architecture of themes and subthemes. This structure of themes will allow easy access to existing paper-based knowledge elements of relevant content. The publication of the information can be made in Intranet page of the Unit or in different web pages in Internet. Each user has to decide if the information will be published as internal information such as bulletin boards, or external information, such as web sites or mailing list of the Unit.

The system will also cooperate with the users of the Bioinformatics unit providing different working files to store information about themes of particular interest for some concrete tasks: publications (books, papers on journals or workshops), presentations (courses, congresses, seminars), projects (projects proposal, technical reports, fellowships).

-Query layer. Queries could be done in terms of authors, themes and subthemes; searching and retrieving access to heterogeneous sources, including Internet sites, paper files, databases and popular formats (MS Office). The result of a query is displayed as a table.

3 Results

BIKMAS employs reasoning techniques to make inferences and provides assistance to support a Bioinformatics research unit. Knowledge of user requirements is an essential part of the software design, checking that the information matches the requirements and is both useful and usable. The knowledge domain needs to be fairly stable; consequently conceptualisation of relevant information and user requirements is an essential part of the software design process [5, 6].

The idea of ontology is to define terms and concepts in a mechanical and computable unit. The result will be a clear classification and mapping of text elements for computers. We have applied this ontological advantage for the classifying and mapping of themes and subthemes in BIKMAS [7, 8].

There have been several attempts to develop Bioinformatics ontologies to exploit biological information. The Gene Ontology (GO) [9] is a controlled vocabulary for annotation of gene products and molecular functions, the biological processes in which they are involved and the cellular locations in which it is found. EcoCyc [10] uses an ontology to specify a database scheme for the *E. coli* metabolism. TAMBIS (Transparent Access to Multiple Bioinformatics information Sources) [11] uses an ontology to allow users to query Bioinformatics databases.

We tried to classify the Bioinformatics field to coordinate information obtained by biomedical studies, biochips experiments and computational methods. To structure and manage information with maximum usefulness we focus the modelling of the knowledge domain in four main components: Biomedical informatics, Applied Biomedical Research, Biochip and Genomic. We built an ontology of themes and subthemes in BIKMAS using a basic framework of classes and slots (Fig. 3).

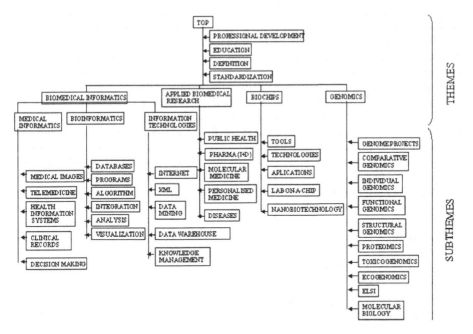

Fig. 3. Classification of the definitions used in the ontology employed in BIKMAS.

We use the Protégé-2000 architecture [14] with ontology-design ideas originated from the literature on objected-oriented design. Each class in the ontology determines the corresponding field that appears in the knowledge acquisition tool and that is used to acquire the instance information. So the user selects theme and subtheme by navigating through the controlled-vocabulary hierarchy.

4   Conclusions

BIKMAS facilitates enormously the task of planning and management of the information to users of a Bioinformatics Unit, even if they don't have a lot of experience. The system collects knowledge from a number of scientific information sources and users can take immediate action in their work processes in a tightly integrated manner.

The system has been designed with open tools and is totally configurable. This makes BIKMAS a general system for knowledge processing that could be easily adaptable to a research group outside the field of Bioinformatics. To design the workflow it was necessary to identify the scientific tasks patterns of the research unit, the effect is a comprehensive, but flexible and continuous process of knowledge management.

The value of BIKMAS as a resource for sharing Bioinformatics information lies not only in the fact that information is organized and distributed, but also in the fact that BIKMAS is an experiment in representation of Bioinformatics knowledge. There is currently no standard data model for Bioinformatics knowledge. BIKMAS determines the most critical areas for information exchange and knowledge capture within a unit of Bioinformatics. It focuses on the priorities of the unit to facilitate the identification of the ways by which the group uses knowledge to perform its routine work. In the design of the system the filters and interactions used in arriving at a decision are analysed.

Future work on BIKMAS will focus in an automatic indexing program to analyse the text of the document determining appropriate index terms either from a controlled vocabulary or from the words contained within the document. In addition BIKMAS could offer a historical file of the work of the Unit that could be exploited with statistical techniques, obtaining interesting temporary ratios (e.g. the proportion of received and discarded information in a concrete theme throughout a period of time).

BIKMAS links knowledge management to action in a scientific unit and it should be integrated in its rutinary activities.

References

1. Abidi, S.R., Cleah. Y.N.: A Convergence of Knowledge Management and Data Mining: Towards "Knowledge-Driven" Strategic Services. 3rd Int. Conference on the Practical Applications of Knowledge Management (PAKeM´2000). Manchester (2000)
2. Fayyad, U., Piatetsky-Shapiro, G., Smyth, P.: The KKD Process for Extracting Useful Knowledge from Volumes of Data. Communications of the ACM. 11(1996) 27-34
3. Jackson, S.E.: Team Composition in Organizational Settings: Issues in Managing and Increasingly Diverse Workforce. In: Worchel, S., Wood, W., Simpson, J. (eds). Group Process and Productivity, Sage Publications, Newbury Park, CA (1992) 138-173
4. Hackman, J.R.: The Design of Work Teams. In: Lorsch, J.W. (eds.): Handbook of Organizational Behaviour Prentice-Hall, Englewood Cliffs, NJ (1987) 315-342.
5. Ould, M.: Strategies for Software Engineering: The Managemet of Risk and Quality. Wiley, Chichester (Wiley series in software engineering practice)(1990)
6. Dix, A., Finlady, J. Abowd, G., Beale, R. (ed.): Human-Computer Interaction. Prentice-Hall. London (1998)
7. Wache, H., Vögele, T., Visser, U., Stuckenschmidt, H., Schuster, G., Neumann, H., Hübner, S.: Ontology-based integration of information. A survey of existing approaches. In Proceedings of IJCAI-01 workshop: Ontologies and information sharing. Seatle, WA. (2001) 108-117
8. Veda, C.S., Debabrata, D., Harald, U., Sundaresan, S. An Ontology-Based Expert System for Database Design. Data and Knowledge Engineering. 28 (1998) 31-46
1. 19. The Gene Ontology Consortium: Gene Ontology: Tool for the Unification of Biology. Nature Genetics. 25 (2000) 25-29
9. Karp, P.D., Riley, M., Saier, M., Paulsen, I.T. Paley, S.M., Pellegrini-Toole, A.: The EcoCyc and MetaCyc Databases. Nucleic Acids Res. 28 (2000) 56-59
10. Baker, P.G., Brass, A., Bechhofer, S., Goble, Paton, N., Stevens, R. TAMBIS: Transparent Access to Multiple Bioinformatics Information Sources. An Overview. In: Proceedings of the Sixth International Conference on Intelligent Systems for Molecular Biology. AAAI Press (1998) 25-34
11. Protege (2000). The Protégé Proyect. http://protégé.standford.edu
12. Rumbaugh, J., Blaha, M., Premerlani, W., Eddy. F., Lorensen, W.: Object –orienting modelling and design. Englewoods Cliffs, New Jersey: Prentice Hall (1991)

Unsupervised Feature Extraction of *in vivo* Magnetic Resonance Spectra of Brain Tumours Using Independent Component Analysis

C. Ladroue[1,2], A.R. Tate[1,2], F.A. Howe[1], and J.R. Griffiths[1]

[1] CR-UK Biomedical Magnetic Resonance Research Group
Department of Biochemistry and Immunology
Cranmer Terrace London SW1 0RE, UK
[2] School of Cognitive and Computing Sciences, University of Sussex, Falmer, Brighton, UK
`chrisla@cogs.susx.ac.uk`

Abstract. We present a method for automatically decomposing magnetic resonance (MR) spectra of different types of human brain tumours into components which directly reflect their different chemical compositions. The automatic analysis of *in vivo* MR spectra can be problematic due to their large dimensionality and the low signal to noise ratio. Principal Component Analysis allows an economic representation of the data but the extracted components themselves may bear little relationship to the underlying metabolites represented by the spectra. The Principal Components can be rotated in order to make them more meaningful but this requires expertise to decide on the transformation. In this study, we use Independent Component Analysis and show that this technique can overcome these two drawbacks and provide meaningful and representative components without requiring prior knowledge.

1 Introduction

[1]H Magnetic Resonance Spectroscopy (MRS) provides a useful addition to MRI for non-invasive diagnosis of brain tumours. The spectra provide biochemical information, which can be used to help distinguish the type of tumour where the radiological diagnosis is ambiguous, as in about 20% of cases. Currently, diagnosis always involves taking a biopsy from the brain, a procedure that is unpleasant and even dangerous for the patient, with a significant number of serious complications and occasional deaths. MRS is completely non-invasive, and our long-term aim is to develop it into a method that will replace biopsy.

At present, however, MRS is not widely used in everyday clinical practice, since measuring the chemical information represented by the peaks in the spectra requires special expertise. Furthermore radiologists are not used to interpreting spectral data.

In order to make MRS more accessible as a clinical tool, we are developing a decision support system that will help radiologists use MRS with little knowledge

H. Yin et al. (Eds.): IDEAL 2002, LNCS 2412, pp. 441–446, 2002.

or expertise ([1]). Clinicians will be able to enter spectra of their own patients into the system. They will be given help with the diagnosis, using a combination of automated classification and a data visualisation technique, which allows comparison with a large database of validated cases.

Since clinicians will be using this system in normal clinical practice, it is essential that all spectral processing is completely automated. Furthermore all results presented must be easy to understand, since our aim is to help the user to extract relevant information from the classifier, rather than providing them with "black box" classifiers that they cannot understand.

There are some fundamental problems with developing an automatic procedure for classifying brain tumours from MR spectra. Firstly, the dimensionality of the spectra is large - the signals can be between 512 and 2048 datapoints, whereas the true dimensionality, determined by the number of metabolites, will be much smaller. Secondly, the signal to noise ratio is low for *in vivo* spectra, meaning that only few of the underlying metabolites will give rise to peaks large enough to be distinguished from the underlying noise.

In this paper we present a method that reduces the number of features to a small number and also produces meaningful components which are directly related to the underlying biochemical composition of the tumours.

1.1   MR Data and Independent Component Analysis

Signal-composed data are commonly analysed with the help of multivariate techniques. Most of them decompose the signals as a linear combination of a small number of signals (Eq. 1). Such a decomposition is not unique and one has to make a choice on the properties of the signals $\mathbf{s}_i$ to make the problem feasible.

$$\mathbf{x} = a_1\mathbf{s}_1 + a_2\mathbf{s}_2 + \cdots + a_d\mathbf{s}_d = \sum_{i=1}^{d} a_i\mathbf{s}_i \qquad (1)$$

A classical way to find those signals $\mathbf{s}_i$ is Principal Component Analysis ([2]). PCA determines the signals that represent most of the data variations. A useful feature of PCA is that it provides an objective means for choosing the number d representative principal components (PC). However, PCs from MR spectra are rarely interpretable in terms of metabolite signals, although rotating them can make them more meaningful - a rotation does not affect the compression rate (Cf. [3] for an application on MR Spectra).

Independent Component Analysis ([4]) also extracts signals $\mathbf{s}_i$ but in a very different fashion. In ICA, signals $\mathbf{s}_i$ are sought which are statistically independent. Statistical independence is approximated by maximising non-Gaussianity, either with kurtosis or negentropy ([5]). Since ICA looks for non-Gaussianity, it is more likely to pick up projections where the data are multi-modal; so on those axes, differences within the data will stand out.

What makes ICA even more attractive for our problem is that it models data in a very similar way to the actual structure of an MR spectrum, which can be considered as the result of a linear combination of signals from individual metabolites. Thus, a spectrum will be written as in eq.1 but with $\mathbf{s}_i$ representing pure metabolites signatures and a_i corresponding to their relative concentration. The only previously reported work applying ICA to single voxel MR data is that of [6], on less complex spectra (long echo spectra, which contain fewer peaks).

1.2   Preliminary Work with ICA on ^{1}H MRS

We began work with ICA on a dataset of artificial spectra, created from a random linear combination of pure metabolite spectra, modified to model the physical phenomena that degrade spectra obtained *in vivo* . This involved randomly broadening the peaks and introduction of Gaussian noise in the range expected for real data. This produced spectra resembling real ones but with the concentrations of all the contributing metabolites accurately known.

Independent Component Analysis of this dataset produced an impractically large number of ICs (about the same as the number of samples) which looked more like Dirac functions than metabolite spectra. Most of the peaks were at the expected locations, but they were shifted by one or two points, seemingly in order to fit a curve. The rest of the ICs just modelled noise. Our conclusions were that this simple method produced too many ICs, was very sensitive to noise, and produced many artefacts.

Two different methods were then investigated to lower the number of ICs. The first involved choosing the ICs that had best discriminative power. However, this was a supervised method and it might have been simpler to select the variables in the first place with respect to the same criterion of separability (Fisher's criterion). In the second method, a cluster analysis of the ICs was performed with the intention of only using one representative signal per cluster. This method was complicated (particularly in the choice of the number of clusters) and gave inconclusive results.

We then decided to use the method of Hyvärinen ([7]), performing an initial PCA to reduce the noise (Cf. next section). This produced much better results. Each IC now looked like a set of Lorentzian peaks (as would be found in a metabolite spectrum) and their number was tractable. Since the method worked on artificial data, we went on to test it on real data.

2   Data and Methods

Four different tumours types, forming three groups, are considered: Meningioma (*mm*), Astrocytoma low grade (*ast2*) and Aggressive tumours, a mixture of Metastases and Glioblastomas (*agg*), plus a fourth group of normal brain spectra acquired from healthy volunteers. The spectra were acquired at St George's Hospital Medical School (SGH, London) and Institut de Diagnòstic per la Imatge (IDI, Barcelona) with different machines (GE and Philips), see table 1 for numbers.

Spectra are normalised so that their Euclidean norm is 1. In order to see if the IC's generalise between centres, only the SGH spectra are used to extract the components.

Table 1. Details of the data used in the experiments. There is a total of 125 spectra and only spectral data within $[4; 0]$ ppm are used, leading to a dimensionality of 200.

	Ast. II	Meningioma	Agg.	Normal brain
SGHMS	$n=10$	$n=11$	$n=24$	$n=14$
IDI	$n=6$	$n=22$	$n=38$	-

Experiments were as follows : a PCA is performed on the (SGHMS) spectra and a number of principal component is selected, to represent a large portion of the data. The spectra are then reconstructed using only those first PCs. The ICA is performed on these new signals and data (from both centers) are expressed as linear combinations (Cf. eq. 1) of the extracted independent components. Box plots corresponding to each IC are examined and the components themselves are examined by an expert spectroscopist, for biochemical interpretation.

3   Results

The selection of the correct number of components is always difficult, but the combination of PCA and ICA appears to be helpful. When we used 5 PCs (enough to represent 85% of the data), 5 ICs were found. When we used 10 (93%) PCs, the program was only able to find 8 ICs, suggesting that the 8 PC's reflected the intrinsic dimensionality. An attempt with 15 starting PCs yielded 13 ICs but the 5 extra PCs did not add any more information: the 7 extra ICs mostly consisted of noise. We then decided to use the eight independent components we previously found.

Figure 1 shows the five (out of eight) independent components extracted that show the most biochemically significant features. Apart from the last one, they are all composed of sharp peaks that can easily be read and interpreted in terms of known metabolites. For example, IC#1 is the signature of lipids and IC#3 contains mostly NAA and Cr and both IC#2 and IC#4 show mI, Cho and Cr but in different relative quantities. When only the principal components are considered, such interpretation is much more difficult - the noise is more prominent and each PC is a mixture of similar metabolites.

After the extraction of the Independent Components, the spectra (from both centres) are written according to eq. 1. Each spectrum is then represented by its scores (a_i of eq. 1). Figure 1 shows the distribution of the scores on each IC for each tumour type.

A number of observations can be made from those plots: 1) On both IC#1 and IC#5, most of the aggressive tumours (agg) separate from the other types, 2) The normal brain spectra separate out from the rest on IC#3 and 3) The box plot corresponding to IC#4 shows good separation between Meningiomas (mm), Astrocytomas ($ast2$) and normal brain spectra.

Thus, the independent components can be used to discriminate between all the tumour types used in this study. Moreover, separations occur on single ICs, suggesting they possess a biochemical function. Such one-dimensional separation

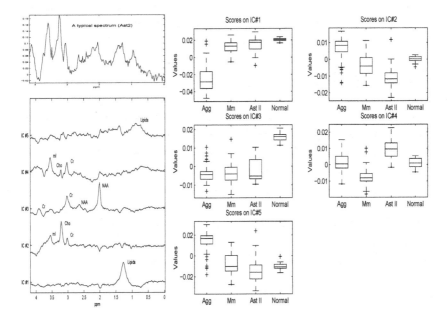

Fig. 1. Independent Components (bottom left) and box plots of the associated scores of the spectra. Cr: Creatine, Cho: Choline, mI: Myo-inositol, NAA: N-acetyl aspartic acid. The left and right edges of a box mark the 25th and 75th percentiles and the line within the box represents the median. The narrow boxes extending to the left and right (whiskers) extend from the quartiles to the farthest observation not farther than 1.5 times the distance between the quartiles. The extreme points are the outliers. A typical spectrum is displayed top left.

is ideal for system like INTERPRET because it provides a clear explanation for the classification. They also are helpful for data mining since they permit to narrow the analysis down to the minimum number of useful variables.

4   Discussion

ICA of MR spectra gives two significant improvements over PCA. Firstly, the individual components show a strong similarity to the metabolite signals associated with particular tissue types. For example IC#3 represents information about the Cr and NAA resonances, not just as the main individual peaks (*i.e.* NAA at 2 ppm and Cr at 3 ppm), but also the smaller components of Cr at 3.9 ppm and NAA at 2.7 ppm. Thus IC#3 is a component that would be expected to have a high value for normal brain spectra since they contain high signals from these biochemicals.

Secondly, the coefficients (Fig. 1) of the ICs appear to automatically provide a certain degree of classification of tissue type. As might be expected from the foregoing discussion, the coefficient of IC#3 discriminates all normal spectra from the tumour spectra. Similarly, IC#1 which represents the lipid component discriminates the aggressive tumours from the relatively benign tumours and the normal brain. The coefficient of IC#4, which represents mI and Cr, appears to separate meningiomas from the other tissues.

In conclusion, ICA seems to provide a method for automatically extracting biochemically relevant features from MR spectra that are characteristic of particular tissue types, and with no need for expert *a priori* knowledge. Furthermore, the IC coefficients allow a degree of classification which could be exploited to give explicit classification to users of decision support tools like INTERPRET. Further studies with NMR spectra from other tumour types are now required to see how far this will generalise.

Acknowledgement. This work was funded by the European Commission (IST-1999-10310). We thank our INTERPRET partners for providing data and Kirstie Opstad for her artificial spectra generating program.

References

1. http://caxbon.uab.es/INTERPRET
2. Fukunaga, K.: Introduction to Statistical Pattern Recognition. Academic Press, Inc, second edition (1990)
3. Howells, S.L.: Maxwell, R.J., and Griffiths, J.R.: Classification of tumour Hnmr spectra by pattern recognition. NMR in Bio-Medicine, (1992) 5:59-64.
4. Hyvarinen, A. and Oja, E: Independent component analysis: Algorithms and applications. Neural Networks, (2000), 13(4-5):411430.
5. Hyvarinen, A.: Survey on independent component analysis. Neural Computing Surveys, (1999) 2:94-128.
6. Lee, Y., Huang, Y.: El-Deredy, W., Lisboa, P., Ards, C., and Harris, P.. Robust methodology for the discrimination of brain tumours from in vivo magnetic resonance spectra. In IEE Proceedings - Science, Measurement and Technology, volume 147, (2000) 309-314.
7. Hyvarinen, A., Sarela, J., and Vigario, R.: Bumps and spikes: Artefacts generated by independent component analysis with insufficient sample size. In Int. Workshop on Independent Component Analysis and Blind Signal Separation (ICA'99),(1999) pages 425-429.

Fuzzy Rule-Based Framework for Medical Record Validation

K. Supekar, A. Marwadi, Y. Lee, D. Medhi

School of Interdisciplinary Computing and Engineering
University of Missouri at Kansas City
{kss2r6, akm7f0, leeyu, dmedhi}@umkc.edu

Abstract. Data cleaning is an important part of the knowledge discovery process. The principal causes of data anomalies include incomplete information, absence of a unique identifier across multiple databases, inconsistent data, existence of data entry errors and logically incorrect data. This situation is further exacerbated while integrating data from multiple, disparate data sources. Since data quality is directly related with the quality of services in data-driven applications, such as medical informatics, a reliable data cleaning solution, which allows rapid and precise detection of invalid data, is needed. Most existing data cleaning solutions are domain specific, time-consuming and do not easily accommodate logical validations. In this paper, we propose a Fuzzy rule-based framework, which is domain independent, flexible and easily accommodates physical as well as logical validations. We have implemented existing cleaning strategies (i.e. Sorted Neighborhood Method), and enhanced them by using state-of-the-art algorithms (i.e. Rete, Bigram). As proof-of-concept, our prototype system was applied to real patient data. Experimental results illustrate that our framework is extensible and allows rapid detection of invalid data with high precision.

1 Introduction

Medical organizations today face the very important challenge of cleaning patient records housed in their systems. Some organizations spend millions of dollars per year to detect data errors [1]. Patient records are highly heterogeneous, widely distributed and fragmented. Individual patient information is scattered throughout many organizations, residing anywhere from primary care physicians' offices to clinical laboratories and specialist centers [12]. According to a survey [8], in 45 health care facilities containing more than 35 million medical records, the duplication rate averaged 11 percent. Invalid medical record discrepancies are even more severe when corporate medical records are connected via community information networks. From the clinical perspective, delivering appropriate patient care requires medical information systems that support the coordination and accessibility of heterogeneous and distributed databases.

Research has pointed out the necessity of a standardized Electronic Patient Record (EPR) and the development of a collaborative medical system [13] providing patient record standardization and integration at an operational level including advanced temporal support, and the aggregation of data into multiple dimensions for qualitative

H. Yin et al. (Eds.): IDEAL 2002, LNCS 2412, pp. 447–453, 2002.
© Springer-Verlag Berlin Heidelberg 2002

analysis. TeleMed [3] developed a distributed medical record system, which deals with instances of multiple medical records, and shares complete medical histories, including prescription, immunization, and referral records with other health care providers. The Synapses (http://www.cs.tcd.ie/synapses/public) and SynEx (http://www.gesi.it/synex) systems focus on data integration for federated medical databases utilizing a Federated Healthcare Record server, which provides integrated access to a record's distributed components. There also exist efficient methods to handle each of these data anomalies (e.g.: AJAX [4] for Duplicate Elimination). There is, however, no provision to combine all these methods into a single framework that can be easily applied independent of the domain.

Data cleaning is an important process in knowledge discovery albeit a computationally expensive and time-consuming process. A report showed that about 80 - 90% of knowledge discovery efforts are for the data cleaning [5]. The cleaning process grows exponentially when very large and heterogeneous databases are involved. Any manual process of data cleaning is laborious, time consuming and itself prone to errors. Intelligent automated cleaning tools are a practical and cost effective way to achieve reasonably accurate data levels in existing data sets [12].

The objective of our research was to build a framework to eliminate inconsistent or redundant information from multiple data sources by either merging or purging. In an attempt to address scalability and efficiency issues associated with large heterogeneous databases, we developed a Fuzzy rule-based data validation framework, called FuzzyKlean. FuzzyKlean is based on a Fuzzy expert system, in which data from multiple sources can be validated through an incremental process and then integrated into a single and general format. It is domain independent, flexible and can easily accommodate logical and physical validations.

2   Motivating Examples

Our research is motivated by the Cardiovascular (CV) Research at the Mid-America Heart Institute (MAHI, http://www.mahi.org), where we were faced with highly heterogeneous databases containing patient information gathered over 20 years of data collection, with new additional information being added every day. One of the challenging tasks the medical data presented was the need for data cleaning. The heterogeneous sources and variance in data quality between the databases made us consider a new framework for data cleaning. For example, in the US an individual's social security number (SSN) is unique, however, many patients aren't willing to provide it at the time of admission, or are unable to provide it due to the emergency nature of their admittance. Soon, many patient records lack this unique identifier. Further, in many cases, the patient may need to go through more than one procedure where the basic information intake is different for different procedures. So when a statistical study is conducted to identify and understand correlations between cross-procedures, data needs to be merged from disparate sources [6]. This leads to a situation where efficient data cleaning mechanisms must be developed before the statistical study can proceed.

Mechanisms capable of dealing with duplicates, missing data, and out-of-range values and determining record usability, erroneous data, logically incorrect data, etc. are used [9]. Performing these tasks at the early stage in the data collection process and storing linked and "sanitary" data in a repository reduce the validation logic required at the time of data extraction and analysis. That is, the sources themselves should be clean prior to being merged at the enterprise level.

When working with the MAHI database we found several obstacles to identifying a patient accurately. One of the largest cardiovascular databases in the region, the MAHI Cardiovascular Database and Outcomes Research Center, contains 26,000 PTCA, 40,000 Nuclear and 8,000 Open Heart Procedures. Listed below are the more common problems we found when it was data cleaned:

- Invalid data: missing entry, missing fields, incomplete data, invalid type, typographical errors, use of abbreviations, misspellings.
- Redundancy and duplication: AKAs (Also known as) and nickname use for the first name, the use of one SSN by multiple family members. Missing Identifiers are related to inadequate software for patient identification and the absence of standards. This problem amplifies the creations of split records like open medical systems with different policies and procedures.
- Dependency inconsistency primarily due to data entry errors and data acquisition errors (e.g., transcription error in the SSN, discrepancies in DOB)
- Evolving data (e.g., change in the last name and hyphenated last name)

3 FuzzyKlean Framework

The FuzzyKlean framework (Fig 1) is composed of three major components (Preprocessing, Rule-based processing, Validation and Verification). In the Preprocessing component, data records are scrubbed of any anomalies using the Sorted Neighborhood method [15] on the base tables. In the Processing component, duplicate (preprocessed) records are detected by an expert system engine as described in the Rete method [2] which is based on a set of Fuzzy JESS rules. In the Validation and Verification component, there are human interventions to decide whether to merge/purge duplicate records [7]. The system was specifically targeted for patient records but can be easily extended for any kind of a dataset due to its rule-based framework.

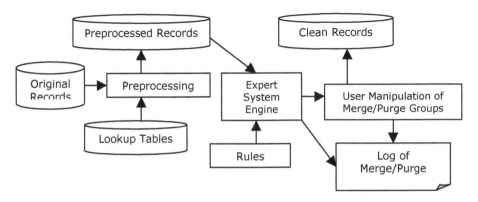

Fig 1. The Architecture of FuzzyKlean

- **Step 1: Preprocessing**

This stage allows patient nicknames to be replaced by their real names. There are occurrences in medical records where patient nicknames are used instead of real names. For example, there are numerous occasions when the nickname "BOB" is used instead of "ROBERT". Alternate use of such nicknames and real names cause multiple patient entries to be present for the same patient. Our FuzzyKlean system allows look-up on such nicknames using a base table consisting of possible nicknames with corresponding real names and replaces these nicknames in the patient dataset. This process greatly enhances the chances of finding duplicates.

Sorting data records in an efficient manner brings likely duplicates into the vicinity of each other. Use of domain independent algorithms [11] expedites the duplicate removal process. The standard method of detecting exact duplicates in a table is to sort the table and then to check if neighboring tuples are identical [15]. We used the approach of comparing nearby records by sliding a window of fixed size over the sorted database. This method [5, 7] significantly reduced the number of comparisons performed.

- **Step 2: Duplicate Detection using FuzzyJESS**

Data cleaning is usually a repetitive process dealing with similar data errors so that representing a repetitive pattern as a rule would be highly useful for effective and efficient data validation. The FuzzyKlean system is based on the Fuzzy rule-based expert system, Fuzzy JESS (http://herzberg.ca.sandia.gov/jess/), which is an extension of the JAVA expert system. FuzzyKlean associates a set of inputs (conditions) and a set of outputs (actions). The FuzzyKlean system applies *Fuzzy rules* to the data in the form of a *knowledge base*. The rules represent the heuristic knowledge of domain experts, and the knowledge base represents an evolving state situation.

FuzzyKlean has some unique features. Firstly, it allows a user to apply distinct weights to the various data fields. These allow one to find duplicates based on the Confidence Factor (CF) assigned to each field. For instance, a user can assign weights on fields like Last Name, First Name, SSN, Date of Birth (DOB) and gender. A CF of 0.9 assigned to the Last Name field means that there is a 90% confidence on the last name being a unique identifier in identifying duplicates. Say, we have two records whose probability of being duplicates is 0.6 (i.e. 60%). Since we associate a confidence of 0.9 with the last name, the overall probability of the two records being duplicates is (0.9 * 0.6*100 = 54%). Secondly, our fuzzy rules find probabilistic duplicates from any dataset. A sample of a Fuzzy JESS rule is shown in Fig 2. Each Fuzzy JESS rule represents IF <conditions> THEN <actions> statements. These rules are heuristic and rely on information obtained from a domain expert. Fuzziness uses the CF to determine probabilistic duplicates. The CF is used to measure the similarity between the indicated base patient record and the retrieved records. The similarity metric relies on a Fuzzy relevance from domain experts.

Thirdly, FuzzyKlean employs the Bigram approach [10] for string comparison. Because pairs of strings often exhibit typographical variation (e.g., Smith versus Smoth), effective string comparison functions are required to address these inconsistencies [14]. Bigrams are known to be a very effective, simply programmed means of dealing with minor typographical errors [10].

The Bigram approach:

a. uses two consecutive letters within a string (e.g., the word "bigram" contains "bi" "ig" "gr" "ra", and "am"),

b. compares two strings and assigns a value between 0 and 1,

c. returns a matched score (i.e., the number of the common bigram divided by the average number of bigrams in the two strings).

```
(defrule checker (basePatient (sex ?x1) (lname ?l1)(fname ?f1) (dob ?dob1) (SSN ? ssn1))
(uncleanPatient (sex ?x2) (lname ?l2) (patient_id ?p2) (legacyid ?leg2)
    (fname ?f2) (middle ?m2) (race ?r2) (SSN ?ssn2) (dob ?dob2)
    (complete ?comp2) (UserName ?uname2) (Modify_Time ?mt2)
    (XrefId ?xref2)) (not (checksex ?x1 ?x2))
        (if (>= ?threshold 0.65) then (assert (dupPatient (sex ?x2) (lname ?l2) (patient_id ?p2)
    (legacyid ?leg2) (fname ?f2) (middle ?m2)
    (race ?r2) (SSN ?ssn2) (dob ?dob2) (complete ?comp2)
    (UserName ?uname2) (Modify_Time ?mt2) (cf ?threshold) (XrefId ?xref2))))) (printout t
\"The records with \" ?l1 \" and \" ?l2 \" match with a threshold of \" ?threshold crlf)
        else (printout t \"The Records \" ?l1 \" and \" ?l2 \" do not match\" crlf)))
```

Fig. 2 An Example of a Fuzzy JESS Rule

Finally, our framework uses templates populated with patient information which form a knowledge base. The rules are then applied to this knowledge base and possible duplicates are found. For the MAHI system, the templates utilized include the Unclean Patient template, Clean Patient template, and Base Patient template. These templates can be created "on-the-fly".

- **Step 3: User's Selection: Merge/Purge Records**

Once the two records are detected as possible duplicates, the merge/purge process is initiated. Two records with a high degree of similarity (high CF) can be merged into a single record. Consider a typical example where there are two records with a matched date of birth and matching last names but there seems to be a typographical error in the first name causing a no-match situation. Decisions regarding records are made based on the information regarding duplicates displayed on a screen. Users make use of this information to decide whether these records should be merged for a consistent, complete and unique record or ignore these records and purge them altogether.

4   Experiments

We tested FuzzyKlean using the MAHI medical patient information databases (http://www.mahi.org). Our testing was performed using Microsoft SQL Server databases on a Pentium4 1.5 GHz machine. The SQL server took a lot of processing time and memory. In both graphs, the x-axis is the test-case number and the y-axis is the number of records. Experimental results illustrate that our framework is extensible and allows rapid detection of invalid data with high precision and efficiency. Fig 3 shows the percentage of probabilistic duplicates shown in the MAHI databases. Fig 4 shows that it took less than 2 minutes to evaluate 10000 records (Test Case 5) with over 96 percent accuracy.

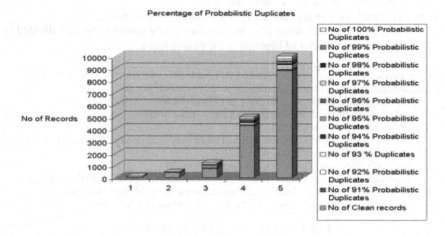

Fig. 3 Experimental Results: Probabilistic Duplicate Analysis

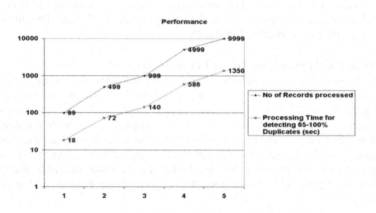

Fig. 4 Experimental Results: FuzzyKlean Performance Analysis

5 Conclusion

Presented here is a fuzzy rule based framework that can efficiently perform data validations. The FuzzyKlean system is based on a fuzzy logic expert system to determine probabilistic data duplicates, increasing the reliability of the data. Experimental results show that our FuzzyKlean framework has the capability of providing fast and high precision duplicate elimination. We are currently working on extending the framework for multiple disparate data sources and metadata.

Acknowledgements. This research was supported in part by the Mid America Heart Institute (MAHI) and University of Missouri Research Board (UMRB). We acknowledge valuable comments from Kelly Kerns, John Spertus, and Jane Vogl.

References

1   Bitton, D., DeWitt, D.J.: Duplicate record elimination in large data files. ACM Transactions on Database Systems, 8(2): 255-65, 1983.

2   Rete, C.F.: A fast algorithm for the many patterns/many objects match problem. Artificial Intelligence, Vol 19. pp. 17-37, 1982.

3   TeleMed: http://www.acl.lanl.gov/TeleMed/NNMRTP/Project.html

4   Galhardas, H., Florescu, D., Shasha, D.: AJAX: An Extensible Data Cleaning Tool , Proc. of ACM SIGMOD Conf. on Management of Data , May , 2000

5   Han, J., Kamber, M.: Data Mining: Concepts and Techniques, Morgan Kaufmann, 1999

6   Hernandez, M.: A generation of band joins and the merge/purge problem. Technical report 005-1995

7   Hernandez, M., Stolfo, S.: The merge/purge problem for large databases. In the proceedings of the ACM SIGMOD International Conference on Management of Data, pp 127-138, 1995.

8   Madison, see http://www.madison-info.com/IDX_Selects_Madison.htm

9   Maletic, I., Marcus, A.: Data Cleansing: Beyond Integrity Analysis, in Proceedings of The Conference on Information Quality, Massachusetts Institute of Technology, 2000, pp. 200-209.

10 Monge, A.E., Elkan, C.P.: The field-matching problem: Algorithms and applications. Proc. of the 2nd Int. Conference on Knowledge Discovery and Data Mining, 1996, pp 267-270.

11 Monge, A.E., Elkan, C.P.: An efficient domain-independent algorithm for detecting approximately duplicate database records, In Proceedings of SIGMOD Workshop on Research Issues on Data Mining and Knowledge Discovery, Tucson, Arizona, 1997.

12 Lee, M., Ling, T.W., Low, W.L.: IntelliClean: A Knowledge Based Intelligent Data Cleaner In Sixth International Conference on Knowledge Discovery and Data Mining, pages 290-294, 2000.

13 Pedersen, T.B., Jensen, C.S.: Research Issues in Clinical Data Warehousing, Proceedings of Tenth International Conference on Scientific and Statistical Database Management, 1998, pp. 43 -52.

14 Porter, E.H., Winkler, W.E.: Approximate String Comparison and its Effect on an Advanced Record Linkage System, Record Linkage Techniques - 1997, 1997, pp. 190-202.

15 Redman, T.: Data Quality for the Information Age, Artech House, 1996.

Classification Learning by Decomposition of Numerical Datasets

Grace J. Hwang and Chun-Chan Tung

Department of Computer Science and Information Engineering
Fu Jen Catholic University, Taipei, Taiwan
{jihwang, andy88}@csie.fju.edu.tw

Abstract. The purpose of a classification algorithm is to predict the class label of a new instance based on the analysis of a training dataset. Many classification algorithms work most naturally with nominal attributes. However, numerical data are very common in real-life applications. In this paper, we present a classification learning for numerical datasets. We adopt the idea of function decomposition, which is an approach used to represent a complex function by simple and smaller subfunctions. We modify the decomposition and apply it to decompose numerical datasets for classification learning. The proposed method is also implemented to evaluate the classification accuracy. The experimental evaluation shows the proposed method is a relatively effective method for classification learning.

1 Introduction

To effectively solve a complex problem, one of the most useful strategies is the technique of "divide-and-conquer". The benefit comes from the fact that a complex problem can be divided into several simple subproblems. In this paper we present a classification method based on function decomposition that inherits the spirit of "divide-and-conquer" and decomposes a complex function into smaller subfunctions.

The function decomposition approach was originally used for the design of switching circuits [1]. Wan and Perkowski [2] modified the approach to decompose incompletely specified switching functions. Luba [3] presented a generalized method for decomposition of multi-valued variables, where each variable is represented by a set of Boolean variables.

Zupan et al. [4] adopted the idea of function decomposition in machine learning. They developed a method to discover a hierarchical concept structure for datasets that contain only nominal-valued attributes and classes. For numerical datasets, Demšal et al. [5] proposed a function decomposition method to construct intermediate concepts for real-valued attributes and classes. In this paper, we develop a classification algorithm for datasets with numerical attributes and nominal-valued classes.

The goal of function decomposition is to replace the initial function with a hierarchy of appropriate subfunctions and variables. Consider a dataset that partially describes a function y = F (X), where X = {x_1, x_2, ... , x_n} is a set of input attributes, and y is the class variable. The decomposition process first divides X into two disjoint subsets A and B, and then defines functions G and H, such that y = H (A, G

H. Yin et al. (Eds.): IDEAL 2002, LNCS 2412, pp. 454–460, 2002.
© Springer-Verlag Berlin Heidelberg 2002

(B)). Note that both functions of G and H are constructed during the process and are not predefined in any way. The decomposition process can be applied further on G and H and so on. As a result of the recursive procedure, a concept hierarchy is generally produced (Fig.1).

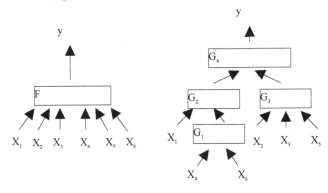

Fig. 1. The initial function (left) and a hierarchy of decomposition functions (right)

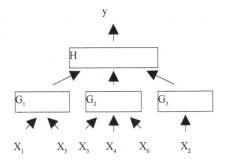

Fig. 2. Two-stage function decomposition

For each decomposition step, the crucial problem is to determine the splitting on the attribute set being considered. For instance, the first function decomposition needs to investigate all possible partitions of X to A and B. An optimal partition is selected to minimize some complexity measure such that the complexity of $y = H (A, G (B))$ is lower than that of $y = F (X)$. A similar problem is occurred on each recursive procedure.

In order to cope with high time complexity of finding an optimal partition for each decomposition step, we propose a heuristic method to divide attributes. The process can be considered as a two-stage function decomposition, whose simple counterpart is shown in Fig. 2. The technique works bottom-up by partitioning the attribute set $X = \{x_1, x_2, \ldots, x_6\}$ into subsets, say $\{x_1, x_5\}$, $\{x_3, x_4, x_6\}$ and $\{x_2\}$, and constructing intermediate decision functions G_1, G_2 and G_3. As a result of this step, all of the attributes are replaced by intermediate decision functions. The last step is to define the final decision function H, which is determined by G_1, G_2 and G_3. In the following section, we will describe the proposed method in detail.

2   Our Decomposition Method

As mentioned in the preceding section, we propose a method of two-stage function decomposition.   Unlike the original function decomposition that partitions the considered attribute set into two disjoint subsets on each recursive decomposition, we partition the whole attribute set into several disjoint subsets for one time only. For each disjoint subset, an intermediate decision function is then determined.   All of these functions are used to construct the final decision function. The process can be stated as the following four steps:

Step 1. Partition the attribute set.
Step 2. Discretize numerical attributes.
Step 3. Construct intermediate decision tables.
Step 4. Determine the final decision table.

The detailed description of each step is described below.

2.1   Partition of the Attribute Set

As we mentioned earlier, we require datasets that consist of numerical attributes only. Therefore, it is natural to consider a statistical technique in the partitioning process. Multivariate methods in statistics such as factor analysis may be considered. Multivariate methods are extremely useful to determine whether massive amounts of data actually contain information, and they also help to summarize the information when it exists. Factor analysis is a multivariate technique and is frequently used to reduce a large number of attributes to a smaller set of uncorrelated groups, called factors. In a factor analysis process, attributes are partitioned into several groups, and the attributes distributed in the same group are more highly related than those attributes in other groups.   Therefore, a subfunction may be made suitably on the basis of the attributes within the same group.   That is, the attribute set of X can be divided into several uncorrelated groups (see Fig. 2). Each of them is then used to construct an intermediate decision function.   For a detailed description of factor analysis, the reader may refer to textbooks of multivariate methods, for instance [6,7].

2.2   Discretization of Numerical Attributes

After splitting the attribute set into several uncorrelated groups, intermediate decision functions will be constructed next.   To derive a new intermediate decision function for a certain group of attributes, we may observe the behavior of attribute values in the group. Since our datasets contain numerical attributes in which each attribute has an infinite domain generally. It is difficult to discover an appropriate concept for an intermediate decision function. One possible solution to deal with the problem is to descretize the numerical attributes.   Discretization is a technique to partition a numerical attribute into a number of intervals and assign each one as a nominal value. A variety of discretization methods have been proposed recently [8]. In our implementation, the method of the equal-frequency-intervals is applied for its simplicity.   The method divides the range of a numerical attribute into a predetermined number of bins, each of them containing the same number of instances.

2.3 Construction of Intermediate Decision Tables

After the discretization, it is ready to define intermediate decision functions as tabular forms. To construct an intermediate decision function on the basis of the attributes within a certain group, we develop a procedure based on the following steps:

(Step3.1) Compute the frequency of each class for each combination of attribute values in the group.
(Step3.2) Find the percentages of the distribution of class labels for each combination of attribute values in the group.
(Step3.3) Build a "binary table", where each entry in the table is either 0 or 1.
(Step3.4) Construct an intermediate decision table for the attributes of this group.

We illustrate the above process by an example. Suppose that a dataset has three numerical attributes x_1, x_2 and x_3 and one class label y with values a and b. After discretization in step 2, assume that x_1 is converted into values 1 and 2, and both x_2 and x_3 are transformed to values 1, 2 and 3. Table 1 shows the resulting discretized dataset. The instances of dataset partially specify a function y = F (x_1, x_2, x_3). If the attributes are partitioned into $A_1 = (x_1, x_2)$ and $A_2 = (x_3)$ in step 1, the goal of step 3 is to construct intermediate decision functions G_1 and G_2 such that the initial function y = F (x_1, x_2, x_3) becomes y = H $(G_1(x_1, x_2), G_2(x_3))$.
    In order to demonstrate the basic working of steps (Step 3.1) – (Step 3.4), the construction for $c_1 = G_1 (x_1, x_2)$ is described. In this case, we only concern the first row of the class labels and the next two rows of attribute values x_1 and x_2 in Table 1. Tables 2 and 3 show how we would proceed after Step 3.1 and Step 3.2.
    Each entry in Table 3 indicates how each combination of attribute values (column values) is related with the class label (row value). A higher percentage implies more related dependence. Therefore, we convert a percentage to be 1 if it exceeds a user-defined threshold•. Otherwise we convert the percentage to be 0. If we setε= 40% in our example, then the resulting "binary table" is shown in Table 4.
    To determine an intermediate decision table, we observe the combination of binary digits for each column. Columns that have the same pattern of binary digits are considered compatible and can be mapped to the same value of c_1. One simple way to generate the values of c_1 is to consider the sequence of binary digits in each column as a binary number and convert it to decimal. The bottom row of Table 4 illustrates the conversion and gives an example of the intermediate decision values of c_1. A similar process would produce $c_2 = G_2 (x_3)$ and is not shown here. The dataset in Table 1 can now be represented by Table 5, in which intermediate decision values c_1 and c_2 replace all attributes in Table 1.

2.4 Determination of the Final Decision Table

The last step of the method is to build a final decision table. The process to determine the final decision table is based on the result of step 3, i.e., Table 5 in our example. The procedure of step 4 is listed as follows.

(Step 4.1) Compute the frequency of each class for each combination of intermediate values.

(Step 4.2) Find the percentages of the distribution of class labels for each combination of intermediate values.

(Step 4.3) Build a final decision table. For each combination of intermediate values, assign the class label with the highest percentage (in the event of a tie, choose one at random).

The processes of Step 4.1 and Step 4.2 are similar to those of Step 3.1 and Step 3.2, respectively. We skip these steps and show the result of Step 4.3 in Table 6.

Table 1. Discretized dataset, in which instances partially describe the function $y = F(x_1, x_2, x_3)$

y	a	b	a	b	a	a	a	a	b	b	a
X_1	1	1	1	1	1	1	1	2	2	2	2
X_2	1	1	2	2	2	3	3	1	2	2	3
X_3	1	2	1	2	3	1	3	1	1	3	1

Table 2. Class frequencies for each combination of attribute values in the group of $\{X_1, X_2\}$

X_1	1	1	1	2	2	2
X_2	1	2	3	1	2	3
a	1	2	2	1	0	1
b	1	1	0	0	2	0
Total	2	3	2	1	2	1

Table 3. Class distributions for each combination of attribute values in the group of $\{X_1, X_2\}$

X_1	1	1	1	2	2	2
X_2	1	2	3	1	2	3
a	50%	67%	100%	100%	0%	100%
b	50%	33%	0%	0%	100%	0%

Table 4. A binary table with column label c_1 for the group of $\{X_1, X_2\}$

X_1	1	1	1	2	2	2
X_2	1	2	3	1	2	3
a	1	1	1	1	0	1
b	1	0	0	0	1	0
c_1	3	2	2	2	1	2

Table 5. An alternative representation of dataset in Table 1

y	a	b	a	b	a	a	a	a	b	b	a
c_1	3	3	2	2	2	2	2	2	1	1	2
c_2	2	1	2	1	2	2	2	2	2	2	2

Table 6. The final decision table

c_1	1	1	2	2	3	3
c_2	1	2	1	2	1	2
y	a	b	b	a	b	a

3 Experimental Results

To test the effectiveness of the proposed method, we compared our approach with C5.0. Both methods were evaluated on 4 well-known datasets from the UCI repository [9]. These four datasets are *Liver*, *Iris*, *Diabetes* and *Heart*. Since our method is restricted to numerical datasets, we extracted numerical attributes from the tested datasets in our evaluation. The evaluation was run for tenfold cross-validation. The initial dataset is divided randomly into 10 parts. Each experiment takes a single part in turn as a test set and remaining 9 parts as a training set.

For each dataset, Table 7 presents the average classification accuracies for both the proposed method and C5.0, and the last column shows the significance of the difference between these two methods for a paired t-test. With respect to the average accuracies shown in columns 2 and 3, our decomposition method outperforms C5.0 for all datasets except *Iris*. From Table 7, we observe a significant increase of performance occurred on *Diabetes* and *Heart* datasets, while no significant difference occurred on *Iris* and *Liver* datasets. It indicates that our method tends to compete well against C5.0.

Table. 7. Classification accuracies

Dataset	Our Method	C5.0	t-test
Diabetes	**80.9 ± 2.9**	71.0 ± 8.4	99.5%
Heart	**81.5 ± 4.3**	72.0 ± 7.9	97.5%
Iris	94.0 ± 8.0	**95.6 ± 5.1**	36.9%
Liver	**67.7 ± 8.9**	63.5 ± 10.3	82.8%

4   Conclusions

The proposed decomposition method provides a new classification algorithm for datasets with numerical attributes and nominal-valued classes. Its important aspects are (a) using factor analysis as a technique for function decomposition and (b) developing systematic ways to construct intermediate and the final decision tables. Experiments show that the proposed method is a relatively effective method for classification learning. Further work may consider the approach to handle noisy data.

References

1.   Curtis, H. A. (1962).   A New approach to the Design of Switching Functions.   Van Nostrand, Princeton, N. J.
2.   Wan, W., Perkowski, M. A.   (1992).   A New Approach to the Decomposition of Incompletely Specified Functions Based on Graph-Coloring and Local Transformations and Its Application to FPGA Mapping. In Proc. Of the IEEE EURO-DAC '92, pages230-235, Hamburg.
3.   Luba, T. (1995). Decomposition of Multiple-Valued Functions. In 25th Intl. Symposium on Multiple-valued Logic, Bloomington, Indiana, pages 256-261.
4.   Zupan, B., Bohanec, M., Bratko, I. and Demšar, J. (1997). Machine Learning by Function Decomposition.   In Proc. Fourteenth International Conference on Machine Learning (ICML-97), pages 421-429, San Mateo, CA.
5.   Demšar, J., Zupan, B., Bohanec, M. and Bratko, I. (1997).   Constructing Intermediate Concepts by Decomposition of Real Functions.   In Proc. European Conference on Machine Learning, ECML-97, pages 93-107, Prague.
6.   Hair, J. Jr., Anderson, R., Tatham, R., and Black, W. (1998). Multivariate Data Analysis, 5th ed. Upper Saddel River, N.J., Prentice-Hall.

7. Johnson, R. and Wichen, D. (1998). Applied Multivariate Statistical Analysis, 4th ed. Upper Saddel River, N.J. Prentice-Hall.
8. Dougherty, J., Kohavi, R. and Shami, M. (1995). Supervised and Unsupervised Discretization of Continuous Features. In Machine Learning: Proceedings of the twelfth International Conference. Morgan kaufmann.
9. Blake, C.L. and Merz. C.J. (1998). UCI Repository of machine learning databases [http://www.ics.uci.edu/~mlearn].

Combining Feature Selection with Feature Weighting for k-NN Classifier

Yongguang Bao[1], Xiaoyong Du[2], and Naohiro Ishii[1]

[1] Department of Intelligence and Computer Science, Nagoya Institute of Technology, Nagoya, 466-8555, Japan
{baoyg, ishii}@egg.ics.nitech.ac.jp
[2] School of Information, Renmin University of China, 100872, Beijing, China
Duyong@mail.ruc.edu.cn

Abstract. The k-nearest neighbor (k-NN) classification is a simple and effective classification approach. However, it suffers from over-sensitivity problem due to irrelevant and noisy features. In this paper, we propose an algorithm to improve the effectiveness of k-NN by combining these two approaches. Specifically, we select all relevant features firstly, and then assign a weight to each one. Experimental results show that our algorithm achieves the highest accuracy or near to the highest accuracy on all test datasets. It also achieves higher generalization accuracy compared with the well-known algorithms IB1-4 and C4.5.

1 Introduction

Nearest neighbor (more precisely, k-nearest neighbor, or k-NN) classifiers have been shown very effective in practice for many problem domains. While the framework of k-NN was originally proposed as a tool for pattern recognition, it is widely used in many applications of intelligent systems such as speech processing, medical diagnosis, molecular biology, and others. It is based on the assumption that if we represent each object as a point in a space, then those points that are close in the space should belong to the same class. Therefore, an unseen point should be classified as the majority class of its k (k≥1) nearest neighbors in the training dataset. However, in its basic form, the k-nearest neighbor algorithm has several weaknesses: 1) large storage is required; 2) selection of k is difficult; 3) it suffers from over-sensitivity to the irrelevant and noisy features.

The k-NN is quite effective when the features of the dataset are equally important, but it is less effective when many of the features are misleading or irrelevant to the classification. There are two basic ways to improve the k-nearest neighbor method. One is feature selection. It selects a subset of features that are critical to a classification task, and removes those that are irrelevant. Aha [3], Cardie [8] *et al.* have reported the improved results in accuracy over the simple k-NN by different feature selections. The other one is feature weighting. It assigns a numerical value between 0 and 1 to each feature as a measure of feature relevancy or importance to improve the accuracy of the simple k-NN. In

H. Yin et al. (Eds.): IDEAL 2002, LNCS 2412, pp. 461–468, 2002.

this direction, many papers (e.g., [2,5,11]) focus on how to compute the weights. Aha [4] has surveyed the work on feature weighting.

Although both feature selection and feature weighting can improve classification accuracy, it is still difficult to predict which one is better for a specific dataset [11]. In some cases, there is distinct difference between these two algorithms. These two ways reflect two extreme viewpoints for feature relevancy to a classification task. The simple k-NN method gives equal weight 1 to all features, as shown in Fig. 1(a). The disadvantage of using the feature selection method is that it treats a feature as completely relevant or irrelevant and set the degree of relevance as either 0 or 1 (Fig. 1(b)). However, the degree of relevance may in fact be a value between 0 and 1. The feature weighting method assigns each feature a weight, which is a real number between 0 and 1 (Fig. 1(c)).

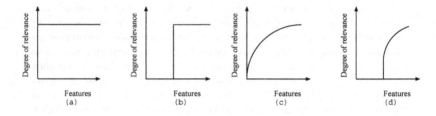

Fig. 1. Feature weighting

In this paper, we focus on a combination of the feature selection and feature weighting method by which only weights of the relevant features are considered. Specifically, we use the feature selection algorithm FS-CBC [6] to select a feature subset firstly, and then assign an information gain (IG) to each selected feature as its weight and set 0 as unselected feature (irrelevant feature) weights (Fig. 1(d)). Experiments have been conducted on 14 datasets from the UCI Machine Learning Repository. The results show that combining feature selection and feature weighting achieves the highest accuracy or near to the highest accuracy on all test datasets. It relaxes the sensitivity of the algorithm to datasets and also reduces the storage requirements by feature selection.

The remainder of this paper is organized as follows: Section 2 introduces how to compute information gain. In Sections 3, we discuss how to select features. Section 4 presents a group of comparison experiments and the empirical results. Concluding remarks are given in the final section.

2   Computation of Information Gain

Information theory answers two fundamental questions in communication theory. One is entropy that is an average measure of uncertainty of a random variable. Let X be a discrete random variable with alphabet A and probability mass function $p(x) = Pr\{X = x\}, x \in \Re$.

Definition 1 (Entropy). *The entropy $H(X)$ of a discrete random variable X is defined by*

$$H(X) = -\sum p(x)log(p(x))$$

The *log* function is to the base 2 and entropy is expressed in bits. For example, the entropy of a fair coin toss is 1 bit. We will use the convention that $0\,log0 = 0$, which is easily justified by continuity since $xlogx \to 0$ as $x \to 0$. Thus adding terms of zero probability does not change the entropy.

Definition 2 (Conditional Entropy). *If $(X,Y) \sim p(x,y)$, then the conditional entropy $H(Y|X)$ is defined as*

$$H(Y|X) = -\sum p(x)H(Y|X = x) = -\sum p(x)\sum p(y|x)log(p(y|x))$$
$$= -\sum\sum p(x,y)log(p(y|x))$$

We now introduce the concept of mutual information, a measure of the amount of information that one random variable contains about another random variable. It is the reduction in the uncertainty of one random variable due to the knowledge of the other.

Definition 3 (Mutual Information). *Consider two random variables X and Y with a joint probability mass function $p(x,y)$ and marginal and probability mass functions $p(x)$ and $p(y)$. The mutual information $I(X,Y)$ is the relative entropy between the joint distribution and the product distribution $p(x)p(y)$, i.e.*

$$I(X,Y) = \sum\sum p(x,y)log(\frac{p(x,y)}{p(x)p(y)})$$

From the definition we have
$$I(X,Y) = H(X) - H(X|Y) = H(Y) - H(Y|X)$$
$I(X,Y)$ is the measure of the dependence between the two random variables. It is symmetric in X and Y and is always nonnegative.

Let X be a class attribute D, and Y a condition attribute A, and we call $I(X,Y)$ the information gain (IG). ID3 [15] uses IG to select features to construct the best decision tree. IG will also be used for feature weighting in our algorithm

3   Feature Selection Based on CORE, Binary Mutual Information, and Class Mutual Information (FS-CBC)

Feature selection can reduce the task's dimensionality when it eliminates irrelevant features and thus improve data quality. Many heuristic methods (e.g., [7,17,15,16]) based on information theory have been proposed for feature selection. Bao *et al.* [6] proposed a hybrid effective algorithm FS-CBC. It selects features based on CORE [14], binary mutual Information and class mutual information. In the following, we give some definitions relevant to algorithm FS-CBC firstly.

Definition 4 (Binary Mutual Entropy). *Let X be a class attribute D, F be a feature and the domain of F be $f_1, f_2, ..., f_m$, for each f_k we can get two classes $F = f_k$ and $F \neq f_k$, and for these two classes we can calculate the mutual information and denote it by $I(X, F, k)$, i.e.*

$$I(X, F, k) = H(X) - p(F = f_k) \times H(X|F = f_k) - p(F \neq f_k) \times H(X|F \neq f_k)$$

We call the maximum of $I(X, F, k)(1 \leq k \leq m)$ binary mutual information of feature F denoted by $BH(x|F)$, i.e.

$$BI(X, F) = \max_{k=1,2,...,m} (I(X, F, k))$$

From the above definition we have the following property.

Proposition 1. *For a binary feature F, we have $BI(X, Y) = I(X, Y)$.*

For the feature set $(S_1, S_2, ..., S_m)$, we know that the values of this set belong to $VS_1 \times VS_2 \times ... \times VS_m$, where VS_k is the domain of feature S_k.

Definition 5 (Class Mutual Informatioy). *Let $S = (S_1, S_2, ..., S_m)$ be a feature set, we take it as a random variable, and its domain is $VS_1 \times VS_2 \times ... \times VS_m$. We call the mutual information of S class mutual informtation and denoted it as $CI(X, S)$, i.e. $CI(X, S) = H(X) - H(X|S)$.*

From the above definition we have the following property.

Proposition 2. *For a single feature set S, we have $CI(X, S) = I(X, S)$.*

Based on rough sets theory [14], CORE is the set of all indispensable features and the most essential part of the information system. The features in CORE must be included whatever in an optimal subset or in an approximate subset. Hence, it is reasonable to select features in CORE firstly. FGMIFS [12] selects the first feature that has the largest information gain ratio. However, it overly reduces the tendency to choose features with more distinct values. Instead, FS-CBC uses the binary mutual information to balance the effect of many values and information gain. So when CORE is empty, the first feature is selected by using the largest binary mutual information. FS-CBC uses the class mutual information to select the next feature in order to consider the previously selected features. Now, we describe our feature selection algorithm in detail, as shown in Fig. 2. Let C be a set of whole condition features, D be a class feature, S be a subset of the selected features, P be a subset of unselected features, and k_0 be a stop criterion which is always set to 0 or a small number.

4   Experiments and Results

For evaluating the effectiveness of our algorithm, the proposed algorithm was compared with some variants of the k-nearest neighbor classification algorithm on the classification accuracy. The data sets used in experiments are downloaded from the UCI Machine Learning Repository [13]. Table 1 shows the basic

In the initial state, set $S = \emptyset$, $P = C$, set stop threshold k_0.

Step 1 Calculate CORE(C,D) and set S=CORE(C,D),

P= C-CORE(C,D);

If $P <> \emptyset$, then go to Step 2;

Otherwise select the first feature:

For each p in P, calculate $BI(D,p)$. Choose p from

P that maximizes $BI(D,p)$;

Set $S = \{p\}$ and $P = P - \{p\}$;

Step 2 Calculate class mutual information k,

$k = CH(D|S)$;

If $k \leq k_0$, then stop.

Step 3 For each p in P, calculate

$V = CI(D, \{p\}S)$;

$M = $ class number $(\{p\}S)$;

Step 4 Choose the feature p with the maximum value V.

If there are two features p and q, and both of them make the

value V maximal, so the one with the smaller class number

M should be selected.

$S = S\{p\}$;

$P = P - \{p\}$;

Step 5 Go back to step 2.

Fig. 2. Algorithm FS-CBC

characteristics of the datasets. The "Train" column shows the size of the total dataset. But for Monk1 and Monk3, the "Train" and "Test" column shows the size of the training data and test data. The "Class" column shows the number of the class. The "Feature" column shows the number of condition features and types (L=Linear, N=Nominal, C=Continuous), and the "noise" column shows the percentage of noise in the total data.

For each dataset (with no test dataset), we use the 5-fold cross validation, i.e., the whole dataset is divided into five subsets. Four of the subsets are used as a training set, and the fifth as the test set. This process is repeated five times, once for each subset being the test set. Then, the average of these five runs is taken as classification accuracy. The stop threshold k_0 in algorithm FS-CBC is 0.

In the simulation, we use k = 3, majority voting, normalized Euclidean distance for linear/continuous attributes and the overlap metric for nominal attributes. For the missing value, we just set it as a new value in process of feature selection and take the greatest possible distance as the distance between object with missing value and other object when computing weight. For continuous attributes, we partition the range of values into a finite number of intervals with equal length, and treat each interval as a distinct value of feature.

To see how our algorithm fares compared with the simple k-nearest neighbor algorithm (k-NN), feature selection (FS) and feature weighting (FW). We con-

Table 1. Basic characteristics of the datasets

Data Set	Train	Test	Class	Feature	Noise
Monk1	124	432	2	L6	
Monk3	122	432	2	L6	5%
LED+noise	200		10	N7	10.14%
LED+17	200		10	N24	
LED+17noise	200		10	N24	8.79%
Breast	699		2	L9	
Vote	435		2	N16	
Credit	690		2	C6N9	
Glass	214		7	C9	
Wine	178		3	C13	
Iris	150		3	C4	
Ionosphere	351		2	C34	
Pima	768		2	C8	
Bupa	345		2	C6	

sider the following four possible combinations of feature selection and feature weighting.

(1) k-NN: also known as the simple k-NN algorithm, which treats all features equally, gives equal weight 1 to all features.

(2) FS: consider only those features selected by the algorithm FS-CBC, which give weight 1 to the selected features and set 0 as unselected feature weights.

(3) FW: assign each feature with the corresponding information gains $I(D, c)$ as their weights.

(4) SW: assign each feature, which is selected by the algorithm FS-CBC, with the corresponding information gains $I(D, c)$ as their weights, and set 0 as unselected feature weights.

To see how SW fares compared with other popular machine learning algorithms, the results of running SW are slao compared with the following systems: C4.5 system (release 8)[16], which is a well-known inductive decision tree algorithm and IB1-4 [1], which are four instance-based learning algorithms.

Table 2. Generalization accuracy of the basic k-NN, FS, FW, SW, IB1-4 and C4.5

Data Set	k-NN	k-NN/D	FW	FS	SW	SFN	IB1	IB2	IB3	IB4	C4.5	C4.5/P
Monk1	73.84	73.84	80.32	100	100	3	73.9	74.2	100	100	76.6	75.7
Monk3	83.33	83.33	95.37	91.67	94.44	4	93.5	93.5	93.5	90.3	92.6	**97.2**
LED+noise	69.64	69.64	69.09	69.64	69.09	7	**72.42**	63.16	69.10	69.80	69.08	69.08
LED+17	64.64	64.64	100	100	100	5	61.16	56.60	50.36	98.52	100	100
LED+17noise	36.35	36.35	**68.93**	55.68	64.17	11.2	33.96	34.92	36.88	62.18	59.12	60.38
Breast	96.13	96.13	96.42	**97.13**	96.84	4	95.26	92.86	95.00	95.82	93.96	93.68
Vote	94.05	94.05	**95.87**	92.43	94.07	8	92.48	91.70	92.14	94.24	93.32	94.94
Credit	82.61	82.75	83.49	82.75	83.49	15	81.48	74.94	83.66	84.64	83.94	**86.56**
Glass	62.94	69.70	70.33	70.46	**72.57**	6	67.70	62.62	63.62	65.88	71.58	71.58
Wine	95.99	94.82	93.64	98.24	**99.41**	4	94.24	87.42	87.04	85.98	93.86	93.86
Iris	96.67	**97.34**	96.67	96.00	96.67	3	96.00	84.00	86.68	88.00	95.00	95.00
Ionosphere	85.47	85.18	86.62	88.32	**89.46**	4.8	86.04	86.32	82.60	80.04	87.46	87.74
Pima	70.45	67.84	71.23	67.84	71.23	8	70.56	67.46	70.02	69.68	72.38	**72.68**
Bupa	62.03	61.16	64.35	61.16	64.35	6	60.58	62.04	58.26	56.54	65.52	**65.82**
Average	76.73	76.91	83.74	83.67	**85.41**	64.76%	77.81	73.70	76.35	81.54	82.46	83.16

Table 2 shows the comparison of generalization accuracy. The "k-NN" column shows average accuracy of classification using the simple k-NN algorithm. For reference, we give the generalization accuracy after the discretization, as column "k-NN/D" for some datasets with continuous features. The columns "FW", "FS", "SW", "IB1", "IB2", "IB3", "IB4", "C4.5" and "C4.5/P" report average accuracy of classification on the discretization data using method FS, FW and SW, IB1-4, C4.5 respectively. The highest accuracy achieved for each dataset is shown in bold type. The average over all datasets are shown at the bottom of the table. The average number of selected condition features in each training data is also shown in the last column "SFN" of Table 2.

As can be seen in Table 2, SW, FS and FW all improve the accuracy of k-NN respectively. Using FS-CBC algorithm to select features increases the average accuracy by 6.94%. Using information gain as the measure of relevance of the features also results in improvement, on the average increasing accuracy 7.01%. Algorithm SW produces a further improvement, achieving the highest or nearly the highest accuracy on all test datasets when compared with FS and FW. It increases accuracy 8.68% as compared with k-NN. The results indicate that combining feature selection with feature weighting can substantially improve the accuracy of k-NN more, while it reduces the storage requirements to 64.76%.

When compared with IB1-4 and C4.5, although there is no algorithm that has the highest accuracy on all the datasets, SW achieves the highest or nearly the highest accuracy. It also has the highest overall average generalization accuracy. Although the results presented above are theoretically limited to this set of applications, the results indicate that SW is a robust and effective classifier that can be successfully applied to a variety of real-world problems.

5   Conclusions

This study shows that combining feature selection and feature weighting is very effective for the k-nearest neighbor classification algorithm by a set of empirical experiments. In our algorithm, we first use class mutual information for feature selection, starting from the rough sets CORE. If CORE is empty we use binary mutual information for the first feature selection. Then we assign an information gain to each selected relevant feature as its weight.

In the experiments on 14 datasets, SW significantly improved the generalization accuracy of k-NN and reduced the storage requirements by feature selection. Compared with the popular learning algorithms IB1-4 and C4.5, SW achieved the highest accuracy or near to the highest accuracy on all test datasets as well as a higher average generalization accuracy.

References

1. D.W. Aha, D. Kibler & M.K. Albert, "Instance-Based Learning Algorithms", Machine Learning, Vol. 6, 1991,pp. 37-66.

2. D.W. Aha, "Tolerating Noisy, Irrelevant and Novel Attributes in Instance-Based Learning Algorithm", International Journal of Man-Machine Studies, Vol.36, No.1, 1992, pp. 267-287.

3. D.W. Aha & R.L. Bankert, "Feature Selection for Case-Based Classification of Cloud Types: An Empirical Comparison", In D.W. Aha (Ed.) Case-Based Reasoning: Papers from the 1994 Worksho ((TR WS-94-10), Menlo Park, CA: AAAI press.

4. D.W. Aha, "Feature Weighting for Lazy Learning Algorithms", In H. Liu & H. Motoda (Eds.) Feature Extraction, Construction and Selection: A Data Mining Perspective, Norwell MA: Kluwer, 1998.

5. N.F. Ayan, "Using Information Gain as Feature Weight", 8th Turkish Symposium on Artificial Intelligence and Neural Networks (TAINN'99), Istanbul, Turkey, June 1999.

6. Y. Bao, X. Du & N. Ishii, "Using Rough Sets and Class Mutual Information for Feature Selection", 6th International Conference on Soft Computing, IIZUKA2000, pp. 452-458.

7. R. Battiti, "Using Mutual Information for Selection Features in Supervised Neural Net Learning," IEEE Trans. On Neural Networks, 5(4), 1994, pp. 537-550.

8. C. Cardie, "A Cognitive Bias Approach to Feature Selection and Weighting for Case-Based Learners", Machine Learning, Vol. 41, 2000, pp. 85-116.

9. T.M. Cover & P.E. Hart, "Nearest Neighbor Pattern Classification", IEEE Transactions on Information Theory, Vol. 13, No.1, 1967, pp. 21-27.

10. T.M. Cover & J.A. Thomas, Elements of Information Theory, 1991.

11. R. Kohavi, P. Langley & Y. Yun, "The Utility of Feature Weighting in Nearest Neighbor Algorithms", ECML-97 (poster).

12. K.C. Lee, "A Technique of Dynamic Feature Selection Using the Feature Group Mutual Information", Third Pacific Asia Conference, PAKDD-99, LNAI 1574, 1999, pp. 138-142.

13. C.J. Merz & P.M. Murphy, 1998, UCI Repository of Machine Learning Databases, Irvine, CA: University of California Irvine, Department of Information and Computer Science, Internet: http://www.ics.uci.edu/ mlearn/MLRepos itory.html.

14. Z. Pawlak, ROUGH SETS (Theoretical Aspects of Reasoning about Data), Kluwer (1991).

15. J.R. Quinlan, "Induction of Decision Trees". Machine Learning 1(1), 1986, pp. 81-106.

16. J.R. Quinlan, C4.5: Programs for Machine Learning, Morgan Kaufmann, 1993.

Pattern Selection for Support Vector Classifiers

Hyunjung Shin and Sungzoon Cho

Department of Industrial Engineering, Seoul National University,
San 56-1, Shillim-Dong, Kwanak-Gu, 151-742, Seoul, Korea
{hjshin72, zoon}@snu.ac.kr

Abstract. SVMs tend to take a very long time to train with a large data set. If "redundant" patterns are identified and deleted in pre-processing, the training time could be reduced significantly. We propose a k-nearest neighbors(k-NN) based pattern selection method. The method tries to select the patterns that are near the decision boundary and that are correctly labeled. The simulations over synthetic data sets showed promising results: (1) By converting a non-separable problem to a separable one, the search for an optimal error tolerance parameter became unnecessary. (2) SVM training time decreased by two orders of magnitude without any loss of accuracy. (3) The redundant SVs were substantially reduced.

1 Introduction

The support vector machine(SVM) methodology introduced in [2], is receiving increasing attention in recent years due to its clear-cut theory and practical performance [3][8]. However, difficulty arises when a large set of training patterns is given. The time and memory requirements to solve the quadratic programming increase almost exponentially since the number of training patterns equals to the number of constraints. Given that "critical" patterns in SVMs are only a few near the decision boundary, most patterns except them could be considered of no use or even harmful.

One way to circumvent this difficulty is to select only the critical patterns. There have been various methods reported in the literature. In [4], the Mahalanobis distance was used between class core and each pattern to find the boundary patterns. In [6], they implement RBF classifiers, somewhat like SVMs, by selecting patterns near the decision boundary. They propose 1-nearest neighbor method in opposite class after class-wise clustering. But this method presumes that the training set should be clean. In [7], the clean patterns near the decision boundary are selected based on the bias and variance of outputs of a network ensemble. This approach is successful in selecting intended and relevant patterns, though it requires additional time for training a network ensemble. A pattern selection approach, specifically designed for SVMs, is proposed in [1]. They conduct k-means clustering on the entire training set first. Then only the centroids are selected for a homogeneous composition(same class label) while all patterns are selected for a mixed composition. Their approach seems to be successful but a difficulty still remains: how to determine k, the number of clusters.

H. Yin et al. (Eds.): IDEAL 2002, LNCS 2412, pp. 469–474, 2002.
© Springer-Verlag Berlin Heidelberg 2002

In this paper, we propose a k-nearest neighbors(k-NN) based method. The idea is to select those patterns with a correct class label near the decision boundary. It is simple and computationally efficient. These are pertinent properties as a preprocessor.

In section 2, the proposed method is introduced with its motives and algorithm in detail. In section 3, simulations over synthetic data sets are shown. In section 4, a conclusion as well as a future research work is given.

2   Proposed Algorithm for Pattern Selection

The proposed method tries to select the patterns that are located near the boundary and are correctly labeled. In order to do that, two quantitative measures are introduced, **"proximity"** and **"correctness"**. First, we introduce proximity. A pattern near the decision boundary tends to have neighbors with mixed class labels. Thus, the entropy of k-nearest neighbors' class labels can estimate the proximity. We select those patterns with "positive" proximity values. Among them, we want to choose only those with a correct class label. We define correctness as k-NN's voting probability to the pattern's correct class label. We select only those patterns whose correctness is larger than a threshold, set to $\frac{1}{J}$ (J is the number of classes) in our experiments. The effect is as follows: among those patterns near the boundary, the pattern whose class label is same as its neighbors' major class label is regarded as a correct pattern near the decision boundary. On the other hand, the pattern whose class label disagrees with its neighbors' major class label is discarded. Fig. 1 shows the conceptual procedure of the proposed approach. By proximity, patterns near the decision boundary are first selected (a→b). Then by correctness only the clean patterns are selected among them (b→c). Fig. 2 presents the algorithm.

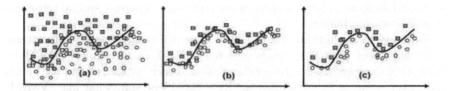

Fig. 1. Conceptual procedure to select the "clean" patterns near the decision boundary.

3   Results

The proposed method was tested on two artificial binary classification problems. All simulations were performed on a PENTIUM PC using the Gunn's SVM MATLAB code [5]. The first problem is a continuous XOR problem. From the four gaussian distributions, a total of 600 training patterns were generated.

1. Find the k nearest neighbors for pattern $\boldsymbol{x}$.
2. For $\boldsymbol{x}$, calculate the voting probabilities of k nearest neighbors over J classes.

$$P_j(\boldsymbol{x}) = \frac{\sum_{i=1}^{k} 1 \text{ if } F_i(\boldsymbol{x})=j}{k}, \quad i = 1,\ldots,k, \quad j = 1,\ldots,J.$$

where $F_i(\boldsymbol{x})$ is the label of the ith nearest neighbor of $\boldsymbol{x}$, $F_i(\cdot) \in \{1,\ldots,J\}$.
$F_0(\boldsymbol{x})$ is defined as the label of $\boldsymbol{x}$ itself.
3. Calculate $\boldsymbol{x}$'s proximity to the decision boundary.
   proximity $(\boldsymbol{x}) = \sum_{j=1}^{J} P_j(\boldsymbol{x}) \log_{|J|} \frac{1}{P_j(\boldsymbol{x})}$.
   In all calculations, 0log0 is defined to be 0.
4. Calculate $\boldsymbol{x}$'s correctness.
   correctness $(\boldsymbol{x}) = P_{j^*}^*(\boldsymbol{x})$ where $j^* = F_0(\boldsymbol{x})$.
5. Apply 1 through 4 to all $\boldsymbol{x}_s$ in the training set.
6. Select the patterns satisfying the following conditions.
   proximity $(\cdot) > 0$ and **correctness** $(\cdot) \geq \frac{1}{J}$.

Fig. 2. Pattern selection algorithm

Because of an overlap between the distributions, there are about 10% innate noise patterns, i.e., having an incorrect class label near the decision boundary.

PROBLEM(A) :   class(1)=$\{(x_1,x_2)\,|N\left(C,0.5^2I\right)$ where $C=(1,1)$ or $(-1,-1)\}$,
class(2)=$\{(x_1,x_2)\,|N\left(C,0.5^2I\right)$ where $C=(-1,1)$or$(1,-1)\}$,
where $-3 \leq x_1 \leq 3$ and $-3 \leq x_2 \leq 3$.

In the second problem, patterns were generated from the two-dimensional uniform distribution, and then class labels were determined by a decision function. In this problem, four different gaussian noises were added on purpose along the decision boundary, i.e., $N(a,b^2)$ where $a =$ point on the decision boundary and $b =$ gaussian width parameter(0.1, 0.3, 0.8, 1.0). Among 500 training patterns, 20% were incorrectly labeled.

PROBLEM(B) :   class(1)=$\{(x_1,x_2)\,|x_2 > \sin\left(3x_1+0.8\right)^2\}$,
class(2)=$\{(x_1,x_2)\,|x_2 \leq \sin\left(3x_1+0.8\right)^2\}$,
where $0 \leq x_1 \leq 1$ and $-2.5 \leq x_2 \leq 2.5$.

The value of k was empirically set as 6 for PROBLEM(A) and 9 for PROBLEM(B). Some other values of k were tried, but such trials did not affect significantly to the SVM performance. Fig. 3 shows both problems (above) and selected patterns (below) after normalization ranged from -1 to 1: Normalization is essential for the better performance of finding the nearest neighbors and of adapting to SVM kernels. The selected patterns shown in white contours are scattered against original ones. From both plots, the proposed method seems to extract relevant patterns from redundant ones for SVMs. Only 9.3% patterns were selected for PROBLEM(A) and 21.8% for PROBLEM(B). The different reduction ratio is due to the difference in densities near the decision boundary.

(a)   (b)

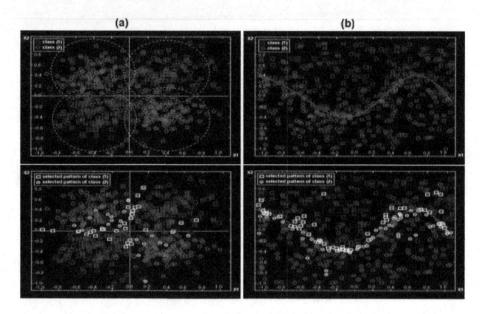

Fig. 3. Original patterns (above) and selected ones (below): (a) PROB(A), (b) PROB(B).

For each problem, 300 test patterns were generated from a statistically identical distribution to its training set. Five RBF kernels with different width parameters($s = 0.25, 0.5, 1, 2, 3$) and five polynomial kernels with different order parameters($p = 1, 2, 3, 4, 5$) were adopted. For SVMs trained with all patterns, various values were tried for the tolerance parameter ($C = 0.1, 1, 5, 10, 20, 100, 1000, \infty$), since the problem under consideration are non-separable. Whereas for SVMs trained with the selected subset of patterns, C was fixed with ∞, since the proposed selection method removed "incorrectly labeled" patterns through converting a non-separable problem into a separable one.

Average performance was compared in terms of the execution time, the number of support vectors and the test error in Table 1. First two columns are ob-

Table 1. SVM Experimental Results

Avg.	PROB(A)			PROB(B)		
	ALL	ALL	SELECTED	ALL	ALL	SELECTED
	($\forall C$)	($C = \infty$)	($C = \infty$)	($\forall C$)	($C = \infty$)	($C = \infty$)
CPU-time(sec)	748.78	2772.97	1.89	430.97	1626.10	5.67
			(=0.88+1.01)			(=0.66+5.01)
No. of patterns	600	600	56	500	500	109
No. of SVs	297.31	385.21	27.00	300.21	380.70	86.20
Test Err.(%)	14.18	15.33	13.70	17.31	18.27	14.53

tained when all training patterns were used. The first column is for all C values we experimented and the second one is for $C = \infty$. The last column is the average results for $C = \infty$ when the selected training patterns were used. The training time with only selected patterns were just 1.89(sec) and 5.67(sec) even including the time taken to execute the proposed selection procedure. For PROBLEM(A), the pattern selection took 0.88(sec) and training SVMs took 1.01(sec). For PROBLEM(B), 0.66(sec) and 5.01(sec) respectively. In the worst case, when one doesn't know the data noise level(it happens almost always), one might set the tolerance parameter $C = \infty$ like in second column. In that case, one should endure 2772.97(sec) and 1626.10(sec) to take the results on such simple artificial problems. Second, in our method, the uppermost number of SVs are bounded by the number of the selected patterns. If the generalization performance is not improved, there is no reason to project input patterns onto too high dimensional feature space even though all calculations are achieved implicitly. Finally, for accuracy, SVMs with selected patterns do not degrade their original performances in both problems. Fig. 4 shows the decision boundaries and margins of SVMs both with all patterns and with the selected patterns. Kernel parameter was

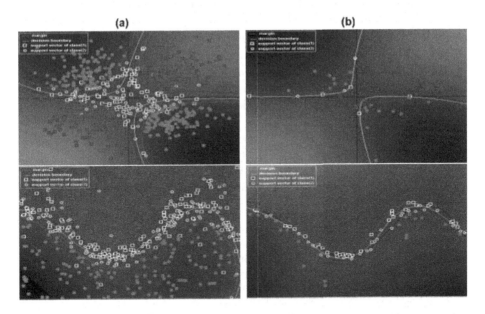

Fig. 4. Decision boundary, margin and SVs, (a) with all patterns and (b) with the selected patterns: the upper figures are for **PROB(A)** with polynomial kernel($p = 3$) and the lower figures are **PROB(B)** with RBF kernel($s = 1$).

fixed at the value which was best performed with all patterns for comparison purpose(for the selected patterns, it is not the best one). From the figures, it is easily seen that the decision boundaries formed using the selected patterns are almost same as those with all patterns. Margins in **(b)** figures are much narrower than those of original margins in **(a)** since noise pattern elimination enabled us to set $C = \infty$. And also the number of support vectors are remarkably smaller in **(b)** figures.

4   Conclusion

We proposed a pattern selection method as a filtering procedure for SVM training. By utilizing k-nearest neighbor method, the patterns with a correct class label near the decision boundary were selected.

The proposed method produced encouraging results as follows. First, the search for an optimal tolerance parameter C is not necessary anymore. Second, SVM execution time decreased two orders of magnitude without any loss of accuracy. Third, by reducing the redundant SVs, the projection onto too high dimensional feature space can be avoided. Our method can be extended to multi-classification problems without any correction.

In this paper, we just demonstrated the proposed method over synthetic data but it is currently applied to over real world problems. Finally, we found that the misclassification error rate of k-NN with a large k seemed to be similar to the noise level which we imposed on the data on purpose. Hence, this approach could be utilized to predict the data noise level ahead of time.

Acknowledgements. This research was supported by Brain Science and Engineering Research Program sponsored by Korean Ministry of Science and Technology and by the Brain Korea 21 Project.

References

1. Almeida, M.B., Braga, A. and Braga J.P.(2000). SVM-KM: speeding SVMs learning with a priori cluster selection and k-means, *Proc. Of the 6th Brazilian Symposium on Neural Networks*, pp. 162–167
2. Boser, B.E., Guyon, I.M. and Vapnik, V.N. (1992). A training algorithm for optimal margin classifiers, *In D. Haussler, Proc. Of the 5th Annual ACM workshop on Computaional Learning Theory*, Pittsborgh, PA:ACM press
3. Burges, C.J.C., (1998). A Tutorial on Support Vector Machines for Pattern Recognition, *Data Mining and Knowledge Discovery*, vol. 2, pp. 121–167
4. Foody, G.M., (1999). The Significance of Border Training Patterns in Classification by a Feedforward Neural Network Using Back Propagation Learning, *International Journal of Remote Sensing*, vol. 20, no. 18, pp. 3549–3562
5. Gunn, S., (1998). Support Vector Machines for Classification and Regression, *ISIS Technical Report*
6. Lyhyaoui, A., Martinez, M., Mora, I., Vazquez, M., Sancho, J. and Figueiras-Vaidal, A.R., (1999). Sample Selection Via Clustering to Construct Support Vector-Like Classifiers, *IEEE Transactions on Neural Networks*, vol. 10, no. 6, pp. 1474–1481
7. Shin, H.J. and Cho, S.Z., (2002). Pattern Selection Using the Bias and Variance of Ensemble, *Journal of the Korean Institute of Industrial Engineers*, (to appear)
8. Vapnik, V., (1999). *The Nature of Statistical Learning Theory*, Springer. 2nd eds

Graphical Features Selection Method

Yuan-chin Ivan Chang[1], Haoran Hsu[2], and Lin-Yi Chou[2]

[1] Academia Sinica, Taipei, Taiwan 11529
ycchang@sinica.edu.tw
[2] Bridgewell Inc., Taipei, Taiwan 10051
{horen_hsu, linyi}@bridgewell.com

Abstract. The performance of a classification process depends heavily on the feature used in it. The traditional features/variables selection schemes are mostly developed from the model fitting point of view, which may not be good or efficient for classification purpose. Here we propose a graphical selection method, which allows us to integrate the information in the test data set, and it is suitable for selection useful features from high dimensional data set. We applied it to the Thrombin data set, which was used in KDD CUP 2001. By using the selected features from our graphical method and a SVM classifier, we obtained the higher classification accuracy than the results reported in KDD Cup 2001.

1 Introduction

People expect to use the data mining methods to analysis huge data sets, which usually has a lot of different types of features. Thus, an efficient feature selection method, which can check and compare all the features at a time, will be highly desirable.

The classification methods are popular analytical tools in many different data mining processes. It is well known that the feature selection plays a crucial role in the classification algorithms, which might determine the final performance of a classifier. In addition, a different selected features may lead us to a totally different classification result. In the multi-variate statistical analysis literature, there are some discussion about dimension reduction for exploration, presentation and many other purposes. Due to the characteristic of variables, we need to transform the original feature to conveniently comparable format. The principal component analysis and projection pursuit are two popular examples. For further detail, we refer to Mardia, Kent and Bibby (1979).

But the traditional statistical tools for feature/variable selection are mostly developed for model fitting purpose, which might not be very efficient for selecting features from a high dimensional data set. How can we efficiently select the most useful features for a particular analysis task is an interesting and important problem.

In this paper, we propose a graphical feature selection method, which is mainly from a classification point of view. The proposed graphical method can be used for comparing many features at a time. It also allows us to integrate not

H. Yin et al. (Eds.): IDEAL 2002, LNCS 2412, pp. 475–480, 2002.

only the information in the training data set, but also the information in the test data set. For discussion purpose, we apply the features selected by our method to the Thrombin data set, which was one of the data set used in KDD CUP 2001. Then using these selected features and some SVM classifiers to classify its test set. The empirical results shows that the accuracy we obtained (or the weighted accuracy) for some cases are much higher than the winner of KDD CUP 2001. For the SVM algorithm we refer readers to Vapnik (1995) and Burges(1998).

2   Feature Selection and Classification

One of the main principle for classification process is to minimize the within-class variation and to maximize the between-class distance, simultaneously. Based on this principle, the variables with larger variation among different classes in the training sets are the most prominent candidate features for classification purpose. If the training and the test data sets are homogeneous, then the feature selected in this way usually will work fine. But, if the test data set and the training data set are not homogeneous; for example, they are from different distributions for the different classes, then it will be very hard to get satisfying results.

On the other hand, if there is already a bunch of test cases available to us, we certainly like to integrate the information of the test set into our feature selection procedure. Because our task is to classify the test data set, not to fit a model for the training set, the features with high variation in the training set but with low variation in the test data set might not be very useful. The reason is obvious, since these features will have little discrimination power for classifying the test data set. Similarly, if the features with large variation in the test set, but not in training set, then they might not be useful, either. Because there are lack of information about these features in the training set. Therefore, it is hard for us to "learn" any enough information for these features from our training process and is unlike to have good classification accuracy in this situation. It follows that to select the features with large variation in both training and test sets might be a selection strategy, and it can be done by comparing the variation of each feature between training and test sets using a scatter-plot. The rest problem is to select a suitable measure of variation for features.

There are many different measurements of variation, which is usually chosen depending on the type of variables as well as the purpose of analysis. For continuous-valued features, the statistical variance is the most popular one for measuring the dispersion from the mean. For categorical variables, the are also many different choices such as Shannon's entropy, the Gini index, etc. The features of the data set, which we are going to used for demonstration, are all binary-valued. Thus, we will first transform original features to probabilities (see Section 3), and then use the Shannon's entropy as our measure of dispersion. Below is a brief summary of the Thrombin data set used in KDD CUP 2001. For detail discussion, we refer readers to the original web page of KDD CUP 2001: http://www.cs.wisc.edu/ dpage/kddcup2001/.

2.1   Thrombin Data Set

According to the set up of KDD CUP 2001, there are 1909 cases in the training set(42 positive), 634 cases in the test set, and 139,351 binary features for each case. We apply our method to the Thrombin data set under the same set up of KDD CUP 2001. We first randomly divided our training data into two subsets: a learning set and a validation set. The classifier is trained using cross-validation method. Since we have a bunch of test cases available, we can also compare the entropy of each feature between the training set and the test set. (We will explain how we compute of Shannon's entropy for this data set in Section 3.) Figure 1 are the entropy scatter plots of (a) Training set versus Test set, and (b) Training set versus Validation set. The red dots are the 2912 selected features (see Section 2.2). The difference of pictures (a) and (b) clearly show that the distributions of entropy in training and test sets are very different. As it was mentioned in Cheng(2001), the data set is not only highly imbalance and high-dimensional, but also different distribution between training and test sets.

Following the ideas we discussed above, we have tried several different features based on the scatter-plots. The red dots in Figure 1 and 2 represent the selected features. Then we apply the SVM algorithm with each selected set of features using Chang and Chen's (2000) SVM algorithm (LIBSVM). The numerical results obtained from them are summarized in Table 1 and 2. Table 2.1 shows the results obtained by using the linear kernel and the last row of Table 2 is the result of Cheng's(2001) Baysian Network (reported in KDD CUP 2001).

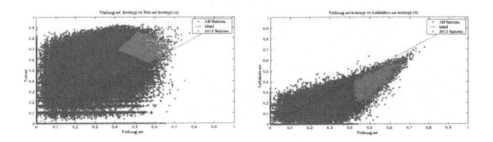

Fig. 1. Feature selected by using Shannon's Entropy

2.2   Numerical Results

In the following tables, the weighted accuracy is the average accuracy of the positive and the negative cases and the "Accuracy" in the last column is the usual global accuracy (i.e. the total number of corrects divided by the total number of test cases). From Table 1, we found that the performance is getting better when the selected features decreasing. For the case with 2912 feature, we actually have slightly better result then Cheng (2001).

When we apply the SVM with radial based kernel function and the same 2912 feature above, we have even better results. The best one in our experiment has achieved a 82% Accuracy (74% weighted accuracy).

In Table 2, we summarize the results of using SVM with the radial based function as its kernel and with different dispersion parameters(g). The features selected are those marked in red dots in all figures. Figure 2 shows some different shape of selected features and their corresponding numerical results are in the last two rows of Table 2.

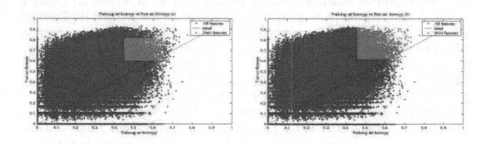

Fig. 2. Using right-upper Corners

Table 1. SVM with Linear Kernel Function

Selected features	Positive	Negative	Weighted accuracy	Accuracy
6287 (SVM Linear)	0.780	0.446	0.613	0.631
5341 (SVM Linear)	0.673	0.630	0.651	0.640
2960 (SVM linear)	0.727	0.624	0.675	0.648
2912 (SVM Linear)	0.646	0.791	0.718	0.757
Cheng's(2001)Baysian Network	0.633	0.736	0.684	0.711

Table 2. SVM with Radial Based Kernel Function

Feature	Dispersion g	Positive	Negative	Weighted accuracy	Accuracy
2912	1	0.720	0.705	0.712	0.721
2912	0.1	0.660	0.781	0.720	0.759
2912	0.01	0.653	0.777	0.715	0.748
2912	0.0001	0.587	0.893	0.740	0.820
2960	0.0001	0.567	0.860	0.714	0.790
2959	0.0001	0.573	0.808	0.691	0.752

3   Shannon's Entropy

The Shannon's entropy is defined as $-\int \log(p(t))dp(t)$, where $p(t)$ denotes a probability density function. For discrete case, it becomes

$$-\sum_t p(t) \log p(t). \tag{1}$$

In data mining, it is very common to encounter variables with discrete values. The Shannon's entropy is a good index to measure the dispersion in this case.

Consider a data set with N subjects and T features. There are different features consist in each subject $s \in N$. Let $f_s(t)$

$$f_s(t) = \frac{n(t)}{\sum_{t'} n(t')}, \tag{2}$$

be the normalized frequency of appearance for the feature t in the subject s, where $n(t)$ is the frequency of the feature t and the summation is the total frequency for all features in the subject s. Then the probability of the feature t in subject s can be defined as

$$P_s(t) = \frac{f_s(t)}{\sum_{s'=1}^{N} f_{s'}(t)}. \tag{3}$$

By the definition of Shannon's entropy, the entropy of the feature t is

$$H(t) = -\frac{1}{\log N} \sum_{s=1}^{N} P_s(t) \log P_s(t). \tag{4}$$

The value of $H(t)$ is restricted in $[0, 1]$ because it is divided by a constant factor $\log N$. (It is actually the relative entropy by using the discrete uniform distribution as its reference distribution.) The $H(t) = 1$ means that the feature t is equally distributed in all subjects and $H(t) = 0$ indicates that the feature t only appears in either one or none of the subjects. The larger the value of $H(t)$, the more subjects contain the feature t. Note that the definition of probability also depends on the population of subjects. Thus, a different set of subjects define different probabilities and entropies of features. The procedure of feature selection is below:

- **Step** 1 Subdivide the whole training cases set into learning and validation parts.
- **Step** 2 Calculate the entropy of each feature for learning, validation and test sets.
- **Step** 3 Plot the scatter plots of entropies for (a)training set versus test set and (b)training set versus validation set.
- **Step** 4 Select promising features from the right-upper corner of the plot of training set versus test set.

The blue dots in pictures represents the entropy for each feature and the red dots is the features selected. In Figure 1, we compute the regression line of training set versus test set and select the upper portion of a pie shape between these two lines.

4   Conclusion

The computation of Shannon's entropy is very fast for discrete variables. Thus, it is suitable for the data set with high dimensional feature space. The above computation does no depend on the information of the true label(class) of each subject. That's why we can take the information in the test set into consideration of our feature selection scheme. With some modification, it can also be applied to the data set with mixture of discrete and continuous variables.

Intuitively, we need to select those features with large variation for training stage. If, in addition, the selected features also have large variations in the test set, then we can expect to have good the classification results. When the training and test sets are homogeneous, there will be no extra information to learn from test set. But if there are some difference between the training and test sets, the method we proposed here can provide us some useful information for feature selection. Although, the comparison here is rather empirical, it provide a good direction for further studies of feature selection. At least, we can notice the difference between the training and test sets in advance, and perhaps, we can plan for some make up procedures for further analysis.

References

1. Burges, Christopher J.C.A (1998) Tutorial on Support Vector Machines for Pattern Recognition, Data Mining and Knowledge Discovery, 2(2), 121–167.
2. Cheng, Jie (2001), KDD CUP 2001 Task 1:Thrombin.
3. Vapnik, V. (1995). The nature of Statistical Learning Theory, New York: Springer Verlag.
4. Chih-Chung Chang and Chih-Jen Lin (2000). LIBSVM – A Library for Support Vector Machines.
5. Mardia, K.V., Kent, J.T. and Bibby, J.M.(1979). Multivariate Analysis. London: Academic Press.
6. Zanette, D. H. Entropic analysis of the role of words in literary texts. Preprint.

Fuzzy-Neural Inference in Decision Trees

Keeley Crockett, Zuhair Bandar, and James O'Shea

The Intelligent Systems Group, Department Of Computing, The Manchester Metropolitan University, Chester Street, Manchester, M1 5GD, UK
Telephone (+44) (0) 161 247 1497
Facsimile (+44) (0) 161 247 1483
K.Crockett@mmu.ac.uk

Abstract. The predominate weakness in the creation of decision trees is the strict partitions which are selected by the induction algorithm. To overcome this problem the theories of fuzzy logic have been applied to generate soft thresholds leading to the creation of fuzzy decision trees, thus allowing cases passing through the tree for classification to be assigned partial memberships down all paths. A challenging task is how these resultant membership grades are combined to produce an overall outcome. A number of theoretical fuzzy inference techniques exist, yet they have not been applied extensively in practical situations and are often domain dependent. Thus the overall classification success of the fuzzy trees has a high dependency on the optimization of the strength of the fuzzy intersection and union operators that are applied. This paper investigates a new, more general approach to combining membership grades using neural-fuzzy inference. Comparisons are made between using the fuzzy-neural approach and the use of pure fuzzy inference trees.

1 Introduction

The original decision tree algorithm, ID3 was developed by Quinlan in the mid eighties and has since [1..3] undergone many improvements: C4, C4.5, See5. The main weakness of the ID3 type algorithm is the limitations on the classification accuracy of the induced tree due to the sharp decision boundaries at each node in the tree. When a crisp decision tree is created from a Training set of data by some induction algorithm it will automatically produce a series of strict partitions in the decision space. This fatality of sharp boundaries is that small changes in attribute values of a case being classified may result in radical changes in classification [4]. This is particularly applicable when an attribute has continuous values

A number of revised algorithms have been proposed which attempt to make the decision tree more robust e.g. fuzzy ID3 [5..8]. These involve splitting the range of a given attribute into intervals and fuzzifying each. However the task of partitioning attributes values is itself fuzzy with the intervals themselves being from an expert's knowledge. Hence this will introduce an additional aspect of uncertainty into the tree. There is a limit to the amount of uncertainty which can be present and if the degree of fuzziness increases above a specific threshold then the tree will become too vague to give the expected performance. Furthermore when an attribute re-occurs at more than one node in the tree different intervals may be required which consequently results in

H. Yin et al. (Eds.): IDEAL 2002, LNCS 2412, pp. 481-486, 2002.
© Springer-Verlag Berlin Heidelberg 2002

the fuzzy rules generated from these decision trees being often more complex than the tree itself. In [10] a new Fuzzy Inference Algorithm (FIA) was proposed which introduces significant fuzziness onto branches of a pre-generated crisp tree in order to use all the data throughout the tree, regardless of it's uncertainty and contradictory nature in the decision process. This algorithm was shown to overcome the weakness of the C4.5 tree family by softening all decision nodes and by combining all information throughout the tree to produce a final decision classification. However, the overall classification success of the fuzzy tree has a high dependency on the optimization of the strength of the fuzzy intersection and union operators that are applied. This paper investigates a new, more general approach to combining membership grades using neural-fuzzy inference.

2   Generating A Fuzzy Decision Tree

The original FIA algorithm [10] involves the application of fuzzy membership functions to all nodes in a pre-generated crisp decision tree. A case passing through the tree will result in all branches in the tree firing to some degree, which is determined by each specific attributes degree of membership in the corresponding fuzzy set. The membership grades associated with every branch within the tree are then combined down each path from root to leaf node using a fuzzy intersection function. Leaf probabilities are then applied to the resultant membership grades, before a fuzzy union function is used to determine the overall outcome.

2.1   Fuzzification

In order to apply fuzzification effectively it is necessary to get the approximate 'right' balance of fuzzification throughout the decision tree. The idea behind FIA is to apply a significant degree of fuzziness to those cases whose attributes lie on the threshold of nodes, whilst at the same time allowing cases with attributes following a strong, definite path to be relatively un-affected by the fuzzification process. This is in contrast to the C4.5 approach, which only truly favors a correct classification when the attributes involved are a significant distance away from the threshold. To aid in this explanation consider the tree in figure 1 with outcomes $o_1...o_s$, which shows a given set of membership grades (μ) for a particular case. A series of high membership grades down one particular path from the root to a leaf node will dominate all the other information present within the tree even though it will still contribute to a degree. A problem occurs when one branch of a node does not dominate over it's pair. Attribute values, which are close to the threshold, are assigned membership grades, which represent the uncertainty, which is naturally present. Maximum uncertainty is represented by a membership grade of 0.5% and is assigned when the attribute value of a particular case equates to the value of the decision threshold, dt. In this scenario, the membership grades of all other branches will have a greater contribution in determining the correct outcome. The larger the tree, the more this becomes apparent.

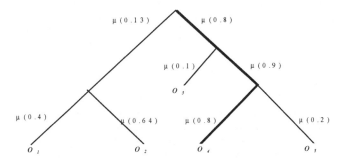

Fig. 1. A Decision Tree With A Strong Path

2.1.1 Linear Membership Functions

Nodes within the crisply generated tree are fuzzified by creating fuzzy regions around each tree node in order to soften the sharp decision thresholds. Each branch with the decision tree was represented by a fuzzy set defined by a membership function. For the purpose of this investigation linear membership functions were applied as defined in (1).

$$L(dm, dn, x) = \begin{bmatrix} 0 \rightarrow x \leq dm \\ \dfrac{x - dm}{dn - dm} \rightarrow dm \leq x \leq dn \\ 1 \rightarrow x \geq dn \end{bmatrix} \tag{1}$$

where dm   generates the zero membership value and is the lower bound of L
defined as $dm = dt - n\sigma$ where n is a real number $n \rightarrow [0, \infty]$ and σ is
the standard deviation.

  dn   generates the complete membership value (the value giving the
maximum membership value) and is the upper bound of L defined as
$dn = dt + n\sigma$ where n is a real number $n \rightarrow [0, \infty]$ and σ is the
standard deviation, and
x is value of Attribute A.

2.1.2 Membership Function Optimisation

To determine sufficient fuzziness for a given tree a Genetic Algorithm (GA) [11] is used. Each set of membership functions are encoded onto a chromosome where each gene will represent a real value *n*, used in the determination of one domain delimiter (dm_i or dn_i). To determine sufficient fuzzifness throughout the tree, the average classification accuracy of the training set is used as fitness function.

2.2 Pure Fuzzy Inference

Significant literature [12.14 has been published concerning the appropriate definitions for intersection and union of fuzzy subsets. For the purposes of this paper, two contrasting fuzzy inference techniques (Table 1) have been selected to combine grades of membership generated by linear membership functions for each attribute down all paths within the tree.

Table 1. Parmeterised Inference Techniques

| Yager | $\mu_{(a \cup b)} = \min[1, (a^{wu} + b^{wu})^{1/wu}]$
 $\mu_{(a \cap b)} = 1 - \min[1, ((1-a)^{wi} + (1-b)^{wi})^{1/wi}]$ | $w_i, w_u \in (0, \infty)$ |
| Dubois & Prade | $\mu_{(a \cup b)} = $

 $\dfrac{a+b-ab-\min(a,b,1-\alpha u)}{\max(1-a,1-b,\alpha u)}$

 $\mu_{(a \cap b)} = \dfrac{ab}{\max(a,b,\alpha i)}$ | $\alpha_i, \alpha_u \in (0,1)$ |

3 Fuzzy Neural Inference

The fuzzy-neural inference process is based around the selection of suitable fuzzy intersection operators from a predefined fuzzy inference technique and then applying the outputs generated at each leaf node to a Back Propagation Feed Forward Neural Network (BP-FFNN) [15] When an input has been applied to a fuzzy decision tree, the membership grades are produced at each branch and a fuzzy intersection operator is used to combine values to produce resultant grades at each of the leaf nodes. The resultant grades are then used as inputs into a BP-FFNN to provide the classification for any given case.

4 Experiments

This investigation will be undertaken using two real world diverse data sets namely Mortgage and Diabetes. The Mortgage data set investigates the possibility of a person acquiring a mortgage and comprises of 8611 records featuring 25 discrete and continuos attributes. (4306 representing a Good Risk and 4305 depicting a Bad Risk). The second set known as Diabetes in Pima Indians investigates whether Pima Indian patients show signs of diabetes and comprises of 768 records featuring 9 continuos attributes (500 Class 1, indicating that a person has diabetes, 268 Class 2 which represents a person who shows no signs of the disease).

4.1 Experiments

Each data set was first partitioned into two sets of randomly selected examples referred to as the Training and Testing sets. It has been previously shown [1] that binary trees produce higher classification accuracy and therefore a binary ID3 tree was created for each data set using the statistical Chi-square pruning technique with a significance level of 0.1%. This produced small highly optimised trees, which produced good classifications with least overfit, compared to trees created with higher significance levels. This prevented bias towards improvement generated from the BP-FFNN or pure fuzzy inference. A GA was applied to the induced tree to optimise the degree of fuzziness at each node, and the parameters of the selected inference technique.

The experiments aim to compare whether outcomes generated using pure fuzzy inference give better performance than using fuzzy membership grades as the inputs into a BP-FFNN. Each fuzzy tree will be used to generate a series of membership grades at the leaf nodes and along with the known classification will be used to train the BP-FFNN. In order to find a good network topology and set of learning parameters, a large number of experiments were undertaken on different permutations of network configurations and learning parameters to determine optimal performance using the fuzzy inputs

4.2 Results

Tables 2 and 3 show the average results of combining membership grades crisp decision trees, fuzzy decision trees (FIA) and Fuzzy-Neural trees (FNI) where %AVG is the average classification accuracy on the unseen test set.

Table 2. Diabetes In Prima Indians

TECHNIQUE	%AVG CRISP	%AVG FIA	%AVG FNI
Dubois & Prade	70.0	75.2	66.1
Yager	70.0	74.3	75.5

Table 3. Mortgage

TECHNIQUE	%AVG CRISP	%AVG FIA	%AVG FNI
Dubois & Prade	67.0	70.7	71.8
Yager	67.0	71.4	71.6

The results in Tables 2 and 3 show improvement when Fuzzy Neural inference is applied to combine membership grades compared with pure fuzzy inference. In Table 2 FIA improves the crisp tree by 5.2% whilst inputs provided by Dubois and Prade's intersection operators into the BP-NN fail to have any impact on performance, producing results, which were poorer than those generated using pure fuzzy inference. Contrasting results however have been obtained for the mortgage data with the results produced using fuzzy-neural inference and Dubois and Prade's technique performing slightly better than Yager's. It was also found that training a BP-NN using fuzzy inputs produced a better classifier than using crisp inputs to the NN.

5   Conclusion

This paper has presented a novel approach, using fuzzy-neural inference to combine membership grades of crisp fuzzy decision trees. The results obtained show that in most cases the BP-FFNN has achieved a better classification accuracy than results obtained using either crisp decision trees or the FIA algorithm. The increase in classification accuracy using fuzzy-neural inference was dependent on both the generic makeup of the dataset and the fuzzy intersection operator used. The weakness of the method is that combining membership grades using parameterized inference techniques and BP-FFNN results in the decision transparency being lost however this is compensated for by the significant increase in accuracy.

References

1. Quinlan J.R, "Probabilistic Decision Trees". In "Machine Learning Volume 3: An AI Approach". (Eds). Kockatoft, Y. Michalshi, R, pp 140-152, 1990.
2. Quinlan, J.R., "Improved Use of Continuous Attributes in C4.5", Journal of Artificial Intelligence Research 4, pp 77-90, 1996.
3. Quinlan, J.R., Is C5.0 Better Than C4.5. Available: http://www.rulequest.com/see5-comparison.html, 2000.
4. Breiman, L., Shang, N., Born Again Trees, ftp.stat.berkeley.edu/pub/users/breiman/, 1997.
5. Tani T. Sakoda, T. Tanaka, K., Fuzzy Modeling by ID3 Algorithm and it's Application to Prediction Of Heater Outlet Temperature, IEEE, pp. 923-930 1992.
6. Umano, M., Okamoto, H., Hatono, I., Tamura, H., Generation of Fuzzy Decision Trees By Fuzzy ID3 Algorithm and it's Application to Diagnosis by Gas in Oil, Japan-U.S.A Symposium, pp. 1445-1450, 1994.
7. Bouchon-Meunier, B., Mamdani, R., "Learning From Imperfect Data", In "Fuzzy Information Engineering A Guided Tour of Applications", Eds. Dubois, D. Prade, H. Yager, R, R, John Wiley and Sons Publishing, pp. 139-148. 1997.
8. Janikow C., Fuzzy Decision Trees: Issues and Methods, IEEE Transactions on Systems, Man, and Cybernetics, pp. 1-14, Vol.28, 1, 1998.
9. Crockett, K.A., Bandar, Z., Soft Decision Trees: A New Approach Using Non-linear Fuzzification, The 9th IEEE International Conference on Fuzzy Systems, May 2000.
10. Crockett, K.A., Bandar, Z., Al-Attar, A A Fuzzy Inference Framework For Induced Decision Trees. ECAI 98. 13th European Conference on Artificial Intelligence, Brighton, UK. Eds. H. Prade. John Wiley & Sons Ltd, pp 425-429, 1998
11. Michalewicz, Z., Genetic Algorithms and Data Structures = Evolution Programs, Second Edition, Springer-Verlag, 1994.
12. Zadeh, L., Fuzzy Sets, Information and Control 8, pp. 338-353, 1965.
13. Yager, R., On a General Class Of Fuzzy Connectives. Fuzzy Sets & Systems 4, 1980.
14. Dubois, D., Prade, H., A Class Of Fuzzy Measures Based On Triangular Norms. Int., J. General Systems 8, 43-61, 1982.
15. Rumelhart, D., Hinton, G., Williams, R., Learning Representations by Back-Propagating Errors, Letters to Nature, Vol. 323, pp. 533-535, 1986.

Decision Tree Based Clustering

Dongsuk Yook

Speech Information Processing Laboratory
Department of Computer Science and Engineering, Korea University
Sungbookgoo Anamdong 5-1, Seoul, Korea 136-701
http://voice.korea.ac.kr
yook@voice.korea.ac.kr

Abstract. A decision tree can be used not only as a classifier but also as a clustering method. One of such applications can be found in automatic speech recognition using hidden Markov models (HMMs). Due to the insufficient amount of training data, similar states of triphone HMMs are grouped together using a decision tree to share a common probability distribution. At the same time, in order to predict the statistics of unseen triphones, the decision tree is used as a classifier as well. In this paper, we study several cluster split criteria in decision tree building algorithms for the case where the instances to be clustered are probability density functions. Especially, when Gaussian probability distributions are to be clustered, we have found that the Bhattacharyya distance based measures are more consistent than the conventional log likelihood based measure.

1 Introduction

In automatic speech recognition, a sound is usually modeled as a context-dependent phone such as a *triphone* which takes into account both the left and the right neighboring phones. In modern speech recognition systems, hidden Markov models (HMMs) are typically utilized for the triphone acoustic modeling. Since there is a large number of triphones, some of them may get too small amount of training data or no data at all if they happen to be absent from the training data. When there is not enough data for some triphones, similar ones can be grouped together to provide sufficient statistics and a representative model can be trained more reliably [4]. The clustering can also be done at a state level rather than at a phone level [2][8]. When a triphone does not occur in the training data, the closest one has to be found among the trained triphones to replace the unseen triphone. The decision tree based clustering techniques [7][3] handle both data insufficiency and unseen triphone problems. A tree is built to serve as a classifier for the states of unseen triphones. At the same time, each leaf node of the tree is generated in an unsupervised way, and all states in each node are clustered to share a common distribution.

Following the famous *Occam's razor* (i.e., prefer the simplest hypothesis that fits the data), the *entropy*-based measure is used to build small trees in the traditional decision tree building algorithm [6]. In building trees to predict unseen triphones, [7] used approximated log likelihood, and [3] used *cross entropy* as the measures for cluster splitting. There is no intuition that the approximated log likelihood based measure will produce

H. Yin et al. (Eds.): IDEAL 2002, LNCS 2412, pp. 487–492, 2002.

small trees. The cross entropy based measure may substitute for the original idea in [6]. However, the cross entropy is not exactly a measure of homogeneity of the distributions in a cluster. Also, it was originally designed for discrete probability density HMMs, and the tree building process becomes complicated when applied to continuous probability density models. In this paper, we consider using the measures based on *Bhattacharyya* distance which is used as a theoretic class separability measure [1]. The Bhattacharyya distance is a more consistent criterion than the log likelihood based measure, especially for Gaussian distributions. It produces small trees following the idea of Occam's razor. Unlike [3], it can be applied to continuous density HMMs that use Gaussian probability density functions.

The organization of this paper is as follows. The approximated log likelihood based approach and the cross entropy based approach are briefly explained in Section 2. In Section 3, the Bhattacharyya distance is reviewed, and several cluster split criteria using the Bhattacharyya distance are introduced. Experimental result and comparison to previous works are followed in Section 4.

2   Log Likelihood and Cross Entropy

A decision tree is built using all k-th states in the triphones of which base phones are the same. There are as many trees as the number of monophones times the number of states in a phone. Each tree is built as in [6];

1. Put k-th state's probability density functions of the triphones that share the same base phone into a root node.
2. For each node, find the split that gives the best value according to the given measure (e.g., log likelihood or cross entropy), and make children nodes using the splits.
3. Repeat the Step 2 while each leaf node has sufficient training data to estimate the distribution reliably.

In this section, we review the two measures used in building the trees; approximated log likelihood [7] and cross entropy [3].

2.1   Approximated Log Likelihood

Let G be a set of all distributions to be clustered in a tree. Assuming that each state of an HMM has one probability density function, G is equivalent to a set of all states to be clustered. The log likelihood of the training utterances U given the set of distributions G can be approximated as follows;

$$L(U|G) = \log P(U|G) \tag{1}$$

$$\propto \sum_{u \in U} \sum_{g \in G} \gamma_{u,g} \log P(u|\bar{g}) \quad , \tag{2}$$

where $\gamma_{u,g}$ (also called *state occupancy*) is the probability of being in the state whose distribution is g when the vector u is observed, given the utterances U and the set of distributions G, and $\bar{g}$ is the representative distribution of the set G. $L(U|G)$ can be rewritten as follows for the Gaussian distribution case;

$$L(U|G) = -\frac{1}{2}\left(n\log(2\pi) + \log(|\Sigma_{\bar{g}}|) + n\right)\sum_{u \in U}\sum_{g \in G}\gamma_{u,g} \quad . \tag{3}$$

The cluster G is affected by common covariance $\Sigma_{\bar{g}}$ and each state's occupancy $\gamma_{u,g}$. The log likelihood increase by partitioning the set G into the subsets G_y and G_n according to some question is defined as

$$\Delta L = L(U|G_y) + L(U|G_n) - L(U|G) \quad . \tag{4}$$

The question that produces maximum ΔL is selected for the set G and it is associated with the decision tree node.

2.2   Cross Entropy

Given a discrete probability distribution g, the entropy of the distribution is defined as

$$E(g) = -\sum_i p_i \log p_i \quad , \tag{5}$$

where p_i is an individual probability entry in the distribution. The cross entropy, known as a measure for determining the distance between two probability distributions g and h, is defined as

$$C(g, h) = \sum_i p_i \log \frac{p_i}{q_i} \quad , \tag{6}$$

where p_i and q_i are individual probability entries in the distributions g and h. The cross entropy decrease introduced by splitting a set of probability distributions G into two subsets G_y and G_n according to some question is defined as

$$\Delta C = P(G_y)C(G_y, G) + P(G_n)C(G_n, G) \tag{7}$$

$$= P(G_y)\sum_i p_{y,i}\log\frac{p_{y,i}}{p_i} + P(G_n)\sum_i p_{n,i}\log\frac{p_{n,i}}{p_i} \tag{8}$$

$$= P(G_y)\sum_i p_{y,i}\log p_{y,i} - P(G_y)\sum_i p_{y,i}\log p_i$$

$$+ P(G_n)\sum_i p_{n,i}\log p_{n,i} - P(G_n)\sum_i p_{n,i}\log p_i \tag{9}$$

$$= E(G) - P(G_y)E(G_y) - P(G_n)E(G_n) \quad . \tag{10}$$

The question that produces maximum ΔC is selected to split the set of distributions G. Equation (10) looks similar to the *information gain* defined in [6]. However, equation (10) does not measure the homogeneity of the instances in a set as in [6], but it reflects the entropy of the distribution itself which is the instance.

The approximated log likelihood based measure is simple and inexpensive in terms of computation time. However, we are not certain whether it produces small decision trees. The cross entropy based measure is an alternative to the information gain, and it tends to favor the splits that produce sharp distributions in each cluster. But, it becomes complicated when applied to continuous probability density HMMs. In the next section, we introduce the Bhattacharyya distance based measures which overcome the above drawbacks.

3   Bhattacharyya Distance Based Measures

The Bhattacharyya distance is a theoretical distance measure between two Gaussian distributions. In this section, several measures based on the Bhattacharyya distance are considered.

3.1   Bhattacharyya Distance

The Bhattacharyya distance between two Gaussian distributions, g and h, is defined as follows [1];

$$B(g,h) = \frac{1}{8}(\mu_g - \mu_h)^T \left[\frac{\Sigma_g + \Sigma_h}{2} \right]^{-1} (\mu_g - \mu_h) + \frac{1}{2} \log \frac{\left| \frac{\Sigma_g + \Sigma_h}{2} \right|}{\sqrt{|\Sigma_g||\Sigma_h|}} \quad , \quad (11)$$

where μ_g and μ_h are the mean vectors and Σ_g and Σ_h are the covariance matrices of the distributions g and h, respectably. The first term in Equation (11) accounts for the difference due to the mean vectors, and the second term gives the separability caused by the covariance matrices. The Bhattacharyya distance for a set of distributions G can be defined as the averaged Bhattacharyya distances of all pairs in the set;

$$B(G) = \sum_{i=1}^{|G|} \sum_{j=i}^{|G|} P(g_i, g_j) B(g_i, g_j) \quad , \quad (12)$$

where $|G|$ is the number of distributions in the set, $P(g_i, g_j)$ is the weight of the pair of distributions g_i and g_j. $P(g_i, g_j)$ can be approximated using the state occupancy, γ, in the previous section. The Bhattacharyya distance decrease by splitting the set G into the subsets G_y and G_n according to some question is defined as

$$\Delta B = B(G) - P(G_y)B(G_y) - P(G_n)B(G_n) \quad , \quad (13)$$

where $P(G_y)$ and $P(G_n)$, the weights of each subset, can be approximated also using the state occupancies. As usual, the question that produces maximum ΔB is selected to split the set of distributions G.

Since the Bhattacharyya distance measures the similarity between two distributions, the subsets splitted by this measure will exhibit homogeneity. Unlike the cross entropy measure, it can be easily applied to continuous probability density HMMs.

3.2 Scatter Matrix

In building recognizers, what one wants is to increase the recognition accuracy after all. One way of achieving this is to use discriminative training algorithms. Applying the same idea, we consider not only the homogeneity of a cluster but also inter-class separability. The following *scatter matrices* [1] are commonly used to measure class separability between the two distributions g and h;

$$M_w(g, h) = P(g)\Sigma_g + P(h)\Sigma_h \tag{14}$$

$$M_b(g, h) = P(g)(\mu_g - \mu)(\mu_g - \mu)^T + P(h)(\mu_h - \mu)(\mu_h - \mu)^T \tag{15}$$

$$D_1(g, h) = tr(M_w M_b^{-1}) \quad , \tag{16}$$

where M_w represents the within-class scatter, M_b represents the between-class scatter, and μ is the common mean. The question that produces minimum scatter value, D_1, can be selected to partition the given set of distributions. However, the scatter value D_1 is an approximation and may not produce a tree that has good unseen triphone prediction capability. In order to emphasize the homogeneity of a class and the discriminative training at the same time, we propose a new measure that combines the Bhattacharyya distance with the idea of class separability.

3.3 Class Separability Using Bhattacharyya Distance

As the within-class scatter is divided by the between-class scatter, the averaged Bhattacharyya distances of two subsets can be divided by the Bhattacharyya distance between the two subsets;

$$D_2 = \frac{P(G_y)B(G_y) + P(G_n)B(G_n)}{B(\bar{g}_y, \bar{g}_n)} \quad , \tag{17}$$

where $\bar{g}_y$ and $\bar{g}_n$ are the representative distributions in the subsets G_y and G_n, respectably. The question that produces the minimum D_2 is selected to partition the given set of distributions.

4 Experiment

We have implemented the measures discussed in the previous sections for the decision tree based clustering algorithm. The performance is measured using triphone recognition accuracy. A speech feature vector used for the experiments is composed of 12 dimensional MFCCs (mel-frequency cepstral coefficients), normalized energy, and their first and second order time derivatives, resulting in a 39 dimensional vector. It is computed every 10 milliseconds using 25 milliseconds long Hamming windowed speech signals. The HMMs of the speech recognizers are built using TIMIT speech corpus [5]. Each system is trained using 3,696 utterances from TIMIT training data, and has approximately 10,000 Gaussian probability density functions. There are 15,421 triphones trained. The systems are evaluated using 1,344 utterances of TIMIT testing data. About 19% of

Table 1. Triphone recognition accuracies using various decision tree building criteria

Measures	Log likelihood	Accuracy (%)
ΔL	-71.15160	75.9
ΔB	-71.42106	74.8
D_1	-71.35892	75.1
D_2	-71.09144	76.0

triphones in the testing set are unseen and must be predicted using the decision trees. Table 1 shows the log likelihood of the training utterances and phone recognition accuracy of testing utterances. Even though the difference is minor, the Bhattacharyya distance based scatter measure shows the highest log likelihood and recognition accuracy. Notice that the log likelihood based approach does not decrease the actual log likelihood of the training utterances as much as D_2 does, which is the Bhattacharyya distance based scatter measure. This may be due to the approximation used in equation (2).

5   Conclusions

Recent speech recognition systems are based on HMMs and use triphones for their acoustic models. Due to the data insufficiency and unseen triphone problems, the probability density functions of the HMMs are clustered using the decision trees. In this paper, we proposed to use the Bhattacharyya distance rather than log likelihood as the measure for cluster splitting. The Bhattacharyya distance based measure is more consistent with the original idea of the Occam's razor. It can be extended to incorporate the class separability measure, and easily applied to the continuous probability densities. The proposed measures and the log likelihood based measure are empirically compared for the performance evaluation, and we have found that the Bhattacharyya distance is a reasonable criterion for the decision tree building algorithms.

References

1. K. Fukunaga. *Introduction to Statistical Pattern Recognition.* Academic Press, 1990.
2. M. Hwang and X. Huang. Shared-distribution hidden Markov models for speech recognition. *IEEE Transactions on Speech and Audio Processing,* 1(4):414–420, October 1993.
3. M. Hwang, X. Huang, and F. Alleva. Predicting unseen triphones with senones. *IEEE Transactions on Speech and Audio Processing,* 4(6):412–419, November 1996.
4. K. Lee. Context-dependent phonetic hidden Markov models for speaker-independent continuous speech recognition. *IEEE Transactions on Acoustics, Speech, and Signal Processing,* 38(4):599–609, April 1990.
5. NIST Speech Disc 1-1.1. *TIMIT Acoustic-Phonetic Continuous Speech Corpus,* October 1990.
6. J. Quinlan. Induction of decision trees. *Machine Learning,* pages 81–106, 1986.
7. S. Young, J. Odell, and P. Woodland. Tree-based state tying for high accuracy acoustic modelling. *DARPA Human Language Technology Workshop,* pages 307–312, March 1994.
8. S. Young and P. Woodland. State clustering in HMM-based continuous speech recognition. *Computer Speech and Language,* 8(4):369–394, 1994.

Usage of New Information Estimations for Induction of Fuzzy Decision Trees

Vitaly G. Levashenko[1, 2] and Elena N. Zaitseva[1]

[1]Dept. of Information Technologies, Belarussian State Economic University, Partizan ave 26, 220672, Minsk, Belarus
levashen @yahoo.com
[2]Dept. of Informatics, Faculty of Management Science and Informatics, University of ilina, Moyzesova 20, 01026, ilina, Slovakia

Abstract. We introduce a technique to compute new summary information estimations (information and entropy) for fuzzy sets. Special features for these estimations are investigated. We give an algorithm for determine various information measures for fuzzy sets and fuzzy decision trees. Finally, we are using our estimations for induction of fuzzy decision trees from a group of training examples.

1 Introduction

Last time an information theoretic approach [1] to solve a number of problems attracts specialists' attention. For instance, enough simple estimation for characteristics of mutual relation between values of attributes can be obtained by using this approach. The estimations of information measures may include: proper and joint information, mutual and conditional information and entropies [2].

J.R. Quinlan was proposed a general top-down mutual information algorithm to design crisp decision trees. Many methods have been developed for induction crisp decision trees [3]. The generalizing ID3 algorithm for fuzzy sets was investigated as Fuzzy ID3 algorithm and its variants [4-11].

The classification task in [4-5] has nominal or numerical values of input and output attributes. Kosko's fuzzy entropy is used to measure the fuzziness of classification by the neuron [6]. The algorithm [7] is processing numerical attributes and its result is two complementary crisp classes only. Y.Yuan and M.Shaw were propose construction a fuzzy decision trees (FDT) in the process of reducing classification *ambiguity* with accumulated fuzzy *evidences* [8]. Their method is used deLuca and Terminy's entropy. The developing of this method was proposed in [9].

In this paper we realized closely unification of methods of Fuzzy Logic and Information Theory. We had used classical Shannon's entropy for obtaining *nonsummary* information estimations [11]. Now we propose to use *summary* information estimations. These estimations are calculated as nonprobabilistic characteristics. The mathematical notation of Shannon's entropy is easier than

---

* This investigation has been supported by the grant Г01M-122 of Fund of Fundamental Researches and grant of Ministry of Education (Republic of Belarus).

H. Yin et al. (Eds.): IDEAL 2002, LNCS 2412, pp. 493-499, 2002.

notation of deLuca and Terminy's entropy. Therefore complexity of offered summary information estimations is less than well-known complexity from [8-9]. The application of *summary* entropy allows reducing the computing costs.

2 Preliminaries of Fuzzy Logic

Definition 1. A fuzzy set A with respect to an universe U is characterized by a *membership function* μ_A: U → [0,1], assign a A-membership degree, $\mu_A(u)$, to each element u in U. $\mu_A(u)$ gives us an estimation of the belonging of u to A [8].

Definition 2. The *cardinality measure* of fuzzy set A is defined by $M(A)=\Sigma_{u\in U}\,\mu_A(u)$, which is the measure of the size of A.

A typical classification problem can be described as follows. A universe of objects U={u} is describe by N training examples and n input attributes A={$A_1,...,A_n$}. Each attribute A_i $(1\leq i\leq n)$ measures some important feature and it presented by group of discrete *linguistic terms* (domain). We assume that each group is a set of m_i $(m_i \geq 2)$ values of fuzzy subsets {$A_{i,1},...,A_{i,j},...,A_{i,m_i}$}.

We will suggest that each object u in the universe is classified by a set of classes (output attributes) B = {$B_1,...,B_b$}. We will suppose that $b=1$ for a simplicity here. We have to find relations between one output attribute B and input attributes $A_1,...,A_n$.

Example 1. An object of Saturday's weather (adopted from [7-8]) is presented with four input attributes: A={A_1,A_2,A_3,A_4} ={*Outlook, Temperature, Humidity, Wind*} and one output attribute B={*Games*}. The membership and cardinality (M) measure of these attributes is given in Table 1.

Table 1. A training set Saturday's weather

No	Outlook			Temp(erature)			Humidity		Windy		Game*		
	Sunny	Cloudy	Rain	Hot	Mild	Cool	Humid	Normal	Windy	NotWin	V	S	W
1.	0.9	0.1	0.0	1.0	0.0	0.0	0.8	0.2	0.4	0.6	0.0	0.8	0.2
2.	0.8	0.2	0.0	0.6	0.4	0.0	0.0	1.0	0.0	1.0	0.6	0.4	0.0
3.	0.0	0.7	0.3	0.8	0.2	0.0	0.1	0.9	0.2	0.8	0.3	0.6	0.1
4.	0.2	0.7	0.1	0.3	0.7	0.0	0.2	0.8	0.3	0.7	0.9	0.1	0.0
5.	0.0	0.1	0.9	0.7	0.3	0.0	0.5	0.5	0.5	0.5	0.0	0.0	1.0
6.	0.0	0.7	0.3	0.0	0.3	0.7	0.7	0.3	0.4	0.6	0.2	0.0	0.8
7.	0.0	0.3	0.7	0.0	0.0	1.0	0.0	1.0	0.1	0.9	0.0	0.0	1.0
8.	0.0	1.0	0.0	0.0	0.2	0.8	0.2	0.8	0.0	1.0	0.7	0.0	0.3
9.	1.0	0.0	0.0	1.0	0.0	0.0	0.6	0.4	0.7	0.3	0.2	0.8	0.0
10.	0.9	0.1	0.0	0.0	0.3	0.7	0.0	1.0	0.9	0.1	0.0	0.3	0.7
11.	0.7	0.3	0.0	1.0	0.0	0.0	1.0	0.0	0.2	0.8	0.3	0.7	0.0
12.	0.2	0.6	0.2	0.0	1.0	0.0	0.3	0.7	0.3	0.7	0.7	0.2	0.1
13.	0.9	0.1	0.0	0.2	0.8	0.0	0.1	0.9	1.0	0.0	0.0	0.0	1.0
14.	0.0	0.9	0.1	0.0	0.9	0.1	0.1	0.9	0.7	0.3	0.0	0.0	1.0
15.	0.0	0.0	1.0	0.0	0.0	1.0	1.0	0.0	0.8	0.2	0.0	0.0	1.0
16.	1.0	0.0	0.0	0.5	0.5	0.0	0.0	1.0	0.0	1.0	0.5	0.5	0.0
M	6.6	5.8	3.6	6.1	5.6	4.3	5.6	10.4	6.5	9.5	4.4	4.4	7.2

*Three symbols V, S and W, denote three sports to play: *Volleyball, Swimming, Weight lifting*

3 Information-Theoretic Learning

We assume that all combinations of values of attributes occur with the certain frequencies. The analysis of these frequencies allows receiving the important features of attributes such as proper information, joint information, condition information and mutual information for a fuzzy subset and their entropy.

3.1 Information and Summary Entropies in Fuzzy Sets

Definition 3. The *proper* information of the value $A_{i,j}$ of the attribute A_i is

$$I(A_{i,j}) = \log N - \log M(A_{i,j}) = \log N + \mathbf{I}(A_{i,j}) \text{ bits,} \tag{1}$$

where log denotes the base 2 logarithm; $(i=1,\dots,n;\ j=1,\dots,m_i)$. $\mathbf{I}(A_{i,j})$ is *summary proper* information of the value $A_{i,j}$.

Definition 4. The *joint* (the unconditional) information of the values $A_{i2,j2}$ of attribute A_{i2} and $A_{i1,j1}$ of attribute A_{i1} is

$$I(A_{i1,j1}, A_{i2,j2}) = \log N - \log M(A_{i1,j1} \times A_{i2,j2}) = \log N + \mathbf{I}(A_{i1,j1}, A_{i2,j2}) \text{ bits,} \tag{2}$$

where $\mathbf{I}(A_{i1,j1}, A_{i2,j2})$ is *summary joint* information.

Definition 5. The *condition* information describes the uncertainty of the value $A_{i2,j2}$ of attribute A_{i2} when the value $A_{i1,j1}$ of attribute A_{i1} is given

$$I(A_{i2,j2}|A_{i1,j1}) = I(A_{i1,j1}, A_{i2,j2}) - I(A_{i1,j1}) = \mathbf{I}(A_{i2,j2}|A_{i1,j1}) \text{ bits,} \tag{3}$$

where $\mathbf{I}(A_{i2,j2}|A_{i1,j1})$ is *summary condition* information of values $A_{i2,j2}$ and $A_{i1,j1}$.

Definition 6. The *mutual* information between the value $A_{i2,j2}$ of attribute A_{i2} and the value $A_{i1,j1}$ of attribute A_{i1} is used as to measure the dependence of the value $A_{i2,j2}$ on the value $A_{i1,j1}$ and vice-versa

$$I(A_{i1,j1}; A_{i2,j2}) = I(A_{i1,j1}) + I(A_{i2,j2}) - I(A_{i2,j2}, A_{i1,j1}) = I(A_{i1,j1}) - I(A_{i1,j1}|A_{i2,j2}) \text{ bits} \tag{4}$$

The mutual information shows as a lot of information (in bits) about values $A_{i1,j1}$ we have found out, if we have determined values of $A_{i2,j2}$ and vice-versa.

Let's generalize previous estimations for all values of attribute. For this purpose we shall generalize concept of information on conception of entropy for fuzzy subsets.

In communication engineering, the entropy of A_i represents the minimum expected number of bits (if we used the base 2 logarithm) required to transmit a value of A_i.

Definition 7. The *summary* entropy of an attribute A_i is

$$H(A_i) = \sum_{j=1}^{m_i} M(A_{i,j}) \times I(A_{i,j}) \text{ bits.} \tag{5}$$

Entropy of input attribute is an average amount of information, which is extracted when we have detected value of this attribute. Entropy of output attribute is an average amount of information, which should be extracted for determination of this output attribute.

Definition 8. The *summary joint* entropy of A_{i2} and A_{i1} is

$$H(A_{i2},A_{i1})= \sum_{j1=1}^{m_{j1}} \sum_{j2=1}^{m_{j2}} M(A_{i1,j1} \times A_{i2,j2}) \times I(A_{i1,j1},A_{i2,j2}) \text{ bits.} \tag{6}$$

Definition 9. The *summary conditional* entropy between attribute A_{i2} and the value $A_{i1,j1}$ (or attribute A_{i1}) is uncertainty of attribute A_{i2} when the value $A_{i1,j1}$ is given

$$H(A_{i2}|A_{i1,j1})= \sum_{j2=1}^{m_{j2}} M(A_{i1,j1} \times A_{i2,j2}) \times I(A_{i2,j2}|A_{i1,j1}) \text{ bits.} \tag{7}$$

$$H(A_{i2}|A_{i1})= \sum_{j1=1}^{m_{j1}} H(A_{i2}|A_{i1,j1}) = H(A_{i1}, A_{i2}) - H(A_{i1}) \text{ bits,} \tag{8}$$

Definition 10. The *summary mutual* information in attribute A_{i1} about attribute A_{i2} and vice versa, that reflects the influence of attribute A_{i1} on the attribute A_{i2} and conversely, the influence of attribute A_{i2} on attribute A_{i1}

$$I(A_{i2};A_{i1}) = H(A_{i2})-H(A_{i2}|A_{i1}) = H(A_{i1})-H(A_{i1}|A_{i2}) = H(A_{i2})+H(A_{i1})-H(A_{i1},A_{i2}) \tag{9}$$

Example 2. The estimations for training set from Table 1 see in Table 2

Table 2. The Summary Conditional Information and Entropy for attribute A_2=Temp (in bits)

Values	$I(A_{2,j})$	I (Game|Temp)			H (Game|Temp)			
$A_{2,j}$		V	S	W	V	S	W	H(Game|Temp) =20,93
Hot	-2,609	1,913	0,886	2,370	3,099	2,925	2,797	H(Game|Hot) =8,820
Mild	-2,485	1,429	2,654	1,090	2,972	2,362	2,868	H(Game|Mild)=8,201
Cool	-2,104	2,619	4,356	0,343	1,833	0,915	1,163	H(Game|Cool)=3,911

3.2 Mutual Summary Information and Entropy for Sequence of Attributes

Let's we have sequence of q input attributes $A_{i1},...,A_{iq}$ and one output attribute B.

Theorem 1. The *summary joint* information of the sequence of values $U_q=\{A_{i1,j1},...,A_{iq,jq}\}$ ($q\geq2$) and B_j ($j=1,...,m_b$) is

$$I(B_j, U_q) = -\log M(B_j \times A_{i1,j1} \times ... \times A_{iq,jq}) \text{ bits.} \tag{10}$$

Theorem 2. The *summary conditional* entropy between attributes B, A_{iq} and the sequence of values $U_{q-1}= \{A_{i1,j1},...,A_{iq-1,jq-1}\}$ of attributes $\{A_{i1},...,A_{iq-1}\}$ is uncertainty of values of output attribute B when the sequence U_{q-1} and values $A_{iq,jq}$ are known

$$H(B|U_{q-1},A_{iq,jq})= \sum_{j=1}^{m_b} M(B_j \times U_q) \times \left(I(B_j,U_q) - I(U_q)\right) \text{ bits} \tag{11}$$

or $H(B|U_{q-1},A_{iq})= \sum_{jq=1}^{m_{iq}} H(B|U_{q-1},A_{iq,jq}) \text{ bits.} \tag{12}$

Theorem 3. The *summary mutual* information in output attribute B about pair attribute A_{iq} and the sequence of values $U_{q-1}=\{A_{i1,j1},...,A_{iq-1,jq-1}\}$ reflects the influence of attribute B on the attribute A_{iq} when sequence U_{q-1} are known.

$$I(B; U_{q-1}, A_{iq})= \sum_{jq=1}^{m_{iq}} \sum_{j=1}^{m_b} M(B_j \times A_{i1,j1} \times ... \times A_{iq,jq}) \times \qquad (13)$$

$$\times \Big(I(B_j, U_{q-1}) + I(A_{iq,jq}, U_{q-1}) - I(B_j, U_{q-1}, A_{iq,jq}) - I(U_{q-1}) \Big) = H(B|U_{q-1}) - H(B|U_{q-1}, A_{iq}).$$

Example 3. For training set in Table 1 information estimations show in Table 3.

Table 3. The Summary Conditional Information and Entropy when values of attribute *Temperature = Hot* is known (in bits)

Values $A_{1,j}$	$I(A_1, Hot)$	I(Game|Hot,Outlook)			H(Game|Hot,Outlook)			H(Game|Temp = Hot, Outlook) = 7,653
		V	S	W	V	S	W	
Sunny	-1,934	1,931	0,636	3,408	1,935	1,564	1,227	4,725
Cloudy	-0,465	1,411	0,990	3,055	0,732	0,688	0,507	1,927
Rain	0,152	3,184	2,614	0,461	0,315	0,384	0,301	1,000

4 The Algorithm of FDT Induction

Let's show using of summary information estimates for FDT induction. We introduce two kind of threshold β and α. Lower β and greatest α may lead to a smaller tree but with lower classification accuracy. Nodes are usually regarded as leaves if:

- the frequency of branch $U_q=\{A_{i1,j1},...,A_{iq,jq}\}$ is less than or equal to a given threshold value α: $I(U_q) \geq -\log \alpha \times N$.
- the relative frequency of one class is greater than or equal to a given threshold value β: $min\ I(B_j|\ U_q) \leq -\log \beta$ for $\forall j=1,...m_b$;

A learning algorithm for construction FDT can be described as follows.

Input Data: The training set (see Table 1). *Attr* $=\{A_1,...,A_n\}$; $q=0$; $U_q = \varnothing$

Output data: FDT.

Tree = *buildTree* $(U_q, Attr)$

{ 1. Calculate *summary condition* entropy Eqs.(8 or 11)

 2. Select attribute with the smallest entropy

    num = argmin $H(B|U_q \cup A_i)$ for $\forall A_i \in Attr$,

 3. Assign current node   Tree $\leftarrow$ node (A_{num}); $Attr = Attr \backslash A_{num}$;

 4. Choose leaves and continue

    for $(\forall A_{num,j})$, $j=1,...,m_{num}$;

    { q++; $U_q = U_{q-1} \cup A_{num,j}$;

      if $(A_{num,j}$ is leaf) Tree $\leftarrow$ leaf $(A_{num,j})$

      else   Recursively construct the sub-trees:

         Tree = *buildTree* $(U_q, Attr)$ }   }

Example 4. For training set in Table 1 we support that α=0,25 and β=0,75.

Step 1. See in Table 2 *summary condition* entropy between input and output attributes.

Step 2. Choose the attribute A_i with minimal entropy: num = argmin $\mathbf{H}(Game|A_i)$ =2.

Step 3. Assign chosen attribute $A_2=Temperature$ to current tree node of FDT.

Step 4. Check up, whether have reached a leaf.

$$min\ \mathbf{I}(A_{2/2})\ for\ \forall j_2 \geq -\log(0,25\times16) = -2\ bits$$

$\mathbf{I}(Hot)$ = -2,609 bits; $\mathbf{I}(Mild)$ =-2,485 bits; $\mathbf{I}(Cool)$ = -2,104 bits (they are not leaf)

$$min\ \mathbf{I}(B_j|A_{2/2})\ for\ \forall j \leq -\log 0,75 = 0,415\ bits$$

$\mathbf{I}(S|Hot)$ = 0,886 bits; $\mathbf{I}(W|Mild)$ = 1,090 bits (they is not leaf);
  $\mathbf{I}(W|Cool)$ = 0,343 bits (it is leaf)

Step 5. Repeat *Step.*1 - *Step.*4 for another three attributes {*Outlook, Humidity* and *Wind*}. Some results are given in Table 3 and Fig.2.
End

5   Conclusion

We have proposed the technique to compute new information estimations for fuzzy sets, which is simple to understand and apply. Our estimations are based on Shannon's information and entropy. The use of these estimations allows precisely estimating mutual influence of attributes. These estimations are tool for analysis of group of training examples.

We have illustrated various algorithmic and computational aspects by a number of examples. We use only one of these estimations (*summary condition* entropy) for induction of FDT. We also apply *summary joint* information for judgment of leaves.

We suppose, that these evaluations will be a basis of algorithms for induction fully optimal FDT in future.

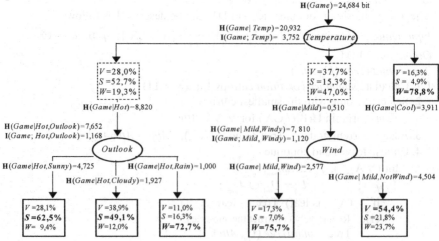

Fig. 2. Induction of FDT

References

1. Cover, T.M.: Elements of Information Theory, Wiley, New York, 1991.
2. Cheushev, V., Shmerko, V., Simovici, D., Yanushkevich, S.: Functional Entropy & Decision Trees. Proc. of the 28th IEEE Int.Symp. on Multiple Valued Logic, Japan, 257-262, (1998)
3. Safavian, S.R., Landgrebe, D.: A Survey of Decision Tree Classifier Methodology, IEEE Trans.Sys.Man Cybernet. 21, pp.660-674, 1991.
4. Weber, R.: Fuzzy-ID3: a Class of Methods for Automatic Knowledge Acquisition, Proc. of the 2nd Int..Conf. on Fuzzy Logic and Neural Networks, Iizuka, Japan, pp. 265-268, 1992.
5. Zeidler, J., Schlosser, M.: Fuzzy Handling of Continous-Valued Attributes in Decision Trees. Proc. of MLNet Familiarization Workshop: Statistics, Machine Learning and Knowledge Discovery in Databases, Heraklion, Greece, pp.41-46, 1995.
6. Kosko, B.: Neural Networks and Fuzzy Systems. Prentice-Hall, Englewood Cliffs, NJ, 1992.
7. Cios, K.J., Sztandera, L.M.: Continuous ID3 Algorithm with Fuzzy Entropy Measures, Proc. of the IEEE Int. Conf. on Fuzzy Systems, San Diego, CA, pp. 469-476, 1992.
8. Yuan, Y., Shaw, M.J.: Induction of Fuzzy Decision Trees, Fuzzy Sets and Systems, 69, pp.125-139, 1995.
9. Wang, X., Chen, B., Qian, G., Ye, F.: On the Optimization of Fuzzy Decision Trees, Fuzzy Sets and Systems, 112, pp.117-125, 2000.
10. Chang, R.L.P., Pavliddis, T.: Fuzzy Decision Tree Algorithms, IEEE Trans. on Systems, Man and Cybernetics, 7, pp. 28-35, 1977.
11. Levashenko, V., Morozevich, A., Zaitseva, E. and Kovalik, S.: Using Information Theoretical Approach for Construction of Fuzzy Decision Trees, Proc. of the 6th Int.Conf. on Information Networks, Systems and Technologies, Minsk, Belarus, pp.164-170, 2001.

Genetic Algorithm Based-On the Quantum Probability Representation[1]

Bin LI[2] and Zhen-quan Zhuang

Laboratory of Quantum Communication and Quantum Computation,
University of Science and Technology of China, Hefei, 230026, China
{binli, zqzhuang}@ustc.edu.cn

Abstract. A genetic algorithm based on the quantum probability representation (GAQPR) is proposed, in which each individual evolves independently; a new crossover operator is designed to integrate searching processes of multiple individuals into a more efficient global searching process; a new mutation operator is also proposed and analyzed. Optimization capability of GAQPR is studied via experiments on function optimization, results of experiments show that, for multi-peak optimization problem, GAQPR is more efficient than GQA[4].

1 Introduction

Research development in quantum computation presents us not only with a tempting perspective of future computational capability [1], but also with inspirations of improving classical algorithms by reconsidering them from a standpoint of quantum mechanics. Genetic algorithm is a well-known heuristic searching algorithm, and has been proved successful in many applications [2]. Research work on merging genetic algorithm and quantum computation has been started by some researchers since 1990's. Only two practical models have been proposed till now.

QIGA (Quantum-Inspired Genetic Algorithm), proposed by Ajit Narayanam, introduces the theory of many universes in quantum mechanics into the implementation of genetic algorithm [3]. The main contribution of [3] is that it proves the efficiency of the strategy that uses multiple colonies to search in parallel, and uses a joint crossover operator to enable the information exchange among colonies.

Kuk-Hyun Han proposed a Genetic Quantum Algorithm (GQA) [4], in which the probability amplitude of qubit was used for the first time to encode the chromosome, and the formula of quantum rotation gate was used to implement the updating of chromosome. GQA is basically a probability algorithm, not a genetic algorithm. All individuals evolve towards one Contemporary Evolutionary Target (CET). Important genetic operators, such as crossover and mutation, are not adopted in it.

---

[1]   The research is supported by the National Natural Science Foundation of China under Grant No. 60171029.

[2]   Bin LI is currently a visiting scholar at Information Systems Institute, Technical University of Vienna, Austria.

H. Yin et al. (Eds.): IDEAL 2002, LNCS 2412, pp. 500–505, 2002.

In this paper, a new Genetic Algorithm based on the Quantum Probability Representation (GAQPR) is proposed, in which each individual has its own Contemporary Evolutionary Target (CET) and evolves independently; a new crossover operator is designed to enable the efficient exchange of evolution information between different individuals. A new mutation operator is also proposed, its effect is studied in experiments. Experiments on two typical function optimization problems prove that, for multi-peak optimization problem, GAQPR is more efficient than GQA.

The remaining part of this paper is organized as follow: section 2 describes the principle and procedure of GAQPR, which includes the introduction of representation and updating strategy of chromosomes, main procedure of GAQPR, and procedures of the new designed crossover and mutation operators. Section 3 is the description of experiment. Section 4 is the conclusion of the whole paper.

2   GAQPR

2.1   Representation and Updating of Chromosomes

In quantum computation, the elementary unit for storing information is a quantum system with two states, called quantum bit (qubit). The key characteristic that makes qubit differ from classical bit is that it can be at the superposition of two quantum states simultaneously. This superposition can be expressed as follow:

$$\varphi = \alpha \,|\, 0 > + \beta \,|\, 1 >, \tag{1}$$

where (α, β) is a pair of complex invariables, called probability amplitude of qubit, which satisfies

$$|\alpha|^2 + |\beta|^2 = 1, \tag{2}$$

$|0>$ and $|1>$ represent two different states of qubit respectively, so one qubit can store the information of both states at the same time.

In GQA, each gene has only two states, so one qubit is enough for encoding one gene. But it is often the case in applications that one gene may have more than two states. In this paper, following the binary coding methods in classical genetic algorithm, we use more than one qubit to encode gene with more than two states. A chromosome is defined as follow:

$$q_j^t = \begin{pmatrix} \alpha_{11}^t & \alpha_{12}^t & \cdots & \alpha_{1k}^t & \alpha_{21}^t & \alpha_{22}^t & \cdots & \alpha_{2k}^t & \alpha_{m1}^t & \alpha_{m2}^t & \cdots & \alpha_{mk}^t \\ \beta_{11}^t & \beta_{12}^t & \cdots & \beta_{1k}^t & \beta_{21}^t & \beta_{22}^t & \cdots & \beta_{2k}^t & \beta_{m1}^t & \beta_{m2}^t & \cdots & \beta_{mk}^t \end{pmatrix}, \tag{3}$$

where q_j^t is the jth chromosome in the colony at generation t, m is the number of genes in a chromosome, and k is the number of qubit used to encode one gene, which can be calculated by function

$$k = ceil(\log_2^n), \tag{4}$$

where n is the state number of each gene, function ceil(x) finds the nearest integer from x towards $+\infty$.

Gene updating follows the formula of quantum rotation gate shown as follow:

$$\begin{pmatrix} \alpha_i' \\ \beta_i' \end{pmatrix} = \begin{pmatrix} \cos(\theta_i) & -\sin(\theta_i) \\ \sin(\theta_i) & \cos(\theta_i) \end{pmatrix} \begin{pmatrix} \alpha_i \\ \beta_i \end{pmatrix}, \tag{5}$$

where (α_i, β_i) is the pair of probability amplitude of the ith qubit in chromosome, $\theta_i = s(\alpha_i \beta_i)\Delta\theta_i$ [4], and the values of $s(\alpha_i, \beta_i)$ and $\Delta\theta_i$ are determined by a predefined strategy shown in table 1. The strategy proposed in [4] is designed for the knapsack problem, which has bias. In this paper we do some adjustment to make it a universal strategy.

Table 1. Tuning strategy of rotation angle

| x_i | b_i | f(x)>f(b) | $\Delta\theta_i$ | $s(\alpha_i, \beta_i)$ | | | |
				$\alpha_i\beta_i>0$	$\alpha_i\beta_i<0$	$\alpha_i=0$	$\beta_i=0$
0	0	False	0	-	-	-	-
0	0	True	0	-	-	-	-
0	1	False	Delta	+1	-1	0	± 1
0	1	True	Delta	-1	+1	± 1	0
1	0	False	Delta	-1	+1	± 1	0
1	0	True	Delta	+1	-1	0	± 1
1	1	False	0	-	-	-	-
1	1	True	0	-	-	-	-

Tuning pace of rotation angle "Delta" may take different values in different opera-tions. For example, in regular evolution operation "Delta" can take the value a little larger than that in crossover operation. This provides an easy way to control the effect of crossover operator.

2.2 Procedure of GAQPR

The procedure of GAQPR is shown as follow:

Begin
1)   t=0
2)   Initialize $Q(t) = \{ q_1^t, q_2^t, ..., q_n^t \}$
3)   For each chromosome q_j^t, apply one measurement to get one solutions p_j^t, cal-culate the fitness of p_j^t, $f(p_j^t)$, store the solution$\{ p_j^t, f(p_j^t) \}$ in T(t,j), which represents the CET of the jth chromosome at next generation t+1.
4)   While (t<Max_Gen) do
5)   Begin
     a)   t=t+1
     b)   For each chromosome q_j^t, apply one measurement to get one solution p_j^t, evaluate p_j^t to get f(p_j^t).
     c)   Update q_j^t for one time according to its CET T(t,j).

    d)   If $f(p'_j) > T(t,j)(2)$, update $T(t,j)$ with $\{ p'_j, f(p'_j) \}$,

    e)   Otherwise, keep $T(t,j)$ unchanged.

    f)   Perform new-designed genetic operator (crossover, mutation) on $Q(t)$.

6)   End

End

Step2) and 3) are the initialization of individuals and their CETs. Step5) to 6) is the evolution procedure of every generation, it can be seen that before step *f)* each chromosome evolves independently, step *f)* implements the interconnection between chromosomes by crossover operator.

2.3 Crossover Operator

In GAQPR, each chromosome represents a superposition of all possible solutions in certain distribution, any operation performed on such chromosome will affect all possible solutions it represents, thus the genetic operators defined on the quantum probability representation have to satisfy the requirement that it must be of the same efficiency to all the possible solutions one chromosome represents.

In classical genetic algorithm, the purpose of crossover is to exchange information between different individuals. In GAQPR, the evolution information of each individual is well contained in its CET, the best solution so far and its fitness. We designed a new crossover operator, shown as below, which satisfies the above requirement.

1) Select two chromosomes from the group randomly with a given probability Pc,

2) Exchange their evolution targets temporarily,

3) Update the two chromosomes according to their new targets for one time,

4) Change back their evolution targets.

Because CET represents the current evolution state of one individual, by exchanging CETs of two individuals, the evolution process of one individual will be influenced by the evolution state of the other one.

2.4 Mutation Operator

The purpose of mutation is to slightly disturb the evolution states of some individuals, to prevent the algorithm from falling into local optimum. The requirement for designing mutation resembles that for designing crossover. As a probing research, we define a single qubit mutation operator, but the thought can be generalized easily to the multiple qubits scenarios. Following is the procedure of mutation operator.

1) Select a set of chromosomes with a given probability Pm.

2) For each chromosome, select a qubit randomly

3) Exchange the position of its pair of probability amplitude, α'_i and β'_i.

Obviously, the mutation operator defined above has the same efficiency to all the superposition states.

3   Experiments and Discussion

Two typical function optimization problems, single-peak function optimization and multi-peak function optimization, are used to test and compare the capability of algorithms. To guarantee the objectivity of the experiment results, every curve illustrated in following figures is the mean of 20 independent experiments.

Function (6) is a single-peak function to be optimized, which is also used as the fitness function of individuals.

$$F_1(x) = 72 - \sum_{i=1}^{n} x_i^2, \quad -5.12 \le x_i \le 5.12 \cdot \tag{6}$$

Fig. 1 shows the performances of GAQPR and GQA. It can be seen that both algorithms are efficient for the single-peak optimization problem.

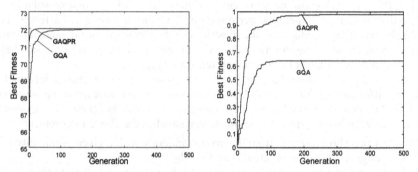

Fig. 1. Performances on single-peak function   **Fig. 2.** Performances on multi-peak function

A variant of Rosenbrock function (7) is used as a multiple-peak function to be optimized, which is also used as the fitness function of individuals.

$$F_2(x) = \frac{1}{1 + \sum_{i=1}^{n-1}(100 \times (x_{i+1} - x_i^2)^2 + (1 - x_i)^2)}, \quad -5 \le x_i \le 5, i = 1,2,\dots,n \cdot \tag{7}$$

Fig. 2 shows the performances of GAQPR and GQA. It can be seen that, for the optimization of function (7), GAQPR is much more efficient than GQA, and that GQA tends to be premature.

To test the effect of the new mutation operator, we introduced only the mutation operator into GQA to optimize the function (7). Fig. 3 shows the results of experiment. It can be seen that, when adopted alone, the new designed mutation operator can help GQA jump out of local optimum efficiently.

We studied also the effect of mutation operator in GAQPR when adopted together with the crossover operator. Fig. 4 shows the performances of GAQPR with various probability of mutation *Pm*. It can be seen that, when works together with crossover operator, the effect of mutation is not so obvious, and the probability *Pm* can't be large, otherwise the performance will decrease. This may be explained as follow: In GAQPR, multiple individuals evolve independently towards multiple different directions simultaneously, this has been able to prevent the algorithms from premature convergence efficiently. When the searching process is converging to the best solution, too many mutation operations will cause the algorithm swing at the neighbor of the best point, and then slow down the speed of convergence.

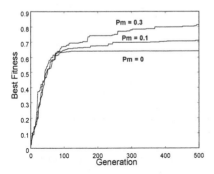
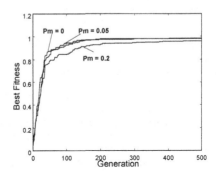

Fig. 3. Performances of GQA
with and without mutation

Fig. 4. Performances of GAQPR
with various probability of mutation

4   Conclusion

Quantum probability representation of chromosome provides the individual with much more powerful global searching capability than that of classical one. In GAQPR, these global searching capabilities of multiple individuals are exploited and integrated by adopting a new searching strategy, which utilizes multiple individuals to search in parallel and uses a new designed crossover operator to implement the communication between individuals. Experiment results prove that, for multi-peak optimization problem, this strategy is more efficient than that of GQA.

References

1. Divincenzo D P, Quantum Computation, Science, 1995, 10, 255~261.
2. Guo-liang Chen, Xu-fa Wang, Zhen-quan Zhuang, Dong-sheng Wang, Genetic algorithm and its applications, people's post and telecommunications press, June 1996. (in Chinese)
3. Narayanan, A. and Moore, M. Quantum inspired genetic algorithms. In Proceedings of the 1996 IEEE International Conference on Evolutionary Computation(ICEC96). IEEE Press. 1996.
4. Kuk-Hyun Han, Jong-Hwan Kim, Genetic Quantum algorithm and its application to Combinatorial Optimization Problem. In IEEE Proceedings of the 2000 Congress on Evolutionary Computation, July 2000, pp. 1354~1360.

A Dynamic Method for Discretization
of Continuous Attributes

Grace J. Hwang and Fumin Li

Department of Computer Science and Information Engineering
Fu Jen Catholic University, Taipei, Taiwan
{jihwang, ted88}@csie.fju.edu.tw

Abstract. A discretization technique converts continuous attribute values into discrete ones. Discretization is needed when classification algorithms require only discrete attributes. It is also useful to increase the speed and the accuracy of classification algorithms. This paper presents a dynamic discretization method, whose main characteristic is to detect interdependencies between all continuous attributes. Empirical evaluation on 12 datasets from the UCI repository shows that the proposed algorithm is a relatively effective method for discretization.

1 Introduction

Discretization is a technique to partition continuous attributes into a number of intervals and map each one as a discrete value. Although continuous data are very common in real-world applications, there are a large number of classification algorithms, which handle only discrete attributes. To use these algorithms when data are continuous, all continuous values must first be converted into discrete values. This triggers the necessity of discretization. The discretization process is also beneficial for some classification algorithms either to increase the speed [1] or to improve accuracy [2]. Therefore, the process of discretization is an essential task for data preprocessing.

Dougherty, Kohavi and Sahami [2] have reviewed a variety of discretization methods and carried out a comparative study. According to their terminology, discretization methods can be classified along three different axes: global vs. local, supervised vs. unsupervised, and static vs. dynamic.

The advantage of global methods as opposed to local methods is the independence from the learning algorithms. A dataset that is discretized by a global method can be used in any classification algorithms that deal with discrete attributes. Supervised methods are expected to lead to better performance compared to unsupervised methods, since the discretization utilizes the information of the class labels. Dougherty, Kohavi and Sahami [2] show that the supervised methods are slightly better than the unsupervised methods. The dynamic methods are believed to be promising since they detect interdependencies between attributes and discretize all attributes concurrently.

H. Yin et al. (Eds.): IDEAL 2002, LNCS 2412, pp. 506-511, 2002.

Based on the above reasons, we attempt to develop a discretization method that is global, supervised and dynamic. The dynamic feature is our primary concern, since most discretization methods to date are static.

This work is related to ChiMerge [3], Chi2 [4] and ConMerge [5]. All of these four methods use the statistical measure, χ^2, in the discretization process. However, our method differs in the following aspects:

1. Our algorithm improves the way in which initial intervals are determined and hence reduces the number of initial intervals.
2. We detect the interdependencies between all continuous attributes by using factor analysis.

2   GroupMerge

The objective of our discretization is to detect the interdependencies between attributes. To meet this aim, multivariate methods in statistics such as factor analysis may be considered. Multivariate methods are extremely useful to determine whether massive amounts of data actually contain information, and they also help to summarize the information when it exists. Factor analysis is a multivariate technique and is frequently used to reduce a large number of attributes to a smaller set of uncorrelated groups, called factors. For a detailed description of factor analysis, the reader may refer to textbooks of multivariate methods, for instance [6,7]. In a factor analysis process, attributes are partitioned into several groups, and the attributes distributed in the same group are more highly related than those attributes in other groups. In other words, the interdependencies may be considered to limit in the attributes within the same group. Therefore, the discretization process can be performed on each group individually. This leads to our proposed algorithm, which we term GroupMerge. A preprocess that partitions all the continuous attributes into different groups is performed first, and then an initialization step and a bottom-up merging process are performed after. The following is the pseudo-code of the GroupMerge.

```
GroupMerge
Preprocess:
        Use the technique of factor analysis to capture interdependencies
        between attributes and partition them into different groups.
FOR each group
Initialization:
    Produce a sorted sequence of attribute values for each attribute within
        the group;
    Divide each sequence into intervals by placing boundary points in it;
Merging process:
        WHILE there are interval pairs to merge DO
        Select an interval pair from the group, where it has the lowest χ² value;
        IF merging the pair does not exceed the inconsistency threshold
        THEN merge the pair into one interval
        ELSE exclude the pair from further merging;
        ENDWHILE
ENDFOR
```

In the initialization step, for each continuous attribute within the group values are sorted and the boundary points are placed to produce initial intervals. A potential cut point is evaluated as the halfway between each successive pair of attribute values in the sorted sequence. A boundary point is a potential cut point that separates intervals of different classes. Fayyad and Irani [8] showed that the minimum of the average class entropy must always be a boundary point.

After the initialization step, an iteration loop called a merging process is executed. This is a bottom-up process that conducts a selection and a test. The selection is based on a criterion that chooses a pair of adjacent intervals from all continuous attributes within the group.

The criterion for merging two adjacent intervals is based on Kerber's ChiMerge [3]. Kerber calculates the χ^2 value for each pair of adjacent intervals and selects the pair with the lowest χ^2 value to merge. χ^2 is a statistical measure used to test the independence of two adjacent intervals. The smallest value of χ^2 indicates the least significant difference between intervals and therefore this pair of intervals is the "best" candidate to merge. The χ^2 value is computed as follows:

$$\chi^2 = \sum_{i=1}^{m} \sum_{j=1}^{k} \frac{(A_{ij} - E_{ij})^2}{E_{ij}},$$

where

$m = 2$ (the 2 intervals being compared),
k = number of classes,
A_{ij} = number of examples in the ith interval, jth class,
N = total number of examples,
E_{ij} = expected frequency of $A_{ij} = (\sum_{j=1}^{k} A_{ij}) * (\sum_{i=1}^{m} A_{ij}) / N,$

An inconsistency test is performed after the selection. The chosen pair from the selection is merged if an inconsistency rate does not exceed a user-defined threshold. Otherwise, the pair is not allowed to be merged and is also excluded from further merging. The merging process is repeated and is terminated when no pairs of intervals can be merged.

An inconsistency in a dataset means there exist some examples having identical attribute values but with different class labels. A set of examples is considered a matching pattern if these examples have same attribute values (no matter what their class labels). An inconsistency count for a matching pattern is the number of examples whose class labels are different with the major class in the pattern set. Let I be the total number of each inconsistency count for each matching pattern in the dataset, and N be the number of the dataset, then the inconsistency rate of the dataset is I/N.

The inconsistency rate is used as a parameter in the algorithm. The inconsistency rate 0% means no matching pattern occurs in the dataset, that is, all examples are consistent. The default value of the inconsistency rate can be determined from the original dataset. The purpose of introducing the inconsistency rate is to assure that the discretized dataset can represent the original one as accurately as possible. Since the inconsistency may be due to the merging process.

Both of the initialization and merging steps are performed in each group individually. The algorithm is terminated when all of the groups in the dataset are done.

3 Empirical Evaluation

To test the effectiveness of GroupMerge in discretizing continuous attribute in datasets, we chose 12 datasets from UCI repository [9]. Table 1 lists some basic characteristics of these datasets. Since GroupMerge is a discretization algorithm, which is a data-preprocessing step in classification algorithms, it is unable to evaluate classification accuracy directly and has to cooperate with a classification algorithm. Therefore, C5.0 [10,11] was chosen to work with GroupMerge for the evaluation. C5.0 is a well-known algorithm and hence further description is not needed. The test was run for tenfold cross-validation. The inconsistency threshold was set at 0% for default in the experiment, since all chosen datasets are consistent. The comparisons of the error rates and tree sizes for the original and discretized datasets are shown in Fig. 1 and Fig. 2, respectively.

With respect to error rates, for all but Australian and Wine, the datasets discretized by GroupMerge performed better when compared to the original datasets. As to tree sizes, for all datasets except Car, Labor and Wine, the datasets discretized by GroupMerge produced smaller sizes than those of the original datasets. The reason why the tree sizes go up for the data sets of Car, Labor and Wine may be due to the 0% inconsistency threshold. The effect of the threshold will be discussed below. From the resulting error rates and tree sizes, the experiment indicates the effectiveness of GroupMerge.

Table 1. Datasets, number of continuous attributes, nominal attributes, classes, and examples

Dataset	Anneal	Australian	Breast-c	Car	Crx	Cleve	Diabetes	Heart	Hepatitis	Iris	Labor	Wine
Cont	6	6	10	8	6	6	8	13	6	4	8	13
Nominal	32	8	0	0	9	7	0	0	13	0	8	0
Classes	6	2	2	3	2	2	2	2	2	3	2	3
Examples	898	690	699	392	690	303	768	270	155	150	57	178

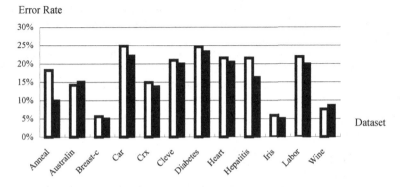

Fig. 1. Comparison of error rates for the original (□) and discretized (■) datasets

Tree Size

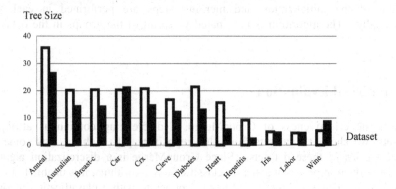

Fig. 2. Comparison of tree sizes for the original (□) and discretized (■) datasets

The default inconsistency threshold is determined from the original dataset. However, the constraint of the inconsistency level may be relaxed to a larger value to allow more interval pairs to be merged, and hence the number of discrete intervals to be reduced. In our experiments, we observed that in general a smaller inconsistency threshold produces smaller error rates and larger tree sizes. There is a trade-off between error rate and tree size: the less the error rate, the more the tree size.

The main characteristic of GroupMerge is that it detects interdependencies between continuous attributes by using factor analysis. Attributes within the same group are considered as they depend on each other, as compared to those in other groups. Therefore, a search for the best interval merging is restricted to the attributes of same group. By using this approach all attributes are considered to discretize in an interdependent way. However, it reduces the searching space from the whole dataset to the group being considered.

To test whether GroupMerge properly captures interdependencies between all attributes, we compared GroupMerge with an approach that did not partition all attributes into groups, i.e., without doing the preprocess in the GroupMerge algorithm. This is in fact a special case of GroupMerge. It considers all attributes in the dataset as interdependent and hence in one group. For both of GroupMerge and the special case without grouping, we found that the results for each tested dataset were very similar. We also evaluated the overall average error rates and tree sizes for the 12 chosen datasets. The average error rates and tree sizes are 15.13% vs. 15.65% and 11.96 vs. 11.02 respectively. This reveals that there is no significant difference between two approaches. This also verifies that GroupMerge properly accounts for interdependencies between all continuous attributes. However, in our experiments GroupMerge is faster. Including the time taken to partition attributes into groups, the GroupMerge usually required only 2/3 of the running time of the special case without grouping.

4   Conclusion

GroupMerge provides a discretization method for classification algorithms. It is a global, supervised and dynamic discretization. GroupMerge is related to ChiMerge

[3], Chi2 [4] and ConMerge [5].   All of these four methods use theχ^2 value as an estimation for merging intervals. In ChiMerge, the stop criterion for the merging process is a user-specified value, χ^2 threshold.   Instead of χ^2 threshold, an inconsistency rate is used in Chi2, ConMerge and GroupMerge.

The main differences between GroupMerge and the other three methods are in twofold.   The first one is the way in which initial intervals are determined.   In a sorted sequence of attributes, ChiMerge, Chi2 and ConMerge put each continuous value into its own interval.   The number of initial intervals for each attribute is therefore the number of distinct values in the attribute. The maximum number of the intervals can be N if the dataset has N examples.   In GroupMerge, the boundary points are placed to divide the range of each attribute into intervals. If there are B boundary points for some attribute, then there are B+1 initial intervals. Therefore, the number of initial intervals in GroupMerge is reduced compared to that of the other three methods. The reduction may be significant if the attribute values are highly relevant to the class labels. The other difference is that GroupMerge detects the interdependencies between all continuous attributes by using factor analysis. This is also the main characteristic of GroupMerge.

Empirical evaluation on 12 datasets from UCI repository shows that GroupMerge is a relatively effective method for discretization.

References

1.   Catlett, J. 1991. On changing continuous attributes into ordered discrete attributes. In Y. Kodratoff, ed., Proceedings of the European Working Session on Learning, Berlin, Germany. Springer-Verlag.
2.   Dougherty, J., Kohavi, R. and Shami, M. 1995.   Supervised and unsupervised discretization of continuous features. In Machine Learning: Proceedings of the twelfth International Conference. Morgan kaufmann.
3.   Kerber, R. 1992. ChiMerge: Discretization of numeric attributes. In Proceedings of the Tenth National Conference on Artificial Intelligence. MIT press.
4.   Liu, H. and Setiono, R. 1997. Feature selection via discretization. In IEEE Transactions on Knowledge and Data Engineering, Vol. 9, No. 4, Pp. 642-645.
5.   Wang, K. and Liu, B. 1998. Concurrent discretization of multiple attributes. In Pacific Rim International Conference on Artificial Intelligence.
6.   Hair, J. Jr., Anderson, R., Tatham, R., and Black, W. 1998. Multivariate Data Analysis, 5th ed. Upper Saddel River, N.J., Prentice-Hall.
7.   Johnson, R. and Wichen, D. 1998. Applied Multivariate Statistical Analysis, 4th ed. Upper Saddel River, N.J., Prentice-Hall.
8.   Fayyad, U. and Irani, K. 1993.   Multi-interval discretization of continuous-valued attributes for classification learning. In 13th International Joint Conference of Artificial Intelligence.
9.   Blake, C.L. and Merz. C.J. 1998.   UCI Repository of machine learning databases [http://www.ics.uci.edu/~mlearn].
10.   Quinlan, J.R. 1993. C4.5: Programs for Machine Learning. Los Altoes, CA, Morgan Kaufman.
11.   RuleQuest Research Data Mining Tools [http://www.relequest.com].

A New Neural Implementation of Exploratory Projection Pursuit

Colin Fyfe and Emilio Corchado

Applied Computational Intelligence Research Unit
The University of Paisley
Scotland
{colin.fyfe, emilio.corchado}@paisley.ac.uk

Abstract. We investigate an extension of the learning rules in a Principal Component Analysis network which has been derived to be optimal for a specific probability density function(pdf). We note that this probability density function is one of a family of pdfs and investigate the learning rules formed in order to be optimal for several members of this family. We show that, whereas previous authors [5] have viewed the single member of the family as an extension of PCA, it is more appropriate to view the whole family of learning rules as methods of performing Exploratory Projection Pursuit(EPP). We explore the performance of our method first in response to an artificial data type, then to a real data set.

1 Introduction

Principal Component Analysis (PCA) is a standard statistical technique for compressing data; it can be shown to give the best linear compression of the data in terms of least mean square error. There are several artificial neural networks which have been shown to perform PCA e.g. [8, 9]. We shall be most interested in a negative feedback implementation [3].

The basic PCA network [3] is described by equations (1)-(3). Let us have an N-dimensional input vector at time t, x(t), and an M-dimensional output vector, y, with W_{ij} being the weight linking input j to output i. η is a learning rate. Then the activation passing and learning is described by

$$y_i = \sum_{j=1}^{N} W_{ij} x_j, \quad \forall i \tag{1}$$

$$e_j = x_j - \sum_{i=1}^{M} W_{ij} y_i \tag{2}$$

$$\Delta W_{ij} = \eta e_j y_i \tag{3}$$

The weights converge to the Principal Component directions.

Exploratory Projection Pursuit (EPP) is a more recent statistical method aimed at solving the difficult problem of identifying structure in high dimensional data. It does this by projecting the data onto a low dimensional subspace in which we search for its

H. Yin et al. (Eds.): IDEAL 2002, LNCS 2412, pp. 512–517, 2002.

structure by eye. However not all projections will reveal the data's structure equally well. We therefore define an index that measures how "interesting" a given projection is, and then represent the data in terms of projections that maximise that index. Now "interesting" structure is usually defined with respect to the fact that most projections of high-dimensional data onto arbitrary lines through most multi-dimensional data give almost Gaussian distributions [2]. Therefore if we wish to identify "interesting" features in data, we should look for those directions onto which the data-projections are as far from the Gaussian as possible.

In this paper, we derive a neural method of performing Exploratory Projection Pursuit from a probabilistic perspective.

2   Maximum Likelihood Hebbian Learning

It has been shown [11] that the learning rule

$$\Delta W_{ij} = \eta \left(x_j y_i - y_i \sum_k W_{kj} y_k \right) \tag{4}$$

can be derived as an approximation to the best linear compression of the data.

Thus we may start with a cost function

$$J(W) = 1^T E\{(\mathbf{x} - W\mathbf{y})^2\} \tag{5}$$

which we minimise to get the rule(4). [5] used the residual in (5) to define a cost function of the residual

$$J = f_1(\mathbf{e}) = f_1(\mathbf{x} - W\mathbf{y}) \tag{6}$$

where $f_1 = \|\cdot\|^2$ is the (squared) Euclidean norm in the standard PCA rule.

We may show [1] that the minimization of J is equivalent to minimizing the negative log probability of the residual, $\mathbf{e}$, if $\mathbf{e}$ is Gaussian.

Let $p(\mathbf{e}) = \dfrac{1}{Z} \exp(-\mathbf{e}^2)$ \hfill (7)

Then we can denote a general cost function associated with this network as

$$J = -\log p(\mathbf{e}) = (\mathbf{e})^2 + K \tag{8}$$

where K is a constant. Therefore performing gradient descent on J we have

$$\Delta W \propto -\frac{\partial J}{\partial W} = -\frac{\partial J}{\partial \mathbf{e}} \frac{\partial \mathbf{e}}{\partial W} \approx \mathbf{y}(2\mathbf{e})^T \tag{9}$$

where we have discarded a less important term (see [7] for details).In general [10], the minimisation of such a cost function may be thought to make the probability of the residuals greater dependent on the pdf of the residuals. Thus if the probability density function of the residuals is known, this knowledge can be used to determine the optimal cost function which in turn gives an optimal learning rule. This suggests a family of learning rules which are derived from a family of zero mean distributions. Let the residual after feedback have probability density function

$$p(\mathbf{e}) = \frac{1}{Z}\exp(-|\mathbf{e}|^p). \tag{10}$$

Then we can denote a general cost function associated with this network as

$$J = -\log p(\mathbf{e}) = |\mathbf{e}|^p + K \tag{11}$$

where K is a constant. Therefore performing gradient descent on J we have

$$\Delta W \propto -\frac{\partial J}{\partial W} = -\frac{\partial J}{\partial \mathbf{e}}\frac{\partial \mathbf{e}}{\partial W} \approx y(p|\mathbf{e}|^{p-1}\ sign(\mathbf{e}))^T \tag{12}$$

where T denotes the transpose of a vector. We would expect that for leptokurtotic residuals (more kurtotic than a Gaussian distribution), values of p<2 would be appropriate, while for platykurtotic residuals (less kurtotic than a Gaussian), values of p>2 would be appropriate. It is a common belief in the ICA community [6] that it is less important to get exactly the correct distribution when searching for a specific source than it is to get an approximately correct distribution i.e. all supergaussian signals can be retrieved using a generic leptokurtotic distribution and all subgaussian signals can be retrieved using a generic platykurtotic distribution. Our experiments will tend to support this belief to some extent but we often find accuracy and speed of convergence are improved when we are accurate in our choice of p.

Therefore the network operation is as before except:

Weight change: $$\Delta W_{ij} = \eta.y_i.sign(e_j)|e_j|^{p-1} \tag{13}$$

[5] described their rule as performing a type of PCA, but this is not strictly true since only the original Hebbian rule (3) actually performs PCA. By maximising the likelihood of the residual with respect to the actual distribution, we are matching the learning rule to the pdf of the residual. We may thus link the method to the standard statistical method of Exploratory Projection Pursuit. Now the nature and quantification of the interestingness is in terms of how likely the residuals are under a particular model of the pdf of the residuals.

3 Results Using Artificial Data Sets

We follow [4] in creating artificial data sets, each of 10 dimensions. All results reported are based on a set of 10 simulations each with different initial conditions. It is our general finding that sphering is necessary to get the most accurate results presented below.

In the first data set, we have 9 Gaussian dimensions and 1 kutotic dimension. The kurtotic dimension are actually samples from a Cauchy distribution which is a distribution which is often used to model noise in spiking neurons. To identify this distribution in the Gaussian mixture, we create our model to maximise the likelihood that the residuals come from a platykurtotic distribution such as

$$p(\mathbf{e}) = \frac{1}{Z}\exp(-|\mathbf{e}|^p)\ \text{with p>2;} \tag{14}$$

Now all the distributions which comprise the independent sources underlying this data set are wrong (in that they do not match the model) but the Cauchy distribution is most wrong (it is a highly leptokurtotic distribution). The mean converged weights over 10 simulations are shown in Table 1 for which we used p=3; in each case the first dimension was the Cauchy distribution and the other 9 were Gaussians. These results were taken after 20 iterations through the data set of 30000 samples though typically over 90 percent convergence occurred after 2 iterations.

Table 1. The mean converged weights over 10 simulations in which the first dimension was the Cauchy distribution and the other 9 were Gaussians.

Dim	1	2	3	4	5	6	7	8	9	10
Weight	0.959	0.006	0.004	0.008	0.005	0.006	0.003	0.005	0.005	0.009

We may equally consider a data set with 9 platykurtotic dimensions and one Gaussian and identify the single Gaussian. We note that this is not a typical data set but it does suggest that this method could usefully be used for denoising. In this case we would use a learing rule with p<2.

4   Minimum Likelihood Hebbian Learning

Just as the Hebbian learning rule has an opposite known as the anti-hebbian rule, we may change our rules so that

$$\Delta W \propto \frac{\partial J}{\partial W} = \frac{\partial J}{\partial \mathbf{e}} \frac{\partial \mathbf{e}}{\partial W} \approx -\mathbf{y}(p \,|\, \mathbf{e} \,|^{p-1} \, sign(\mathbf{e}))^T \qquad (15)$$

Now we may argue that, in doing so, we are aiming to minimise the likelihood of the residual given the current model. In detail, if the residual has probability density function

$$p(\mathbf{e}) = \frac{1}{Z} \exp(- \,|\, \mathbf{e} \,|^{p}) . \qquad (16)$$

and we denote the general cost function associated with this network as

$$J = -\log p(\mathbf{e}) = \,|\, \mathbf{e} \,|^{p} + K \qquad (17)$$

where K is a constant, we may perform gradient ascent on J to get

$$\Delta W \propto \frac{\partial J}{\partial W} = \frac{\partial J}{\partial \mathbf{e}} \frac{\partial \mathbf{e}}{\partial W} \approx -y(p \,|\, \mathbf{e} \,|^{p-1} \, sign(\mathbf{e}))^T \qquad (18)$$

We are thus using our learning rules to make the residuals as unlikely as possible under the current model assumptions (determined by the p parameter). Thus when we have 9 Gaussian dimensions and 1 platykurtotic dimension we get similar results to those of the last section (with p=3 in our minimum likelihood rule). By identifying and removing the platykurtotic dimension we are leaving a residual which has 0 kurtosis.

Note that with Minimum Likelihood Hebbian learning we are using the correct model for the distribution that we are seeking but minimising the probability of the residual being taken from this distribution. Thus we find and extract this distribution.

5 Experiments Using a Real Data Set

Our next data set is from a scientific study of various forms of algae some of which have been manually identified. Each sample is recorded as a 18 dimensional vector representing the magnitudes of various pigments. Some algae have been identified as belonging to specific classes which are numbered 1 to 9. Others are as yet unclassified and these are labelled 0. Figure 1 shows a projection of this data set onto the first two Principal Components. We can see that some separation of the classes has been achieved. However Figure 2 shows a projection of the same data set onto the filters found using Minimum Likelihood Hebbian learning with p=1; a rather better separation of the individual classes has been found.

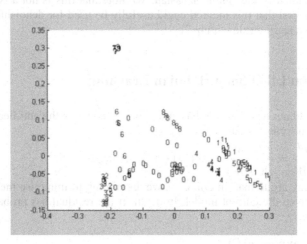

Fig. 1. Projection of the algae data set onto the first two principal components.

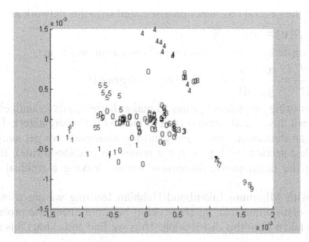

Fig. 2. Projection of the algae data set onto the first two filters found using Minimum Likelihood Hebbian Learning with p=1.

6 Conclusions

In conclusion, we have derived a family of learning rules based on the probability density function of the residuals. This family of rules may be called Hebbian in that all use a simple multiplication of the output of the neural network with some function of the residuals after feedback. The power of the method comes from the choice of an appropriate function. In particular, we showed how to choose a function to maximise the likelihood of the residuals under particular models of probability density functions. We now see that both the original PCA rule and the ·-insensitive rule [5] are merely particular cases of this class of rules. We have also shown that the rules are more akin to Exploratory Projection Pursuit and prefer to call them Maximum Likelihood Hebbian learning, believing that '·-insensitive PCA' does not do justice to the power of the method. We have also shown how powerful Minimum Likelihood Hebbian learning is and indeed that this is, in some sense, even more closely related to EPP: the real power of these learning rules is in the context of exploratory data analysis.

A reviewer has pointed out that, if we know the error model, we could consider an MLP in autoassociative mode which would make the hidden units a form of feature detectors. This is true and the current study links these two strands of neural network development – supervised and unsupervised – rather explicitly. These are powerful new tools for the data mining community and should take their place along with existing exploratory methods.

References

1. Bishop, C.M, Neural Networks for Pattern Recognition, Oxford, 1995.
2. Diaconis, P. and Freedman D., Asymptotics of Graphical Projections. The Annals of Statistics. 12(3): 793-815, 1984.
3. Fyfe, C., "PCA Properties of Interneurons", From Neurobiology to Real World Computing, Proceedings of International Conference on Artificial on Artificial Neural Networks, ICAAN 93, pages 183-188, 1993.
4. Fyfe, C. and Baddeley, R. Non-linear Data Structure Extraction using Simple Hebbian Learning, Biological Cybernetics,72(6), 533-541,1995.
5. Fyfe, C. and MacDonald, D.,·-Insensitive Hebbian learning, Neurocomputing, 2001
6. Hyverinnen, A. Complexity Pursuit: Separating interesting components from time series. Neural Computation, 13: 883-898, 2001.
7. Karhunen, J. and Joutsensalo, J., Representation and Separation of Signals Using Non-linear PCA Type Learning, Neural Networks, 7:113-127, 1994.
8. Oja, E., Neural Networks, Principal Components and Subspaces, International Journal of Neural Systems, 1:61-68, 1989.
9. Oja, E., Ogawa, H., Wangviwattana, J., Principal Components Analysis by Homogeneous Neural Networks, part 1, The Weighted Subspace Criterion, IEICE Transaction on Information and Systems, E75D: 366-375,May 1992.
10. Oimola, A.J. and. Scholkopf, B. A Tutorial on Support Vector Regression. Technical Report NC2-TR-1998-030, NeuroCOLT2 Technical Report Series, Oct.1998.
11. Xu L., Least Mean Square Error Reconstruction for Self-Organizing Nets", Neural Networks, Vol. 6, pp. 627-648, 1993.

A General Framework for a Principled Hierarchical Visualization of Multivariate Data

Ata Kabán[1], Peter Tiňo[2], and Mark Girolami[3]

[1] Department of Information Systems, Eötvös Loránd University, Budapest, Hungary
ata@ullman.inf.elte.hu
[2] Neural Computing Research Group, Aston University, Birmingham B4 7ET, UK
tinop@aston.ac.uk
[3] School of Information & Communication Technology, University of Paisley
mark.girolmi@paisley.ac.uk

Abstract. We present a general framework for interactive visualization and analysis of multi-dimensional data points. The proposed model is a hierarchical extension of the latent trait family of models developed in [4] as a generalization of GTM to noise models from the exponential family of distributions. As some members of the exponential family of distributions are suitable for modeling discrete observations, we give a brief example of using our methodology in interactive visualization and semantic discovery in a corpus of text-based documents. We also derive formulas for computing local magnification factors of latent trait projection manifolds.

1 Introduction

The topographic visualization of multi-dimensional data has been an important method of data analysis and data mining [1,4,5]. Hierarchical extensions of topographic visualization methods [2,7,9] have been developed for capturing informative aspects of the data in a more flexible manner: successive 2-D plots are interactively constructed to account for the level of detail required by the user. In particular, hierarchical GTM [9] has been proposed as a statistically principled construction of local non-linear projection manifolds. However, by imposing a Gaussian noise model in the original GTM, the hierarchical GTM is restricted to continuous data types. Similar tools are needed for other data types, such as discrete data. Application examples may include organization of digital libraries encoded in binary and/or count-based arrays.

Building upon the latent trait models [4] — a generalization of GTM to noise models from the exponential family of distributions - we develop a general probabilistic framework for interactive hierarchical visualization of multi-dimensional data sets in a top-down fashion. Some members of the exponential family of distributions are suitable for modeling discrete observations and we briefly elaborate upon the possibility of using our methodology in interactive visualization and semantic discovery in collections of text-based documents.

We also give formulas for computing local geometric properties, namely magnification factors, of latent trait projection manifolds, which, due to the smooth

H. Yin et al. (Eds.): IDEAL 2002, LNCS 2412, pp. 518–523, 2002.

character of the latent trait mapping, can be computed using the tools of differential geometry. Magnification factors provide potentially valuable additional visual information regarding the structure of the data and may aid the user to better understand the visualization plot and provide useful hints in the process of interactive construction of deeper levels of the hierarchy (see [1,9]).

2   Probabilistic Model of Hierarchic Visualization

2.1   Latent Trait Models

The latent trait model [4] is a generalized version of GTM capable of modeling outcomes from the exponential family of distributions.

Consider an L-dimensional latent space, which, for visualization purposes is typically a bounded 2-D Euclidean domain, e.g. $[-1,1] \times [-1,1]$. The aim is to represent, using the latent space, multi-dimensional data points $\{d_n\}_{n=1..N}$, such that the "important" structural characteristics are revealed. For tractability reasons, the latent space is discretized into a regular grid of K latent points $x_1, ... x_K$ (which are analogous to the nodes of the SOM [5]). The uniform latent space prior distribution is a mixture of delta functions and so $p(d)$ can be evaluated as $p(d) = \sum_{k=1}^{K} p(d|x_k)p(x_k)$.

The conditional distribution over the data is modeled as a member of the exponential family in a parameterized functional form

$$p_G(d_n|x_k, A) = \exp\left\{ f_A(x_k)d_n - G(f_A(x_k)) \right\} p_0(d_n), \qquad (1)$$

where $G(\cdot)$ denotes the cumulant function, $d_n \in \mathcal{R}^T$ denotes the n-th observed data point, $n = 1 : N$, $x_k \in \mathcal{R}^L$ is the k-th sample from a uniformly distributed latent variable over the continuous visualization space $[-1,1]^2$, $k = 1 : K$, and the nonlinearity $f(.)$ is (conveniently) chosen to be of the form $f_A(x_k) = A\phi(x_k)$, where $A \in \mathcal{R}^{T \times M}$ is a parameter matrix and $\phi(.) = (\phi_1(.), ..., \phi_M(.))^T, \phi_m(.) : \mathcal{R}^L \to \mathcal{R}$ is a set of M non-parametric nonlinear smooth basis functions (typically RBFs). This formulation allows for a convenient formalism which includes a principled treatment of discrete observations. Projection of a data point d in the latent space is obtained as the mean of the posterior distribution over the latent space, given the observation d. Details regarding the derivation of an EM-based parameter estimation algorithm and application examples for some of the discrete members of this model family can be found in [4].

2.2   Hierarchical Latent Trait Models

When dealing with large and complex data sets, a single global visualization plot is often not sufficient. Therefore we introduce a hierarchical mixture extension of the latent trait model family. A set of latent trait projections is arranged in a tree structure in a recursive top-down fashion [2,3,9]: provided that one has already trained models up to level $\ell - 1$ (by convention, the *root*'s level is 1), training of the ℓ-th level models proceeds on the data indicated by the user as "regions of interest" on the previous level parent plot (see [2,9]).

Denote by c_r the indicator variables for tree nodes at level r. In particular, $c_1 = root$. $c_{1:r} = (c_1, c_2, ..., c_r)$ denotes a path from the *root* to a level-r node identified by c_r. Given a particular node $\mathcal{N}$ at level r, i.e. $c_r = \mathcal{N}$, there is only one path $c_{1:r}$ in the tree from the *root* to $\mathcal{N}$, such that $c_r = \mathcal{N}$.

The expectation of the *complete* data likelihood of an ℓ-level hierarchical model, under the *joint* posterior density of latent variables $c_{1:\ell}$ and $\boldsymbol{x}_k$ is

$$Q^{(\ell)} = \sum_{n=1}^{N} \sum_{c_{1:\ell}} \sum_{k} p(c_{1:\ell}|\boldsymbol{d}_n)p(\boldsymbol{x}_k|c_\ell, \boldsymbol{d}_n) \log \{p(c_{1:\ell})p(\boldsymbol{x}_k|c_\ell)p(\boldsymbol{d}_n|\boldsymbol{x}_k, \boldsymbol{A}, c_\ell)\},$$

where the tree-structure leads to the following recursive decompositions:

$$p(c_{1:\ell}|\boldsymbol{d}_n) = p(c_{1:\ell-1}|\boldsymbol{d}_n)p(c_\ell|c_{\ell-1}, \boldsymbol{d}_n) \quad \text{and} \quad p(c_{1:\ell}) = p(c_{1:\ell-1})p(c_\ell|c_{\ell-1}).$$

Maximizing $Q^{(\ell)}$ under the constraints $\sum_k p(\boldsymbol{x}_k|c_\ell) = 1$ and $\sum_{c_\ell} p(c_\ell|c_{\ell-1}) = 1$, we obtain the following updates for the parameters (**M-step**)

$$p(c_\ell|c_{\ell-1}) = \frac{\sum_{n=1}^{N} p(c_{1:\ell-1}|\boldsymbol{d}_n)p(c_\ell|c_{\ell-1}, \boldsymbol{d}_n)}{\sum_{n=1}^{N} p(c_{1:\ell-1}|\boldsymbol{d}_n)} \tag{2}$$

$$\boldsymbol{g}(\boldsymbol{A\Phi})\boldsymbol{G}^{(\ell)}\boldsymbol{\Phi}^T = \boldsymbol{D}\boldsymbol{R}^{(\ell)T}\boldsymbol{\Phi}^T, \qquad p(\boldsymbol{x}_k|c_\ell) = \frac{1}{N} \sum_{n=1}^{N} r_{kn}^{(\ell)} \tag{3}$$

where $r_{kn}^{(\ell)} = p(c_{1:\ell-1}|\boldsymbol{d}_n)p(c_\ell|c_{\ell-1}, \boldsymbol{d}_n)p(\boldsymbol{x}_k|c_\ell, \boldsymbol{d}_n)$, $\boldsymbol{R}^{(\ell)} = (r_{kn}^{(\ell)})_{k=1:K, n=1:N}$, $\boldsymbol{G}^{(\ell)}$ is a diagonal matrix with elements $g_{kk}^{(\ell)} = \sum_{n=1}^{N} r_{kn}^{(\ell)}$, $\boldsymbol{\Phi}$ is an $M \times K$ matrix the k-th column of which is $\boldsymbol{\phi}(\boldsymbol{x_k})$ and $\boldsymbol{D}$ is the data matrix. The factor $p(c_{1:\ell-1}|\boldsymbol{d}_n)$ is the posterior "inherited" from the previous level. For consistency of the training equations, we adopt the convention that $p(c_1|\boldsymbol{d}_n) \equiv 1$, $p(c_1|c_0) \equiv 1$ and $p(c_0|\boldsymbol{d}_n) \equiv 1$. The (non-linear) inverse link function $\boldsymbol{g}(.)$ is the derivative of the cumulant function $G(.)$ [6]. In general, non-linear optimization techniques are needed to solve for $\boldsymbol{A}$ in (3). Posterior estimates over the hidden variables are computed using the "old" values of the parameters (**E-step**)

$$p(c_\ell|c_{\ell-1}, \boldsymbol{d}_n) = \frac{p(c_\ell|c_{\ell-1})p(\boldsymbol{d}_n|c_\ell)}{\sum_{c'_\ell} p(c'_\ell|c_{\ell-1})p(\boldsymbol{d}_n|c'_\ell)} \tag{4}$$

$$p(\boldsymbol{x}_k|c_\ell, \boldsymbol{d}_n) = \frac{p(\boldsymbol{x}_k|c_\ell)p(\boldsymbol{d}_n|\boldsymbol{x}_k, c_\ell, \boldsymbol{A})}{\sum_{k'} p(\boldsymbol{x}_{k'}|c_\ell)p(\boldsymbol{d}_n|\boldsymbol{x}_{k'}, c_\ell, \boldsymbol{A})} \tag{5}$$

At each level, the E and M steps are iterated until convergence to a local optimum.

3   Local Geometric Analysis of the Latent Trait Manifolds

The probabilistic latent trait model defines a density model (1), using a smooth mapping from the latent space into the 'data space' (projection space) $\boldsymbol{z} : \mathcal{R}^L \rightarrow$

$\mathcal{R}^T$, $z(x) = g(A\Phi(x))$, where $g()$ is the the inverse link function. We refer to the image of the latent space under z as the *projection manifold* [9]. For visualization purposes, $L = 2$, and so the projection manifold is a 2-D surface embedded in the data space $\mathcal{R}^T$.

The term *magnification factor* [1] refers to the degree of stretching/compression of the latent space when embedded into the data space. Consider a Cartesian coordinate system defined in the latent space and the corresponding curvilinear coordinate system on the projection manifold. The local magnification factor corresponding to a latent space point x_0 is the ratio between the areas of an infinitesimal rectangle in the latent Cartesian space and its image (under z) in the projection manifold. It is computed as ([1]) $\sqrt{|T(x_0)|}$, where $|T(x_0)|$ is the determinant of the metric tensor $T(x_0) = \Gamma^T \Gamma$ [9], with Γ denoting (the transpose of) the Jacobian of the mapping z. In our case

$$\Gamma = \frac{\partial z(x_0)}{\partial x} = \frac{\partial g(A\phi(x_0))}{\partial x} = QAV, \qquad (6)$$

where $V = \left(\frac{\partial \phi_m(x)}{\partial x_l}|_{x=x_0}\right)_{m=1:M, l=1:L}$. The Fisher information matrix $Q = \left(\frac{\partial g_{t'}(y)}{\partial y_t}|_{y=A\phi(x_0)}\right)_{t'=1:T, t=1:T}$ happens to be the identity matrix only in the special case of the original GTM with spherical Gaussian noise model. In this case the magnification factors derived here coincide with those previously obtained for the original GTM model [1].

4   Hierarchical Visualization of Text Documents

We demonstrate our system on an interactive visualization of a text-collection formed by 10 topic classes from the newsgroups[1] text corpus. 800 instances were taken from each topic. The instances were binary encoded over a dictionary of $T = 300$ words [8]. The initial preprocessing, word-stemming and removal of 'stop-words' was done using the Bow toolkit[2]. To account for binary encoding, the Bernoulli noise model was employed at the expert nodes of our model, i.e. the cumulant function had the form $G(A\Phi(x)) = \log\{1 + exp(A\Phi(x))\}$. The latent (topics') space has been discretized into a $K = 15 \times 15$ grid, and $M = 16$ spherical RBF basis functions of unit width were positioned on a regular 4×4 grid. An example of hierarchically organized projection plot of the posterior means is shown in Figure 1. The *root* plot contains a dense cluster with overlapping projection classes and is recursively detailed at deeper levels of the hierarchy. The level of detail in the leaf plots is solely dictated by the user and his idea of "interesting" areas in the data space.

In the case of the Bernoulli model, the proximity of local regions of the low-dimensional projection manifold to vertices of the T-dimensional hypercube

---

[1] http://www.cs.cmu.edu/textlearning
[2] http://www-2.cs.cmu.edu/mccalum/bow/

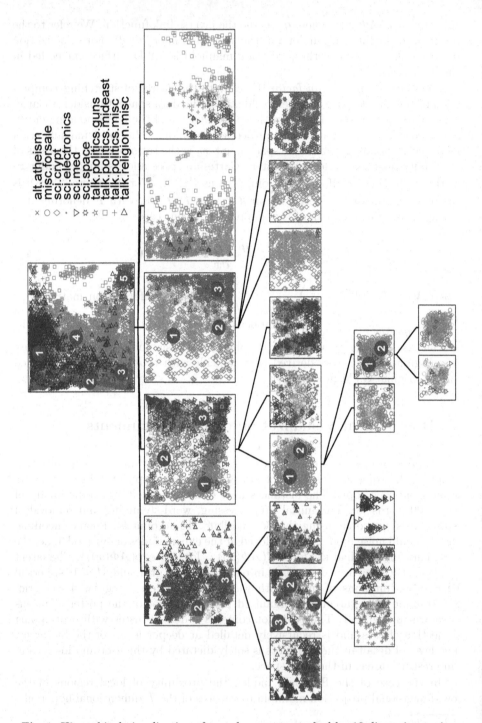

Fig. 1. Hierarchical visualization of text documents marked by 10 discussion topics.

$\{0,1\}^{T}$ determines what areas of the latent space will be devoted to which keyword occurrences. Hence, when two documents are mapped to neighboring positions in the latent plane, but the area between them is characterized by high magnification factors, the user can infer that the two documents correspond to different clusters. This leads recursively to ("semantically-driven") selection of regions of interest for more and more detailed plots on lower levels of the visualization hierarchy. Other tools aimed at improving our understanding of the plots, like listing the most probable dictionary words for each latent point $\mathbf{x_k}$ [4], are also incorporated in the system.

5 Conclusions

We have developed a statistically principled general framework for interactive visualization and analysis of multi-dimensional data in a hierarchical manner and generalized the local geometric analysis of projection manifolds (magnification factors) to accommodate for non-Gaussian members of the exponential noise model family. We demonstrated a topic-driven interactive visualization of a real-world text corpus.

Acknowledgements. P. Tiňo is supported by the BBSRC grant BIO/12093 and Pfizer Research. A. Kabán and M. Girolami has been funded by re:source, The Council for Museums Archives and Libraries, Grant Number RE/092.

References

1. C. Bishop, M. Svensén, and C. Williams, "Magnification factors for the SOM and GTM algorithms," in *Proceedings 1997 Workshop on Self-Organizing Maps, Helsinki, Finland*, 1997.
2. C. Bishop and M. E. Tipping, "A Hierarchic Latent Variable Model for data Visualization. *IEEE Transactions on Pattern Analysis and Machine Intelligence*, 20(3), pp. 281–293, 1998.
3. M. I. Jordan, "Hierarchical Mixture of Experts and the EM Algorithm". *Neural Computation*, (6), pp.181–214, 1994.
4. A. Kabán and M. Girolami, "A combined latent class and trait model for the analysis and visualization of discrete data," *IEEE Transactions on Pattern Analysis and Machine Intelligence*, 23(8), pp. 859 -872, 2001.
5. T. Kohonen, *Self-organized formation of topographically correct feature maps*. Biological Cybernetics, vol.43, pp. 59–69, 1982.
6. P. McCullagh and L. Nelder, *Generalized Linear Models*. Chapman and Hall, 1985.
7. R. Miikkulainen, *Script recognition with hierarchical feature maps* Connection Science, vol.2, pp. 83–101,1990.
8. Sahami, *Using Machine Learning to Improve Information Access*, PhD Thesis, Stanford University, 1998.
9. P. Tiňo and I. Nabney, "Constructing localized non-linear projection manifolds in a principled way: hierarchical generative topographic mapping," *IEEE Transactions on Pattern Analysis and Machine Intelligence*, in print.

Chinese Character Recognition- Comparison of Classification Methodologies

Sameer Singh[1], Adnan Amin[2], and K.C. Sum[2]

[1]Department of Computer Science, University of Exeter, Exeter, UK
[2]School of Computer Science and Engineering, UNSW, Sydney, Australia

Abstract. In this paper we propose the use of dominant point method for Chinese character recognition. We compare the performance of three classifiers on the same inputs; a statistical linear classifier, a machine learning C4.5 classifier, and a fuzzy nearest neighbour method of classification. Such a comparison highlights the degree of advantage of correct recognition method for our problem.

1 Introduction

Unlike alphabetic and one-dimensional western languages such as English, Chinese characters are well known two-dimensional and non-alphabetic [1]. There are several major problems with Chinese character recognition using automated methods: Chinese characters are distinct and ideographic, the character size is very large, and a lot of structurally similar characters exist in the character set. Thus, classification criteria are difficult to generate. Several different techniques are used for Chinese character recognition. According to Lee [2] these can be categorized as follows: (i) Coarse Classification and Candidate Selection: in which the input character matches the reference character in a database. Two approaches have been proposed to address this issue: Coarse Classification [3,4]; Heirarchical Systems [5-7]. (ii) Statistical Approaches use a set of characteristic measurements usually called "global features" extracted from the characters to identify characters by partitioning the feature space [8-10]. Structural approaches express characters as compositions of structural primitives such as lines, curves, and loops, and then identify the characters by matching representations of its primitives with those of a reference character, or by parsing the representation according to sets of syntactic rules [11]. Structural approaches fall into three categories: Methods based on line segments [12-15]; Methods based on strokes [17-22]; Methods based on radicals [23-25]. In this paper we describe a method which is based on dominant points in a character image. We compare the performance and results of three classifier on the same data; statistical linear classifier, a machine learning C4.5 system, and a fuzzy nearest neighbor method of classification.

H. Yin et al. (Eds.): IDEAL 2002, LNCS 2412, pp. 524-530, 2002.

2 Dominant Point Algorithm

This paper is based on the dominant point algorithm summarised as follows:

2.1 Digitization and Preprocessing

The first step of our system is digitization in which the real image is transformed into binary image using 300 dpi scanner and the size of the character is approximately 30mm x 30mm. Next a prethinning algorithm is used in this paper similar to that which appears in [26] to reduce the noise that the binarization process yields. We have chosen Jang and Chin's one-pass parallel thinning algorithm [27] because it gives skeletons with few spurious branches. After thinning, the maximum circle technique proposed by Liao and Huang [28] is used to remove the spurious branches. After removing spurious branches, the next step is to extract strokes from the image. An algorithm implementing a 3x3 window is used to trace along the path of the skeleton, recording the Freeman codes (0 E, 1 NE, 2 N, 4 W, 5 SW, 6 S, 7 SE) [29] along the path. The Freeman code simply attaches a number to each of the eight major points of the compass and the orientation of a line segment is characterized by this number. We then apply a stroke segmentation technique, using inner products of line segments [30] to join line segments into strokes. The result of the stroke segmentation is the input to feature extraction block.

2.2 Feature Extraction

The feature extraction steps involve smoothing of the Freeman code, and extraction of primitives. Smoothing is needed to reduce the noise and removes the redundancy of the Freeman code. In this project we have used a total of six primitives (Figure 1) extracted by using the *dominant point* method. These primitives are based on the shape of the strokes.

▬	Horizontal	╱	Slash
▌	Vertical	⌐	Corner
╲	Backslash	●	Dot

Fig: 1: Primitive features used in this project.

A number of dominant point detection algorithms have been proposed in the past. These algorithms have been summarized and compared by Teh and Chin [31]. However, in character recognition, the requirements of a good dominant point detection algorithm are slightly different from those of algorithms for general usage.

In character recognition, we do not have to identify all dominant points. We only need to identify points with very sharp curvature. Based on this requirement, we were inspired by the Rosenfeld-Johnston algorithm [32]. The basic concept of the algorithm is to calculate the curvature of each point in the line, then the points with the local maximum in curvature are designated as dominant points. However, the initial results were not satisfactory. Due to the irregularity of lines, we detected too many dominant points in line segments. After analyzing results of the dominant point extraction, we found that most undesirable dominant points were due to small irregularities of the chain code pattern. From this observation, we implemented a simple merging algorithm. The basic concept is to try to merge segments that are really short with their adjacent long segments. Then we check the long segment. If there are two long segments of the same type, then we merge them together. The formal algorithm is described in [38]. We calculate the probability of a stroke being horizontal, vertical, backslash, slash, or dot. The equations for this calculation are detailed in [38]. These probabilities are used in the form of a feature vector on the basis of which different characters can be differentiated.

3   Classifier Systems

In this paper, we compare three classifier systems. The linear discriminant analysis [33] is the most basic classification system, the C4.5 is decision tree based classifier and we finally use a fuzzy nearest neighbour classifier. In our experiments, a total of twelve features are used for training the three types of classifiers discussed next. The first six feature variables record the presence or absence of the six primitives discussed in the previous section Horizontal…Dot, i.e. these can be 0 to represent absence or 1 to show presence. The next six feature variables represent the stroke probability of these primitives in sequence and it is computed as shown in the previous section. These are continuous variables and are statistically normalised for a balanced contribution to the classification process. Statistical classification was performed using cross-validation Stone[34].

3.1   Discriminant Analysis

In order to appreciate the ability of dominant point features to discriminate between Chinese characters using cross-validation, we selected a random sample of 100 different types of characters from the original set of 500 characters under consideration (40 samples for each class). With cross-validation using the leave-one-out method, the recognition rate so achieved as 86.7% which further strengthens our argument that features extracted using the proposed technique are good discriminators across different types of handwritten Chinese characters. The results for 200 characters showed 85% correct recognition rate. The analysis used here yielded a classification rate of 84.45% for a total of 500 Chinese characters (40 samples for each character). This result strongly supports the usefulness of the *dominant point* method for characterising Chinese characters even with LDA.

3.2 Machine Learning C4.5

In C4.5, Quinlan uses a modified version of the entropy measure from information theory [35,36]. In this study, the decision tree generated from the training data, using C4.5, is used to classify characters. We get an average result of 86.58% accurate recognition. A more detailed analysis is shown in Table 1. We measure how well the system performance improves as we increase the number of samples. For this we first select 100 characters (4000 samples) at random from the overall data and then perform six fold cross validation. For each trial (fold), the misclassification rates are quoted. As it can be observed, as the number of characters increase, the average misclassification rate drops and the confidence intervals decrease showing more confidence in our results.

3.3 Fuzzy Nearest Neighbour Method

A fuzzy classifier system based on proximity measures for membership computation has been used [37]. For a given test pattern X, the fuzzy classifier computes the membership of X in different classes $C_1, ... C_j ... C_m$ where $1 = j = m$. The test pattern is allocated to a class for which the membership function yields the maximum value. The overall process may be mathematically explained as: Consider an unknown pattern X represented by a point in a multi-dimensional space Ω_X consisting of m pattern classes $C_1 ... C_m$. Let $R_1 ... R_j ... R_m$ be the reference vectors where R_j associated with C_j contains h_j number of prototypes such that, $R_j^{(l)} \in R_j$, $l = 1, 2, ... h_j$

$$\mu_j^{'}(X) = [1 + \{d(X, R_j^{(l)})/F_d\}^{F_e}]^{-1.0}$$

where $\mu_j^{'}(X)$ is the membership of X in class C_j as determined through the class sample l, and $d(X, R_j^{'})$ is the distance between X and $R_j^{'}$. In eqn. (1), F_e and F_d are positive constants that determine the degree of fuzziness in membership space hence specifying the degree of skew of the possibility distribution. For the fuzzy method, we again use the leave-one-out method for the recognition of Chinese characters.

Table 1. Error rates for learning trials

Trial	100 chars error rate %	Confidence interval	200 chars error rate %	Confidence interval	500 chars error rate %	Confidence Interval
1	8.6	±0.93	10.2	±0.7	12.5	±0.49
2	8.7	±0.92	10.5	±0.72	12.6	±0.49
3	9.0	±0.91	12.3	±0.76	12.9	±0.49
4	10.1	±0.99	13.0	±0.83	13.6	±0.50
5	11.0	±1.02	13.3	±0.78	14.1	±0.51
6	11.9	±1.07	14.9	±0.83	14.7	±0.52
Avg. Error rate %	9.9	±0.97	12.3	±0.77	13.4	±0.5

We find that the recognition performance is superior for a smaller number of different Chinese characters as shown in Figure 2 . Here, the recognition rate is higher for a data set with only 200 different Chinese characters compared to 500 different characters. We find that the best performance of the fuzzy classifier is obtained when $F_d = 1$ and $F_e = 1$. As the value of F_e increased, the recognition rate falls slowly by roughly 2% for every rise in its integer value. We find that an increase in the constant F_d makes no difference in the recognition performance of the system for different values of F_e. The recognition rates on tests are compared in Table 2.

Table2. Comparison of Recognition Rates % with Discriminant Analysis, C4.5 and FNN methods

Characters	DA	C4.5	FNN
100	86.7	90.0	97.6
200	85.0	87.6	98.3
500	84.5	86.6	94.0

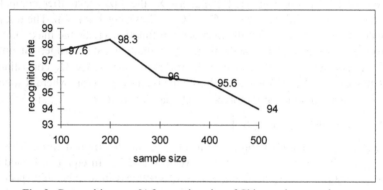

Fig. 2. Recognition rate % for varying size of Chinese character data set.

4 Conclusions

This paper discussed the performance of three classifiers on the same inputs used for Chinese character recognition; a statistical linear classifier; a decision tree C4.5 system, and a fuzzy nearest neighbor method of classification for the recognition of handwritten Chinese characters. In this paper we make one important discovery: the appropriate selection of a classifier system is important for achieving good results. We expect that our findings will be used by other researchers to investigate whether a similar trend is observed with international databases.

References

1. Kanal, J., Liu, Y. and Nagy, G.: An OCR-Oriented overview of idographic writing systems, Handbook of Character Recognition and Document Image Analysis, Ed. H. Bunke and P. S. P Wang, World Scientific, pp. 285-304, 1997.
2. Lee, H.J.: Chinese character recognition in Taiwan, Handbook of Character Recognition and Document Image Analysis, Ed. H. Bunke and P.Wang, W. Scientific, pp.331-355, 1997.
3. Cheng, H.D. and Wang, J.F.: Preclassification for handwritten Chinese character recognition by a peripheral shape coding method, Pattern Recognition 26, pp. 711-719, 1993.
4. Cheng, R.H. Lee, C.W. and Chen, Z.: Preclassification of handwritten Chinese character recognition based on basic stroke substructures, Proc. 4th International workshop on Frontiers in Handwritten Recognition, Taiwan, pp. 176-184, 1994.
5. Kumamoto, T., Toraichi, K., Horiuchi, T., Yamamoto, K. and Yamada, H.: On Speeding candidate selection in handprinted Chinese character recognition, Pattern Recognition 24, pp.793-799, 1991.
6. Tung, C.H., Lee, H.J. and Tsai, J.Y.: Multistage pre-candidate selection in handwritten Chinese character recognition systems, Pattern Recognition 27, pp. 1093-1102, 1994.
7. Lin, T.Z. and Fan, K.C.: Coarse classification of on-line Chinese character via structure feature-based method, Pattern Recognition 27, pp. 1365-1378, 1994.
8. Huang, J.S. and Chung, M.L.: Separating similar complex Chinese characters by Walsh transform, Pattern Recognition, pp. 425-428, 1987.
9. Tu, T.Y. and Ma, Y.L.: Character recognition by stochastic sectionalgram approach, Pattern Recognition, 21, pp. 593-601, 1988.
10. Li, T.F., and Yu, S.S.: Hand printed Chinese character recognition using the probability distribution feature, IJPRAI Journal, 8, pp. 1241-1258, 1994.
11. Fu, K.S.: Syntactic (linguistic) pattern recognition in digital pattern recognition, Ed. K. S. Fu , New York Springer-Verlag, 1980
12. Lee, H.J. and Chen, B.: Recognition of handwritten Chinese characters via short line segments, Pattern Recognition 25, pp. 543-552, 1992.
13. Cheng, F.H., Hsu, W.H. and Kuo, M.C.: Recognition of handprinted Chinese character via stroke relaxation, Pattern Recognition 26, pp. 579-593, 1993.
14. Hsieh, A.J., Fan, K.C. and Fan, T.I., Bipertite weighted matching for on-line handwritten Chinese character recognition, Pattern Recognition 28, pp. 143-151, 1995.
15. Chou, S.L. and Tsai, W.H.: Recognition of handwritten Chinese character by stroke-segment matching using an iteration scheme, IJPRAI Journal, 5, pp. 175-197, 1991.
16. Lin, C.K., Fan, K.C. and Lee, F.T.P.: On-line recognition by deviation-expansion model and dynamic programming matching, Pattern Recognition, 26, pp. 259-268, 1993.
17. Cheng, F.H., Hsu, W.H. and Chen, M.Y.: Recognition of handwritten Chinese characters by modified Hough transform, IEEE Trans. PAMI-6, pp. 386-405, 1989.
18. Cheng, F.H., Hsu, W.H., and Chen, C.A.: Fuzzy approach to solve the recognition problem of handwritten Chinese characters, Pattern Recognition 33, pp. 475-484, 1990.
19. Wang, A.B., Huang, J.S. and Fan, K.C.: Recognition of handwritten Chinese characters by modified relaxation methods, Image and Vision Computing 12, pp. 509-522, 1994.
20. Chen, L.H. and Leih, J.R.: Handwritten character recognition using a 2-layer randomgraph model by relation matching, Pattern Recognition 23, pp. 1189-1205, 1990.
21. Hsieh, C.C. and Lee, H.J.: A probabilistic stroke-based Viterbi algorithm for handwritten Chinese characters recognition, IJPRAI Journal, 7, pp. 329-352, 1993.
22. Tsay, Y.T. and Tsai, W.H.: Attributed string matching by split-and-merge for on-line Chinese character recognition, IEEE Trans. PAMI-15, pp. 180-185, 1993.

23. Cheng, F.H. and Hsu, W.H.: Radical extraction from handwritten Chinese characters by background thinning methods, IEEE Trans. IECE **E71**, pp. 88-98, 1988.
24. Liao, C.W. and Huang, J.S.: A transformed invariant matching algorithm for handwritten Chinese character recognition, Pattern Recognition **23**, pp. 1167-1188, 1990.
25. Cheng, F.H. and Hsu, W.H.: Radical extraction by background thinning method for handwritten Chinese characters, Proc. Int. Conf. on Chinese Computing, pp.175-182, 1987.
26. Amin, A. and Al-Sadoun, H.B.: Handprinted Arabic character recognition system using an artificial neural network, Pattern Recognition, **28**(4), 663-675, 1996.
27. Jang, B.K. and Chin, R.T.: One-pass parallel thinning: analysis, properties, and quantitative evaluation, IEEE Trans. PAMI-**14**, 1129-1140, 1992.
28. Liao, C.W. and Huang, J.S.: Stroke segmentation by Bernstein-Bezier curve fitting, Pattern Recognition **23**, pp. 475-484, 1990.
29. Freeman, H.: On the encoding of arbitrary geometric configurations, IEEE Trans. Electronic Computers **EC-10**, 260-268, 1968.
30. Cheng, F.H. and Hse, W.H.: Three stroke extraction methods for recognition of handwritten Chinese characters, Proc. Int. Conf. Chinese Computing, Singapore, 191-195, 1986.
31. The, C.H. and Chin, R.T. On the Detection of Dominant Points in Digital Curves, IEEE PAMI-**11**, 859-872, 1989.
32. Rosenfeld, A. and Johnston, E.: Angle detection on digital curves, IEEE Trans. Computers **C-22**, 875-878, 1973.
33. Huberty, C.J.: Applied discriminant analysis, Wiley- Statistics, 1994.
34. Stone, M.: Cross-validatory choice and assessment of statistical predictions, Journal of the Royal Statistical Society. **36**: 111-147, 1974.
35. Quinlan, J.R.: C4.5; Programs for machine learning, Morgan Kauffman, 1993.
36. Quinlan, J.R.: Discovering rules for a large collection of examples, Edinburgh, 1979.
37. Pal, S.K. and Majumder, D.D.: Fuzzy mathematical approach to pattern recognition, John Wiley, 1986.
38. Amin, A. and Singh, S.: Recognition of hand-printed Chinese characters using decision trees/machine learning C4.5 system, Pattern Analysis and Applications, 1(2):130-141, 1998.

Lempel-Ziv Coding in Reinforcement Learning

Kazunori Iwata[1] and Naohiro Ishii[2]

[1] Dept. of Systems Science, Graduate School of Informatics, Kyoto University
Yoshida-Honmachi, Sakyo-ku, Kyoto, 606-8501, Japan
kiwata@sys.i.kyoto-u.ac.jp
[2] Dept. of Intelligence and Computer Science, Nagoya Institute of Technology
Gokiso-cho, Showa-ku, Nagoya, 466-8555, Japan
ishii@ics.nitech.ac.jp

Abstract. In this paper, we propose a new measure within the framework of reinforcement learning, by describing a model of an information source as a representation of a learning process. We confirm in experiments that Lempel-Ziv coding for a string of episode sequences provides a quality measure to describe the degree of complexity for learning. In addition, we discuss functions comparing expected return and its variance.

1 Introduction

Consider that an agent learns an optimal policy to choose an action in an unknown environment without a supervisor's support. Examples of agents include an autonomous robot, a controller, and an intelligent system. Reinforcement learning is an effective framework to describe a general process that consists of interactions with an environment. First, we review the framework of reinforcement learning having a discrete system in time and state space. Let $T = \{t \mid t = 0, 1, 2, \cdots\}$ denote the discrete time steps. Let $\mathcal{S}$ be a finite set of possible states of the environment, let $\mathcal{A}$ be a finite set of possible actions, and let $\Re$ be the real numbers. At each step t, the agent senses the current state $s_t \in \mathcal{S}$, then chooses an action $a_t \in \mathcal{A}(s_t)$, where $\mathcal{A}(s_t)$ denotes the set of the actions that can be performed in the state s_t. The performed action a_t changes the current state s_t to the next state $s_{t+1} \in \mathcal{S}$. The environment gives a scalar reward $r_{t+1} \in \Re$ as the value of the state transition. This interaction produces a sequence of state, action, and reward: $s_1 r_1 a_1 s_2 r_2 a_2 \cdots$. Let us call it an "episode sequence". The goal of an agent's task is to learn the optimal policy $\pi^* : \mathcal{S} \to \mathcal{A}$, that maximizes the following expected return over time:

$$R_t = r_{t+1} + \gamma r_{t+2} + \gamma^2 r_{t+3} + \cdots = \sum_{k=0}^{\infty} \gamma^k r_{t+k+1} \tag{1}$$

where r_{t+1} is called the "immediate reward", and $r_{t+2}, r_{t+3}, \cdots$ are called the "delayed reward". The parameter γ is the discount factor that controls the relative value between immediate and delayed rewards. Thus, reinforcement learning uses a scalar value called reward to formulate an agent's goal. This is a notable feature which realizes a flexible description of the goal.

H. Yin et al. (Eds.): IDEAL 2002, LNCS 2412, pp. 531–537, 2002.

2   Source Coding

Learning is closely connected with information theory. We will begin by considering information theory, especially source coding. Shannon and Weaver [1] defined information as a stochastic concept in communication, and quantified it by "bit" as an unit. They also established a mathematical theory for communication within the limits of channel capacity. Data compression in the field of source coding has been attempted to achieve the shortest description length of a random variable by an information source. Shannon's code assignment $\ell(x) = -\lceil \log_2 p(x) \rceil$ provides the best data compression of an i.i.d. source with a known probability distribution $p(x)$. If we can sufficiently investigate to identify the parameters of the probability distribution, then a good data compressor (encoder and decoder) can be achieved. However, in many cases, it is impossible to know the parameters, because of cost or time limitations. This drives us to the question about what compression can be achieved if the probability distribution is unknown. The answer is in universal coding such as Lempel-Ziv coding. With a large amount of data, universal coding can be an asymptotic optimal compressor without knowing the parameters of the probability distribution. The process of universal coding that generates "code" as compressed data is not essentially different from a learning process that generates "knowledge" as compressed experience. Thus, a good learner is also a good data compressor.

2.1   Description as a Model of Information Source

Suppose the process of interactions between agent and environment follows a Markov Decision Process (MDP), that the probabilistic structure is composed of three probability distributions: the agent's policy

$$\pi(a_t \mid s_1 r_1 a_1 \cdots s_t r_t) = \Pr(a_t \mid s_1 r_1 a_1 \cdots s_t r_t), \tag{2}$$

the transition probability distribution

$$p(s_{t+1} \mid s_1 r_1 a_1 \cdots s_t r_t a_t) = \Pr(s_{t+1} \mid s_1 r_1 a_1 \cdots s_t r_t a_t), \tag{3}$$

and the reward probability distribution

$$r(r_{t+1} \mid s_1 r_1 a_1 \cdots s_t r_t a_t s_{t+1}) = \Pr(r_{t+1} \mid s_1 r_1 a_1 \cdots s_t r_t a_t s_{t+1}) \tag{4}$$

Let $\Re_0$ be the properly discrete real numbers. Let x be the injective mapping from $\mathcal{S} \cup \mathcal{A} \cup \Re_0$ to the finite source alphabets $\mathcal{X} = \{0, 1, 2, \cdots, J-1\}$[1]. We will use the notation x_1^n to denote the mapped episode sequence:

$$\underbrace{x(s_1)x(r_1)x(a_1)x(s_2)x(r_2)x(a_2)\cdots}_{n} = x_1 x_2 x_3 x_4 x_5 x_6 \cdots x_n = x_1^n \tag{5}$$

---

[1] The elements of $\mathcal{X}$ will do as long as they have a distinct order. Here, we will use a non-negative integer in order to give a brief account.

We will call it a "string". Then, the three probability distributions are transformed into one probability distribution Q on alphabet $\mathcal{X}$ as follows.

$$\left. \begin{array}{l} \pi(a_t \mid s_1 r_1 a_1 \cdots s_t r_t) \\ p(s_{t+1} \mid s_1 r_1 a_1 \cdots s_t r_t a_t) \\ r(r_{t+1} \mid s_1 r_1 a_1 \cdots s_t r_t a_t s_{t+1}) \end{array} \right\} \xrightarrow{\mathcal{S} \cup \mathcal{A} \cup \mathfrak{R}_0 \to \mathcal{X}} Q(x_i \mid x_1^{i-1}) = \Pr(x_i \mid x_1^{i-1}) \quad (6)$$

When the probability distribution depends on the last observed k symbols, let us call the process a k-th order MDP (k-MDP). The probability of a string x^n is given by

$$Q(x^n) = \prod_i^n Q(x_i \mid x_{i-k}^{i-1}) \quad (7)$$

It is noted that the representation of k-MDP is more general than that of conventional reinforcement learning [2], and includes it as well. Thus, the process of interactions are regarded as a model of an information source given by Q. Therefore, to specify the information source is the same as knowing the probabilistic structure of the process. We will specify the information source by coding the string of episode sequences so that the coding removes redundancy and gives a short description. The achievement of the ideal minimum coding rate (entropy rate) means that we know the probabilistic structure perfectly; that is, an optimal policy can be achieved. As a property of the learning process, the entropy rate is connected to the degree of complexity of the probabilistic structure. The more complex it is, the more difficult it is to achieve the optimal policy, and the larger episode the agent needs. In addition, the coding rate shows how much the agent specifies the probabilistic structure. It is possible for it to be a quality measure for a partially trained agent. In the framework of reinforcement learning, we wish to work the coding sequentially. Then, we note the adaptive coding algorithm due to Lempel-Ziv.

2.2   Lempel-Ziv Complexity

Now let us begin to just look the string $x_1 x_2 x_3 \cdots$ produced by an information source. Without thinking of the probabilistic structure behind the string, let us find "rules". This idea is closer to pattern matching rather than estimation, which most conventional reinforcement learning algorithms have done. Consider that the string is sequentially parsed into phrases that no two phrases are identical. Let us give the name "distinct parsing" to this parsing. For example, when parsing 1010, 1-0-10 is distinct, but 10-10 is not distinct. The numbers of distinct parsings are decided by complexity of a string called the Lempel-Ziv complexity [3].

Definition 1 (Lempel-Ziv Complexity). *Lempel-Ziv complexity $c_{LZ}(x^n)$ is the number of phrases in a distinct parsing that all the phrases are as short as possible.*

There are two versions of Lempel-Ziv algorithms that give a distinct parsing. One is based on the incremental parsing [4], and another is based on the recursive property of an ergodic source [5]. In this paper, we will use the former. The algorithm is standard in the field of data compression, because of its simplicity and efficiency. The function of the Lempel-Ziv algorithm is also desirable from an aspect of reinforcement learning, as will be discussed later.

2.3   Incremental Parsing of String

We will consider that a string is sequentially parsed into phrases that have not appeared earlier. Suppose the following parsing of a given string x_1^n is done by applying the Lempel-Ziv algorithm.

$$x_1^n = \underbrace{x_1, \cdots, x_{n_1}}_{x_1^{n_1}}, \underbrace{x_{n_1+1}, \cdots, x_{n_2}}_{x_{n_1+1}^{n_2}}, \cdots, \underbrace{x_{n_{p-1}+1}, \cdots, x_{n_p}}_{x_{n_{p-1}+1}^{n_p}}, \underbrace{x_{n_p+1}, \cdots, x_n}_{x_{n_p+1}^{n}}$$

$$= w_1, w_2, \cdots, w_p, w_{p+1} \tag{8}$$

where $w_j = x_{n_{j-1}+1}^{n_j}$, and $w_i \neq w_j$ $(i \neq j)$ for $1 \leq i, j \leq p$. The phrase w_{p+1} denotes the remnant of the string left over from parsing.

Lempel-Ziv Algorithm: Now consider the j-th parsing so that we get the phrase w_j. We look along the string $x_{n_{j-1}+1}^n$ until we come to the shortest phrases that have not been appeared before. This entails the following procedure. First, the phrases corresponding to the earlier parsed phrases $w_1, w_2, \cdots, w_{j-1}$ are picked up from the prefix of the remaining string. Let w_{k_j} $(1 \leq k_j \leq j - 1)$ be the longest phrase among the phrases that are picked up, and let $l_{k_j} = n_{k_j} - n_{k_j-1}$ be its length. If not found, then $k_j = 0$ and $l_{k_j} = 0$. Next,

- if $n_{j-1} + l_{k_j} < n$, then $w_j = w_{k_j} x_{n_j} = x_{n_{j-1}+1}^{n_j}$, where $n_j = n_{j-1} + l_{k_j} + 1$.
- else if $n_{j-1} + l_{k_j} = n$, then $w_j = w_{k_j} = x_{n_{j-1}+1}^{n_j}$, where $n_j = n$, and finished.

Note all phrases w_j are the union of the prefix w_{k_j} that has already appeared and the alphabet x_{n_j}. It is clear that the distinct parsing is unique, and we can recover the source string x_1^n from the pairs (k_j, x_{n_j}), the location k_j of the prefix and the last alphabet x_{n_j}.

We then translate the pair (k_j, x_{n_j}) to an integer value as follows.

$$z_j = k_j J + x_{n_j} \tag{9}$$

By $0 \leq k_j \leq j - 1$ and $0 \leq x_{n_j} \leq J - 1$, z_j holds $0 \leq z_j \leq jJ - 1$. We thus need $L_j = \lceil \log_2 jJ \rceil$ bits to describe z_j, and $\sum_{j=1}^{p+1} L_j$ bits to describe the string x_1^n. It is clear that the source string is recovered without error. The coding rate converges to the entropy rate under the condition that the source is a stationary ergodic process [6].

Table 1. Total Codeword Length (bit)

domain	Figure 1 domain	Figure 2 domain	Figure 3 domain
total codeword length	4468.864	5589.834	5428.422

3   Experiments

We will verify that the Lempel-Ziv coding for a string of episode sequences gives a quality measure to describe the degree of complexity for learning in the framework. For simplicity without loss of generality, we take up three domains of a Markov decision process (see Figures 1, 2, and 3). In these figures, the circle and the narrow arrow are the state of the environment and the state transition, respectively. The number associated with each narrow arrow denotes the probability of the state transition, and the alphabet ("a" and "b") denotes the action. The wide arrow with the number "10" represents the scalar reward. During each episode, the agent begins at the initial state "S", and is allowed to perform actions until it reaches the goal state "G". The agent learns by the tabular version of one-step Q-learning [7], where the learning rate $\alpha_{n(s,a)} = 0.1(100 + 1)/(100 + n(s,a))$ and the discount factor $\gamma = 1$. The notation $n(s,a)$ denotes the number of times that the state-action (s,a) has been tried. As a strategy of action selection, we employs the following ε-greedy method, where $\varepsilon_m = \ln(m)/7$.

ε-greedy method: Let m be the number of episodes. With probability ε_m, the agent chooses the best action with a largest expected value. On the other hand, the agent randomly chooses an action with probability $1 - \varepsilon_m$.

At the end of an episode, the Lempel-Ziv algorithm is applied to the string of episode sequences that have been observed. The alphabet size is $J = 10$ in the Figures 1 and 2 domains, and $J = 11$ in the Figure 3 domain. One trial consists of 100 episodes. Table 1 shows the total codeword length per trial, averaged over 1000 trials. Figure 4 also shows the codeword length per step, that is, the coding rate. Let us consider the degree of complexity for learning in Figures 1 and 2. It is hard to learn the optimal policy in the Figure 2 domain as compared with the Figure 1 domain because the values of the expected return between action "a" and "b" are closer. This means that the agent requires more trial-and-errors to make sure of a better action. Table 1 and Figure 4 show how well the Lempel-Ziv

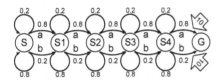

Fig. 1. Shortcut Domain1

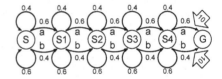

Fig. 2. Shortcut Domain2

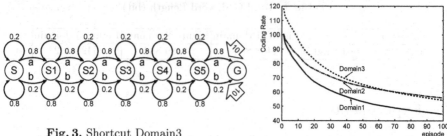

Fig. 3. Shortcut Domain3

Fig. 4. Coding Rate

algorithm detects complexity due to values that are close. As these indicate, the Lempel-Ziv algorithm detects the complexity. Next, let us consider the degree of complexity for learning in the Figure 3 domain as compared with the Figure 1 domain. The Figure 3 domain is more complex than the Figure 1 domain, because the number of states is larger. According to Table 1 and Figure 4, we can confirm that the complexity on the size of the domain leads to an increase of the total codeword length and the coding rate. It follows from what has been mentioned that the Lempel-Ziv algorithm provides a quality guide to measure complexity with respect to learning.

4   Discussions and Conclusions

In short, the codeword length shows how often some specific phrases occur in the episode sequence. The more frequent a shorter one is, and the easier it is to learn. The codeword length is decided by the Lempel-Ziv complexity c_{LZ} and the size J of the alphabet $\mathcal{X}$, as mentioned in Section 2. We can also see from a reinforcement learning view point that the Lempel-Ziv algorithm includes the function of the quantification for complexity due to the following points.

Uncertainty of transition and reward. The agent suffers from an uncertainty of an expected return in the domain that the number of transitions are large and the entropy on the transition probability is high. It is not efficient to compress the string in this case. Consequently, the codeword length becomes long and the fall in the coding rate is slow. The same applies to the reward.

Closeness between action values. When the values between the actions are close, it is difficult for an agent to decide which action is better. This case does not lead to a large drop in the coding rate, because of the high entropy.

Size of set. A large domain is hard to learn. If the size of $\mathcal{S} \cup \mathcal{A} \cup \Re_0$ is large, then the alphabet J is large. Therefore, the value of the coding rate is high, especially at the beginning.

Variance has recently attracted attention for measuring the uncertainty of an expected return, and has been applied to risk-avoiding control [8]. At first sight, the codeword length and variance seem to be the same. The codeword length is similar in function of the above uncertainty to the variance. However, the variance does not include the functions of the closeness and size given above. In brief, the codeword length is a measure of complexity for learning, and the variance is a measure of uncertainty. They are distinct, and one is not necessarily better than the other.

As has been discussed, the codeword length of a string contains some new points that conventional measures such as expected return and its variance can not include, yet the algorithm is particularly simple and does not need tuning. More importantly, the coding rate shows an asymptotic optimal rate (approaching the entropy rate of an ergodic source) without knowing the source. These advantages provide a wide application including the efficient control for the exploitation-exploration dilemma, generalization on the state space, and detection for a change of an environment.

In this paper, we proposed a new measure within the framework of reinforcement learning, by describing a model of an information source as a representation of a learning process. Unlike conventional measures based on bootstrapping, the idea comes from pattern matching, and connects to the entropy rate of an ergodic source. We confirmed that the Lempel-Ziv coding for a string of episode sequences provides a quality measure to describe the degree of complexity for learning from an aspect of reinforcement learning.

Acknowledgements. We gratefully acknowledge the helpful discussions held with Assistant Professor Kazushi Ikeda at Graduate School of Informatics, Kyoto University. This study is supported in part by a Grant-in-Aid for Scientific Research from the Ministry of Education of Japan.

References

1. Shannon, C.E., Weavor, W.: The Mathematical Theory of Communication, University of Illinois Press, (1949), Urbana.
2. Sutton, R.S., Barto, A.G.: Reinforcement Learning: An Introduction, MIT Press, 1998, Adaptive Computation and Machine Learning, Cambridge, Massachusetts, http://envy.cs.umass.edu/ rich/book/the-book.html,
3. Lempel, A., Ziv, J.: On the Complexity of Finite Sequences, IEEE Transactions on Information Theory, (1976) vol. IT-22,1 75-81
4. Ziv, J., Lempel, A.: Compression of Individual Sequences via Variable-Rate Coding", IEEE Transactions on Information Theory, (1978), IT-24, 5 530–536
5. Ziv, J., Lempel, A.: A Universal Algorithm for Sequential Data Compression, IEEE Transactions on Information Theory, (1977), IT-23, 3 337-343
6. Han, T.S., Kobayashi, K.: Mathematics of Information and Coding, American Mathematical Society, (2002),Vol 203, Translations of Mathematical Monographs
7. Watkins, C.J.C.H., Dayan, P.: Technical Note: Q-learning, Machine Learning, (1992), vol. 8, 279-292, Kluwer Academic
8. Sato, M., Kobayashi S.: Average-Reward Reinforcement Learning for Variance Penalized Markov Decision Problems, Machine Learning: Proceedings of the 18th International Conference, (2001) 473-480, San Francisco, Calif.

Efficient Face Extraction Using
Skin-Color Model and a Neural Network

Jong-Bae Kim, Chae-Hyun Moon, and Hang-Joon Kim

Dept. of Computer Engineering, Kyungpook National University
1370, Sangyuk-dong, Pook-gu, Dea-gu, 702-701, Korea
{kjblove,chmoon,hjkim}@ailab.knu.ac.kr

Abstract. In this paper, we present a method to efficiently extract a human's face from a given image sequence. The method consists of two steps: image segmentation and facial region extraction. In the image segmentation, the input frames are segmented using watershed algorithms segmenting the frame into an appropriate set of arbitrary regions. In the facial region extraction, the facial regions are extracted by integrating the results of facial region detection using a skin-color model and the results of facial region identification using a Neural Network (NN). The results of the image segmentation and facial region extraction are integrated to provide facial regions with accurate and closed boundaries. In our experiments, the presented method detected 92.2% of the faces and the average run time ranged from 0.31 to 0.48 sec per frame.

1 Introduction

Automatic detection and extraction of facial regions make some major applications possible, including content-based coding of video sequences, video indexing and recognition or identification of faces. In the MPEG-4 and 7 content, human faces can be used to index and search images and videos, classify video scenes and extract human faces from the background [1]. Above all, the extraction of a facial region provides a content-based representation of the image so that it can be used for encoding, manipulation, indexing and face recognition purposes.

Until now, various techniques and algorithms have been proposed to detect and extract the human face. The model-based approach was proposed by Govindaraju *et al.* [2] where the face was defined as interconnected arcs that represent chins and hairlines. The knowledge-based approach to detect human faces in complex backgrounds was proposed by Yang and Huang [3]. Other approaches include temple-based, Neural Network-based and example-based, which have been studied by many researchers. These methods, however, are all computationally expensive and some can only deal with frontal views, thus allowing for little variation in size and viewpoint. Although research on face extraction has been pursued at a feverish pace, there are still many problems yet to be fully and convincingly solved. This is because the level of difficulty of the problem depends highly on the complexity level of the image content and its applications. To solve these problems, color-based face detection has

H. Yin et al. (Eds.): IDEAL 2002, LNCS 2412, pp. 538–543, 2002.
© Springer-Verlag Berlin Heidelberg 2002

recently become a direction that has exhibited better performance [3, 5]. Currently, one approach makes use of skin-color to directly identify the human face, while another employs color as a feature to partition an image into a set of homogeneous regions. However, when using skin-color only to detect human faces, it is impossible to detect faces with accurate and closed boundaries since skin-colors occur not only in faces but also in backgrounds.

In this paper, we present a face extraction method with accurate and closed boundaries using watersheds, a skin-color model and a NN. The presented method consists of two steps: image segmentation and facial region extraction. In the image segmentation, the input image is segmented into several initial regions using a watershed algorithm. In the facial region extraction, the facial regions are extracted from the results of the image segmentation using a skin-color model and a NN. After candidate face detection, we employed a chain-code based approach to remove the loosely connected pixels of the detected regions and a morphological operator to fill-in on the hold of the detected regions. A general outline of the presented method procedure is presented in Fig. 1.

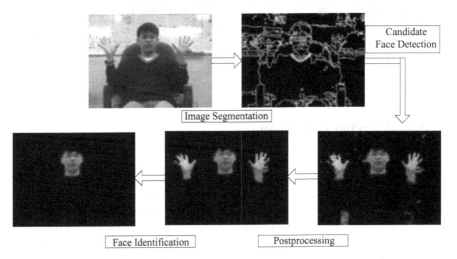

Fig. 1. The main steps for our face extraction algorithm

2   Image Segmentation

An image is segmented through the application of a watershed transformation based on the gradient image. Watersheds are traditionally defined in terms of the drainage patterns of rainfall. Regions of terrain that drain to the same points are defined to be part of the same watershed. This same description can be applied to images by viewing intensity as height. In this case, the image gradient is used to predict the direction of the drainage. By following the image gradient downhill from each point in the image, the set of points which drains to each local intensity minimum can be identified.

These disjointed regions are called the watersheds of the image. Similarly, the gradients can be followed uphill to the local intensity maximum in the image, defining the inverse watersheds of the image [4].

The watershed algorithm consists of initialization and flooding. Initialization puts the location of all pixels in a queue corresponding to the interior of a region in the marker. These pixels have the highest priority because they belong to their respective regions. Next, flooding assigns pixels to regions following a region growing procedure [4]. Fig. 2 shows the region segmentation of a watershed transform. Fig. 2 (a) is the original image of 'Claire', (b) is the gradient image using the Canny operator, (c) is a result of region segmentation by watershed transformation and (d) is the simplified image that has average color values within segmented regions. Here, flat regions larger than 100 pixels are extracted as intensity marks.

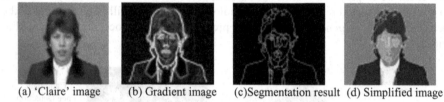

(a) 'Claire' image   (b) Gradient image   (c)Segmentation result   (d) Simplified image

Fig. 2. Image segmentation of the watershed transformation

3   Facial Region Extraction

Facial regions are extracted by integrating the results of candidate facial region detection using a skin-color model and the results of facial region identification using a NN. The skin-color model characterizes the skin colors of human faces. Fig. 3 shows the color distribution of human faces obtained from 200 test images in chromatic color space. As shown in Fig. 3, the color distribution of human faces is clustered in a small area of chromatic color space and can be approximated by 2D-Gaussian distribution [5]. This is a three-dimensional plot with r and g forming a chrominance plane. The occurrence of each r and g in the image gives the values along the vertical axis. The histogram of the skin-color is illustrated in Fig. 3(a). Fig. 3(b) shows the mean and covariance matrix of the skin-color model obtained from 200 sample images. A skin-color model is represented by a 2D-Gaussain model with a mean vector $\mathbf{m}$ and covariance matrix Σ, where $\mathbf{m} = (\vec{r}, \vec{g})$ with

$$\vec{r} = \frac{1}{N}\sum_{i=1}^{N} r_i \; , \; \vec{g} = \frac{1}{N}\sum_{i=1}^{N} g_i \; , \; \Sigma = \begin{bmatrix} \sigma_r^2 & p_{X,Y}\sigma_g\sigma_r \\ p_{X,Y}\sigma_r\sigma_g & \sigma_g^2 \end{bmatrix} \qquad (1)$$

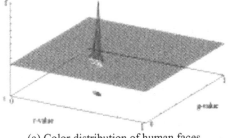

Parameters	Values
μ_r	117.588
μ_g	79.064
σ_r^2	24.132
$\rho_{X,Y}\sigma_g\sigma_r$	-10.085
$\rho_{X,Y}\sigma_r\sigma_g$	-10.085

(a) Color distribution of human faces   (b) Actual 2D-Gaussian parameters

Fig. 3. Color distribution of human faces and actual 2D-Gaussian parameters

After facial region detection, NN is used to extract real facial regions in the detected candidate facial regions. For the NN input, we use the gray-level information of the detected facial regions, normalizing the size of the detected facial regions to 30×30 pixels for the NN. The network is trained using the standard error back-propagation algorithm. To train the NN, we used mirror images to create a total of 687 positive patterns (non-face: 470, face: 217), along with 530 negative patterns. Once we computed the feature vectors for both the positive and negative patterns, we used these to train the NN classifier. A NN consists of three layers: an input layer of 900 units; a hidden layer of 350 units; and an output layer of 3 units. Each layer is fully connected to the next. Fig. 4 shows the structure of the NN-based identifier for facial region identification.

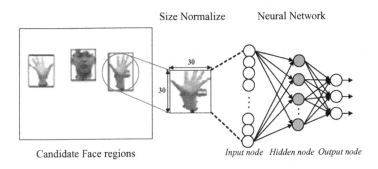

Candidate Face regions   Input node Hidden node Output node

Fig. 4. The structure of NN-based face identification

4   Experimental Results

To evaluate the performance of the presented method, simulation was carried out on the frames of 'Claire', 'Akiyo', 'Foreman' and our room, and the frame size was 352 × 288. The experiments were performed on a Pentium IV 1.4Ghz PC with an algorithm that was implemented using Matlab 5.3. The image segmentation processing of each image took 0.39 sec on average. The time depended on the number and size of facial regions present in the image. To show the robustness of the presented method, we performed a noise sensitivity test. Table 1 gives the percentages of correct facial region detection versus the increasing Gaussian noise. As the rate of noise increased, the rate of correct location decreased. However, the presented method shows 85% average for correct location of facial regions in the Gaussian noise 20% added images. Although the results of watershed image segmentation are over-segmented because of the great number of minima and various noise contributions the information within an image or its gradient, the segmentation results well preserved the boundary of objects. These results demonstrate the robustness of the presented method with regard to noise. From the experimental results, we know that the rough position of the facial region is determined. This proves the presented method is robust against noise of degraded images, tilting and rotation of the head as well as the presence of complex back-grounds. Fig. 5a and b shows the face extraction results. As a result of face extraction, the average facial region extraction ratio is 92.2%.

Table 1. The error probability of the face detection (%)

Gaussian noise (%)	0	10	20	30
Akiyo #2	3.5	7.2	14.6	22.2
Claire #5	3.7	10.2	13.6	23.7
Foreman #11	2.0	9.6	15.2	28.3

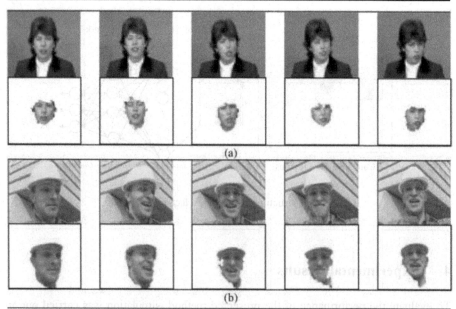

Fig. 5 *a.* Face extraction results. (a) and (b) are 'Claire' and 'Foreman' video sequences (top) and face extraction results (bottom)

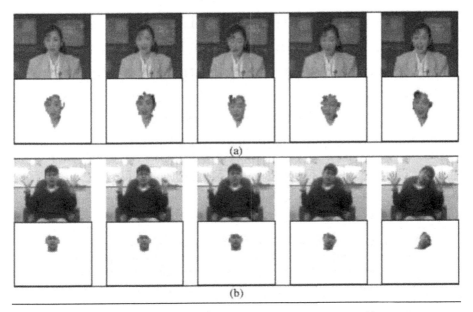

Fig. 5 *b*. Face extraction results. (a) and (b) are 'Akyio' and our room video sequences

5   Conclusions

An efficient method for human face extraction using a skin-color model and NN are described in this paper. The procedure for complete method consists of two steps: image segmentation and facial region extraction. The results of the image segmentation and facial region extraction are integrated to provide more accurate segmentation of the facial regions. As shown in the simulation results, the presented method generates accurate and closed boundaries of human face extraction results, which makes region- or object-based coding more efficient. It can also significantly reduce the computational cost of face detection while improving detection accuracy.

References

1. Wang, H. and Chang, S. F.: A Highly Efficient System for Automatic Face Region Detection in MPEG Video, IEEE Trans. Circuit Syst. Video Tech., Vol. 7, No. 4 (1997) 615-628
2. Yang, G. and Huang, T. S.: Human face detection in a complex background, Pattern Recognition, Vol. 27, No. 1, (1994) 53-63
3. Greensapn, H., Goldberger, J. and Eshet, I.: Mixture model for face-color modeling and segmentation, Pattern Recognition Letters, Vol. 22, No. 14 (2001) 1525-1536
4. Vincent, L. and Soile, P.: Watersheds in digital space: An efficient algorithm based on immersion simulation, IEEE Trans. PAMI., Vol. 13, No. 6, (1998) 583-598
5. Hsu, R. L., Mottalev, M. A., Jain, A. K.: Face detection in color images, in proc. Int. Conf. Image Processing, Vol. 1 (2001) 1046-1049

Feature Weights Determining of Pattern Classification by Using a Rough Genetic Algorithm with Fuzzy Similarity Measure

Shan Ding and Naohiro Ishii

Department of Intelligence and Computer Science,
Nagoya Institute of Technology,
Gokiso-cho, Showa-ku, Nagoya 466, Japan
{ding, ishii}@egg.ics.nitech.ac.jp

Abstract. The classification problem is one of the typical problems encountered in data mining and machine learning. In this paper, a rough genetic algorithm (RGA) is applied to the classification problem in an undetermined environment based on a fuzzy distance function by calculating attribute weights. The RGA, a genetic algorithm based on rough values, can complement the existing tools developed in rough computing. Computational experiments are conducted on benchmark problems downloaded from UCI machine learning databases. Experimental results, compared with the usual GA [1] and C4.5 algorithms, verify the efficiency of the developed algorithm. Furthermore, the weights acquired by the proposed learning method are applicable not only to fuzzy similarity functions but also to any similarity functions. As an application, a new distance metric called weighted discretized value difference metric (WDVDM) is proposed. Experimental results show that WDVDM is an improvement on the discretized value difference metric (DVDM).

1 Introduction

The NN method is the basis of many applications of case-based reasoning systems [2] [3]. It is extremely simple to implement and is open to a wide variety of variations. On the other hand, it suffers from the existence of noisy attributes. Simpler metrics may fail to capture the complexity of the problem domains, and as a result, may not perform well. One way to diminish the influence of noisy attributes is to calculate the attribute weights and attach weights to the attributes to further modify the distance in degrees of similarity.

In this paper, we present rough genetic algorithms (RGA) to calculate attribute weights from similarity information which is generated from training sets. Rough set theory [4] provides an important complement to fuzzy set theory in the field of soft computing. The RGA, a genetic algorithm based on rough values, can complement the existing tools developed in rough computing. Lingras and Davies [5] provided a simple example to demonstrate the practical applications of RGA to Information Retrieval (IR). However, their findings are of little help in pattern classification. First, their fail to address the effectiveness

H. Yin et al. (Eds.): IDEAL 2002, LNCS 2412, pp. 544–550, 2002.

of the precision that plays an such important role in evaluating a rough individual. Second, the adaptability of the distance measurements is not proved. The example they give is too simple to demonstrate the effectiveness of RGA. In this paper, we developed this method specifically to help solve the classification problem. A fuzzy distance function is defined that can be useful for determining the degree of similarity between two rough individuals. As its one of comparison algorithms, a conventional GA [1] is used to determine real-valued parameters for comparison with RGA. The other comparison algorithms (C4.5 algorithms) are used to show the efficiency of the developed algorithm as a reference for our algorithm.

Furthermore, the weights learned by our developed learning methods are applicable not only to fuzzy similarity functions but also to any other similarity function. As an application, a new distance metric called a weighted discretized value difference metric (WDVDM) is proposed. Experimental results show that WDVDM is an improvement on discretized value difference metric (DVDM).

The remainder of this paper is organized as follows: in Section 2 the problem is defined, and the background knowledge about the similarity function is provided. Section 3 discusses in detail our RGA approach and our experimental tests. In Section 4, a new distance metric based on a discretized value difference metric (DVDM) is proposed, and experimental tests are carried out. Some concluding remarks follow in Section 5.

2   Problem Description

2.1   Qualitative Similarity Information and Condition

Let recorders are formed of n attributes and one output class. If the recorders x and y are in the same output class, we say that the recorder x is similar to y. We call the given similarity information *Qualitative Similarity Information* (QSI) [1] which denotes whether or not recorder x is similar to recorder y. Let $w = (w_1, w_2, \cdots, w_n)$ denote a weight vector, where $w_i(i = 1, 2, \cdots, n)$ is the weight assigned to feature f_i. Let $s_w(\mathrm{x, y})$ be a similarity function which calculates the degree of similarity between recorders x and y using the weight vector w. The problem is to find a weight vector w and a threshold $\alpha(0 < \alpha < 1)$, which satisfy the following *Qualitative Similarity Condition*(QSC). For each chosen recorder pair (x, y), if x is similar to y, then $s_w(x, y) < \alpha$; otherwise $s_w(x, y) \geq \alpha$.

It should be noted that there does not exist a single w and α satisfying that condition. We add the following condition to w to reduce the search space. $\forall x, y$ and any w, $\exists w' = \{w'_1, w'_2 \cdots, w'_n\}$, $s_w(x, y) = s_{w'}(x, y)$, where $w' = w/\sum_{i=1}^{n} w_i$ (note that almost all of the similarity functions have this type of property).

2.2   Fuzzy Similarity Measure

In order to learn feature weights for similarity, we use a nonlinear similarity function based on fuzzy integrals [6]. The importance of attributes is reflected in the attribute weights which will be used in determining the fuzzy measure for calculating the fuzzy integrals. This nonlinear similarity function for training set is used for our experiments. In fact, the attribute weights learned by RGA can also be used in Euclidean distance functions [2].

3   Rough Genetic Algorithm for QSI

3.1   Rough Genetic Algorithm (RGA)

In this subsection, we describe the genetic algorithm to calculate w and α. It is called the Rough Genetic Algorithm (RGA). In a RGA, the value of each gene is specified by setting lower and upper bounds:

$$x = (\underline{x}, \overline{x}),$$

where $\underline{x}$ is the lower bound and $\overline{x}$ the upper bound of x. The weight vector can easily be represented as a rough individual by specifying that both the lower and upper bounds must be equal to the gene values.

Coding weight vector. A weight vector can be encoded by a string of real numbers where the ith one is the weight assigned to the ith feature. The threshold of the individual is added to the end of the string. In this paper, a rough individual r is a string of rough genes r_i:

$$r = (r_i | 1 \leq i \leq n, 0 \leq r_i \leq 1)$$

A rough gene r_i can be viewed as a pair of conventional genes, one for the lower bound, called the lower gene($\underline{r_i}$), and the other for the upper bound, called the upper gene($\overline{r_i}$):

$$r_i = (\underline{r_i}, \overline{r_i})$$

As discussed in Section 2, we add the condition $\sum_{i=1}^{n}(\underline{r_i} + \overline{r_i}) = 2$ to reduce the search space.

Evaluation. When evaluating an individual, we must change each rough gene into its conventional one. The process is as follows:

```
for(i=0; i<(2×AttriNum) − 1;i+ = 2){
    k=(int)i/2;
    individual[k]=(r[i]+r[i+1])/2;
}
```

The fitness value of an individual is taken as the satisfaction degree of QSI, i.e., R_{QSI}/R, where R_{QSI} is the number of the sets of two recorders which satisfy QSC using weight vector w and α representing the individual, and R is the number of chosen sets of two recorders. The fitness value of a population is the maximum fitness value of individuals in it.

Selection. All individuals in the population are sorted by their fitness values, and the first individual is the fittest. The operation is performed as described elsewhere [7] in details.

Crossover. Lingras and Davies [5] proposed two genetic operations called *union* and *intersection*. They are defined as follows.
Let r=$(r_i|1 \leq i \leq n)$ and s=$(s_i|1 \leq i \leq n)$ be two rough individuals defined as strings of rough genes r_i and s_i, respectively. The *union* operation denoted by the symbol $\bigcup$, is given as follows:

$$r \cup s = (r_i \cup s_i|1 \leq i \leq n), where$$
$$r_i \cup s_i = (min(\underline{r_i}, \underline{s_i}), max((\overline{r_i}, \overline{s_i})).$$

The intersection operation, denoted by the symbol $\bigcap$, is given as follows:

$$r \bigcap s = (r_i \bigcap s_i|1 \leq i \leq n), where$$
$$r_i \bigcap s_i = (min(min(\overline{r_i}, \overline{s_i}), max(\underline{r_i}, \underline{s_i})), max(min(\overline{r_i}, \overline{s_i}), max(\underline{r_i}, \underline{s_i})))$$

For the threshold, set the average value of those in two parents of the offspring.

Mutation. If both of the two genes chosen to be mutated are weights then randomly exchange a gene for another different one, or replace a gene pair (g_1, g_2) with a new one (g_1', g_2'), where $g_1 + g_2 = g_1' + g_2'$ for keeping the sum of weights unchanged.
    In this operation, it is necessary to check each attribute(x) in an individual to keep $\overline{x} \geq \underline{x}$.

Differentiation of the same individuals. After crossover and mutation, the differentiation of the same individuals will be carried out for individuals in the population. Mutations will be induced in the individual if there are other same ones in the generation until it is different from all of the other individuals.

GA parameters. The population size is $2N_w$, where N_w is the number of attributes. The probability of mutation is 0.8. The two kinds of rough crossover operations are selected by probability 0.5. The cutoff criterion is taken to be $200N_w$ individual evaluations.
    The overall pseudo-code procedure of RGA is outlined as a generational genetic algorithm procedure. Changed the top of rough individual of the last generations into conventional one just the same as in evaluation, the weight vector of attributes can be obtained by RGA. The same parameters and evaluation method are used by the usual GA.

3.2   Simulation and Test I

The developed RGA and the real-coded GA for QSI are implemented using C language on the SunOS 5.6 with Pentium III 600 MHz and tested on 10 datasets downloaded from UCI machine learning databases. The correct rates reported

Table 1. Results of test I

Data Set	RGA	GA	C4.5 (Before)	C4.5 (After)	C4.5 (Rules)
Annealing	0.938 ± 0.012	0.922 ± 0.023	**0.967 ± 0.013**	0.95 ± 0.008	0.94 ± 0.024
BreastCancer-Wisconsin	**0.958 ± 0.007**	0.946 ± 0.015	0.943 ± 0.012	0.944 ± 0.012	0.951 ± 0.011
Dermatology	0.965 ± 0.013	0.928 ± 0.018	0.973 ± 0.008	**0.975 ± 0.008**	0.972 ± 0.011
Glass	**0.912 ± 0.046**	0.899 ± 0.045	0.641 ± 0.06	0.653 ± 0.077	0.623 ± 0.08
Monk1	**1 ± 0**	0.99 ± 0.003	0.766	0.714	1
Monk2	**75.2 ± 0.078**	0.746 ± 0.081	0.653	0.603	0.662
Monk3	0.937 ± 0.005	0.93 ± 0.012	0.926	0.829	**0.963**
Iris	**0.928 ± 0.017**	0.928 ±0.021	0.881 ± 0.015	0.881 ± 0.015	0.881 ± 0.018
Vote	**0.97 ± 0.006**	0.97 ± 0.008	0.971	0.931	0.948
Wine	**0.949 ± 0.041**	0.933 ± 0.025	0.861 ± 0.046	0.859 ± 0.046	0.854 ± 0.045
Average	**0.932**	0.918	0.858	0.834	0.879

in Table 1 are the average values of 10 trials obtained by RGA (RGA), the real-coded GA (GA), and C4.5 algorithms including a before-pruning algorithm ("Before"), after-pruning algorithm ("After") and rules algorithm ("Rules"), respectively.

From Table 1, we have the following observations:

1. Experimental results show the average accuracy of all datasets obtained by RGA is the highest among all the algorithms.
2. To deal with the datasets including only continuous attributes, GAs are better than C4.5 algorithms.
3. Compared with the C4.5 rules algorithm, the number of wins, ties, and losses between the correct rates of RGA and the real-coded GA are 6/1/3 and 6/0/4, respectively. It is shown that the RGA effectiveness is superior to both the real-coded GA and C4.5 algorithms.

Considering that an algorithm that dominates the other algorithms in all datasets does not exist, the effectiveness of the developed method is confirmed by the experiments. The execution time of GAs is decided by the amount of similarity information. It is better to select the representative information to calculate when the size of the training dataset is very large.

4   Application of Weight Vector

4.1   Weighted Discretized Value Difference Metric

According to the different role (weight) which each attribute has in the classification problem (in a training data set), the weight of each attribute in the distance function is decided. Based on their algorithm and DVDM, we propose a new distance metric call Weighted Discretized Value Difference Metric (WD-VDM). In this Section, we apply the calculated weight vector to the discretized value difference metric (DVDM) described by Wilson and Martinez [8].

$$WDVDM(x,y) = \sum_{a=1}^{m} w_a |vdm_a(d_a(x_a), d_a(y_a))|^2$$

where w_a is calculated from similarity information provided by RGA, and vdm_a is described as before.

4.2   Simulation and Test II

The developed RGA and the WDVDM are also implemented using C language on the SunOS 5.6 with Pentium III 600 MHz and tested on 10 datasets downloaded from UCI machine-learning databases. The datasets and correct rates are listed in Table 2. Datasets generated in Test I are used.

Table 2. Results of test II

Data Set	Inst	test	WDVDM	DVDM
Annealing	400	150	**0.933± 0.009**	0.933 ± 0.01
BreastCancer-Wisconsin	489	210	0.949 ± 0.005	**0.95± 0.008**
Dermatology	256	110	0.977± 0.019	**0.986± 0.011**
Glass	150	64	**0.541 ± 0.09**	0.476 ± 0.09
Monk1	124	432	**1 ± 0**	0.879 ± 0.015
Monk2	169	432	**0.749 ± 0.039**	0.745± 0.054
Monk3	122	432	**0.94 ± 0.011**	0.938 ± 0.011
Iris	105	46	**0.928± 0.026**	0.924± 0.027
Vote	300	135	**0.967 ± 0.004**	0.963 ± 0.006
Wine	125	53	**0.804± 0.061**	0.70 ± 0.083
Average			**0.879**	0.849

Experimental results of Table 2 show that WDVDM on average has a higher accuracy than the DVDM algorithm, indicating that the proposed WDVDM improves the accuracy of the DVDM.

5   Concluding Remarks

In this paper, a rough genetic algorithm (RGA) that deduces attribute weights from similarity information is developed. A nonlinear similarity function based on fuzzy integrals is used as the distance function. Ten sets of benchmark problems downloaded from UCI machine-learning datasets are tested. Compared with the real-coded genetic algorithm and the C4.5 algorithms, including C4.5 before and after pruning algorithms and the C4.5 rules algorithm, the developed RGA obtains the best results on average. The effectiveness of the developed method is confirmed by the experiments. Furthermore, the attribute weights calculated by the proposed RGA are applied to the discretized value difference metric (DVDM), and a new distance metric called weighted discretized value difference metric (WDVDM) is proposed. Computational experiments show WDVDM is superior to the DVDM algorithm.

References

1. Y. Wang and N. Ishii, *"Learning Feature Weights from Similarity Information,"* International Journal on Artificial Intelligence Tools, Vol. 7, No. 1, pp 31-41, 1998.
2. C. Stanfill and D. Waltz, *"Toward Memory-Based Reasoning,"* Communication of ACM, 29:1213-1229, 1986.
3. S. Wess, K. D. Althoff, and G. Derwand, *"Using k-d Trees to Improve the Retrieval Step in Case-Based Reasoning,"* In Topics in Case-Based Reasoning, First European Workshop, EWCBR-93, pp 167-181 Berlin, 1993.

4. Z. Pawlak, *Rough Sets: Theoretical Aspects of Reasoning About Data,* Kluwer Academic Publishers, Dordrecht 1991.
5. P. Lingras and C. Davies, *"Rough Genetic Algorithm,"* 7th International Workshop, New Directions in Rough Sets, Data Mining, and Granular-soft Computing, Japan, pp. 38–46, 1999.
6. M. Sugeno, *"Fuzzy Measure and Fuzzy Integral,"(in Japanese)* Trans. of the Society of Instrument and Control Engineers, 8(2): 218-226, 1972.
7. S. Ding and N. Ishii, *"An Online Genetic Algorithm for Dynamic Steiner Tree Problem,"* 2000 IEEE International Conference on Industrial Electronics, Control and Instrumentation. pp. 812–817, 2000.
8. D. R. Wilson and T. R. Martinez, *"Improved Heterogeneous Distance Functions,"* Journal of Artificial Intelligence Research, 11:1-34, 1997.

Recursive Form of the Discrete Fourier Transform for Two-Dimensional Signals

Zümray Dokur and Tamer Ölmez

Department of Electronics and Communication Engineering,
Istanbul Technical University, Istanbul, Turkey
zumray@ehb.itu.edu.tr

Abstract. In this paper, recursive fast Fourier transform is presented for two-dimensional signals. When applying to real-time analysis, the computational efficiency is highly improved by integrating a recursive procedure. The recursive procedure highly reduces the number of complex arithmetic operations, and provide detailed spectral analysis for one or two-dimensional signals.

In the first stage, the recursive algorithm is realized for one-dimensional signals. Then, recursive fast Fourier transform is presented for two-dimensional signals. The advantages of the recursive algorithm are presented by giving examples for one and two-dimensional signals.

1 Introduction

In past years, time-frequency signal representation such as the short-time Fourier transform (STFT), the short-time Hartley transform and the Wigner distribution, have received considerable attention as powerful tools for analysing a variety of signals and systems [1,2,3]. In particular, if the frequency content is time varying, as in non-stationary signals, these approaches are very attractive. In applications of spectral analysis such as speech processing and the detection or estimation of a narrow band spectral peak, the spectral content over a small portion of the band or even at arbitrary frequencies is required.

Not long after the key contribution to digital spectral analysis, the development of the fast Fourier transform (FFT) by Cooley and Tukey [4], Halberstein [5] proposed the idea of evaluating the successive DFTs using the recursive computation. Bongiovanni presented the formulated procedure, which allowed a moving size M to be any integer power of 2; nonetheless, M is no greater than the frame size [6]. Several algorithms for efficient computation of moving-frame DFTs have been developed thereafter [7].

2 Recursive Procedures of the Fourier Transform

In the paper, the moving size M is selected as one. The recursive procedure for the succeeding DFT process uses sequence samples from $x(1)$ to $x(N-1)$, which are computed for the previous window. Fig. 1. shows the previous and succeeding windows for recursive procedure.

H. Yin et al. (Eds.): IDEAL 2002, LNCS 2412, pp. 551–556, 2002.

The results obtained from one-dimensional signals are extended into the analysis of two-dimensional signals.

2.1   Recursive Procedure for One-Dimensional Signals

Let $X(k)$ denote the N-point DFT of non-stationary long-term sequence $x(n)$. Since the running Fourier spectrum is updated at a rate of one sample point (M=1), $X(k)$ is given by the following equation:

$$X(k) = x(0)e^{\frac{-j2\pi k.0}{N}} + x(1)e^{\frac{-j2\pi k.1}{N}} + \ldots\ldots + x(N-1)e^{\frac{-j2\pi k(N-1)}{N}}. \tag{1}$$

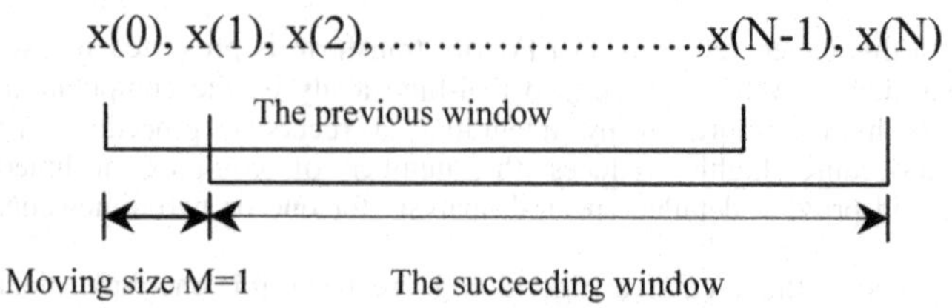

$$x(0),\ x(1),\ x(2),\ldots\ldots\ldots\ldots\ldots\ldots,x(N\text{-}1),\ x(N)$$

Moving size M=1   The succeeding window

Fig. 1. The previous and succeeding windows for the recursive procedure

The succeeding DFT becomes as follows:

$$X'(k) = x(1+M)e^{\frac{-j2\pi k.0}{N}} + \ldots + x(N+M-1)e^{\frac{-j2\pi k(N-2)}{N}} + x(N+M)e^{\frac{-j2\pi k(N-1)}{N}}. \tag{2}$$

In the analysis, moving size M is selected as 1. Let us subtract the first term of the summation in equation (1) from $X(k)$,

$$X(k) - x(0)e^{\frac{-j2\pi k.0}{N}} = x(1)e^{\frac{-j2\pi k.1}{N}} + \ldots\ldots + x(N-1)e^{\frac{-j2\pi k(N-1)}{N}} \tag{3}$$

and then, multiply equation (3) by $e^{\frac{+j2\pi k.1}{N}}$:

$$e^{\frac{+j2\pi k.1}{N}} \cdot \left(X(k) - x(0)e^{\frac{-j2\pi k.0}{N}} \right) = x(1)e^{\frac{-j2\pi k.0}{N}} + \ldots\ldots + x(N-1)e^{\frac{-j2\pi k(N-2)}{N}}. \tag{4}$$

Let us subtract the last term of $X'(k)$ in equation (2) from $X'(k)$,

$$X'(k) - x(N)e^{\frac{-j2\pi k(N-1)}{N}} = x(1)e^{\frac{-j2\pi k.0}{N}} + \ldots\ldots + x(N-1)e^{\frac{-j2\pi k(N-2)}{N}} \tag{5}$$

and equate the left side of equation (4) to that of equation (5):

$$X'(k) - x(N)e^{\frac{-j2\pi k(N-1)}{N}} = X(k)\cdot e^{\frac{j2\pi k}{N}} - x(0)\cdot e^{\frac{j2\pi k}{N}} ; \quad e^{\frac{-j2\pi k(N-1)}{N}} = e^{\frac{+j2\pi k}{N}}$$

$$X'(k) = e^{\frac{j2\pi k}{N}} \cdot \left(X(k) + x(N) - x(0) \right). \tag{6}$$

There exists a class of algorithms, called the fast Fourier transform (FFT), which requires $O(N \times \log_2 N)$ operations for the succeeding DFT, where one operation is a real multiplication and a real addition. Equation (6) requires one multiplication and two addition operations for a single term of the succeeding DFT (for M=1). The overall computation requires O(N) multiplication and O(2N) addition operations.

2.2   Recursive Procedure for Two-Dimensional Signals

In this paper, two different recursive procedures are formulated depending on the moving direction of a sub-image (for M=1). Fig. 2 shows the sub-image moved along n1 axis. Two square regions (shown by bold borders) represent the $x(n_1,n_2)$ and $x(n_1+1,n_2)$ sub-images, where the sub-image $x(n_1+1,n_2)$ is shown by dark gray.

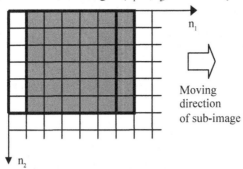

Fig. 2. Sub-image moved along the n_1 axis

The two-dimensional DFT of an $N_1 \times N_2$ sub-image ($x(n_1,n_2)$) is a separable transform defined as follows:

$$X(k_1,k_2) = \sum_{n_1=0}^{N_1-1} \sum_{n_2=0}^{N_2-1} x(n_1,n_2).e^{\frac{-j2\pi k_1 n_1}{N_1}} e^{\frac{-j2\pi k_2 n_2}{N_2}} \qquad W_1 = e^{\frac{-j2\pi}{N_1}} \qquad W_2 = e^{\frac{-j2\pi}{N_2}}$$

$$X(k_1,k_2) = x(0,0).W_1^{k_1 0} \cdot W_2^{k_2 0} + x(0,1).W_1^{k_1 0} \cdot W_2^{k_2 1} + \ldots\ldots \\ + x(N_1-1,N_2-1).W_1^{k_1(N_1-1)} \cdot W_2^{k_2(N_2-1)} \tag{7}$$

The succeeding 2D-DFT becomes

$$X(k_1,k_2) = \sum_{n_1=0}^{N_1-1} \sum_{n_2=0}^{N_2-1} x(n_1+1,n_2).e^{\frac{-j2\pi k_1 n_1}{N_1}} e^{\frac{-j2\pi k_2 n_2}{N_2}}$$

$$X'(k_1,k_2) = x(1,0).W_1^{k_1 0} \cdot W_2^{k_2 0} + x(1,1).W_1^{k_1 0} \cdot W_2^{k_2 1} + \ldots\ldots \\ + x(N_1,N_2-1).W_1^{k_1(N_1-1)} \cdot W_2^{k_2(N_2-1)} \tag{8}$$

Let us subtract the terms belonging to $x(0, n_2)$ in equation (7) from $X(k_1,k_2)$,

$$X(k_1,k_2) - \sum_{n_2=0}^{N_2-1} x(0,n_2) \cdot W_1^{k_1 0} \cdot W_2^{k_2 n_2} = \sum_{n_1=1}^{N_1-1}\sum_{n_2=0}^{N_2-1} x(n_1,n_2).e^{\frac{-j2\pi k_1 n_1}{N_1}} e^{\frac{-j2\pi k_2 n_2}{N_2}} \tag{9}$$

and then, multiply equation (9) by $W_1^{-k_1}$;

$$W_1^{-k_1}\left[X(k_1,k_2) - \sum_{n_2=0}^{N_2-1} x(0,n_2) \cdot W_1^{k_1 0} \cdot W_2^{k_2 n_2} \right] = \sum_{n_1=1}^{N_1-1}\sum_{n_2=0}^{N_2-1} x(n_1,n_2) . W_1^{k_1(n_1-1)} . W_2^{k_2 n_2} \quad (10)$$

Now, let us subtract the terms belonging to $x(N_1, n_2)$ in equation (8) from $X'(k_1,k_2)$,

$$X'(k_1,k_2) - \sum_{n_2=0}^{N_2-1} x(N_1,n_2) W_1^{k_1(N_1-1)} \cdot W_2^{k_2 n_2} = \sum_{n_1=0}^{N_1-2}\sum_{n_2=0}^{N_2-1} x(n_1+1,n_2) . W_1^{k_1 n_1} . W_2^{k_2 n_2} \quad (11)$$

and equate the left side of equation (10) to that of equation (11):

$$W_1^{-k_1}\left[X(k_1,k_2) - \sum_{n_2=0}^{N_2-1} x(0,n_2) \cdot W_2^{k_2 n_2} \right] = X'(k_1,k_2) - \sum_{n_2=0}^{N_2-1} x(N_1,n_2) \cdot W_1^{k_1(N_1-1)} \cdot W_2^{k_2 n_2}$$

$$X'(k_1,k_2) = W_1^{-k_1}\left[X(k_1,k_2) - \sum_{n_2=0}^{N_2-1} x(0,n_2) \cdot W_2^{k_2 n_2} + \sum_{n_2=0}^{N_2-1} x(N_1,n_2) \cdot W_2^{k_2 n_2} \right]. \quad (12)$$

For the sub-window moved along n2 axis, recursive procedure is formulated as follows:

$$X'(k_1,k_2) = W_2^{-k_2}\left[X(k_1,k_2) - \sum_{n_1=0}^{N_1-1} x(n_1,0) \cdot W_1^{k_1 n_1} + \sum_{n_1=0}^{N_1-1} x(n_1,N_2) \cdot W_1^{k_1 n_1} \right]. \quad (13)$$

Two-dimensional fast Fourier transform requires $O(N_1 \times N_2 \times Log_2 N_1)$ operations for the succeeding DFT, where one operation is a real multiplication and a real addition.

For the recursive algorithm, firstly, the second and third terms in square brackets of equation (12) are computed and stored for all k_2 values. These processes require $O(2 \times N_2 \times N_2)$ multiplication operations. And then, $W_1^{k_1}$ is multiplied by the term in the square brackets of equation (12). This process requires $O(N_1 \times N_2)$ multiplication operations. Thus, the overall computation requires $O(N_1 \times N_2 + 2 \times N_2 \times N_2)$ multiplication operations.

For $N_2 = 1$, equation (12) is defined as follows:

$$X'(k_1,1) = W_1^{-k_1}\left[X(k_1,1) - x(0,0) \cdot W_2^{k_2 0} + x(N_1,0) \cdot W_2^{k_2 0} \right]. \quad (14)$$

For $N_1 = 1$, equation (13) is defined as follows:

$$X'(1,k_2) = W_2^{-k_2}\left[X(1,k_2) - x(0,0) \cdot W_1^{k_1 0} + x(0,N_2) \cdot W_1^{k_1 0} \right]. \quad (15)$$

It is observed that equation (6) has a similar form with equations (14) and (15).

3 Computer Simulations

For the analysis of one-dimensional signals, a signal with four different frequency components at four different time intervals is given as an example in order to determine the starting and ending times of the bursts. The signal is sampled at 2048 Hz, and contains 2048 data. The interval of 171 to 190 msec. has a 400 Hz sinusoid, the interval of 195 to 215 msec. has a 200 Hz sinusoid, the interval of 732 to 747 msec. has a 300 Hz sinusoid, and finally the interval 879 to 898 msec. has a 100 Hz sinusoid. In the analysis, a window of 128 samples is formed. Fig. 3 shows the STFS obtained by the recursive procedure. It is observed that the recursive procedure gives more detailed spectral analysis by consuming less computational time.

The results obtained from one-dimensional signals are extended to the analysis of two-dimensional signals. As an example, in texture processing, textures and their boundaries can be determined by analysing the Fourier spectrum. By choosing the moving size M as 1, changes in the Fourier spectrum will be observed in detail.

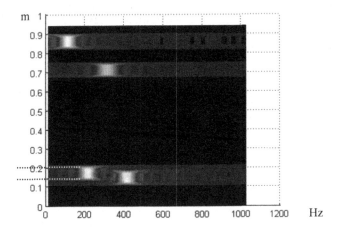

Fig. 3. The STFS obtained by the recursive procedure

As an application to image processing, the ultrasound image of kidney cyst is segmented by using the ISOM network developed in a previous study [8]. The kidney cyst image is shown in Fig. 4.a. The only difference from the previous study is to move the sub-image over the entire image, instead of splitting the entire image into square blocks. Feature vectors are formed by using 2D-DFT of the sub-images. Training set consists of the feature vectors formed by moving the sub-image over the entire ultrasound image.

Threshold value determines the number of classes (tissues) in the ultrasound image. Threshold is selected as 60000 (the same as in the previous study). Size of the sub-image is selected as 4×4 pixels. For 100 sub-images, the consumed times by using recursive process and the standart DFT are 8 and 40 seconds, respectively. Ultrasound image of kidney cyst in Fig. 4.b is segmented into five tissues.

In this study, the recursive 2D-DFT algorithm enables us to analyse the Fourier spectrum in detail. Hence, better classification performance is achieved by using the recursive algorithm.

All simulations are performed on Pentium III-450 MHz PC using MATLAB 6.0.

4 Conclusion

In the analysis of one-dimensional signals, the starting and ending times of bursts can be determined easily, assuming that the moving window does not contain the same frequency content at disconnected locations in the window. In Fig. 3, it is observed that the durations of the four frequencies in the Fourier spectrum are longer than the values explained in the section of Computer Simulations. The ending times of bursts are easily obtained as t_2 from Fig. 3. However, the starting time of a burst is found by adding the t_1 value appeared in Fig. 3 to the duration of the moving window. This analysis enables us to find the starting and ending times of bursts in detail.

In the previous study [8], we developed a novel method for the segmentation of ultrasound images. Splitting the entire image into square blocks decreased the performance of the classification process. In this study, by moving the sub-image over the entire image, the boundaries of textures are determined in detail. However, this process increases the overall computational time. By using the recursive algorithm, the consumed times for training and classification processes are decreased.

In this study, the recursive two-dimensional Fourier transform is developed for general-purpose image processing applications. The recursive algorithm can be used as a pre-process for pattern recognition applications or texture processing.

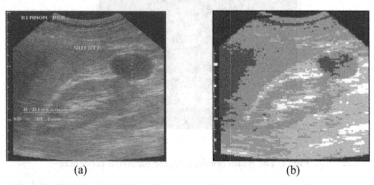

(a)   (b)

Fig. 4.(a) Ultrasound image of kidney cyst, (b) segmented image by the ISOM.

References

1.   Claasen, T.A.C.M., Mecklenbruker W.F.G.: The Wigner Distribution – A Tool for Time-Frequency Signal Analysis, Part I: Continuous-Time Signals; Part II: Discrete-Time Signals. Phillips J. Research 35, pp. 217-259, (1980) pp. 276-300.
2.   Liu, J.-C., Lin, H.-C.: Short-Time Hartley Transform. IEE Processing 44, (1995) 211-222.
3.   Portnoff, M.R.: Representation of Digital Signals and Systems Based on the Short-Time Fourier Transform. IEEE Trans. Acoust. Speech Signal Process., 28(1), (1980) 55-69.
4.   Cooley, J.W., Tukey, J.W.: An Algorithm for Machine Computation of Complex Fourier Series. Math. Comput. 19, (1965) 297-301.
5.   Halberstein, H.J.: Recursive, Complex Fourier Analysis for Real-Time Application. Proc. IEEE (lett.) 54, (1966) 903.
6.   Bongiovanni, G., Corsini, P., Frosini, G.: Procedures for Computing the Discrete Fourier Transform on Staggered Blocks. IEEE Trans. Acoust. Speech Signal Process. ASSP-24 (2), (1976) 132-137.
7.   Lo, P.-C., Lee, Y.-Y.: Real-Time Implementation of the Moving FFT Algorithm. Signal Processing (79), (1999) 251-259.
8.   Kurnaz, M.N., Dokur, Z., Ölmez, T.: Segmentation of Ultrasound Images by Using an Incremental Self-Organized Map. 23rd Ann. Int. Con. of the IEEE-EMBS, (2001).

Viseme Recognition Experiment Using Context Dependent Hidden Markov Models

Soonkyu Lee and Dongsuk Yook

Speech Information Processing Laboratory
Department of Computer Science and Engineering, Korea University
Sungbookgoo Anamdong 5-1, Seoul, Korea 136-701
http://voice.korea.ac.kr
{mudwall,yook}@voice.korea.ac.kr

Abstract. Visual images synchronized with audio signals can provide user-friendly interface for man machine interactions. The visual speech can be represented as a sequence of visemes, which are the generic face images corresponding to particular sounds. We use HMMs (hidden Markov models) to convert audio signals to a sequence of visemes. In this paper, we compare two approaches in using HMMs. In the first approach, an HMM is trained for each triviseme which is a viseme with its left and right context, and the audio signals are directly recognized as a sequence of trivisemes. In the second approach, each triphone is modeled with an HMM, and a general triphone recognizer is used to produce a triphone sequence from the audio signals. The triviseme or triphone sequence is then converted to a viseme sequence. The performances of the two viseme recognition systems are evaluated on the TIMIT speech corpus.

1   Introduction

With the recent advances in computer and multimedia technologies, audio-to-visual conversion becomes an important area for efficient multimedia communications. In multimedia environments, using both sounds and images is a natural and efficient way to communicate between men and machines. Images synchronized with sounds can transfer information more reliably than sounds alone can. Audio-to-visual conversion techniques can help to create speaking facial images from speech data. The speech data is converted to a sequence of visemes, which are the visual equivalent of phonemes. From the viseme sequence, its corresponding facial images can be synthesized. The audio-to-visual conversion techniques can be applied to many areas such as human-computer interaction, videophone, and character animation. In this paper, we will focus on the viseme recognition from audio data.

Several methods have been proposed to handle the audio-to-visual conversion problem. In VQ (vector quantization) based methods, a codebook that represents entire acoustic space of speech feature vectors is created during training process. A testing speech feature vector is classified as one of the codeword in the codebook, and the images corresponding to the codeword are selected for the visual image synthesis [4]. This method is simple to implement and easy to train. However, the error in quantization can cause extra classification errors. Another approach uses artificial neural networks [1]. Some neural networks such as TDNN (time-delay neural

H. Yin et al. (Eds.): IDEAL 2002, LNCS 2412, pp. 557-561, 2002.

network) [10] can make use of contextual information and learn very complex classification functions. In some experiments for speech processing [8][10], neural networks show very high classification accuracy and some robustness to noises. However, the training process is computationally too expensive especially for a large amount of training data. The third approach uses HMM (hidden Markov models) [6]. It assumes that the speech signal can be modeled by the Markov process. The parameters of HMMs are estimated during training process from a large amount of training corpus. The testing speech is scored against the HMMs and the most likely model sequence is selected for the given speech signals [5]. The most likely phoneme sequence can be computed in this way, and it can be easily converted to the corresponding viseme sequence. The HMM-based speech recognition is one of popular methods because of its relatively high recognition accuracy and trainability using a large amount of data. In this paper, we compare two approaches in building viseme recognizers using HMMs. The first approach uses an HMM for each triviseme, while a general triphone recognizer is utilized in the second approach.

Table 1. Phonemes and visemes in English language.

Phone classes	Phonemes	Example words	Visemes	Phone classes	Phonemes	Example words	Visemes
Stops	b	bee	B	Front	ae	bat	AE
	d	day	D		eh	bet	AE
	g	gay	G		ih	bit	IH
	k	key	G		iy	beet	IH
	p	pea	B	Mid	aa	bott	AA
	t	tea	D		ah	but	AH
Affricates	ch	choke	CH		ao	bought	AO
	jh	joke	CH		er	bird	ER
Fricatives	dh	then	D	Back	uh	book	UH
	f	fin	F		uw	boot	UH
	s	sea	D	Diphthongs	aw	bout	AA,UH
	sh	she	CH		ay	bite	AA,IH
	th	thin	D		ey	bait	AE,IH
	v	van	F		ow	boat	AO,UH
	z	zone	D		oy	boy	AO,IH
	zh	azure	CH	Silence	h#		#
Nasals	m	mom	B				
	n	noon	G				
	ng	sing	G				
Glides	l	lay	G				
	r	ray	R				
	w	way	R				
	y	yacht	G				
Whisper	hh	hay	G				

(a) Consonants   (b) Vowels and silence

The rest of this paper is organized as follows. In Section 2, we review the visual speech unit called viseme, and describe the viseme recognition systems using HMMs. Some experimental results of the systems are analyzed in Section 3. Section 4 concludes the paper with some suggestions to the future works.

2   Viseme Recognition

A *viseme* is a unit of visual speech. A generic facial image or lip shape is associated with a viseme in order to represent a particular sound. Fisher [2] introduced the word viseme, which is a compound word of "visual" and "phoneme". A viseme can be used to describe a set of phonemes visually.   It can help to increase speech recognition accuracy for both human and machines by visually recognizing the shape of speakers' lip movements [3][7]. There are many-to-one mappings from phonemes to visemes. Table 1 shows the typical 40 phonemes including silence used in English language. The viseme mapping is shown in the last column of the table. We named each viseme after one of the phoneme that maps to the viseme.   For example, phonemes /b/, /m/, and /p/ belong to viseme /B/. According to the shape of mouth and placement of tongue, we grouped the 40 phonemes into 14 visemes. The lip shapes of 6 consonant visemes and 7 vowel visemes are shown in Figures 1 and 2, respectably. The viseme names are shown above the lip images, and the phonemes are shown below the images.

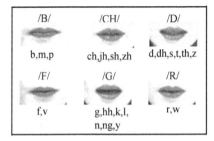
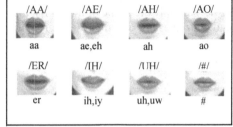

Fig. 1. The 6 consonant visemes.   **Fig. 2.** The 7 vowel visemes and 1 silence viseme.

One of distinguishing characteristics of speech is that it is dynamic.   Even within a small segment such as a phoneme, the speech sound changes gradually. The previous phones affect the beginning of the current phone, the middle portion of the phone is relatively stable, and the following phones affect the end of the phone. The temporal information of speech feature vectors plays an important role in recognition process. In order to handle the dynamic characteristics of speech for automatic speech recognition, a sound is usually modeled as a context-dependent phone such as a *triphone* that takes into account both the left and right neighboring phones.   For a viseme recognizer, each *triviseme*, which considers its left and right neighboring visemes, is modeled using an HMM with multiple Gaussian distribution functions per state.   Another way of using HMMs for viseme recognition is utilizing a phoneme recognizer. A general triphone recognizer can be trained in the similar way as the triviseme recognizer. In this approach, the audio signals are first converted into a sequence of triphones. Then, the triphone sequence is mapped to a viseme sequence using Table 1.   In the next section, we show some viseme recognition experiments using these approaches.

3   Experimental Results

A speech feature vector used for the experiments is composed of 12 dimensional MFCCs (mel-frequency cepstral coefficients), normalized energy, and their first and second order time derivatives, resulting in a 39 dimensional vector. It is computed every 10 milliseconds using 25 milliseconds long Hamming windowed speech signals. The HMMs are trained using 3,696 utterances from TIMIT training data [9]. For the first approach described in the previous section, 14×13×14 triviseme and 1 silence HMMs are created. For the triphone recognizer, 40×39×40 triphone and 1 silence HMMs are trained. All HMMs are modeled using 3-state left-to-right HMM. In total, the first and the second systems have both about 16,000 Gaussian distributions. 1,344 utterances from the testing portion of TIMIT are used for evaluation.

The baseline triviseme recognition system shows 22.7% viseme recognition error rate. The baseline triphone recognizer shows 22.8% phoneme recognition error rate, which corresponds to viseme error rate of 17.4% when converted into viseme sequences using Table 1. In order to reduce the viseme error rate, we merge similar viseme classes according to their mouth shapes. First, we split /er/ into /ah/ and /r/, and merge them with the existing /ah/ and /r/, respectably. By doing this for the triphone-based system, the error rate is reduced to 16.9%. Second, we group visemes /CH/ and /D/ together, and /AE/, /AH/, and /IH/ together. The error rate is reduced to 13.3%. Not only the shape of mouth but also the confusion matrices shown in Figures 3 and 4 motives this and the rest of groupings. The x axes in Figures 3 and 4 are the reference visemes and the y axes are the recognized visemes. For example, a lot of viseme /IH/'s are classified as visemes /AH/ or /AE/ in both Figures 3 and 4.

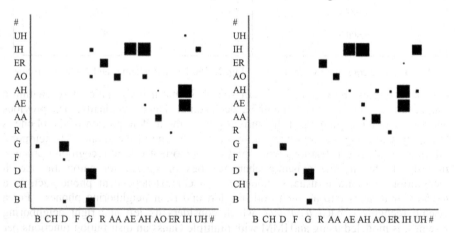

Fig. 3. Confusion matrix: Triviseme-based.   **Fig. 4.** Confusion matrix: Triphone-based.

We keep merging the viseme classes until there are only 3 classes left; consonant, vowel, and silence. That is, /CH/ and /G/ are merged, and /AE/ and /UH/ are merged, resulting in 11.6% error rate. Further error reduction is obtained by merging /B/ and /CH/, /B/ and /R/, /AE/ and /AO/, /B/ and /F/, /AA/ and /AE/ successively. The error rates are reduced to 10.7%, 9.6%, and 7.6%, respectably. The comparison of the triviseme-based and the triphone-based systems in this experiment is summarized in Table 2.

Compared to using monoviseme or monophone based systems, the triviseme or triphone based systems reduce the error rate by 34% relatively on the average.

Table 2. The triviseme-based and the triphone-based systems with varying viseme sets.

Merge	Number of visemes	Triviseme-based	Triphone-based
Baseline	14	22.7	17.4
er ⟶ ah+r	13	21.8	16.9
CH+D, AE+AH+IH	10	19.8	13.3
CH+G, AE+UH	8	19.3	11.6
B+CH	7	18.8	10.7
B+R, AE+AO	5	-	9.6
B+F, AA+AE	3	-	7.6

4   Conclusions

The audio-to-visual conversion is becoming an important area of interests as the multimedia communication environments become popular. Automatic conversion of audio signals to the visual speech units can help to create natural dynamic images of speaking faces. In this paper, we studied the viseme recognizers, which produce a sequence of viseme symbols in text from speech waveforms. We compared two approaches in using HMMs for the viseme recognition. The first approach is based on the triviseme recognizer, where each triviseme is model with a single HMM. The second approach uses a general phoneme recognizer. The audio signals are recognized as a sequence of triphone, and it is converted into a viseme sequence. The performances of the two approaches have been evaluated using TIMIT speech data. We have found that the triphone-based approach is superior probably because it can handle the detail characteristic of phonemes individually. The error rates can vary from 17.4% to 7.6% depending on the viseme sets used.

References

1. Choi, K., Hwang, J.: Baum-Welch HMM inversion for audio-to-visual conversion, IEEE International Workshop on Multimedia Signal Processing, pp. 175-180, 1999.
2. Fisher, C.: Confusions among visually perceived consonants, Journal on Speech and Hearing Research, vol. 11, pp. 796-804, 1968.
3. Grant, K., Walden, B., Seitz, P.: Auditory-visual speech recognition by hearing-impaired subjects: consonant recognition, sentence recognition, and auditory-visual integration, Journal of Acoustic Society of America, vol. 103, pp. 2677-2690, 1998.
4. Morishima, S., Harashima, H.: A media conversion from speech to facial image for intelligent man-machine interface, IEEE Journal on selected areas in communications, vol. 9, no. 4, pp. 594-600, 1991.
5. Rabiner, L.: A tutorial on hidden Markov models and selected applications in speech recognition, Proceedings of the IEEE, vol. 77, no. 2, pp. 257-286, 1989.
6. Rao, R., Chen, T.: Mersereau, R., Audio-to-visual conversion for multimedia communication, IEEE Transaction on Industrial Electronics, vol. 45, no. 1, pp. 15-22, 1998.
7. Rogozan, A., Delelise, P.: Adaptive fusion of acoustic and visual sources for automatic speech recognition, Speech Communication, vol. 26, pp. 149-161, 1998.
8. Tamura, S., Waibel, A.: Noise reduction using connectionist models, IEEE International Conference on Acoustics, Speech, and Signal Processing, pp. 553-556, 1988.
9. TIMIT: Acoustic-phonetic continuous speech corpus, Nist Speech Disc 1-1.1, October 1990.
10. Waibel, A., Hanazawa, T., Hinton, G., Shikano, K., Lang, K.: Phoneme recognition using time-delay neural networks, IEEE Transactions on Acoustics, Speech, and Signal Processing, vol. 37, no. 3, pp. 328-339, 1989.

Stave Extraction for Printed Music Scores

Hidetoshi Miyao

Shinshu University, 4-17-1 Wakasato, Nagano 380–8553, JAPAN
miyao@cs.shinshu-u.ac.jp

Abstract. In this paper, a satisfactory method is described for the extraction of staff lines in which there are some inclinations, discontinuities, and curvatures. The extraction calls for four processes: (1) Extraction of specific points on a stave on vertical scan lines, (2) Connection of the points using DP matching, (3) Composition of stave groups using labeling, and (4) Extraction and adjustment of the edges of lines. The experiment resulted in an extraction rate of 99.4% for 71 printed music scores that included lines with some inclinations, discontinuities, and curvatures.

1 Introduction

Databases are necessary when applying computers to the field of music. Optical music recognition systems are fast and easy to use. Many algorithms have been proposed for music recognition, and most of them extract staff lines in the first stage since the positions of staff lines are used to determine the positions for other musical symbols and their sizes. Therefore, stave extraction greatly influences the extraction rate of other musical symbols.

Ideally, staff lines are a set of five straight horizontally drawn parallel lines. However, scanned images of staff lines may contain inclinations, curvatures, and discontinuities. An algorithm for extracting staff lines should be useful to overcome the irregularities. An algorithm should be able to distinguish between staff lines and the many other horizontal notations used in music, such as slurs, ties, and ledger lines.

In order to extract staff lines, many algorithms have been proposed[1]. Fujinaga[2] applied a method for horizontal projection of an image and extracted distinct peaks of the profile as the vertical positions of the staff lines. The method is easy to use; however, it is inadequate for coping with the inclination and curvature of the lines. An inclination of only 0.4 degrees causes deterioration in the projection profile[3]. To cope with staff lines that incline slightly, Kato[4] applied a method of horizontal and vertical projection to only local areas in which the edges of the staff lines were assumed to exist. The staff lines were then represented by the extracted edges. This method functions while permitting a slight inclination of the staff lines, but it is inadequate for dealing with large inclinations and curvatures in the lines. Miyao[5] proposed a stave extraction method using a Hough Transform. This method extracts lines with large inclinations and discontinuities, but it does not cope with curvature. Carter[6] used a Line

H. Yin et al. (Eds.): IDEAL 2002, LNCS 2412, pp. 562–568, 2002.

Adjacency Graph to extract them. This method copes with slight curvature and inclination of staff lines, but it places a heavy load on a computer because all the image pixels must be searched.

The purpose of this work is to obtain a high extraction rate for staff lines that have slight inclinations, discontinuities, and curvatures, while searching specific areas of a music score image.

2   Stage-1: Extraction of Candidate Points

To determine the width and height of staff lines in scans of printed music, the black and white run-lengths are measured by scanning 10 vertical lines that divide the images into equal areas. The maximum value of a histogram for the black run-length is then regarded as the average thickness of a staff line ($awid$), while the white one is considered as the average distance between each staff line ($aintv$)[4].

The whole image is also divided into equal areas by some vertical scan lines (set to 35($=Scdiv$) scan lines in the experiment). If the black run-length on the scan lines is within the range of $awid \pm Lad$(set to 2 dots in the experiment), the center of the run-length would be extracted as a candidate point that is considered to be an intersection of a staff line and a scan line. At this point, some intersections of scan lines and staff lines that had been overlooked and some extra points that are not located on the staff lines can also be included in the candidate points.

3   Stage-2: Connection of Candidate Points Using DP Matching

Dynamic Programming (DP) matching is used to connect the extracted candidate points on two adjacent scan lines, p_k and p_{k+1} ($1 \le k \le Scdiv - 2$), in Fig. 1. This method produces the most feasible one-to-one matching for a 2-pattern series without changing the pattern order, and it can permit patterns with missing and extra points.

The series of candidate points on scan lines p_k and p_{k+1} are represented by $\{a_1, a_2, \cdots, a_I\}$ and $\{b_1, b_2, \cdots, b_J\}$, shown in Fig. 1, respectively. When the pattern series $\{a_1, a_2, \cdots, a_i\}$ and $\{b_1, b_2, \cdots, b_j\}$ are matched most feasibly, the accumulated distance $g(i, j)$ is calculated as follows:

$$Initial\ values\ :\ \begin{cases} g(0,0) = 0 \\ g(i,0) = g(i-1,0) + 1, & for\ 1 \le i \le I \\ g(0,j) = g(0,j-1) + 1, & for\ 1 \le j \le J \end{cases} \tag{1}$$

$$Recurrence\ formula: \\ g(i,j) = min\left\{g(i-1,j-1) + d(i,j), g(i-1,j) + 1, g(i,j-1) + 1\right\}, \tag{2}$$

where $d(i, j)$ means a distance between patterns a_i and b_j that is determined based on whether there is a staff line between points a_i and b_j. Its value is assigned to be 0 if the following two conditions are satisfied; otherwise, it is 2.

Condition 1: If an average angle of the linked lines for the previous area (between p_{k-1} and p_k) is referred to as pr_ang, the inclination of the line through the two specified points is within a range $pr\_ang \pm Sang$(set to 1 degree in the experiment). If the angle pr_ang has not yet been determined, an angle $\pm Pang$ (set to 20 degrees in the experiment) is used.

Condition 2: The rate of black pixels on the line between the two specified points is more than a certain threshold value $Brate$ (set to 90% in the experiment). In order to manage the slight curvature, 3 dots were used as the thickness of any point on the line. If there is at least one black pixel in the 3 vertical dots, the center point is regarded as a black pixel.

Using the above formulas, the accumulated distance $g(I, J)$ is calculated. The one-to-one matching between the 2-pattern series is obtained by backtracking the calculation process, and the side-linked line between the candidate points is produced.

Some overlooked points occur, as mentioned above, because of the musical symbols superimposed above the staff lines, such as the solid note heads shown in Fig. 1. To interpolate them, the following process is applied to all candidate points a_p not having a right-hand link on the scan line p_k. The position of the overlooked point b_p is predicted to be the intersection of the scan line p_{k+1} and the line (dashed line shown in Fig. 1) that is drawn based on the coordinates of a_p and the average angle of the extracted linked line in this area. If the points a_p and b_p satisfy Condition 2 above, point b_p would be added as a new candidate point on line p_{k+1}, and a side-linked line between them would be produced.

After completing the process from the scan line p_1 to $p_{Scdiv-2}$, some overlooked points may also exist in the left-hand side of the music. Therefore, the same interpolation process is applied to points that do not have a left-hand link in the direction from $p_{Scdiv-2}$ to p_1.

Since the points not having a link are not regarded as points on the staff lines, they are deleted.

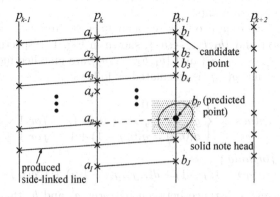

Fig. 1. Connection of candidate points

4   Stage-3: Composition of Stave Groups Using Labeling

The composition method is described in this chapter along with the candidate points that belong to one stave group.

The points on the real staff lines must be aligned vertically with the same space that is almost equal to $aintv + awid$. Making use of this feature, for every 5 consecutive points on each scan line, if all four spaces between the adjacent two points are within $aintv + awid \pm (aintv + awid) \cdot Gapw$ (set to 0.15 in the experiment), these points are regarded as the points that belong to the same stave group, and are thus linked vertically.

Next, the labeling method is applied to all of the linked points. After completing the labeling process, the points in the same staff lines have the same label number and make up a stave group. The system memorizes all of the vertical step numbers in the staff lines for all of the points, as shown in Fig. 2.

Musical symbols with horizontal lines, such as ties, slurs, or ledgers, can produce an extra link on the upper or lower sides of the stave groups. To remove them, for the stave groups that have more than 5 steps, the following process is used. The number of side links for the uppermost and lowermost steps is counted (the number of links is 2 for step 1 and 1 for step 7), as shown in Fig. 2. Comparing the two counters, the step with the fewer links is deleted. This process is continued until the number of steps is equal to 5 (In Fig. 2, the points belonging to steps 1 and 7 are deleted). On the other hand, if the step number for a stave group is lower than 5, the stave group is deleted.

Finally, lacks of the side link are interpolated for each step in the same stave group (shown as dashed lines in Fig. 2). As a result, 5 polygonal lines represent a stave group.

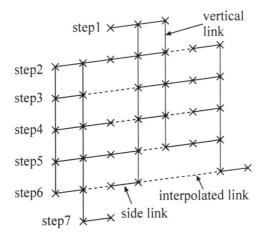

Fig. 2. Candidate points having same label

5   Stage-4: Extraction and Adjustment of the Edges of Staff Lines

At this point, the terminal of the side link does not coincide with the edge point of the staff lines. An accurate extraction method is described for the edge points.

To extract left-side edge points, for the left terminals of all the side links, the following process is used. First, if the left terminal belongs to the scan line p_k, the average angle of all the side links between scan lines p_k and p_{k+1} is calculated, and a line is drawn from the terminal based on the calculated angle. Next, the lines are scanned from the terminal toward the left side. If the black pixels are broken, the position is regarded as a left edge of a staff line. In fact, in order to cope with a slight curvature, the thickness of any point on a line was 3 vertical dots. If there is at least one black pixel among the 3 vertical dots, the center point is regarded as a black pixel. For the right terminal of all the side links, the right edge points are extracted in the same manner.

Blurs with ink and discontinuities of the line may produce uneven positions in the side direction for the extracted edge points. To adjust them, the following process is used for all of the edge points. At first, the average angle for all the side links is calculated as an angle avg. For the 2 left edge points in the same stave group, if the angle of the line that connects the 2 points is within the angle $avg+90$[degree]$\pm Rang$ (set to 5 degrees in the experiment), the counters corresponding to the 2 points are increased by one. For all combinations of 2 edge points, the above process is used, and then the edge point having the largest counter is set to be a standard edge point. Next, the line with the angle $avg+90$[degree] is drawn from the standard edge point as a base line, as shown in Fig. 3. If 4 lines are drawn with the angle avg from the 4 edge points, except for the standard edge point (represented by $line_1$ to $line_4$ in Fig. 3), the 4 intersections of the base line and the 4 lines become adjusted new edge points. The adjustment for all of the right edge points is executed in the same manner.

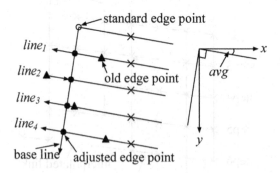

Fig. 3. Adjustment of edge points

6   Experimental Results and Discussion

In the experiments, 71 music scores printed on A4 sheets were used. They were published by 5 different publishers and include various types of scores, such as piano and orchestra. The number of staff lines in one sheet varies from 30 to 140 lines. The total stave group is 859; in other words, there are 4,295 staff lines.

Each score was scanned by an image scanner with a resolution of 300 dpi as a binary image. Eleven scores (665 staff lines) had a skew with an angle from 1 to 5 degrees; the other 60 scores (3,630 staff lines) had a skew of less than 1 degree. For all the staff lines, the number of lines with a curvature was 327, and the number of discontinuity parts was 206.

In total, 4,268 staff lines (99.4%) were accurately extracted. Accurate line extraction means that all the extracted side-link lines completely overlap real staff lines and all the edge positions are located within a 5-dot area around the real edge. Not a single staff line was overlooked.

In the observation of several scores used in the experiments, for the stage-1 process (extraction of candidate points), about 85% of the points were extracted properly, and about 10% of the points appeared excessive. For stage-2 (connection of the points), almost 100% of the links were detected. That means that about 15% of the overlooked points in stage-1 were interpolated properly. After this stage, about 2% of the extra links remained. Next, stage-3 (composition of stave groups) was able to delete almost all of the extra links and make the stave groups properly. From this observation, it is considered that each stage process is quite functional.

For all the scores used in the experiments, there were a few errors, which are described bellow:

(1) One stave group, appearing on a guitar chord, was detected excessively.
(2) The positions of two detected staff lines were mismatched.
(3) The positions of 15 detected edge points were mismatched.
(4) One stave group was divided into two stave groups.

In a case in which many solid note heads or note beams are aligned horizontally on the same staff line, there will be a lack of candidate points in a large area. Therefore, stage-2 has to interpolate many consecutive overlooked points. This may produce a mismatch between a predicted position and a real one. That is why the above error (2) occurred. In stage-1, if there is not one candidate point for a staff line, stage-2 cannot recover the overlooked points; as a result, the stave group that the overlooked points belong to cannot be extracted. However, a case such as this one was not encountered in this experiment. Stages 1 and 2 were conducted with almost perfect precision.

The system functioned well with the lines that included discontinuities because, when stage-2 produced a link between candidate points, the threshold value *Brate* was introduced in order to allow the line to have slight discontinuities. The value indicates the rate of black pixels on a link line. If the value decreases, more discontinuities can be allowed. If there were many discontinuities around the edge points, the edge positions were not detected completely since the points were detected by tracing black pixels. That is why all of the error

(3) occurred. However, when at least 2 or 3 edge points were properly detected, stage-4 enabled the adjustment of the other edge positions that were wrong. In the experiments, since many edge positions were wrong and then adjusted, the stage-4 process proved effective for these blurred edge points.

This system is also considered to be satisfactory for curvatures because 317 lines were extracted properly for the 327 lines that had some curvature. In stages 1 and 2, the large divided number *Scdiv*, the large angle range *Sang*, and the thickened scan line contributed to the good results. However, if there were lines with a large curvature, the side-linked lines could not be properly produced. As a result, a stave group might then be divided into a few groups, such as in error (4). The lines skewed up to 5 degrees did not affect the accuracy of the experimental results, which indicates that this method would also work for them.

7   Conclusions

In order to obtain a high extraction rate for staff lines that have slight inclinations, discontinuities, and curvatures by searching local areas of an image, the following processes were proposed: (1) Extraction of specific points on a stave on vertical scan lines, (2) Connection of the points using DP matching, (3) Composition of stave groups using labeling, and (4) Extraction and adjustment of edges. For 4,295 staff lines, including those with inclinations of up to 5 degrees, some discontinuities, and some curvatures in various kinds of scores, an extraction rate of 99.4% (4,268 lines) was obtained. No staff lines were overlooked, either. As shown by this result, this method can be used to satisfactorily obtain staff line positions.

References

1. Blostein, D., Baird, H.: A Critical Survey of Music Image Analysis. in Structured Document Image Analysis, eds. Baird, H., Bunke, H., Yamamoto, K., Springer-Verlag (1992) 405–434
2. Fujinaga, I.: Optical Music Recognition Using Projections. Master's thesis, McGill University, Faculty of Music, Montreal, Canada (1988)
3. Bainbridge, D., Bell, T.: The Challenge of Optical Music Recognition. Computers and the Humanities **35** (2001) 95–121
4. Kato, H., Inokuchi, S.: A Recognition System for Printed Piano Music Using Musical Knowledge and Constraints. in Structured Document Image Analysis, eds. Baird, H., Bunke, H., Yamamoto, K., Springer-Verlag (1992) 435–455
5. Miyao, H., Ejima, T., Miyahara, M., Kotani, K.: Symbol Recognition for Printed Piano Scores Based on Musical Knowledge. IEICE Trans., vol.J75-D-II, **11** (1992) 1848–1855 (in Japanese)
6. Carter, N.P.: Automatic Recognition of Printed Music in the Context of Electronic Publishing. PhD thesis, University of Surrey, Depts. of Physics and Music (1989)

Scaling-Up Model-Based Clustering Algorithm by Working on Clustering Features*

Huidong Jin[1], Kwong-Sak Leung[1], and Man-Leung Wong[2]

[1] Department of Computer Sci. & Eng., The Chinese University of Hong Kong
Shatin, N.T., Hong Kong
{hdjin, ksleung}@cse.cuhk.edu.hk
[2] Department of Information Systems, Lingnan University
Tuen Mun, Hong Kong
mlwong@ln.edu.hk.

Abstract. In this paper, we propose EMACF (Expectation-Maximization Algorithm for Clustering Features) to generate clusters from data summaries rather than data items directly. Incorporating with an adaptive grid-based data summarization procedure, we establish a scalable clustering algorithm: gEMACF. The experimental results show that gEMACF can generate more accurate results than other scalable clustering algorithms. The experimental results also indicate that gEMACF can run two order of magnitude faster than the traditional expectation-maximization algorithm with little loss of accuracy.

1 Introduction

Clustering is the unsupervised classification of data items into meaningful clusters based on similarity or density. Given a data set $X = (\mathbf{x}_1, \mathbf{x}_2, \cdots, \mathbf{x}_N)$, the model-based clustering algorithms assume that each data item $\mathbf{x}_i = [x_{1i}, x_{2i}, \cdots, x_{1i}]^T$ is drawn from a finite mixture model Φ of K distributions: $p(\mathbf{x}_i|\Phi) = \sum_{k=1}^{K} p_k \phi(\mathbf{x}_i|\theta_k)$. Here p_k is the mixing proportion for the kth cluster. In this paper, we concentrate on Gaussian mixture model. That is, the component density function $\phi(\mathbf{x}_i|\theta_k)$ is of the form $\phi(\mathbf{x}_i|\theta_k) = \frac{\exp\left\{-\frac{1}{2}(\mathbf{x}_i-\mu_k)^T \Sigma_k^{-1}(\mathbf{x}_i-\mu_k)\right\}}{(2\pi)^{\frac{D}{2}}|\Sigma_k|^{\frac{1}{2}}}$ where μ_k is a mean vector, Σ_k is a covariance matrix, D is the dimensionality of the data set.

The Expectation-Maximization (EM) algorithm, an effective and popular technique for selecting mixture models, maximizes iteratively the log-likelihood $L(\Phi) = \log\left[\prod_{i=1}^{N} p(\mathbf{x}_i|\Phi)\right]$. However, the EM algorithm has to read each data item many times since it reads each data item within each iteration of E-step and M-step. This prohibits it from handling large sets, especially when they are too

---

* The work was partially supported by RGC Earmarked Grant for Research CUHK 4212/01E of Hong Kong.

H. Yin et al. (Eds.): IDEAL 2002, LNCS 2412, pp. 569–575, 2002.
© Springer-Verlag Berlin Heidelberg 2002

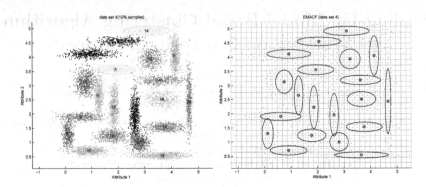

Fig. 1. (a). A data set with 100,000 data items in 20 clusters (b). the clusters generated by EMACF. A dot indicates a data item in (a) and a clustering feature in (b). The center 'o' (or '+') and its corresponding solid (or dotted) ellipse indicate the mean and a contour of a generated (or original) component Gaussian distribution.

large to fit into main memory. There are much research work to accelerate the convergence but most of them still need multiple scans of the whole data set [3,4]. The scalable model-based clustering algorithm in [1] only scans through a whole data set once. But it invokes its core algorithm, ExEM (Extended EM), multiple times to sum up the data set before generating a mixture model. Furthermore, ExEM has no convergence guarantee.

Our idea for scaling-up model-based clustering algorithms is first to partition the large data set into mutually exclusive subclusters which only contain similar data items. Each subcluster is summarized into a data summary. Then we will propose a new model-based clustering algorithm to generate clusters from data summaries directly.

2   Adaptive Data Summarization Procedure

Before discussing how to summarize a data set effectively, we need to choose a proper data summary representation. Although different forms of data summaries may be used to describe a subcluster of data items [1,4], they may be derived from a Clustering Feature (CF), which is originally used in [6]. In fact, under the assumption that attributes are independent in this paper, a clustering feature is a sufficient statistics of the subcluster if data items distribute normally. A clustering feature is denoted by $\mathbf{s}_m = \{n_m, \nu_m, \gamma_m\}$ $(m = 1, ..., M)$. Here n_m is the cardinality of the mth subcluster; $\nu_m = \frac{1}{n_m} \sum_{\text{the } m^{th} \text{subcluster}} \mathbf{x}_i$ is the mean; $\gamma_m = (\gamma_{1m}, \gamma_{2m}, ..., \gamma_{Dm})^T$ is the diagonal vector of the matrix $\Gamma_m = \frac{1}{n_m} \sum_{\text{the } m^{th} \text{ subcluster}} \mathbf{x}_i \mathbf{x}_i^T$, which indicates the second moment of the mth subcluster.

There are many approaches to summarize data sets. We employ an intuitive and simple grid-based approach. Basically, the data space is partitioned into mutually exclusive subspace and data items within same subspace form a subcluster. We use grid to partition the data space and partition each attribute into multiple segments. Thus, the data space is partitioned into many cells and data items within a same cell are quite similar to each other. Each cell may have a unique number to identify itself. To reduce the memory requirement, we only store the clustering features for these non-empty cells in a CF-array. In our implementation, the length of the CF-array is $\min(30^D, 300\ 0)$ empirically. The index of a clustering feature is determined by a hash function based on its cell number. When a new data item comes, starting from the hash index, we look for an entry in the CF-array to assimilate the data item by updating the clustering feature. This entry may be empty or already be occupied by the associated cell. When the CF-array is full, the smallest width of cells is doubled, and pairs of neighboring cells are merged into bigger ones to release some memory for forthcoming data items. The cell width may increase gradually to make better use of main memory. In addition, when it reconstructs a new CF-array, only the clustering features in the old CF-array are involved. Therefore, the procedure merely scans through the whole data sets once. For the data set shown in Fig. 1 (a), the procedure can generate 656 non-empty clustering features as plotted in Fig. 1(b).

3   An EM Algorithm for Clustering Features

For each subcluster, the second moment γ_m may represent data dispersion within a subcluster. Taking account of the second moment directly in the clustering algorithms, we may generate more accurate results. On the other hand, the Gaussian mixture models contain the second moment too. This enables us to embody entire clustering features explicitly in our new algorithm.

For each data item $\mathbf{x}_i$ in the mth subcluster, we give a 'density function' to approximate the normal distribution, specified as follows:

$$\psi(\mathbf{x}_i \in m^{th}\ \text{subcluster}|\theta_k) \triangleq \psi(\mathbf{s}_m|\theta_k) = \prod_{d=1}^{D} \frac{\exp\left\{-\frac{1}{2\sigma_{dk}}(\gamma_{dm} - 2\mu_{dk}\nu_{dm} + \mu_{dk}^2)\right\}}{(2\pi)^{\frac{1}{2}}\sigma_{dk}^{\frac{1}{2}}}.$$

It is a normal density function when $\gamma_{dm} = \nu_{dm}^2$. With this function, the probability of a data item $\mathbf{x}_i$ explicitly depends on which subcluster it belongs to. It is only implicitly relevant with its values. The function enables us to treat data items in a subcluster in the same way, so we can just store the clustering features to reduce lots of memory usage as well as execution time. In addition, intuitively, if the second moment γ_m is small, that is, data items are quite dense, the subcluster has more influence on clustering. This accords with the model-based clustering principle to locate clusters in dense regions.

With this density function, the probability for a data item $\mathbf{x}_i$ in the mth subcluster under the mixture model is $p(\mathbf{x}_i \in \text{the } m^{th} \text{ subcluster}|\Psi) \triangleq$ $p(\mathbf{s}_m|\Psi) = \sum_{k=1}^{K} p_k\psi(\mathbf{s}_m|\mu_k, \sigma_k)$. Then the log-likelihood is given as $L(\Psi) =$

Table 1. The clustering accuracy of 6 clustering algorithms on 10 data sets.

Data Set	#N	#D	#K	gEMACF	gExEM	gEMAWS	iEM	SampiEM	IBS
1	60000	2	6	**0.962**	0.934	0.942	0.960	0.958	0.836
2	480000	2	16	**0.885**	0.882	0.819	0.855	0.827	0.671
3	100000	2	9	**0.785**	0.676	0.782	0.748	0.745	0.553
4	100000	2	20	0.851	0.847	0.739	**0.858**	0.846	0.632
5	120000	2	31	0.893	0.854	0.819	**0.905**	0.875	0.697
6	120000	2	41	**0.873**	0.865	0.727	0.871	0.839	0.657
7	100000	3	10	0.911	**0.917**	0.854	0.892	0.770	0.676
8	100000	4	10	**0.931**	0.927	0.920	0.930	0.925	0.825
9	100000	5	10	**0.868**	0.816	0.820	0.856	0.843	0.741
10	100000	6	10	**0.934**	**0.934**	0.800	0.904	0.896	0.690
Average				**0.889**	0.865	0.822	0.878	0.853	0.698

$\sum_{m=1}^{M} n_m \log p(\mathbf{s}_m | \Psi)$. Based on these definitions, we derive the EM algorithm for Clustering Features (EMACF) based on the general EM algorithm [3].

1. **E-step:** Given the mixture model parameters $\Psi^{(j)}$, compute the membership $r_{mk}^{(j)}$ for each subcluster:

$$r_{mk}^{(j)} = \frac{p_k^{(j)} \psi(\mathbf{s}_m | u_k^{(j)}, \sigma_k^{(j)})}{\sum_{i=1}^{K} p_i^{(j)} \psi(\mathbf{s}_m | u_k^{(j)}, \sigma_k^{(j)})}. \tag{1}$$

2. **M-step:** Given $r_{mk}^{(j)}$, update the mixture model parameters for $k = 1, ..., K$:

$$p_k^{(j+1)} = \frac{1}{N} \sum_{m=1}^{M} n_m r_{mk}^{(j)}, \tag{2}$$

$$\mu_k^{(j+1)} = \frac{\sum_{i=1}^{M} n_m r_{mk}^{(j)} \nu_m^{(j)}}{\sum_{m=1}^{M} n_m r_{mk}^{(j)}} = \frac{\sum_{i=1}^{M} n_m r_{mk}^{(j)} \nu_m^{(j)}}{N \cdot p_k^{(j+1)}}, \tag{3}$$

$$\sigma_k^{(j+1)} = \frac{\sum_{m=1}^{M} n_m r_{mk}^{(j)} \left[\gamma_m - 2\mu_k^{(j)} \circledast \nu_m + \mu_k^{(j)} \circledast \mu_k^{(j)} \right]}{N \cdot p_k^{(j+1)}} \tag{4}$$

where $\circledast$ indicates the array multiplication.

The algorithm ends when the log-likelihood values $L(\Psi^{(j)})$ changes little. This criterion is certainly reachable as supported by the convergence theorem [2]. It is easy to see that the computation complexity of EMACF is $O(MKD)$ if the loop is terminated after perdefined number of iterations.

4   Experiments

Now, we compare our proposed algorithm with other scalable clustering algorithms. Working on the clustering features generated by the adaptive grid-based data summarization procedure, EMACF may form a scalable clustering algorithm, identified as gEMACF below. If the second moment γ_m in EMACF is replaced by $v_m \circledast v_m$, EMACF is simplied into an EM Algorithm for Weighted Samples (EMAWS). That scalable algorithm is denoted by gEMAWS. Similarly, if the ExEM algorithm works on the clustering features [1], we can construct a scalable algorithm: gExEM. We also compare gEMACF with the Inverse Biased Sampling (IBS) algorithm. It is a typical implementation of density-biased sampling algorithm, which outperforms BIRCH on skewed data sets [5]. To highlight the scalability of these algorithms, we also compare them with the traditional EM algorithm. It is denoted by iEM, where i indicates that attributes are independent as in EMACF and ExEM. SampiEM stands for iEM working on 5% random samples. We include it because sampling is a common strategy for scaling-up data mining algorithms [1,5]. All algorithms were implemented with MATLAB and ran on a Sun Enterprise E4500. The results were averaged on 10 runs.

Table 1 illustrates the clustering accuracy of these 6 algorithms on 10 data sets. These data sets are generated according to 10 random mixture models whose parameters are given in columns 2, 3, and 4. The data size ranges from 6,400 to 480,000 and their dimensionality ranges from 2 to 6. Fig. 1(a) illustrates the fourth data set. The clustering accuracy indicates the proportion of data items that are correctly clustered with respect to the original mixture models. Observed from the table, gEMACF generates better clustering results than the others do except data sets 4, 5 and 7 where gEMACF performs sightly worse. Fig.1(b) illustrates a mixture model generated by gEMACF which well describes the data set in Fig.1(a). The clustering accuracy of gEMACF ranges from 78.5% to 96.2%. On average, the clustering accuracy of gEMACF, gExEM, gEMAWS, SampiEM and iEM algorithm are 88.9%, 86.5%, 82.2%, 85.3% and 87.8% respectively. The gEMACF algorithm can generate more accurate results. It is interesting to see that gEMACF performs even slightly better than the iEM algorithm. This partially because that the smaller number of clustering features may cause smaller number of local maxima in the log-likelihood space. The gEMACF algorithm performs much better than SampiEM because sampling usually introduces some biases. The average clustering accuracy for the distance-based clustering algorithms, IBS, is much worse than that of the model-based clustering algorithms. Because all mixture models involved are so skew that they are not suitable for the distance-based clustering algorithm.

Fig.2 illustrates the execution time for the 6 clustering algorithms on 8 4-dimensional data sets. All data sets have 10 clusters. Observed from the figure, the execution time of gEMACF, gExEM, gEMAWS and IBS increases slowly while iEM and SampiEM increases more quickly with the size of data set. The first 4 algorithms take similar execution time and all scale up well with large data sets. Because the data summarization procedure takes longer time than

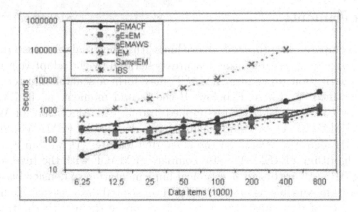

Fig. 2. Execution time on 8 4-dimensional data sets.

sampling for the first 3 small data sets, the first four algorithms execute slightly slower than SampiEM. However, for the last three large data sets, the difference between gEMACF and SampiEM/iEM becomes quite significant. For example, gEMACF only takes about 1344 seconds for the largest data set with 800,000 data items. It runs 3 times faster than SampiEM which needs 4050 seconds. Moreover, the traditional algorithm, iEM, failed to generate mixture models for the data set after executing for two days. Even for the data set with 400,000 data times, iEM needs about 110,245 seconds to generate a mixture model for the data set. The gEMACF algorithm only takes about 775 seconds which is about 142.7 times faster than iEM. For these data sets, the smallest speedup of gEMACF is obtained for the smallest data set with a value of 2.4. Thus, gEMACF is much faster than the traditional EM algorithm.

5   Conclusion

The EMACF (Expectation-Maximization Algorithm for Clustering Features) algorithm has been proposed to make better use of clustering features. It guarantees to converge. We have examined its performance by incorporating it with an adaptive grid-based data summarization procedure to construct a scalable algorithm: gEMACF. The experimental results have shown that the gEMACF algorithm can run two order of magnitude faster than the traditional EM algorithm. It can generate clustering results more accurate than other scalable model-based clustering algorithms with similar computation resources. It is subject to our future research on integrating with other data summarization procedure to establish scalable clustering algorithms for high-dimensional data sets. Another interesting direction of this work is to establish other model-based clustering algorithms on data summaries of complicated data sets.

References

1. P. Bradley, U. Fayyad, and C.R. Reina. Clustering very large databases using EM mixture models. In *Proceedings of 15th International Conference on Pattern Recognition*, volume 2, pages 76–80, 2000.
2. Huidong Jin, Kwong-Sak Leung, and Man-Leung Wong. An expectation-maximization algorithm working on data summary. In *Second International Workshop on Intelligent Systems Design and Applications*, Mar. 2002. Accepted.
3. Geoffrey J. McLachlan and Thriyambakam Krishnan. *The EM Algorithm and Extensions*. John Wiley & Sons, Inc., New York, 1997.
4. A. Moore. Very fast EM-based mixture model clustering using multiresolution KD-trees. In *Advances in Neural Information Processing Systems 11*, pages 543–549. The MIT Press, 1999.
5. Christopher R. Palmer and Christos Faloutsos. Density biased sampling: An improved method for data mining and clustering. In *Proceedings of ACM SIGKOD International Conference on Management of data*, pages 82–92, 2000.
6. Tian Zhang, Raghu Ramakrishnan, and Miron Livny. BIRCH: An efficient data clustering method for very large databases. *SIGMOD Record: Proc. ACM SIGMOD Int. Conf. Management of Data*, 25(2):103–114, June 4 - June 6 1996.

A New Approach to Hierarchically Retrieve MPEG Video

Yang Liu, Huanqiang Zhang, and Zhimei Wu

Institute of Software, Chinese Academy of Sciences
Zhongguancun, Beijing, China
{liuyang, zhq, wzm}@iscas.ac.cn

Abstract. Many researchers have devoted into video retrieval research and given lots of efficient video retrieval algorithms. Most of past algorithms were done in pixel domain, which needed lots of decoding calculations. What's more, the same matching algorithm was used to all the video clips, which also wasted many unnecessary calculations. This paper presents a new approach to hierarchically retrieve video by example video in MPEG compressed domain. Firstly, the dct_dc_size field in I frames is analyzed to filter out the obviously different video clips quickly, and then the precise matching analysis of DC image is used to get the final retrieval result. Our experiment results show that this approach needs a few calculations and has high precision ratio.

1 Introduction

With the more application of multimedia technology and the great development of computer technology, more and more researchers have devoted into video retrieval research and given lots of efficient video retrieval algorithms [1],[2],[3]. Video retrieval is different from text retrieval completely, and it is not same as image retrieval in some ways, because image retrieval only needs to analyze the features in one single image separately, but video retrieval needs to analyze specific features in some continuous frames.

Video retrieval by example clip is the process of retrieving the video clips that are most similar to the given video example. Some specific features of example video should be distilled firstly, and then those features are compared with the corresponding features of every video clip in the database. We divide the video retrieval algorithms into two kinds. For the first kind of algorithm, the analysis process, for example color and object edge features comparison, is done in pixel domain. Most of early retrieval algorithms belonged to this kind, which has been rapidly developed in the last decade. For the second kind of algorithm, the analysis process, for example DC coefficient and flow field features comparison, is done in compressed domain. The research about the second kind of algorithm is relatively less. Because this kind of algorithm does not need to fully decode the compressed data, it needs a few calculations, which is very useful for large video database retrieval and real time retrieval. On the other hand, the same matching algorithm was used to the completely different and basically similar video clips in the same way. In fact, the obviously different video clips can be filtered out by simple analysis, but for

H. Yin et al. (Eds.): IDEAL 2002, LNCS 2412, pp. 576-581, 2002.

the basically similar video clips, more precise analysis is needed. Few video retrieval methods have considered this. References [4] and [5] have surveyed the current main retrieval algorithms.

This paper presents a new hierarchical video retrieval approach by example video for MPEG I or MPEG II video. Firstly, we use dct_dc_size field in I frames to filter out the obviously different video clips quickly, and then we use DC image matching analysis to get the final retrieval result. At the same time, we will revise the original dct_dc_size analysis algorithm.

This paper is organized as follows: The detailed retrieval principle will be discussed in section 2. The experimental results are shown in section 3. The final section will present our conclusion.

2   Our Retrieval Principle

2.1   Overview of Our Retrieval Approach

Different from text data, there are many similar standards for video data. What kind of compared features to be used determines the performance of retrieval approach.. While choosing compared features, we mainly consider the following standards: 1) needed calculations; 2) needed memory; 3) ability of distinguishing different videos. The compared features that our approach uses are based on the original fields in MPEG video data. They only need a few calculations and memory and have good distinguishing ability.

In video database, the similar video clips are only a small part, so we do not need to precisely compare all of them. We can only use dct_dc_size field in I frame to filter out most of the completely different video clips. This is the first stage of our retrieval approach, then in order to get the final results, we use DC image matching analysis.

2.2   Quickly Filter by Analyzing dct_dc_size Field

According to MPEG standard [6], there is one I frame in every GOP (Group of Picture). I frame mainly includes DC coefficient and AC coefficients of every block. It is an important feature in video analysis and is widely used. What exists in MPEG video data is not the DC real value, but the DC difference between the two adjacent blocks. Adding the current DC difference to the DC value of reference block can get the DC value of current block. MPEG standard also defines the specific conditions, where the DC value of reference block is zero, for example at the beginning of every slice. The main intention is to increase the compressed proportion. The more detailed principle of DC difference can be found in MPEG standard [6]. Figure 1 gives the DC value reference mode of four luminance blocks in macroblock (i, j), where the digitals and arrows denote the reference orders. The meaning of other characters in this figure will be given later.

From the above discussion, we can know that the DC difference is proportional to the average of difference between the two adjacent blocks. The DC difference of similar video must be similar, so DC difference is also an important compared feature in video analysis. In MPEG video data, the dct_dc_size field is used to denote the coded length of the DC difference. The larger the DC difference is, the larger the coded length is, so dct_dc_size value can indicate the range of the DC difference value. The study about this feature is very little in the past. We only find that reference [7] has used this feature to segment video into shots and gotten good performance.

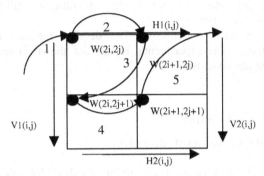

Fig.1. DC value reference mode of the four blocks in macroblock (i, j)

We use diff(i) to denote the value range of the DC difference when dct_dc_size is equal to i. According to MPEG standard [6], diff(i) is $\pm(2^{i-1}, 2^i - 1)$. Reference [7] has used dct_dc_size value as the compared feature value directly. This has the following two problems: 1) it has omitted quantization coefficient and positive or negative properties of DC difference 2) it has not considered that dct_dc_size value only denotes the coded length, not the real difference value. For example, diff(8) - diff(7) must be greater than diff(3) - diff(2) obviously. It will be error to use the dct_dc_size value as compared feature. To solve the above problems, we define the following weighted feature value for block (x,y):

$$W(x,y)= \begin{cases} 0 & i=0; \\ Q(x,y)*\text{sign}(diff(x,y))\,\text{int}\left((2^{i-1}+2^i-1)\Big/2\right) & i \geq 1; \end{cases} \quad (1)$$

where $w(x,y)$ is the weighted feature value of block(x, y) and $Q(x, y)$ is the quantization coefficient. $sign(diff(x,y))$ is positive sign or negative sign according to the MSB (Most Significant Bit) of the actual DC difference data, which is behind the dct_dc_size field in MPEG data. int() denotes the integer operation.

For the macroblock (i, j) in figure 1, based on the above definition, we define the following weighted feature values, which are more reasonable than reference [7]:

The horizontal feature value $H1(i,j)$ between block(2i+1,2j) and block(2i, 2j):

$$H1(i,j) = W(2i+1, 2j) \quad (2)$$

The horizontal feature value $H2(i,j)$ between block (2i+1,2j+1) and block (2i, 2j+1):

$$H2(i,j) = W(2i+1, 2j+1) \quad (3)$$

The vertical feature value $V1(i,j)$ between block (2i,2j+1) and block (2i, 2j):

$$V1(i,j) = W(2i+1, 2j) + W(2i, 2j+1) \qquad (4)$$

The vertical weighted feature value $V2(i,j)$ between block $(2i+1,2j+1)$ and block $(2i+1, 2j)$:

$$V2(i,j) = W(2i, 2j+1) + W(2i+1, 2j+1) \qquad (5)$$

The feature value $G(i,j)$ between the first block of macroblock (i,j) and the last block of macroblock$(i-1,j)$:

$$G(i,j) = W(2i, 2j) \qquad (6)$$

The total weighted feature value $T(i,j)$ of macroblock(i, j):

$$T(i,j) = H1(i,j) + H2(i,j) + V1(i,j) + V2(i,j) + G(i,j) \qquad (7)$$

Based on the above defined weighted feature values, we can get the similarity between I frames in example video and I frames in compared video. We define the following expression for the frame difference:

$$D(k) = \frac{\sum_{j=0}^{N-1}\sum_{i=0}^{M-1} \left| Tr(i,j) - Tc(i,j) \right|}{\sum_{j=0}^{N-1}\sum_{i=0}^{M-1} \left| Tr(i,j) \right|} \qquad (8)$$

where $D(k)$ is frame difference value between the kth I frame in example video and the kth I frame in compared video, $Tr(i,j)$ and $Tc(i,j)$ separately sign the weighted feature value of the macroblock (i,j) in the kth frame in example video and that in compared video. We assume that the video resolution is $16M*16N$.

Next, we can calculate the average value of frame difference between all I frames. We define the following inequation to determine whether example video is similar to compared video:

$$\frac{\sum_{k=0}^{S-1} D(k)}{S} \leq \eta 1 \qquad (9)$$

where S is the number of I frame in example video. $\eta 1$ is the threshold that is used to determine whether example video is similar to compared video. We can suitably adjust the value of $\eta 1$ to control the retrieval precision. Normally, $\eta 1$ should be smaller than 2 when the video resolution is $352*288$.

2.3   Get Final Results by Analyzing DC Image

The above retrieval process only ensures that retrieval results are roughly similar to example video. Because the proportion of I frame data in the MPEG video is very small. In fact, we can use the above basic principle of revised I frame retrieval algorithm to retrieve the JPEG image. On the other hand, retrieval process needs to locate the beginning and end frame. It will be obviously deficient to only use I frame. We need use other type frame in this retrieval stage.

We will use stricter matching algorithm than the first retrieval stage. Precise matching analysis of DC image is applied. We can regard DC image as the approximate epitome of the original frame. We can get their similarity to original example video by analyzing the similarity of their corresponding DC images. The DC image of I frame can be formed directly in MPEG compressed domain. The DC image of B frame and P frame can be formed using the algorithm in reference [8].

The coefficients of DC images in example video and those in compared video can form different matrixes separately. We will compute the matrix distance to get their similarity. We use the Euclidean Distance to measure the matrixes distance. For the frame difference of DC image, we define the following expression:

$$B(k) = \sqrt{\sum_{q=0}^{N-1}\sum_{p=0}^{M-1}(Er(p,q) - Ec(p,q))^2} \tag{10}$$

Where $B(k)$ is difference value. $Er(p,q)$ and $Ec(p,q)$ separately sign DC value of the pixel (p,q) in the kth frame in example DC image and that in compared DC image. We assume that the video resolution of the DC image is M*N.

Next, we calculate average difference value of all DC images. We define the following inequation to determine whether they are similar:

$$\frac{1}{T}\sum_{k=0}^{T-1}B(k) \le \eta 2 \tag{11}$$

where T is the frame number in example video. $\eta 2$ is the threshold that is used to determine whether they are similar. We can suitably adjust the value of $\eta 2$ to control the retrieval precision.

3   Experimentation

In order to test the performance of our retrieval approach, we refer to the experimentation ways of other retrieval approaches. We download 62 football shoot clips from ftp://202.38.126.48. All of them are compressed in MPEG-1 standard. They include 12106 frames, whose video resolution is 352*288. We use the video clip showed in figure 2 as example video, which includes 30 frames.

Fig. 2. Example clips of our experimentation

Every video clip is compared with example video using our presented approach. It only needs a few decoded calculations and simple comparison operations. The calculation of our retrieval approach is fewer than that of real time MPEG fully decoding. The real time MPEG video stream can be retrieved.

We get similarity degree by computing the frame difference. Figure 3 (a)–(d) gives four retrieval results according to similarity degree from large to small.

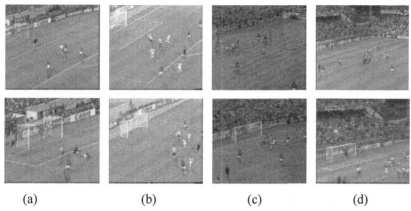

(a)   (b)   (c)   (d)

Fig.3. Retrieval results of our experimentation

4 Conclusion

This paper presents a new hierarchical video retrieval approach for MPEG video. It is not necessary to fully decode the MPEG compressed data, so it needs a few calculations. The real time video can be retrieved using our retrieval approach. What's more, it has high retrieval precision through two retrieval stages. On the other hand, we revise the original dct_dc_size analysis algorithm.

References

1. Zhang H J et al.:Video parsing retrieval and browsing: an integrated and content-based solution. Proc. ACM Multimedia '95. San Francisco, CA. (1995), 15-24
2. Jain A K, Vailaya A, Xiong W.: Query by video clip. Multimedia Systems: Special Issue on Video Libraries, 7(5), (1995), 369-384
3. Xiaoming Liu, Yueting Zhuang.:A new approach to retrieve video by example video clip. ACM Multimedia 99. Florida, USA, (1999)
4. Atsuo Y, Tadao I : Survey on content-based retrieval for multimedia databases. IEEE Tran. On Knowledge and Data Engineering, 11(1), (1999), 81-93
5. Veltkamp C, Tanase M.: Content-based image retrieval systems: a survey. Technical Report of University Utrecht, (2000), NO: UU-CS-2000, 34
6. Joint Technical Committee ISO/IEC JTC 1. : ISO/IEC 13818-2 information technology – Genecic coding of moving pictures and associasted audio information video" May 1996
7. Won C S, Park D K, Yoo S J: Extracting image features from MPEG-2 compressed stream. Storage and Retrieval for Image and Video Databases VI , Vol. 3312, (1998) 426-435
8. Yeo B L, Liu B.: On the extraction of DC sequence from MPEG compressed video. In: Proceedings of International Conference on Image Processing, Vol. II, (1995), 260-263

Alpha-Beta Search Revisited

Paul Parkins and John A. Keane

Department of Computation, UMIST, Manchester, UK.
p.parkins@pindar.com jak@co.umist.ac.uk

Abstract. An algorithm, *Aspiration Scout/MTD(f)*, is derived from an analysis of alpha-beta $(\alpha\text{-}\beta)$ tree search. When compared to its predecessors, it results in an average 10.1% reduction in search effort with a best case of 17.4%.

1 Introduction

This paper derives a game-playing algorithm that combines properties of earlier $\alpha\text{-}\beta$ search efforts, and out-performs its predecessors. Game-playing programs consist of a *search engine* that generates and searches a tree[1], and an *evaluation function* called at leaf nodes to identify the game's value at that node. In a game represented in this n-ary tree form, a search is performed on the game-tree to evaluate its value: at each *leaf* node, calculate the value for the player whose turn it is to move; at each *interior* node, take the value of the 'best' sub-node, where even levels correspond to player 1's turn, odd levels to player 2's turn. The 'best' sub-node is determined by finding the maximum (at even-level nodes) or minimum (at odd-level nodes) sub-node value depending on whose turn it is (hence the name *minimax*).

The basic evaluation function here calculates the value of a position using two factors: the 'material' in the position and a 'positional bonus' based on domain information. A quiescence search is used to ensure that only stable positions (where the opponent cannot make a move that alters the position's value significantly) are evaluated.

Minimax computes the value of a position p by searching the entire tree (to a given depth) rooted at p. Various enhancements allow deeper searches within given time constraints to improve accuracy and quality of the decision: (1) *algorithmic enhancements* attempt to prove that certain sub-trees need not be searched; (2) *graph enhancements* exploit the graph properties of the search space by saving information about searched nodes, to be used if those nodes are re-searched. As the minimal graph is significantly smaller than the minimal tree [2], there is potential for building graphs smaller than the minimal tree; (3) *move ordering enhancements:* the size of the search tree built largely depends on the order in which branches are considered at interior nodes. If the move leading to the best minimax score is considered first at each interior node, the tree built will be minimal (though this may not be the minimal *graph*). If the

---

[1] The search space is usually referred to as a tree, however in games such as chess and draughts it is actually a directed acyclic graph (DAG). Programs search a dynamically unfolding DAG.

H. Yin et al. (Eds.): IDEAL 2002, LNCS 2412, pp. 582–587, 2002.

branches are considered in worst to best order, the tree built will be maximal. As the difference between these extremes is large, it is crucial to obtain a good ordering of branches at interior nodes [3].

The structure of this paper is as follows: section 2 considers game-tree search algorithms, section 3 discusses the innovation developed here, section 4 analyses the new algorithm's performance, and section 5 presents conclusions.

2 Game-Tree Search

Compared to full minimax search, α-β search evaluates fewer leaf nodes before returning the correct value by trading exact knowledge for a 'good enough' answer. In general, α-β returns immediately from a node if a value returned to it is better than the value of a node an even number of levels above in the tree because this proves that the rest of the node's branches could not affect the result at that ancestor node. The algorithm is passed two parameters: (1) β is the minimum value of nodes an even number of levels above in the tree (i.e. the value which causes a cutoff if exceeded); and (2) α stores this value for nodes an odd number of levels above.

The branching factor is usually quite large, thus cutoff effects due to α-β can be very pronounced; in addition, the branches pruned could be entire sub-trees. Therefore, α-β can substantially reduce the size of the tree searched, and enhance performance significantly. Best-case α-β search (i.e. on a perfectly ordered tree) only searches $O(B^{D/2})$ instead of B^D leaves, where B is the branching factor and D is the depth [1]. This allows significant additional depth to the search within the same time constraints.

Scout is similar to α-β, except that a *test* is performed on each non-first child node instead of a full search. A test is an empty-window search that returns a boolean result: either the value is better or worse than the estimate. If the test proves that the non-first child *is not* better than the first child, a full search was unnecessary, otherwise it proves that the non-first child *is* better, and that child must be searched to find its true value. When the α-β window is smaller more of the tree is likely to be pruned, thus, a test is typically much cheaper to execute than a full search. When tests succeed less work is required, however when tests fail the child must be searched additionally, thus more work is needed. Scout relies heavily on move ordering – assuming that non-first children are not going to be as good as the first.

In a normal α-β search, to ensure the correct value is found (i.e. to avoid pruning an important value at the root), α-β is usually called at the root node with a search window of (α=-∞) and (β=+∞). *Aspiration* α-β algorithms use an artificially narrow window centred around the expected value [4]. If the search result falls within the window, the correct value will have been found with less search effort. If the search fails, the child must be re-searched with a wider window to find the true value.

A related approach performs *all* searches with a minimal window (i.e. as tests). *MTD(f)* uses an initial estimate for the position and converges on the correct value. Typically, between 5 and 15 tests are performed before finding the correct value.

3 Search Enhancements

The next section presents a new algorithm, *Aspiration Scout/MTD(f)*, that has been derived combining properties of its predecessors, along with various enhancements.

Algorithmic: *Aspiration Scout/MTD(f)* is given below (Fig. 1). The `Window` parameter specifies the window for the initial search on line 4. In normal Aspiration α-β, this would typically be half a pawn in chess and half a draught in draughts. Using a stable evaluation function, the initial estimate for a search is often very close to the true value. Thus, the call to Aspiration Scout is made with an *ultra*-narrow window.

```
1   Aspiration_Scout/MTDf( Pos, Depth, Guess, Window )
2       Alpha:= Guess - Window
3       Beta:= Guess + Window
4       BestMove:= Scout( Pos, Depth, Alpha, Beta )
5       If BestMove.Score <= α then
6           BestMove:= MTDf( Pos, Depth, BestMove.Score )
7       End if
8       If BestMove.Score >= Beta then
9           BestMove:= AlphaBeta( Pos, Depth, WIN - 1, WIN )
10      End if
11      If BestMove.Score >= WIN then
12          BestMove:= MTDf( Pos, Depth, BestMove.Score )
13      End if
14      Return BestMove
15  End Asp_Scout_MTDf
```

Fig 1: Pseudo-code for *Aspiration Scout/MTD(f)*.

Most of the tree cutoff in a test would also be cutoff in this search, thus, it retains most of the efficiency of performing a test. If the initial call to Aspiration Scout returns a correct result, this avoids much unnecessary search effort: In contrast, Aspiration α-β is called with a much larger window (hence a much larger tree is searched), and MTD(f) requires more searches to converge to the *exact* value. If the initial search fails here, it acts as the first test in the MTD(f) algorithm's series of tests to converge to the true value. This gives efficient convergence to the true value if the initial search fails, and is much more effective than widening the window as Aspiration α-β does.

If the initial search fails low (the result is less than α) then convergence to the true value using MTD(f) *must* be executed. If the search fails high (the result is greater than β) then the value is greater than expected, and the MTD(f) search is not strictly necessary – unless a win is possible, in that case an MTD(f) search *is* needed to find the true value. To determine if MTD(f) search is necessary in a fail-high situation, the algorithm performs a test on the win boundary.

Graph exploitation: In a DAG search space, different move sequences may lead to the same position. Large portions of the tree traversed may be eliminated by recognising previously visited nodes [2]. A *transposition table* acts as a cache of previous searches. Before performing a search at a node, the table is interrogated for previous search results relevant to the current node. If the information is sufficient (i.e. calculated to sufficient depth) the search result is returned, otherwise the information is used to improve the subsequent search. MTD(f)-like algorithms, involving multiple re-searching of positions, require efficient storage of previous searches.

Enhanced Transposition Cutoff (ETC) enables maximum information re-use. Before performing a search at an interior node, ETC consults the transposition table for each possible position arising from the node. This may result in finding an immediate cutoff before any (potentially wasted) searching is even performed. This scheme maximises the use of information in the table: in effect, in a left-to-right search, ETC encourages sub-trees in the right part of the tree to transpose in to the left [2].

If relevant stored information is not as 'reliable' as desired (i.e. not searched to sufficient depth previously), the stored 'best' move from the previous search is searched first. Schaeffer [3] states that as this move was previously best (albeit for a shallower search) there is a high probability it is the best for the current depth and should be tried first. However the previous 'best' move may not be the best move, i.e. another move may cause a quicker cutoff. Here the probability of the stored move being the best move is considered, rather than blindly forcing the stored move to always be searched first. In this approach, the stored move is made *more likely* rather than *forced* to be searched first, taking further advantage of other move ordering heuristics. Therefore, a highly successful move throughout the rest of the tree, which may also be a 'better' move at this node, may be tried before the stored move.

Move ordering: Schaeffer [3] shows that the *iterative deepening, history heuristic* and transposition table enhancements account for over 99% of the possible reductions in tree size for all known enhancements. For example, domain-knowledge based move ordering is shown to be inferior to the domain-independent history heuristic technique.

Iterative deepening is used to improve move ordering within the tree, especially at the root where consequences of poor ordering are most costly. It is also useful both when the search is constrained by time as the search can be terminated at any instant with the best move *so far* returned, and it gives a good initial estimate of the score that, to be efficient, algorithms such as Aspiration α-β and MTD(f) require. Starting with a very shallow depth, a series of successively deeper searches is performed.

The history heuristic maintains information regarding correlation of moves and their success. For each sufficient move found (i.e. one that causes a cutoff, or, if no cutoff occurs, the best move), its *history score* is increased. If a move is consistently sufficient, it achieves a high score quickly. Before searching at an interior node, moves are ordered based on their history scores. The history heuristic is generated as the tree is searched, i.e. it adapts to conditions encountered within the search.

The *history weight* is the value by which a sufficient move's history score is increased. Greater weight is given to results obtained from deeper searches as they are more reliable, and information about sufficient moves closer to the root are more likely to be useful throughout the tree than moves near leaves. The history weight used in practice is 2^{depth}, although other schemes are possible [3].

Making a stored move *more likely* rather than *forced* to be searched first, is implemented by inflating the history score based on a set multiplier. Therefore, it is possible for a highly successful move to 'out-score' the transposition table suggested move, and therefore be searched before it. However, if the scores for each of the moves were initially similar, the stored move will be searched first due to its inflated score.

4 Performance

A number of representative draughts test positions were used to analyse performance. The new algorithm often excels in quiet test positions (as positions in this domain usually are), where the initial estimate is highly accurate. The use of a disproportional number of non-quiet test positions biases the results to other algorithms; however, the efficiency of the new algorithm is such that it outperforms the other algorithms.

The following search performance metrics were used: *execution time* (ET) measures elapsed CPU time of a search, while *node count* (NC) measures all nodes in the tree searched, including interior and leaf nodes (and leaf evaluation sub-tree nodes).

Aspiration Scout/MTD(f) (see Fig. 2 and 3) has the best performance for both ET and NC at depths 15 and 17[2]. The transposition table, ETC and history heuristic enhancements account for most of the possible reductions in tree size. ETC gives a significant (18.8%) increase in efficiency. Incorporating probability in the use of Transposition Table suggested move ordering gives a 5.5% reduction in tree size.

Comparing the best existing algorithm, MTD(f), to the combination of *Aspiration Scout/MTD(f)* and the use of probability within transposition table move ordering, the innovations here result in an average reduction of search effort by 10.1%, and a best case of 17.4%, based on depth 13 and 15 serial searches over the test positions. The worst case still reduces the tree relative to MTD(f) by 3.8%.

5 Conclusions

This paper has re-visited alpha-beta search and the domain of draughts game-playing. A new algorithm, *Aspiration Scout/MTD(f)*, that combines aspects of its predecessors, results in an average 10.1% reduction in search effort with a best case of 17.4%.

Further work includes more in-depth testing, development of a more advanced evaluation function, and more intelligent machine learning to allow re-use of previous experience. Legal move generation is relatively expensive and performed at every internal node, thus, a scheme of efficiently generating only moves that will be searched would give a significant benefit. Exploiting the irregular branching factor for move ordering to encourage the cheapest cutoff (see [2]) is also of interest.

---

[2] The following were evaluated: *Minimax, α-β Aspiration Scout, Aspiration α-β Scout, SSS*, DUAL*, MTD(f), Aspiration Scout/MTD(f),* and *Aspiration α-β/MTD(f),* developed here that makes an initial call to α-β rather than to Scout; its performance is worse than MTD(f).

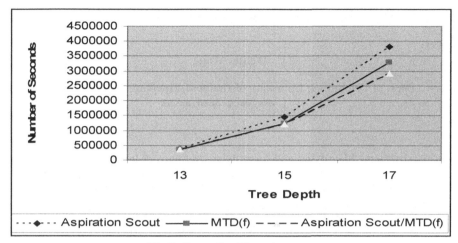

Fig 2: Execution Time Average

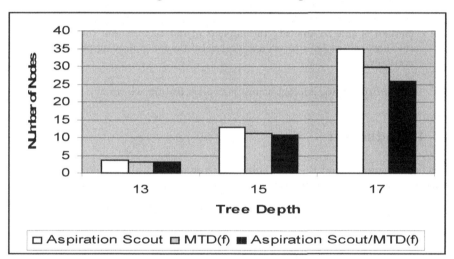

Fig 3: Node Count Average

References

1. Eppstein, D.: Strategy and Board Game Programming Lecture Notes, 1997 http://www.ics.uci/~eppstein/180a/s97.html.
2. Plaat, A., et al: Exploiting Graph Properties of Game Trees, AAAI, 1996.
3. Schaeffer, J.: The History Heuristic and Alpha-Beta Enhancements in Practice, IEEE Transactions on Pattern Analysis and Machine Intelligence, Vol. 11, 1989.
4. Schaeffer, J., Plaat, A.: New Advances in Alpha-Beta Searching, Proceedings of the 24th ACM Computer Science Conference, 1996.

Quantifying Relevance of Input Features

Wenjia Wang

Dept. of Computing, University of Bradford, Bradford, BD7 1DP, UK.
w.j.wang@scm.brad.ac.uk

Abstract. Identifying and quantifying relevance of input features are particularly useful in data mining when dealing with ill-understood real-world data defined problems. The conventional methods, such as statistics and correlation analysis, appear to be less effective because the data of such type of problems usually contains high-level noise and the actual distributions of attributes are unknown. This papers presents a neural-network based method to identify relevant input features and quantify their general and specified relevance. An application to a real-world problem, i.e. osteoporosis prediction, demonstrates that the method is able to quantify the impacts of risk factors, and then select the most salient ones to train neural networks for improving prediction accuracy.

Keywords: Data mining, neural networks, feature selection

1 Introduction

It is fairly common that the data collected from real-world problems may contain, apart from other kinds of noises, some less important or redundant, or even completely irrelevant inputs. Then a normal practice is to decide what features or which subsets of the inputs or all the inputs should be used by problem-solving techniques. Unnecessary input features included in a data set not only increase the cost of resources for data collection and processing, but also can seriously degrade performance of a problem-solving technique. Therefore, There is a need for correctly and efficiently identifying the relevance of features against a given output target. In this paper the general problem particularizes to which set of features to use as neural network inputs in order to optimize network performance. This encompasses issues of both efficiency and accuracy.

Some feature selection techniques, such as the sensitivity analysis based methods [1] the functional analysis [2] the ARD (Automatic Relevance Determination) model [3], the neural net clamping [4] and the weight-product [5], etc. have emerged from the field of neural computing. The comparative study on some of these methods, i.e. ARD and the weight-product, together with a standard statistical technique as a baseline, has been described in details in our previous paper [6]. This paper presents further developments on the technique as well as the measures defined for evaluating performance of the feature ranking techniques in terms of stability and consistency. Specifically, the measures of

H. Yin et al. (Eds.): IDEAL 2002, LNCS 2412, pp. 588–593, 2002.

'distance' and the weighted dissimilarity between rankings have been proposed. A standard statistical similarity measure – Spearman's correlation is used as a reference baseline. The effectiveness of feature-ranking will be assessed primarily by the test performance of multilayer perceptron networks (MLPs) trained with the selected feature sets. The developed technique has been applied to a real-world medical problem, i.e. osteoporosis prediction, in which the relevance of all the risk factors are quantified and the most relevant risk factors are selected for prediction. The effectiveness of feature ranking and selection is tested and compared.

2 Quantifying Feature Relevance

The technique we developed [4] [6] relies on the observation that the degradation of the generalization performance of a trained neural network when the information content of a particular feature in all test patterns is removed will reflect the relevance of that input feature with respect to the network's computational task.

A feature-ranking exercise then consists of testing a trained neural network to obtain the baseline generalization performance; retesting with one feature in every test pattern clamped to a fixed value and recording the new generalization performance; repeating this clamp-and-retest cycle for each feature of the test patterns. Finally, the sets of generalization performances, relative to the baseline performance, ordered in terms of extent of deterioration gives the relevance ranking of the features — the largest performance decrease indicates the most relevant feature. The term *impact ratio* is defined below for quantitatively representing the relevance of features when applying the clamping technique.

General Relevance: Given a data set for a classification problem with n input features, $\{x_i, i = 1, .., n\}$, and a finite number of target categories, the impact ratio $\xi(x_i)$ of input feature x_i is defined as:

$$\xi(x_i) = 1 - \frac{g(\mathbf{x}|_{x_i=\bar{x}_i})}{g(\mathbf{x})} \qquad i = 1, ..., n. \tag{1}$$

where $\mathbf{x} = [x_1, x_2, ..., x_n]^T$, $g(\mathbf{x})$ is the generalisation performance of the neural net, and $g(\mathbf{x}|_{x_i=\bar{x}_i})$ is the clamped generalisation performance of the net when input x_i is clamped to its mean $\bar{x}_i$. By this definition, a higher value of $\xi(x_i)$ indicates a higher relevance for input x_i with respect to the output.

If the interest is the impact of individual input features to a specific outcome class, the definition below can apply.

Specified Relevance: Given a classification problem with n input features, $\{x_i, i = 1, .., n\}$, and m target categories, $\{c_j, j = 1, ..., m\}$, the relevance of feature x_i associated with outcome class c_j, $\xi(x_i, c_j)$, is then defined as:

$$\xi(x_i, c_j) = 1 - \frac{g(\mathbf{x}|_{x_i=\bar{x}_i}, c_j)}{g(\mathbf{x}, c_j)} \qquad i = 1, ..., n, \qquad j = 1, ..., m. \tag{2}$$

where $g(\mathbf{x}, c_j)$ is the generalisation performance of the neural net for class c_j, and $g(\mathbf{x}|_{x_i=\bar{x}_i}, c_j)$ is the clamped generalisation performance of the net for class c_j when input x_i is clamped to its mean $\bar{x}_i$.

The clamping technique can be extended from clamping individual features to combined subsets of the features. It is not necessary to train the nets every time for each size of feature subsets, but only to train a net (or a set of nets) with all the features and then to perform the clamping for various combinations of features. In this way it is possible to carry out the exhaustive clamping for all possible combinations (2^n) of n features if necessary. Then the relevance of all feature-subsets can be ranked. The one with highest value of the impact will be an optimal subset of features.

The clamping technique can be further extended to general problems other than classifications by simply substituting the generalisation measure with other type of performance measures accordingly, e.g. using the mean squared error (MSE) for regression problems.

3   Measures of Ranking Performance

The performance of a ranking technique is evaluated in two perspectives, i.e. stability and effectiveness. Assume that $P = \{...p_i...\}$ and $Q = \{...q_i...\}$ are the two rankings generated by a ranking method for n input factors, where p_i denotes the position of input x_i in ranking P, q_i the position of x_i in ranking Q, then the stability and the effectiveness are defined as follows:

(a) Stability and consistency: We proposed two quantitative measures, i.e. mean 'distance' D and the weighted dissimilarity β [6] to evaluate stability and consistence of a ranking method. If the rankings produced by a specific ranking technique have a short 'distance', $d_i = p_i - q_i$, on average and smaller mean dissimilarity β (together with a small standard deviation) the technique is considered to be stable and consistent.

A normalised weighted similarity measure is introduced here, modified from Spearman's correlation coefficient, ρ. The Spearman's correlation is a commonly used nonparametric statistical measure of similarity between paired rankings, and is calculated by

$$\rho_s = 1 - \frac{6\sum_{i=1}^n d_i^2}{n(n^2 - 1)} \tag{3}$$

When $\rho_s = 1$ means that two rankings are exactly same, $\rho_s = -1$, two rankings in reverse order, and $\rho_s = 0$ indicates no correlation between two rankings. Tables exist for obtaining the significance levels of other values of ρ_s. However, it only calculates linear correlation between two rankings and treats all features equally without considering their relative positions in the ranks. In practice it is more important to know whether those factors ranked highly by one technique are also ranked highly by another. Or in terms of feature selection, the position changes of high-ranked features in both rankings will have stronger effect than the position changes of low-ranked features.

The weighted similarity measure γ was specially defined to reflect these changes by putting larger weight to a high-ranked feature in a ranking than to one in a lower position of the ranking. The normalised weighted similarity is defined as,

$$\gamma = \begin{cases} 1 - \frac{2}{n+1} \sum_{i=1}^{n} \frac{\|p_i - q_i\|}{(p_i + q_i)} & \text{if } n = even \\ \\ 1 - \frac{2(n-1)}{n^2} \sum_{i=1}^{n} \frac{\|p_i - q_i\|}{(p_i + q_i)} & \text{if } n = odd \end{cases} \qquad (4)$$

A large γ represents a high similarity between the two rankings. When $\gamma = 1$, a maximum similarity means that the two rankings are identical. $\gamma = 0$, the minimum similarity, indicates that the factors are ranked in inverse order in the two rankings.

In this study we produced a set of N rankings with each technique in order to reliably measure the stability of the different ranking methods. Then the above measures are calculated for each possible pair within the ranking sets and the mean and standard deviation are quoted for the $N(N-1)/2$ pairs. In our experiments, the number of repetitions, N, is 9 unless otherwise stated.

(b) Effectiveness - it is defined by measuring the test performance of neural nets trained with the most salient features selected from different ranking techniques in turn. A ranking technique is considered effective to the extent that a selected feature subset produces neural nets that generalise well compared with those trained on the full feature set and on randomly selected subsets.

4   Identifying Risk Factors of Osteoporosis

The developed technique has been tested on a number bench marks and compared with other neural net based methods in our previous research [4], [6], [7]. Here presents an application to osteoporosis prediction problem. The data collected from over 700 cases contains 31 risk factors that were initially identified by the medical experts as relevant to the disease. The outcome is a diagnostic decision, i.e. osteoporotic or non-osteoporotic, based on the T-score from an ultrasound scanner on the patient's heel. Identification of the most salient risk factors, out of these 31 factors, will assist doctors to detect the disease in its earlier stage. The data set was randomly partitioned into 3 subsets for training, validating and testing respectively. Multiple experiments were conducted by shuffling the data before each repetition.

Figure 1 illustrates the clamped generalisations of a neural net trained with all input factors that are clamped one by one. Four factors, i.e. Kyphosis, FH, Backpain and OesDef, are singled out from others and therefore they are identified as the four most salient risk factors. Based on these results the general relevance–impact ratio, of 31 risk factors, are calculated using Equation 1. Then the most relevant 10, 15 and 20 factors are selected to constitute the corresponding data subsets for training and testing of predictors – neural nets.

Figure 2 shows the comparisons of the testing performance of the nets trained with different number of features selected separately by each ranking technique,

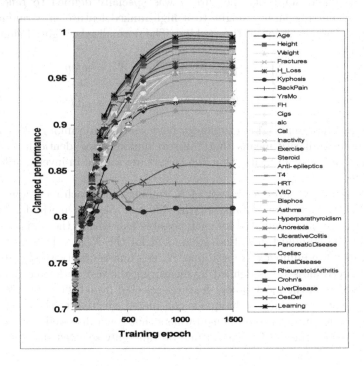

Fig. 1. Ranking curves of the factors of osteoporosis as the neural network learning goes on. Note that the y-axis is the clamped generalisation performance – an inverse proportion to the defined relevance. Thus the curves plotted at the bottom are most relevant, and the top ones the least salient.

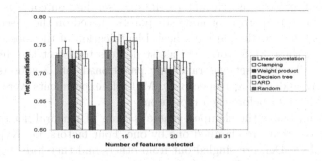

Fig. 2. The test performance of nets trained on variously selected subsets of osteoporosis features compared with performance on the full feature set.

plus a random ranking. It clearly shows that the all ranking techniques performed better than random feature selection. The nets trained by using the top 10 and 15 features chosen by clamping technique tested better than those of the nets trained using the features selected by the other methods. The decision-tree heuristic also did quite well, only slightly worse than clamping. ARD achieved similar results in 20 features group. The weight-product method was always the worst in non-random feature selection techniques.

5   Conclusion

This paper describes a neural net based approach for identifying and quantifying relevance of input features. Two types of relevance, the general relevance and specified relevance, are explicitly defined for quantifying the salience of risk factors. The technique is applied to osteoporosis problem and the results are compared with other neural-net based methods, i.e. the weight-product and automatic relevance determination, a conventional one – linear correlation analysis, and random-ranking in terms of effectiveness and consistency.

In general, the technique we developed performs better at identifying most relevant risk factors as well as eliminating irrelevant factors. More importantly, it is relatively consistent when dealing with real-world noisy data, and able to effectively reduce dimensionality of data set and to improve performance of problem-solving methods.

Acknowledgements. This research is funded by the EPSRC (GR/K78607 and GR/R86041), UK.

References

1. Utans, J. and Moody, J. (1991), Selecting neural network architecture via the prediction risk: application to corporate bond rating prediction. in D. S. Tourentzky, ed., 'Proc. 1st Int. Conf. on AI Applications on Wall Street', IEEE Computer Society Press, Los Atlamitos, CA.
2. Gedeon, T. (1997), 'Data mining of inputs: analysis magnitude and functional measures', Int. J. of Neural Networks 8, 209–218.
3. MacKay, D. (1998), 'Bayesian methods for supervised neural networks'. Handbook of mind theory and neural networks, Editor, M. Irbib, MIT press, 144-149.
4. Wang, W., Jones, P. & Partridge, D. (1998), Ranking pattern recognition features for neural networks. S. Singh, ed., Advances in Patterns Recognation, Springer, 232–241.
5. Tchaban, T. et al. (1998), 'Establishing impacts of the inputs in a feedforward network', Neural Computing and Applications 7, 309–317.
6. Wang, W., Jones, P. and Partridge, D. (2000), 'Assessing the impact of input features in a feedforward network'. Neural Computing and Applications, Vol.9, 101–112.
7. Wang, W. et al. (2001), 'A comparative study of feature salience rankingtechniques' Neural Computation 13(7), 1602–1623. MIT Press

Author Index